Structural Analysis of Discrete Data with Econometric Applications

Structural Analysis of Discrete Data with Econometric Applications

edited by
Charles F. Manski
and Daniel McFadden

The MIT Press
Cambridge, Massachusetts
London, England

This book was set in Times Roman by Komiyama Printing Co. and printed and bound by Halliday Lithograph in the United States of America.

Library of Congress Cataloging in Publication Data
Main entry under title:

Structural analysis of discrete data with econometric applications.

Includes bibliographies and indexes.
1. Econometrics. I. Manski, Charles F. II. McFadden, Daniel.
III. Title: Discrete data with econometric applications.
HB139.S79 330′.028 81-1450
ISBN 0-262-13159-5 AACR2

Contents

List of Contributors

Robert B. Avery
Carnegie-Mellon University
Pittsburgh, Pa.

Moshe Ben-Akiva
Massachusetts Institute
of Technology
Cambridge, Mass.

Stephen R. Cosslett
Northwestern University
Evanston, Ill.

Gregory W. Fischer
Carnegie-Mellon University
Pittsburgh, Pa.

Jerry A. Hausman
Massachusetts Institute
of Technology
Cambridge, Mass.

James J. Heckman
University of Chicago
Chicago, Ill.

Lung-Fei Lee
University of Minnesota
Minneapolis, Minn.

Steven R. Lerman
Massachusetts Institute
of Technology
Cambridge, Mass.

Charles F. Manski
Hebrew University
Jerusalem, Israel

Daniel McFadden
Massachusetts Institute
of Technology
Cambridge, Mass.

Daniel Nagin
Carnegie-Mellon University
Pittsburgh, Pa.

Dale J. Poirier
University of Toronto
Toronto, Canada

Peter Schmidt
Michigan State University
East Lansing, Mich.

Thawat Watanatada
International Bank for
Reconstruction and Development
Washington, D.C.

David A. Wise
Harvard University
Cambridge, Mass.

Preface

The chapters in this volume are all original and previously unpublished major research contributions made by econometricians to the structural analysis of discrete data. Two factors led to our decision to organize this volume.

First, we feel that the piecemeal publication in the journals of new research in this field has made it difficult for econometricians not actively working on discrete data problems to overview the existing state of knowledge and the present frontiers of research. Coordinated publication of the basic findings in this new subject should lower the cost of entry into the field and speed dissemination of recent research into the graduate econometrics classroom.

Second, as the econometric literature on discrete data analysis has grown, and its contributions have matured, we have increasingly wished to communicate the concerns and results of this literature to the wider community of researchers involved in the structural analysis of discrete data, both in applied economics and in disciplines outside economics. As the editors' introduction to this volume emphasizes, there exist important interconnections between the econometric literature on discrete data and the work in statistics, biometrics, psychometrics, sociometrics, and other disciplines on discrete data analysis. We have tried to organize this volume so that readers from outside economics as well as applied economists will recognize the connections between the problems they face and the issues addressed in econometric analysis of discrete data and will find the results obtained here useful in their work.

Submissions of papers for possible publication in the volume were solicited by the editors in the spring of 1978. We are grateful to R. Avery, M. Ben-Akiva, S. Cosslett, G. Duncan, D. Gillen, J. Hausman, J. Heckman, L. Lee, S. Lerman, D. Nagin, D. Poirier, P. Schmidt, B. Singer, R. Westin, and D. Wise, each of whom reviewed one or more papers.

The editors and many of the contributors in this volume have benefited greatly from exchanges of results at a series of workshops on the econometric analysis of discrete data sponsored by the National Science Foundation. The editors wish to thank Carnegie-Mellon University, the University of California, Berkeley, and the University of Chicago for providing facilities for these workshops.

Editors' Introduction

This volume deals with parametric statistical inference on structural conditional probability models in which some or all of the endogenous variables are discrete valued. Within this broad theme the models posed and inferential questions addressed arise out of each author's work in econometric analysis. Taken together, these chapters provide a methodological foundation for the analysis of economic problems involving discrete data and chart the current frontiers of this subject. Some chapters are also relevant to other literatures concerned with structural analysis of discrete data: biometrics, psychometrics, sociometrics, discrete multivariate analysis, and applied subjects such as finance, marketing, geography, and transportation. Workers in these areas will recognize that econometric methods for discrete data analysis have benefited from their own literatures. This volume is intended to be useful not only for econometricians but also for the wider community of researchers involved in the structural analysis of discrete data.

In econometrics, research on models with discrete endogenous variables has two primary sources: discrete choice analysis, the study of behavior in situations where decision makers must select from finite sets of alternatives, and discrete simultaneous system modeling, the study of economic processes which may be described by systems of equations in which some endogenous variables are structurally or observationally discrete.

Discrete Choice Analysis

The canonical discrete choice model has the form $P(i \mid \mathbf{z})$, where i is an alternative in a finite choice set $\mathbf{C}$, $\mathbf{z}$ is a real vector characterizing the choice set and decision maker, and P gives the conditional probability that in the choice context characterized by $\mathbf{z}$ alternative i will be selected. The econometric literature on discrete choice generally assumes that P has been specified up to a real parameter vector $\boldsymbol{\theta}$, in which case we write $P(i \mid \mathbf{z}, \boldsymbol{\theta})$. The concerns of the literature are (1) formulation of models $P(i \mid \mathbf{z}, \boldsymbol{\theta})$ consistent with rational choice behavior and tractable, (2) inference on the parameters $\boldsymbol{\theta}$ from observations of the choices made by samples of decision makers, and (3) application of estimated probabilistic choice models to predict the behavior of populations of decision makers in given choice contexts, such as occupation, travel mode, labor force participation, or migration to new locations.

Econometric discrete choice analysis has numerous connections with other literatures. In particular the notion of a probabilistic discrete choice model originates in psychometrics with the work of Thurstone (1927) on the probit random utility model. The modern psychometric literature on probabilistic choice, as exemplified by Luce (1959), Luce and Suppes (1965), and Tversky (1972), has greatly influenced econometric model specification. Conversely, the chapters in this volume by McFadden and by Fischer and Nagin should prove of interest to psychometricians.

McFadden generalizes the Luce (1959) strict utility model and demonstrates that the generalization is consistent with an underlying random utility model of specified form. He also offers a constructive approach to the problem, first addressed by Block and Marschak (1960), of determining when an arbitrary probabilistic choice model has a random utility interpretation.

Fischer and Nagin present intriguing empirical evidence on the usefulness of the random coefficients multinomial probit model as a probabilistic description of behavior. The multinomial probit model is an important generalization of the familiar binary probit model. Lerman and Manski address computational issues associated with the calculation of multinomial probit probabilities as well as of more general choice probability forms.

Stripped of its behavioral interpretation, a probabilistic discrete choice model is simply a multinomial or quantal response model. Quantal response models have long found use in biometrics, particularly in bioassay. Indeed the biometric literature on statistical inference in such models, as developed early on by Berkson (1944) and later by Finney (1971), Cox (1970) and others, provided the initial inferential tools for discrete choice analysis.

Recent developments in the statistical analysis of discrete choice should be very valuable to biometricians. The canonical discrete choice model presumes an extant population of decision makers $\mathbf{T}$, each member τ of whom must select an alternative $i \in \mathbf{C}$ and each of whom has his choice context characterized by an attribute vector $\mathbf{z} \in \mathbf{Z}$, $\mathbf{Z}$ being the attribute space. The joint distribution of choices and attributes in the population is described by the generalized density $f(i, \mathbf{z}) = P(i \mid \mathbf{z}, \boldsymbol{\theta})p(\mathbf{z})$, where p is the marginal attribute distribution.

The primary inferential approach investigated in the literature is natural observation rather than experimentation: a sample of decision makers, each with associated choice and attributes, is drawn from **T** by a specified sampling rule, and $\boldsymbol{\theta}$ is estimated from this sample of observations. Taken together, the chapters by Manski and McFadden and by Cosslett in this volume provide a quite general, rigorous treatment of sample design and estimation using natural observations. In particular they consider maximum likelihood and pseudomaximum likelihood approaches to the estimation of $\boldsymbol{\theta}$ under sampling processes in which the population is stratified into choice-attribute subsets and observations are drawn at random within the subpopulations defined by these subsets.

The focus of the discrete choice literature on inference from natural observations follows in part from the difficulties associated with experimentation in human populations. While much of the biometric literature is concerned with animal populations where experimentation is possible, many biometric investigations concern human populations where natural observation may often be the only feasible inferential approach. Given this, the Manski-McFadden and Cosslett chapters seem to us quite relevant to biometric practice. (For example, case-control sampling of the biometric literature is closely related to what is termed choice-based sampling here.)

The relationship between discrete choice analysis and the statistical literature on discrete multivariate analysis is also close. Consider again the population model $f(i, \mathbf{z})$, which is the starting point for discrete multivariate analysis as well as for formal discrete choice analysis. The feature of the discrete choice problem that distinguishes it from the general analysis of discrete data is the postulate that the conditional probability $P(i \mid \mathbf{z})$ belongs to a known parametric family and reflects an underlying link from $\mathbf{z}$ to i that will continue to hold even if the marginal distribution $p(\mathbf{z})$ changes. This postulate motivates our decomposition of $f(i, \mathbf{z})$ into the form $f(i, \mathbf{z}) = P(i \mid \mathbf{z}, \boldsymbol{\theta})p(\mathbf{z})$.

In general, given a population with a probability distribution $f(i, \mathbf{z})$, one might in the absence of any knowledge of the process relating i's to $\mathbf{z}$'s obtain a random sample and directly examine the joint distribution $f(i, \mathbf{z})$. This exploratory data analysis approach is exemplified by the literature on associations in contigency tables, where it is assumed that **Z** is finite. See, for example, Goodman and Kruskal (1954), Haberman (1974), and Bishop, Fienberg, and Holland (1975).

Alternatively, if one believes that the elements of **C** index conceptually distinct populations of **z** values, then the natural analytic approach is to decompose $f(i, \mathbf{z})$ into the product $f(i, \mathbf{z}) = q(\mathbf{z} \mid i)Q(i)$, where $q(\mathbf{z} \mid i)$

gives the distribution of **z** within the population indexed by i and $Q(i)$ is the proportion of the population with this index. This is the approach taken in discriminant analysis. There prior knowledge allows the analyst to specify $q(\mathbf{z} \mid i)$ up to a parametric family, and a sample suitable for estimating the unknown parameters is obtained from the subpopulation i. See, for example, Anderson (1959), Warner (1963), and Kendall and Stuart (1976).

Clearly discrete choice analysis, or more generally quantal response modeling, falls within and not outside the general statistical analysis of discrete data. This fact has sometimes been obscured because statisticians have analyzed via contingency tables or discriminant functions populations where the relation between i's and **z**'s is more appropriately modeled using the quantal response decomposition of $f(i, \mathbf{z})$. Some examples are given in the chapter by Manski and McFadden.

Where the quantal response decomposition is in fact appropriate, the discrete choice literature makes practical contributions that should interest statisticians. First, it offers a variety of useful forms for the response probability $P(i \mid \mathbf{z}, \boldsymbol{\theta})$. The statistical literature appears to us excessively preoccupied with log-linear forms. (Note, however, that the multinomial logit model used in many discrete choice analyses is log-linear.) Second, it offers a range of sample designs and estimation methods for $\boldsymbol{\theta}$ and highlights the value of auxiliary information in the estimation process. Many of the technical results on sample design and estimation achieved in the discrete choice literature have not been explored by statisticians. Perhaps calling attention to the relations and distinctions among the contigency table, quantal response and discriminant analysis approaches to discrete data analysis will lead statisticians to examine more carefully which approach is the most appropriate in applications.

A further symbiosis has existed between choice analysis and mobility studies in sociometrics, geography, and regional science. Sociometricians have for some time applied descriptive Markov-modeling approaches to study the way individuals move within organizations and across space. See, for example, Blumen, Kogan, and McCarthy (1955), Ginsberg (1972), and Stewman (1976). In contrast, the discrete choice literature has generally confined its attention to static modeling. To workers in both econometrics and sociometrics, it has become increasingly apparent that the development of dynamic discrete choice models would constitute a significant advance over both the descriptive dynamic models of mobility studies and the structural static models of present discrete choice analysis.

An important step in this direction is taken by Heckman. In his work mobility arises as the outcome of sequences of choices made by individuals over time. The choice process may be behaviorally dynamic (exhibit true state dependence, in Heckman's terms), observationally dynamic (exhibit spurious state dependence), or both. A focus of Heckman's analysis is the development of inferential procedures for distinguishing true from spurious state dependence. A second focus is on the statistical problems that arise when one's observation of a dynamic choice process does not provide a complete history of the process.

A chapter that will be of interest to urban geographers, regional economists, and socioeconometricians pursuing mobility studies is by Ben-Akiva and Watanatada. These authors address the problem of characterizing the spatial distribution of destination alternatives faced by trip makers and the way trip makers choose among these destinations. Their MIT-TRANS modeling approach, which incorporates a continuous endogenous variable logit choice model, should be applicable to the analysis of intraurban residential and business location.

Discrete Simultaneous Systems Modeling

The literature on discrete simultaneous systems modeling is a natural outgrowth of the long-standing concern in econometrics with the estimation of linear model systems. Consider the two-equation linear system,

$$y_1 = \beta_1 y_2 + x_1\gamma_1 + \varepsilon_1,$$
$$y_2 = \beta_2 y_1 + x_2\gamma_2 + \varepsilon_2,$$

where the distribution of $(\varepsilon_1, \varepsilon_2)$, conditioned on (x_1, x_2), is multivariate normal with mean zero and covariance matrix $\boldsymbol{\Sigma}$. A major theme of the literature on discrete systems is to investigate ways to estimate the parameters $(\beta_1, \beta_2, \gamma_1, \gamma_2, \boldsymbol{\Sigma})$ when an economic process is described by the two-equation (or a similar multi-equation) system but observations are influenced by discrete events involving y_1 and y_2.

To start with some relatively simple cases, Tobin (1958) and Amemiya (1973) examine estimators for γ_1 in the situation where $\beta_1 = 0$, x_1 is always observed but y_1 is observed only when $y_1 > \alpha_1$, a constant. Gronau (1974) and Heckman (1976) analyze the version of this situation in which $y_1 \leqq \alpha_1$ implies that neither y_1 nor x_1 is observed. The latter problem is one of truncated sampling; the former has been termed the tobit case.

In another type of problem $\beta_1 = \beta_2 = 0$, x_1 and x_2 are always observed, y_1 and y_2 are not observed, but the event $y_1 > y_2$ is observed. The reader familiar with discrete choice analysis will recognize that this is the observational situation faced when one attempts to infer preferences from choices. That is, if y_1 and y_2 are random utilities for alternatives 1 and 2, a decision-maker's choice of alternative 1 over 2 implies only that $y_1 > y_2$. See, for example, McFadden (1973) or Manski (1975).

A third class of problems that has received much attention is switching regression. Here (y_1, x_1) is observed if and only if $y_1 < y_2$; otherwise $(y_2, x_2)$is observed. Switching regressions, which have been studied by Fair and Jaffee (1972), Maddala and Nelson (1974), and by others, arise naturally in the analysis of markets in disequilibrium.

A great many variants and generalizations of observational problems have been identified and studied in recent years. Lee offers a unified framework for posing and resolving such problems. In particular Lee demonstrates that an estimation approach proposed by Amemiya (1978, 1979) in specific contexts can be usefully applied to a broad range of discrete observational conditions.

A second chapter by Hausman and Wise examines the sampling process used in data collection for a recent social experiment and presents alternative estimation methods appropriate under that process. Ostensibly the sampling process followed is endogenous censored sampling, in which a random sample is first drawn and then some observations are deleted, based on a discrete condition related to the value of endogenous variables. Hausman and Wise clarify some subtle distinctions among various stratified and censored sampling processes, which superficially appear quite similar, and develop tractable estimators.

Poirier in an interesting applied chapter analyzes various aspects of physician behavior. His behavioral model involves both discrete choice and linear model aspects. In the sampling process generating his data, the physicians' discrete choice determines what variables from the linear system are observed. Also the procedure by which physicians were drawn into the sample itself is choice based. Poirier's handling of this myriad of complexities demonstrates the power of discrete choice analysis and discrete simultaneous modeling as applied tools.

Recently the literature on discrete simultaneous modeling has developed a second major theme. Consider the two-equation mixed discrete-linear system,

$$y_1 = \beta_1 y_2 + \beta_1^* y_2^* + x_1 \gamma_1 + \varepsilon_1,$$
$$y_2 = \beta_2 y_1 + \beta_2^* y_1^* + x_2 \gamma_2 + \varepsilon_2,$$

where $y_1^* = 1$ if $y_1 > \alpha_1$, $y_1^* = 0$ otherwise, $y_2^* = 1$ if $y_2 > \alpha_2$, $y_2^* = 0$ otherwise, and ε is the same as before. This system is qualitatively different from the one posed earlier because discrete transformations of the endogenous variables are part of the system structure. Consequently the system now does not have a linear reduced form.

Even when observational problems do not exist, parameter estimation in models such as the mixed discrete-linear system poses difficulties. See Amemiya (1974) and Heckman (1978) for relevant analyses. The paper by Schmidt sets out several classes of mixed discrete-linear model systems. Schmidt finds that in each model internal consistency requires that a set of more or less restrictive parameter constraints be satisfied. Since these constraints often have no apparent economic interpretation, his results call into question the appropriateness of some of the model structures that have been posed in the literature.

Avery deals with estimation of a mixed discrete-linear system in the presence of discrete observational problems. Avery's concern is with the measurement of racial differences in consumer credit demand and supply. His model assumes that a household's durable demand is a function of, among other things, its observed credit, which is itself the minimum of its unobserved demand for and supply of credit. His work illustrates the concerns of the discrete simultaneous modeling literature, and his empirical results are of substantive interest.

It will be noticed that, in discussing the papers in this volume that contribute to the discrete simultaneous modeling literature, we have not developed connections with other literatures as we did in our treatment of discrete choice analysis. This asymmetry arises because the simultaneous equations field has as a whole developed largely within econometrics. Certainly connections with other disciplines exist. In particular the reduced form of a linear simultaneous system is the multivariate regression model widely studied in statistics. Recursive simultaneous equations models are the path analysis models of sociometrics. Simultaneous systems models with unobserved (latent) exogenous variables are the factor analytic models of psychometrics. However, we are unaware of systematic efforts to go beyond the obvious similarities of the models used in econometrics and other disciplines and search for approaches that can be productively transferred between subjects. We hope the readers of this volume will be motivated to further research that integrates the methods in various disciplines for structural analysis of discrete data.

References

Amemiya, T. 1973. Regression Analysis When the Dependent Variable is Truncated Normal. *Econometrica*. 41: 997–1016.

Amemiya, T. 1974. Multivariate Regression and Simultaneous Equation Models When the Dependent Variables are Truncated Normal. *Econometrica*. 42: 999–1012.

Amemiya, T. 1978. The Estimation of a Simultaneous Equation Generalized Probit Model. *Econometrica*. 46: 1193–1205.

Amemiya, T. 1979. The Estimation of a Simultaneous Equation Tobit Model, *International Economic Review*.

Anderson, T. W. 1958. *An Introduction to Multivariate Statistical Analysis*. New York: Wiley.

Berkson, J. 1944. Application of the Logistic Function to Bio-Assay. *Journal of the American Statistical Association*. 39: 357–365.

Bishop, Y., S. Fienberg, and P. Holland. 1975. *Discrete Multivariate Analysis*, Cambridge, Mass.: MIT Press.

Block, H., and J. Marschak. 1960. Random Orderings and Stochastic Theories of Response. In *Contributions to Probability and Statistics*, ed. I. Olkin. Stanford, Calif.: Stanford University Press.

Blumen, A., M. Kogan, and J. McCarthy. 1955. *The Industrial Mobility of Labor as a Stochastic Process*. Ithaca, N. Y.: Cornell University Press.

Cox, D. 1970. *Analysis of Binary Data*. London: Methuen.

Fair, R., and D. Jaffee. 1972. Methods of Estimation for Markets in Disequilibrium. *Econometrica*. 40: 497–514.

Finney, D. 1971. *Probit Analysis*. New York: Cambridge University Press.

Ginsberg, R. 1972. Incorporating Causal Structure and Exogenous Information with Probabilistic Models with Special Reference to Choice, Gravity, Migration and Markov-Chains. *Journal of Mathematical Sociology*. 2: 83–101.

Goodman, L., and W. Kruskal. 1954. Measures of Association for Cross-Classifications. *Journal of the American Statistical Association*. 49: 732–764.

Gronau, R. 1974. Wage Comparisons—A Selectivity Bias. *Journal of Political Economy*. 82: 1119–1143.

Haberman, S. 1974. *The Analysis of Frequency Data*. Chicago: University of Chicago Press.

Heckman, J. 1976. The Common Structure of Statistical Models of Truncation, Sample Selection and Limited Dependent Variables and a Simple Estimator for Such Models. *Annals of Economic and Social Measurement*. 5: 475–492.

Heckman, J. 1978. Dummy Endogenous Variables in a Simultaneous Equations System. *Econometrica*. 46: 931–959.

Kendall, M., and J. Stuart. 1976. *Advanced Theory of Statistics*, vol. 3. New York: Hafner.

Luce, R. 1959. *Individual Choice Behavior*. New York: Wiley.

Luce, R., and P. Suppes. 1965. Preference, Utility and Subjective Probability. In *Handbook of Mathematical Psychology*, ed. R. Luce, R. Bush, and E. Galanter, vol. 3, pp. 249–410. New York: Wiley.

Maddala, G. S., and F. Nelson. 1974. Maximum Likelihood Methods for Markets in Disequilibrium. *Econometrica*. 42: 1013–1030.

Manski, C. 1975. Maximum Score Estimation of the Stochastic Utility Model of Choice. *Journal of Econometrics*. 3: 205–228.

McFadden, D., 1973. Conditional Logit Analysis of Qualitative Choice Behavior. In *Frontiers in Econometrics*. ed. P. Zarembka. New York: Academic Press.

Stewman, S. 1976. Markov Models of Occupational Mobility: Theoretical Development and Empirical Tests. *Journal of Mathematical Sociology*. 6: 201–278.

Thurstone, L. 1927. A Law of Comparative Judgment. *Psychological Review*. 34: 273–286.

Tobin, J. 1958. Estimation of Relationships for Limited Dependent Variables. *Econometrica*. 26: 24–36.

Tversky, A. 1972. Elimination by Aspects: A Theory of Choice. *Psychological Review*. 79: 281–299.

Warner, S. 1963. Multivariate Regression of Dummy Variates Under Normality Assumptions. *Journal of the American Statistical Association*. 58: 1054–1063.

I STATISTICAL ANALYSIS OF DISCRETE PROBABILITY MODELS

1 Alternative Estimators and Sample Designs for Discrete Choice Analysis

Charles F. Manski and Daniel McFadden

1.1 Introduction

In many scientific studies using evidence from uncontrolled experiments, interest centers on a postulated causal influence from the attributes and environment of subjects to their responses. The structure of the postulated relationship can be revealed with appropriate statistical methods.

This chapter examines alternative sample designs and estimators for causal models in the case that the set of possible responses is finite—these are termed *quantal response* or *discrete choice* models.[1] The causal relationships are assumed to be specified a priori up to finite parameter vectors.

Recently considerable progress has been made in the development of tractable, statistically sound estimators for particular probabilistic choice models in the context of particular sampling processes. See, for example, McFadden (1973), Westin (1974), Manski (1975), and Manski and Lerman (1977). A considerable empirical literature has also developed. In the area of transportation decisions see Domencich and McFadden (1975) and Lerman and Ben-Akiva (1976). For work on educational choices see Kohn, Manski, and Mundel (1976) and Radner and Miller (1975). Bureaucratic behavior has been studied by McFadden (1976a). A comprehensive survey of methodological and empirical work through mid-1976, both published and unpublished, is provided by McFadden (1976b).

Concentrating as it has on the study of special models and sampling processes, the literature on discrete choice analysis has not until now included any investigation of the general quantal response model estimation problem. On the other hand the statistical literature on the analysis of discrete data (Bishop et al. 1975, Haberman 1974, Goodman and Kruskal 1954) has largely ignored the special opportunities introduced by the presence of an a priori causal structure. This void has prevented a full appreciation of the statistical properties of the estimation methods now

Research was supported in part by the National Science Foundation, through grants SOC72-05551-AO2 and SOC75-22657, to the University of California, Berkeley. Portions of this paper were written while the second author was an Irving Fisher Visiting Professor of Economics at Yale University. We have benefited from discussions with Stephen Cosslett. We claim sole responsibility for errors. This chapter was first circulated during May 1976, and has undergone several revisions.

1. The assumption of a finite response set is inessential for many conclusions in this paper.

routinely used in empirical work. It also has artificially constrained the set of sampling processes and estimators used empirically. Finally, it has obscured the relations between the concerns and methods of quantal response analysis and those of other statistical literatures analyzing discrete data.

The importance of a general theory of quantal response analysis is best illustrated by a series of examples:

1. A study of death rates following surgery under various anesthetics assumes a causal link from anesthetic (and other variables such as patient age, sex, type of operation) to death rate.[2] The objective of the study is to identify high-risk anesthetics by patient type and forecast the impact on death rates of changes in policy for the administration of anesthetics. A sample is first drawn of all patients dying in a selected institution and then of a control group of other surgical patients from the institution. A log-linear probability model is fitted and used to test for the presence of anesthetic effects.[3]

2. A study of college choice by high school seniors assumes a causal link from personal characteristics (SAT, parent's income) and college attributes (cost, distance, quality) to observed choice.[4] The object of the study is to forecast the impact of changing tuition on college enrollments. A random sample of high school seniors in selected states is drawn, and a multinominal logit model is fitted and used to predict enrollments.[5]

3. A study of transportation mode-choice assumes a causal link from travel times and costs, as well as personal characteristics, to choice of auto or bus to work.[6] The object of the study is to predict mode splits in response to changes in bus service. A random sample of households in an urban area is surveyed, and a discriminant analysis is applied to the auto-using and bus-using subpopulations.[7]

The common thread of these examples is the postulate of a causal link between explanatory variables and a response variable and the objective of predicting the impact on responses of changes in explanatory variables. The examples differ in their sample designs, estimation methods, and, as

2. Bishop and Mosteller (1969).
3. Bishop, Fienberg, and Holland (1975).
4. Kohn, Manski, and Mundel (1976).
5. McFadden (1973).
6. McGillvrey (1970). A medical study with this structure is the Framingham study of coronary disease; see Truett, Cornfield, and Kannel (1967).
7. Kendall and Stuart (1976, chapter 44) and T. Anderson (1958).

will be clarified later, in the appropriateness of their estimation methods for the sample designs utilized.

For the purposes of this chapter the quantal response problem can be defined by a finite set $\mathbf{C} = \{1, \ldots, M\}$ of mutually exclusive alternative responses, a space of attributes $\mathbf{Z}$, assumed to be a measurable subset of a finite-dimensional Euclidean space, a probability density, $p(\mathbf{z})$, $[\mathbf{z} \in \mathbf{Z}]$, giving the distribution of attributes in the population, and a *response probability*, or *choice probability*, $P(i \mid \mathbf{z}, \boldsymbol{\theta}^*)$, specifying the conditional probability of selection of alternative $i \in \mathbf{C}$, given attributes $\mathbf{z} \in \mathbf{Z}$.[8] Prior knowledge of causal structure is assumed to allow the analyst to specify the response model $P(i \mid \mathbf{z}, \cdot\,)$ up to a parameter vector $\boldsymbol{\theta}^*$ contained in a subset $\boldsymbol{\Theta}$ of a finite-dimensional Euclidean space. The analyst's problem is to estimate $\boldsymbol{\theta}^*$ from a suitable sample of subjects and their associated responses.

The probability density of $(i, \mathbf{z})$ pairs in the population is given by

$$f(i, \mathbf{z}) = P(i \mid \mathbf{z}, \boldsymbol{\theta}^*) p(\mathbf{z}), \quad [(i, \mathbf{z}) \in \mathbf{C} \times \mathbf{Z}]. \tag{1.1}$$

The analyst can draw observations of $(i, \mathbf{z})$ pairs from $\mathbf{C} \times \mathbf{Z}$ according to one of various sampling rules. The problem of interest is first, given any sampling rule, to determine how $\boldsymbol{\theta}^*$ may be estimated and second to assess the relative advantages of alternative sampling rules and estimation methods.

The data layout can be visualized using a contingency table, as illustrated in figure 1.1. Throughout this paper, we assume an infinite population and sampling with replacement. Then an observation $(i, \mathbf{z})$ occurs in the population with frequency $f(i, \mathbf{z})$. The row sums give the marginal distribution of attributes $p(\mathbf{z})$, while the column sums give the population shares of responses $Q(i)$. The joint frequency $f(i, \mathbf{z})$ can be written either in terms of the conditional probability of i given $\mathbf{z}$ (the choice probability) or, by Bayes' law, in terms of the conditional probability of $\mathbf{z}$ given i,

8. More formally, assume there exists a probability space $(\mathbf{T}, \mathscr{A}, \lambda)$ of subjects and a measurable mapping F from $\mathbf{T}$ into $\mathbf{C} \times \mathbf{Z}$, where $(\mathbf{Z}, \mathscr{Z}, \nu)$ is a subset of a finite-dimensional Euclidean space with measure ν. Define a measure π on $(\mathbf{Z}, \mathscr{Z})$: for $\mathbf{W} \in \mathscr{Z}$, $\pi(\mathbf{W}) = \lambda\{\mathbf{t} \in \mathbf{T}: F(\mathbf{t}) \in \mathbf{C} \times \mathbf{W}\}$. Assume π absolutely continuous with respect to ν, and let $p(\mathbf{z})$ be the density on $\mathbf{Z}$ satisfying $\pi(\mathbf{W}) = \int_{\mathbf{W}} p(\mathbf{z}) \nu(d\mathbf{z})$. Similarly define a measure ϕ on $\mathbf{C} \times \mathbf{Z}$: for $\mathbf{A} \in 2^{\mathbf{C}} \otimes \mathscr{Z}$, $\phi(\mathbf{A}) = \lambda(\{\mathbf{t} \in \mathbf{T}: F(\mathbf{t}) \in \mathbf{A}\})$, assume ϕ absolutely continuous with respect to $\sigma \otimes \nu$, where σ is a counting measure on $\mathbf{C}$, and write $\phi(\mathbf{A}) = \int_{\mathbf{A}} f(i, \mathbf{z})\, \sigma(di) \nu(d\mathbf{z})$. Define $P(i \mid \mathbf{z}) = f(i, \mathbf{z})/p(\mathbf{z})$ to be the conditional probability of i given $\mathbf{z}$. Assume $P(i \mid \mathbf{z}) = P(i \mid \mathbf{z}, \boldsymbol{\theta}^*)$ is known a priori up to a parameter vector $\boldsymbol{\theta}^*$.

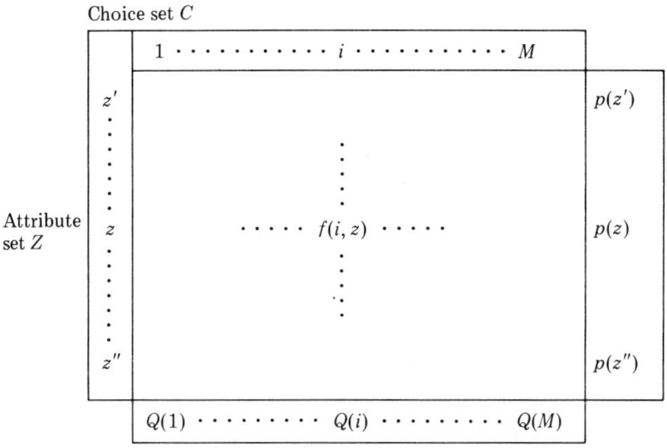

Figure 1.1
Contingency table layout for the population

$$q(\mathbf{z} \mid i, \boldsymbol{\theta}^*) = \frac{f(i, \mathbf{z})}{Q(i)} = \frac{P(i \mid \mathbf{z}, \boldsymbol{\theta}^*) p(\mathbf{z})}{Q(i)},$$

where

$$Q(i) = \sum_{\mathbf{z} \in \mathbf{Z}} f(i, \mathbf{z}) = \sum_{\mathbf{z} \in \mathbf{Z}} P(i \mid \mathbf{z}, \boldsymbol{\theta}^*) p(\mathbf{z}).$$ [9]

The feature of the quantal response problem which distinguishes it from the general analysis of discrete data is the postulate that the response probability $P(i \mid \mathbf{z}, \boldsymbol{\theta}^*)$ belongs to a known parametric family and reflects an underlying link from $\mathbf{z}$ to i which will continue to hold even if the distribution $p(\mathbf{z})$ of the explanatory variables changes.[10]

In general, given a population with a probability distribution specified by $f(i, \mathbf{z})$, one might in the absence of any knowledge of the process relating i's to $\mathbf{z}$'s obtain a random sample from $\mathbf{C} \times \mathbf{Z}$ and directly examine the

9. If $\mathbf{Z}$ is not countable, the summation becomes integration, i.e.,

$$Q(i) = \int_{\mathbf{Z}} f(i, \mathbf{z}) \nu(d\mathbf{z}) = \int_{\mathbf{Z}} P(i \mid \mathbf{z}, \boldsymbol{\theta}^*) p(\mathbf{z}) \nu(d\mathbf{z}).$$

We shall employ summation notation throughout this chapter, leaving to the reader the obvious substitution of integrals with respect to the measure ν on $\mathbf{Z}$, or with respect to the measure $\sigma \otimes \nu$ on $\mathbf{C} \times \mathbf{Z}$, as appropriate.

10. This postulate is fundamental to the concept of "scientific explanation." If the response probability function is invariant over populations with different distributions of attributes, then it defines a "law" which transcends the character of specific sets of data. Otherwise the model provides only a device for summarizing data and fails to provide a key ingredient of "explanation"—predictive power.

joint distribution $f(i, \mathbf{z})$. This exploratory data analysis approach is exemplified by the literature on associations in contingency tables, where it is assumed that $\mathbf{Z}$ is finite. See, for example, Goodman and Kruskal (1954), Haberman (1974), and Bishop, Fienberg, and Holland (1975).

Alternately, if one believes that the elements of $\mathbf{C}$ index conceptually distinct populations of $\mathbf{z}$ values, then the natural analytical approach is to decompose $f(i, \mathbf{z})$ into the product $f(i, \mathbf{z}) = q(\mathbf{z} \mid i)Q(i)$, where $q(\mathbf{z} \mid i)$ gives the distribution of $\mathbf{z}$ within the population indexed by i and $Q(i)$ is the proportion of the population with this index. This is the approach taken in discriminant analysis. There, prior knowledge allows the analyst to specify $q(\mathbf{z} \mid i)$ up to a parametric family, and a sample suitable for estimating the unknown parameters is obtained from the subpopulation i. See, for example, Anderson (1958), Warner (1963), and Kendall and Stuart (1976).

Finally, when a well-defined process generates a value from $\mathbf{C}$ given any $\mathbf{z} \in \mathbf{Z}$, then the decomposition $f(i, \mathbf{z}) = P(i \mid \mathbf{z}, \boldsymbol{\theta}^*)p(\mathbf{z})$ is appropriate. This decomposition, and the attendant focus on the structural relation embodied in $P(i \mid \mathbf{z}, \boldsymbol{\theta}^*)$, is clearly the natural one for the analysis of choice data.[11] A separate and interesting question is whether specific parametric models permit estimation of the parameter vector $\boldsymbol{\theta}^*$ of $P(i \mid \mathbf{z}, \boldsymbol{\theta}^*)$ from convenient parameterizations of $f(i, \mathbf{z})$ or $q(\mathbf{z} \mid i)$.[12]

The present chapter attempts to provide a general theory of estimation for quantal response models. The scope of our investigation is as follows: we consider the problem of estimating $\boldsymbol{\theta}^*$ from stratified samples of $(i, \mathbf{z})$ observations. A stratified sampling process is one in which the analyst establishes a finite or countable set $\mathbf{B}$ indexing strata. A stratum $\mathbf{b} \in \mathbf{B}$ is defined by a measurable subset $\mathbf{A_b} \subseteq \mathbf{C} \times \mathbf{Z}$.[13] The analyst establishes a sample size for stratum $\mathbf{b}$ by design, or by sampling from a suitable probability distribution over $\mathbf{B}$. To obtain an $(i, \mathbf{z})$ observation from

11. Interest in the structural approach to discrete data analysis predates modern choice analysis by at least forty years, in Thurstone's (1927) development of the probit model. Later extensive contributions were made in the field of bioassay. See in particular Cox (1970) and Finney (1971).

12. It is well known, for example, that a multinomial logit model of the response probability function is consistent, in the presence of suitable parameter restrictions, with a log-linear model of $f(i, \mathbf{z})$ or with a multivariate normal model of $q(\mathbf{z} \mid i, \boldsymbol{\theta}^*)$. Hence estimation of these models may provide convenient alternatives to direct estimation of the multinomial logit model, *provided* the parameter restrictions implied by the response probability model are imposed. See McFadden (1976c).

13. Formally, $\mathbf{A_b} \in 2^{\mathbf{C}} \otimes \mathscr{Z}$. The definition of stratified sampling used here is more general than a common usage in which the $\mathbf{A_b}$, $\mathbf{b} \in \mathbf{B}$ form a partition of $\mathbf{C} \times \mathbf{Z}$. We allow the stratum subsets $\mathbf{A_b}$ to overlap.

stratum $\mathbf{B}$, the analyst samples at random from within $\mathbf{A_b}$. A *random sample* is the special case $\mathbf{B} = \{1\}$ and $\mathbf{A}_1 = \mathbf{C} \times \mathbf{Z}$.

Within the class of all stratification rules two symmetric types of stratification are of particular statistical and empirical interest. In exogenous sampling the analyst partitions $\mathbf{Z}$ into subsets $\mathbf{Z_b}$, $\mathbf{b} \in \mathbf{B}$ and lets $\mathbf{A_b} = \mathbf{C} \times \mathbf{Z_b}$. In endogenous or choice based sampling he partitions $\mathbf{C}$ into subsets $\mathbf{C_b}$, $\mathbf{b} \in \mathbf{B}$ and lets $\mathbf{A_b} = \mathbf{C_b} \times \mathbf{Z}$. Less formally, in exogenous sampling the analyst selects decision makers and observes their choices, while in choice-based sampling the analyst selects alternatives and observes decision makers choosing them. In figure 1.1 "fine partition" exogenous sampling corresponds to stratifying on rows and then sampling randomly from each row, while fine partition choice-based sampling corresponds to stratifying on columns and then sampling randomly from each column.

Section 1.2 formally introduces the general stratified sampling process and specifies the likelihood of an observation obtained through an arbitrary stratification or drawn via an exogenous or choice-based sampling rule. Comparison of the various likelihood forms suggests that the problem of parameter estimation in choice-based samples will differ qualitatively from the estimation problem in exogenous samples.

Because of its generality of application and classical asymptotic efficiency properties, maximum likelihood estimation provides a natural focus for our study.[14] In sections 1.3 through 1.7 we make a detailed statistical examination of maximum likelihood estimation of $\boldsymbol{\theta}^*$ in both exogenous and choice-based samples. We find that application of maximum likelihood is wholly classical in exogenous samples. In choice-based samples, however, the form and properties of the maximum likelihood estimate (MLE) depend crucially on whether the analyst has available certain prior information, namely, the marginal distributions $p(\mathbf{z})$ and $Q(i)$. Some interesting results also emerge concerning the value of prior knowledge of the marginal distributions in reducing the asymptotic variance of the estimates. Section 1.8 contains a discussion of estimation in general stratified samples.

14. An additional reason for our focusing on maximum likelihood derives from the nonexperimental nature of empirical choice studies in economics. Empirical studies typically draw samples of observations of real-world decisions rather than of decisions made in controlled settings. The resultant inability to obtain repetitive observations of choices for given values of the attributes $\mathbf{z}$ prevents the use of estimators that require repetitions for effectiveness. (Some such estimators are Berkson's method and minimum chi-square. See Amemiya 1976.)

The question of optimal sample design inevitably must be raised in an investigation such as ours. Unfortunately the nonlinear structure inherent in all choice models has prevented our making much progress on this problem. In particular, given almost any interesting class of designs and reasonable definition of optimality, selection of the best design within the class requires prior knowledge of $\boldsymbol{\theta}^*$, the parameters to be estimated. Hence an explicitly Bayesian approach to the design problem seems necessary. The present paper does not take on this task. Instead we limit ourselves to a general discussion of the optimal design problem and to a listing of the few classical results we have been able to obtain. These matters constitute the subject of section 1.9.

Basic asymptotic properties for the estimators presented in the text can be found in the appendixes concluding this chapter.

1.2 The Likelihood of an Observation under Alternative Stratified Sampling Processes

In this section we describe a general stratified process for drawing observations from $\mathbf{C} \times \mathbf{Z}$, and the associated likelihood of observations. As before, let $\mathbf{B}$ be a finite or countable set indexing strata and $\mathbf{A_b}$ a measurable subset of $\mathbf{C} \times \mathbf{Z}$ for each $\mathbf{b} \in \mathbf{B}$. We assume that the analyst draws an a priori fixed sample size of N observations by independent sampling with replacement. We assume that the analyst takes an observation by first drawing a stratum $\mathbf{b}$ from a probability distribution H on $\mathbf{B}$.[15] Then he draws an observation $(i, \mathbf{z})$ at random from $\mathbf{A_b}$.[16]

15. Under this protocol the stratum subsample sizes are random, with a multinomial distribution with probabilities $H(\mathbf{b})$. An immediate generalization, left to the reader, is to allow the distributions of subsample sizes to vary with N, with a limiting distribution H. The alternative protocol of fixing subsample sizes leads to likelihood functions with the same kernels, and hence to the same estimators, as the case of random subsample sizes. With a mild abuse of the definition of likelihood, the analysis for random subsample sizes can be applied to the case of fixed subsample sizes, with the $H(\mathbf{b})$ interpreted as fixed sampling proportions.
16. More generally one can characterize a stratum $\mathbf{b}$ by a *censoring rule* $\xi_{\mathbf{b}}(i, \mathbf{z})$ which specifies the probability that a vector $(i, \mathbf{z})$ will be retained in the sample, given its occurrence in the population and the protocol for recording observations from stratum $\mathbf{b}$. Then the likelihood of *observing* the vector $(i, \mathbf{z})$, given stratum $\mathbf{b}$, is $f(i, \mathbf{z})\, \xi_{\mathbf{b}}(i, \mathbf{z}) / \Sigma_{\mathbf{C} \times \mathbf{Z}} f(j, \mathbf{y}) \xi_{\mathbf{b}}(j, \mathbf{y})$. We restrict our attention to the case where $\xi_{\mathbf{b}}$ is the indicator function for the set $\mathbf{A_b}$, corresponding to random sampling within $\mathbf{A_b}$.

Under this stratified sampling procedure the likelihood of drawing stratum $\mathbf{b}$ and observation $(i, \mathbf{z}) \in \mathbf{A_b}$ is[17]

$$\lambda(i, \mathbf{z}, \mathbf{b}) = \frac{f(i, \mathbf{z}) H(\mathbf{b})}{\sum_{\mathbf{A_b}} f(j, \mathbf{y})} = \frac{P(i \mid \mathbf{z}, \boldsymbol{\theta}^*) p(\mathbf{z}) H(\mathbf{b})}{\sum_{\mathbf{A_b}} P(j \mid \mathbf{y}, \boldsymbol{\theta}^*) p(\mathbf{y})}. \tag{1.2}$$

It is important to point out that while every $(\mathbf{B}, H)$ pair and associated family of subsets $\mathbf{A_b}$ defines a unique stratified sampling process, and hence a unique likelihood function, distinct sampling processes may yield the same likelihood function. In particular consider any pseudorandom sample in which the sets $\mathbf{A_b}$ partition $\mathbf{C} \times \mathbf{Z}$ and $H(\mathbf{b}) = \Sigma_{\mathbf{A_b}} f(j, \mathbf{y})$ for all $\mathbf{b} \in \mathbf{B}$. From (1.2) the true likelihood for each process in this class has the form associated with random sampling,

$$\lambda_r(i, \mathbf{z}) = f(i, \mathbf{z}) = P(i \mid \mathbf{z}, \boldsymbol{\theta}^*) p(\mathbf{z}). \tag{1.3}$$

Consider now an exogenous sampling process, where we establish in $\mathbf{Z}$ a collection of measurable subsets $\mathbf{Z_b}$, $\mathbf{b} \in \mathbf{B}$, and let $\mathbf{A_b} = \mathbf{C} \times \mathbf{Z_b}$.[18] Then the likelihood of drawing stratum $\mathbf{b} \in \mathbf{B}$ and observation $(i, \mathbf{z}) \in \mathbf{A_b}$ under exogenous stratified sampling has the general form

$$\lambda_e(i, \mathbf{z}, \mathbf{b}) = P(i \mid \mathbf{z}, \boldsymbol{\theta}^*) g(\mathbf{z} \mid \mathbf{b}) H(\mathbf{b}), \tag{1.4}$$

where

$$g(\mathbf{z} \mid \mathbf{b}) = \frac{p(\mathbf{z})}{\sum_{\mathbf{Z_b}} p(\mathbf{y})}.$$

17. We impose the regularity condition that there is a positive probability of observations from each stratum, that is $\Sigma_{\mathbf{A_b}} f(i, \mathbf{z}) H(\mathbf{b}) > 0$ for each $\mathbf{b} \in \mathbf{B}$. By definition $\lambda(i, \mathbf{z}, \mathbf{b}) = 0$ for $(i, \mathbf{z}) \notin \mathbf{A_b}$. We also assume that the stratum from which each observation $(i, \mathbf{z})$ is drawn is recorded. Otherwise the likelihood of $(i, \mathbf{z})$ is the sum of the probabilities of $(i, \mathbf{z})$ being drawn from each stratum.

18. A note regarding the definition of $\mathbf{Z}$ and $\mathbf{B}$ may be useful for practitioners. Often in exogenous sampling the stratification is based on attributes which do not directly influence choice. For example, we may partition a population according to residence and sample people at varying rates across areas. Formally the "residential area" attributes can be incorporated into the definition of $\mathbf{z}$ even if choice probabilities are assumed to depend on this attribute only trivially. Then $\mathbf{B}$ corresponds to a partition of $\mathbf{Z}$, and knowledge of $\mathbf{z}$ is sufficient to identify the stratum $\mathbf{b}$ from which it is drawn.

An important simple case is "fine stratification" of $\mathbf{Z}$, with $\mathbf{B} = \mathbf{Z}$, implying $g(\mathbf{z} \mid \mathbf{b}) = 1$ if $\mathbf{z} = \mathbf{b}$ and zero otherwise. Then, letting $g(\mathbf{z}) = H(\mathbf{b})$ for $\mathbf{b} = \mathbf{z}$, the likelihood is[19]

$$\lambda_e(i, \mathbf{z}) = P(i \mid \mathbf{z}, \boldsymbol{\theta}^*) g(\mathbf{z}).$$

In deriving results for exogenous stratified sampling, we limit our analysis to the fine stratification case, leaving the obvious generalization to the reader.

The derivation of the choice-based sampling likelihood is analogous, but the resulting expression is quite different. In choice-based sampling we establish a family $\mathbf{C_b}$ of subsets of $\mathbf{C}$ for $\mathbf{b} \in \mathbf{B}$ and let $\mathbf{A_b} = \mathbf{C_b} \times \mathbf{Z}$. Then the likelihood of drawing stratum $\mathbf{b}$ and observation $(i, \mathbf{z}) \in \mathbf{A_b}$ is

$$\lambda_c(i, \mathbf{z}, \mathbf{b}) = \frac{P(i \mid \mathbf{z}, \boldsymbol{\theta}^*) p(\mathbf{z}) H(\mathbf{b})}{Q(\mathbf{b} \mid \boldsymbol{\theta}^*)}, \tag{1.5}$$

where

$$Q(\mathbf{b} \mid \boldsymbol{\theta}^*) = \sum_{\mathbf{C_b} \times \mathbf{Z}} P(j \mid \mathbf{y}, \boldsymbol{\theta}^*) p(\mathbf{y}).$$

Comparison of equations (1.2), (1.4), and (1.5) indicates the qualitative difference between the exogenous and choice-based sampling likelihoods and the nature of both of these relative to the general stratified expression. In exogenous sampling, when the likelihood is considered a function of the unknown parameters $\boldsymbol{\theta}^*$, the kernel is the choice probability function $P(i \mid \mathbf{z}, \boldsymbol{\theta})$, $\boldsymbol{\theta} \in \boldsymbol{\Theta}$, regardless of the manner in which $\mathbf{Z}$ is stratified or the probability measure H imposed. In choice-based samples, on the other hand, the kernel is $P(i \mid \mathbf{z}, \boldsymbol{\theta}) / Q(\mathbf{b} \mid \boldsymbol{\theta})$, since the marginal distribution Q is dependent on $\boldsymbol{\theta}^*$.[20] In general stratified sampling the kernel is the expression $P(i \mid \mathbf{z}, \boldsymbol{\theta}) / S(\mathbf{b} \mid \boldsymbol{\theta})$, where $S(\mathbf{b} \mid \boldsymbol{\theta}) = \Sigma_{\mathbf{A_b}} P(j \mid \mathbf{y}, \boldsymbol{\theta}) p(\mathbf{y})$.

We note for later use the special cases in which exogenous and choice-based processes yield random samples from $\mathbf{C} \times \mathbf{Z}$. The exogenous

19. This likelihood form is the same as would be obtained in a stimulus response experimental setting in which the analyst presents subjects with choice sets and observes their responses. In this context the distribution $g(\mathbf{z})$ characterizes the experimental design.

20. If the relation between Q and $\boldsymbol{\theta}^*$ is ignored, the choice-based sampling kernel reduces to the exogenous sampling one. It might be thought that ignoring this relation would lower the efficiency of estimators for $\boldsymbol{\theta}^*$ but not affect their consistency. In fact recognition of the relation turns out to be generally necessary for consistency, and the choice-based sampling kernel cannot be reduced to the exogenous sampling one. See in particular section 1.5.

sampling likelihood takes the form (1.3) if $\mathbf{B} = \mathbf{Z}$ and $H(\mathbf{z}) = p(\mathbf{z})$. In choice-based samples we require $H(\mathbf{b}) = Q(\mathbf{b} \mid \boldsymbol{\theta}^*)$ for each $\mathbf{b} \in \mathbf{B}$. It is important to recognize that, while the true likelihood of exogenous and choice-based sampling observations are identical when the above conditions are met, the respective likelihood function kernels remain distinct.

1.3 Estimation of the Choice Model Parameters

Assume now that a sequence of observations $\mathbf{x} = (i_n, \mathbf{z}_n), n = 1, \ldots, \infty$, is drawn by independent sampling according to a fixed stratified rule. Given a sample consisting of the first N of such observations, we should like to estimate the choice model parameters $\boldsymbol{\theta}^*$.

For reasons set forth earlier we shall focus attention on maximum likelihood estimation of $\boldsymbol{\theta}^*$. Furthermore we shall limit the formal investigation of estimation to samples obtained by exogenous or choice-based stratifications. Consideration of these two forms of stratification is sufficient to illuminate the important statistical and computational issues that arise within the general class of stratified rules.[21] Moreover the great empirical usefulness of the exogenous and choice-based sampling processes makes their examination of interest per se.

Within the class of choice-based stratifications, we shall, for notational simplicity, explicitly consider only those for which $\mathbf{B} = \mathbf{C}$, so that $\mathbf{C}_i = [i]$, all $i \in \mathbf{C}$. In this case the choice-based sampling likelihood has the form

$$\lambda_c(i, \mathbf{z}) = \frac{P(i \mid \mathbf{z}, \boldsymbol{\theta}^*) p(\mathbf{z}) H(i)}{Q(i)}. \tag{1.6}$$

Extension of our results from this fine partition of $\mathbf{C}$ to stratifications involving aggregations of alternatives is straightforward.

Inspection of the choice-based sampling likelihood, given in equation (1.5), suggests that in choice-based samples the estimation of $\boldsymbol{\theta}^*$ requires, or at least is facilitated by, prior knowledge of the marginal distributions $p(\mathbf{z})$, $\mathbf{z} \in \mathbf{Z}$ and $Q(i)$, $i \in \mathbf{C}$. On the other hand, in exogenous samples, it appears from equation (1.4) that such prior knowledge should be of little, if any, consequence. A major thrust of our work is to clarify the role that knowledge of the p and $\mathbf{Q}$ distributions actually plays in the estimation of $\boldsymbol{\theta}^*$, both in exogenous and in choice-based samples. We examine, in turn,

21. See section 1.8.

estimation in four informational situations: section 1.4, p and $\mathbf{Q}$ both known; section 1.5, p known and $\mathbf{Q}$ unknown; section 1.6, p unknown and $\mathbf{Q}$ known; section 1.7, p and $\mathbf{Q}$ both unknown.[22]

Certain assumptions used in the statistical proofs will be maintained throughout the analysis. These are as follows:

ASSUMPTION 1.1 (Positivity): For each $(i, \mathbf{z}) \in \mathbf{C} \times \mathbf{Z}$, either $P(i \mid \mathbf{z}, \boldsymbol{\theta}) > 0$ for all $\boldsymbol{\theta} \in \boldsymbol{\Theta}$ or $P(i \mid \mathbf{z}, \boldsymbol{\theta}) = 0$ for all $\boldsymbol{\theta} \in \boldsymbol{\Theta}$.

ASSUMPTION 1.2 (Identifiability): For each $\boldsymbol{\theta} \in \boldsymbol{\Theta}$ such that $\boldsymbol{\theta} \neq \boldsymbol{\theta}^*$, there exists $\mathbf{A} \subset \mathbf{C} \times \mathbf{Z}$ such that $\Sigma_{\mathbf{A}} P(j \mid \mathbf{y}, \boldsymbol{\theta}) p(\mathbf{y}) \neq \Sigma_{\mathbf{A}} P(j \mid \mathbf{y}, \boldsymbol{\theta}^*) p(\mathbf{y})$. Moreover the stratified sampling process satisfies the conditions $\bigcup_{\mathbf{b} \in \mathbf{B}} \mathbf{A}_{\mathbf{b}} = \mathbf{C} \times \mathbf{Z}$, and for each $\mathbf{b} \in \mathbf{B}$, $\Sigma_{\mathbf{A}_{\mathbf{b}}} P(j \mid \mathbf{y}, \boldsymbol{\theta}^*) p(\mathbf{y}) > 0$ and $H(\mathbf{b}) > 0$.

ASSUMPTION 1.3 (The parameter space): The space $\boldsymbol{\Theta} \subset \mathbf{R}^K$ is compact. Furthermore there exists an open set $\boldsymbol{\Theta}'$ in $\mathbf{R}^K$ such that $\boldsymbol{\theta}^* \in \boldsymbol{\Theta}' \subset \boldsymbol{\Theta}$.

ASSUMPTION 1.4 (The attribute space): The space $\mathbf{Z} \subset \mathbf{R}^J$ is compact.

ASSUMPTION 1.5 (Regularity): $P(i \mid \mathbf{z}, \boldsymbol{\theta})$ is continuous in $\mathbf{C} \times \mathbf{Z} \times \boldsymbol{\Theta}$. Furthermore for each $(i, \mathbf{z}) \in \mathbf{C} \times \mathbf{Z}$ such that $P(i \mid \mathbf{z}, \boldsymbol{\theta}^*) > 0$, this function is three times continuously differentiable for all $\boldsymbol{\theta}$ in a neighborhood of $\boldsymbol{\theta}^*$. Let $\mathbf{R}$ denote the $K \times M$ matrix with columns

$$\sum_{\mathbf{z}} \frac{\partial P(i \mid \mathbf{z}, \boldsymbol{\theta}^*)}{\partial \boldsymbol{\theta}} p(\mathbf{z}),$$

22. While our present concern is theoretical, it is certainly relevant to ask whether prior knowledge of p or $\mathbf{Q}$ is likely to be available in practice.

It appears knowledge of $\mathbf{Q}$ is quite often obtainable. For example, the $\mathbf{Q}$ distribution appropriate to a study of travel mode choices can be determined from aggregate traffic count data by mode. Similarly for a study of college choices freshmen enrollment figures by school yield the necessary marginal distribution of choices. Finally, in a nonchoice quantal response context, consider the problem of modeling the incidence of cancer within a population. Here $\mathbf{Q}$ is given by the crude fraction of the relevant population contracting the disease. Statistics such as the above are often readily available in published sources.

In contrast, knowledge of p seems to be rarely in the possession of the analyst. In applications the attributes $\mathbf{z}$ are usually multidimensional transformations of detailed raw population attributes. Knowledge of the joint distribution of such attributes is generally quite difficult to obtain.

Beyond these cases it is of interest to explore the consequences of partial information on p or $\mathbf{Q}$ (e.g., knowledge of some marginal distributions of p or of some components of $\mathbf{Q}$), or of sampling information on these distributions. This topic has been investigated by Cosslett in chapter 2.

where M represents the number of alternatives in $\mathbf{C}$. Then rank $\mathbf{R} = \min(K, M-1)$.

Other assumptions used in particular contexts will be introduced as necessary.[23]

1.4 Estimation with p and $\mathbf{Q}$ Both Known

Assume that both p and $\mathbf{Q}$ are a priori known. Under exogenous sampling a maximum likelihood estimate will be any solution to the problem

$$\max_{\boldsymbol{\theta} \in \boldsymbol{\Theta}_0} \sum_{n=1}^{N} \ln P(i_n \mid \mathbf{z}_n, \boldsymbol{\theta}), \tag{1.7}$$

where $\boldsymbol{\Theta}_0 = \{\boldsymbol{\theta} \in \boldsymbol{\Theta} \mid Q(i) = \Sigma_{\mathbf{Z}} P(i \mid \mathbf{z}, \boldsymbol{\theta}) p(\mathbf{z}),\ i \in \mathbf{C}\}$ and where terms of the log likelihood not belonging to its kernel have been suppressed.

Under fine partition choice-based sampling, the criterion will be

$$\max_{\boldsymbol{\theta} \in \boldsymbol{\Theta}_0} \left\{ \sum_{n=1}^{N} \ln P(i_n \mid \mathbf{z}_n, \boldsymbol{\theta}) - \sum_{n=1}^{N} \ln \sum_{\mathbf{Z}} P(i_n \mid \mathbf{z}, \boldsymbol{\theta}) p(\mathbf{z}) \right\}. \tag{1.8}$$

But $\boldsymbol{\theta} \in \boldsymbol{\Theta}_0$ implies $Q(i) = \Sigma_{\mathbf{Z}} P(i \mid \mathbf{z}, \boldsymbol{\theta}) p(\mathbf{z})$, all $i \in \mathbf{C}$. Hence (1.8) reduces to

$$\max_{\boldsymbol{\theta} \in \boldsymbol{\Theta}_0} \sum_{n=1}^{N} \ln P(i_n \mid \mathbf{z}_n, \boldsymbol{\theta}), \tag{1.9}$$

23. A brief description of the role of each of the five maintained assumptions may be helpful:

Assumption 1.1 implies that the support of the likelihood function is independent of $\boldsymbol{\theta}$, both in exogenous and in choice-based samples. This assumption is necessary to use standard methods to prove consistency. Note that the assumption provides a way to deal with alternatives that are unavailable to decision makers. For such $(i, \mathbf{z})$ pairs simply set $P(i \mid \mathbf{z}, \boldsymbol{\theta}) = 0$, all $\boldsymbol{\theta} \in \boldsymbol{\Theta}$.

Assumption 1.2 states that the choice model $P(i \mid \mathbf{z}, \boldsymbol{\theta}^*)$ is observationally distinguishable from all other models of the form $P(i \mid \mathbf{z}, \boldsymbol{\theta})$, $\boldsymbol{\theta} \neq \boldsymbol{\theta}^*$, and that the sampling process is such that $\boldsymbol{\theta}^*$ is identified.

Assumption 1.5 and the second part of assumption 1.3 are used in demonstrating asymptotic normality for the various estimators. In general these assumptions are innocuous.

Assumption 1.4 and the first parts of assumptions 1.3 and 1.5 are used in consistency proofs. These assumptions can be substantially weakened if additional structure is imposed on the choice probabilities $P(i \mid \mathbf{z}, \boldsymbol{\theta})$ and the marginal distribution p. In particular it is possible to develop proofs that allow one to assume that $\boldsymbol{\Theta} = \mathbf{R}^K$ and $\mathbf{Z} = \mathbf{R}^J$.

a form identical to exogenous sampling criterion (1.7). Hence (1.7) is the maximum likelihood estimator under either exogenous or choice-based sampling.

The estimator (1.7) is a constrained maximum likelihood estimator of the type examined by Aitchison and Silvey (1958). Such constrained estimators are certain to be consistent for $\boldsymbol{\theta}^*$ if the relevant unconstrained estimators, those maximizing over $\boldsymbol{\Theta}$, can be shown to be consistent. The latter estimators are treated in section 1.5 and are proved to be consistent in appendix 1.11. Given consistency, asymptotic normality for both the constrained and unconstrained estimators can be demonstrated using assumptions 1.3 and 1.5; see appendix 1.12.

Let $\mathbf{J}_e$ and $\mathbf{J}_c$ be the exogenous and choice-based sampling asymptotic information matrices.[24] That is,

$$\mathbf{J}_e = \sum_{\mathbf{Z}} \sum_{i \in \mathbf{C}} P(i \mid \mathbf{z}, \boldsymbol{\theta}^*) g(\mathbf{z}) \frac{\partial \ln P(i \mid \mathbf{z}, \boldsymbol{\theta}^*)}{\partial \boldsymbol{\theta}} \frac{\partial \ln P(i \mid \mathbf{z}, \boldsymbol{\theta}^*)}{\partial \boldsymbol{\theta}'}; \tag{1.10}$$

$$\mathbf{J}_c = \sum_{\mathbf{Z}} \sum_{i \in \mathbf{C}} \frac{P(i \mid \mathbf{z}, \boldsymbol{\theta}^*) p(\mathbf{z}) H(i)}{Q(i)} \frac{\partial \ln P(i \mid \mathbf{z}, \boldsymbol{\theta}^*)}{\partial \boldsymbol{\theta}} \frac{\partial \ln P(i \mid \mathbf{z}, \boldsymbol{\theta}^*)}{\partial \boldsymbol{\theta}'}$$
$$- \sum_{i \in \mathbf{C}} H(i) \frac{\partial \ln \sum_{\mathbf{Z}} P(i \mid \mathbf{z}, \boldsymbol{\theta}^*) p(\mathbf{z})}{\partial \boldsymbol{\theta}} \frac{\partial \ln \sum_{\mathbf{Z}} P(i \mid \mathbf{z}, \boldsymbol{\theta}^*) p(\mathbf{z})}{\partial \boldsymbol{\theta}'}. \tag{1.11}$$

Let M be the number of alternatives in $\mathbf{C}$, and define the $K \times M$ matrix $\mathbf{R}$ by

$$\mathbf{R} = \left[\frac{\partial \sum_{\mathbf{Z}} P(i \mid \mathbf{z}, \boldsymbol{\theta}^*) p(\mathbf{z})}{\partial \boldsymbol{\theta}} \right]_{i=1}^{M}. \tag{1.12}$$

By assumption 1.5 the rank of $\mathbf{R}$ is $\rho(\mathbf{R}) = \min(K, M - 1)$. Define $\hat{\mathbf{R}}$ to be a $K \times \rho(\mathbf{R})$ matrix whose columns are linearly independent columns of $\mathbf{R}$. Then the exogenous and choice-based sampling asymptotic covariances can be shown to be

$$\mathbf{V}_e = \mathbf{J}_e^{-1} - \mathbf{J}_e^{-1} \hat{\mathbf{R}} (\hat{\mathbf{R}}' \mathbf{J}_e^{-1} \hat{\mathbf{R}})^{-1} \hat{\mathbf{R}}' \mathbf{J}_e^{-1}, \tag{1.13}$$
$$\mathbf{V}_c = \mathbf{J}_c^{-1} - \mathbf{J}_c^{-1} \hat{\mathbf{R}} (\hat{\mathbf{R}}' \mathbf{J}_c^{-1} \hat{\mathbf{R}})^{-1} \hat{\mathbf{R}}' \mathbf{J}_c^{-1}, \tag{1.14}$$

24. When the stratification of $\mathbf{Z}$ in exogenous sampling is not fine, $g(\mathbf{z})$ is replaced by $g(\mathbf{z} \mid \mathbf{b}) H(\mathbf{b})$, and there is an additional summation over $\mathbf{B}$.

and $\rho(\mathbf{V}_e) = \rho(\mathbf{V}_c) = K - \rho(\hat{\mathbf{R}}) = K - \rho(\mathbf{R})$.[25] Note that, when $\rho(\mathbf{R}) = K$, the constraint equations have a unique solution for $\boldsymbol{\theta}^*$, and $\mathbf{V}_e = \mathbf{V}_c = \mathbf{0}$. In many applications the response probability model is specified to include "alternative-specific" parameters. In general there will be $M - 1$ independent parameters of this type, implying $\rho(\mathbf{R}) = M - 1 \leqq K$, and $\rho(\mathbf{V}_e) = \rho(\mathbf{V}_c) = K + 1 - M$.

Although the estimation criteria (1.7) and (1.9) are identical and the matrices $\mathbf{V}_e$ and $\mathbf{V}_c$ have the same rank, these two matrices are generally not equal. Equality of the two covariances, implying equivalence of the MLE asymptotic distributions under exogenous and choice-based sampling, should be expected only when both processes yield random samples. For here, and only here, are the exogenous and choice-based sampling likelihoods identical. Equality of $\mathbf{V}_e$ and $\mathbf{V}_c$ can in fact be demonstrated in this special case.[26] More generally the structure of $\mathbf{V}_e$ depends on the sampling distribution g, and the structure of $\mathbf{V}_c$ depends on the distribution H. We defer until section 1.9 further discussions of these structures.

Given specified exogenous or choice-based sampling processes, and assuming that the requisite prior information is available, the criteria (1.7) or (1.9), respectively, provide asymptotically efficient estimators for $\boldsymbol{\theta}^*$. Unfortunately the use of these estimators will often not be computationally practical because characterization of the parameter space $\boldsymbol{\Theta}_0$ requires solution of complicated constraint equations.[27] When this problem arises,

25. For equations (1.13) and (1.14) to be meaningful, $\mathbf{J}_e$ and $\mathbf{J}_c$ must be nonsingular. A crucial, necessary condition for such nonsingularity is provided by assumption 1.2. Given this and the regularity implied by assumption 1.5, nonsingularity of $\mathbf{J}_e$ follows.

26. To show this, first recall that $\rho(\mathbf{R}) = K$ implies $\mathbf{V}_e = \mathbf{V}_c = 0$ trivially. If $\rho(\mathbf{R}) < K$, let $\mathbf{D}$ be a $K \times (K - \rho(\mathbf{R}))$ matrix of rank $K - \rho(\mathbf{R})$ such that $\mathbf{R}'\mathbf{D} = \mathbf{O}$. Then $\mathbf{V}_e$ and $\mathbf{V}_c$ can be written in the forms

$$\mathbf{V}_e = \mathbf{D}(\mathbf{D}'\mathbf{J}_e\mathbf{D})^{-1}\mathbf{D}';$$
$$\mathbf{V}_c = \mathbf{D}(\mathbf{D}'\mathbf{J}_c\mathbf{D})^{-1}\mathbf{D}'.$$

See Rao (1973, p. 77, prob. 33) for this result.

Note that in random exogenous sampling, $g(\mathbf{z}) = p(\mathbf{z})$, all $\mathbf{z}$, while in random choice-based sampling, $H(i) = Q(i)$, all $i \in \mathbf{C}$. It is easy to show that, when the exogenous and choice-based samples are both random, equations (1.10) and (1.11) have the following relation: $\mathbf{J}_c = \mathbf{J}_e - \mathbf{R}\mathbf{A}^{-1}\mathbf{R}'$, where $\mathbf{R}$ was defined in (1.12) and $\mathbf{A}$ is the $M \times M$ diagonal matrix with diagonal elements $\mathbf{Q}$. It now follows that in random samples

$$\mathbf{V}_c = \mathbf{D}[\mathbf{D}'(\mathbf{J}_e - \mathbf{R}\mathbf{A}^{-1}\mathbf{R}')\mathbf{D}]^{-1}\mathbf{D}' = \mathbf{D}(\mathbf{D}'\mathbf{J}_e\mathbf{D})^{-1}\mathbf{D}' = \mathbf{V}_e.$$

27. See Manski and Lerman (1977) for a discussion relevant to this problem. Within this chapter see section 1.6 for a tractable approximation to the constraint equations that does not involve the distribution p.

it may be preferable to use one of the simpler, but less efficient, estimators to be introduced in sections 1.5 through 1.7.

1.5 Estimation with p Known and Q Unknown

When the marginal distribution p is known, but $\mathbf{Q}$ is not, the exogenous and choice-based sampling likelihood functions are those given in (1.7) and (1.8), respectively, but the maximization is over the full parameter space $\boldsymbol{\Theta}$ rather than the constrained set $\boldsymbol{\Theta}_0$. That is, in exogenous samples we have

$$\max_{\theta \in \boldsymbol{\Theta}} \sum_{n=1}^{N} \ln P(i_n \mid \mathbf{z}_n, \boldsymbol{\theta}), \tag{1.15}$$

and in choice-based samples

$$\max_{\theta \in \boldsymbol{\Theta}} \sum_{n=1}^{N} \ln P(i_n \mid \mathbf{z}_n, \boldsymbol{\theta}) - \sum_{n=1}^{N} \ln \sum_{\mathbf{Z}} P(i_n \mid \mathbf{z}, \boldsymbol{\theta}) p(\mathbf{z}). \tag{1.16}$$

Here in contrast to the situation in section 1.4 the exogenous and choice-based MLE's are clearly distinct. It should be apparent from the form of the exogenous sampling likelihood, given in (1.4), that in exogenous samples the MLE remains that expressed in (1.15) if either or both of p and $\mathbf{Q}$ are unknown. Hence for exogenous samples the informational cases in sections 1.6 and 1.7 will introduce no considerations beyond those relevant in this section. For choice-based samples, on the other hand, the cases in the following two sections will be seen to raise a number of new and analytically interesting issues.

Given assumptions 1.1 through 1.5, the estimators (1.15) and (1.16) can each be proved consistent and asymptotically normal within their respective sampling regimes. See appendixes 1.11 and 1.12 for the relevant proofs. The asymptotic covariance matrices are the inverted information matrices $\mathbf{J}_e^{-1}$ and $\mathbf{J}_c^{-1}$, respectively, from equations (1.10) and (1.11).

As in section 1.4 no general relation exists between the two covariance structures, but one does exist when both the exogenous and choice-based rules yield random samples. In this special case we have already stated that

$$\mathbf{J}_c^{-1} = [\mathbf{J}_e - \mathbf{R}\mathbf{A}^{-1}\mathbf{R}']^{-1},$$

where $\mathbf{R}$ was defined in (1.12) and $\mathbf{A}$ is the $M \times M$ diagonal matrix with diagonal elements $\mathbf{Q}$. The matrix $\mathbf{R}\mathbf{A}^{-1}\mathbf{R}'$ is positive semidefinite with rank

$\rho(\mathbf{R}) = \min(K, \; M-1)$. This implies that $\mathbf{J}_c^{-1} - \mathbf{J}_e^{-1}$ is positive semidefinite and non-null. Because the exogenous and choice-based sampling true likelihoods are identical, in a random sample both estimators (1.15) and (1.16) are consistent for $\boldsymbol{\theta}^*$. It follows that, when the sample is random, criterion (1.15) is statistically preferable to criterion (1.16) in large samples. This choice is sensible on computational grounds as well.

The option to estimate $\boldsymbol{\theta}^*$ either through (1.15) or through (1.16) is limited to the random sample situation. In other than random samples the estimator (1.15) is inconsistent when applied to a choice-based sample. This result, proved in Manski and Lerman (1977), has an interesting implication. In forming the choice-based sampling likelihood function one cannot in general treat $Q(i), i \in \mathbf{C}$, as a set of free parameters and ignore the set of equations relating $\mathbf{Q}$ to $\boldsymbol{\theta}^*$. Treatment of $\mathbf{Q}$ as a function of $\boldsymbol{\theta}$ is necessary for consistency, not simply useful for efficiency.

1.6 Estimation with p Unknown and Q Known

It was pointed out earlier that in empirical contexts prior knowledge of the marginal distribution p is not likely to be available. We have also noted that in exogenous samples the MLE for $\boldsymbol{\theta}^*$ in the absence of such prior knowledge remains that given in (1.15). Therefore in this section and the next we shall focus on the empirically important and analytically interesting problem of estimating $\boldsymbol{\theta}^*$ in choice-based samples when p is not known.

In the case where p is characterized by a finite vector of unknown parameters, joint maximum likelihood estimation of $\boldsymbol{\theta}$ and p is entirely classical, satisfying

$$\max_{(\boldsymbol{\theta}, \tilde{p}) \in \boldsymbol{\Theta} \times \mathscr{P}_0} \sum_{n=1}^{N} \ln \frac{P(i_n \mid \mathbf{z}_n, \boldsymbol{\theta}) \tilde{p}(\mathbf{z}_n)}{\sum_{\mathbf{y} \in \mathbf{Z}} P(i_n \mid \mathbf{y}, \boldsymbol{\theta}) \tilde{p}(\mathbf{y})}, \tag{1.17}$$

subject to

$$Q(i) = \sum_{\mathbf{Z}} P(i \mid \mathbf{z}, \boldsymbol{\theta}) \tilde{p}(\mathbf{z}), \quad i \in \mathbf{C}, \tag{1.18}$$

where $\mathscr{P}_0$ is the (finite-dimensional) space of admissible probability distributions $\tilde{p}$. This case always holds if the attribute space $\mathbf{Z}$ is finite. Then the data can be formatted in a finite contingency table, with $\tilde{p}$ an unknown multinomial distribution. The large statistical literature on analysis of contingency tables, particularly the log-linear probability model (Bishop et al. 1975), provides methods for this problem. Alternately p may be restricted to a finite-dimensional family on nonfinite attribute spaces by imposing a priori distributional assumptions. Important cases in the literature are the restriction of p to be multivariate normal on $\mathbf{Z} = \mathbf{R}^J$ (see McFadden-Reid 1975) or to be a finite mixture of multivariate normal distributions, as assumed in discriminant analysis (see Ladd 1966, Warner 1963, McFadden 1976c).

When p is not restricted to a finite-dimensional space, it is no longer obvious that solutions to (1.17) will exist and be computationally tractable, or will enjoy the asymptotic properties associated with classical maximum likelihood estimators. However, several estimators that do not involve p and are statistically and computationally appealing have been found for this problem, including a nonclassical maximum likelihood estimator.

The first estimator developed for this problem was the "weighted" exogenous sampling MLE (WESML) of Manski and Lerman (1977). Here the criterion is

$$\max_{\boldsymbol{\theta} \in \boldsymbol{\Theta}} \sum_{n=1}^{N} w(i_n) \ln P(i_n \mid \mathbf{z}_n, \boldsymbol{\theta}), \tag{1.19}$$

where $w(i) = Q(i)/H(i), i \in \mathbf{C}$, are known positive weights. This estimator was shown by Manski and Lerman to be consistent for $\boldsymbol{\theta}^*$ and asymptotically normal under assumptions 1.1 through 1.5. Appendixes 1.11 and 1.12 restate these results. Cosslett, chapter 2, has shown subsequently that a more efficient estimator results in (1.19) if one uses the weights $w_N(i) = Q(i)N/N_i$, where N_i is the number of observations in stratum i.[28]

The asymptotic covariance matrix for the estimator with weights $w(i)$ is

$$\mathbf{V}_c = \mathbf{A}^{-1}\mathbf{B}\mathbf{A}^{-1}, \tag{1.20}$$

where

$$\mathbf{A} = \sum_{\mathbf{Z}} \sum_{i \in \mathbf{C}} P(i \mid \mathbf{z}, \boldsymbol{\theta}^*) \frac{\partial \ln P(i \mid \mathbf{z}, \boldsymbol{\theta}^*)}{\partial \boldsymbol{\theta}} \frac{\partial \ln P(i \mid \mathbf{z}, \boldsymbol{\theta}^*)}{\partial \boldsymbol{\theta}'} p(\mathbf{z}),$$

$$\mathbf{B} = \sum_{\mathbf{Z}} \sum_{i \in \mathbf{C}} P(i \mid \mathbf{z}, \boldsymbol{\theta}^*) \frac{Q(i)}{H(i)} \frac{\partial \ln P(i \mid \mathbf{z}, \boldsymbol{\theta}^*)}{\partial \boldsymbol{\theta}} \frac{\partial \ln P(i \mid \mathbf{z}, \boldsymbol{\theta}^*)}{\partial \boldsymbol{\theta}'} p(\mathbf{z}).$$

28. Note that the weights w_N can be used even if H is unknown and that $w_N(i)$ converges almost surely to $w(i) = Q(i)/H(i)$. The covariance matrices for both cases follow by application of lemma 5, appendix 1.12.

In a random sample $Q(i) = H(i)$ for $i \in \mathbf{C}$, the estimators (1.15) and (1.19) are identical, and $\mathbf{V}_c = \mathbf{J}_e^{-1}$. A significant advantage of the weighted estimator is its computational simplicity—existing exogenous sampling maximum likelihood computer programs are easily modified to yield the WESML estimate and its asymptotic variance matrix.

A second approach to the estimation of $\boldsymbol{\theta}^*$, yielding a nonclassical maximum likelihood estimator, has been developed by Cosslett in chapter 2. Suppose $\mathbf{z}$ is countable, and the constrained optimization problem (1.17) is considered over the set $\mathscr{P}$ of all probability distributions on $\mathbf{z}$. Cosslett has shown that, if the conditions for a Langrangian representation of the constrained optimization problem (1.17) are satisfied, then (1.17) is equivalent to the problem

$$\max_{\boldsymbol{\theta} \in \boldsymbol{\Theta}} \min_{\mathbf{m} \in \Delta_N} \sum_{n=1}^{N} \ln\left[\frac{P(i_n \mid \mathbf{z}_n, \boldsymbol{\theta})}{\sum_{i \in \mathbf{C}} m(i) P(i \mid \mathbf{z}_n, \boldsymbol{\theta})}\right], \tag{1.21}$$

where

$$\Delta_N = \left\{\mathbf{m} \in \mathbf{R}^M \,\middle|\, \sum_{i \in \mathbf{C}} m(i) Q(i) = 1 \quad \text{and} \quad \sum_{i \in \mathbf{C}} m(i) P(i \mid \mathbf{z}_n, \boldsymbol{\theta}) > 0 \quad \text{for} \quad n = 1, \ldots, N\right\}. \tag{1.22}$$

Thus (1.21) provides a nonclassical maximum likelihood estimator of $\boldsymbol{\theta}^*$. A related estimator is obtained by replacing $\boldsymbol{\Delta}_N$ in (1.21) by the positive simplex

$$\boldsymbol{\Delta} = \left\{\mathbf{m} \in \mathbf{R}^M \,\middle|\, \sum_{i \in \mathbf{C}} m(i) Q(i) = 1 \quad \text{and} \quad m(i) > 0 \quad \text{for} \quad i \in \mathbf{C}\right\}. \tag{1.23}$$

The substitution of $\boldsymbol{\Delta}$ for $\boldsymbol{\Delta}_N$ can be shown to leave unchanged the asymptotic distribution of the estimator (1.21).

Cosslett has shown the estimator given by (1.21) to be consistent and asymptotically normal under assumptions 1.1 through 1.5. The Lagrangian multipliers $m(i)$ satisfy

$$m(i) \xrightarrow{\text{a.s.}} \frac{H(i)}{Q(i)}. \tag{1.24}$$

The asymptotic covariance matrix of the estimator is

$$\mathbf{V} = [\mathbf{A}_{\theta\theta} - \mathbf{A}_{\theta\mathbf{m}} \mathbf{A}_{\mathbf{mm}}^{-1} \mathbf{A}'_{\theta\mathbf{m}}]^{-1}, \tag{1.25}$$

where

$$\mathbf{A}_{\alpha\beta} = -\sum_{i \in \mathbf{C}} \sum_{\mathbf{z} \in \mathbf{Z}} p(\mathbf{z}) \frac{H(i)}{Q(i)} P(i \mid \mathbf{z}, \theta^*) \frac{\partial^2}{\partial\alpha\partial\beta'} \ln \frac{P(i \mid \mathbf{z}, \theta)}{\sum_{j \in \mathbf{C}} m(j) P(j \mid \mathbf{z}, \theta)}, \tag{1.26}$$

with α and β equal to θ or $\mathbf{m} = (m(1), \ldots, m(M-1))$.[29] Since $\mathbf{A}_{\mathbf{mm}}$ is negative definite, and $\mathbf{A}_{\theta\mathbf{m}}$ is in general non-null, the matrix $\mathbf{A}_{\theta\theta}^{-1}$ is larger than $\mathbf{V}$, in the sense that $\mathbf{A}_{\theta\theta}^{-1} - \mathbf{V}$ is non-null and positive semidefinite.

A third approach to the estimation of θ^* not requiring knowledge of p begins with the identity

$$p(\mathbf{z}) = \sum_{j \in \mathbf{C}} Q(j) q(\mathbf{z} \mid j), \tag{1.27}$$

where, it will be recalled, the conditional distribution q is defined by $f(i, \mathbf{z}) = P(i \mid \mathbf{z}, \theta^*) p(\mathbf{z}) = Q(i) q(\mathbf{z} \mid i)$.

Observe first that if both of the distributions $\mathbf{Q}$ and q were a priori known, the value θ^* could be determined directly as the unique solution to the set of equations

$$P(i \mid \mathbf{z}, \theta) = \frac{Q(i) q(\mathbf{z} \mid i)}{\sum_{j \in \mathbf{C}} Q(j) q(\mathbf{z} \mid j)}, \quad \text{for } (i, \mathbf{z}) \in \mathbf{C} \times \mathbf{Z}. \tag{1.28}$$

We note that the uniqueness of θ^* as the solution to these equations is guaranteed by assumption 1.2 and that the solution does not require the sample data $(i, \mathbf{z})_n$, $n = 1, \ldots, N$.

In general the distribution q, like p, will not be a priori known.[30]

29. The constraint $\Sigma_{i \in \mathbf{C}} m(i) Q(i) = 1$ is used to eliminate $m(M)$ prior to differentiation. The derivative is evaluated at θ^* and $m(i) = H(i)/Q(i)$.

30. In a recent paper Carroll and Relles (1976) assumed that the distributions $q(\mathbf{z} \mid j)$, $j \in \mathbf{C}$, each fall within the multivariate normal family (see also Warner 1963). Given what is assumed to be a random sample of observations, they estimate the parameters for each such distribution and subsequently estimate the choice probabilities by

$$\hat{P}(i \mid \mathbf{z}, \theta^*) = \frac{Q(i) \hat{q}(\mathbf{z} \mid i)}{\sum_{j \in \mathbf{C}} Q(j) \hat{q}(\mathbf{z} \mid j)},$$

where $\hat{q}(\mathbf{z} \mid j)$ is the estimate for $q(\mathbf{z} \mid j)$ and $\hat{P}(i \mid \mathbf{z}, \theta^*)$ is the estimated choice

Nevertheless the identity (1.27) can be used advantageously. Observe that for each $\boldsymbol{\theta} \in \boldsymbol{\Theta}$ and $i \in \mathbf{C}$ we can write

$$\sum_{\mathbf{Z}} P(i \mid \mathbf{z}, \boldsymbol{\theta}) p(\mathbf{z}) = \sum_{j \in \mathbf{C}} Q(j) \sum_{\mathbf{Z}} P(i \mid \mathbf{z}, \boldsymbol{\theta}) q(\mathbf{z} \mid j). \tag{1.29}$$

Now for each i and $\boldsymbol{\theta}$ the sum $\Sigma_{\mathbf{Z}} P(i \mid \mathbf{z}, \boldsymbol{\theta}) q(\mathbf{z} \mid j)$ can be interpreted as the expectation of $P(i \mid \mathbf{z}, \boldsymbol{\theta})$ with respect to the distribution $q(\mathbf{z} \mid j)$, which is the distribution of $(j, \mathbf{z})$ pairs drawn at random from the subpopulation $\{j\} \times \mathbf{Z}$. But this is exactly the process by which observations are drawn in choice-based sampling. It follows that, if we let $\mathbf{N}(j)$ be that subset of our sample in which alternative j is selected, and let $N_j = |\mathbf{N}(j)|$, then the expression $1/N_j \, \Sigma_{m \in \mathbf{N}(j)} P(i \mid \mathbf{z}_m, \boldsymbol{\theta})$ is the sample mean of independent observations on $P(i \mid \mathbf{z}, \boldsymbol{\theta})$ when $\mathbf{z}$ is drawn according to the distribution $q(\mathbf{z} \mid j)$. As $N \to \infty$, $N_j/N \xrightarrow{\text{a.s.}} H(j) > 0$ for each $j \in \mathbf{C}$, so $N_j \xrightarrow{\text{a.s.}} \infty$. Hence by the strong law of large numbers, as $N \to \infty$,

$$\begin{aligned} \sum_{j \in \mathbf{C}} \frac{Q(j)}{N_j} \sum_{m \in \mathbf{N}(j)} P(i \mid \mathbf{z}_m, \boldsymbol{\theta}) &\xrightarrow{\text{a.s.}} \sum_{j \in \mathbf{C}} Q(j) \sum_{\mathbf{Z}} P(i \mid \mathbf{z}, \boldsymbol{\theta}) q(\mathbf{z} \mid j) \\ &= \sum_{\mathbf{Z}} P(i \mid \mathbf{z}, \boldsymbol{\theta}) p(\mathbf{z}). \end{aligned} \tag{1.30}$$

The relation (1.30) suggests two estimators for $\boldsymbol{\theta}^*$. First, recalling the criterion (1.9), we might consider solutions to the following problem:

$$\max_{\boldsymbol{\theta} \in \boldsymbol{\Theta}} \sum_{n=1}^{N} \ln P(i_n \mid \mathbf{z}_n, \boldsymbol{\theta}), \tag{1.31}$$

subject to

$$Q(i) = \sum_{j \in \mathbf{C}} \frac{Q(j)}{N_j} \sum_{m \in \mathbf{N}(j)} P(i \mid \mathbf{z}_m, \boldsymbol{\theta}), \quad i \in \mathbf{C}. \tag{1.32}$$

probability.

The problem with this approach is that when the joint distribution $f(i, \mathbf{z})$ is decomposed into the product structure $f(i, \mathbf{z}) = P(i \mid \mathbf{z}, \boldsymbol{\theta}^*) p(\mathbf{z})$, the conditional distribution $q(\mathbf{z} | j)$ is only a derived distribution defined by the relation

$$q(\mathbf{z} \mid j) = \frac{P(i \mid \mathbf{z}, \boldsymbol{\theta}^*) p(\mathbf{z})}{Q(j)}.$$

It follows that in the absence of knowledge of $\boldsymbol{\theta}^*$, we cannot in general a priori place q within the normal or any other parametric family. See McFadden (1976c) for a detailed discussion of the circumstances in which restriction of q to the normal family can be justified.

Second, as an approximation to the criterion (1.16) consider

$$\max_{\theta\in\Theta} \sum_{n=1}^{N} \left[\ln P(i_n \mid \mathbf{z}_n, \theta) - \ln\left[\sum_{j\in\mathbf{C}} \frac{Q(j)}{N_j} \sum_{m\in\mathbf{N}(j)} P(i_n \mid \mathbf{z}_m, \theta)\right]\right]. \tag{1.33}$$

The criterion (1.31) can be reformulated as a Lagrangian problem

$$\max_{\theta\in\Theta} \min_{\mathbf{m}\in\mathbf{R}^M} \sum_{n=1}^{N} \left[\ln P(i_n \mid \mathbf{z}_n, \theta) - m(i_n) \ln\left[\sum_{j\in\mathbf{C}} \frac{Q(j)}{N_j Q(i_n)} \sum_{k\in N(j)} P(i_n \mid \mathbf{z}_k, \theta)\right]\right], \tag{1.34}$$

while (1.33) can be rewritten as the criterion (1.34) with fixed $m(i) = 1$, $i \in \mathbf{C}$.

Under assumptions 1.1 through 1.5 appendixes 1.11 and 1.12 show that the estimator (1.33) is consistent for θ^* and asymptotically normal. The asymptotic properties of (1.31) are not developed here.

Our fourth method for estimating θ^* in the absence of p is quite straightforward. Consider the likelihood under choice-based sampling of observing an alternative i, *conditioned* on an attribute observation $\mathbf{z}$. It follows from (1.5) that this is

$$\lambda_c(i \mid \mathbf{z}) = \frac{\lambda_c(i, \mathbf{z})}{\sum_{j\in\mathbf{C}} \lambda_c(j, \mathbf{z})} = \frac{P(i \mid \mathbf{z}, \theta^*) H(i)/Q(i)}{\sum_{j\in\mathbf{C}} P(j \mid \mathbf{z}, \theta^*) H(j)/Q(j)}. \tag{1.35}$$

Observe that (1.35) does not explicitly involve the distribution p. This suggests estimating θ^* via the conditional MLE

$$\max_{\theta\in\Theta} \sum_{n=1}^{N} \ln \frac{P(i_n \mid \mathbf{z}_n, \theta) H(i_n)/Q(i_n)}{\sum_{j\in\mathbf{C}} P(j \mid \mathbf{z}_n, \theta) H(j)/Q(j)}. \tag{1.36}$$

Note that this criterion results from replacing the undetermined multipliers $m(i)$ in the nonclassical maximum likelihood estimator (1.21) by their probability limits $H(i)/Q(i)$.

Given knowledge of $\mathbf{Q}$ and of the sampling distribution H, the estimator (1.36) is consistent and asymptotically normal for θ^* under assumptions 1.1 through 1.5.[31] See appendixes 1.11 and 1.12 for the relevant proofs. The

31. Cosslett, chapter 2, has shown that a more efficient version of the estimator (1.36) is obtained by replacing H by the empirical subsample frequencies, N_i/N.

conditional MLE has an asymptotic covariance matrix $\mathbf{V}_c$ equal to the inverse of the conditional likelihood information matrix,

$$\mathbf{V}_c^{-1} = \sum_{\mathbf{Z}} p(\mathbf{z}) \sum_{i \in \mathbf{C}} P(i \mid \mathbf{z}, \boldsymbol{\theta}^*) \frac{H(i)}{Q(i)} \frac{\partial \ln P(i \mid \mathbf{z}, \boldsymbol{\theta}^*)}{\partial \boldsymbol{\theta}} \frac{\partial \ln P(i \mid \mathbf{z}, \boldsymbol{\theta}^*)}{\partial \boldsymbol{\theta}'}$$

$$- \sum_{\mathbf{Z}} q(\mathbf{z}) \frac{\partial \ln \left[\sum_{j \in \mathbf{C}} P(j \mid \mathbf{z}, \boldsymbol{\theta}^*) H(j)/Q(j) \right]}{\partial \boldsymbol{\theta}} \cdot$$

$$\frac{\partial \ln \left[\sum_{j \in \mathbf{C}} P(j \mid \mathbf{z}, \boldsymbol{\theta}^*) H(j)/Q(j) \right]}{\partial \boldsymbol{\theta}'}, \tag{1.37}$$

where

$$q(\mathbf{z}) = \sum_{i \in \mathbf{C}} \frac{P(i \mid \mathbf{z}, \boldsymbol{\theta}^*) p(\mathbf{z}) H(i)}{Q(i)}$$

is the marginal likelihood of $\mathbf{z}$ under choice-based sampling. Note also that $\mathbf{V}_c = \mathbf{A}_{\theta\theta}^{-1}$, from (1.26), implying that this estimator is in general less efficient than the estimator given by (1.21).

In the special case of a random sample we have $\Sigma_{j \in \mathbf{C}} P(j \mid \mathbf{z}, \boldsymbol{\theta}) H(j)/Q(j) = \Sigma_{j \in \mathbf{C}} P(j \mid \mathbf{z}, \boldsymbol{\theta}) = 1$ for all $\mathbf{z} \in \mathbf{Z}, \boldsymbol{\theta} \in \boldsymbol{\Theta}$. Hence the estimator (1.36) reduces to the exogeneous sampling MLE (1.15).

All of the estimators (1.19), (1.21), (1.23), (1.33), and (1.36) are computationally tractable, consistent, and asymptotically normal. The weighted estimator (1.19) and conditional estimator (1.36) avoid the introduction of nuisance parameters; (1.19) is particularly easy to compute using existing programs.[32] The nonclassical maximum likelihood estimators, (1.21) or (1.23), are strictly more efficient than the others in large samples. We conclude that, when solution of the saddle-point problem required by (1.21) is computationally feasible, this estimator is the most desirable. In the presence of computational constraints, (1.19) or (1.36) appear best. The remaining estimators are only of theoretical interest.

32. Note that the implicit relation between $\mathbf{Q}$ and $\boldsymbol{\theta}^*$ is not utilized in the estimator (1.36). Nor was it employed in defining the weighted estimator (1.19). Nevertheless both estimators are consistent. This contrasts with the situation faced in estimators (1.9) and (1.16). There consistency required that the relation between $\mathbf{Q}$ and $\boldsymbol{\theta}^*$ be recognized.

1.7 Estimation with p and Q Both Unknown

In this section we consider the estimation of $\boldsymbol{\theta}^*$ when the analyst's specification of the parametric choice model $P(i \mid \mathbf{z}, \cdot)$ constitutes his only prior knowledge of the distribution f over $\mathbf{C} \times \mathbf{Z}$. While this level of prior information is certainly sufficient to estimate $\boldsymbol{\theta}^*$ in exogenous samples, it is not immediately clear that the choice model parameters should be estimable in choice-based samples. Interestingly we have found that consistent estimation is generally still possible in this context.

To obtain suitable estimators, we have considered the criteria (1.19), (1.33), and (1.36) introduced in section 1.6 and have sought to determine whether any of these might be adapted for use when $\mathbf{Q}$ is not known.[33] In particular two adaptations have been investigated. First, we have explored treating $Q(i)$, $i \in \mathbf{C}$, as a set of free parameters and maximizing the objective functions (1.19), (1.33), and (1.36) jointly over $\boldsymbol{\theta}$ and $\mathbf{Q}$ values. Second, we have considered using the equations

$$Q(i) = \sum_{j \in \mathbf{C}} \frac{Q(j)}{N_j} \sum_{n \in \mathbf{N}(j)} P(i \mid \mathbf{z}_n, \boldsymbol{\theta}), \tag{1.38}$$

$i \in \mathbf{C}$, to solve for $\mathbf{Q}$ as a function of $\boldsymbol{\theta}$ and then to maximize the section 1.6 objective functions over $\boldsymbol{\theta}$.

Let $\boldsymbol{\Pi}$ denote a closed subset of the unit simplex in $\mathbf{R}^M$ such that $\mathbf{Q} \in \boldsymbol{\Pi}$. Three criteria for joint estimation of $\boldsymbol{\theta}$ and $\mathbf{Q}$ are

$$\max_{(\boldsymbol{\theta}, \mathbf{Q}) \in \boldsymbol{\Theta} \times \boldsymbol{\Pi}} \frac{1}{N} \sum_{n=1}^{N} \frac{\tilde{Q}(i_n)}{H(i_n)} \ln P(i_n \mid \mathbf{z}_n, \boldsymbol{\theta}); \tag{1.39}$$

$$\max_{(\boldsymbol{\theta}, \mathbf{Q}) \in \boldsymbol{\Theta} \times \boldsymbol{\Pi}} \frac{1}{N} \sum_{n=1}^{N} \ln P(i_n \mid \mathbf{z}_n, \boldsymbol{\theta}) - \frac{1}{N} \sum_{n=1}^{N} \ln \left[\sum_{j \in \mathbf{C}} \frac{\tilde{Q}(j)}{N_j} \sum_{m \in \mathbf{N}(j)} P(i_n \mid \mathbf{z}_m, \boldsymbol{\theta}) \right]; \tag{1.40}$$

$$\max_{(\boldsymbol{\theta}, \mathbf{Q}) \in \boldsymbol{\Theta} \times \boldsymbol{\Pi}} \frac{1}{N} \sum_{n=1}^{N} \ln \frac{P(i_n \mid \mathbf{z}_n, \boldsymbol{\theta}) H(i_n) / \tilde{Q}(i_n)}{\sum_{j \in \mathbf{C}} P(j \mid \mathbf{z}_n, \boldsymbol{\theta}) H(j) / \tilde{Q}(j)}. \tag{1.41}$$

33. We do not consider the criterion (1.31) because in the absence of knowledge of $\mathbf{Q}$ this reduces to the estimator (1.15) which is known to be inconsistent in choice-based samples.

Of these three estimators only (1.41) is generally consistent for the augmented parameter vector $(\boldsymbol{\theta}^*, \mathbf{Q})$. To see why this is so, we examine the limiting behavior of each of the above objective functions. For estimator (1.39), as $N \to \infty$, we have

$$\frac{1}{N} \sum_{n=1}^{N} \frac{\tilde{Q}(i_n)}{H(i_n)} \ln P(i_n \mid \mathbf{z}_n, \boldsymbol{\theta})$$

$$\xrightarrow{\text{a.s.}} \sum_{i \in \mathbf{C}} \tilde{Q}(i) \sum_{\mathbf{Z}} \frac{P(i \mid \mathbf{z}, \boldsymbol{\theta}^*)}{Q(i)} p(\mathbf{z}) \ln P(i \mid \mathbf{z}, \boldsymbol{\theta}).$$

Observe that this limiting form is linear in $\tilde{\mathbf{Q}}$. Therefore its maximum over $\boldsymbol{\Theta} \times \boldsymbol{\Pi}$ must occur at one of the vertices of the simplex $\boldsymbol{\Pi}$. Also for each $i \in \mathbf{C}$ the sum

$$\sum_{\mathbf{Z}} \frac{P(i|\mathbf{z}, \boldsymbol{\theta}^*) p(\mathbf{z})}{Q(i)} \ln P(i|\mathbf{z}, \boldsymbol{\theta})$$

will not generally be maximized at $\boldsymbol{\theta} = \boldsymbol{\theta}^*$. Hence (1.39) cannot be consistent for either $\boldsymbol{\theta}^*$ or $\mathbf{Q}$.

For estimator (1.40) the limiting objective function is

$$\sum_{\mathbf{Z}} \sum_{i \in \mathbf{C}} \frac{P(i|\mathbf{z}, \boldsymbol{\theta}^*) p(\mathbf{z}) H(i)}{Q(i)} \ln P(i|\mathbf{z}, \boldsymbol{\theta})$$

$$- \sum_{i \in \mathbf{C}} H(i) \ln \left[\sum_{j \in \mathbf{C}} \tilde{Q}(j) \sum_{\mathbf{Z}} P(i|\mathbf{z}, \boldsymbol{\theta}) q(\mathbf{z}|j) \right].$$

In this expression let $\boldsymbol{\theta} = \boldsymbol{\theta}^*$, and consider the expression as a function of $\tilde{\mathbf{Q}}$. Clearly the value within $\boldsymbol{\Pi}$ minimizing the second term, and hence maximizing the expression as a whole, depends on the sampling distribution H. Thus $\tilde{\mathbf{Q}} = \mathbf{Q}$ will not generally be the maximizing value, and the estimator (1.40) cannot generally be consistent.

Consider now the conditional MLE (1.41). The limiting objective function here can be written as

$$\sum_{\mathbf{Z}} q(\mathbf{z}) \sum_{i \in \mathbf{C}} \frac{P(i|\mathbf{z}, \boldsymbol{\theta}^*) H(i)/Q(i)}{\sum_{j \in \mathbf{C}} P(j \mid \mathbf{z}, \boldsymbol{\theta}^*) H(j)/Q(j)} \ln \frac{P(i \mid \mathbf{z}, \boldsymbol{\theta}) H(i)/\tilde{Q}(i)}{\sum_{j \in \mathbf{C}} P(j \mid \mathbf{z}, \boldsymbol{\theta}) H(j)/\tilde{Q}(j)},$$

where $q(\mathbf{z})$ is the marginal density of $\mathbf{z}$ under choice-based sampling. One can show that for every $\mathbf{z} \in \mathbf{Z}$, the second sum in the above expression is maximized at $(\boldsymbol{\theta}, \tilde{\mathbf{Q}}) = (\boldsymbol{\theta}^*, \mathbf{Q})$. Thus the expression as a whole is maximized at this point. Consistency is proved by showing that this maximum is unique and the convergence of the objective function (1.41) to its expectation is uniform in $\boldsymbol{\theta}$ and $\mathbf{Q}$; see appendix 1.11. Generally assumptions 1.1 through 1.5 guarantee that these conditions are met. However, there exists an empirically important class of choice models for which assumption 1.2 does not ensure uniqueness of the maximum. These are models of the form

$$P(i|\mathbf{z}, \boldsymbol{\theta}) = \frac{\delta_i F(i, \mathbf{z}, \boldsymbol{\phi})}{\sum_{j \in \mathbf{C}} \delta_j F(j, \mathbf{z}, \boldsymbol{\phi})},$$

where $\boldsymbol{\theta} = (\boldsymbol{\phi}, \delta_j, j \in \mathbf{C})$ and F is a positive-valued function.[34] It is easy to see that, if the choice model has this form, then in estimator (1.41) all parameter pairs $(\delta_j, \tilde{Q}(j))$ yielding the same value for $\delta_j / \tilde{Q}(j)$ are observationally equivalent.[35] Assumption 1.2 is strengthened in appendix 1.11 so as to exclude models of this form and thereby guarantee consistency of (1.41).

Cosslett's argument in chapter 2 shows that (1.41) is the nonclassical MLE for the case considered in this section. Consider the criterion (1.17), without side constraints, and with $\tilde{p}$ any discrete probability distribution. The set of first-order conditions for maximization in $\tilde{p}$ is

$$\frac{s_N(\mathbf{z})}{\tilde{p}(\mathbf{z})} - \frac{\sum_{i \in \mathbf{C}} H(i) P(i|\mathbf{z}, \boldsymbol{\theta})}{\sum_{\mathbf{y} \in \mathbf{Z}} P(i|\mathbf{y}, \boldsymbol{\theta}) \tilde{p}(\mathbf{y})} = 0, \tag{1.42}$$

for $\mathbf{z} \in \mathbf{Z}$, where $s_N(\mathbf{z})$ is the proportion of the sample where attribute value $\mathbf{z}$ is observed. Letting

$$m(i) = \frac{H(i)}{\sum_{\mathbf{y} \in \mathbf{Z}} P(i|\mathbf{y}, \boldsymbol{\theta}) \tilde{p}(\mathbf{y})}, \tag{1.43}$$

in (1.42), one can write

34. An important model within this class is the multinomial logit model having "alternative-specific" dummy variables.
35. In models of this form the parameters $\boldsymbol{\phi}$ may be consistently estimated. It is only the δ and $\mathbf{Q}$ parameters that cannot be identified.

$$\tilde{p}(\mathbf{z}) = \frac{s_N(\mathbf{z})}{\sum_{i \in \mathbf{C}} m(i) P(i|\mathbf{z}, \boldsymbol{\theta})}. \tag{1.44}$$

Substituting this expression in (1.17) yields the criterion

$$\max_{\boldsymbol{\theta} \in \boldsymbol{\Theta}} \max_{\mathbf{m} \in \mathbf{R}_+^M} \sum_{n=1}^{N} \ln \frac{P(i_n|\mathbf{z}_n, \boldsymbol{\theta}) m(i_n)}{\sum_{j \in \mathbf{C}} m(j) P(j|\mathbf{z}_n, \boldsymbol{\theta})}, \tag{1.45}$$

where terms independent of $\boldsymbol{\theta}$ and $\mathbf{m}$ have been dropped. The maximum can be achieved at $\mathbf{m} \in \boldsymbol{\Pi}$, by homogeneity, yielding (1.41), with $m(i) = H(i)/\tilde{Q}(i)$. Hence (1.41) is the nonclassical MLE for the case of p and $\mathbf{Q}$ unknown.

When (1.41) is consistent, it is asymptotically normal (see appendix 1.12), with an asymptotic covariance matrix

$$\mathbf{V}_c = (\mathbf{A}_{\boldsymbol{\theta\theta}} - \mathbf{A}_{\boldsymbol{\theta}\mathbf{m}} \mathbf{A}_{\mathbf{mm}}^{-1} \mathbf{A}_{\mathbf{m}\boldsymbol{\theta}})^{-1}, \tag{1.46}$$

where

$$\mathbf{A}_{\boldsymbol{\alpha\beta}} = -\sum_{i \in \mathbf{C}} \sum_{\mathbf{z} \in \mathbf{Z}} p(\mathbf{z}) \frac{H(i)}{Q(i)} P(i|\mathbf{z}, \boldsymbol{\theta}^*) \frac{\partial^2}{\partial \boldsymbol{\alpha} \partial \boldsymbol{\beta}'} \frac{P(i|\mathbf{z}, \boldsymbol{\theta}) m(i)}{\sum_{j \in \mathbf{C}} P(j \mid \mathbf{z}, \boldsymbol{\theta}) m(j)}, \tag{1.47}$$

with $\boldsymbol{\alpha}$, $\boldsymbol{\beta}$ equal to $\boldsymbol{\theta}$ or $\mathbf{m} = (m(1), \ldots, m(M-1))$ and $m(M)$ eliminated using the constraint $\Sigma_{i \in \mathbf{C}}\, m(i) = 1$.

A second approach to estimation when neither p nor $\mathbf{Q}$ is known begins with the constraint equations $Q(i) = \Sigma_{j \in \mathbf{C}} Q(j)/N_j \Sigma_{n \in \mathbf{N}(j)} P(i|\mathbf{z}_n, \boldsymbol{\theta})$, $i \in \mathbf{C}$, introduced in equation (1.32). Previously we have used these equations to constrain $\boldsymbol{\theta}$ given prior knowledge of $\mathbf{Q}$. Here we propose employing them to solve for $\mathbf{Q}$ as a function of $\boldsymbol{\theta}$.

To characterize the hypothesized solution vector $\mathbf{Q}_N(\boldsymbol{\theta}) = (Q_N(i|\boldsymbol{\theta}), i \in \mathbf{C})$, observe that for each $\boldsymbol{\theta} \in \boldsymbol{\Theta}$, the constraint equations can be written in the form $\mathbf{Q}_N(\boldsymbol{\theta}) = \mathbf{A}_N(\boldsymbol{\theta}) \mathbf{Q}_N(\boldsymbol{\theta})$, where $\mathbf{A}_N(\boldsymbol{\theta})$ is the $M \times M$ matrix whose typical elements are $a_{ij}^N(\boldsymbol{\theta}) = 1/N_j \Sigma_{n \in \mathbf{N}(j)} P(i|\mathbf{z}_n, \boldsymbol{\theta})$. The matrix $\mathbf{A}_N(\boldsymbol{\theta})$ has for every $\boldsymbol{\theta} \in \boldsymbol{\Theta}$ the properties $a_{ij}^N(\boldsymbol{\theta}) \geqq 0$, for all $i, j \in \mathbf{C}$, and $\Sigma_{i \in \mathbf{C}}\, a_{ij}^N(\boldsymbol{\theta}) = 1$, for each $j \in \mathbf{C}$. That is, $\mathbf{A}_N(\boldsymbol{\theta})$ is a stochastic matrix. It follows that $\mathbf{A}_N(\boldsymbol{\theta})$ has the maximal characteristic root $\delta = 1$, implying that the equations $\mathbf{Q}_N(\boldsymbol{\theta}) = \delta \mathbf{A}_N(\boldsymbol{\theta}) \mathbf{Q}_N(\boldsymbol{\theta})$ have a solution for $\delta = 1$. Assumption 1.1 ensures that with probability one, the matrix $\mathbf{A}_N(\boldsymbol{\theta})$ is positive and hence irreducible. It then follows from the Frobenius theorem (see Gantmacher 1959, vol. 2, p. 53) that the characteristic vector corresponding to the root $\delta = 1$ is positive and unique. Therefore the solution $\mathbf{Q}_N(\boldsymbol{\theta})$ must be this characteristic vector, scaled so as to satisfy the constraint $\Sigma_{i \in \mathbf{C}} Q_N(i|\boldsymbol{\theta}) = 1$.

Consider now the solution $\mathbf{Q}(\boldsymbol{\theta})$ to the set of equations $\mathbf{Q}(\boldsymbol{\theta}) = \mathbf{A}(\boldsymbol{\theta})\mathbf{Q}(\boldsymbol{\theta})$, where $\mathbf{A}(\boldsymbol{\theta}) = \operatorname{plim}_{N \to \infty} \mathbf{A}_N(\boldsymbol{\theta}) = (\Sigma_{\mathbf{z}} P(i|\mathbf{z}, \boldsymbol{\theta}) q(\mathbf{z}|j); i, j \in \mathbf{C})$. Observe that at $\boldsymbol{\theta} = \boldsymbol{\theta}^*$ these equations have the solution $\mathbf{Q}(\boldsymbol{\theta}^*) = \mathbf{Q}$ and that for each $\boldsymbol{\theta} \in \boldsymbol{\Theta}$

$$\mathbf{Q}_N(\boldsymbol{\theta}) \xrightarrow{\text{a.s.}} \mathbf{Q}(\boldsymbol{\theta}) \quad \text{as} \quad N \to \infty.$$

While estimators (1.39) and (1.40) are not consistent when maximized over $\boldsymbol{\Theta} \times \boldsymbol{\Pi}$, appendix 1.11 establishes that they are when maximized over $\boldsymbol{\Theta}$, with $\tilde{\mathbf{Q}}$ treated as a parameter and the substitution $\tilde{\mathbf{Q}} = \mathbf{Q}_N(\boldsymbol{\theta})$ made in the first order conditions.[36] We rewrite these estimators as

$$\max_{\theta \in \boldsymbol{\Theta}} \sum_{n=1}^{N} \frac{\tilde{Q}(i_n)}{\mathbf{H}(i_n)} \ln P(i_n|\mathbf{z}_n, \boldsymbol{\theta}) \tag{1.48}$$

$$\max_{\theta \in \boldsymbol{\Theta}} \sum_{n=1}^{N} \left[\ln P(i_n|\mathbf{z}_n, \boldsymbol{\theta}) - \ln \left[\sum_{j \in \mathbf{C}} \frac{\tilde{Q}(j)}{N_j} \sum_{m \in \mathbf{N}(j)} P(i_n|\mathbf{z}_m, \boldsymbol{\theta}) \right] \right] \tag{1.49}$$

with $\tilde{Q}(i) = Q_N(i \mid \boldsymbol{\theta})$, $i \in \mathbf{C}$, substituted in the first-order conditions.

1.8 Estimation in a General Stratified Sample

Recall from (1.2) the expression for the likelihood under a general stratified sampling process $(\mathbf{B}, H)$ of drawing a stratum $\mathbf{b} \in \mathbf{B}$ and an observation $(i, \mathbf{z}) \in \mathrm{A}_{\mathbf{b}}$,

$$\lambda(i, \mathbf{z}, \mathbf{b}) = \frac{P(i|\mathbf{z}, \boldsymbol{\theta}^*) p(\mathbf{z}) H(\mathbf{b})}{S(\mathbf{b}|\boldsymbol{\theta}^*)}, \tag{1.50}$$

where $S(\mathbf{b}|\boldsymbol{\theta}^*) = \Sigma_{\mathbf{A}_\mathbf{b}} P(j|\mathbf{y}, \boldsymbol{\theta}^*) p(\mathbf{y})$.

This general form and the more special choice-based sampling likelihood appear structurally similar, with $S(\mathbf{b}|\boldsymbol{\theta}^*)$ replacing $Q(i|\boldsymbol{\theta}^*)$. In fact most of our results on estimation in choice-based samples extend directly to the general stratified context.

36. The estimator (1.41) will of course continue to be consistent when maximized over the constrained set rather than $\boldsymbol{\Theta} \times \boldsymbol{\Pi}$.

Consider first the case in which the distributions p and $s(\mathbf{b}) = S(\mathbf{b}|\boldsymbol{\theta}^*)$ are a priori known. The maximum likelihood estimator is

$$\max_{\boldsymbol{\theta} \in \boldsymbol{\Theta}_0} \sum_{n=1}^{N} \ln P(i_n|\mathbf{z}_n, \boldsymbol{\theta}), \tag{1.51}$$

where $\boldsymbol{\Theta}_0 = \{\boldsymbol{\theta} \in \boldsymbol{\Theta} \text{ and } s(\mathbf{b}) = \Sigma_{\mathbf{A}_\mathbf{b}} P(j \mid \mathbf{y}, \boldsymbol{\theta}) p(\mathbf{y}), \mathbf{b} \in \mathbf{B}\}$. If p is known but $s(\mathbf{b})$ is not, the MLE is

$$\max_{\boldsymbol{\theta} \in \boldsymbol{\Theta}} \sum_{n=1}^{N} \ln P(i_n|\mathbf{z}_n, \boldsymbol{\theta}) - \sum_{\mathbf{B}} N_\mathbf{b} \ln \sum_{\mathbf{A}_\mathbf{b}} P(j|\mathbf{y}, \boldsymbol{\theta}) p(\mathbf{y}). \tag{1.52}$$

The estimators (1.51) and (1.52) are straightforward generalizations of (1.9) and (1.16), respectively. It is easy to show that under assumptions 1.1 through 1.5 the former estimators have the same asymptotic statistical properties as the latter.

When the distribution p is unknown, but $\mathbf{s}$ is known, a nonclassical maximum likelihood estimator analogous to (1.21) can be derived. Let $\mathbf{A}_\mathbf{b}(\mathbf{z}) = \{i|(i, \mathbf{z}) \in \mathbf{A}_\mathbf{b}\}$. The estimator is

$$\max_{\boldsymbol{\theta} \in \boldsymbol{\Theta}} \min_{\mathbf{m} \in \Delta} \sum_{n=1}^{N} \ln \frac{P(i_n|\mathbf{z}_n, \boldsymbol{\theta})}{\sum_{\mathbf{b} \in \mathbf{B}} m(\mathbf{b}) \sum_{j \in \mathbf{A}_\mathbf{b}(\mathbf{z}_n)} P(j|\mathbf{z}_n, \boldsymbol{\theta})}, \tag{1.53}$$

where $\boldsymbol{\Delta} = \{\mathbf{m}(\mathbf{b}), \mathbf{b} \in \mathbf{B} \mid \Sigma_\mathbf{b} m(\mathbf{b}) s(\mathbf{b}) = 1\}$.

Suppose the sampling process has the property that $\bigcup_\mathbf{B} \mathbf{A}_\mathbf{b}(\mathbf{z}) = \mathbf{C}$ for each $\mathbf{z} \in \mathbf{Z}$. Then this problem admits a weighted exogenous sampling MLE

$$\max_{\boldsymbol{\theta} \in \boldsymbol{\Theta}} \sum_{n=1}^{N} w(i_n, \mathbf{z}_n) \ln P(i_n \mid \mathbf{z}_n, \boldsymbol{\theta}), \tag{1.54}$$

where

$$w(i, \mathbf{z}) = \left[\sum_{\substack{\mathbf{b} \in \mathbf{B} \\ i \in \mathbf{A}_\mathbf{b}(\mathbf{z})}} \frac{N_b}{N s_b} \right]^{-1}$$

A conditional maximum likelihood estimator for the case of p unknown and $\mathbf{s}$ known is

$$\max_{\theta \in \Theta} \sum_{n=1}^{N} \ln \frac{P(i_n \mid \mathbf{z}_n, \theta) N_{\mathbf{b}_n}/s_{\mathbf{b}_n}}{\sum_{c \in \mathbf{B}} (N_c/s_c) \sum_{j \in \mathbf{A}_c(\mathbf{z}_n)} P(j|\mathbf{z}_n, \theta)}. \tag{1.55}$$

Under the stated assumptions, the estimators (1.53) through (1.55) are in general consistent for θ^* and asymptotically normal. The method of proof mirrors that used in demonstrating these properties for the three analogous choice-based sampling estimators (1.21), (1.19), and (1.36).

If neither **s** nor p is known, a generally consistent asymptotically normal estimator is the conditional MLE

$$\max_{(\theta, \tilde{\mathbf{s}}) \in \Theta \times \Pi} \sum_{n=1}^{N} \ln \frac{P(i_n \mid \mathbf{z}_n, \theta) N_{\mathbf{b}_n}/\tilde{s}(\mathbf{b}_n)}{\sum_{\mathbf{c} \in \mathbf{B}} (N_{\mathbf{c}}/\tilde{s}(\mathbf{c})) \sum_{j \in \mathbf{A}_c(\mathbf{z}_n)} P(j \mid \mathbf{z}_n, \theta)}, \tag{1.56}$$

where Π is a closed subset of the unit simplex containing **s**.

It is also possible to generalize to this case the estimators based on the approximation introduced in (1.29) and (1.30). For any stratification **B** write

$$p(\mathbf{y}) \equiv \sum_{\mathbf{b} \in \mathbf{B}} s(\mathbf{b}) q(\mathbf{y} \mid \mathbf{b}), \quad \mathbf{y} \in \mathbf{Z}, \tag{1.57}$$

where $q(\mathbf{y} \mid \mathbf{b}) \equiv \Sigma_{i \in \mathbf{A_b(y)}} P(i \mid \mathbf{y}, \theta^*) p(\mathbf{y})/s(\mathbf{b})$ is the conditional distribution of $\mathbf{y}$ given that the pair $(i, \mathbf{y})$ is drawn from $\mathbf{A_b}$.
We can write

$$s(\mathbf{c}) = \sum_{\mathbf{A_c}} P(j \mid \mathbf{y}, \theta) p(\mathbf{y}) = \sum_{\mathbf{b} \in \mathbf{B}} s(\mathbf{b}) \sum_{\mathbf{A_c}} P(j \mid \mathbf{y}, \theta) q(\mathbf{y} \mid \mathbf{b}), \tag{1.58}$$

for each $\mathbf{c} \in \mathbf{B}$ and $\theta \in \Theta$.

Let $N_{\mathbf{b}}$ denote the number of sample points in $\mathbf{b} \in \mathbf{B}$ and $N_{\mathbf{b}}(\mathbf{y})$ denote the number of these sample points with $\mathbf{z}_n = \mathbf{y}$. If $N_{\mathbf{b}} \to \infty$, the strong law of large numbers implies that for each $\mathbf{b} \in \mathbf{B}$

$$\sum_{\mathbf{A_b}} P(j \mid \mathbf{y}, \theta) \frac{N_{\mathbf{b}}(\mathbf{y})}{N_{\mathbf{b}}} \xrightarrow{\text{a.s.}} \sum_{\mathbf{A_b}} P(j \mid \mathbf{y}, \theta) q(\mathbf{y} \mid \mathbf{b}). \tag{1.59}$$

Hence the approximate relation

$$s(\mathbf{c}) = \sum_{\mathbf{b} \in \mathbf{B}} s(\mathbf{b}) \sum_{\mathbf{A_c}} P(j \mid \mathbf{y}, \theta) \frac{N_{\mathbf{b}}(\mathbf{y})}{N_{\mathbf{b}}} \tag{1.60}$$

can be used in general stratified sampling analogues of the estimators

(1.31), (1.33), (1.48), and (1.49). The covariance matrices for all the general stratified estimators above can be calculated by application of lemma 5 in appendix 1.12.

To conclude this section we reiterate earlier remarks on the special status enjoyed by exogenous samples within the class of all stratifications. It is only in exogenous samples that the terms $\Sigma_{\mathbf{A}_b} P(j \mid \mathbf{y}, \boldsymbol{\theta}) p(\mathbf{y})$, $\mathbf{b} \in \mathbf{B}$, reduce to expressions not involving $\boldsymbol{\theta}$. Hence it is only in such samples that the likelihood function kernel takes the simple form $P(i \mid \mathbf{z}, \boldsymbol{\theta})$. This simplification differentiates the parameter estimation problem in exogenous samples from that encountered under all other stratified sampling rules.

1.9 Selection of a Sample Design and Estimation Method

Sample designs and estimation methods differ in terms of sampling and computation costs and precision of parameter estimates. Cost comparisons are situation-specific, and only a few general observations can be made. Comparison of the precision of alternative estimators can be made for large samples using the asymptotic covariance matrices of the estimators. In a few cases the difference of two covariance matrices is positive semidefinite for all possible parameter vectors, and a uniform ranking can be made. More generally rankings will depend on the true parameter vector and on the true distribution of explanatory variables. Then rankings of designs and estimators will usually require a Bayesian approach utilizing a priori beliefs on the distributions of parameters, perhaps based on pilot samples and previous studies. A systematic treatment of this approach lies outside the scope of this chapter.

Consider sampling costs. In general, substantial economies can be achieved by stratifications designed to make it easier to locate and observe subjects. For example, exogenous cluster sampling, in which respondents are clustered geographically, reduces interviewer access time. Stratification on other exogenous variables, such as employer, may also reduce the cost of locating the subject. In many applications choice-based sampling greatly simplifies location. For example, subjects choosing alternative colleges or travel modes can be sampled economically at the site of choice. Choice-based sampling has the greatest potential economy in applications where some responses are rare (e.g., choice of a seldom used travel mode, or mortality from a surgical procedure with a low mortality rate) or are difficult to observe accurately in an exogenously drawn sample (e.g., a retrospective history of criminal activity).

Considerations of computation cost are relatively unimportant in the choice of an estimation method from those considered in this paper. The primary component of computation costs for these estimators, the evaluation of response probabilities at all sample points, will be common to all.

These estimators in general require iterative solution of a system of nonlinear equations. Estimators with auxiliary parameters, such as (1.21) and (1.41), may require more iterations than those involving $\boldsymbol{\theta}$ alone. Estimators (1.7) and (1.9), requiring computation of expected values over $\mathbf{Z}$ for the constraint equations, may impose a large added computational burden, as may estimators (1.48) and (1.49) requiring determination of the Frobenius characteristic vector of an $M \times M$ matrix at each iteration.

Consider the precision of estimates obtained by alternative methods from alternative sample designs. Note first that the level of precision, and possibly the ranking of alternative methods, will depend on the prior information available on the marginal distributions p and $\mathbf{Q}$. We shall assume the state of this information is fixed. However, it should be noted that in practice the question of drawing observations on p or $\mathbf{Q}$ at some cost in order to utilize more efficient estimators of the response probability function may be an important part of the overall design decision.

First consider alternative exogenous sampling processes. Unless both p and $\mathbf{Q}$ are known, the maximum likelihood estimator (1.15) applies, with an asymptotic covariance matrix given by the inverse of the information matrix $\mathbf{J}_e$ in (1.10). Stratification influences this matrix via the distribution $g(\mathbf{z})$. The simplest case is that of experimental design where $g(\mathbf{z})$ is in effect chosen directly by the analyst. When both p and $\mathbf{Q}$ are known, the estimator (1.7) applies, with the asymptotic covariance matrix $\mathbf{V}_e$ in (1.13). The only result on sample design we have obtained at this level of generality is that an exogenous design dominates a second for the estimator (1.15) if and only if it does so for the estimator (1.7).[37]

To illustrate the problem of exogenous design, we consider the example of two alternatives, a single parameter θ and explanatory variable z, and a

37. A design α *dominates* a design β if $\mathbf{J}_e(\beta)^{-1} - \mathbf{J}_e(\alpha)^{-1}$ is positive semidefinite (p.s.d.). To establish the conclusion, note that α dominates β iff $\mathbf{J}_e(\alpha) - \mathbf{J}_e(\beta)$ is p.s.d. From note 26, $\mathbf{V}_e = \mathbf{D}(\mathbf{D}'\mathbf{J}_e\mathbf{D})^{-1}\mathbf{D}'$ for a matrix $\mathbf{D}$ determined independently of the design. Then $\mathbf{V}_e(\beta) - \mathbf{V}_e(\alpha) = \mathbf{D}[(\mathbf{D}'\mathbf{J}_e(\beta)\mathbf{D})^{-1} - (\mathbf{D}'\mathbf{J}_e(\alpha)\mathbf{D})^{-1}]\mathbf{D}'$ p.s.d. $\Leftrightarrow (\mathbf{D}'\mathbf{J}_e(\beta)\mathbf{D})^{-1} - (\mathbf{D}'\mathbf{J}_e(\alpha)\mathbf{D})^{-1}$ p.s.d. $\Leftrightarrow \mathbf{D}'\mathbf{J}_e(\alpha)\mathbf{D} - \mathbf{D}'\mathbf{J}_e(\beta)\mathbf{D}$ p.s.d. $\Leftrightarrow \mathbf{J}_e(\alpha) - \mathbf{J}_e(\beta)$ p.s.d.

binary logit model $P(1 \mid z, \theta^*) = 1/(1 + e^{-\theta^* z})$, where $\theta^* \neq 0$. Then

$$J_e = \int_{-\infty}^{+\infty} z^2 \frac{e^{-\theta^* z}}{(1 + e^{-\theta^* z})^2} g(z)\,dz = \frac{1}{\theta^{*2}} \int_0^1 \left(\ln \frac{P}{1 - P}\right)^2 P(1 - P)h(P)\,dP,$$

where the second integral is obtained by the transformation of variables $P = 1/(1 + e^{-\theta^* z})$, and h is the distribution of P. The expression $(\ln P/(1 - P))^2 P(1 - P)$ is maximized at P (or $1 - P$) equal to 0.9168. Hence the most efficient design would be one in which z is concentrated at values giving $P(1 \mid z, \theta^*) = 0.9168$ or 0.0832; note that the corresponding z values will depend on the true parameter value θ^*.

Consider now choice-based sample designs. Cosslett investigates in chapter 2 the efficiency of alternative choice-based sample designs and estimators for binary probit, logit, and arctan models with a single explanatory variable. All three models have the form $P(1 \mid z, \theta) = \psi(\theta z)$, where

$$\psi(y) = \begin{cases} \dfrac{1}{\sqrt{2\pi}} \displaystyle\int_{-\infty}^{y} e^{-x^2/2}\,dx & \text{for probit,} \\[2ex] \dfrac{1}{(1 + e^{-y})} & \text{for logit,} \\[2ex] \dfrac{1}{2} + \dfrac{1}{\pi} \tan^{-1} y & \text{for arctan.} \end{cases} \tag{1.61}$$

Choice-based sample designs vary in the proportion of the sample $H(1)$ drawn from the subpopulation choosing alternative 1. The optimal sample design for any estimator is determined by the value of $H(1)$ which minimizes the asymptotic variance of the estimator. Cosslett finds that equal shares designs are relatively robust, giving asymptotic efficiencies close to those obtainable using an optimal design. For the case with Q known and p unknown he finds that the nonclassical maximum likelihood estimator (1.21) is considerably more efficient than the most efficient forms of the estimators (1.19) and (1.36). The last two estimators are comparable in efficiency for many parameter values.

1.10 Conclusion

This chapter has established that the parameters of a choice probability function can be estimated consistently under a variety of stratified sampling procedures. However, the estimator used must be appropriate to the sampling scheme adopted. Practical estimators have been developed for two common sampling methods, exogenous stratification and choice-based sampling, for alternative information conditions on marginal distributions.

Three applications of quantal response models were given as examples. From the results the following conclusions can be drawn:

1. Only the study of college choice parameterizes the response probability function directly, postulating a multinomial logit model. However, the parameterizations in the remaining two examples imply, indirectly, a multinomial logit response probability. In the study of survival rates following surgery, the log-linear model is a direct parameterization of $f(i, \mathbf{z})$, with the schematic form

$$\ln f(i,\mathbf{z}) = \lambda + \alpha_{\mathbf{z}} + \gamma_i + \beta_i'\mathbf{z}, \tag{1.62}$$

with $\mathbf{z}$ assumed finite. This implies

$$P(i \mid \mathbf{z}, \boldsymbol{\theta}) = \frac{e^{\gamma_i + \beta_i'\mathbf{z}}}{\sum_{j\in\mathbf{C}} e^{\gamma_j + \beta_i'\mathbf{z}}}, \tag{1.63}$$

where $\boldsymbol{\theta} = [\gamma_j, \beta_j, j \in \mathbf{C}]$. This is a general multinomial logit form.

The study of transportation mode-choice postulates the posterior distributions $q(\mathbf{z} \mid i)$ to be multivariate normal with means μ_i and common covariance matrix $\boldsymbol{\Sigma}$. Then

$$P(i \mid \mathbf{z}) = \frac{q(\mathbf{z} \mid i)Q(i)}{\sum_{j\in\mathbf{C}} q(\mathbf{z} \mid j)Q(j)}$$

has the form (1.63) with $\beta_i' = \boldsymbol{\mu}_i'\boldsymbol{\Sigma}^{-1}$ and $\gamma_i = \ln Q(i) - 1/2\ \boldsymbol{\mu}_i'\boldsymbol{\Sigma}^{-1}\boldsymbol{\mu}_i$. If either the log-linear joint or the multivariate normal posterior specification is correct, then direct maximum likelihood estimation of these forms, taking into account the sample likelihood resulting from the sampling scheme, should yield consistent estimates of the response probability parameters in (1.63). It should be noted, however, that these specifications, which place a priori restrictions on the distribution of $\mathbf{z}$, may be false even when a direct specification of the response probability in the form (1.63) is correct.[38] In this sense direct parameterization of the response probability function should be more "robust" than indirect specifications. When the response probability function is specified directly to be multinomial logit, but with a more restrictive parameterization than (1.63), the indirect estimation of parameters fitting the log-linear model or by discriminant analysis will not provide efficient estimators even if the conditions for consistency are met; see McFadden (1976c).

2. In light of the preceding paragraph one might assume that each of the three studies takes as its primary parameterization a multinomial logit response probability. Then one can ask whether the estimation method each uses provides consistent estimates of the logit parameters, given the sample design. For the studies of college choice and travel mode, exogenous random sampling is used, and the preceding argument establishes consistency of the estimators under standard regularity conditions. Consider the study of survival following surgery, which uses a choice-based sample. The estimation procedure applies maximum likelihood to $f(i, \mathbf{z})$, without adjustments for the sampling stratification. The likelihood function then converges in probability to

$$L = \sum_{i \in \mathbf{C}} \sum_{\mathbf{z} \in \mathbf{Z}} q(\mathbf{z} \mid i, \boldsymbol{\theta}^*) H(i) \ln f(i, \mathbf{z}, \boldsymbol{\theta})$$

$$= \sum_{i \in \mathbf{C}} \sum_{\mathbf{z} \in \mathbf{Z}} \frac{P(i \mid \mathbf{z}, \boldsymbol{\theta}^*) p(\mathbf{z}) H(i)}{Q(i)} \ln f(i, \mathbf{z}, \boldsymbol{\theta}),$$

where $\boldsymbol{\theta} = ((\gamma_i, \boldsymbol{\beta}_i), (\alpha_o), \boldsymbol{\lambda})$ and $\boldsymbol{\theta}^*$ denotes the true value. Then

$$L = \sum_{\mathbf{z} \in \mathbf{Z}} \left[\sum_{j \in \mathbf{C}} P(j \mid \mathbf{z}, \boldsymbol{\theta}^*) \frac{H(j)}{Q(j)} \right] p(\mathbf{z})$$

$$\sum_{j \in \mathbf{C}} \frac{P(i \mid \mathbf{z}, \boldsymbol{\theta}^*) H(i)/Q(i)}{\sum_{j \in \mathbf{C}} P(j \mid \mathbf{z}, \boldsymbol{\theta}^*) H(j)/Q(j)} \left[\ln P(i \mid \mathbf{z}, \boldsymbol{\theta}) + \ln p(\mathbf{z}) \right]$$

38. When $\mathbf{Z}$ is finite, a saturated log-linear model is "true" in the sense that it describes observations perfectly. However, when the set $\mathbf{Z}$ is made finite by dichotomizing or restricting variables, or when the log-linear model is restricted to exclude some interactions, misspecification is possible.

$$= \sum_{\mathbf{z} \in \mathbf{Z}} \left[\sum_{j \in \mathbf{C}} P(j \mid \mathbf{z}, \boldsymbol{\theta}^*) \frac{H(i)}{Q(j)} \right] p(\mathbf{z})$$

$$\cdot \sum_{j \in \mathbf{C}} \frac{e^{\gamma_i^* + \ln(H(i)/Q(i)) + \boldsymbol{\beta}^{*\prime}_i \mathbf{z}}}{\sum_{j \in \mathbf{C}} e^{\gamma_j^* + \ln(H(j)/Q(j)) + \boldsymbol{\beta}^{*\prime}_j \mathbf{z}}} \ln \frac{e^{\gamma_i + \boldsymbol{\beta}'_i \mathbf{z}}}{\sum_{j \in \mathbf{C}} e^{\gamma_j + \boldsymbol{\beta}'_j \mathbf{z}}}$$

$$+ \sum_{\mathbf{z} \in \mathbf{Z}} \left[\sum_{j \in \mathbf{C}} P(j \mid \mathbf{z}, \boldsymbol{\theta}^*) \frac{H(j)}{Q(j)} \right] p(\mathbf{z}) \ln p(\mathbf{z}).$$

This function is maximized at $\boldsymbol{\beta}_i = \boldsymbol{\beta}_i^*$ and $\gamma_i = \gamma_i^* + \ln\ H(i)/Q(i)$. Applying the consistency theorems in appendix 1.11, one concludes that the study estimates the parameter vectors $\boldsymbol{\beta}_i^*$ in the multinomial logit response function consistently but gives inconsistent estimates of the "alternative-specific" parameters γ_i. This is a property unique to response probability functions with multiplicative alternative-specific effects; see Manski and Lerman (1977).

3. In the college choice and travel mode studies, the use of choice-based sampling offers a substantial potential economy in locating and observing subjects. With stratification, infrequently observed alternatives can be over sampled to achieve a reduction in variance of the estimators for fixed total sample size. This chapter provides consistent, computationally tractable estimators for these stratified sampling procedures.

1.11 Appendix: Consistency of the Estimators

In this section we demonstrate consistency for the estimators (1.7), (1.9), (1.15), (1.16), (1.19), (1.33), (1.36), (1.41), (1.48), and (1.49). All of these estimators have the form

$$\max_{\boldsymbol{\phi} \in \boldsymbol{\Phi}} \frac{1}{N} \sum_{n=1}^{N} g_N(i_n, \mathbf{z}_n, \boldsymbol{\phi}), \tag{1.64}$$

where g_N is a real function defined on $\mathbf{C} \times \mathbf{Z} \times \boldsymbol{\Phi}$ and $\boldsymbol{\Phi}$ is a parameter space. For estimators (1.15), (1.16), (1.19), (1.33), (1.36), (1.48), and (1.49), $\boldsymbol{\Phi} = \boldsymbol{\Theta}$. For estimators (1.7) and (1.9), $\boldsymbol{\Phi} = \boldsymbol{\Theta}_0$, while for (1.41), $\boldsymbol{\Phi} = \boldsymbol{\Theta} \times \boldsymbol{\Pi}$. In estimators (1.7), (1.9), (1.15), (1.16), (1.19), (1.36), and (1.41) the function g_N does not vary with N, but in (1.33), (1.48) and (1.49) it does.

Consistency proofs for all of the above estimators may be based on the following lemma of Amemiya (1973):

LEMMA 1.1. Let $f_N(\mathbf{x}, \boldsymbol{\phi})$, $N = 1, \ldots, \infty$ be a sequence of measurable functions on a measurable space $\mathbf{X}$ and for each $\mathbf{x} \in \mathbf{X}$, a continuous function for $\boldsymbol{\phi} \in \boldsymbol{\Phi}$, $\boldsymbol{\Phi}$ being compact. Then there exists a sequence of measurable functions $\boldsymbol{\phi}_N(\mathbf{x})$, $N = 1, \ldots, \infty$ such that $f_N(\mathbf{x}, \boldsymbol{\phi}_N(\mathbf{x})) = \sup_{\boldsymbol{\phi} \in \boldsymbol{\Phi}} f_N(\mathbf{x}, \boldsymbol{\phi})$ for all $\mathrm{x} \in \mathbf{X}$ and $N = 1, \ldots, \infty$. Furthermore, if for almost every $\mathbf{x} \in \mathbf{X}$, $f_N(\mathbf{x}, \boldsymbol{\phi})$ converges to $f(\boldsymbol{\phi})$ uniformly for all $\boldsymbol{\phi} \in \boldsymbol{\Phi}$, and if $f(\boldsymbol{\phi})$ has a unique maximum at $\boldsymbol{\phi}^* \in \boldsymbol{\Phi}$, then $\boldsymbol{\phi}_N$ converges to $\boldsymbol{\phi}^*$ for almost every $\mathbf{x} \in \mathbf{X}$.

A key step in the consistency demonstration is to show that for each of our estimators the maximand $N^{-1} \sum_{n=1}^{N} g_N(i_n, \mathbf{z}_n, \boldsymbol{\phi})$ almost surely converges to a function $f(\boldsymbol{\phi})$ as $N \to \infty$ and that the convergence is uniform in $\boldsymbol{\phi}$. To show this regularity property, the following result of Jennrich (1969) will be repeatedly used:

LEMMA 1.2. Let μ be a probability measure over a Euclidean space $\mathbf{S}$, let $\boldsymbol{\Phi}$ be a compact subset of a Euclidean space, and let $g(\mathbf{s}, \boldsymbol{\phi})$ be a continuous function of $\boldsymbol{\phi}$ for each $\mathbf{s} \in \mathbf{S}$ and a measurable function of $\mathbf{s}$ for each $\boldsymbol{\phi} \in \boldsymbol{\Phi}$. Assume also that $|g(\mathbf{s}, \boldsymbol{\phi})| \leq \alpha(\mathbf{s})$ for all $\mathbf{s}, \boldsymbol{\phi}$, and some μ-integrable α. For any sequence $\mathbf{x} = \mathbf{s}_1, \mathbf{s}_2, \ldots$ let $f_N(\mathbf{x}, \boldsymbol{\phi}) = \sum_{n=1}^{N} g(\mathbf{s}_n, \boldsymbol{\phi})/N$, and let $\mathbf{X}$ be the set of all sequences $\mathbf{x}$. If sequences $\mathbf{x}$ are drawn as random samples from $\mathbf{S}$, then for almost every realized such sequence, as $N \to \infty$,

$$f_N(\mathbf{x}, \boldsymbol{\phi}) \to E(g(\mathbf{s}, \boldsymbol{\phi})) \equiv f(\boldsymbol{\phi})$$

uniformly for all $\boldsymbol{\phi} \in \boldsymbol{\Phi}$.

Finally the crucial substantive step in proving consistency is to show that the limiting maximand $f(\boldsymbol{\phi})$ achieves its unique maximum at the "true" parameter value $\boldsymbol{\phi}^* \in \boldsymbol{\Phi}$. For this purpose the following parametric form of the classical information inequality will be used (see, for example, Rao 1973, p. 59):

LEMMA 1.3. Let $g(\mathrm{s}, \boldsymbol{\phi})$ be a real valued function over a space $\mathbf{S} \times \boldsymbol{\Phi}$ such that g is integrable with respect to a measure μ over $\mathbf{S}$ and $g(\mathbf{s}, \boldsymbol{\phi}) \geq 0$, all $\mathbf{s} \in \mathbf{S}$, $\boldsymbol{\phi} \in \boldsymbol{\Phi}$. Let $\boldsymbol{\phi}^*$ be an element of $\boldsymbol{\Phi}$ such that $g(\mathbf{s}, \boldsymbol{\phi}^*) > 0$ for almost every $\mathbf{s} \in \mathbf{S}$ and $\int_{\mathbf{S}} (g(\mathbf{s}, \boldsymbol{\phi}^*) - g(\mathbf{s}, \boldsymbol{\phi}))\, d\mu \geq 0$, all $\boldsymbol{\phi} \in \boldsymbol{\Phi}$. Then the expression

$$f(\boldsymbol{\phi}) = \int_{\mathbf{S}} g(\mathbf{s}, \boldsymbol{\phi}^*) \ln g(\mathbf{s}, \boldsymbol{\phi})\, d\mu$$

attains its maximum at $\boldsymbol{\phi} = \boldsymbol{\phi}^*$. The maximum is unique if, for every $\boldsymbol{\phi} \in \boldsymbol{\Phi}$

such that $\boldsymbol{\phi} \neq \boldsymbol{\phi}^*$, there exists an $\mathbf{S}_{\phi} \subset \mathbf{S}$ such that

$$\int_{\mathbf{S}_\phi} g(\mathbf{s},\boldsymbol{\phi})\,d\mu \neq \int_{\mathbf{S}_\phi} g(\mathbf{s},\boldsymbol{\phi}^*)\,d\mu.$$

From these preliminaries consistency for each of our estimators may be demonstrated. In what follows assumptions 1.1 through 1.5 are maintained throughout. Easily verified technical conditions required to use lemma 1.1 through 1.3 are generally omitted. For the sake of conciseness the abstract functional notation of equation (1.64) and lemmas 1.1 through 1.3 is often used. Finally the letter K designates a nonessential constant appearing in certain expressions.

Estimators (1.7) and (1.9)

These are constrained versions of estimators (1.15) and (1.16), respectively. Since $\boldsymbol{\theta}^* \in \boldsymbol{\Theta}_0 \subset \boldsymbol{\Theta}$, consistency of (1.15) guarantees that of (1.7), and consistency of (1.16) guarantees that of (1.9).

Estimator (1.15)

$g_N(i,\mathbf{z},\boldsymbol{\phi}) = \ln P(i \mid \mathbf{z},\boldsymbol{\theta}),\ \boldsymbol{\Phi} = \boldsymbol{\Theta}.$

1. By lemma 1.2, as $N \to \infty$,

$$f_N(\mathbf{x},\boldsymbol{\phi}) \xrightarrow{\text{a.s.}} f(\boldsymbol{\phi}) \equiv \sum_{\mathbf{Z}} g(\mathbf{z}) \sum_{i\in\mathbf{C}} P(i \mid \mathbf{z},\boldsymbol{\theta}^*) \ln P(i \mid \mathbf{z},\boldsymbol{\theta})$$

uniformly over $\boldsymbol{\Theta}$.

2. By lemma 1.3 $f(\boldsymbol{\phi})$ is uniquely maximized at $\boldsymbol{\phi} = \boldsymbol{\theta}^*$.

3. Hence by lemma 1.1 (1.15) is consistent for $\boldsymbol{\theta}^*$.

Estimator (1.16)

$$g_N(i,\mathbf{z},\boldsymbol{\phi}) = \ln P(i \mid \mathbf{z},\boldsymbol{\theta}) - \ln \sum_{\mathbf{y}} P(i \mid \mathbf{y},\boldsymbol{\theta}) p(\mathbf{y}), \quad \boldsymbol{\Phi} = \boldsymbol{\Theta}.$$

1. By lemma 1.2, as $N \to \infty$,

$$f_N(\mathbf{x},\boldsymbol{\phi}) \xrightarrow{\text{a.s.}} f(\boldsymbol{\phi}) \equiv \sum_{i\in\mathbf{C}} H(i) \sum_{\mathbf{Z}} \frac{P(i \mid \mathbf{z},\boldsymbol{\theta}^*) p(\mathbf{z})}{Q(i)}$$

$$\cdot \ln \frac{P(i \mid \mathbf{z},\boldsymbol{\theta}) p(\mathbf{z})}{\sum_{\mathbf{y}} P(i \mid \mathbf{y},\boldsymbol{\theta}) p(\mathbf{y})} + K$$

uniformly over $\boldsymbol{\Theta}$.

2. Recall that $Q(i) = \Sigma_{\mathbf{y}} P(i \mid \mathbf{y}, \boldsymbol{\theta}^*)p(\mathbf{y})$. By lemma 1.3 then $f(\boldsymbol{\phi})$ is uniquely maximized at $\boldsymbol{\phi} = \boldsymbol{\theta}^*$.

3. By lemma 1.1 (1.16) is consistent for $\boldsymbol{\theta}^*$.

Estimator (1.19)

$$g_N(i, \mathbf{z}, \boldsymbol{\phi}) = \frac{Q(i)}{H(i)} \ln P(i \mid \mathbf{z}, \boldsymbol{\theta}), \quad \boldsymbol{\Phi} = \boldsymbol{\Theta}.$$

1. By lemma 1.2, as $N \to \infty$,

$$f_N(\mathbf{x}, \boldsymbol{\phi}) \xrightarrow{\text{a.s.}} f(\boldsymbol{\phi}) \equiv \sum_{\mathbf{z}} p(\mathbf{z}) \sum_{i \in \mathbf{C}} P(i \mid \mathbf{z}, \boldsymbol{\theta}^*) \ln P(i \mid \mathbf{z}, \boldsymbol{\theta})$$

uniformly over $\boldsymbol{\Theta}$.

2. By lemma 1.3 $f(\boldsymbol{\phi})$ is uniquely maximized at $\boldsymbol{\phi} = \boldsymbol{\theta}^*$.

3. By lemma 1.1 (1.19) is consistent for $\boldsymbol{\theta}^*$.

Estimator (1.33)

$$g_N(i, \mathbf{z}, \boldsymbol{\phi}) = \ln P(i \mid \mathbf{z}, \boldsymbol{\theta}) - \ln B_N(i \mid \boldsymbol{\theta}),$$

where

$$B_N(i \mid \boldsymbol{\theta}) = \sum_{j \in \mathbf{C}} \frac{Q(j)}{N_j} \sum_{m \in N(j)} P(i \mid \mathbf{z}_m, \boldsymbol{\theta}), \quad \boldsymbol{\Phi} = \boldsymbol{\Theta}.$$

By lemma 1.2, as $N \to \infty$,

$$\frac{1}{N} \sum_{n=1}^{N} \ln P(i_n \mid \mathbf{z}_n, \boldsymbol{\theta}) \xrightarrow{\text{a.s.}} \sum_{i \in \mathbf{C}} H(i) \sum_{\mathbf{z}} \frac{P(i \mid \mathbf{z}, \boldsymbol{\theta}^*)p(\mathbf{z})}{Q(i)} \ln P(i \mid \mathbf{z}, \boldsymbol{\theta})$$

uniformly over $\boldsymbol{\Theta}$.

Consider

$$\frac{1}{N} \sum_{n=1}^{N} \ln B_N(i_n \mid \boldsymbol{\theta}) = \sum_{i \in \mathbf{C}} \frac{N_i}{N} \ln B_N(i \mid \boldsymbol{\theta}).$$

Lemma 1.2 implies that, as $N \to \infty$,

$$\frac{1}{N_j} \sum_{m \in N(j)} P(i \mid \mathbf{z}_m, \boldsymbol{\theta}) \xrightarrow{\text{a.s.}} \sum_{\mathbf{z}} \frac{P(j \mid \mathbf{z}, \boldsymbol{\theta}^*)p(\mathbf{z})}{Q(j)} P(i \mid \mathbf{z}, \boldsymbol{\theta})$$

uniformly over $\boldsymbol{\Theta}$. Hence, as $N \to \infty$, $B_N(i \mid \boldsymbol{\theta}) \xrightarrow{\text{a.s.}} \Sigma_{\mathbf{z}} P(i \mid \mathbf{z}, \boldsymbol{\theta}) p(\mathbf{z})$ uniformly over $\boldsymbol{\Theta}$. Now observe that by assumptions 1.1 through 1.5 there exists $\delta > 0$ such that $\Sigma_{\mathbf{z}} P(i \mid \mathbf{z}, \boldsymbol{\theta}) p(\mathbf{z}) > \delta$ for all $\boldsymbol{\theta} \in \boldsymbol{\Theta}$ and $i \in \mathbf{C}$. From this, from the uniform convergence of B_N, and from the concavity of the log function it follows that for any ε such that $\delta > \varepsilon > 0$, there exists $\bar{N}$ such that

$$\left| \ln B_N(i \mid \boldsymbol{\theta}) - \ln \sum_{\mathbf{z}} P(i \mid \mathbf{z}, \boldsymbol{\theta}) p(\mathbf{z}) \right| < \left| \ln \left(\sum_{\mathbf{z}} P(i \mid \mathbf{z}, \boldsymbol{\theta}) p(\mathbf{z}) - \varepsilon \right) - \ln \left(\sum_{\mathbf{z}} P(i \mid \mathbf{z}, \boldsymbol{\theta}) p(\mathbf{z}) \right) \right| < |\ln(\delta - \varepsilon) - \ln \delta|$$

almost surely for all $N > \bar{N}$ and $\boldsymbol{\theta} \in \boldsymbol{\Theta}$. That is, $\ln B_N(i \mid \boldsymbol{\theta})$ converges almost surely uniformly. Hence

$$\sum_{i \in \mathbf{C}} \frac{N_i}{N} \ln B_N(i \mid \boldsymbol{\theta}) \xrightarrow{\text{a.s.}} \sum_{i \in \mathbf{C}} H(i) \ln \sum_{\mathbf{z}} P(i \mid \mathbf{z}, \boldsymbol{\theta}) p(\mathbf{z}),$$

and finally

$$f_N(\mathbf{x}, \boldsymbol{\phi}) \xrightarrow{\text{a.s.}} f(\boldsymbol{\phi}) \equiv \sum_{i \in \mathbf{C}} H(i) \sum_{\mathbf{z}} \frac{P(i \mid \mathbf{z}, \boldsymbol{\theta}^*) p(\mathbf{z})}{Q(i)} \cdot \ln \frac{P(i \mid \mathbf{z}, \boldsymbol{\theta}) p(\mathbf{z})}{\sum_{\mathbf{z}} P(i \mid \mathbf{y}, \boldsymbol{\theta}) p(\mathbf{y})} + K$$

uniformly in $\boldsymbol{\Theta}$.

Consistency of the estimator (1.33) then follows from that of (1.16).

Estimator (1.36)

$$g_N(i, \mathbf{z}, \boldsymbol{\phi}) = \ln \frac{P(i \mid \mathbf{z}, \boldsymbol{\theta}) H(i)/Q(i)}{\sum_{j \in \mathbf{C}} P(j \mid \mathbf{z}, \boldsymbol{\theta}) H(j)/Q(j)}, \quad \boldsymbol{\Phi} = \boldsymbol{\Theta}.$$

1. By lemma 1.2, as $N \to \infty$,

$$f_N(\mathbf{x}, \boldsymbol{\phi}) \xrightarrow{\text{a.s.}} f(\boldsymbol{\phi})$$

$$\equiv \sum_{\mathbf{z}} q(\mathbf{z}) \sum_{i \in \mathbf{C}} \frac{P(i \mid \mathbf{z}, \boldsymbol{\theta}^*) H(i)/Q(i)}{\sum_{j \in \mathbf{C}} P(j \mid \mathbf{z}, \boldsymbol{\theta}^*) H(j)/Q(j)} \ln \frac{P(i \mid \mathbf{z}, \boldsymbol{\theta}) H(i)/Q(i)}{\sum_{j \in \mathbf{C}} P(j \mid \mathbf{z}, \boldsymbol{\theta}) H(j)/Q(j)}$$

uniformly over $\boldsymbol{\Theta}$. Here

$$q(\mathbf{z}) \equiv \sum_{j \in \mathbf{C}} \frac{P(j \mid \mathbf{z}, \boldsymbol{\theta}^*) p(\mathbf{z})}{Q(j)} H(j).$$

2. By lemma 1.3 $f(\boldsymbol{\phi})$ is uniquely maximized at $\boldsymbol{\phi} = \boldsymbol{\theta}^*$.

3. Consistency then follows from lemma 1.1.

Estimator (1.41)

$$g_N(i, \mathbf{z}, \boldsymbol{\phi}) = \ln \frac{P(i \mid \mathbf{z}, \boldsymbol{\theta}) H(i)/\tilde{Q}(i)}{\sum_{j \in \mathbf{C}} P(j \mid \mathbf{z}, \boldsymbol{\theta}) H(j)/\tilde{Q}(j)}, \qquad \boldsymbol{\Phi} = \boldsymbol{\Theta} \times \boldsymbol{\Pi}.$$

1. Observe first that if $\boldsymbol{\Pi}$ is taken to be the closed unit simplex, then $g_N(i, \mathbf{z}, \boldsymbol{\phi})$ is not suitably bounded, so lemma 1.2 cannot be applied. Recall, however, that there exists $\delta > 0$ such that $\Sigma_{\mathbf{Z}} P(i \mid \mathbf{z}, \boldsymbol{\theta}) p(\mathbf{z}) > \delta$, all $i \in \mathbf{C}$, $\boldsymbol{\theta} \in \boldsymbol{\Theta}$. Hence $Q(i) > \delta$, all $i \in \mathbf{C}$, and we may take $\boldsymbol{\Pi}$ to be the compact set $\boldsymbol{\Pi} = [\tilde{\mathbf{Q}}: \Sigma_{i \in \mathbf{C}} \tilde{Q}(i) = 1, \tilde{Q}(i) \geqq \delta, \text{ all } i \in \mathbf{C}]$. Now lemma 1.2 implies that, as $N \to \infty$,

$$f_N(\mathbf{x}, \boldsymbol{\phi}) \xrightarrow{\text{a.s.}} f(\boldsymbol{\phi}) \equiv \sum_{\mathbf{Z}} q(\mathbf{z}) \sum_{i \in \mathbf{C}} \frac{P(i \mid \mathbf{z}, \boldsymbol{\theta}^*) H(i)/Q(i)}{\sum_{j \in \mathbf{C}} P(j \mid \mathbf{z}, \boldsymbol{\theta}^*) H(j)/Q(j)} \cdot \ln \frac{P(i \mid \mathbf{z}, \boldsymbol{\theta}) H(i)/\tilde{Q}(i)}{\sum_{j \in \mathbf{C}} P(j \mid \mathbf{z}, \boldsymbol{\theta}) H(j)/\tilde{Q}(j)}$$

uniformly over $\boldsymbol{\Theta} \times \boldsymbol{\Pi}$.

2. By lemma 1.3 $f(\boldsymbol{\phi})$ has a maximum at $\boldsymbol{\phi} = (\boldsymbol{\theta}^*, \mathbf{Q})$. However, assumptions 1.1 through 1.5 do not ensure uniqueness. The following strengthening of assumption 1.2 does guarantee uniqueness.

ASSUMPTION **1.2′**: For each $(\boldsymbol{\theta}, \tilde{\mathbf{Q}}) \in \boldsymbol{\Theta} \times \boldsymbol{\Pi}$ such that $(\boldsymbol{\theta}, \tilde{\mathbf{Q}}) \neq (\boldsymbol{\theta}^*, \mathbf{Q})$, there exists $\mathbf{A} \subset \mathbf{C} \times \mathbf{Z}$ such that

$$\sum_{\mathbf{A}} q(\mathbf{z}) \frac{P(i \mid \mathbf{z}, \boldsymbol{\theta}) H(i)/\tilde{Q}(i)}{\sum_{j \in \mathbf{C}} P(j \mid \mathbf{z}, \boldsymbol{\theta}) H(j)/\tilde{Q}(j)} \neq \sum_{\mathbf{A}} q(\mathbf{z}) \frac{P(i \mid \mathbf{z}, \boldsymbol{\theta}^*) H(i)/Q(i)}{\sum_{j \in \mathbf{C}} P(j \mid \mathbf{z}, \boldsymbol{\theta}^*) H(j)/Q(j)}.$$

Moreover, the stratified sampling process satisfies $\Sigma_{\mathbf{A_b}} P(j \mid \mathbf{y}, \boldsymbol{\theta}^*) p(\mathbf{y}) > 0 \Rightarrow H(\mathbf{b}) > 0$ for each $\mathbf{b} \in \mathbf{B}$, and $\bigcup_{\mathbf{b} \in \mathbf{B}} \mathbf{A_b} = \mathbf{C} \times \mathbf{Z}$.

3. Lemma 1.1 then implies consistency of (1.41).

Estimator (1.48)

$$g_N(i, \mathbf{z}, \boldsymbol{\phi}) = \frac{Q_N(i \mid \boldsymbol{\theta})}{H(i)} \ln P(i \mid \mathbf{z}, \boldsymbol{\theta})$$

where $\mathbf{Q}_N(\boldsymbol{\theta}) = \mathbf{A}_N(\boldsymbol{\theta})\mathbf{Q}_N(\boldsymbol{\theta})$, and $\mathbf{A}_N(\boldsymbol{\theta})$ is an $M \times M$ matrix with typical element

$$a_{ij}^N(\boldsymbol{\theta}) = \frac{1}{N_j} \sum_{n \in \mathbf{N}(j)} P(i \mid \mathbf{z}_n, \boldsymbol{\theta}), \quad \boldsymbol{\Phi} = \boldsymbol{\Theta}.$$

The key step in establishing consistency of this estimator is to determine the limiting behavior, as $N \to \infty$, of $\mathbf{Q}_N(\boldsymbol{\theta})$.

First, observe that by lemma 1.2, as $N \to \infty$,

$$a_{ij}^N(\boldsymbol{\theta}) \xrightarrow{\text{a.s.}} \sum_{\mathbf{z}} \frac{P(j \mid \mathbf{z}, \boldsymbol{\theta}^*)p(\mathbf{z})}{Q(j)} P(i \mid \mathbf{z}, \boldsymbol{\theta}) \equiv a_{ij}(\boldsymbol{\theta})$$

uniformly over $\boldsymbol{\Theta}$. Therefore $\mathbf{A}_N(\boldsymbol{\theta}) \xrightarrow{\text{a.s.}} \mathbf{A}(\boldsymbol{\theta})$ uniformly, where $\mathbf{A}(\boldsymbol{\theta})$ has typical element $a_{ij}(\boldsymbol{\theta})$.

Next, recall from the text that $(\mathbf{A}(\boldsymbol{\theta}) - \mathbf{I})$ has rank $M - 1$, and that $\mathbf{Q}(\boldsymbol{\theta})$ is the unique solution to the set of equations $(\mathbf{A}(\boldsymbol{\theta}) - \mathbf{I})\mathbf{Q}(\boldsymbol{\theta}) = 0$ and $[1 \ldots 1]\mathbf{Q}(\boldsymbol{\theta}) = 1$. It follows that, if we define $\hat{\mathbf{A}}(\boldsymbol{\theta})$ to be an $M \times M$ matrix whose first $M - 1$ rows are linearly independent rows of $(\mathbf{A}(\boldsymbol{\theta}) - \mathbf{I})$, and whose last row is a vector of ones, then $\hat{\mathbf{A}}(\boldsymbol{\theta})$ has full rank and $\mathbf{Q}(\boldsymbol{\theta}) = \hat{\mathbf{A}}(\boldsymbol{\theta})^{-1} (0, \ldots, 0, 1)'$.

Similarly define $\hat{\mathbf{A}}_N(\boldsymbol{\theta})$ for each N and observe that, since $\hat{\mathbf{A}}_N(\boldsymbol{\theta}) \xrightarrow{\text{a.s.}} \hat{\mathbf{A}}(\boldsymbol{\theta})$ uniformly, $\hat{\mathbf{A}}_N(\boldsymbol{\theta})$ is almost surely nonsingular for N sufficiently large. For such N then $\mathbf{Q}_N(\boldsymbol{\theta}) = \hat{\mathbf{A}}_N(\boldsymbol{\theta})^{-1} (0, \ldots, 0, 1)'$. Now note that for large N, $\mathbf{Q}_N(\boldsymbol{\theta}) - \mathbf{Q}(\boldsymbol{\theta}) = (\hat{\mathbf{A}}_N(\boldsymbol{\theta})^{-1} - \hat{\mathbf{A}}(\boldsymbol{\theta})^{-1}) (0, \ldots, 0, 1)'$ and that each element of $\hat{\mathbf{A}}_N(\boldsymbol{\theta})^{-1}$ is a product of elements of $\hat{\mathbf{A}}_N(\boldsymbol{\theta})$ divided by the determinant $|\hat{\mathbf{A}}_N(\boldsymbol{\theta})|$. Since for each $i, j \in \mathbf{C}$, $a_{ij}^N(\boldsymbol{\theta}) \xrightarrow{\text{a.s.}} a_{ij}(\boldsymbol{\theta})$ uniformly, it follows that $\hat{\mathbf{A}}_N(\boldsymbol{\theta})^{-1} \xrightarrow{\text{a.s.}} \hat{\mathbf{A}}(\boldsymbol{\theta})^{-1}$ uniformly. Hence $\mathbf{Q}_N(\boldsymbol{\theta}) \xrightarrow{\text{a.s.}} \mathbf{Q}(\boldsymbol{\theta})$ uniformly, the desired limiting property.

The simple method of proving global consistency using lemma 1.3 cannot be employed for the estimator (1.48) since the first-order condition it satisfies is evaluated at the argument $\tilde{\mathbf{Q}} = \mathbf{Q}_N(\boldsymbol{\theta})$ which depends on $\boldsymbol{\theta}$. However, a direct argument using lemma 1.1 can be used to prove a weaker form of consistency: given an identification condition, there exists a neighborhood of the true parameter vector in which (1.48) has a unique root, and this root converges almost surely to the true parameter vector. Note that this result does not rule out the existence of nonlocal inconsistent roots.

The gradient of (1.48) is

$$\mathbf{h}_N(\boldsymbol{\theta}) = \frac{1}{N}\sum_{n=1}^{N}\frac{Q_N(i_n\mid\boldsymbol{\theta})}{H(i_n)}\frac{\partial\ln P(i_n\mid\mathbf{z}_n,\boldsymbol{\theta})}{\partial\boldsymbol{\theta}}$$

$$= \sum_{i\in\mathbf{C}}\frac{N_i}{N}\frac{Q_N(i\mid\boldsymbol{\theta})}{H(i)}\left(\frac{1}{N_i}\sum_{n\in\mathbf{N}(i)}\frac{\partial\ln P(i\mid\mathbf{z}_n,\boldsymbol{\theta})}{\partial\boldsymbol{\theta}}\right).$$

Applying lemma 1.2 to the term in parentheses,

$$\mathbf{h}_N(\boldsymbol{\theta}) \xrightarrow{\text{a.s.}} \mathbf{h}(\boldsymbol{\theta}) \equiv \sum_{\mathbf{z}}\sum_{i\in\mathbf{C}} p(\mathbf{z})\frac{Q(i\mid\boldsymbol{\theta})}{Q(i)}P(i\mid\mathbf{z},\boldsymbol{\theta}^*)\frac{\partial\ln P(i\mid\mathbf{z},\boldsymbol{\theta})}{\partial\boldsymbol{\theta}},$$

uniformly over $\boldsymbol{\Theta}$. Recall that $\mathbf{Q}(\boldsymbol{\theta})$ satisfies

$$Q(i\mid\boldsymbol{\theta}) = \sum_{j\in\mathbf{C}}\sum_{\mathbf{z}}\frac{P(j\mid\mathbf{z},\boldsymbol{\theta}^*)\,P(i\mid\mathbf{z},\boldsymbol{\theta})\,p(\mathbf{z})}{Q(j)}Q(j\mid\boldsymbol{\theta})$$

and $Q(i\mid\boldsymbol{\theta}^*) = Q(i)$. Hence

$$Q(i)\frac{\partial\ln Q(i\mid\boldsymbol{\theta}^*)}{\partial\boldsymbol{\theta}} = \sum_{j\in\mathbf{C}}\gamma_{ij}\frac{\partial\ln Q(j\mid\boldsymbol{\theta}^*)}{\partial\boldsymbol{\theta}} + \sum_{\mathbf{z}}p(\mathbf{z})\frac{\partial P(i\mid\mathbf{z},\boldsymbol{\theta}^*)}{\partial\boldsymbol{\theta}},$$

with $\gamma_{ij} = \sum_{\mathbf{z}}p(\mathbf{z})\,P(i\mid\mathbf{z},\boldsymbol{\theta}^*)\,P(j\mid\mathbf{z},\boldsymbol{\theta}^*)$.

The Jacobian of $\mathbf{h}(\boldsymbol{\theta})$ evaluated at $\boldsymbol{\theta}^*$ is

$$\frac{\partial\mathbf{h}(\boldsymbol{\theta}^*)}{\partial\boldsymbol{\theta}'} = \sum_{\mathbf{z}}\sum_{i\in\mathbf{C}}p(\mathbf{z})\,P(i\mid\mathbf{z},\boldsymbol{\theta}^*)\frac{\partial^2\ln P(i\mid\mathbf{z},\boldsymbol{\theta}^*)}{\partial\boldsymbol{\theta}\,\partial\boldsymbol{\theta}'}$$

$$+ \sum_{\mathbf{z}}\sum_{i\in\mathbf{C}}p(\mathbf{z})\,P(i\mid\mathbf{z},\boldsymbol{\theta}^*)\frac{\partial\ln P(i\mid\mathbf{z},\boldsymbol{\theta}^*)}{\partial\boldsymbol{\theta}}\frac{\partial\ln Q(i\mid\boldsymbol{\theta}^*)}{\partial\boldsymbol{\theta}'}$$

$$= -\sum_{\mathbf{z}}\sum_{i\in\mathbf{C}}p(\mathbf{z})\,P(i\mid\mathbf{z},\boldsymbol{\theta}^*)\frac{\partial\ln P(i\mid\mathbf{z},\boldsymbol{\theta}^*)}{\partial\boldsymbol{\theta}}\frac{\partial\ln P(i\mid\mathbf{z},\boldsymbol{\theta}^*)}{\partial\boldsymbol{\theta}'}$$

$$+ \left(\frac{\partial\ln\mathbf{Q}(\boldsymbol{\theta})}{\partial\boldsymbol{\theta}'}\right)'(\hat{\mathbf{Q}} - \boldsymbol{\Gamma})\left(\frac{\partial\ln\mathbf{Q}(\boldsymbol{\theta})}{\partial\boldsymbol{\theta}'}\right),$$

where $\hat{\mathbf{Q}}$ is a diagonal matrix with elements $Q(i)$, $\mathbf{\Gamma}$ is the symmetric matrix with coefficients γ_{ij}, and we have used the identity $\Sigma_i \; P(i \mid \mathbf{z}, \boldsymbol{\theta}) \equiv 1$ and the equations defining $\partial \ln \mathbf{Q}(i \mid \boldsymbol{\theta})/\partial \boldsymbol{\theta}$. We make the identifying assumption as follows.

ASSUMPTION 1.2″: $\partial \mathbf{h}(\boldsymbol{\theta}^*)/\partial \boldsymbol{\theta}'$ is nonsingular.
Then the function $f(\boldsymbol{\theta}) = -\mathbf{h}(\boldsymbol{\theta})'\mathbf{h}(\boldsymbol{\theta})$ has a local maximum $f(\boldsymbol{\theta}^*) = 0$ which is unique in a neighborhood of $\boldsymbol{\theta}^*$, and lemma 1.1 establishes that within this neighborhood $\mathbf{h}_N(\boldsymbol{\theta})$ has a unique root $\hat{\boldsymbol{\theta}}_N$ which converges almost surely to $\boldsymbol{\theta}^*$.

As was the case for estimator (1.41), models with multiplicative alternative-specific parameters, such as the multinomial logit model, are not fully identified when $\mathbf{Q}$ is unknown and will fail to satisfy assumption 1.2″. We conjecture that assumption 1.2′, plus a regularity condition that the rank of $\partial \mathbf{h}(\boldsymbol{\theta})/\partial \boldsymbol{\theta}$ be constant in a neighborhood of $\boldsymbol{\theta}^*$, imply assumption 1.2″, with $\partial \mathbf{h}(\boldsymbol{\theta}^*)/\partial \boldsymbol{\theta}$ negative definite. We have verified this for two alternative choice sets.

Estimator (1.49)

The gradient for this estimator is

$$\mathbf{h}_N(\boldsymbol{\theta}) = \frac{1}{N} \sum_{n=1}^{N} \left\{ \frac{\partial \ln P(i_n \mid \mathbf{z}_n, \boldsymbol{\theta})}{\partial \boldsymbol{\theta}} - \sum_{j \in \mathbf{C}} \frac{Q_N(j \mid \boldsymbol{\theta})}{Q_N(i_n \mid \boldsymbol{\theta})} \frac{1}{N_j} \sum_{m \in \mathbf{N}(j)} \frac{\partial P(i_n \mid \mathbf{z}_m, \boldsymbol{\theta})}{\partial \boldsymbol{\theta}} \right\},$$

satisfying

$$\mathbf{h}_N(\boldsymbol{\theta}) \xrightarrow{\text{a.s.}} \mathbf{h}(\boldsymbol{\theta}) = \sum_{i \in \mathbf{C}} \frac{H(i)}{Q(i)} \sum_{\mathbf{z}} p(\mathbf{z})\, P(i \mid \mathbf{z}, \boldsymbol{\theta}^*) \frac{\partial \ln P(i \mid \mathbf{z}, \boldsymbol{\theta})}{\partial \boldsymbol{\theta}} - \sum_{i \in \mathbf{C}} \frac{H(i)}{Q(i \mid \boldsymbol{\theta})} \sum_{j \in \mathbf{C}} \frac{Q(j \mid \boldsymbol{\theta})}{Q(j)} \cdot \sum_{\mathbf{z}} p(\mathbf{z})\, P(j \mid \mathbf{z}, \boldsymbol{\theta}^*) \frac{\partial P(i \mid \mathbf{z}, \boldsymbol{\theta})}{\partial \boldsymbol{\theta}}.$$

Then $\mathbf{h}(\boldsymbol{\theta}^*) = \mathbf{0}$, and an argument identical to that for (1.48) establishes that, if this gradient satisfies assumption 1.2″, then (1.49) has a locally unique root that converges almost surely to $\boldsymbol{\theta}^*$.

1.12 Appendix: Asymptotic Normality

Under assumptions 1.1 through 1.5 all of the estimators just proved consistent have associated with them first-order asymptotic normal distributions. In each case the relevant asymptotic distribution can be found by application of the following two lemmas:

LEMMA **1.4:** Let the assumptions of lemma 1.1 be satisfied. Furthermore let $f_N(\mathbf{x},\cdot) \in \mathbf{C}^2(\boldsymbol{\Phi})$ for almost all $\mathbf{x} \in \mathbf{X}$ and $f(\cdot) \in \mathbf{C}^2(\boldsymbol{\Phi})$. Let $(\mathbf{r}:\boldsymbol{\Phi} \to \mathbf{R}^J) \in \mathbf{C}^2(\boldsymbol{\Phi})$ with $\mathbf{r}(\boldsymbol{\phi}^*) = \mathbf{0}$ and $\mathbf{R} = \partial \mathbf{r}(\boldsymbol{\phi}^*)/\partial \boldsymbol{\phi}$ of full rank. Let $\hat{\boldsymbol{\phi}}_N(\mathbf{x})$, $N = 1, \ldots, \infty$, be a sequence of solutions to the problems max $f_N(\mathbf{x}, \boldsymbol{\phi})$ subject to $\mathbf{r}(\boldsymbol{\phi}) = \mathbf{0}$. Finally suppose that $\boldsymbol{\phi}^* \in \text{int}\ \boldsymbol{\Phi}$, that $\mathbf{F} = \partial^2 f(\boldsymbol{\phi}^*)/\partial\boldsymbol{\phi}\partial\boldsymbol{\phi}'$ is nonsingular, and that $\sqrt{N}\,(\partial f_N(\mathbf{x}, \boldsymbol{\phi}^*)/\partial \boldsymbol{\phi}) \xrightarrow{\text{a.d.}} \mathcal{N}(\mathbf{0}, \boldsymbol{\Delta})$. Then

$$\sqrt{N}\,(\hat{\boldsymbol{\phi}}_N - \boldsymbol{\phi}^*) \xrightarrow{\text{a.d.}} \mathcal{N}\,(0, \boldsymbol{\Omega}^{-1}\boldsymbol{\Delta}\boldsymbol{\Omega}^{-1}),$$

where

$$\boldsymbol{\Omega}^{-1} = \mathbf{F}^{-1} - \mathbf{F}^{-1}\mathbf{R}(\mathbf{R}'\mathbf{F}^{-1}\mathbf{R})^{-1}\mathbf{R}'\mathbf{F}^{-1}.$$

PROOF: Lemma 1.1 implies that $[\hat{\boldsymbol{\phi}}_N]$ exists and that, as $N \to \infty$, $\hat{\boldsymbol{\phi}}_N \xrightarrow{\text{a.s.}} \boldsymbol{\phi}^*$. Hence for N sufficiently large $\hat{\boldsymbol{\phi}}_N \in \text{int}\ \boldsymbol{\Phi}$ and $\partial\,\mathbf{r}(\hat{\boldsymbol{\phi}}_N)/\partial\boldsymbol{\phi}$ has full rank a.s. By the classical Lagrangian theorem there then exists a.s. a unique $\hat{\boldsymbol{\lambda}}_N \in \mathbf{R}^J$ such that

$$\frac{\partial f_N(\mathbf{x}, \hat{\boldsymbol{\phi}}_N)}{\partial \boldsymbol{\phi}} + \frac{\partial \mathbf{r}(\hat{\boldsymbol{\phi}}_N)}{\partial \boldsymbol{\phi}}\hat{\boldsymbol{\lambda}}_N = 0.$$

Moreover as $N \to \infty$, $\hat{\boldsymbol{\lambda}}_N \xrightarrow{\text{a.s.}} \boldsymbol{\lambda}^* = 0$. This last follows because

$$\frac{\partial f_N(\mathbf{x}, \hat{\boldsymbol{\phi}}_N)}{\partial \boldsymbol{\phi}} \xrightarrow{\text{a.s.}} \frac{\partial f(\boldsymbol{\phi}^*)}{\partial \boldsymbol{\phi}} = \mathbf{0}$$

and

$$\frac{\partial \mathbf{r}(\hat{\boldsymbol{\phi}}_N)}{\partial \boldsymbol{\phi}} \xrightarrow{\text{a.s.}} \frac{\partial \mathbf{r}(\boldsymbol{\phi}^*)}{\partial \boldsymbol{\phi}}$$

which has full rank.

A Taylor's expansion around $(\boldsymbol{\phi}^*, \boldsymbol{\lambda}^*)$ of the first-order conditions for maximization of $f_N(\mathbf{x}, \boldsymbol{\phi})$ subject to $\mathbf{r}(\boldsymbol{\phi}) = \mathbf{0}$ yields $\mathbf{0} = \mathbf{A}_N \mathbf{y}_N + \mathbf{b}_N$, where

$$\mathbf{A}_N = \left[\begin{array}{c:c} \dfrac{\partial^2 f_N(\mathbf{x}, \tilde{\boldsymbol{\phi}}_N)}{\partial\boldsymbol{\phi}\partial\boldsymbol{\phi}'} + \sum_{j=1}^{J} \tilde{\lambda}_j \dfrac{\partial^2 \mathbf{r}_j(\tilde{\boldsymbol{\phi}}_N)}{\partial\boldsymbol{\phi}\partial\boldsymbol{\phi}'} & \dfrac{\partial \mathbf{r}(\hat{\boldsymbol{\phi}}_N)}{\partial\boldsymbol{\phi}} \\ \hdashline \dfrac{\partial \mathbf{r}(\tilde{\boldsymbol{\phi}}_N)}{\partial\boldsymbol{\phi}'} & \mathbf{0} \end{array}\right]$$

$$\mathbf{y}_N = \begin{bmatrix} \hat{\boldsymbol{\phi}}_N - \boldsymbol{\phi}^* \\ \hat{\boldsymbol{\lambda}}_N - \boldsymbol{\lambda}^* \end{bmatrix} \qquad \mathbf{b}_N = \begin{bmatrix} \dfrac{\partial f_N(\mathbf{x}, \boldsymbol{\phi}^*)}{\partial\boldsymbol{\phi}} + \sum_{j=1}^{J} \lambda_j^* \dfrac{\partial \mathbf{r}_j(\boldsymbol{\phi}^*)}{\partial\boldsymbol{\phi}} \\ \mathbf{0} \end{bmatrix},$$

and where $(\tilde{\boldsymbol{\phi}}, \tilde{\boldsymbol{\lambda}})$ lies on the line segment connecting $(\hat{\boldsymbol{\phi}}_N, \hat{\boldsymbol{\lambda}}_N)$ with $(\boldsymbol{\phi}^*, \boldsymbol{\lambda}^*)$. Recall that $\boldsymbol{\lambda}^* = \mathbf{0}$, and let $N \to \infty$. Then

$$\mathbf{A}_N \xrightarrow{\text{a.s.}} \begin{bmatrix} \mathbf{F} & \mathbf{R} \\ \mathbf{R}' & \mathbf{0} \end{bmatrix}$$

and

$$\sqrt{N}\begin{bmatrix} \hat{\boldsymbol{\phi}}_N - \boldsymbol{\phi}^* \\ \hat{\boldsymbol{\lambda}}_N \end{bmatrix} \xrightarrow{\text{a.s.}} \begin{bmatrix} \mathbf{F} & \mathbf{R} \\ \mathbf{R}' & \mathbf{0} \end{bmatrix}^{-1} \begin{bmatrix} -\sqrt{N}\dfrac{\partial f_N(\mathbf{x}, \boldsymbol{\phi}^*)}{\partial\boldsymbol{\phi}} \\ \mathbf{0} \end{bmatrix}$$

Finally observe that

$$\begin{bmatrix} \mathbf{F} & \mathbf{R} \\ \mathbf{R}' & \mathbf{0} \end{bmatrix}^{-1} = \begin{bmatrix} \boldsymbol{\Omega}^{-1} & \mathbf{B} \\ \mathbf{B}' & \mathbf{D} \end{bmatrix},$$

where $\mathbf{D} = -(\mathbf{R}'\mathbf{F}^{-1}\mathbf{R})^{-1}$ and $\mathbf{B} = -\mathbf{F}^{-1}\mathbf{R}\mathbf{D}$. Thus $\sqrt{N}(\hat{\boldsymbol{\phi}}_N - \boldsymbol{\phi}^*) \xrightarrow{\text{a.d.}} \mathcal{N}(\mathbf{0}, \boldsymbol{\Omega}^{-1}\boldsymbol{\Delta}\boldsymbol{\Omega}^{-1})$.

LEMMA 1.5: Let the assumptions of lemma 1.4 be satisfied and also those of lemma 1.2 except that

$$f_N(\mathbf{x}, \boldsymbol{\phi}) = \sum_{n=1}^{N} g(\mathbf{s}_n, \boldsymbol{\phi}, \mathbf{h}_N(\boldsymbol{\phi}))/N,$$

where $\mathbf{h}_N(\boldsymbol{\phi}) = \Sigma_{n=1}^{N} \mathbf{e}(\mathbf{s}_n, \boldsymbol{\phi})/N$, $\mathbf{e} \in \mathbf{C}^2(\boldsymbol{\Phi}, \mathbf{R}^L)$, and $g \in \mathbf{C}^2(\boldsymbol{\Phi})$. Suppose

$$\mathbf{h}(\boldsymbol{\phi}^*) = \int \mathbf{e}(\mathbf{s}, \boldsymbol{\phi}^*)\, d\mu,$$

$$\mathbf{V}_g = \int \frac{\partial g(\mathbf{s}, \boldsymbol{\phi}^*, \mathbf{h}(\boldsymbol{\phi}^*))}{\partial \boldsymbol{\phi}} \frac{\partial g(\mathbf{s}, \boldsymbol{\phi}^*, \mathbf{h}(\boldsymbol{\phi}^*))}{\partial \boldsymbol{\phi}'}\, d\mu,$$

$$\mathbf{V}_e = \int \mathbf{e}(\mathbf{s}, \boldsymbol{\phi}^*) \cdot \mathbf{e}(\mathbf{s}, \boldsymbol{\phi}^*)'\, d\mu - \mathbf{h}(\boldsymbol{\phi}^*) \cdot \mathbf{h}(\boldsymbol{\phi}^*)',$$

$$\mathbf{W} = \int \frac{\partial^2 g(\mathbf{s}, \boldsymbol{\phi}^*, \mathbf{h}(\boldsymbol{\phi}^*))}{d\boldsymbol{\phi}\, d\mathbf{h}'}\, d\mu$$

all exist and are finite. Let

$$\mathbf{V}_{eg} = \int \mathbf{e}(\mathbf{s}, \boldsymbol{\phi}^*) \frac{\partial g(\mathbf{s}, \boldsymbol{\phi}^*, \mathbf{h}(\boldsymbol{\phi}^*))}{\partial \boldsymbol{\phi}'}\, d\mu.$$

Then

$$\sqrt{N} \frac{\partial f_N(\mathbf{x}, \boldsymbol{\phi}^*)}{\partial \boldsymbol{\phi}} \xrightarrow{\text{a.d.}} \mathcal{N}(\mathbf{0}, \boldsymbol{\Delta}),$$

where $\boldsymbol{\Delta} = \mathbf{V}_g + \mathbf{W}\mathbf{V}_{eg} + \mathbf{V}_{eg}'\mathbf{W}' + \mathbf{W}\mathbf{V}_e\mathbf{W}'$.

PROOF: A Taylor's expansion around $\mathbf{h}(\boldsymbol{\phi}^*)$ yields

$$\begin{aligned}
\sqrt{N} \frac{\partial f_N(\mathbf{x}, \boldsymbol{\phi}^*)}{\partial \boldsymbol{\phi}} &= \frac{1}{\sqrt{N}} \Bigg[\sum_{n=1}^{N} \frac{\partial g(\mathbf{s}_n, \boldsymbol{\phi}^*, \mathbf{h}(\boldsymbol{\phi}^*))}{\partial \boldsymbol{\phi}} \\
&\quad + \frac{\partial^2 g(\mathbf{s}_n, \boldsymbol{\phi}^*, \tilde{\mathbf{h}}_N(\boldsymbol{\phi}^*))}{\partial \boldsymbol{\phi} \partial \mathbf{h}'} (\mathbf{h}_N(\boldsymbol{\phi}^*) - \mathbf{h}(\boldsymbol{\phi}^*)) \Bigg] \\
&= \left[\frac{1}{\sqrt{N}} \sum_{n=1}^{N} \frac{\partial g(\mathbf{s}_n, \boldsymbol{\phi}^*, \mathbf{h}(\boldsymbol{\phi}^*))}{\partial \boldsymbol{\phi}} \right] \\
&\quad + \left[\frac{1}{N} \sum_{n=1}^{N} \frac{\partial^2 g(\mathbf{s}_n, \boldsymbol{\phi}^*, \tilde{\mathbf{h}}_N(\boldsymbol{\phi}^*))}{\partial \boldsymbol{\phi} \partial \mathbf{h}'} \right] \\
&\quad \cdot \left[\frac{1}{\sqrt{N}} \left(\sum_{n=1}^{N} \mathbf{e}(\mathbf{s}_n, \boldsymbol{\phi}^*) - \mathbf{h}(\boldsymbol{\phi}^*) \right) \right],
\end{aligned}$$

where $\tilde{\mathbf{h}}_N(\boldsymbol{\phi}^*)$ lies on the line segment connecting $\mathbf{h}_N(\boldsymbol{\phi}^*)$ with $\mathbf{h}(\boldsymbol{\phi}^*)$.

As $N \to \infty$,

$$\frac{1}{N}\sum_{n=1}^{N}\frac{\partial^2 g(\mathbf{s}_n, \boldsymbol{\phi}^*, \tilde{h}_N(\boldsymbol{\phi}^*))}{\partial\boldsymbol{\phi}\partial\mathbf{h}'} \xrightarrow{\text{a.s.}} \mathbf{W}.$$

Observe that by lemma 1.4

$$\int\frac{\partial g(\mathbf{s}, \boldsymbol{\phi}^*, \mathbf{h}(\boldsymbol{\phi}^*))}{\partial\boldsymbol{\phi}}\,d\mu = \frac{\partial f(\boldsymbol{\phi}^*)}{\partial\boldsymbol{\phi}} = 0.$$

It therefore follows from the multivariate Lindberg-Levy theorem that, as $N \to \infty$,

$$\frac{1}{\sqrt{N}}\begin{bmatrix}\displaystyle\sum_{n=1}^{N}\frac{\partial g(\mathbf{s}_n, \boldsymbol{\phi}^*, \mathbf{h}(\boldsymbol{\phi}^*))}{\partial\boldsymbol{\phi}} \\ \displaystyle\sum_{n=1}^{N}(\mathbf{e}(\mathbf{s}_n, \boldsymbol{\phi}^*) - \mathbf{h}(\boldsymbol{\phi}^*))\end{bmatrix} \xrightarrow{\text{a.d.}} \mathcal{N}\left(\mathbf{0}, \begin{bmatrix}\mathbf{V}_g & \mathbf{V}'_{eg} \\ \mathbf{V}_{eg} & \mathbf{V}_e\end{bmatrix}\right).$$

Hence

$$\sqrt{N}\frac{\partial f_N(\mathbf{x}, \boldsymbol{\phi}^*)}{\partial\boldsymbol{\phi}} \xrightarrow{\text{a.d.}} \mathcal{N}(\mathbf{0}, \boldsymbol{\Delta}).$$

It may easily be verified that under assumptions 1.1 through 1.5, each of the estimators (1.7), (1.9), (1.15), (1.16), (1.19), (1.33), (1.36), (1.41), (1.48), and (1.49) satisfies the assumptions of lemmas 1.4 and 1.5 and hence has an associated first-order normal asymptotic distribution. For all estimators except (1.7) and (1.9) the constraint equations are the trivial ($\mathbf{r}: \boldsymbol{\Phi} \to \mathbf{R}^0$) so that the matrix $\boldsymbol{\Omega}^{-1}$ simplifies to $\boldsymbol{\Omega}^{-1} = \mathbf{F}^{-1}$. For all estimators except (1.33), (1.48), and (1.49) the range space of the function $\mathbf{e}$ is the empty set, so that the matrix $\boldsymbol{\Delta}$ simplifies to $\boldsymbol{\Delta} = \mathbf{V}_g$. For all estimators except (1.19) and (1.48), $\mathbf{F} = -\mathbf{V}_g$, allowing further simplification of the covariance matrix expression.

References

Aitchison, J. A., and S. Silvey. 1958. Maximum Likelihood Estimation of Parameters Subject to Constraint. *Annals of Mathematical Statistics*. 29: 813–828.

Amemiya, T. 1973. Regression Analysis When the Dependent Variable is Truncated Normal. *Econometrica*. 41: 997–1016.

Amemiya, T. 1976. The Maximum Likelihood, the Minimum Chi-Square, and the Non-Linear Weighted Least Squares Estimator in the General Qualitative Response Model. *Journal of the American Statistical Association*. 71: 347–351.

Anderson, T. W. 1958. *An Introduction to Multivariate Statistical Analysis*. New York: Wiley.

Bishop, Y., S. Fienberg, and P. Holland. 1975. *Discrete Multivariate Analysis*. Cambridge, Mass.: MIT Press.

Bishop, Y., and F. Mosteller. 1969. Smoothed Contingency Table Analysis. In *The National Halothane Study*, ed. J. Bunker. Washington, D.C.: Government Printing Office.

Carroll, S., and D. Relles. 1976. A Bayesian Model of Choice Among Higher Education Institutions. RAND Corporation report R-2005-NIE/LE. Santa Monica, Calif.

Cox, D. 1970. *Analysis of Binary Data*. London: Methuen.

Domencich, T., and D. McFadden. 1975. *Urban Travel Demand: A Behavioral Analysis*. Amsterdam: North-Holland.

Finney, D. 1971. *Probit Analysis*. New York: Cambridge University Press.

Gantmacher, F. 1959. *The Theory of Matrices*. London: Chelsea.

Goodman, L., and W. Kruskal. 1954. Measures of Association for Cross Classifications. *Journal of the American Statistical Association*. Vol. 49, pp. 732–764.

Haberman, S. 1974. *The Analysis of Frequency Data*. Chicago: University of Chicago Press.

Kendall, M., and J. Stuart. 1976. *Advanced Theory of Statistics*, vol. 3. New York: Hafner.

Kohn, M., C. Manski, and D. Mundel. 1976. An Empirical Investigation of Factors Influencing College Going Behavior. *Annals of Economic and Social Measurement*. 5: 391–419.

Ladd, G. 1966. Linear Probability Functions and Discriminant Functions. *Econometrica*. 34: 873–885.

Lerman, S., and M. Ben-Akiva. 1976. A Disaggregate Behavioral Model of Automobile Ownership. *Transportation Research Record*, 569: 34–55.

Manski, C. 1975. Maximum Score Estimation of the Stochastic Utility Model of Choice. *Journal of Econometrics*. 3: 205–228.

Manski, C., and S. Lerman. 1977. The Estimation of Choice Probabilities from Choice-Based Samples. *Econometrica*. 45: 1977–1988.

McFadden, D. 1973. Conditional Logit Analysis of Qualitative Choice Behavior. In *Frontiers in Econometrics*, ed. P. Zarembka. New York: Academic Press.

McFadden, D. 1976a. The Revealed Preferences of a Government Bureaucracy, Part II: Evidence. *Bell Journal of Economics*. 7: 55–72.

McFadden, D. 1976b. Quantal Choice Analysis: A Survey. *Annals of Economic and Social Measurement*. 5: 363–390.

McFadden, D. 1976c. A Comment on Discriminant Analysis "versus" Logit Analysis. *Annals of Economic and Social Measurement*. 5:

McFadden, D., and F. A. Reid. 1975. Aggregate Travel Demand Forecasting from Disaggregated Behavioral Models. *Transportation Research Record*, 534: 24–37.

McGillvrey, R. 1970. Demand and Choice Models of Modal Split. *Journal of Transport Economics and Policy*. 4: 192–207.

Rao, C. R. 1973. *Linear Statistical Inference and Its Application*. New York: Wiley.

Radner, R., and L. Miller. 1975. *Demand and Supply in U.S. Higher Education*. New York: McGraw-Hill.

Thurstone, L. 1927. A Law of Comparative Judgement. *Psychological Review*. 34: 273–286.

Warner, S. 1963. Multivariate Regression of Dummy Variates under Normality Assumptions. *Journal of the American Statistical Association*. 58: 1054–1063.

Westin, R. 1974. Predictions from Binary Choice Models. *Journal of Econometrics*. 2: 1–16.

2 Efficient Estimation of Discrete-Choice Models

Stephen R. Cosslett

2.1 Introduction

In this chapter we consider maximum likelihood estimation of discrete-choice models when the sample of observations is choice-based. Unlike a random sample in which the probability of being included is the same for all individuals, a choice-based sample is designed so that the probability of being included depends on which choice the individual made; that is, the sample is stratified on an endogenous variable. This type of sampling is appropriate when some alternatives of particular interest are infrequently chosen.

There are two aspects of this problem: the choice of estimators and the design of samples. As far as estimation is concerned, the nonrandom nature of the sample is a liability—it is more difficult to get consistent and asymptotically efficient estimates of the parameters of a choice model from a choice-based sample than from a random sample. The first part of this chapter develops a systematic method for obtaining estimators with these properties. The proofs of consistency and asymptotic efficiency are somewhat lengthy and technical; in particular the question of asymptotic efficiency involves problems that appear not to have been addressed in the econometric or statistical literature. Details of these proofs are therefore presented elsewhere (Cosslett 1978, 1981). Using this method, maximum likelihood estimators are derived for several nonrandom sampling procedures. Some of these sampling procedures have been investigated previously by Manski and Lerman (1977) and by Manski and McFadden, chapter 1; some of the estimators obtained in chapter 1 are the same as the corresponding maximum likelihood estimators and thus are asymptotically efficient.

When sample design is concerned, however, the nonrandom sample becomes an asset. Once a suitable estimator is available, a properly

This research was supported in part by the Alfred P. Sloan Foundation, through grant 74-12-8 to the Department of Economics, University of California, Berkeley, in part by the National Science Foundation through grant SOC75-22657 to the University of California, Berkeley, and in part by the University of California. An earlier version of this chapter was presented at the NBER-NSF Conference on Decision Rules and Uncertainty, Carnegie-Mellon University, April 1978.

I have benefited from discussion with C. Manski, T. Amemiya, and R. Radner, and especially from valuable advice, comments, and suggested improvements from D. McFadden.

designed choice-based sample can often provide more precise estimates than can a random sample of the same total size. Equivalently, if estimates are required to some specified level of precision, use of a choice-based sample can often reduce the size (and cost) of the sample.[1] The selection of sample design is illustrated by numerical calculations for some simple choice models. From computed values of the asymptotic variances of different estimators and different sampling schemes, we obtain a qualitative picture of the effects of (1) using a choice-based sample rather than a random sample, (2) varying the relative sizes of the alternative-specific subsamples in a choice-based sample, (3) prior knowledge of the proportions of the whole population that choose each alternative, and (4) using suboptimal, but computationally simpler, estimators, such as the Manski-Lerman estimator (Manski and Lerman 1977).

2.2 Discrete Choice Models

A discrete choice model specifies probabilities $P(i|\mathbf{z}, \boldsymbol{\theta})$ for each of a set of alternatives $\{i\}$ among which an individual can choose. The exogenous variables $\mathbf{z}$ describe observed attributes of the individual and of the alternatives available to him, and are supposed to be causal variables affecting the choice. The parameters $\boldsymbol{\theta}$ are to be estimated from the observed choices of a sample of individuals. The method of estimation depends on the functional form of $P(i \mid \mathbf{z}, \boldsymbol{\theta})$, on the way in which the sample was drawn, and on the extent of prior knowledge of the distribution of the exogenous variables $\mathbf{z}$. Predictions of choice probabilities can then be made for different populations, or for the same population following changes in some external variables, or even following the introduction of entirely new alternatives.

A review of discrete choice models and their application is given by McFadden (1976), with further discussion by Manski and McFadden in chapter 1 and by McFadden in chapter 5.[2] As an example, in the case that provided the starting point for this research, the alternatives are the modes of transportation available for traveling from home to work, such as car,

1. Two related papers address the questions of sample design and estimation from choice-based samples: Manski and McFadden, chapter 1, and Lerman and Manski (1978).
2. Any discrete response or outcome can be analyzed, not necessarily choice. In such cases the terminology "qualitative response" or "quantal response" is more appropriate than "discrete choice" or "probabilistic choice."

bus, subway, or car pool; the attributes of the individual are socioeconomic characteristics such as family income and home location; and typical attributes of the alternatives are the times and costs of each mode.[3]

The estimation procedures described in the following sections can be applied to quite general probability models $P(i \mid \mathbf{z}, \boldsymbol{\theta})$, subject only to some mild regularity and identifiability conditions. Only a few probability models, however, have been found useful in econometric applications, regardless of whether the sample is random, stratified, or choice-based. The tasks of specification and estimation may be quite intractable unless the form of the probabilities is very much restricted. Thus the only probability models used in practice are the well-known logit and probit models. The nested logit model, a special case of the generalized extreme value model developed by McFadden (1978) (see also Williams 1977 and Daly and Zachary 1979), has also been used recently.[4] These models can all be derived from an underlying random utility maximization model with a linear additive utility function (see McFadden 1973, 1978); but they are still useful and convenient parametrizations even when utility maximization or stochastic thresholds are not appropriate as underlying models.

Besides the general form of each estimator, we shall also give the particular form that it takes when the choice probabilities are specified by a multinomial logit model. Because of the special properties of the logit model, the estimator in this case is often greatly simplified. The multinomial logit form of the probabilities is

$$P(i \mid \mathbf{z}, \boldsymbol{\theta}) = \frac{\exp V_i(\mathbf{z}, \boldsymbol{\theta})}{\sum_{j=1}^{M} \exp V_j(\mathbf{z}, \boldsymbol{\theta})}, \tag{2.1}$$

where M is the number of alternatives. The actual specification of $V_i(\mathbf{z}, \boldsymbol{\theta})$ does not matter here: it is just a summary statistic or index number

3. Another type of application uses repeated observations on the same individuals, as for example in studies of unemployment, of labor-force participation (Heckman, chapter 3), or of welfare dependency, where now the probability $P[i(t) \mid \mathbf{z}(t), \boldsymbol{\theta}]$ is conditioned on the previous outcome $i(t-1)$ as well as on $\mathbf{z}$. Panel data of this kind may be analyzed in terms of a "dynamic" discrete state model, invovling time-dependent transitions between the different states. Choice-based sampling in such cases, however, can lead to additional complications which are not covered in the present work.

4. The estimator derived here (see section 2.14) has been applied in estimating a nested logit model of transportation mode choice (McFadden, chapter 5) from an enriched choice-based sample (Cosslett 1978).

representing the attractiveness or desirability of alternative i. In the random utility maximization model it is the average utility (for all subjects with the same characteristics $\mathbf{z}$) of alternative i. In practice it generally has the linear form (used also in the probit and nested logit models)

$$V_i(\mathbf{z}_i, \boldsymbol{\theta}) = \sum_{\alpha} z_{i\alpha}\theta_\alpha = \mathbf{z}_i \cdot \boldsymbol{\theta}, \tag{2.2}$$

for $i = 1, \ldots, M$, where the subvector of exogenous variables $\mathbf{z}_i$ is supposed to contain attributes of alternative i, and socioeconomic characteristics of the individual, but not attributes of the other alternatives. When specifying the model, one generally includes a full set of alternative-specific dummy variables (one fewer than the number of alternatives), and some further simplifications occur in the case of the logit model with a full set of alternative dummies.[5]

2.3 Stratified Sampling and Choice-Based Sampling

Three types of sampling procedure are of interest here: random sampling, stratified sampling, and choice-based sampling. A random sample is self-explanatory and is typified by the household survey in which households are selected randomly within some geographical area.

In stratified sampling the population is first classified in subsets on the basis of one or more exogenous variables; a random sample is then drawn from each group, but different groups are sampled at different rates. Thus in a study of choice of transportation mode for travel between home and work, one might want to sample suburban residents at a higher rate than city center residents (provided that residence location is not an endogenous variable in the choice model). As another example, the study may be designed to determine the significance, if any, of one particular exogenous variable (such as educational background) in determining the response probabilities; one might therefore select a sample which is more or less homogeneous in the other exogenous variables.

In choice-based sampling, on the other hand, the classification of the population into subsets to be sampled is based instead on the choices or outcomes: for each alternative a random sample is drawn of those individuals who chose that alternative. This may be considered as an *endogenous* sampling process, as opposed to the *exogenous* stratification

5. A dummy variable on alternative j is a variable $z_{i\alpha}$ such that $z_{j\alpha} = 1$ and $z_{i\alpha} = 0$ for $i \neq j$.

just described. Thus in a study of transportation mode choice one might select for interview, say, 200 subjects using each mode (bus, rapid transit, car, car pool, etc.) rather than rely on a random household survey in which the proportion of subjects using some modes may well be very small (e.g., for the Los Angeles area only a few percent would be found to travel by bus). In a study of consumer behavior, a sample might be drawn from those consumers who actually bought the product in question and supplied personal information on a so-called warranty card. (In this last case some information on the characteristics of the whole population of consumers is also needed.)

Consider another example of choice-based sampling: in the study of the incidence of some disease, one would examine, say, 100 subjects hospitalized with the disease plus another 100 unaffected persons from the general population. In the epidemiological literature, this type of sampling is referred to as a "case-control," or "case-referent," study, as opposed to an exogenously sampled cohort study; see, for example, Seigel and Greenhouse (1973) and Miettinen (1976). One should note, however, that the term "case-control" is often used to describe studies where the samples are not only choice-based but also *matched* on one or more exogenous variables. Thus in a study of the effects of coffee drinking on heart disease, for example, one might first study 100 persons with heart disease and then find a sample of 100 unaffected subjects with the same composition by, say, age, race, sex and residential area as the affected sample. One then looks for any signficant difference in the coffee-drinking habits of the two samples, the confounding effects of the matched variables having been reduced or eliminated. This type of sampling can also be analyzed by the methods described in this chapter. But in econometric work, with which we are primarily concerned here, the problem is generally tackled with some form of multivariate analysis rather than by matching.

There are also more complicated sampling procedures, involving stratification on both exogenous and endogenous variables at the same time. These will not be considered here, but a formalism for describing more general types of stratification is given by Manski and McFadden, chapter 1. The term "stratified sampling" will be reserved for the case where all the variables defining the subsamples are exogenous; all other stratifications will be referred to as choice-based sampling.[6]

6. This differs from the terminology of Manski and McFadden in chapter 1, who use stratified sampling to refer to all stratifications—endogenous, exogenous, or mixed.

Choice-based sampling appears to have been first considered by Warner (1963); see also Warner (1967).[7] More recently, Lerman and Manski (1975, 1978) have discussed in some detail t reasons for considering choice-based sampling, in the context of transportation demand. As is apparent from the examples we have given, advantages may be gained from efficient sample design (shared to some extent with stratified sampling). A very large random sample may be needed to provide useful information on infrequently chosen alternatives, and it may not be possible by stratifying on exogenous variables to find individuals with a high probability of selecting those alternatives. In addition random surveys involving household interviews tend to be expensive in comparison with on-board and similar surveys where problems such as identifying the subpopulation of interest and making initial contact (possibly for later interview by telephone or mail) are less severe. Partly for this reason large household surveys are sometimes updated by subsequent small-scale, choice-based surveys, but consistent methods of integrating these samples have not always been clear.

As shown by Lerman and Manski (1975), and by Manski and Lerman (1977), (1) estimation from stratified samples does not present any new problems, since the maximum-likelihood techniques that have been developed for particular choice models in the case of random sampling continue to yield consistent, efficient estimates of the parameters $\boldsymbol{\theta}$ in the case of stratified sampling, but (2) these estimation procedures lead to inconsistent (and thus asymptotically biased) estimates in choice-based sampling, a fact not always recognized in empirical applications. This leads to the problem of obtaining maximum likelihood estimators for choice-based samples.

In practice a purely choice-based sample of the kind we have described is not likely to be useful. If a logit model is used for the choice probabilities, and if the model contains alternative-specific dummy variables, then the coefficients of the model are not identifiable from a purely choice-based sample (Manski and Lerman 1977). If a probit model is specified instead, it is in theory identifiable from a purely choice-based sample, but in fact the coefficients of the dummy variables will be poorly determined—identifiability rests on the assumption that the true probabilities are exactly represented by the probit form. Alternative-specific dummies are always necessary in practice, to allow for the effects of unobserved attributes.

7. Warner's subsequent analysis was based on discriminant analysis rather than on a probabilistic choice model.

The underlying reason for this identifiability problem with purely choice-based samples is the lack of information about the choices and independent variables in the population as a whole. The leads us to consider *hybrid* sampling procedures, in which a choice-based sample is combined with additional survey data or statistics taken from a random sample of the entire population under study. A comparatively small amount of this additional information may be sufficient. Two examples of hybrid sampling procedures are the following:

1. Enriched sample. A random sample is *enriched* by addition of a choice-based sample for one or more alternatives that occur infrequently but are of interest in the analysis. For example, a study of the probability of unemployment might reinforce a random sample of labor-force participants by a sample of persons currently drawing unemployment benefits. The combined sample is then used for estimation.
2. Prior knowledge of the aggregate shares. One may know the proportions of the whole population that select each alternative, that is, the aggregate demand for each of the alternatives. For example, one might have data giving the total number of people traveling to work in some city by each mode: car, bus, rail, and so on. If the known aggregate shares are incorporated as a constraint in the estimation procedure, a purely choice-based sample is identifiable.

In the next four sections a number of hybrid sampling procedures that appear to be of practical value are listed and defined more precisely. These are the sampling schemes for which we shall derive maximum likelihood estimators.

2.4 Generalized Choice-Based Sample

As a generalization of the choice-based sampling procedure, one may take each choice-based subsample to be a random sample on some subset of the full set of chosen alternatives, not necessarily on a single alternative. Three special cases of this sampling scheme have already been mentioned: the purely choice-based sample, the enriched sample, and the random sample. As an example of the more general scheme, consider a rail travel demand study in which two of the alternatives have the traveler parking his car at the railroad station and the traveler taking a taxi to the station (plus two analogous alternatives for, say, air travel). A choice-based subsample of rail travelers would then consist of a random sample on two modes out of four.

Suppose the entire sample is made up of S subsamples, labeled by s, with $s = 1, \ldots, S$. Subsample s is a random sample drawn from those cases where the chosen alternative is in the set $\mathscr{J}(s)$. This set $\mathscr{J}(s)$ is a subset of the full set of alternatives $\{1, \ldots, M\}$. The various subsets $\mathscr{J}(s)$ need not be mutually exclusive. There is no loss of generality in assuming that the subsets $\mathscr{J}(s)$ are all different, because observations from two surveys with the same sampling rule can be combined into a single subsample.

A purely choice-based sample is given by the special case

$$\mathscr{J}(1) = \{1\}, \quad \mathscr{J}(2) = \{2\}, \ldots, \quad \mathscr{J}(M) = \{M\},$$

with $S = M$. A random sample is given by the trivial case

$$\mathscr{J}(1) = \{1, \ldots, M\},$$

with $S = 1$. A simple enriched sample, with enrichment on only one alternative, is given by

$$\mathscr{J}(1) = \{1\}, \quad \mathscr{J}(2) = \{1, 2, \ldots, M\},$$

with $S = 2$. Note that an enriched sample can be considered from two points of view: as a random sample in which the number of cases with rarely chosen alternatives is increased by adding choice-based subsamples, so as to improve the quality of the estimates, or conversely, as a choice-based sample (possibly not including all alternatives) to which a random subsample has been added, thus providing enough information about the population as a whole to make the model identifiable.

A generalized choice-based sample will not always allow a choice probability model to be estimated. A certain amount of overlapping between the sets $\mathscr{J}(s)$ is needed. For a logit model with a full set of alternative-specific dummy variables, sufficient conditions for identifiability are[8]

1. All alternatives are included, namely,

$$\bigcup_{s=1}^{S} \mathscr{J}(s) = \{1, 2, \ldots, M\}. \tag{2.3}$$

8. It is also assumed that each subsample s is sufficiently large that all the alternatives in $\mathscr{J}(s)$ are actually observed.

2. The subsets $\mathscr{I}(s)$ cannot be grouped into two (or more) mutually exclusive sets of alternatives, that is, if $\mathscr{S}_1$ and $\mathscr{S}_2$ are any two nonempty subsets of $\{1, \ldots, S\}$ such that

$$\mathscr{S}_1 \bigcup \mathscr{S}_2 = \{1, \ldots, S\},$$

then

$$\left(\bigcup_{s \in \mathscr{S}_1} \mathscr{I}(s)\right) \cap \left(\bigcup_{s \in \mathscr{S}_2} \mathscr{I}(s)\right) \neq \phi. \tag{2.4}$$

In most cases, however, a simpler condition for identifiability will be assumed: let one of the subsamples be a random sample of the whole population.

2.5 Sample with Known Aggregate Shares

Besides sample design the estimation procedure also depends on the extent of existing information about the distribution of the exogenous variables $\mathbf{z}$ in the sampled population. One may possibly know the functional form of the distribution $\mu(\mathbf{z})$, or the proportions Q_i of the whole population that select each alternative i, or have both pieces of information. Knowledge of Q_i comes from data on the aggregate demand for each alternative, or the total incidence of each outcome, which is often available in published statistics. For $\mu(\mathbf{z})$, however, one requires the joint distribution of what may be a large number of variables, which, even if known empirically, may be rather difficult to express in an explicit parametric form. Even if the form of $\mu(\mathbf{z})$ were known, its inclusion in the estimation procedure would lead to serious practical difficulties: for example, multidimensional integrals of the form $\int d\mathbf{z}\, \mu(\mathbf{z}) P(i \mid \mathbf{z}, \boldsymbol{\theta})$ would have to be performed for every evaluation of the objective function and its derivatives in the iteration procedure. For these reasons we will suppose that the explicit form of $\mu(\mathbf{z})$ is not known. There are then only two sources of information on this distribution: sample observations of the variables $\mathbf{z}$; and, indirectly, the marginal proportions Q_i (when available).

As mentioned, the constraints imposed by known aggregate shares can allow one to estimate an otherwise unidentifiable choice model from a purely choice-based sample.[9] But knowledge of the Q_i improves the quality

9. Use of a purely choice-based sample in conjunction with a priori knowledge of the mode split appears to have been first proposed by Warner (1963).

of estimates for other sampling schemes too, such as random and enriched samples. When the Q_i are known, the essential difference between estimation from choice-based samples and from random (or stratified) samples disappears. Consequently the problem of estimation subject to the constraints imposed by the Q_i can be handled independently of the problems raised by nonrandom sampling: an estimator will be derived that is applicable to both random and choice-based samples when the Q_i are known.

2.6 Aggregate Shares Estimated from an Auxiliary Sample

In this case the aggregate shares Q_i are not known in advance, but they are estimated from an auxiliary random survey in which the subject's choice is determined (but not data on the exogenous variables). Such a survey should be comparatively inexpensive: for example, a random telephone survey asking a single question might well suffice (Lerman and Manski 1975). Knowledge of the aggregate shares can considerably improve the precision of the parameter estimates, even from a random survey; thus an auxiliary survey may, depending on circumstances, be more productive than increasing the size of the main sample, given a fixed sampling budget.

If the auxiliary sample is large enough, the statistical error in determining the Q_i from it can be ignored, and this case reduces to the previous case in section 2.5. The estimator obtained for the present case is applicable when the auxiliary sample is smaller than, or of a size comparable to, the main sample.

2.7 Supplemented Sample

A choice-based sample is supplemented by the addition of a random sample which provides observations of the exogenous variables but not of the actual choices. (This is the reverse of the previous case in section 2.6, where the auxiliary sample provides observations of the choices but not of the exogenous variables.) An example of a supplementary sample is the public use sample of the U.S. census. Other types of independent variable might be obtained, for example, from an existing large-scale survey of psychological attitudes. The survey must, however, provide individual observations rather than aggregate or marginal totals. A purely choice-based sample, when supplemented in this way, allows one to estimate a choice model that would otherwise be unidentifiable.

It is even possible in some cases to estimate from a choice-based sample where not all the choices are observed. An example is a market research type of survey, where data are gathered on consumers who buy some particular product but not on those who do not buy. If the same exogenous variables are observed in a random sample of the whole population, then a choice model can be estimated, even though the random survey is not concerned with purchases of the product in question. A maximum likelihood estimator will be given also for this case.

2.8 General Considerations in Maximum Likelihood Estimation

In a random sample the likelihood of observing a case with characteristics $\mathbf{z}$ and chosen alternative i is

$$f(i,\mathbf{z} \mid \boldsymbol{\theta}) = P(i \mid \mathbf{z},\boldsymbol{\theta})\mu(\mathbf{z}), \tag{2.5}$$

continuing the notation of section 2.2 where $\mu(\mathbf{z})$ is the density function for the distribution of the independent variables. The log likelihood for a sample of size N is therefore

$$L_N(\boldsymbol{\theta}) = \sum_{n=1}^{N} \ln P(i_n \mid \mathbf{z}_n, \boldsymbol{\theta}) + \sum_{n=1}^{N} \ln \mu(\mathbf{z}_n), \tag{2.6}$$

where $\mathbf{z}_n$ and i_n are the characteristics and choice of case n.[10] Maximization of $L_N(\boldsymbol{\theta})$ with respect to $\boldsymbol{\theta}$ involves only the first sum, which is independent of $\mu(\mathbf{z})$, and thus a maximum likelihood estimate $\hat{\boldsymbol{\theta}}_N$ can be obtained without any knowledge of $\mu(\mathbf{z})$. Given sufficient conditions on the regularity of the probability functions $P(i \mid \mathbf{z}, \boldsymbol{\theta})$, one may then apply the classical proofs of consistency and asymptotic efficiency of the maximum likelihood estimator (for example, as given by Rao 1973). Specific types of probabilistic choice model have been treated by McFadden (1973), Hausman and Wise (1978), and others (for a review see McFadden 1976). The corresponding maximization algorithms have been implemented in generally efficient and stable computer programs.

For stratified sampling the log likelihood differs from that of equation (2.6) only in the second sum. Let $\mu_s(\mathbf{z})$ be the probability density of $\mathbf{z}$ in subpopulation s, and let $s(n)$ denote the subpopulation (stratum) from

10. The abbreviation $\mathbf{z}_n$ represents $(z_{i\alpha})_n$, where $(z_{i\alpha})$ is the matrix of exogenous variables, explained in section 2.2, corresponding to individual n.

which case n was drawn; then $\mu(\mathbf{z}_n)$ is replaced by $\mu_{s(n)}(\mathbf{z}_n)$ in equation (2.6). Since maximization with respect to $\boldsymbol{\theta}$ involves only the first term, the maximum likelihood estimators are the same as in random sampling.[11]

Next consider a purely choice-based sample. The choice $i(n)$ is now fixed by the sample design. Within each subsample, the relevant likelihood is the probability of observing $\mathbf{z}$, given the choice i. By application of Bayes' rule for conditional probabilities, this likelihood is[12]

$$f(\mathbf{z} \mid i, \boldsymbol{\theta}) = \frac{P(i \mid \mathbf{z}, \boldsymbol{\theta})\mu(\mathbf{z})}{Q(i \mid \boldsymbol{\theta})}, \tag{2.7}$$

where the marginal choice probabilities are

$$Q(i \mid \boldsymbol{\theta}) = \int d\mathbf{z}\, \mu(\mathbf{z}) P(i \mid \mathbf{z}, \boldsymbol{\theta}). \tag{2.8}$$

The actual proportions Q_i, which may or may not be observed, are thus $Q_i = Q(i \mid \boldsymbol{\theta}^*)$ for a very large total population, $\boldsymbol{\theta}^*$ being the "true" values of the parameters. Evidently, the log likelihood $L_N(\boldsymbol{\theta})$ corresponding to equation (2.7) can no longer be separated into a sum of terms involving only $\boldsymbol{\theta}$ and only $\mu(\mathbf{z})$.

Maximum likelihood estimation for a choice-based sample therefore involves maximizing not only over the discrete paraters $\boldsymbol{\theta}$ of the choice model but also over the space of unknown density functions $\mu(\mathbf{z})$, or rather, over the corresponding probability distributions. This problem does not satisfy the conditions for the classical proofs that the maximum likelihood estimator is consistent and asymptotically efficient; it does not even satisfy the conditions of Kiefer and Wolfowitz (1956) for consistency in the presence of infinitely many incidental parameters. One must therefore proceed step by step, as follows:

1. Derive the estimator, guided by the maximum likelihood approach. The problem must be reduced to a maximization over a finite set of discrete parameters before the estimation can be carried out. There is no general theory to guarantee that the resulting estimator will be asymptotically efficient or even consistent; however, the fact that it is a maximum likelihood estimator provides the motivation for proceeding to the next two steps.

2. Prove that the estimator is consistent, by direct attack. A consistent

11. Thus knowledge of $\mu(\mathbf{z})$ does not improve the estimates of $\boldsymbol{\theta}$ in a stratified sample.

12. See Manski and Lerman (1977). The likelihood for a generalized choice-based sample is given in section 2.10.

estimator $\hat{\boldsymbol{\theta}}_N$ is one that converges in probability to the true value $\boldsymbol{\theta}^*$ as N becomes large.

3. Prove that the estimator is asymptotically efficient. There are two parts to the proof (see Cosslett 1978, 1981): first, a lower bound is established on the variance of any unbiased estimator, closely analogous to the Cramér-Rao lower bound; and second, the estimator is shown to be asymptotically normally distributed with a variance equal to this lower bound.

2.9 Notation for a General Choice-Based Sample

The following notation will be used to describe generalized choice-based samples and the estimators and their asymptotic covariances:
N = the total number of cases,
N_i = the observed number of cases choosing alternative i, $i = 1, \ldots, M$,
$\tilde{N}_s$ = the number of cases in subsample s, for $s = 1, \ldots, S$,
$H_i = N_i/N$,
$\tilde{H}_s = \tilde{N}_s/N$,
Q_i = the proportion of the population choosing alternative i,
$\tilde{Q}_s = \Sigma_{i \in \mathscr{J}(s)} Q_i$.
In terms of a choice model with specified probabilities $P(i \mid \mathbf{z}, \boldsymbol{\theta})$, we define

$$P(\mathscr{J}(s) \mid \mathbf{z}, \boldsymbol{\theta}) = \sum_{j \in \mathscr{J}(s)} P(j \mid \mathbf{z}, \boldsymbol{\theta}), \tag{2.9}$$

$$Q(\mathscr{J}(s) \mid \boldsymbol{\theta}) = \sum_{j \in \mathscr{J}(s)} Q(j \mid \boldsymbol{\theta}) = \int d\mathbf{z}\, \mu(\mathbf{z})\, P(\mathscr{J}(s) \mid \mathbf{z}, \boldsymbol{\theta}), \tag{2.10}$$

and

$$\bar{P}(\mathbf{z}, \boldsymbol{\theta}) = \sum_{s=1}^{S} \frac{\tilde{H}_s}{\tilde{Q}_s} P(\mathscr{J}(s) \mid \mathbf{z}, \boldsymbol{\theta}), \tag{2.11}$$

with $Q(j \mid \boldsymbol{\theta})$ given by equation (2.8).

The following notation will also be useful:

$$\delta_{ij} = \begin{cases} 1 & \text{if } i = j, \\ 0 & \text{otherwise;} \end{cases}$$
$$\eta_{is} = \begin{cases} 1 & \text{if } i \in \mathscr{J}(s), \\ 0 & \text{otherwise;} \end{cases} \tag{2.12}$$

and

$$h_{ij} = \sum_{s=1}^{S} \frac{\tilde{H}_s}{\tilde{Q}_s^2} \eta_{is} \eta_{js}. \tag{2.13}$$

Note that the expected value of H_i, the proportion of the total sample choosing alternative i, is

$$\bar{H}_i \equiv E[H_i] = Q_i \sum_{s=1}^{S} \frac{\tilde{H}_s}{\tilde{Q}_s} \eta_{is}, \tag{2.14}$$

and an alternate expression for $\bar{P}(\mathbf{z}, \boldsymbol{\theta})$ in equation (2.11) is therefore

$$\bar{P}(\mathbf{z},\boldsymbol{\theta}) = \sum_{i=1}^{M} \frac{\bar{H}_i}{Q_i} P(i \mid \mathbf{z},\boldsymbol{\theta}). \tag{2.15}$$

The following abbreviated notation will also be used:

$$\begin{cases} \langle F(\mathbf{z})\rangle \equiv \int F(\mathbf{z})\mu(\mathbf{z})\,d\mathbf{z}, \\ P_i \equiv P(i \mid \mathbf{z},\boldsymbol{\theta}^*), \\ P(s) \equiv P(\mathscr{J}(s) \mid \mathbf{z},\boldsymbol{\theta}^*), \\ \bar{P} \equiv \bar{P}(\mathbf{z},\boldsymbol{\theta}^*). \end{cases} \tag{2.16}$$

We assume that $Q_i > 0$ for all i and that every alternative is included in at least one of the subsamples (see equation 2.3); thus we almost always have $H_i > 0$ for sufficiently large N.

2.10 The Likelihood Function for Choice-Based Samples

We first consider the case of a generalized choice-based sample (section 2.4) for which the aggregate shares Q_i are not known. Special cases of this include purely choice-based samples and enriched samples. Subsample s is a random sample of those subjects whose choice is in the subset of alternatives $\mathscr{J}(s)$.

The likelihood for a single observation in subsample s is now

$$f(i,\mathbf{z} \mid \mathscr{J}(s),\boldsymbol{\theta}) = \frac{P(i \mid \mathbf{z},\boldsymbol{\theta})\mu(\mathbf{z})}{Q(\mathscr{J}(s) \mid \boldsymbol{\theta})} \eta_{is}, \tag{2.17}$$

and so the log likelihood for the sample is

$$L_N(\boldsymbol{\theta};\mu) = \sum_{n=1}^{N} \ln P(i_n \mid \mathbf{z}_n, \boldsymbol{\theta}) + \sum_{n=1}^{N} \ln \mu(\mathbf{z}_n)$$
$$- \sum_{s=1}^{S} \tilde{N}_s \ln \left\{ \int d\mathbf{z}\, \mu(\mathbf{z}) P(\mathscr{I}(s) \mid \mathbf{z}, \boldsymbol{\theta}) \right\} \tag{2.18}$$

The log likelihood is to be maximized over all possible parameter values $\boldsymbol{\theta}$ and probability densities $\mu(\mathbf{z})$. If one attempts to maximize with respect to $\mu(\mathbf{z})$, it is apparent that the resulting empirical density $\hat{\mu}(\mathbf{z})$ will have all its weight concentrated at the observed data points $\{\mathbf{z}_n\}$. We therefore replace $\mu(\mathbf{z})$ by a discrete density with weight $w_n > 0$ at each data point $\mathbf{z}_n$. The appropriate likelihood is then

$$L_N(\boldsymbol{\theta};\mathbf{w}) = \sum_{n=1}^{N} \ln P(i_n \mid \mathbf{z}_n, \boldsymbol{\theta}) + \sum_{n=1}^{N} \ln w_n$$
$$- \sum_{s=1}^{S} \tilde{N}_s \ln \left\{ \sum_{m=1}^{N} w_m P(\mathscr{I}(s) \mid \mathbf{z}_m, \boldsymbol{\theta}) \right\}. \tag{2.19}$$

This is to be maximized over $\boldsymbol{\theta} \in \boldsymbol{\Theta}$ and $\mathbf{w} \in \mathbf{W}$, where $\mathbf{W}$ is the unit simplex

$$\mathbf{W} = \left\{ \mathbf{w} \mid w_n \geqslant 0 \quad \text{and} \quad \sum_{n=1}^{N} w_n = 1 \right\}. \tag{2.20}$$

Note that this procedure corresponds to replacing the (unknown) cumulative probability distribution of $\mathbf{z}$ by the empirical distribution[13]

$$F_N(\mathbf{z}) = \sum_{n:\,\mathbf{z}_n \geqslant \mathbf{z}} w_n.$$

It is noted by Kiefer and Wolfowitz (1956) that the empirical distribution is the maximum likelihood estimate of an unknown distribution function. When the sample is random, the weights are of course all equal to $1/N$. In the present case the sampling is nonrandom, and the weights associated with different observations will in general be unequal.

Although the problem has been reduced to parametric form, equation (2.19), the number of parameters increases with the number of observations. The next step is to reduce further the maximization to a fixed number of parameters.

13. If $\mathbf{x}$ and $\mathbf{y}$ are vectors with components x_α, y_α ($\alpha = 1, \ldots, K$), then $\mathbf{x} \leq \mathbf{y}$ means that all K inequalities $x_\alpha \leq y_\alpha$ hold.

2.11 Maximization of the Likelihood

First, $L_N(\boldsymbol{\theta};\mathbf{w})$ is maximized with respect to $\mathbf{w}$ at some fixed, arbitrary value of $\boldsymbol{\theta} \in \boldsymbol{\Theta}$. It is straightforward to show that the upper bound,

$$L_N(\boldsymbol{\theta};\mathbf{w}) < \sum_{n=1}^{N} \ln P(i_n \mid \mathbf{z}_n, \boldsymbol{\theta}) + \ln w_0 - N \ln p_0, \tag{2.21}$$

follows from the regularity conditions assumed for the probability functions (see assumptions 2.2 and 2.4 in appendix 2.26). In equation (2.21), w_0 is the smallest component of $\mathbf{w}$, and p_0 is a positive lower bound on the probabilities $P(i \mid \mathbf{z}, \boldsymbol{\theta})$. It follows that there is a maximum in int $\mathbf{W}$. Since $L_N(\boldsymbol{\theta};\mathbf{w})$ is continuous and differentiable for $\mathbf{w} \in$ int $\mathbf{W}$, the maximum is given by a solution of the equations for a stationary point[14]

$$\frac{\partial L_N}{\partial w_n} \equiv \frac{1}{w_n} - \sum_{s=1}^{S} \frac{\tilde{N}_s P(\mathscr{I}(s) \mid \mathbf{z}_n, \boldsymbol{\theta})}{\sum_{m=1}^{N} w_m P(\mathscr{I}(s) \mid \mathbf{z}_m, \boldsymbol{\theta})} = 0. \tag{2.22}$$

At any solution of equation (2.22) the matrix of second derivatives $\partial^2 L_N / \partial w_n \partial w_m$ is negative definite when restricted to $\mathbf{W}$, that is, every stationary point is a maximum. Because of the bound (2.21), which tends to $-\infty$ at the boundaries of $\mathbf{W}$, there cannot be two (or more) maxima in int $\mathbf{W}$ without an intervening saddle point; thus there is only one maximum. As a result the required maximum in w is given by a unique solution of equation (2.22).

Making the substitution

$$\lambda(s, \boldsymbol{\theta}) = \frac{\tilde{H}_s}{\sum_{m=1}^{N} w_m P(\mathscr{I}(s) \mid \mathbf{z}_m, \boldsymbol{\theta})}, \tag{2.23}$$

we obtain the concentrated likelihood function

$$L_N(\boldsymbol{\theta}) = \sum_{n=1}^{N} \ln \frac{\lambda(s_n, \boldsymbol{\theta}) P(i_n \mid \mathbf{z}_n, \boldsymbol{\theta})}{\sum_{s=1}^{S} \lambda(s, \boldsymbol{\theta}) P(\mathscr{I}(s) \mid \mathbf{z}_n, \boldsymbol{\theta})} - \sum_{s=1}^{S} \tilde{N}_s \ln \tilde{N}_s, \tag{2.24}$$

14. Since $L_N(\boldsymbol{\theta};\mathbf{w})$ is homogeneous in $\mathbf{w}$ of degree zero, the additional constraint $\Sigma_n w_n = 1$ does not affect the first-order conditions in equation (2.22).

where s_n is the subsample containing case n. In equation (2.24), the weight factors λ are the solution of the constraint equations

$$\frac{\tilde{N}_s}{\lambda(s,\boldsymbol{\theta})} = \sum_{n=1}^{N} \frac{P(\mathcal{J}(s) \mid \mathbf{z}_n, \boldsymbol{\theta})}{\sum_{t=1}^{S} \lambda(t,\boldsymbol{\theta}) P(\mathcal{J}(t) \mid \mathbf{z}_n, \boldsymbol{\theta})}, \tag{2.25}$$

for $s = 1, \ldots, S$ (obtained by substituting for w_n from equation 2.22 into equation 2.23), together with the normalization condition

$$\frac{1}{N} \sum_{n=1}^{N} \frac{1}{\sum_{n=1}^{S} \lambda(s,\boldsymbol{\theta}) P(\mathcal{J}(s) \mid \mathbf{z}_n, \boldsymbol{\theta})} = 1 \tag{2.26}$$

(obtained by substituting for w_n from equation 2.22 in the condition $\Sigma_n w_n = 1$). The weight factors $\mathbf{w}$ have now disappeared from the problem. Because equation (2.22) has a unique solution for $\mathbf{w} \in \mathbf{W}$, it follows that equation (2.25) likewise has a unique solution for $\boldsymbol{\lambda} \in \boldsymbol{\Lambda}_\theta$, where $\boldsymbol{\Lambda}_\theta$ is the set of weight factors $\boldsymbol{\lambda} \geq \mathbf{0}$ that also satisfy equation (2.26).

This can be reformulated in a much more convenient form, as follows. We maximize the "pseudolikelihood" function

$$\tilde{L}_N(\boldsymbol{\theta}, \lambda) = \sum_{n=1}^{N} \ln \frac{\lambda(s_n) P(i_n \mid \mathbf{z}_n, \boldsymbol{\theta})}{\sum_{s=1}^{S} \lambda(s) P(\mathcal{J}(s) \mid \mathbf{z}_n, \boldsymbol{\theta})}, \tag{2.27}$$

over $\boldsymbol{\lambda} \in \boldsymbol{\Lambda}_\theta$, where $\boldsymbol{\lambda}$ is now considered as a vector of M independent variables, rather than a function of $\boldsymbol{\theta}$. This equivalence follows from the fact that the first-order conditions for a stationary point of $\tilde{L}_N(\boldsymbol{\theta}, \boldsymbol{\lambda})$ are the same as equation (2.25), and the matrix of second derivatives $\partial^2 \tilde{L}_N(\boldsymbol{\theta}, \boldsymbol{\lambda})/\partial\lambda(s)\partial\lambda(t)$ is negative definite at any stationary point when restricted to $\boldsymbol{\lambda} \in \boldsymbol{\Lambda}_\theta$. Thus $\tilde{L}_N(\boldsymbol{\theta}, \boldsymbol{\lambda})$ has a unique maximum in $\boldsymbol{\lambda} \in \boldsymbol{\Lambda}_\theta$, at which point it is equal to the concentrated likelihood of equation (2.24), apart from a constant term independent of $\boldsymbol{\theta}$. Note that the number of weight factors is now M (the number of alternatives) instead of N (the number of observations).

Maximum likelihood estimation for a choice-based sample therefore reduces to the problem of finding $\hat{\boldsymbol{\theta}}_N$ and $\hat{\boldsymbol{\lambda}}_N$, such that

$$\tilde{L}_N(\hat{\boldsymbol{\theta}}_N, \hat{\boldsymbol{\lambda}}_N) = \max_{\boldsymbol{\theta} \in \boldsymbol{\Theta},\, \boldsymbol{\lambda} \in \boldsymbol{\Lambda}_{\boldsymbol{\theta}}} \tilde{L}_N(\boldsymbol{\theta}, \boldsymbol{\lambda}), \tag{2.28}$$

where the pseudolikelihood $\tilde{L}_N(\boldsymbol{\theta}, \boldsymbol{\lambda})$ is given by equation (2.27). $\tilde{L}_N(\boldsymbol{\theta}, \boldsymbol{\lambda})$ is called a pseudolikelihood because in general it is not equal to the likelihood $L_N(\boldsymbol{\theta}; \mathbf{w})$; the only equality that holds between them is

$$\max_{\mathbf{w} \in \mathbf{W}} L_N(\boldsymbol{\theta}; \mathbf{w}) = \max_{\boldsymbol{\lambda} \in \boldsymbol{\Lambda}_{\boldsymbol{\theta}}} \tilde{L}_N(\boldsymbol{\theta}, \boldsymbol{\lambda}).$$

The subsidiary condition $\boldsymbol{\lambda} \in \boldsymbol{\Lambda}_{\boldsymbol{\theta}}$ is inconvenient in that the normalization condition, equation (2.26), depends on $\boldsymbol{\theta}$. But since $\tilde{L}_N(\boldsymbol{\theta}, \boldsymbol{\lambda})$ is homogeneous of degree zero in $\boldsymbol{\lambda}$, the normalization condition has no effect on the maximization problem. In practice therefore, one can impose an arbitrary normalization. A convenient normalization is to fix a weight factor, say, $\lambda(S) = \tilde{H}_S$, and then maximize over

$$\boldsymbol{\lambda} \in \boldsymbol{\Lambda}(S) \equiv \{\boldsymbol{\lambda} \mid \lambda(s) \geq 0 \quad \text{and} \quad \lambda(S) = \tilde{H}_S\}. \tag{2.29}$$

If only estimates of $\boldsymbol{\theta}$ are required, this is all that is needed. If estimates of the aggregate shares $\tilde{Q}_s$ are also wanted, then the weight factors $\hat{\boldsymbol{\lambda}}_N$ have to be rescaled by a factor $\hat{\kappa}_N$ to satisfy the normalization condition, equation (2.26); see section 2.13.

2.12 Asymptotic Properties of the Unconstrained Estimator

If the exogenous space $\mathbf{Z}$ is discrete with a finite set of values, then $\hat{\boldsymbol{\theta}}_N$ as given by equation (2.28) is the classical maximum likelihood estimator, and its consistency is assured by assumptions 2.1 through 2.5 given in appendix 2.26. In fact, even if $\mathbf{Z}$ consists of a countable (rather than finite) discrete set of points, the results of Kiefer and Wolfowitz (1956) establish consistency of $\hat{\boldsymbol{\theta}}_N$. Since a continuous distribution can be approximated arbitrarily well by a discrete distribution, and since the pseudolikelihood (2.27) is a function only of the observations and of the parameters of the choice model, this suggests that the result must be valid also for $\mathbf{Z}$ continuous. However, the usual proofs of consistency of the maximum likelihood estimator require assumptions which, even though of very general applicability, do not hold in the present case. In particular, note that while the estimated empirical distribution of $\mathbf{z}$ converges weakly to the true distribution, the pseudolikelihood in equation (2.27) does not converge to the expectation of the true likelihood.

It is therefore necessary to establish directly the consistency of estimators obtained from equation (2.28). The proof follows a method due to Manski and Lerman (1977), and used by them to prove consistency of the weighted exogenous sample maximum likelihood estimator for choice-based sampling.[15] A few technical modifications are needed to apply the proof here (for details see Cosslett 1978, 1981). One finds that

$$\hat{\boldsymbol{\theta}}_N \rightarrow \boldsymbol{\theta}^*$$

$$\hat{\kappa}_N \hat{\lambda}_N(s) \rightarrow \frac{\tilde{H}_s}{\tilde{Q}_s} \qquad \text{(a.s.).} \tag{2.30}$$

This provides an interpretation of the parameters $\boldsymbol{\lambda}$, that is, the weights $\hat{\boldsymbol{\lambda}}_N$ are estimates of the ratios of the sample choice proportions to the population choice proportions. The weights $\boldsymbol{\lambda}$ may thus be viewed as correction factors, applied to the probabilities that hold for random sampling. With the normalization condition $\lambda(S) = \tilde{H}_S$, we also have

$$\hat{\kappa}_N \rightarrow \kappa \equiv \frac{1}{\tilde{Q}_S}. \tag{2.31}$$

Once consistency has been shown, one may readily establish asymptotic normality by standard methods: $L_N(\boldsymbol{\theta}, \boldsymbol{\lambda})$ is expanded in a Taylor series about the true parameter point using the differentiability conditions of assumption 2.7. This is followed by application of the Lindberg-Lévy form of the central limit theorem (e.g., see section 2c.5 of Rao 1973). Positive definiteness of the information matrix corresponding to the pseudolikelihood function follows from assumption 2.8, and from the identifiability conditions of equations (2.3) and (2.4). (For details, see Cosslett 1981.)

We next consider the asymptotic covariance matrix of the estimates $\hat{\gamma}$, where we define for brevity the composite parameter $\gamma = [\boldsymbol{\theta}, \boldsymbol{\lambda}]$. If we denote the log of the pseudolikelihood for a single observation by

$$\tilde{l}(i, \mathbf{z} \mid s, \gamma) = \ln \frac{\lambda(s) P(i \mid \mathbf{z}, \boldsymbol{\theta})}{\sum_{t=1}^{S} \lambda(t) P(\mathscr{I}(t) \mid \mathbf{z}, \boldsymbol{\theta})}, \tag{2.32}$$

15. The method is based on one originally developed by Amemiya (1973) to prove consistency of the maximum likelihood estimator for the truncated normal distribution.

and denote expectations with respect to i and $\mathbf{z}$ in subsample s by

$$E_s[F] \equiv \sum_{i \in \mathscr{I}(s)} \int d\mathbf{z}\, \mu(\mathbf{z}) \frac{1}{\tilde{Q}_s} P(i \mid \mathbf{z}, \boldsymbol{\theta}) F(i, \mathbf{z}), \tag{2.33}$$

then the asymptotic covariance matrix of $\hat{\gamma}_N$ is

$$\mathbf{V} = \mathbf{J}^{-1} \mathbf{M} \mathbf{J}^{-1}, \tag{2.34}$$

where

$$\begin{aligned} J_{\alpha\beta} &= E\left[-\frac{1}{N} \frac{\partial^2 \tilde{L}_N}{\partial \gamma_\alpha \partial \gamma_\beta} \right] \\ &= \sum_{s=1}^{S} \tilde{H}_s E_s\left[-\frac{\partial^2 \tilde{l}(s, \gamma^*)}{\partial \gamma_\alpha \partial \gamma_\beta} \right] \end{aligned} \tag{2.35}$$

and

$$\begin{aligned} M_{\alpha\beta} &= E\left[\frac{1}{N} \frac{\partial \tilde{L}_N}{\partial \gamma_\alpha} \frac{\partial \tilde{L}_N}{\partial \gamma_\beta} \right] \\ &= \sum_{s=1}^{S} \tilde{H}_s \left\{ E_s\left[\frac{\partial \tilde{l}(s, \gamma^*)}{\partial \gamma_\alpha} \frac{\partial \tilde{l}(s, \gamma^*)}{\partial \gamma_\beta} \right] - E_s\left[\frac{\partial \tilde{l}(s, \gamma^*)}{\partial \gamma_\alpha} \right] E_s\left[\frac{\partial \tilde{l}(s, \gamma^*)}{\partial \gamma_\beta} \right] \right\}. \end{aligned} \tag{2.36}$$

Because of the normalization condition $\lambda(S) = \tilde{H}_S$, the variables are $\boldsymbol{\theta}$ and $\lambda(1), \ldots, \lambda(S-1)$, and $\mathbf{J}$ and $\mathbf{M}$ are $(K + S - 1) \times (K + S - 1)$ square matrices. The assumptions in appendix 2.26, as well as the identifiability conditions of equations (2.3) and (2.4), ensure that $\mathbf{J}$ is positive definite and $\mathbf{M}$ is positive semidefinite.

From equations (2.35) and (2.36), we find that

$$\mathbf{M} = \mathbf{J} - \mathbf{J} \begin{pmatrix} \mathbf{0} & \mathbf{0} \\ \mathbf{0} & \mathbf{G} \end{pmatrix} \mathbf{J}, \tag{2.37}$$

where the $(S-1) \times (S-1)$ submatrix $\mathbf{G}$ is given by

$$G_{tt'} = \frac{1}{\kappa^2} \left(\frac{\tilde{H}_t}{\tilde{Q}_t^2} \delta_{tt'} + \frac{1}{\tilde{H}_S} \cdot \frac{\tilde{H}_t}{\tilde{Q}_t} \frac{\tilde{H}_{t'}}{\tilde{Q}_{t'}} \right). \tag{2.38}$$

Therefore we have

$$\mathbf{V} = \mathbf{J}^{-1} - \begin{pmatrix} \mathbf{0} & \mathbf{0} \\ \mathbf{0} & \mathbf{G} \end{pmatrix}. \tag{2.39}$$

If the information matrix $\mathbf{J}$ is partitioned according to $\gamma = [\boldsymbol{\theta}, \boldsymbol{\lambda}]$,

$$\mathbf{J} = \begin{pmatrix} \mathbf{A} & \mathbf{B} \\ \mathbf{B}' & \mathbf{C} \end{pmatrix}, \tag{2.40}$$

then

$$A_{\alpha\beta} = \left\langle \sum_{i=1}^{M} \frac{\bar{H}_i}{Q_i} \frac{1}{P_i} \frac{\partial P_i}{\partial \theta_\alpha} \frac{\partial P_i}{\partial \theta_\beta} - \frac{1}{\bar{P}} \frac{\partial \bar{P}}{\partial \theta_\alpha} \frac{\partial \bar{P}}{\partial \theta_\beta} \right\rangle, \tag{2.41}$$

$$B_{\alpha s} = \kappa \left\langle \frac{\partial P(s)}{\partial \theta_\alpha} - \frac{P(s)}{\bar{P}} \frac{\partial \bar{P}}{\partial \theta_\alpha} \right\rangle, \tag{2.42}$$

$$C_{st} = \kappa^2 \left\{ \frac{\tilde{Q}_s^2}{\tilde{H}_s} \delta_{st} - \left\langle \frac{P(s) P(t)}{\bar{P}} \right\rangle \right\} \tag{2.43}$$

(see equations 2.14 through 2.16 for notation).

The sample estimate of the variance $(1/N)\hat{\mathbf{V}}$ is obtained from the obvious estimator

$$\hat{J}_{\alpha\beta} = -\frac{1}{N} \frac{\partial^2 L_N(\hat{\boldsymbol{\theta}}_N, \hat{\boldsymbol{\lambda}}_N)}{\partial \gamma_\alpha \partial \gamma_\beta}, \tag{2.44}$$

assuming of course that N is large enough for asymptotic results to be valid to a good approximation.

The asymptotic covariance matrix for $\boldsymbol{\theta}$ alone is

$$\mathbf{V}_{\theta\theta} = (\mathbf{A} - \mathbf{B}\mathbf{C}^{-1}\mathbf{B}')^{-1}, \tag{2.45}$$

which is independent of the normalization of $\boldsymbol{\lambda}$. A lower bound, analogous to the Cramér-Rao lower bound, can be obtained for the covariance matrix of an estimator of $\boldsymbol{\theta}$; this is briefly discussed in appendix 2.27, while details of the derivations are given elsewhere (Cosslett 1978, 1981). The lower bound is in fact equal to $N^{-1}\,\mathbf{V}_{\theta\theta}$, so the estimator $\hat{\boldsymbol{\theta}}_N$ obtained by maximizing the pseudolikelihood is asymptotically efficient.

2.13 Estimation of Aggregate Shares

From the estimated weight factors $\hat{\boldsymbol{\lambda}}_N$, one can obtain estimates of the aggregate shares $\tilde{Q}_s$, although the primary goal was to estimate $\boldsymbol{\theta}$. To estimate $\tilde{Q}_s$ we need the absolute rather than relative values of the weights; we need the scale factor $\hat{\kappa}$ such that $\hat{\kappa}\hat{\boldsymbol{\lambda}}_N$ satisfies the normalization condition of equation (2.26). Thus we have

$$\hat{\kappa} = \frac{1}{N} \sum_{n=1}^{N} \left[\sum_{s=1}^{S} \hat{\lambda}(s) P(\mathscr{I}(s) \mid \mathbf{z}_n, \hat{\boldsymbol{\theta}}) \right]^{-1} \tag{2.46}$$

For some sample designs there is a simplification. If there is an identity of the form

$$\sum_{s=1}^{S} k_s P(\mathscr{I}(s) \mid \mathbf{z}, \boldsymbol{\theta}) \equiv k_0, \tag{2.47}$$

where the coefficients k are constants, then from equations (2.25) and (2.26)

$$\hat{\kappa} = \frac{1}{k_0} \sum_{s=1}^{S} k_s \frac{\tilde{H}_s}{\hat{\lambda}(s)}. \tag{2.48}$$

For example, in a purely choice-based sample we have

$$\sum_{s=1}^{S} P(\mathscr{I}(s) \mid \mathbf{z}, \boldsymbol{\theta}) = \sum_{i=1}^{M} P(i \mid \mathbf{z}, \boldsymbol{\theta}) = 1,$$

and so

$$\hat{\kappa} = \sum_{i=1}^{M} \frac{H_i}{\hat{\lambda}(i)};$$

while for an enriched sample (with $s = S$ corresponding to the random subsample) we have

$$P(\mathscr{I}(S) \mid \mathbf{z}, \boldsymbol{\theta}) = 1,$$

so that $\hat{\kappa} = 1$.

The asymptotic covariance matrix for $(\hat{\boldsymbol{\theta}}, \hat{\kappa}\hat{\boldsymbol{\lambda}})$ is then given by

$$\mathbf{U} = \mathscr{W}'\mathbf{V}\mathscr{W}, \tag{2.49}$$

where

$$\mathscr{W} = \begin{pmatrix} \mathbf{I} & \mathbf{0} \\ \mathbf{0} & \mathscr{V} \end{pmatrix} \tag{2.50}$$

is a $(K+S-1) \times (K+S)$ matrix with

$$\mathscr{V}_{st} = E\left[\frac{\partial \hat{\kappa}(\boldsymbol{\theta}, \boldsymbol{\lambda})}{\partial \lambda(s)} \lambda(t) + \kappa \delta_{st}\right]$$

$$= \kappa \left\{ \delta_{st} - \frac{k_s}{k_0} \frac{\tilde{Q}_s^2}{\tilde{H}_s} \frac{\tilde{H}_t}{\tilde{Q}_t} \right\} \tag{2.51}$$

for $s = 1, \ldots, S-1$ and $t = 1, \ldots, S$. The corresponding sample estimate is just

$$\hat{\mathscr{V}}_{st} = \hat{\kappa}\delta_{st} - \frac{k_s}{k_0} \frac{\hat{\lambda}(t)}{\hat{\lambda}(s)^2}. \tag{2.52}$$

If there is no identity of the form (2.47), we have to fall back on the more complicated normalization (2.46).[16]

Despite appearances the covariance matrix $\mathbf{U}$ is actually symmetric in the index $s = 1, \ldots, S$. An explicitly symmetric form can also be obtained, starting from a symmetric normalization of the weight factors, such as $\Sigma_s \lambda(s) = 1$. The expression given in (2.49) may be more useful in practice, however, because $\mathbf{V}$ is closely related to the inverse of the Hessian encountered in the maximization of $\tilde{L}_N$ (see equation 2.39).

2.14 The Unconstrained Maximum Likelihood Estimator

To summarize the preceding results, the maximum likelihood estimator $(\hat{\boldsymbol{\theta}}_N, \hat{\boldsymbol{\lambda}}_N)$ is obtained by maximizing the pseudolikelihood

$$\tilde{L}_N(\boldsymbol{\theta}, \boldsymbol{\lambda}) = \sum_{n=1}^{N} \ln \frac{\lambda(s_n) P(i_n \mid \mathbf{z}_n, \boldsymbol{\theta})}{\sum_{s=1}^{S} \lambda(s) P(\mathscr{I}(s) \mid \mathbf{z}_n, \boldsymbol{\theta})} \tag{2.53}$$

over $\boldsymbol{\theta} \in \boldsymbol{\Theta}$ and $\boldsymbol{\lambda} \in \Lambda(S)$, as given by equation (2.29). $\hat{\boldsymbol{\lambda}}_N$ is then rescaled with the factor $\hat{\kappa}_N$ discussed in section 2.13. If we let $N \to \infty$ with the relative subsample sizes $\tilde{H}_s$ held fixed, then $(\hat{\boldsymbol{\theta}}_N, \hat{\kappa}_N \hat{\boldsymbol{\lambda}}_N)$ is a consistent estimator of $(\boldsymbol{\theta}^*, \{\tilde{H}_s/\tilde{Q}_s\})$. The asymptotic covariance matrix $\mathbf{U}$ of $(\hat{\boldsymbol{\theta}}_N, \hat{\kappa}_N \hat{\boldsymbol{\lambda}}_N)$ is given by equations (2.49) and (2.39); the matrices appearing in these expressions can be estimated from sample data via equations (2.52) and (2.44).

16. See Cosslett (1978) for the asymptotic covariance matrix in this case.

Two important special cases of equation (2.53) are the enriched sample with $S = 2$ and the purely choice-based sample. In the enriched sample with $S = 2$, if cases $1, \ldots, \tilde{N}_1$ are in the choice-based subsample ($s = 1$) and cases $\tilde{N}_1 + 1, \ldots, N$ in the random subsample ($s = 2$), then

$$\tilde{L}_N(\boldsymbol{\theta}, \lambda) = \sum_{n=1}^{N_1} \ln \left\{ \frac{\lambda P(i_n \mid \mathbf{z}_n, \boldsymbol{\theta})}{\lambda P(\mathscr{I}(1) \mid \mathbf{z}_n, \boldsymbol{\theta}) + \tilde{H}_2} \right\}$$

$$+ \sum_{n=N_1+1}^{N} \ln \left\{ \frac{P(i_n \mid \mathbf{z}_n, \boldsymbol{\theta})}{\lambda P(\mathscr{I}(1) \mid \mathbf{z}_n, \boldsymbol{\theta}) + \tilde{H}_2} \right\}, \qquad (2.54)$$

where we put $\lambda(1) = \lambda$, $\lambda(2) = \tilde{H}_2$ and use the identity $P(\mathscr{I}(2) \mid \mathbf{z}, \boldsymbol{\theta}) = 1$. Note that a term in the summation corresponding to an observation in the random subsample is *not* the same as the likelihood of an observation in a random sample. Heuristically speaking, this is because an observation from the random subsample conveys some information about the distribution of $\mathbf{z}$: in a purely random sample this information is of no value in estimating $\boldsymbol{\theta}$, but in the present case it enhances the value of the information contained in an observation from the choice-based subsample.

In the purely choice-based sample,

$$\tilde{L}_N(\boldsymbol{\theta}, \boldsymbol{\lambda}) = \sum_{n=1}^{N} \ln \frac{\lambda(i_n) P(i_n \mid \mathbf{z}_n, \boldsymbol{\theta})}{\sum_{j=1}^{M} \lambda(j) P(j \mid \mathbf{z}_n, \boldsymbol{\theta})} \qquad (2.55)$$

This estimator $\hat{\boldsymbol{\theta}}_N$ was previously given by Manski (1976; see Manski and McFadden, chapter 1) for purely choice-based samples. The derivation given here shows that (1) it is a special case of the estimator (2.53), which thus extends the result of Manski and McFadden to generalized choice-based samples, including enriched samples, (2) it is the maximum likelihood estimator, so one is motivated to prove that is indeed asymptotically efficient, and (3) a general method is available for deriving maximum likelihood estimators in other cases where the likelihood is complicated by an unknown probability distribution, such as sampling schemes with known aggregate shares, with auxiliary samples, or with supplementary samples (see sections 2.5 through 2.7).

Maximization of the pseudolikelihood can generally be achieved by fairly straightforward modification of existing computer routines for maximum likelihood estimation of specific models. In the case of the probit model, the main computational cost involves evaluation of the $P(i \mid \mathbf{z}, \boldsymbol{\theta})$, so the transformation involved in equation (2.53) does not add materially to the cost.

The special case of the logit model is treated separately in section 2.15. An application of the estimator to the nested logit model (McFadden, chapter 5) is given by Cosslett (1978). The simplifications found in the ordinary logit model do not occur for the nested logit model, and it is necessary to work directly with the pseudolikelihood of equation (2.53).

2.15 The Logit Model as a Special Case

In the case of the logit model, $\tilde{L}_N(\boldsymbol{\theta}, \boldsymbol{\lambda})$ reduces to a form very similar to the original log likelihood for random samples: the denominator in the multinomial logit form, equation (2.1), is independent of the choice and so cancels from the ratio of weighted probabilities in equations (2.53).

Let $\boldsymbol{\theta} = (\boldsymbol{\phi}, \mathbf{d})$, where $\mathbf{d} = (d_1, \ldots, d_M)$ are the coefficients of alternative-specific dummy variables (subject to some linear constraint, e.g., $d_M = 0$). We then denote the log likelihood for a logit model with *random* sampling by $L_N(\boldsymbol{\phi}, \mathbf{d})$. There are two interesting cases where the pseudolikelihood $\tilde{L}_N(\boldsymbol{\theta}, \boldsymbol{\lambda})$ can be reduced exactly to the log likelihood for random sampling:

1. For a purely choice-based sample, equation (2.55) reduces to

$$\tilde{L}_N(\boldsymbol{\phi}, \mathbf{d}, \boldsymbol{\lambda}) = L_N(\boldsymbol{\phi}, \{d_i + \ln \lambda(i)\}). \tag{2.56}$$

Thus one can estimate $\boldsymbol{\phi}$ consistently by proceeding as if the sample were random, but the dummy coefficients d_i and the aggregate share ratios H_i/Q_i cannot be separately identified (see Manski and McFadden, chapter 1, and Manski and Lerman 1977). This sampling scheme cannot therefore be used for logit model estimation unless estimates of $\mathbf{d}$ are not needed, or one is confident enough in the explanatory power of the observed exogenous variables not to require dummies, or the mode splits Q_i are known in advance. In the last case, however, a better estimator is available (which will be described in section 2.19).

2. For a logit model with a full set of alternative dummies, in a general choice-based sampling scheme (assumed to be identifiable), we have

$$\tilde{L}_N(\boldsymbol{\phi}, \mathbf{d}, \boldsymbol{\lambda}) = L_N(\boldsymbol{\phi}, \mathbf{d}') + \sum_{s=1}^{S} \tilde{N}_s \ln \lambda(s) - \sum_{j=1}^{M} N_j \ln \left\{ \sum_{s=1}^{S} \eta_{js} \lambda(s) \right\}, \tag{2.57}$$

where new dummy coefficients $\mathbf{d}'$ are defined by

$$d_i' = d_i + \ln\left(\sum_{s=1}^{S} \eta_{is} \lambda(s) \right) \tag{2.58}$$

The pseudolikelihood is thus separable into two parts: the first involves only $\boldsymbol{\phi}$ and $\mathbf{d}'$, which can be estimated as if from a random sample, while the second involves only $\boldsymbol{\lambda}$. Maximization of just the last two terms in equation (2.57) gives $\hat{\lambda}(s)$; this preliminary calculation is relatively easy because these terms do not involve the individual observations $\{i_n, \mathbf{z}_n\}$ but only the subsample sizes and the numbers of subjects choosing each alternative. $\hat{\boldsymbol{\lambda}}$ is now also a set of correction terms for transforming the estimated dummy coefficients $\hat{\mathbf{d}}'$ into consistent estimators $\hat{\mathbf{d}}$, via equation (2.58).

As an example, consider estimation of a logit model from an enriched sample with one choice-based subsample. $\hat{\lambda}$ is obtained by maximizing

$$\tilde{N}_1 \ln \lambda - \sum_{j \in \mathscr{J}(1)} N_j \ln (\lambda + \tilde{H}_2)$$

(in the notation of equation 2.54), which gives

$$\hat{\lambda} = \frac{\tilde{H}_1 \tilde{H}_2}{\sum_{j \in \mathscr{J}(1)} H_j - \tilde{H}_1}.$$

Thus $\tilde{H}_1/\hat{\boldsymbol{\lambda}}$ is the proportion of subjects in the random sample who choose the alternatives on which the enriching subsample is based, which is, in fact, an obvious estimator of $\tilde{Q}_1$. The dummy coefficients corresponding to alternatives in the enriching subsample are then corrected (from the values given by the random-sampling estimator) by subtracting $\ln \hat{\boldsymbol{\lambda}}$.

2.16 Estimation with Known Aggregate Shares

We now consider the estimation of a generalized choice-based sample when the aggregate choice proportions Q_i are known in advance, perhaps from published statistics. This is the case discussed in section 2.5. It is assumed that all the Q_i are given (i.e., $M - 1$ constraints); analogous estimators can be obtained when only some of the aggregate shares are known.

The log likelihood is now

$$L_N(\boldsymbol{\theta}, \mu) = \sum_{n=1}^{N} \ln P(i_n \mid \mathbf{z}_n, \boldsymbol{\theta}) + \sum_{n=1}^{N} \ln \mu(\mathbf{z}_n) - \sum_{s=1}^{S} \tilde{N}_s \ln \tilde{Q}_s, \tag{2.59}$$

where μ and $\boldsymbol{\theta}$ are subject to the constraints

$$\int d\mathbf{z}\mu(\mathbf{z}) P(i \mid \mathbf{z}, \boldsymbol{\theta}) = Q_i. \tag{2.60}$$

The last term in equation (2.59) is constant and can be dropped before maximizing. As a result the log likelihood does not explicitly depend on the sampling scheme. The form of the estimator will therefore be independent of whether the sample is random, purely choice-based, enriched, and the like. (The asymptotic covariance matrix still depends on the sampling scheme, however, because it involves expected values taken over the different subsamples.)

As before, replacement of $\mu(\mathbf{z})$ by an empirical distribution with weight factors w_n leads to the likelihood

$$L_N(\boldsymbol{\theta}; \mathbf{w}) = \sum_{n=1}^{N} \ln P(i_n \mid \mathbf{z}_n, \boldsymbol{\theta}) + \sum_{n=1}^{N} \ln w_n, \tag{2.61}$$

to be maximized over $\boldsymbol{\theta} \in \boldsymbol{\Theta}$ and $\mathbf{w} \in \mathbf{W}$ (given by equation 2.20), subject to the constraints[17]

$$\sum_{n=1}^{N} w_n P(i \mid \mathbf{z}_n, \boldsymbol{\theta}) = Q_i, \quad i = 1, \ldots, M. \tag{2.62}$$

We have assumed that the constraints are consistent, which is to say that positive weight vectors $\mathbf{w}$ satisfying equation (2.62) do in fact exist. In general this is true only for certain values of $\boldsymbol{\theta}$, termed "admissible" values of $\boldsymbol{\theta}$. Let $\boldsymbol{\Theta}_N^{(A)} \subseteq \boldsymbol{\Theta}$ be the set of admissible $\boldsymbol{\theta}$, and let $\hat{\boldsymbol{\theta}}_N$, $\hat{\mathbf{w}}_N$ be the parameter

17. Only $M - 1$ of these constraints are independent if $\mathbf{w} \in \mathbf{W}$, but summation of equation (2.62) over i yields $\Sigma_n w_n = 1$. Hence we can drop the explicit normalization condition $\mathbf{w} \in \mathbf{W}$ and impose instead the M constraints in equation (2.62) together with the condition $\mathbf{w} > \mathbf{0}$.

values that maximize equation (2.61) over $\boldsymbol{\theta} \in \boldsymbol{\Theta}_N^{(A)}$ and $\mathbf{w} \in \mathbf{W}$ subject to equation (2.62). Then for the present we assume that $\hat{\boldsymbol{\theta}}_N \in \operatorname{int} \boldsymbol{\Theta}_N^{(A)}$ exists and consider only admissible values of $\boldsymbol{\theta}$. The question of inconsistent constraints is considered in section 2.17.

Consider the maximization over $\mathbf{w}$, at some fixed $\boldsymbol{\theta} \in \boldsymbol{\Theta}_N^{(A)}$. Obviously $L_N(\boldsymbol{\theta}; \mathbf{w})$ is bounded above, because $w_n < 1$. The region $\mathbf{W}$ is bounded, while $L_N(\boldsymbol{\theta}; \mathbf{w}) \to -\infty$ at the boundary of $\mathbf{W}$, and thus a maximum exists in int $\mathbf{W}$. The matrix of second derivatives $\partial^2 L_N(\boldsymbol{\theta}; \mathbf{w})/\partial w_i \partial w_j$ is negative definite, so the unconstrained likelihood $L_N(\boldsymbol{\theta}; \mathbf{w})$ is strictly concave in $\mathbf{w}$; since equations (2.62) are linear in $\mathbf{w}$, $L_N(\boldsymbol{\theta}; \mathbf{w})$ remains strictly concave in $\mathbf{w}$ when subject to the constraints. We conclude that the maximum in $\mathbf{w}$ is unique and is given by a unique solution of the equations for a stationary value of the Lagrange function

$$\mathscr{L}_N(\boldsymbol{\theta}; \mathbf{w}, \boldsymbol{\lambda}) = L_N(\boldsymbol{\theta}; \mathbf{w}) - N \sum_{j=1}^{M} \lambda(j) \left\{ \sum_{n=1}^{N} w_n P(j \mid \mathbf{z}_n, \boldsymbol{\theta}) - Q_j \right\}, \qquad (2.63)$$

with Lagrange multipliers $\lambda(j)$, $j = 1, \ldots, M$. Stationary values are given by

$$\frac{1}{w_n} = N \sum_{j=1}^{M} \lambda(j) P(j \mid \mathbf{z}_n, \boldsymbol{\theta}). \qquad (2.64)$$

It then follows that maximization of $L_N(\boldsymbol{\theta}; \mathbf{w})$ over $\mathbf{w}$ subject to (2.62) is equivalent to minimizing the dual objective function $\tilde{L}_N^{(1)}(\boldsymbol{\theta}, \boldsymbol{\lambda})$ over $\boldsymbol{\lambda}$.[18] This is obtained from $\mathscr{L}_N(\boldsymbol{\theta}; \mathbf{w}, \boldsymbol{\lambda})$ by substituting for $\mathbf{w}$ from the first-order conditions (2.64), giving

$$\tilde{L}_N^{(1)}(\boldsymbol{\theta}, \boldsymbol{\lambda}) = \sum_{n=1}^{N} \ln \frac{P(i_n \mid \mathbf{z}_n, \boldsymbol{\theta})}{\sum_{j=1}^{M} \lambda(j) P(j \mid \mathbf{z}_n, \boldsymbol{\theta})} + N \sum_{j=1}^{M} \lambda(j) Q_j, \qquad (2.65)$$

where a constant term has been dropped. The range of $\boldsymbol{\lambda}$ corresponding to $\mathbf{w} > \mathbf{0}$ is

18. This equivalence between the original constrained maximization and the minimization of $\tilde{L}_N^{(1)}(\boldsymbol{\theta}, \boldsymbol{\lambda})$ with respect to $\boldsymbol{\lambda}$ can also be shown directly.

$$\boldsymbol{\Delta}_{(1)} = \left\{ \boldsymbol{\lambda} \,\middle|\, \sum_{j=1}^{M} \lambda(j) P(j \mid \mathbf{z}_n, \boldsymbol{\theta}) > 0, \quad n = 1, 2, \ldots, N \right\}. \tag{2.66}$$

The matrix of second derivatives $\partial^2 \tilde{L}_N^{(1)}/\partial\lambda(i)\partial\lambda(j)$ is positive definite, provided that the probabilities $P(i \mid \mathbf{z}_n, \boldsymbol{\theta})$, considered as M N-dimensional vectors, are linearly independent. (From assumption 2.6 it can be shown that this is true with probability approaching one as $N \to \infty$.) The required minimum is therefore unique.

This is equivalent to minimizing the simpler expression

$$\tilde{L}_N^{(2)}(\boldsymbol{\theta}, \boldsymbol{\lambda}) = \sum_{n=1}^{N} \ln \frac{P(i_n \mid \mathbf{z}_n, \boldsymbol{\theta})}{\sum_{j=1}^{M} \lambda(j) P(j \mid \mathbf{z}_n, \boldsymbol{\theta})} \tag{2.67}$$

over $\boldsymbol{\lambda} \in \boldsymbol{\Delta}_{(1)}$, subject to the constraint

$$\sum_{i=1}^{M} \lambda(i) Q_i = 1. \tag{2.68}$$

This equivalence is easily verified by comparing the first-order conditions for the two minimization problems.[19] Thus maximum likelihood estimation when the Q_i are known reduces to finding $\hat{\boldsymbol{\theta}}_N$ and $\hat{\boldsymbol{\lambda}}_N$, such that

$$\tilde{L}_N^{(2)}(\hat{\boldsymbol{\theta}}_N, \hat{\boldsymbol{\lambda}}_N) = \max_{\boldsymbol{\theta} \in \boldsymbol{\Theta}_N^{(A)}} \{ \min_{\boldsymbol{\lambda} \in \boldsymbol{\Delta}_{(2)}} \tilde{L}_N^{(2)}(\boldsymbol{\theta}, \boldsymbol{\lambda}) \}, \tag{2.69}$$

where the pseudolikelihood $\tilde{L}_N^{(2)}(\boldsymbol{\theta}, \boldsymbol{\lambda})$ is given by equation (2.67) and

$$\boldsymbol{\Delta}_{(2)} = \left\{ \boldsymbol{\lambda} \mid \boldsymbol{\lambda} \in \boldsymbol{\Delta}_{(1)} \text{ and } \sum_{i=1}^{M} \lambda(i) Q_i = 1 \right\}, \tag{2.70}$$

with $\boldsymbol{\Delta}_{(1)}$ given by equation (2.66).

2.17 Consistency of the Constraint Equations

Let $\boldsymbol{\Theta}^{(A)}$ be the set of $\boldsymbol{\theta}$ for which the population constraint equations (2.60) are satisfied by some probability measure $\mu(\mathbf{z})$. Similarly $\boldsymbol{\Theta}_N^{(A)}$ is the set of $\boldsymbol{\theta}$

19. If the first-order equations for the constrained minimization of $\tilde{L}_N^{(2)}$ are multiplied by $\boldsymbol{\lambda}(i)$ and summed over i, the Lagrange multiplier is found to equal N.

for which the sample constraint equations (2.62) are satisfied by some positive weight vector $\mathbf{w}$. Clearly $\mathbf{\Theta}_N^{(A)} \subseteq \mathbf{\Theta}^{(A)}$.

There does not appear to be any straightforward method of determining $\mathbf{\Theta}_N^{(A)}$ for a given sample. The question of interest is therefore how the estimation procedure fails when $\boldsymbol{\theta}$ is "inadmissible." This can occur in the following cases:

1. $\mathbf{\Theta}^{(A)}$ may be empty. This could arise if the model is badly misspecified, or if the aggregate shares Q_i are determined for a population that is not really the same as that from which the main sample is drawn.

2. Even if $\mathbf{\Theta}^{(A)}$ is not empty, $\mathbf{\Theta}_N^{(A)}$ may be empty for a finite sample. The probability of this tends to zero as $N \to \infty$.

3. Even if $\mathbf{\Theta}_N^{(A)}$ is not empty, it is not known in advance, and we might choose inadmissible values of $\boldsymbol{\theta}$ (except in the special case $\mathbf{\Theta}_N^{(A)} = \mathbf{\Theta}$) in attempting to find $\hat{\boldsymbol{\theta}}_N$ and $\hat{\boldsymbol{\lambda}}_N$. This is obviously the case of most concern.[20]

If $\boldsymbol{\theta}^*$ is the "true" value of $\boldsymbol{\theta}$, then by definition $\boldsymbol{\theta}^* \in \mathbf{\Theta}^{(A)}$, so from now on we may assume $\mathbf{\Theta}^{(A)} \neq \phi$. One can then establish the following results (see Cosslett 1978 for further details): (1) $\mathbf{\Theta}_N^{(A)} \to \mathbf{\Theta}^{(A)}$ as $N \to \infty$; (2) $\mathbf{\Theta}^{(A)}$ is an open set; and (3) $\mathbf{\Theta}_N^{(A)}$ is an open set for large enough N. Results 1 and 3 hold for almost all sequences $\{\mathbf{z}_n\}$. Note that assumptions 2.5 and 2.6 are required (see appendix 2.26), as well as the assumption that $P(i \mid \mathbf{z}, \boldsymbol{\theta})$ is continuous in $\mathbf{z}$ (for almost all $\mathbf{z}$).

Suppose $\tilde{\boldsymbol{\theta}}_N$ is a consistent estimator of $\boldsymbol{\theta}^*$. We shall see that $\hat{\boldsymbol{\theta}}_N$ is in fact a consistent estimator too. From the results above $\boldsymbol{\theta}^*$, $\tilde{\boldsymbol{\theta}}_N$, and $\hat{\boldsymbol{\theta}}_N$ are all in $\mathbf{\Theta}_N^{(A)}$ for large enough N (a.s.), and thus any consistent $\tilde{\boldsymbol{\theta}}_N$ is a good candidate for a starting value of $\boldsymbol{\theta}$.

The following result can be established (Cosslett 1978): the constraint equations (2.62) are inconsistent if and only if $\tilde{L}_N^{(2)}(\boldsymbol{\theta}, \boldsymbol{\lambda})$ has no minimum for $\boldsymbol{\lambda} \in \mathbf{\Delta}_{(2)}$, which is the case if and only if $\mathbf{\Delta}_{(2)}$ is unbounded. This is not immediately useful, since there appears to be no simple test for unboundedness of $\mathbf{\Delta}_{(2)}$. But it indicates how the estimation procedure fails if $\boldsymbol{\theta}$ is inadmissible: the attempt to minimize $\tilde{L}_N^{(2)}(\boldsymbol{\theta}, \boldsymbol{\lambda})$ over $\boldsymbol{\lambda}$ will lead to a diverging sequence of values of $\boldsymbol{\lambda}$.

2.18 Asymptotic Properties with Known Aggregate Shares

For discrete variables $\mathbf{z}$ the estimator $\hat{\boldsymbol{\theta}}_N$ given by equations (2.69) and (2.67) is the classical maximum likelihood estimator, which is known to be

20. In cases 1 and 2 maximum likelihood estimation cannot be used.

consistent and asymptotically efficient. A direct proof of consistency, applicable to both discrete and continuous variables $\mathbf{z}$, is given elsewhere (see Cosslett 1978). The result is

$$\hat{\boldsymbol{\theta}}_N \to \boldsymbol{\theta}^*,$$
$$\hat{\lambda}_N(i) \to \frac{\bar{H}_i}{Q_i} \qquad \text{(a.s.),} \tag{2.71}$$

where $\bar{H}_i$, the expected proportion of the total sample who choose alternative i, is given by equation (2.14). The asymptotic limit of the Lagrange multipliers $\hat{\lambda}(i)$ does not in principle provide any new information since the Q_i are already known, but, when used in conjunction with an estimate of the covariance matrix, it does provide a check on the validity of the estimation procedure.

The estimates are asymptotically normally distributed. As before, the asymptotic covariance matrix is of the form

$$\mathbf{V} = \mathbf{J}^{-1}\mathbf{M}\mathbf{J}^{-1},$$

with $\mathbf{J}$ and $\mathbf{M}$ defined by equations (2.35), (2.36), and (2.33). The differences from the previous case (where $\mathbf{Q}$ was unknown) are: first, that the pseudolikelihood for a single observation is now

$$\tilde{l}(i, \mathbf{z} \mid s, \gamma) = \ln \frac{P(i \mid \mathbf{z}, \boldsymbol{\theta})}{\sum_{j=1}^{M} \lambda(j) P(j \mid \mathbf{z}, \boldsymbol{\theta})} \tag{2.72}$$

instead of equation (2.32); and, second, the estimates $\hat{\boldsymbol{\lambda}}(i)$ satisfy the linear constraint (2.68) instead of the normalization condition $\hat{\boldsymbol{\lambda}}(S) = \tilde{H}_S$. Equation (2.68) is therefore used to eliminate one of the multipliers, say, $\boldsymbol{\lambda}(M)$, before differentiating the expression (2.72).

If the matrices $\mathbf{J}$ and $\mathbf{M}$ are partitioned according to the decomposition $[\boldsymbol{\theta}, \boldsymbol{\lambda}]$, they are found to have the forms

$$\mathbf{J} = \begin{pmatrix} \mathbf{A} & \mathbf{B}_Q \\ \mathbf{B}'_Q & -\mathbf{C}_Q \end{pmatrix} \tag{2.73}$$

and

$$\mathbf{M} = \begin{pmatrix} \mathbf{A} & \mathbf{0} \\ \mathbf{0} & \mathbf{C}_Q \end{pmatrix} - \mathbf{J} \begin{pmatrix} \mathbf{0} & \mathbf{0} \\ \mathbf{0} & \mathbf{G}_Q \end{pmatrix} \mathbf{J}. \tag{2.74}$$

The submatrix $\mathbf{A}$ is the same as in the case of unknown $\mathbf{Q}$ (see equation 2.41). The submatrices $\mathbf{B}_Q$, $\mathbf{C}_Q$, and $\mathbf{G}_Q$ are given by

$$(B_Q)_{\alpha i} = \left\langle \left(\frac{\partial P_i}{\partial \theta_\alpha} - \frac{Q_i}{Q_M} \frac{\partial P_M}{\partial \theta_\alpha} \right) - \left(P_i - \frac{Q_i}{Q_M} P_M \right) \frac{1}{\bar{P}} \frac{\partial \bar{P}}{\partial \theta_\alpha} \right\rangle, \tag{2.75}$$

$$(C_Q)_{ij} = \left\langle \frac{1}{\bar{P}} \left(P_i - \frac{Q_i}{Q_M} P_M \right) \left(P_j - \frac{Q_j}{Q_M} P_M \right) \right\rangle, \tag{2.76}$$

and

$$(G_Q)_{ij} = h_{ij} - \frac{\bar{H}_i \bar{H}_j}{Q_i Q_j}, \tag{2.77}$$

with h_{ij} given by equation (2.13). We therefore have

$$\mathbf{V} = \begin{pmatrix} (\mathbf{A} + \mathbf{B}_Q \mathbf{C}_Q{}^{-1} \mathbf{B}'_Q)^{-1} & \mathbf{0} \\ \mathbf{0} & (\mathbf{C}_Q + \mathbf{B}'_Q \mathbf{A}^{-1} \mathbf{B}_Q)^{-1} - \mathbf{G}_Q \end{pmatrix}. \tag{2.78}$$

Note that $\mathbf{V}_{\theta\theta}$ has improved from $(\mathbf{A} - \mathbf{B}\mathbf{C}^{-1}\mathbf{B}')^{-1}$ when $\mathbf{Q}$ was unknown (equation 2.45) to $(\mathbf{A} + \mathbf{B}_Q \mathbf{C}_Q^{-1} \mathbf{B}'_Q)^{-1}$ now that $\mathbf{Q}$ is known.[21]

Sample estimates of the submatrices $\mathbf{A}$, $\mathbf{B}_Q$, and $\mathbf{C}_Q$ are obtained as before from $\hat{\mathbf{J}}$, given by equation (2.44), except that the pseudolikelihood $\tilde{L}_N$ is of course replaced by $\tilde{L}_N^{(2)}$ as defined in equation (2.67).

A lower bound on the covariance matrix of $\hat{\boldsymbol{\theta}}$, analogous to the Cramér-Rao lower bound, can be obtained also in the case of known aggregate shares (see Cosslett 1978). This lower bound is again equal to $N^{-1}\,\mathbf{V}_{\theta\theta}$, so that the estimator $\hat{\boldsymbol{\theta}}_N$ is asymptotically efficient.

2.19 The Constrained Maximum Likelihood Estimator

To summarize the results in sections 2.16 through 2.18, the maximum likelihood estimator $\hat{\boldsymbol{\theta}}_N$ is obtained from the pseudolikelihood

$$\tilde{L}_N^{(2)}(\boldsymbol{\theta}, \boldsymbol{\lambda}) = \sum_{n=1}^{N} \ln \frac{P(i_n \mid \mathbf{z}_n, \boldsymbol{\theta})}{\sum_{j=1}^{M} \lambda(j) P(j \mid \mathbf{z}_n, \boldsymbol{\theta})} \tag{2.79}$$

by minimizing over $\boldsymbol{\lambda} \in \boldsymbol{\Delta}_{(2)}$ and maximizing over $\boldsymbol{\theta} \in \boldsymbol{\Theta}_N^{(A)}$. The region $\boldsymbol{\Delta}_{(2)}$ is given by equation (2.70): it is the region where $\Sigma_j \lambda(j) Q_j = 1$ and where the

21. Since $\mathbf{C}$ and $\mathbf{C}_Q$ are positive definite, the old $\mathbf{V}_{\theta\theta}$ exceeds the new $\mathbf{V}_{\theta\theta}$ by a positive semidefinite matrix.

denominator in equation (2.79) is positive for every observation. $\boldsymbol{\Theta}_N^{(A)}$ is the region where the constraint equations (2.62) can be satisfied for some $\mathbf{w} > \mathbf{0}$; if $\boldsymbol{\theta}$ is not in $\boldsymbol{\Theta}_N^{(A)}$, then $\boldsymbol{\Delta}_{(2)}$ is unbounded, and the minimization will fail, with a divergent sequence of $\boldsymbol{\lambda}$ giving ever-decreasing values of $\tilde{L}_N^{(2)}(\boldsymbol{\theta}, \boldsymbol{\lambda})$.

If $N \to \infty$ with the relative subsample sizes held fixed, then $\hat{\boldsymbol{\theta}}_N$ is a consistent estimator of $\boldsymbol{\theta}^*$, and $\hat{\lambda}_N(i)$ converges in probability to the known ratio $\bar{H}_i/Q_i$. The asymptotic covariance matrix of $\hat{\boldsymbol{\theta}}_N$ and $\hat{\lambda}_N(1), \ldots, \hat{\lambda}_N(M-1)$ is given by equation (2.78). The submatrices appearing in this expression can again be estimated from the sample value of the Hessian matrix at convergence.

As before, actual computation of the estimates will involve modifying existing routines to carry out the transformation from the random sample likelihood to the pseudolikelihood. However, more substantial changes are now required because the stationary value is a saddle-point, rather than a maximum, in the combined parameter space. The only practical method of locating the saddle-point appears to be to solve all the first-order conditions for a stationary point as a set of simultaneous nonlinear equations.[22] This is evidently less efficient than the hill-climbing techniques that can be used when the stationary point is known to be a maximum.

The subsidiary condition $\boldsymbol{\lambda} \in \boldsymbol{\Delta}_{(2)}$ should not present any problems. The linear constraint (2.68) can be imposed explicitly. At the boundaries of $\boldsymbol{\Delta}_{(2)}$ both the pseudolikelihood and its gradient become infinite, so any reasonably effective search algorithm will stay inside $\boldsymbol{\Delta}_{(2)}$ if it starts there.

The condition $\boldsymbol{\theta} \in \boldsymbol{\Theta}_N^{(A)}$ is more serious. We require a starting value of $\boldsymbol{\theta}$ in $\boldsymbol{\Theta}_N^{(A)}$, but $\boldsymbol{\Theta}_N^{(A)}$ is unknown. (If $\boldsymbol{\Theta}_N^{(A)}$ is disjoint, we may have to start in that part containing the maximand $\hat{\boldsymbol{\theta}}_N$.) A suitable starting point is suggested by the fact that $\hat{\boldsymbol{\lambda}}_N$ has a known asymptotic probability limit: set $\lambda(i) = \bar{H}_i/Q_i$, the limiting value, and maximize the pseudolikelihood with respect to $\boldsymbol{\theta}$ at this value of $\boldsymbol{\lambda}$. Call the maximand $\tilde{\boldsymbol{\theta}}_N$. Then $\boldsymbol{\theta} = \tilde{\boldsymbol{\theta}}_N$ and $\lambda(i) = \bar{H}_i/Q_i$ are used as starting values for the search algorithm to find a stationary point.

In fact $\tilde{\boldsymbol{\theta}}_N$ is one form of the Manski-McFadden estimator for this problem (Manski and McFadden, chapter 1). It is known to be consistent. Thus, according to the results in section 2.17, $\tilde{\boldsymbol{\theta}}_N \in \boldsymbol{\Theta}_N^{(A)}$ for large enough N (almost always), and therefore $(\tilde{\boldsymbol{\theta}}_N, \{\bar{H}_i/Q_i\})$ is a very promising starting

22. Existing saddle-point routines, for example, those designed for Kuhn-Tucker type problems, are applicable only when the objective function is linear in Lagrange parameters, which is not the case here.

point. We note that an alternative form of the Manski-McFadden estimator, using the sample values H_i instead of their expectations $\bar{H}_i$ (see appendix 2.28), has a slightly better asymptotic variance, and so may provide a better starting point.

But $\hat{\boldsymbol{\theta}}_N$ should be an improvement over $\tilde{\boldsymbol{\theta}}_N$ in that: (1) if we are not using a logit model with a full set of alternative dummies, $\tilde{\boldsymbol{\theta}}_N$ is in general not asymptotically efficient;[23] and (2) by testing whether there is in fact a stationary value in $\boldsymbol{\lambda}$, the estimation procedure provides a check against inconsistent constraints. There is also a method of avoiding the problem of inconsistent constraints altogether where the Q_i are considered as sample statistics from an auxiliary sample rather than as a priori constraints (see section 2.21).

2.20 Estimation of the Logit Model with Known Aggregate Shares

As in the case of the unconstrained estimator, there is a drastic simplification in the case of the logit model with a full set of alternative-specific dummies. In the notation introduced in section 2.15, we have

$$\tilde{L}_N^{(2)}(\phi, \mathbf{d}, \boldsymbol{\lambda}) = L_N(\phi, \mathbf{d}') - \sum_{i=1}^{M} N_i \ln \lambda(i), \tag{2.80}$$

with

$$d_i' = d_i + \ln \lambda(i). \tag{2.81}$$

Maximization over $\boldsymbol{\theta} = (\boldsymbol{\phi}, \mathbf{d}')$ just involves the term $L_N(\boldsymbol{\phi}, \mathbf{d}')$ and so is the same as for a random sample. Minimization over $\boldsymbol{\lambda}$, subject to equation (2.68), is trivial and yields $\lambda(i) = H_i/Q_i$. Therefore in this case both the constrained maximum likelihood estimator and the Manski-McFadden estimator (see appendix 2.28) reduce to the ordinary maximum likelihood logit estimator, apart from a correction term $\ln(H_i/Q_i)$ to be subtracted from the estimated dummy coefficients $\hat{d}_i'$.[24]

23. We have the somewhat counter-intuitive result that a better estimate of $\boldsymbol{\theta}$ is obtained by using sample estimates $\hat{\lambda}(i)$ for the weight factors than is obtained by using the "true" values $\bar{H}_i/Q_i$.

24. It follows that the Manski-McFadden estimator is asymptotically efficient in this case.

2.21 Estimation with Aggregate Shares Inferred from an Auxiliary Sample

Estimation from a generalized choice-based sample plus an auxiliary sample is discussed in section 2.6. It differs from the case of known aggregate shares, considered in sections 2.16 through 2.19, only in that the Q_i are not given a priori; rather they are estimated with the aid of an auxiliary random survey in which subjects are asked which alternative they chose. No other data is collected in the auxiliary survey.[25]

Let there be N_0 cases in the auxiliary sample, and define

$$H_0 = N_0/N,$$

where N is the number of cases in the main sample (as before). Let $\mathcal{N}_i$ be the number of subjects in the auxiliary sample who chose alternative i. If cases $1, \ldots, N$ are in the main sample, and cases $N+1, \ldots, N+N_0$ in the auxiliary sample, the log likelihood can be written as

$$\begin{aligned} L_N(\boldsymbol{\theta};\mu) = {} & \sum_{n=1}^{N} \ln P(i_n \mid \mathbf{z}_n, \boldsymbol{\theta}) + \sum_{n=1}^{N} \ln \mu(\mathbf{z}_n) \\ & - \sum_{s=1}^{S} \tilde{N}_s \ln \left\{ \int d\mathbf{z}\, \mu(\mathbf{z}) P(\mathscr{I}(s) \mid \mathbf{z}, \boldsymbol{\theta}) \right\} \\ & + \sum_{j=1}^{M} \mathcal{N}_j \ln \left\{ \int d\mathbf{z}\, \mu(\mathbf{z}) P(j \mid \mathbf{z}, \boldsymbol{\theta}) \right\}. \end{aligned} \tag{2.82}$$

A maximum likelihood estimator may then be found by essentially the same method as in sections 2.11 and 2.16. Details of the derivation (Cosslett 1978) will be omitted, and we shall just give the resulting estimator.

The pseudolikelihood is given by

$$\begin{aligned} \tilde{L}_N(\boldsymbol{\theta}, \xi, \boldsymbol{\lambda}) = {} & \sum_{n=1}^{N} \ln \frac{\xi(s_n) P(i_n \mid \mathbf{z}_n, \boldsymbol{\theta})}{\sum_{s=1}^{S} \xi(s) P(\mathscr{I}(s) \mid \mathbf{z}_n, \boldsymbol{\theta}) + \sum_{j=1}^{M} [1 - \lambda(j)] P(j \mid \mathbf{z}_n, \boldsymbol{\theta})} \\ & - \sum_{j=1}^{M} \mathcal{N}_j \ln \lambda(j). \end{aligned} \tag{2.83}$$

25. Lerman and Manski (1975) refer to such a survey as a supplementary survey.

There are now two sets of weight factors: $\lambda(j)$, $j = 1, \ldots, M$, and $\xi(s)$, $s = 1, \ldots, S$. The estimators are determined by

$$\tilde{L}_N(\hat{\boldsymbol{\theta}}_N, \hat{\xi}_N, \hat{\boldsymbol{\lambda}}_N) = \max_{\boldsymbol{\theta}} \left\{ \max_{\xi, \boldsymbol{\lambda}} \text{s.v.}\, \tilde{L}_N(\boldsymbol{\theta}, \xi, \boldsymbol{\lambda}) \right\}, \tag{2.84}$$

where max s.v. stands for maximum stationary value. For the pseudolikelihood $\tilde{L}_N(\boldsymbol{\theta}, \xi, \boldsymbol{\lambda})$, the stationary value in $(\xi, \boldsymbol{\lambda})$ is not necessarily unique: if there are several stationary values, we take the one at which $\tilde{L}_N(\boldsymbol{\theta}, \xi, \boldsymbol{\lambda})$ is largest.[26] The quantity $\hat{\xi}_N$ is not really independent but is given in terms of $\hat{\boldsymbol{\lambda}}_N$ by the identity

$$\frac{\tilde{N}_s}{\hat{\xi}(s)} = \sum_{j=1}^{M} \eta_{js} \frac{\mathcal{N}_j}{\hat{\lambda}(j)}. \tag{2.85}$$

If we let $N \to \infty$, with H_0 and $\{\tilde{H}_s\}$ fixed, then

$$\begin{aligned} &\hat{\boldsymbol{\theta}}_N \to \boldsymbol{\theta}^*, \\ &\hat{\lambda}_N(i) \to H_0, \\ &\hat{\xi}_N(s) \to \frac{\tilde{H}_s}{\tilde{Q}_s} \qquad \text{(a.s.).} \end{aligned} \tag{2.86}$$

Although the stationary value in the weight factors is not necessarily unique, it does always exist—there is no problem analogous to that of inconsistent constraints, which can arise in the case of known aggregate shares. In particular, note that the present estimator is *not* equivalent to using the estimated value $\hat{Q}_i = \mathcal{N}_i/N_0$ in the constrained maximum likelihood estimator of section 2.19. In principle therefore the problem of inconsistent constraints can be avoided by treating the given values Q_i as preliminary estimates from an auxiliary sample of size N_0, setting $\mathcal{N}_i = N_0 Q_i$, and then using the estimator given by equations (2.83) and (2.84). Of course in many cases this is how known values of Q were measured in the first place—even if N_0 is not known, a rough estimate should be adequate here.[27] Against this we have to weigh the practical difficulty of estimating

26. The maximum stationary value may in some cases be a saddle-point or even a local minimum.
27. An incorrectly specified N_0 leads to estimates that are consistent but no longer asymptotically efficient.

from equation (2.84) when the equations for a stationary value may have multiple solutions.

2.22 Asymptotic Variance of the Auxiliary Sample Estimator

As with the other maximum likelihood estimators already considered, the asymptotic covariance matrix has the form given by equations (2.34) through (2.36). There are two differences. First, some of the observations are in the auxiliary sample, which we treat as a special subsample with $s = 0$. For this subsample expectations are given by

$$E_0[F] = \sum_{i=1}^{M} Q_i F(i) \tag{2.87}$$

instead of by equation (2.33). Corresponding to equation (2.32), the pseudolikelihood for a single observation is

$$\tilde{l}(i \mid s = 0, \gamma) = -\ln \lambda(i) \tag{2.88}$$

for the auxiliary sample, and

$$\tilde{l}(i, \mathbf{z} \mid s, \gamma) = \ln \frac{\xi(s) P(i \mid \mathbf{z}, \boldsymbol{\theta})}{\sum_{s=1}^{S} \xi(s) P(\mathscr{J}(s) \mid \mathbf{z}, \boldsymbol{\theta}) + \sum_{j=1}^{M} [1 - \lambda(j)] P(j \mid \mathbf{z}, \boldsymbol{\theta})} \tag{2.89}$$

for the regular subsamples.

The second difference arises from the identity (2.85), which means that we need consider the covariance of the estimates $\hat{\boldsymbol{\theta}}_N$ and $\hat{\boldsymbol{\lambda}}_N$ only. Consequently $\partial\tilde{l}/\partial\gamma$ has not only an explicit dependence on $\boldsymbol{\lambda}$ but also an indirect dependence via $\boldsymbol{\xi}$, which is a function of $\boldsymbol{\lambda}$ given by equation (2.85). The appropriate expressions for $\mathbf{J}$ and $\mathbf{M}$ are found to be

$$J_{\alpha\beta} = \sum_{s=0}^{S} \tilde{H}_s E_s\left[-\frac{\partial^2 \tilde{l}(s, \gamma^*)}{\partial\gamma_\alpha \partial\gamma_\beta} - \sum_{t=1}^{S} \frac{\partial^2 \tilde{l}(s, \gamma^*)}{\partial\gamma_\alpha \partial\xi(t)} \frac{\partial\xi(t)}{\partial\gamma_\beta}\right], \tag{2.90}$$

where $\partial\xi(t)/\partial\gamma_\beta$ is evaluated at the true parameter values and

$$M_{\alpha\beta} = \sum_{s=0}^{S} \tilde{H}_s \left\{ E_s\left[\frac{\partial\tilde{l}(s, \gamma^*)}{\partial\gamma_\alpha} \frac{\partial\tilde{l}(s, \gamma^*)}{\partial\gamma_\beta}\right] - E_s\left[\frac{\partial\tilde{l}(s, \gamma^*)}{\partial\gamma_\alpha}\right] E_s\left[\frac{\partial\tilde{l}(s, \gamma^*)}{\partial\gamma_\beta}\right] \right\}. \tag{2.91}$$

In this formulation $\mathbf{J}$ is not symmetric, and we have

$\mathbf{V} = \mathbf{J}^{-1}\mathbf{M}(\mathbf{J}^{-1})'$.

From equations (2.90) and (2.91) we have

$$\mathbf{J} = \begin{pmatrix} \mathbf{A}_{\alpha\beta} & \mathbf{B}_{\alpha i} - (\mathbf{Bh})_{\alpha i}\dfrac{Q_i}{H_0} \\ \mathbf{B}_{\alpha i} & -\mathbf{C}_{ij} + (\mathbf{Ch})_{ij}\dfrac{Q_j}{H_0} - \dfrac{Q_i}{H_0}\delta_{ij} \end{pmatrix} \tag{2.92}$$

and

$$\mathbf{M} = \begin{pmatrix} \mathbf{A}_{\alpha\beta} - (\mathbf{BhB}')_{\alpha\beta} & (\mathbf{BhC})_{\alpha i} \\ (\mathbf{ChB}')_{i\alpha} & \mathbf{C}_{ij} - (\mathbf{ChC})_{ij} + \dfrac{Q_i\delta_{ij} - Q_iQ_j}{H_0} \end{pmatrix}, \tag{2.93}$$

where (for this estimator only)

$$A_{\alpha\beta} = \left\langle \sum_{i=1}^{M} \frac{\bar{H}_i}{Q_i}\frac{1}{P_i}\frac{\partial P_i}{\partial\theta_\alpha}\frac{\partial P_i}{\partial\theta_\beta} - \frac{1}{\tilde{P}}\frac{\partial\tilde{P}}{\partial\theta_\alpha}\frac{\partial\tilde{P}}{\partial\theta_\beta}\right\rangle, \tag{2.94}$$

$$B_{\alpha i} = \left\langle \frac{\partial P_i}{\partial\theta_\alpha} - \frac{P_i}{\tilde{P}}\frac{\partial\tilde{P}}{\partial\theta_\alpha}\right\rangle, \tag{2.95}$$

$$C_{ij} = \left\langle \frac{P_iP_j}{\tilde{P}}\right\rangle, \tag{2.96}$$

with

$$\tilde{P} \equiv \sum_{s=1}^{S} \xi(s)P(\mathscr{I}(s)\mid \mathbf{z},\boldsymbol{\theta}) + \sum_{j=1}^{M} [1 - \lambda(j)]P(j\mid \mathbf{z},\boldsymbol{\theta}). \tag{2.97}$$

The matrix $(\mathbf{h}_{ij})$ is given by equation (2.13).

A proof of asymptotic efficiency has not yet been established for the auxiliary sample estimator, but it is anticipated that one will follow along the same lines as existing proofs (Cosslett 1978, 1981) for the estimators given in sections 2.14 and 2.19.

2.23 Special Cases of the Auxiliary Sample Estimator

There are two special cases of interest where the maximum likelihood estimator given in section 2.22 for auxiliary samples can be somewhat simplified:

1. When the main sample is purely choice-based, the maximum likelihood estimator is

$$\tilde{L}_N(\hat{\boldsymbol{\theta}}_N, \hat{\boldsymbol{\lambda}}_N) = \max_{\boldsymbol{\theta}} \left\{ \max_{\boldsymbol{\lambda}} \text{ s.v. } \tilde{L}_N(\boldsymbol{\theta}, \boldsymbol{\lambda}) \right\}, \tag{2.98}$$

where (for this case only)

$$\tilde{L}_N(\boldsymbol{\theta}, \boldsymbol{\lambda}) = \sum_{n=1}^{N} \ln \frac{\lambda(i_n) P(i_n \mid \mathbf{z}_n, \boldsymbol{\theta})}{\sum_{j=1}^{M} [1 + \zeta_j \lambda(j)] P(j \mid \mathbf{z}, \boldsymbol{\theta})} - \sum_{j=1}^{M} \mathcal{N}_j \ln \lambda(j), \tag{2.99}$$

with

$$\zeta_j = \begin{cases} 1 & \text{if } N_j > \mathcal{N}_j, \\ 0 & \text{if } N_j = \mathcal{N}_j, \\ -1 & \text{if } N_j < \mathcal{N}_j. \end{cases} \tag{2.100}$$

Thus if $N_i = \mathcal{N}_i$ for some alternative, the corresponding weight factor $\lambda(i)$ disappears from $\tilde{L}_N$, and so can be ignored in the estimation procedure. While the stationary value is a minimum for those $\lambda(i)$ with $\zeta_i = -1$, the sign of the second differential is in general indefinite for the remaining weight factors. The weight factors $\boldsymbol{\lambda}$ have been redefined in deriving equation (2.99) from (2.83), and the asymptotic limit of $\hat{\lambda}_N(i)$ is now $|(H_i/Q_i) - H_o|$.

2. When the probability model is a logit model with a full set of alternative dummies, there is a drastic simplification. In terms of the log likelihood for a random sample, $L_N(\boldsymbol{\phi}, \mathbf{d})$, see section 2.15, we have

$$\tilde{L}_N(\boldsymbol{\theta}, \boldsymbol{\xi}, \boldsymbol{\lambda}) = L_N(\boldsymbol{\phi}, \mathbf{d}') - \sum_{j=1}^{M} N_j \ln \left\{ 1 - \lambda(j) + \sum_{s=1}^{S} \eta_{js} \xi(s) \right\} + \sum_{s=1}^{S} \tilde{N}_s \ln \xi(s) - \sum_{j=1}^{M} \mathcal{N}_j \ln \lambda(j), \tag{2.101}$$

where the composite dummy variable coefficients $\mathbf{d}'$ are related to the true coefficients $\mathbf{d}$ by

$$d_i' = d_i + \ln\left\{1 - \lambda(i) + \sum_{s=1}^{S} \eta_{is}\xi(s)\right\}, \tag{2.102}$$

with $\xi(s)$ given as a function of $\boldsymbol{\lambda}$ by equation (2.85).

Then $\hat{\boldsymbol{\lambda}}_N$ and $\hat{\boldsymbol{\xi}}_N$ are obtained by finding the stationary values of the last three terms in equation (2.101); although nonlinear simultaneous equations in $\boldsymbol{\lambda}$ have to be solved, the main sample data $\{i_n, \mathbf{z}_n\}$ are not involved. Estimates $\hat{\boldsymbol{\theta}}_N \equiv [\hat{\boldsymbol{\phi}}_N, \hat{\mathbf{d}}_N']$ are obtained from $L_N(\boldsymbol{\phi}, \mathbf{d}')$, as if the sample were random, and the estimated dummy variable coefficients are then corrected according to equation (2.102), using the estimates $\hat{\boldsymbol{\lambda}}_N$ and $\hat{\boldsymbol{\xi}}_N$.

2.24 Estimation with a Supplementary Sample

In addition to the main sample, the generalized choice-based sample, one can have a supplementary sample consisting of individual observations of the exogenous variables but not of the subjects' choices—for example, a census tape (see section 2.7). Unlike the other sampling schemes considered earlier, a supplementary sample allows one to estimate at least some of the parameters of a choice model even when the main sample does not cover all the alternatives—for example, it may consist only of subjects who bought some particular product or service. Although a census tape does not identify buyers and nonbuyers, the information it provides on the distribution of the exogenous variables may be enough to identify the model.

Let there be N_0 cases in the supplementary sample and N cases in the main sample, and again define

$$H_0 = \frac{N_0}{N}.$$

If cases $1, \ldots, N$ are in the main sample, and cases $N+1, \ldots, N+N_0$ in the supplementary sample, then the log likelihood is

$$L_N(\boldsymbol{\theta};\mu) = \sum_{n=1}^{N} \ln P(i_n \mid \mathbf{z}_n, \boldsymbol{\theta}) + \sum_{n=1}^{N+N_0} \ln \mu(\mathbf{z}_n)$$

$$- \sum_{s=1}^{S} \tilde{N}_s \ln \left\{ \int d\mathbf{z}\, \mu(\mathbf{z})\, P(\mathscr{I}(s) \mid \mathbf{z}, \boldsymbol{\theta}) \right\}. \tag{2.103}$$

A maximum likelihood estimator can be derived by the same methods as before: $(\hat{\boldsymbol{\theta}}_N, \hat{\boldsymbol{\lambda}}_N)$ is given by

$$\tilde{L}_N(\hat{\boldsymbol{\theta}}_N, \hat{\boldsymbol{\lambda}}_N) = \max_{\boldsymbol{\theta} \in \boldsymbol{\Theta}} \max_{\boldsymbol{\lambda} > 0} \tilde{L}_N(\boldsymbol{\theta}, \boldsymbol{\lambda}), \tag{2.104}$$

where the pseudolikelihood is

$$\tilde{L}_N(\boldsymbol{\theta}, \boldsymbol{\lambda}) = \sum_{n=1}^{N} \ln \frac{\lambda(s_n) P(i_n \mid \mathbf{z}_n, \boldsymbol{\theta})}{\sum_{s=1}^{S} \lambda(s) P(\mathscr{I}(s) \mid \mathbf{z}_n, \boldsymbol{\theta}) + H_0}$$

$$- \sum_{n=N+1}^{N+N_0} \ln \left\{ \sum_{s=1}^{S} \lambda(s) P(\mathscr{I}(s) \mid \mathbf{z}_n, \boldsymbol{\theta}) + H_0 \right\}. \tag{2.105}$$

The estimators can be shown to be consistent:

$$\hat{\boldsymbol{\theta}}_N \to \boldsymbol{\theta}^*,$$

$$\hat{\lambda}_N(s) \to \frac{\tilde{H}_s}{\tilde{Q}_s} \qquad \text{(a.s.)}, \tag{2.106}$$

as $N \to \infty$ with H_0 and $\{\tilde{H}_s\}$ fixed. Asymptotic normality then follows by standard methods, and asymptotic efficiency can be proved along the same lines as in the case of the generalized choice-based estimator (Cosslett 1978). Unlike previous cases there is no special simplification when $P(i \mid \mathbf{z}, \boldsymbol{\theta})$ corresponds to a logit model with alternative dummies.

The asymptotic covariance matrix is again of the form given by equations (2.34) through (2.36), except that the sums over s are extended to cover the supplementary sample, say, $s = 0$. Expectations over this special subsample are given by

$$E_0[F(\mathbf{z})] = \int F(\mathbf{z}) \mu(\mathbf{z})\, d\mathbf{z} \tag{2.107}$$

instead of equation (2.33). The pseudolikelihood for an observation in the supplementary sample is

$$\tilde{l}(\mathbf{z} \mid s = 0, \gamma) = -\ln\left\{\sum_{t=1}^{S} \lambda(t) P(\mathcal{J}(t) \mid \mathbf{z}, \boldsymbol{\theta}) + H_0\right\}, \tag{2.108}$$

while for the remaining subsamples it is

$$\tilde{l}(i, \mathbf{z} \mid s, \gamma) = \ln \frac{\lambda(s) P(i \mid \mathbf{z}, \boldsymbol{\theta})}{\sum_{t=1}^{S} \lambda(t) P(\mathcal{J}(t) \mid \mathbf{z}, \boldsymbol{\theta}) + H_0} \tag{2.109}$$

The matrix **J** is then the same as for a general choice-based sample without a supplementary sample (equations 2.40 through 2.43), except that $\bar{P}$ is replaced by $\tilde{P} = \bar{P} + H_0$, and κ is omitted from equations (2.42) and (2.43). The expression for **M**, equation (2.37), is now changed to

$$\mathbf{M} = \mathbf{J} - \mathbf{J}\begin{pmatrix} \mathbf{0} & \mathbf{0} \\ \mathbf{0} & \mathbf{G} \end{pmatrix}\mathbf{J} - \mathbf{M}_0, \tag{2.110}$$

where **G** is given by equation (2.38) and

$$\mathbf{M}_0 = H_0 \begin{bmatrix} \left\langle \frac{1}{\tilde{P}} \frac{\partial \tilde{P}}{\partial \theta_\alpha} \right\rangle \left\langle \frac{1}{\tilde{P}} \frac{\partial \tilde{P}}{\partial \theta_\beta} \right\rangle & \left\langle \frac{1}{\tilde{P}} \frac{\partial \tilde{P}}{\partial \theta_\alpha} \right\rangle \left\langle \frac{P(t)}{\tilde{P}} \right\rangle \\ \left\langle \frac{1}{\tilde{P}} \frac{\partial \tilde{P}}{\partial \theta_\beta} \right\rangle \left\langle \frac{P(s)}{\tilde{P}} \right\rangle & \left\langle \frac{P(s)}{\tilde{P}} \right\rangle \left\langle \frac{P(t)}{\tilde{P}} \right\rangle \end{bmatrix} \tag{2.111}$$

Finally, consider a case where not all alternatives are sampled: suppose the main sample consists entirely of subjects who have chosen alternative 1. For all other estimators considered, the "information matrix" **J** would be zero. When the estimator also incorporates the data from a supplementary sample, however, the asymptotic covariance matrix for $\boldsymbol{\theta}$ is given by

$$\mathbf{V}_{\theta\theta} = \frac{1}{H_0}\left\{\left\langle \frac{(\partial P_1/\partial \theta_\alpha)(\partial P_1/\partial \theta_\beta)}{P_1(P_1 + Q_1 H_0)} \right\rangle - \left\langle \frac{\partial P_1/\partial \theta_\alpha}{P_1 + Q_1 H_0} \right\rangle \left\langle \frac{\partial P_1/\partial \theta_\beta}{P_1 + Q_1 H_0} \right\rangle \left\langle \frac{P_1}{P_1 + Q_1 H_0} \right\rangle^{-1} \right\}^{-1} \tag{2.112}$$

In general this matrix will be nonsingular, provided we omit parameters that do not enter $P(1 \mid \mathbf{z}, \boldsymbol{\theta})$, and thus the model should be identifiable for at least a subset of the parameters.

2.25 Comparison of Estimators and Sample Designs

A qualitative picture of the relative efficiency of different estimators and sample designs can be obtained by numerical studies of simple choice models. For design of an actual sample—if the option were available—these calculations would of course be repeated with realistic models and parameter values appropriate to the case being studied. There are three main questions of interest:

1. Asymptotic bias. If the problem of consistently estimating a choice probability model from a choice-based sample is ignored, and the model is estimated by conventional means as if it were random, then what is the magnitude of the bias in the estimators?

2. Sample design. Given a consistent estimator, how does the asymptotic variance depend on the sample design, with respect to the relative subsample sizes and prior knowledge of the aggregate shares?

3. Choice of estimator. Several different estimators are available for choice-based samples, some asymptotically efficient and some not (see Manski and McFadden, chapter 1). In particular, when the aggregate shares are known, there are three estimators of interest: the constrained maximum likelihood estimator derived in sections 2.16 through 2.19; the Manski-McFadden estimator (chapter 1, equation 1.36); and the WESML or Manski-Lerman estimator (Manski and Lerman 1977, see also appendix 2.28). How do these estimators compare, asymptotically, for different ratios of subsample sizes and aggregate shares?

Some results will be given for three particularly simple cases: the probit, logit, and arctangent models, in each case with two alternatives and one exogenous variable z. The sample is taken to be a purely choice-based sample. We consider different values of the parameter θ, different mean values of z, and different relative sizes of the subsamples, as well as the optimal sample design for each value of θ in each model. The utility function is just $z\theta$ for alternative 1. The probability functions are as follows:

1. Probit model

$$P(1 \mid z, \theta) = \frac{1}{\sqrt{2\pi}} \int_{-\infty}^{z\theta} \exp\left(-\frac{1}{2}x^2\right) dx. \tag{2.113}$$

2. Logit model

$$P(1 \mid z, \theta) = \frac{1}{1 + \exp(-z\theta)}. \tag{2.114}$$

3. Arctangent model

$$P(1 \mid z, \theta) = \frac{1}{2} + \frac{1}{\pi} \tan^{-1}(z\theta). \tag{2.115}$$

The distribution of the exogenous variable $\mu(z)$ was taken to be the normal distribution $N(m, \frac{1}{2})$. Calculations were carried out for two values of the mean $m = 1$ and $m = 2$. For comparability of the different probability models, the biases and asymptotic variances were calculated at specified values of Q_1 rather than of θ. The following values of Q_1 were used: with $m = 1$, $Q_1 = 0.5, 0.75, 0.9$; and with $m = 2$, $Q_1 = 0.5, 0.75, 0.9, 0.95, 0.99, 0.995$. The larger values of Q_1 are not used when $m = 1$ because for this distribution of z they cannot be realized by any probability function $P(i \mid z, \theta)$.

In calculating the asymptotic bias when a choice-based sample is estimated as if it were random, we also include an alternative-specific dummy variable on alternative 1: the utility $z\theta$ is replaced by $z\theta + \phi$, where ϕ is also to be estimated. (The true value ϕ^* is taken to be zero.) This is because, in the case of the logit model, the bias is known to be confined to alternative dummies, and can be explicitly calculated in terms of Q (see sections 2.15 and 2.20). The questions of interest thus apply only to the other two models: to what extent is the bias absorbed in the coefficient of the dummy variable, and is this bias well approximated by the corresponding correction in the logit model? The asymptotic variance calculations, on the other hand, were carried out without a dummy variable, using the models given by equations (2.113) through (2.115) as they stand.

Note that questions of bias and relative efficiency in small samples have not yet been considered for these estimators and sample designs and might present a picture quite different from the asymptotic results.

Tables 2.1 (probit model) and 2.2 (arctangent model) present the results on asymptotic bias when the choice-based sample is estimated as if it were random, using the maximum likelihood estimator. The true value θ^* is also given in each case. In all cases ϕ^* is zero. Three sample designs are considered: $H_1 = 1/4$, $1/2$, and $3/4$. In the logit model there is no asymptotic bias in θ, while the asymptotic bias in ϕ is given explicitly by

Table 2.1
Asymptotic bias for choice-based sample estimated as a random sample

Probit model		$H_1 = 0.25$	$H_1 = 0.5$	$H_1 = 0.75$
m = 1				
$Q_1 = 0.5, \quad \theta^* = 0$				
	$\hat{\theta}$	0	0	0
	$\hat{\phi}$	−0.675	0	0.675
	ϕ_1	−0.689	0	0.689
$Q_1 = 0.75, \quad \theta^* = 0.768$				
	$\hat{\theta}$	0.781	0.808	0.768
	$\hat{\phi}$	−1.32	−0.690	0
	ϕ_1	−1.32	−0.659	0
$Q_1 = 0.9, \quad \theta^* = 3.03$				
	$\hat{\theta}$	3.31	3.28	3.18
	$\hat{\phi}$	−1.90	−1.29	−0.646
	ϕ_1	−1.84	−1.23	−0.614
m = 2				
$Q_1 = 0.5, \quad \theta^* = 0$				
	$\hat{\theta}$	0	0	0
	$\hat{\phi}$	−0.675	0	0.675
	ϕ_1	−0.689	0	0.689
$Q_1 = 0.75, \quad \theta^* = 0.348$				
	$\hat{\theta}$	0.349	0.368	0.348
	$\hat{\phi}$	−1.34	−0.710	0
	ϕ_1	−1.34	−0.671	0
$Q_1 = 0.9, \quad \theta^* = 0.719$				
	$\hat{\theta}$	0.832	0.854	0.809
	$\hat{\phi}$	−2.11	−1.48	−0.759
	ϕ_1	−1.91	−1.27	−0.636
$Q_1 = 0.95, \quad \theta^* = 1.01$				
	$\hat{\theta}$	1.28	1.29	1.22
	$\hat{\phi}$	−2.66	−2.04	−1.30
	ϕ_1	−2.26	−1.64	−1.03
$Q_1 = 0.99, \quad \theta^* = 2.05$				
	$\hat{\theta}$	2.84	2.79	2.69
	$\hat{\phi}$	−3.71	−3.07	−2.38
	ϕ_1	−3.04	−2.46	−1.87
$Q_1 = 0.995, \quad \theta^* = 3.12$				
	$\hat{\theta}$	4.21	4.14	4.03
	$\hat{\phi}$	−3.95	−3.34	−2.67
	ϕ_1	−3.43	−2.84	−2.25

$$\phi_0 = \ln \left\{ \frac{H_1 (1 - Q_1)}{Q_1 (1 - H_1)} \right\}.$$

In table 2.2, the values of ϕ_0 are given for comparison with the asymptotic estimates $\hat{\phi}$. In the case of the probit model we find empirically that a better approximation to the bias in ϕ is given by the following ad hoc correction to the bias term from the logit model:

$$\phi_1 = \frac{\phi_0 \cdot \theta^* [\text{probit}]}{\theta^* [\text{logit}]}.$$

The values of ϕ_1 are given for comparison in table 2.1, with the limiting value $\phi_0 \cdot \sqrt{2\pi}/4$ when $\theta^* = 0$. From table 2.1 we see that for moderate values of Q_1 (up to 0.75) the bias in $\hat{\theta}$ is less than 10%, but it increases with Q_1—for $m = 2$ and $H_1 = 0.5$ it reaches 27% at $Q_1 = 0.95$ and 33% at $Q_1 = 0.995$. Smaller, but not negligible, differences are found between $\hat{\phi}$ and ϕ_1, also increasing with Q_1. In the arctangent model, table 2.2, the bias is already large (30% or more) for $Q_1 = 0.75$, while at larger values of Q_1 we find that $\hat{\theta}$ is only a fraction of the true value θ^*. The arctangent model is, however, known to be somewhat pathological for extreme values of the mode split. Generally the bias in $\hat{\theta}$ is upward in the probit model and downward in the arctangent model. It is clear from table 2.1 that results on asymptotic bias in the logit model remain only approximately true when carried over to the probit model. Although it is speculative to generalize from this simple example to the multivariate, multialternative case, biases of 30% or more could well occur if the choice-based nature of the sample is ignored.

In tables 2.3 through 2.5 we compare the asymptotic covariances of $\hat{\theta}$ for different estimators and sample designs. Three sampling schemes are considered: choice-based sampling with known Q; choice-based sampling with Q unknown; and random sampling. In each of the choice-based sampling schemes three different designs are given for the relative subsample sizes: (1) a pseudorandom sample, in which the subsample sizes are proportional to the population shares $H_i = Q_i$, (2) equal subsample sizes $H_1 = 1/2$, and (3) subsample sizes chosen so as to minimize the asymptotic variance of $\hat{\theta}$. The optimizing values of H_1 for the third design are also given in these tables; the optimal design depends on which estimator is used. Note that, when Q is known, the choice-based estimator with $H_i = Q_i$ has the same asymptotic variance as the estimator for a

Table 2.2
Asymptotic bias for choice-based sample estimated as a random sample

Arctangent model		$H_1 = 0.25$	$H_1 = 0.5$	$H_1 = 0.75$
m = 1				
$Q_1 = 0.5$, $\theta^* = 0$				
	$\hat{\theta}$	0	0	0
	$\hat{\phi}$	−1.0	0	1.0
	ϕ_0	−1.10	0	1.10
$Q_1 = 0.75$, $\theta^* = 1.34$				
	$\hat{\theta}$	1.02	0.949	1.34
	$\hat{\phi}$	−1.97	0.807	0
	ϕ_0	−2.20	−1.10	0
$Q_1 = 0.9$, $\theta^* = 15.4$				
	$\hat{\theta}$	3.30	4.82	8.48
	$\hat{\phi}$	−2.64	−1.67	−0.944
	ϕ_0	−3.30	−2.20	−1.10
m = 2				
$Q_1 = 0.5$, $\theta^* = 0$				
	$\hat{\theta}$	0	0	0
	$\hat{\phi}$	−1.0	0	1.0
	ϕ_0	−1.10	0	1.10
$Q_1 = 0.75$, $\theta^* = 0.534$				
	$\hat{\theta}$	0.486	0.366	0.534
	$\hat{\phi}$	−1.97	−0.710	0
	ϕ_0	−2.20	−1.10	0
$Q_1 = 0.9$, $\theta^* = 1.80$				
	$\hat{\theta}$	0.636	0.533	0.815
	$\hat{\phi}$	−2.23	−0.985	−0.423
	ϕ_0	−3.30	−2.20	−1.10
$Q_1 = 0.95$, $\theta^* = 3.89$				
	$\hat{\theta}$	0.679	0.594	0.935
	$\hat{\phi}$	−2.28	−1.06	−0.562
	ϕ_0	−4.04	−2.94	−1.85
$Q_1 = 0.99$, $\theta^* = 24.9$				
	$\hat{\theta}$	0.863	0.866	1.43
	$\hat{\phi}$	−2.48	−1.37	−0.987
	ϕ_0	−5.69	−4.60	−3.50
$Q_1 = 0.995$, $\theta^* = 72.0$				
	$\hat{\theta}$	1.14	1.32	2.26
	$\hat{\phi}$	−2.71	−1.75	−1.46
	ϕ_0	−6.39	−5.29	−4.19

Table 2.3
Asymptotic efficiency of choice-based sample designs and estimators

Probit model	Pseudorandom design, $H_1 = Q_1$	Equal shares, $H_1 = 1/2$	Optimal design	Optimal value of H_1
m = 1				
$Q_1 = 0.75$				
Q known				
MLE	61.5%	84.6%	100.0%	0.17
MM	25.0	41.7	45.8	0.33
WESML	25.0	44.1	49.8	0.32
Q unknown				
MLE	5.8	7.8	7.8	0.46
Random	13.0			
$Q_1 = 0.9$				
Q known				
MLE	26.2%	89.2%	100.0%	0.29
MM	24.7	86.6	97.3	0.29
WESML	24.7	54.0	55.2	0.57
Q unknown				
MLE	17.6	39.1	39.6	0.43
Random	22.3			
m = 2				
$Q_1 = 0.75$				
Q known				
MLE	87.1%	95.0%	100.0%	0.13
MM	18.6	26.1	26.5	0.44
WESML	18.6	35.3	46.8	0.22
Q unknown				
MLE	0.4	0.6	0.6	0.49
Random	3.1			
$Q_1 = 0.9$				
Q known				
MLE	62.1%	95.2%	100.0%	0.30
MM	22.9	62.3	64.9	0.37
WESML	22.9	88.6	94.9	0.37
Q unknown				
MLE	1.3	3.6	3.7	0.45
Random	6.3			
$Q_1 = 0.95$				
Q known				
MLE	40.7%	95.5%	100.0%	0.34
MM	17.4	79.7	83.8	0.35
WESML	17.4	89.8	89.8	0.51

Table 2.3
(continued)

Probit model	Pseudorandom design, $H_1 = Q_1$	Equal shares, $H_1 = 1/2$	Optimal design	Optimal value of H_1
Q unknown				
MLE	1.6	7.5	7.6	0.43
Random	6.1			
$Q_1 = 0.99$				
Q known				
MLE	9.5%	96.9%	100.0%	0.38
MM	5.9	95.7	98.9	0.38
WESML	5.9	45.5	53.3	0.71
Q unknown				
MLE	1.4	17.8	17.8	0.46
Random	3.4			
$Q_1 = 0.995$				
Q known				
MLE	4.5%	98.4%	100.0%	0.42
MM	3.6	98.2	99.8	0.42
WESML	3.6	24.6	33.1	0.79
Q unknown				
MLE	1.4	23.0	23.0	0.49
Random	2.6			

random sample, so there is no separate entry in the table for random sampling with known Q.

For choice-based sampling with known Q, two other estimators are considered, as alternatives to the maximum likelihood estimator (MLE): the Manski-McFadden estimator (MM) and the WESML estimator (see appendix 2.28). These are of interest because, although in general not asymptotically efficient, they are relatively easy to compute.

As a basis for comparison, consider the maximum likelihood estimator for known Q with optimal sample design. The tabulated values are *asymptotic efficiencies*, defined as the asymptotic variance of this maximum likelihood estimator with optimal design divided by the asymptotic variance of the estimator and sample design in question.[28] (Results are not given for $Q_1 = 0.5$ because in this case var $\hat{\theta} = 0$ when Q is known.) The general features of the results are as follows.

28. This method of presentation was proposed by McFadden. In general, when θ is unknown, the optimal design cannot be determined, and the efficiency level 1 is unobtainable.

Table 2.4
Asymptotic efficiency of choice-based sample designs and estimators

Logit model	Pseudorandom design, $H_1 = Q_1$	Equal shares, $H_1 = 1/2$	Optimal design	Optimal value of H_1
m = 1				
$Q_1 = 0.75$				
Q known				
MLE	60.6%	83.9%	100.0%	0.14
MM	24.6	40.9	45.0	0.33
WESML	24.6	42.3	46.6	0.34
Q unknown				
MLE	4.8	6.2	6.2	0.50
Random	11.8			
$Q_1 = 0.9$				
Q known				
MLE	25.6%	88.0%	100.0%	0.28
MM	23.8	85.0	96.7	0.28
WESML	23.8	51.8	52.8	0.57
Q unknown				
MLE	16.0	31.2	31.2	0.49
Random	21.2			
m = 2				
$Q_1 = 0.75$				
Q known				
MLE	86.7%	94.5%	100.0%	0.09
MM	19.8	27.6	28.0	0.44
WESML	19.8	37.5	49.3	0.22
Q unknown				
MLE	0.3	0.4	0.4	0.50
Random	2.9			
$Q_1 = 0.9$				
Q known				
MLE	62.2%	94.3%	100.0%	0.26
MM	24.8	64.1	66.9	0.37
WESML	24.8	88.9	91.9	0.41
Q unknown				
MLE	0.8	1.8	1.8	0.50
Random	5.2			
$Q_1 = 0.95$				
Q known				
MLE	41.5%	94.7%	100.0%	0.30
MM	18.7	79.4	83.6	0.34
WESML	18.7	85.0	85.6	0.54

Table 2.4
(*continued*)

Logit model	Pseudorandom design, $H_1 = Q_1$	Equal shares, $H_1 = 1/2$	Optimal design	Optimal value of H_1
Q unknown				
MLE	0.9	3.4	3.4	0.50
Random	4.9			
$Q_1 = 0.99$				
Q known				
MLE	9.0%	95.0%	100.0%	0.35
MM	5.6	93.1	98.3	0.35
WESML	5.6	41.7	48.9	0.71
Q unknown				
MLE	0.9	8.9	8.9	0.50
Random	2.7			
$Q_1 = 0.995$				
Q known				
MLE	3.9%	95.7%	100.0%	0.37
MM	3.0	95.3	99.6	0.37
WESML	3.0	21.8	29.0	0.79
Q unknown				
MLE	1.0	12.9	12.9	0.51
Random	2.1			

1. Knowledge of Q greatly improves the precision of the estimates, as can be seen from the low efficiency of the estimators for unknown Q. We should note, however, that knowledge of Q_1 should have greatest impact for a one-variable model without an alternative-specific dummy and in general the value of this information will be less. In particular the very small relative efficiency at moderate values of Q_1 is related to the fact that in this model $\hat{\theta}$ is necessarily zero if Q_1 is known to be 0.5, that is, the relative efficiency is zero when $Q_1 = 0.5$. This artificial situation will not occur in more complex models.

2. At moderate values of the mode split (e.g., $Q_1 = 0.75$) the Manski-McFadden and WESML estimators are comparable and are considerably less efficient than the maximum likelihood estimator. For intermediate values of Q_1 (e.g., $Q_1 = 0.9$ to 0.95 for $m = 2$) the efficiency of the WESML estimator increases and comes close to that of the maximum likelihood estimator. (For $m = 1$, not enough values of Q_1 have been tabulated for this effect to be apparent). At larger values of Q_1 the efficiency of the WESML

Table 2.5
Asymptotic efficiency of choice-based sample designs and estimators

Arctangent model	Pseudorandom design, $H_1 = Q_1$	Equal shares, $H_1 = 1/2$	Optimal design	Optimal value of H_1
m = 1				
$Q_1 = 0.75$				
Q known				
MLE	53.2%	75.7%	100.0%	0
MM	20.8	36.0	40.1	0.32
WESML	20.8	31.3	31.9	0.43
Q unknown				
MLE	2.5	2.6	2.7	0.62
Random	8.1			
$Q_1 = 0.9$				
Q known				
MLE	19.3%	74.0%	100.0%	0.10
MM	18.2	71.1	92.9	0.16
WESML	18.2	32.4	34.2	0.62
Q unknown				
MLE	10.3	8.8	11.4	0.79
Random	15.6			
m = 2				
$Q_1 = 0.75$				
Q known				
MLE	83.5%	91.3%	100.0%	0
MM	28.0	38.6	39.3	0.41
WESML	28.0	50.8	59.9	0.29
Q unknown				
MLE	0.08	0.09	0.09	0.55
Random	1.8			
$Q_1 = 0.9$				
Q known				
MLE	52.9%	84.0%	100.0%	0
MM	32.2	74.0	82.3	0.23
WESML	32.2	53.3	57.3	0.64
Q unknown				
MLE	0.04	0.04	0.05	0.73
Random	1.7			
$Q_1 = 0.95$				
Q known				
MLE	27.0%	78.1%	100.0%	0
MM	16.1	73.8	87.9	0.15
WESML	16.1	32.2	37.4	0.70

Table 2.5
(*continued*)

Arctangent model	Pseudorandom design, $H_1 = Q_1$	Equal shares, $H_1 = 1/2$	Optimal design	Optimal value of H_1
Q unknown				
MLE	0.04	0.03	0.04	0.83
Random	1.1			
$Q_1 = 0.99$				
Q known				
MLE	2.2%	64.4%	100.0%	0
MM	1.7	63.7	93.9	0.06
WESML	1.7	8.2	10.5	0.76
Q unknown				
MLE	0.04	0.03	0.05	0.94
Random	0.5			
$Q_1 = 0.995$				
Q known				
MLE	0.8%	59.8%	100.0%	0
MM	0.7	59.6	97.0	0.03
WESML	0.7	4.7	6.0	0.80
Q unknown				
MLE	0.05	0.03	0.06	0.96
Random	0.4			

estimator declines, and it is rapidly overtaken by the Manski-McFadden estimator. For large values of Q_1 the Manski-McFadden estimator is virtually indistinguishable from an asymptotically efficient estimator.

3. The efficiency of the equal-shares sample design is not very much less than the efficiency of the optimal sample design, for all the estimators considered and for both known Q and unknown Q (except for large values of Q_1 in the arctangent model). This holds even when the optimal value of H_1 is not close to 0.5. The optimal value of H_1 depends of course on the unknown true values of the parameters. This result, however, suggests that (1) efficiency is not very sensitive to the sample design if H_1 is reasonably close to its optimal value, so that low-grade estimates of the parameter values (e.g., from analysis of a preliminary survey) could be used to determine a good approximation to the optimal design, and (2) if the parameter values are uncertain, a reasonable rule of thumb is to use equal shares.

Table 2.6 compares the relative efficiency of choice-based sampling with equal shares versus random sampling, using maximum likelihood esti-

Table 2.6
Relative efficiency of maximum likelihood estimators for equal shares, choice-based sample versus random sample

	Q_1	Q known	Q unknown
Probit			
$m = 1$	0.75	1.38	0.60
	0.9	3.40	1.75
$m = 2$	0.75	1.09	0.19
	0.9	1.53	0.57
	0.95	2.35	1.23
	0.99	10.2	5.30
	0.995	21.7	8.83
Logit			
$m = 1$	0.75	1.38	0.53
	0.9	3.44	1.47
$m = 2$	0.75	1.09	0.16
	0.9	1.52	0.35
	0.95	2.28	0.69
	0.99	10.5	3.28
	0.995	24.7	6.26
Arctan			
$m = 1$	0.75	1.42	0.32
	0.9	3.83	0.56
$m = 2$	0.75	1.09	0.05
	0.9	1.59	0.02
	0.95	2.90	0.03
	0.99	29.0	0.06
	0.995	74.5	0.10

mation in both cases. The cases of known Q and unknown Q are considered separately. The table gives the *relative efficiencies*, defined as the asymptotic variance of the maximum likelihood estimator for a random sample divided by the corresponding asymptotic variance for the choice-based sample. Thus a tabulated value exceeding one means that the choice-based sample is more efficient than a random sample of the same total size. When Q is known, the choice-based design is always more efficient than the random sample. The results for all three models are remarkably similar. The more extreme the mode split (the larger the value of Q_1), the greater is the relative efficiency of the choice-based design. When Q is unknown, random sampling is more efficient for the arctangent model, and for smaller values of Q_1 in the other models; for large values of Q_1 in the probit and logit models the relative efficiency of the choice-based design is still substantial, however.

The improvement can be quite significant: a relative efficiency of 10 means that the precision can be improved by a factor of $\sqrt{(10/r)}$ for a fixed sampling budget, where r is the cost of collecting an observation in the choice-based sample relative to a random sample.

2.26 Appendix: Conditions on the Choice Probability Model

Of the following assumptions some are stronger than strictly necessary for proofs of consistency of maximum likelihood estimators. They are, however, generally satisfied in practical applications and allow expeditious proofs.

ASSUMPTION **2.1**: The choice set $\mathbf{C}$ (of alternatives i) is finite.

ASSUMPTION **2.2**: $\mathbf{z} \in \mathbf{Z}$ and $\boldsymbol{\theta}^* \in \text{int}\, \boldsymbol{\Theta}$, where $\mathbf{Z}$ and $\boldsymbol{\Theta}$ are given closed, bounded subsets of Euclidean spaces.

ASSUMPTION **2.3**: The model is identifiable: if $\boldsymbol{\theta} \neq \boldsymbol{\theta}^*$ and $\boldsymbol{\theta} \in \boldsymbol{\Theta}$, there is a region $\boldsymbol{\Omega} \subseteq \mathbf{Z}$, such that

$$\int_{\boldsymbol{\Omega}} d\mathbf{z}\, \mu(\mathbf{z})\, P(i \mid \mathbf{z}, \boldsymbol{\theta}) \neq \int_{\boldsymbol{\Omega}} d\mathbf{z}\, \mu(\mathbf{z})\, P(i \mid \mathbf{z}, \boldsymbol{\theta}^*) \tag{2.116}$$

for at least one choice alternative i included in the sampling procedure.

ASSUMPTION 2.4: $P(i \mid \mathbf{z}, \boldsymbol{\theta})$ is strictly positive for $\mathbf{z} \in \mathbf{Z}$, $\boldsymbol{\theta} \in \boldsymbol{\Theta}$. This condition may be relaxed slightly, so as to allow $P(i \mid \mathbf{z}, \boldsymbol{\theta})$ to be zero for all $\boldsymbol{\theta}$ for any specified set of values of $(i, \mathbf{z})$: this covers the situation where choice i is unavailable at certain values of $\mathbf{z}$ (Manski and McFadden, chapter 1). We assume here, however, that the remaining set of $\mathbf{z}$ is still closed.

ASSUMPTION 2.5: $P(i \mid \mathbf{z}, \boldsymbol{\theta})$ is continuous in $\boldsymbol{\theta}$ for $\boldsymbol{\theta} \in \boldsymbol{\Theta}$.

To show consistency of the estimator for the case of known aggregate shares, a further assumption is needed.

ASSUMPTION 2.6: The $P(i \mid \mathbf{z}, \boldsymbol{\theta})$ are linearly independent, that is, there exists no set of nonzero constants $\{a_j(\boldsymbol{\theta}), j = 1, \ldots, M\}$, such that

$$\sum_{j=1}^{M} a_j(\boldsymbol{\theta}) P(j \mid \mathbf{z}, \boldsymbol{\theta}) = 0 \tag{2.117}$$

for almost all $\mathbf{z}$.[29] This is to hold for all $\boldsymbol{\theta}$, except possibly for an exceptional set of $\boldsymbol{\theta}$ which is nowhere dense and does not contain $\boldsymbol{\theta}^*$. Assumption 2.6 does not hold when all the variables are alternative-specific dummies, but in that case the coefficients $\boldsymbol{\theta}$ are fully determined by the aggregate shares Q_i, and an estimator is not needed.

For establishing asymptotic covariance properties, two more assumptions are needed.

ASSUMPTION 2.7: The first two derivatives of $P(i \mid \mathbf{z}, \boldsymbol{\theta})$ with respect to $\boldsymbol{\theta}$ exist and are continuous in $\boldsymbol{\theta}$, for $\boldsymbol{\theta}$ in some neighborhood of $\boldsymbol{\theta}^*$ and for all $\mathbf{z} \in \mathbf{Z}$.

ASSUMPTION 2.8: The K derivatives $\partial P(i \mid \mathbf{z}, \boldsymbol{\theta}^*)/\partial \theta_\alpha$ $(\alpha = 1, \ldots, K)$ are linearly independent on $\mathbf{C} \times \mathbf{Z}$, that is, there is no nonzero vector $\mathbf{k}$, such that

$$\sum_{\alpha=1}^{K} k_\alpha \frac{\partial P(i \mid \mathbf{z}, \boldsymbol{\theta}^*)}{\partial \theta_\alpha} = 0 \tag{2.118}$$

for all i and z (except possibly for a subset of $\mathbf{Z}$ with zero measure μ).

In practice the only difficulty that may occur is verification of the identifiability assumption. There are apparently no general criteria for identifiability in nonlinear models, and the question must be studied on a case-by-case basis. One method that is sometimes applicable is to establish

29. This means for all $\mathbf{z} \in \mathbf{Z}'$, where $\mathbf{Z}' \subseteq \mathbf{Z}$ is such that $\int_{\mathbf{Z}'} \mu(\mathbf{z}) d\mathbf{z} = 1$.

the negative-definiteness of the expectation of the matrix of second derivatives of the likelihood function at $\boldsymbol{\theta} = \boldsymbol{\theta}^*$ (Rothenberg 1971). Sufficient identifiability conditions for the multinomial logit model have been given by McFadden (1973).

In discussing identifiability from choice-based samples, we assumed that the model was already identifiable in the sense of assumption 2.3, that the probability of it not being identifiable from a random sample tends to zero as the sample size becomes large.

2.27 Appendix: Derivation of Asymptotic Properties

We give here a very brief discussion of the methods by which consistency, asymptotic normality, and asymptotic efficiency may be proved for the estimators given in sections 2.14 and 2.19 (see Cosslett 1978, 1981 for details of the proofs).

The proof of consistency does not involve any essentially different methods from those used by Amemiya (1973) to prove consistency of the maximum likelihood estimator for the truncated normal distribution, and by Manski and Lerman (1977) to prove consistency of the weighted exogenous sample maximum likelihood estimator for a purely choice-based sample. Manski and McFadden, chapter 1, have also proved consistency of a number of other estimators by a similar procedure.

The proof basically involves three steps: (1) to show that the expected value of the pseudolikelihood has a unique maximum at $\gamma = \gamma^*$, (2) to show that the pseudolikelihood converges uniformly to its expected value, and (3) to conclude that the point at which the pseudolikelihood is maximized, $\hat{\gamma}_N$, converges to the point at which its expected value is maximized, γ^*. The case of known aggregate shares is complicated by the fact that the minimization over $\boldsymbol{\lambda}$ and the maximization over $\boldsymbol{\theta}$ have to be considered separately. A technical problem arises here: it cannot immediately be shown that the minimum over $\boldsymbol{\lambda}$ lies within the domain of uniform convergence, and a slight extension of Amemiya's lemma 3 (Amemiya 1973) is needed (see Cosslett 1978).

Given consistency, the proof of asymptotic normality is fairly standard Since enough assumptions have already been made to establish uniform convergence of the pseudolikelihood, we need only assumption 2.7 on the derivatives of $P(i \mid \mathbf{z}, \boldsymbol{\theta})$ with respect to $\boldsymbol{\theta}$, rather than Cramér type conditions involving third derivatives (e.g., see Amemiya 1973 for the appropriate treatment). The only substantive point is to establish positive-definiteness of the information matrix **J**, as defined in sections 2.12 and 2.18.

The proof of asymptotic efficiency, on the other hand, does require a special approach because the usual derivation of the Cramér-Rao bound (e.g., see Rao 1973) is applicable only to a finite set of parameters. There are problems in defining an information matrix when the number of parameters is infinite, or, worse yet, when the estimation problem involves an unknown function. A brief outline of the method, in the case of unknown aggregate shares, is as follows. First, we consider two statistics: a vector $\mathbf{t}_1$ which is an unbiased estimator of $\boldsymbol{\theta}$ and t_2 which is an unbiased estimator of $\int d\mathbf{z}\mu(\mathbf{z})\phi(\mathbf{z})$, assuming here that $\mu(\mathbf{z})$ is continuous. The test function $\phi(\mathbf{z})$ is arbitrary, except for normalization conditions,

$$\int d\mathbf{z}\phi(\mathbf{z}) = 0, \qquad \int d\mathbf{z}\,[\phi(\mathbf{z})]^2 = 1, \tag{2.119}$$

and some mild regularity conditions. A lower bound on the variance of $\hat{\theta}_1$, say, can be established by essentially the same method as is used to derive the Cramér-Rao bound; the only difference is that differentiation of t_2 with respect to the parameter of which it is an estimate is replaced by functional differentiation with respect to $\phi(\mathbf{z})$, subject to the conditions imposed by equation (2.119). We then have to search the space of test functions ϕ for one that gives a maximal lower bound: this is done using the calculus of variations to find a stationary value with respect to $\phi(\mathbf{z})$. The resulting lower bound on the covariance matrix is found to be the same as V_{11}, equation (2.45). This is the required result because θ_1 could be taken as an arbitrary linear combination of the actual parameters.

If the aggregate shares are known, we consider instead just the statistic $\mathbf{t}_1$. But instead of partial differentiation with respect to θ, we subject it to simultaneous variations of the form

$$\begin{cases} \boldsymbol{\theta} \to \boldsymbol{\theta} + \delta\boldsymbol{\theta}; \\ \mu \to \mu(1 + \boldsymbol{\xi}'\,\delta\boldsymbol{\theta}), \end{cases} \tag{2.120}$$

such that the aggregate shares $Q_i = \int d\mathbf{z}\mu(\mathbf{z})P(i \mid \mathbf{z}, \boldsymbol{\theta})$ remain unchanged for $i = 1, \ldots, M$. For any suitable $\boldsymbol{\xi}(\mathbf{z}, \boldsymbol{\theta})$ this leads to a Cramér-Rao-like lower bound on, say, var $(\hat{\theta}_1)$. Then a $\boldsymbol{\xi}(\mathbf{z}, \boldsymbol{\theta})$ is found that yields a maximal lower bound: this bound is in fact equal to V_{11} given in equation (2.78), as required.

2.28 Appendix: Alternative Estimators for Generalized Choice-Based Samples with Known Aggregate Shares

Two other consistent estimators have been proposed for choice-based samples when the aggregate shares Q_i are known: the Manski-McFadden estimator (see Manski and McFadden, chapter 1, equation 1.36) and the Manski-Lerman, or WESML (weighted exogenous sample maximum likelihood), estimator (Manski and Lerman 1977; also chapter 1, equation 1.19). These can immediately be extended to generalized choice-based samples. For reference we give here the corresponding pseudolikelihoods and asymptotic covariance matrices.

1. The Manski-McFadden estimator is the value of $\boldsymbol{\theta}$ that maximizes

$$\tilde{L}_N(\boldsymbol{\theta}) = \sum_{n=1}^{N} \ln \frac{\dfrac{H_{i(n)}}{Q_{i(n)}} P(i_n \mid \mathbf{z}_n, \boldsymbol{\theta})}{\sum_{j=1}^{M} \dfrac{H_j}{Q_j} P(j \mid \mathbf{z}_n, \boldsymbol{\theta})}, \tag{2.121}$$

over $\boldsymbol{\theta} \in \boldsymbol{\Theta}$, where $i(n)$ is the alternative chosen by subject n. Note that the weights involve the sample choice proportions H_i rather than their expected values $\bar{H}_i$.[30] This estimator is asymptotically efficient in the case of the logit model with a full set of alternative-specific dummies (in which case it is identical to the constrained maximum likelihood estimator), but in general its asymptotic covariance is not optimal. It is, however, relatively easy to compute.

Its asymptotic covariance matrix is

$$\mathbf{V}^{[MM]} = \mathbf{A}^{-1} - \mathbf{A}^{-1}\mathbf{B}_Q \mathbf{G}^{[MM]} \mathbf{B}'_Q \mathbf{A}^{-1}, \tag{2.122}$$

where $\mathbf{A}$ and $\mathbf{B}_Q$ are given by equations (2.41) and (2.75) and

$$G_{ij}^{[MM]} = \frac{\bar{H}_i}{Q_i^2}\delta_{ij} - \frac{\bar{H}_i \bar{H}_j}{Q_i Q_j}. \tag{2.123}$$

2. The WESML estimator is the value of $\boldsymbol{\theta}$ that maximizes

$$\tilde{L}_N(\boldsymbol{\theta}) = \sum_{n=1}^{N} \frac{Q_{i(n)}}{H_{i(n)}} \ln \{ P(i_n \mid \mathbf{z}_n, \boldsymbol{\theta}) \}, \tag{2.124}$$

30. For a purely choice-based sample $H_i = \bar{H}_i$. But in general use of $\bar{H}_i$ rather than H_i results in a less efficient estimator, both for the Manski-McFadden and the WESML estimators.

over $\boldsymbol{\theta} \in \boldsymbol{\Theta}$. Its asymptotic covariance matrix is

$$\mathbf{V}^{[W]} = \mathbf{J}^{-1}\mathbf{M}\mathbf{J}^{-1}, \tag{2.125}$$

where

$$\mathbf{J} = \sum_{i=1}^{M} \left\langle \frac{1}{P_i} \frac{\partial P_i}{\partial \theta} \frac{\partial P_i}{\partial \theta'} \right\rangle \tag{2.126}$$

and

$$\mathbf{M} = \sum_{i=1}^{M} \left\{ \frac{Q_i}{\bar{H}_i} \left\langle \frac{1}{P_i} \frac{\partial P_i}{\partial \theta} \frac{\partial P_i}{\partial \theta'} \right\rangle - \frac{1}{\bar{H}_i} \left\langle \frac{\partial P_i}{\partial \theta} \right\rangle \left\langle \frac{\partial P_i}{\partial \theta'} \right\rangle \right\} \tag{2.127}$$

This differs from the covariance matrix given by Manski and Lerman (1977) for a purely choice-based sample, because we have adopted a different sampling scheme in which the subsample sizes $\tilde{N}_s$ are fixed in advance (are not themselves random variables).

The WESML estimator is not asymptotically efficient, except in the special case $Q_i = \bar{H}_i$, $i = 1, \ldots, M$.

References

Amemiya, T. 1973. Regression Analysis when the Dependent Variable is Truncated Normal. *Econometrica*. 41: 997–1016.

Cosslett, S. 1978. Efficient Estimation of Discrete Choice Models from Choice-Based Samples. Ph. D. dissertation. Department of Economics, University of California, Berkeley.

Cosslett, S. 1981. Maximum Likelihood Estimator for Choice-Based Samples. *Econometrica* (forthcoming).

Daly, A., and S. Zachary. 1979. Improved Multiple Choice Models. In *Identifying and Measuring the Determinants of Mode Choice*, D. Hensher and O. Dalvi eds. London: Teakfield.

Hausman, J. A., and D. A. Wise. 1978. A Conditional Probit Model for Qualitative Choice: Discrete Data Decisions Recognizing Interdependence and Heterogeneous Preferences. *Econometrica*. 46: 403–420.

Kiefer, J., and J. Wolfowitz. 1956. Consistency of the Maximum Likelihood Estimator in the Presence of Infinitely Many Incidental Parameters. *Annals of Mathematical Statistics*. 27: 887–906.

Lerman, S., and C. Manski. 1975. Alternative Sampling Procedures for Disaggregate Choice Model Estimators. *Transportation Research Record*. 592: 24–28.

Lerman, S. R., and C. F. Manski. 1978. Sample Design for Discrete Choice Analysis of Travel Behavior. Report presented at NBER-NSF Conference on Decision Rules and Uncertainty, Carnegie-Mellon University, Pittsburgh.

Manski, C., and S. Lerman. 1977. The Estimation of Choice Probabilities from Choice-Based Samples. *Econometrica*. 45: 1977–1988.

McFadden, D. 1973. Conditional Logit Analysis of Qualitative Choice Behavior. In *Frontiers in Econometrics*, ed. P. Zarembka. New York: Academic Press.

McFadden, D. 1976. Quantal Choice Analysis: A Survey. *Annals of Economic and Social Measurement*. 5: 363–390.

McFadden, D. 1978. Modelling the Choice of Residential Location. In *Spatial Interaction Theory and Planning Models*, A. Karlquist et al., eds. Amsterdam: North Holland.

Miettinen, O. S. 1976. Estimability and Estimation in Case-Referent Studies. *American Journal of Epidemiology*. 103: 226–235.

Rao, C. R. 1973. *Linear Statistical Inference and its Applications*. New York: Wiley.

Rothenberg, T. 1971. Identification in Parametric Models. *Econometrica*. 39: 577–592.

Seigel, D. G., and S. W. Greenhouse. 1973. Multiple Relative Risk Functions in Case-Control Studies. *American Journal of Epidemiology*. 97: 324–331.

Warner, S. L. 1963. Multivariate Regression of Dummy Variates under Normality Assumptions. *Journal of the American Statistical Association*. 58: 1054–1063.

Warner, S. L. 1967. Asymptotic Variances for Dummy Variate Regression under Normality Assumptions. *Journal of the American Statistical Association*. 62: 1305–1314.

Williams, H. C. L. 1977. On the Formation of Travel Demand Models and Economic Evaluation Measures of User Benefit. *Environment and Planning*. *A*9: 285–344.

II DYNAMIC DISCRETE PROBABILITY MODELS

3 Statistical Models for Discrete Panel Data

James J. Heckman

3.1 Introduction

This chapter formulates a general dynamic model for the analysis of discrete panel data that can be used to analyze the structure of discrete choices made over time. A rich group of discrete time-discrete outcome stochastic processes is generated by imposing restrictions on the general model developed here. Markov models, renewal processes, Pólya schemes, Bernoulli models, and other familiar stochastic processes emerge as special cases of this model. The model is sufficiently flexible to accommodate time-varying explanatory variables, quite general serial correlation patterns for unobservable variables, and complex structural economic interrelationships among decisions taken at different times.

The analysis in this chapter generalizes previous work by McFadden (1976) and others that considers consumer choice among a collection of discrete alternatives at a point in time. The models considered here focus on relationships among choices over time, or more generally, intertemporal relationships among discrete variables.

The procedures proposed here are used to investigate the following important problem: in a variety of contexts, such as in the study of the incidence of accidents (Bates and Neyman 1951), labor force participation (Heckman and Willis 1977) and unemployment (Layton 1978), it is often noted that individuals who have experienced the event under study in the past are more likely to experience the event in the future than are individuals who have not experienced the event. The conditional probability that an individual will experience the event in the future is a function of past experience. There are two distinct explanations for this empirical regularity.

One explanation is that as a consequence of experiencing an event, preferences, prices or constraints relevant to future choices are altered. In

This research was supported by NSF Grant SOC 77-27136, Grant 10-P-90748/9-01 from the Social Security Administration, and a Fellowship from the J. S. Guggenheim Memorial Foundation. Discussions with Tom MaCurdy have been valuable at all stages of the work. I have also benefited from comments by Gary Chamberlain, Chris Flinn, Zvi Griliches, Jan Hoem, Samuel Kotz, Charles Manski, Jerzy Neyman, Marc Nerlove, Guillherme Sedlacek, Donald Waldman and David Wise. I retain responsibility for any errors that remain. The first draft of this chapter circulated in July, 1977. I have benefited from assorted comments received at seminars at Harvard-MIT (the Joint Econometrics Workshop), The University of Iowa, Columbia University, the University of Wisconsin, and the University of Chicago.

this case past experience has a genuine behavioral effect in the sense that an otherwise identical individual who did not experience the event would behave differently in the future than an individual who experienced the event. This explanation applies even in an environment of perfect certainty so that all relevant information is available to the individual but not necessarily to the observing economist. Structural relationships of this sort give rise to true state dependence, as defined in this chapter.

A second explanation for the phenomenon is that individuals may differ in their propensity to experience the event. If individual differences are correlated over time, and if these differences are not properly controlled, previous experience may appear to be a determinant of future experience solely because it is a proxy for temporally persistent unobservables that determine choices. Improper treatment of unmeasured variables gives rise to a conditional relationship between future and past experience that is termed spurious state dependence.

The problem of distinguishing between spurious and true state dependence is somewhat analogous to the familiar problem of estimating a distributed lag model in the presence of serial correlation (Griliches 1966, Malinvaud 1970, Nerlove 1978). It is also closely related to previous work on the mover-stayer model that appears in the literature on discrete stochastic processes (Goodman 1961, Singer and Spilerman 1976).

This substantive problem is of considerable practical interest. Two examples are offered to illustrate this point. The first is drawn from recent work in the theory of unemployment. Phelps (1972) has argued that short-term economic policies that alleviate unemployment tend to lower aggregate unemployment rates in the long run by preventing the loss of work-enhancing market experience. His argument rests on the assumption that unemployment has a real and lasting effect on the future probability of unemployment of the currently unemployed. Cripps and Tarling (1974) maintain the opposite view in their analysis of the incidence and duration of unemployment. They assume that individuals differ in their propensity to experience unemployment and in their unemployment duration times and that differences cannot be fully accounted for by measured variables. They further assume that the actual experience of having been unemployed or the duration of past unemployment does not affect future incidence or duration. Hence in their model short-term economic policies have no effect on long-term unemployment. The model developed in this chapter is sufficiently flexible to accommodate both views of unemployment and can be used to test the two competing theories.

As another example, recent work on the dynamics of female labor supply assumes that entry and exit from the labor force can be described by a Bernoulli probability model (Heckman and Willis 1977). This view of female labor supply dynamics ignores considerable evidence that work experience raises wage rates and hence that such experience may raise the probability that a woman works in the future, even if initial entry into the work force is determined by a random process. The general model outlined in this chapter extends the econometric model of Heckman and Willis by permitting (1) unobservable variables that determine labor force choices to be freely correlated, in contrast with the rigid permanent-transitory error scheme for the unobservables assumed in their model, (2) observed explanatory variables to change over time and (3) previous work experience to determine current participation decisions. Empirical work based on the general model developed in this chapter (Heckman 1978b, 1981) reveals that these three extensions are important in correctly assessing the determinants of female labor supply and in developing models that can be used in policy simulation analysis.

Since this chapter is long, and a number of new ideas are developed in it, an outline of the topics covered is in order. The first sections discuss the general model proposed here. This model is an extension of previous work by the author (1978a) that incorporates dummy endogenous variables into a simultaneous equation system. This chapter extends that framework to develop a very general choice theoretic model for the analysis of discrete decisions made over time. Many different discrete time-discrete outcome stochastic processes are developed as special cases of a more general model.

The models considered here are based on the notion that discrete outcomes are generated by continuous variables that cross thresholds. In certain applications these continuous variables correspond to well-defined economic concepts. For example, in the work of Domencich and McFadden (1975) the continuous variables that generate discrete choices are differences in utilities of possible choices. In work on labor supply the continuous variable that generates labor force participation is the difference between market wages and reservation wages (Heckman and MaCurdy 1980).

The main novelty in this chapter comes in the treatment of consumer decision making over time. With the exception of the few papers mentioned here, previous work has only considered consumer decision making at a point in time. This chapter develops a flexible statistical model that considers the relationship between current choices (or discrete outcomes) and choices (or outcomes) in other periods. Variation in the specification of the interrelationship among choices (or outcomes) in different periods gives rise to a variety of stochastic processes. For example, if choices made last period are the only prior choices relevant to current choice, a first-order Markov model is generated. If the entire history of the process is relevant to current decision making, as is assumed in certain human capital models in labor economics, a Pólya process (Feller 1957, Johnson and Kotz 1977) emerges. If the current continuous duration in one state is a determinant of the decision to remain in or exit the state, a renewal process is generated that captures the essence of many models of firm specific investment recently advanced in the literature on worker turnover (Jovanovic 1978).

In formulating any econometric model, the treatment of unobservables is an important ingredient of the specification. This chapter extends previous work on estimating discrete stochastic processes by permitting the unobservables that generate the stochastic process to be freely correlated over time. Within the context of the models considered here, previous work assumes the unobservables that generate the underlying continuous variables that cross thresholds (and thus generate discrete outcomes) follow a "components of variance" scheme. Virtually all of the available literature on discrete data stochastic processes (implicitly) defines heterogeneity in this way. This chapter broadens the definition of heterogeneity to allow for more general correlation patterns among the unobservables. The greater generality of the model developed here permits the analyst to relax the (implicit) assumption—maintained in previous work—that the unmeasured variables that determine discrete outcomes are a combination of an immutable person specific component and a temporally independently identically distributed component. Unobservables are permitted to be characterized by a more general scheme so that conventional specifications of heterogeneity can be tested against more general models.

A major advantage of the models for discrete stochastic processes that are developed in this chapter is that they are sufficiently flexible to accommodate the introduction of time-varying explanatory variables. This feature improves on previous models advanced in the literature in which explanatory variables cannot be introduced at all, or special assumptions on their structure must be invoked—such as their assumed constancy over time.

Another advantage of the models presented here is that they are computationally tractable and hence useful in practical work. This is especially true of the factor analytic schemes and fixed effect schemes discussed in sections 3.5 and 3.6. The random factor model is the discrete data analogue of the MIMIC model of Joreskog and Goldberger (1975). The fixed effect probit model is a conditional version of the random factor model. Both models are very simple to compute but neither is without its limitations. These limitations are discussed briefly in the text and are spelled out in greater detail in the appendix and in chapter 4. The appendix also develops more general factor analytic schemes than those presented in the text.

Special cases of the general model that are likely to be of practical interest are developed in sections 3.3 through 3.10. Markov models, renewal models, Bernoulli models, "latent Markov" models, Pólya processes, and other schemes emerge as restricted versions of the general model. Very general types of population heterogeneity for unobserved variables are considered. Comparisons are made among models in terms of data requirements, identification criteria, and implications for runs patterns.

One important topic is only briefly covered in this chapter: the problem of initial conditions. In formulating any stochastic process with structural dependence among time-ordered outcomes, it is necessary to initialize the process. In much applied work in social science this problem is treated somewhat casually. Typically the initial conditions or the relevant presample history of the process are assumed to be predetermined or exogenous. This assumption is valid only if the unobservables that generate the process are serially independent or if a genuinely new process is (fortuitously) observed at the beginning of the sample at the analyst's disposal, and the relevant presample history is unrelated to the unobservables that generate the process in the sample period. Neither assumption is very appealing in applied work.

If the process has been in operation prior to the time it is sampled (e.g., a labor force participation process for middle-age women), and the unobservables that generate the process are serially correlated, the standard treatment of initial conditions results in biased and inconsistent parameter estimates. The confluence of heterogeneity and true (structural) state dependence leads to an important and neglected problem. Because of the importance of the problem, it is given special treatment in chapter 4.

Sections 3.12 through 3.15 are devoted to a discussion of the concepts of heterogeneity and state dependence. These concepts are defined, and their applicability to models of perfect foresight and models of uncertainty is discussed. The limitations of the multivariate probit framework for measuring separate effects of heterogeneity and state dependence are considered. The main points raised in these sections are (1) the concepts of heterogeneity and state dependence do not require the multivariate probit framework for their definition, but the multivariate probit framework is sufficiently flexible to permit empirical discrimination between the two concepts; (2) analogies between the classical time-series problem of discriminating between a distributed lag model and a serial correlation model and the problem of discriminating between heterogeneity and state dependence in a discrete data model, while of some heuristic value, are not precise and, if pushed too far, are misleading; (3) the concept of structural state dependence defined here is applicable to an environment of perfect certainty, in which there is no revision of plans, as well as to an environment of imperfect certainty, or an environment of stimulus-response conditioning of the sort considered by mathematical psychologists.

3.2 A Framework for Analyzing Dynamic Choice

All of the statistical models considered in this chapter are based on the following ideas: the analyst has access to a random sample of I individuals. On each of these persons there is a record that registers the presence or absence of an event under study in each of T equispaced time periods. The event occurs in period t for individual i if and only if a continuous latent random variable $Y(i, t)$ crosses a threshold, assumed to be zero for convenience. The event occurs, and dummy variable $d(i, t) = 1$ if and only if $Y(i, t) \geq 0$. Otherwise the event does not occur and $d(i, t) = 0$. The model developed in this chapter is confined to only two states, although it can readily be extended to accommodate more states.

Introducing a latent continuous random variable into the analysis simplifies the analysis, links the current work to previous work in econometrics, and provides a natural framework for formulating choice theoretic econometric models. Several examples are offered.

In an analysis of the labor force participation of women, $Y(i, t)$ may be interpreted as the difference between the lifetime utility of woman i at time t if she is in the labor force at t and her lifetime utility if she does not participate, the assumption being that she chooses the best sequence of lifetime labor force participation in the remainder of her lifetime given participation or nonparticipation in t. In an analysis of the purchase of consumer durables, $Y(i, t)$ may be interpreted as the difference between lifetime utility if consumer i purchases a durable at time t and lifetime utility if he does not. In both of these examples it is natural to assume that the difference in utilities is a continuous latent random variable (McFadden 1976). In analyses of labor market search decisions or female labor supply decisions (Heckman and MaCurdy 1980), it is sometimes natural to formulate a model in terms of the difference between reservation wages and offered market wages. If this difference is positive in period t, an individual chooses to continue searching (or remain out of the labor force) in the period. In certain cases it is possible to observe the continuous random variable that generates the discrete random variable $\varepsilon(i, t)$ so that $Y(i, t)$ is more than a theoretical construct. For example, if a person is classified to be in poverty ($d(i, t) = 1$) when income at time $t(E(i, t))$ is below some cutoff value C, the latent variable that generates the dynamics of poverty status is $Y(i, t) = C - E(i, t)$ (Fase 1971).

Random variable $Y(i, t)$ may be decomposed into two components: a purely stochastic disturbance component, $\varepsilon(i, t)$, and a function of exogenous, predetermined, and measured endogenous variables that affect current choices, $V(i, t)$. $V(i, t)$ may or may not be independent of $\varepsilon(i, t)$. We may write

$$Y(i,t) = V(i,t) + \varepsilon(i,t), \tag{3.1}$$

$$Y(i,t) \geq 0 \quad \text{iff} \quad d(i,t) = 1, \tag{3.2}$$
$$Y(i,t) < 0 \quad \text{iff} \quad d(i,t) = 0.$$

The distribution of the $d(i, t)$, $t = 1, \ldots, T$, $i = 1, \ldots, I$, is generated by the distributions of $\varepsilon(i, t)$ and $V(i, t)$. To simplify the argument in this chapter, it is assumed throughout much of the discussion that the $\varepsilon(i, t)$ are jointly normally distributed when a distributional assumption is required so that this model is similar to the multivariate probit model of Ashford and Sowden (1970) as extended by Amemiya (1975), Domencich and McFadden (1975) and the author (1978a). Alternative specifications of $V(i, t)$ and $\varepsilon(i, t)$ give rise to a variety of interesting and important models useful in the analysis of discrete panel data.

In sections 3.3 through 3.12 content is given to the terms $V(i, t)$ and $\varepsilon(i, t)$ in equation (3.1). The next section presents a very general model and some intuitive motivation for its constituent terms. Sections 3.4 through 3.12 deal with specific versions of the model in much greater detail.

3.3 The General Model

In this section content is given to the model of equations (3.1) and (3.2). $Y(i, t)$ is assumed to be a linear function of exogenous variables, $\mathbf{Z}(i, t)$, lagged values of $Y(i, t)$, and past outcomes $d(i, t')$, $t' \leq t$. The general model considered in this chapter may be written as

$$Y(i,t) = \mathbf{Z}(i,t)\boldsymbol{\beta} + \sum_{j=1}^{\infty} \gamma(t-j,t)\,d(i,t-j) + \sum_{j=1}^{\infty} \lambda(j,t-j) \prod_{l=1}^{j} d(i,t-l) + G(L)\,Y(i,t) + \varepsilon(i,t), \tag{3.3}$$

$i = 1, \ldots, I$, $t = 1, \ldots, T$, where $G(0) = 0$ and $G(L)$ is a general lag operator of order K, $[G(L) = g_1 L + g_2 L^2 + \cdots + g_K L^K$, $L^K Y(i, t) = Y(i, t - K)]$, $d(i, t) = 1$ iff $Y(i, t) \geq 0$, $d(i, t) = 0$ otherwise, and initial conditions $d(i, t')$, $t' = 0, -1, \ldots$, $Y(i, t')$, $t' = 0, -1, \ldots$, are assumed to be fixed outside of the model. The term $\varepsilon(i, t)$ is a normally distributed disturbance with mean zero. The distribution of vector $\boldsymbol{\varepsilon}(i) = (\varepsilon(i, 1), \ldots, \varepsilon(i, T))$ is fully characterized by the assumption

$$\boldsymbol{\varepsilon}(i) \sim N(\mathbf{0}, \boldsymbol{\Sigma}),$$

where Σ is a $T \times T$ positive definite covariance matrix. No assumption about stationarity of the disturbances is imposed. Random sampling is assumed across people, so that $\boldsymbol{\varepsilon}(i)$ is independent of $\boldsymbol{\varepsilon}(i')$, $i \neq i'$, $i, i' = 1, \ldots, I$. The components of vector $\mathbf{Z}(i, t)$ are assumed to be distributed independent of $\boldsymbol{\varepsilon}(i)$, so that these variables are exogenous.

The first term on the right-hand side of equation (3.3) represents the effect of exogenous variables on current utility comparisons. Vector $\mathbf{Z}(i, t)$ may include past exogenous variables, current exogenous variables, and expectations of future exogenous variables that determine current choices. In principle the $\boldsymbol{\beta}$ parameters may depend on time, but this generality is foregone in this chapter.

The second term on the right-hand side of the equation represents the effect of the entire past history of the process on current choice. This term is assumed to be finite. To capture the idea that the effect of a past event on current choice may depend on the time period in which the event occurred as well as on the current time period, the coefficients on past events are assumed to be functions of the current period, t, and the period in which the event occurred, $t-j$. This characterization of the effect of the past on current choices is consistent with depreciation and the notion that the values of exogenous variables at the time events occur as well as current values of exogenous variables modify the effect of previous choices on current choices. Various restrictions imposed on the coefficients $\gamma(t-j, t)$ generate a variety of interesting stochastic processes.[1]

The third term on the right-hand side represents the cumulative effect on current choices of the most recent continuous experience in a state. This term is introduced to capture the notion that, once an individual is in a state, an accumulation process begins. For example, in human capital theory specific capital may be accumulated and accumulation continues until the individual leaves the state, at which time the state specific capital is lost. This term generates a renewal process (see Karlin and Taylor 1975) of the sort considered by Jovanovic (1978). It is assumed to be finite. In principle one could generalize this term to allow for depreciation and other forms of time dependence. Moreover, one could introduce another term representing state specific capital that is accumulated when an individual is in the state corresponding to $d(i, t)=0$. These generalizations are not pursued in this chapter.

The fourth term in the equation is introduced to capture the notion of habit persistence. This term represents the effect of *previous relative evaluations of the two states* on current choices. This term captures the essential idea in Coleman's "latent Markov" model (Coleman 1964) in which prior propensities to select a state rather than prior occupancy of a state determine the current probability that a state is occupied.

The information that $Y(i, t) \geq 0$ is equivalent to the information that $Y(i, t)/\sigma(t, t)^{1/2} \geq 0$. For notational convenience it is useful to work with the normalized latent variables.

1. This term could be augmented to include the effect of future outcomes of the process on current choice. Structural dependence of this sort, while unfamiliar in the literature on applied probability, naturally arises in economic models of life cycle decision making under perfect certainty of the sort considered by Polachek (1975). If the range of the j subscript on the second term is changed to range from -1 to $-\infty$, this sort of dependence can be captured by the model. A certain technical difficulty arises if both forward and past dependence are introduced in the model simultaneously. This difficulty is discussed in note 26.

The general model may be summarized in a compact expression that is useful in computational work as well as in the theoretical analysis. Array the $d(i,t)$, $t = 1, \ldots, T$ into a $1 \times T$ vector $\mathbf{d}(i) = (d(i,1), \ldots, d(i,T))$. Define $V(i,t)$ as the right-hand side of equation (3.3) exclusive of the disturbance term

$$V(i,t) = \mathbf{Z}(i,t)\boldsymbol{\beta} + \sum_{j=1}^{\infty} \gamma(t-j,t)\,d(i,t-j)$$

$$+ \sum_{j=1}^{\infty} \lambda(j,t-j) \prod_{l=1}^{j} d(i,t-l) + G(L)\,Y(i,t). \tag{3.4}$$

The $V(i,t)$ may be normalized by $\sigma(t,t)^{1/2}$. Thus $\tilde{V}(i,t) = V(i,t)/\sigma(t,t)^{1/2}$ Array the $\tilde{V}(i,t)$ into a $1 \times T$ vector, $\tilde{\mathbf{V}}(i)$,

$$\tilde{\mathbf{V}}(i) = [\tilde{V}(i,1), \ldots, \tilde{V}(i,T)]. \tag{3.5}$$

For convenience the vectors of exogenous variables may be collected into a super vector $\mathbf{Z}(i)$, where $\mathbf{Z}(i) = (\mathbf{Z}(i,1), \mathbf{Z}(i,2), \ldots, \mathbf{Z}(i,T))$.

The correlation matrix $\tilde{\boldsymbol{\Sigma}}$ is derived from the covariance matrix $\boldsymbol{\Sigma}$ by the equation

$$\tilde{\boldsymbol{\Sigma}} = (\text{diag}\ \boldsymbol{\Sigma}^{-1})^{1/2}\,\boldsymbol{\Sigma}\,(\text{diag}\ \boldsymbol{\Sigma}^{-1})^{1/2},$$

where diag $\boldsymbol{\Sigma}$ is the diagonal matrix formed from the diagonal of $\boldsymbol{\Sigma}$.

Letting $\boldsymbol{\iota}$ denote a $1 \times T$ vector of ones, the probability of $\mathbf{d}(i)$, given $\mathbf{Z}(i,t)$, $t = 1, \ldots, T$ and the nonstochastic initial conditions specified below, equation (3.3) may be written as

$$\text{Prob}\,[\mathbf{d}(i) \mid \mathbf{Z}(i), d(i,0), d(i,-1), \ldots, Y(i,0), Y(i,-1), \ldots]$$

$$= F\{\tilde{V}(*)(2\mathbf{d}(i) - \boldsymbol{\iota});\ \tilde{\boldsymbol{\Sigma}}(*)[(2\mathbf{d}(i)) - \boldsymbol{\iota})'(2\mathbf{d}(i) - \boldsymbol{\iota})]\}, \tag{3.6}$$

where $F(\mathbf{a}; \tilde{\boldsymbol{\Sigma}})$ is the cumulative distribution function of a T-variate standardized multivariate normal random variable with correlation matrix $\tilde{\boldsymbol{\Sigma}}$ evaluated at an upper limit by vector $\mathbf{a}$, and where $(*)$ denotes the operation of a Hadamard product.[2] Expression (3.6) is a simple, shorthand summary of all of the possible probabilities associated with the 2^T possible values of $\mathbf{d}(i)$ that exploits the symmetry of the multivariate normal density.

2. A Hadamard product of two vectors $\mathbf{a}(*)\mathbf{b}$ is defined as a vector $\mathbf{C} = \mathbf{a}(*)\mathbf{b}$, where $(C_i) = (a_i b_i)$. A Hadamard product of two matrices $\mathbf{C} = \mathbf{A}(*)\mathbf{B}$ is defined by $(C_{ij}) = (a_{ij} b_{ij})$; e.g., see Rao (1973).

Given specific values for the exogenous variables, and given the initial conditions, the sample likelihood function may be written as

$$\mathscr{L} = \prod_{i=1}^{I} \text{Prob}[\mathbf{d}(i) \mid \mathbf{Z}(i,1), \ldots, \mathbf{Z}(i,T), d(i,0), d(i,-1),$$
$$\ldots, Y(i,0), Y(i,-1), \ldots]. \tag{3.7}$$

Maximizing the log likelihood produces estimators that are consistent, asymptotically normally distributed, and efficient.

To make the discussion more specific, and also to link the general model with previous work, it is helpful to consider the variety of special cases that arise from the general model by imposing restrictions on the coefficients and the admissible distribution of the error term in equation (3.7). In investigating these models, we consider the following issues of model identification: (1) What are the data requirements for the estimation of each model? In particular, when can cross section data be used to characterize fully a dynamic process? If cross section data cannot be so used, what information about the dynamic process can be retrieved from a cross section? (2) From observed sequences of discrete events (runs patterns) is it possible to infer the underlying stochastic process that generates the data?

We consider a sequence of models which are specializations of the general model starting with the simplest and most familiar: a Bernoulli model.

3.4 An Independent Trials Bernoulli Model

Let $V(i, t) = \bar{V}$, and assume that $\varepsilon(i, t)$ is independently identically distributed, iid. Each person has the same probability of experiencing the event $(d(i, t) = 1)$ in each period:

$$\text{Prob}[\varepsilon(i,t) \geq -\bar{V}] = \Phi\left(\frac{\bar{V}}{\sigma_\varepsilon}\right) = \bar{P}, \tag{3.8}$$

where

$$E(\varepsilon(i,t)^2) = \sigma_\varepsilon^2,$$

Φ is the cumulative distribution function of a standard normal random variable, and the symmetry of Φ is exploited ($\Phi(b) = 1 - \Phi(-b)$).[3]

Average continuous duration in the state ($d(i,t) = 1$) is $\bar{P}/(1 - \bar{P})$. From data on duration in the state, one can determine $\bar{P}$ uniquely. In a panel of T periods, the expected number of periods in the state for any person is $\bar{P}T$ with variance $\bar{P}(1 - \bar{P})T$. $\bar{P}$ can be consistently estimated from a single cross section or from a long time series on one person by the method of maximum likelihood. If the cross section and panel samples are the same size, estimators are equally efficient.

In T trials, the probability of J successes ($\Sigma d(i,t) = J$) and $T - J$ failures in a particular order is

$$\bar{P}^J (1 - \bar{P})^{T-J}.$$

The random variables $d(i,t)$, $t = 1, \ldots, T$, are exchangeable, in the sense that the probability of any sequence with J successes in T trials is the same as any other sequence with the same number of successes in the same number of trials.

This model can be modified to take account of measured differences in personal characteristics. If $V(i, t)$ is assumed to be a linear function of known exogenous variables ($\mathbf{Z}(i,t)$) distributed independent of $\varepsilon(i,t)$, one may write

$$V(i,t) = \mathbf{Z}(i,t)\boldsymbol{\beta}. \tag{3.9}$$

Depending on the content of the $\mathbf{Z}(i,t)$ regressor vector, one can generate a nonstationary time inhomogeneous stochastic process at the micro level (e.g., $\mathbf{Z}(i,t)$ may include "age" or "calendar time" variables). Provided that there is sufficient variation in the sample regressors, so that the cross product matrix for the data is nonsingular, and the expectation of the Hessian of the log likelihood is negative definite at true parameter values, one can estimate the parameters of the model from a cross section of individuals or a time series on a single person.[4]

3. If $\varepsilon(i, t)$ is distributed logit, Φ would be the cumulative distribution of the logit. Obviously $\varepsilon(i, t)$ may have *any* distribution, and Φ is the corresponding distribution of the standardized variate. However, for nonsymmetric variates the notation in the text would have to be altered in an obvious way.

4. For example, if education is included as a regressor in $\mathbf{Z}(i, t)$, and education does not change over the sample period, a time series for one person would not yield estimates of the effect of education on the probability of experiencing the event. If there are year effects, data from a single cross section would not permit estimation of the year effect.

Of course, if the $\mathbf{Z}(i, t)$ change over the sample period, the exchangeability property of the model disappears. Depending on the distribution of the exogenous variables, runs patterns with identical numbers of successes may have different probabilities.

The assumption that the $\varepsilon(i, t)$ are identically distributed can be relaxed. Suppose that the disturbances are independent (over time and people) but come from different distributions in different time periods. For example, suppose that

$$E(\varepsilon(i,t)^2) = \sigma(t,t),$$

so that the variance is different in each time period and the underlying disturbance is nonstationary. In this case the probability that $d(i, t) = 1$ given $\mathbf{Z}(i, t)$ is

$$\text{Prob}[\varepsilon(i,t) \geq -\mathbf{Z}(i,t)\boldsymbol{\beta}] = \Phi[\mathbf{Z}(i,t)\tilde{\boldsymbol{\beta}}(t)], \tag{3.10}$$

where

$$\tilde{\boldsymbol{\beta}}(t) = \frac{\boldsymbol{\beta}}{\sigma(t,t)^{1/2}}.$$

The probability that $d(i, t) = 0$ given $\mathbf{Z}(i, t)$ is the complement of this probability. Subject to the identification conditions previously stated, if the analyst has access to a series of successive cross sections, he can estimate $\tilde{\boldsymbol{\beta}}(t) = \boldsymbol{\beta}/\sigma(t,t)^{1/2}, t = 1, \ldots, T$ by applying probit analysis to each cross section. In this case it is clearly possible to estimate the ratio of variances in successive cross sections. Of course this procedure requires that $\boldsymbol{\beta}$ be time invariant.

The likelihood function for this model is a special case of the general likelihood function given in equation (3.7):[5]

$$\mathscr{L} = \prod_{i=1}^{I} \text{Prob}[\mathbf{d}(i) \mid Z(i)] = \prod_{i=1}^{I} \prod_{t=1}^{T} \Phi\{[\mathbf{Z}(i,t)\tilde{\boldsymbol{\beta}}(t)][2d(i,t) - 1]\}. \tag{3.11}$$

5. Clearly, if $\varepsilon(i, t)$ is assumed to be logit distributed, or generated by any other symmetric (around zero) distribution, equation (3.11) applies with Φ as the relevant cumulative distribution function. The modification of (3.11) for asymmetric random variables is straightforward.

3.5 A Random Effect Bernoulli Model and One-Factor Schemes

Unobserved temporally correlated error components are now introduced into the analysis. Such components are often termed heterogeneity in the applied literature on stochastic processes. Initially it is assumed that individuals all have the same values for the time invariant exogenous variables so that $V(i, t) = \bar{V}$. Also it is assumed initially that $\varepsilon(i, t)$ has a components of variance structure:

$$\varepsilon(i,t) = \tau(i) + U(i,t), \tag{3.12}$$

where $U(i, t)$ is iid with mean zero and variance σ_U^2 and $\tau(i)$ is distributed independent of the $U(i, t)$.

Individual i has a fixed component $\tau(i)$. Given $\tau(i)$, the probability that person i experiences an event at time $t(d(i, t) = 1)$ is

$$\begin{aligned}\text{Prob}[\varepsilon(i,t) \geq -\bar{V} \mid \tau(i)] &= \text{Prob}[U(i,t) \geq -(\tau(i) + \bar{V})] \\ &= P(\tau(i)) = \Phi\left[\frac{\tau(i) + \bar{V}}{\sigma_U}\right]\end{aligned} \tag{3.13}$$

The mean probability in the population is

$$\begin{aligned}\bar{P} &= \text{Prob}[\varepsilon(i,t) \geq -\bar{V}] = \textstyle\int \text{Prob}[U(i,t) \geq -(\tau(i) + \bar{V})] f(\tau) d\tau \\ &= \Phi\left[\frac{\bar{V}}{(\sigma_U^2 + \sigma_\tau^2)^{1/2}}\right],\end{aligned} \tag{3.14}$$

where $f(\tau)$ is the frequency distribution of τ, and where $\text{Prob}[U(i, t) \geq -(\tau(i) + \bar{V})]$ is shorthand for the probability that $U(i, t)$ exceeds minus $(\tilde{\tau}(i) + \bar{V})$ given $\tilde{\tau}(i)$ and $\bar{V}$—a shorthand notation that will be used in the rest of this chapter. The mean probability in the population $\bar{P}$, and hence $\Phi[\bar{V}/(\sigma_U^2 + \sigma_\tau^2)^{1/2}]$, can be estimated from a single cross section by ordinary probit analysis. At least two years of panel data must be obtained to estimate the correlation coefficient between $\varepsilon(i, t)$ and $\varepsilon(i, t')$, $t \neq t'$. This is known as the intraclass correlation coefficient, $\rho = \sigma_\tau^2/(\sigma_\tau^2 + \sigma_U^2)$. Using probit analysis, the expected number of periods in the state, $\bar{P}T$, can be estimated, but at least two periods of panel data are required to estimate the population variance, $(\int P(\tau)(1 - P(\tau))f(\tau)d\tau)T$, unless $f(\tau)$ is degenerate $(\sigma_\tau^2 = 0)$.

Maximum likelihood estimators of $\bar{P}$ based on a single cross section are consistent estimators of $\bar{P}$ as the cross section sample size I becomes large.

Unlike the situation in the preceding model, maximum likelihood estimators based on a long time series on one person or a large cross section at a point in time estimate different parameters. If both samples become large, the first sample estimates $(\bar{V} + \tau(i))/\sigma_U$ while the second sample estimates $\bar{V}/(\sigma_U^2 + \sigma_\tau^2)^{1/2}$. The first sample is conditioned on a specific value of $\tau(i)$, so that τ is a fixed effect indistinguishable from $\bar{V}$. The second sample is not conditioned on a specific value of $\tau(i)$.

As a consequence of Jensen's inequality the average duration in the state cannot be estimated from cross section data, because expected continuous duration in the state satisfies the following inequality:

$$E_\tau((1 - P(\tau)) \sum_{j=0}^{\infty} jP(\tau)^j) = E_\tau\left(\sum_{j=1}^{\infty} P(\tau)^j \right) \geq \sum_{j=1}^{\infty} \bar{P}^j,$$

where E_τ denotes expectation with respect to the density of τ, $f(\tau)$. Estimates of the average duration based on an estimated cross section probability (an estimate of $\bar{P}$) understate the average length of duration in the state.

Panel data can be used to estimate a separate $P(\tau(i))$ for each person by the method of maximum likelihood. This estimate is consistent as T becomes large. The estimated probabilities can be used to generate consistent estimators of the average duration in a state for each person: insert the estimated $P(\tau(i))$ into the mathematical formula for average duration.[6]

The probability of J successes $(\Sigma d(i, t) = J)$ and $T - J$ failures is the same for any sequence with J successes in any order. To see this, note that conditional on $\tau(i)$ the model in this section is the same as in the preceding section. Removing the conditioning (by integrating out $\tau(i)$), leads to the probability of J successes and $T - J$ failures in a particular sequence as

$$\int P(\tau)^J (1 - P(\tau))^{T-J} f(\tau)\, d\tau.$$

As in a case without heterogeneity, any of the $\binom{T}{J}$ sequences with J successes have the same probability.

It is possible to account for measured differences in personal characteristics in exactly the same way as is done in the model presented in the preceding section. If $V(i, t)$ is assumed to be a linear function of known exogenous variables, one may write

6. This example illustrates the point that panel data can be used to relax the ergodicity assumption maintained in much work in stationary time-series analysis.

$$V(i,t) = \mathbf{Z}(i,t)\boldsymbol{\beta}. \tag{3.15}$$

Under the identification conditions specified in section 3.3, $\boldsymbol{\beta}$ is estimable. This model has been estimated by Heckman and Willis (1975). Using maximum likelihood, they estimate $\boldsymbol{\beta}$ and ρ under the normalizing assumption that $\sigma_\tau^2 + \sigma_U^2 = 1$. This final assumption may be relaxed. Exactly as in the model of the preceding section it is possible to permit the disturbance variances to differ among time periods and estimate the ratio among disturbance variances in different periods. Thus a nonstationary version of the model can be estimated. If the $\mathbf{Z}(i, t)$ are permitted to vary arbitrarily, and disturbance variances are permitted to assume a free structure, the exchangeability property of the random effects model disappears.

Defining the probability of a given sequence of events given $\mathbf{Z}(i)$ for the random effect model is straightforward. For convenience it is useful to work with the standardized value of τ, $\tilde{\tau} = (\tau/\sigma_\tau)$, which has mean zero and variance one. Define $\tilde{\boldsymbol{\beta}}$ as $\boldsymbol{\beta}/\sigma_U$. In this notation the probability of sequence $\mathbf{d}(i)$ given $\mathbf{Z}(i)$ is

$$\text{Prob}[\mathbf{d}(i) \mid \mathbf{Z}(i)]$$

$$= \int_{-\infty}^{\infty} \prod_{t=1}^{T} \Phi\left\{\left[\mathbf{Z}(i,t)\tilde{\boldsymbol{\beta}} + \tilde{\tau}\left(\frac{\rho}{1-\rho}\right)^{1/2}\right][2d(i,t) - 1]\right\} f(\tilde{\tau})\, d\tilde{\tau}, \tag{3.16}$$

where $f(\tilde{\tau})$ is the density of the standard normal distribution and $\rho < 1$.[7] Subject to the given identification conditions maximum likelihood estimators of $\tilde{\boldsymbol{\beta}}$ and ρ are consistent and efficient. The likelihood formed from the product of the probabilities is relatively easy to compute since it involves only one numerical integration per observation of products of cumulative normal error functions which are available on most computers.

7. The probability that $d(i, t) = 1$ given $\mathbf{Z}(i, t)$ and $\tau(i)$ is

$$\text{Prob}[U(i, t) \geq -\mathbf{Z}(i, t)\boldsymbol{\beta} - \tau(i)] = \text{Prob}\left[\frac{U(i, t)}{\sigma_U} \geq -\mathbf{Z}(i, t)\frac{\boldsymbol{\beta}}{\sigma_U} - \frac{\tau(i)}{\sigma_U}\right].$$

Since $\tilde{\boldsymbol{\beta}} = \boldsymbol{\beta}/\sigma_U$, and since $\sigma_\tau/\sigma_U = (\rho/1-\rho)^{1/2}$, this probability is

$$\text{Prob}\left[\frac{U(i, t)}{\sigma_U} \geq -\mathbf{Z}(i, t)\tilde{\boldsymbol{\beta}} - \left(\frac{\rho}{1-\rho}\right)^{1/2}\tilde{\tau}(i)\right] = \boldsymbol{\Phi}\left[\mathbf{Z}(i, t)\tilde{\boldsymbol{\beta}} + \left(\frac{\rho}{1-\rho}\right)^{1/2}\tilde{\tau}(i)\right].$$

Removing the conditioning on $\tilde{\tau}(i) = \tau(i)/\sigma_\tau$, which in this context is equivalent to

The components of variance error specification can be generalized to a one-factor scheme. This generalization leads to a discrete data analogue of the MIMIC model of Joreskog and Goldberger (1975). One-factor representations of the cumulative normal integral have been considered by Gupta (1963) and others (see the references in Johnson and Kotz 1972, vol. 4, pp. 47–50). In this model the disturbance is written as

$$\varepsilon(i,t) = \alpha(t)\tau(i) + U(i,t), \tag{3.17}$$

$t = 1, \ldots, T$, $i = 1, \ldots, I$, where $\tau(i)$ is distributed independent of $U(i, t)$, $E(\tau(i)) = E(U(i, t)) = 0$, and $E(U(i, t)^2) = \sigma_U(t, t) > 0$, $E(\tau(i)^2) = \sigma_\tau^2$. The components of variance structure is a special case of this scheme with $\alpha(t) = 1$ and $\sigma_U(t, t) = \sigma_U$ for all t.

Before elaborating the one-factor model, it is useful to introduce some notation that simplifies the exposition. It is analytically convenient to work with the square root of the proportion of the variance of disturbance $\varepsilon(i, t)$, $t = 1, \ldots, T$, that is explained by the factor $\tau(i)$, defined as $\tilde{\alpha}(t)$, where

$$\tilde{\alpha}(t) \equiv \frac{\alpha(t)\sigma_\tau}{(\alpha^2(t)\sigma_\tau^2 + \sigma_U(t,t))^{1/2}}.$$

(Positive values of square roots are used.) In this notation the correlation between disturbances in periods t and t' for a randomly selected person is

$$\sigma(t,t') = 1, \quad t = t',$$

$$\sigma(t,t') = \tilde{\alpha}(t)\tilde{\alpha}(t'), \quad t \neq t'.$$

It is also convenient to define $\eta(t)$, the ratio of permanent to transitory variance, by

$$\eta(t) \equiv \left[\frac{\tilde{\alpha}(t)^2}{1 - \tilde{\alpha}(t)^2}\right]^{1/2} = \left[\frac{\alpha(t)^2\sigma_\tau^2}{\sigma_U(t,t)}\right]^{1/2}.$$

integrating out $\tau(i)$, leads to

$$\text{Prob}[d(i, t) = 1 \mid \mathbf{Z}(i)] = \int_{-\infty}^{\infty} \Phi\left(\mathbf{Z}(i, t)\tilde{\boldsymbol{\beta}} + \left(\frac{\rho}{1-\rho}\right)^{1/2} \tilde{\tau}\right) f(\tilde{\tau})\, d\tilde{\tau}.$$

The probability of any sequence of events conditional on $\tilde{\tau}(i)$ can be expressed as the product of cumulative distributions (see the kernel of the integral of equation 3.16). Removing the conditioning (integrating out $\tilde{\tau}$) leads to the expression in the text.

Clearly neither $\tilde{\tau}$ nor $U(i, t)/\sigma_U$ is restricted to be a normal random variable.

Thus $\eta(t)$ is the ratio of the standard deviation of the permanent component to the standard deviation of the transitory component in $\varepsilon(i, t)$.

Finally, it is notationally convenient to work with the normalized coefficient vector $\tilde{\boldsymbol{\beta}}(t)$, defined as

$$\tilde{\boldsymbol{\beta}}(t) \equiv \frac{\boldsymbol{\beta}}{\sigma_U(t,t)^{1/2}}.$$

In this notation the probability that $d(i, t) = 1$ given $\mathbf{Z}(i, t)$, and $\tau(i)$ is

$$\begin{aligned}\text{Prob}[d(i,t) = 1 \mid \mathbf{Z}(i,t), \tau(i)] \\ &= \text{Prob}[U(i,t) \geq -\mathbf{Z}(i,t)\boldsymbol{\beta} - \alpha(t)\tau(i) \mid \tau(i), \mathbf{Z}(i,t)] \\ &= \Phi[\mathbf{Z}(i,t)\tilde{\boldsymbol{\beta}}(t) + \eta(t)\tilde{\tau}(i)],\end{aligned} \tag{3.18}$$

where $\tilde{\tau}(i)$ is the standardized $\tau(i)$ variable and $|\eta(t)| < \infty$.[8] For proof of this proposition see appendix 3.18. This expression corresponds to the probability that $d(i, t) = 1$ in the components of variance model; $\eta(t)$ corresponds to $(\rho/(1-\rho))^{1/2}$.

The probability of $\mathbf{d}(i)$ given $\mathbf{Z}(i)$ for the one-factor model is

$$\text{Prob}[\mathbf{d}(i) \mid \mathbf{Z}(i)]$$

$$= \int_{-\infty}^{\infty} \prod_{t=1}^{T} \Phi\{[\mathbf{Z}(i,t)\tilde{\boldsymbol{\beta}}(t) + \eta(t)\tilde{\tau}][2d(i,t) - 1]\} f(\tilde{\tau})\, d\tilde{\tau}. \tag{3.19}$$

Subject to the normalization restriction $\sigma_U(1, 1) = 1$, it is possible to maximize the sample likelihood to estimate $\boldsymbol{\beta}$, $\sigma_U(t, t)$, $t = 2, \ldots, T$, and the $\eta(t)$, $t = 1, \ldots, T$, for $T \geq 3$.[9,10] The $\eta(t)$, $t = 1, \ldots, T$, are uniquely identified up to a sign change for the entire set of values (e.g., see Lawley and Maxwell 1971). From these parameters it is possible to identify $\alpha(t)\sigma_\tau$, $t = 1, \ldots, T$, given the normalization $\sigma_U(1, 1) = 1$ and the estimates of $\sigma_U(t, t)$, $t = 2, \ldots, T$.

8. The final assumption is relaxed in appendix 3.18.

9. The choice of $\sigma_U(1, 1) = 1$ is arbitrary. One could normalize any of the $\sigma_U(j, j)$ to unity, or one could normalize $\alpha(1)\sigma_\tau = 1$ (or any $\alpha(j)\sigma_\tau$).

10. This restriction is familiar in factor analysis (e.g., see Joreskog and Goldberger 1975).

An alternative normalization sets $\alpha(1)\sigma_\tau = 1$. In this case it is possible to estimate $\boldsymbol{\beta}$, $\sigma_U(t, t)$, $t = 1, \ldots, T$, and the $\eta(t)$, $t = 1, \ldots, T$, for $T \geq 3$.[11,12]

Further results on the one-factor model and generalizations to higher factor schemes are given in appendix 3.18.

In the one-factor model the random variables $d(i, t)$, $t = 1, \ldots, T$, are not exchangeable even if $\mathbf{Z}(i, t)\boldsymbol{\beta} = \bar{V}$ unless the period specific factor-loading coefficients are identical ($\alpha(t) = \alpha$, $t = 1, \ldots, T$) and the variances of the unique components are equal ($\sigma_U(t, t) = \sigma_U$), conditions which generate the simple random effect model.

The one-factor model permits the generalization of the unobserved heterogeneity concept beyond the components of variance scheme initially suggested in this section. Other generalizations of the heterogeneity concept are considered in section 3.7. Both the one-factor and components of variance models are simply computed, since they require only one numerical integration of products of cumulative normal functions which are already available on most computers.

11. The statements about identification of parameters made in the text are readily verified. An intuitive argument is as follows: For $T \geq 3$ it is possible to estimate the correlation matrix of the unobservables $\tilde{\boldsymbol{\Sigma}}$, by multivariate probit analysis. From the estimated correlation matrix it is possible to estimate $\tilde{\alpha}(t)$, $t = 1, \ldots, T$, up to a sign change for the entire set of values of these parameters. From cross section probit analysis applied to each of the T cross sections, one can estimate

$$\tilde{\tilde{\boldsymbol{\beta}}}(t) = \frac{\boldsymbol{\beta}}{(\alpha^2(t)\sigma_\tau^2 + \sigma_U(t, t))^{1/2}},$$

$t = 1, \ldots, T$. From the ratio of the coefficients in $\boldsymbol{\beta}(t)$ to the corresponding coefficients in $\tilde{\tilde{\boldsymbol{\beta}}}(t')$, it is possible to estimate

$$\frac{[\alpha^2(t)\sigma_\tau^2 + \sigma_U(t, t)]^{1/2}}{[\alpha^2(t')\sigma_\tau^2 + \sigma_U(t', t')]^{1/2}}$$

for all t and t'. Set $\sigma_U(1, 1) = 1$. From the estimated value of $\tilde{\boldsymbol{\alpha}}(1)$ one can estimate $\alpha(1)\sigma_\tau$, and hence $\boldsymbol{\beta}$. From the ratio of the coefficients in $\tilde{\tilde{\boldsymbol{\beta}}}(t)$ to the corresponding coefficients in $\tilde{\tilde{\boldsymbol{\beta}}}(1)$ one can estimate $(\alpha^2(t)\sigma_\tau^2 + \sigma_U(t, t))^{1/2}$, $t = 2, \ldots, T$. This piece of information in conjunction with $\tilde{\boldsymbol{\alpha}}(t)$ is sufficient to identify $\alpha(t)\sigma_\tau$, and hence $\sigma_U(t, t)$, $t = 2, \ldots, T$.

An alternative normalization sets $\alpha(1)\sigma_\tau = 1$. From the estimated value of $\tilde{\boldsymbol{\alpha}}(1)$ one can estimate $\sigma_U(1, 1)$, and hence $\boldsymbol{\beta}$, and proceed, following the logic of the case in which $\sigma_U(1, 1) = 1$, to estimate $\alpha(t)\sigma_\tau$, and hence $\sigma_U(t, t)$, $t = 2, \ldots, T$.

12. For $T = 2$ it is necessary to normalize $\eta(1) = 1$ and $\sigma_U(1, 1) = 1$ (obviously 2 can be substituted for 1). This follows from well-known results in factor analysis; any two-period model can be one-factor analyzed. In this case $\eta(2) = (\rho/1 - \rho)$.

An alternative normalization is $\eta(1) = \eta(2) = (\rho/1 - \rho))^{1/2}$.

Note finally that in either the components of variance model or the one-factor model it is not necessary to assume that $\tau(i)$ or $U(i, t)$ are normal variates to write down the expression given in equations (3.16) and (3.19). The only assumption required is that the density of $U(i, t)$ be symmetric, and even this condition can easily be relaxed at the cost of minor notational inconvenience. An example of non-normal factor analysis for continuous data is found in the work of Mandelbrot (1962).

The one-factor model may be generalized in several ways. First, the period specific components may have zero variance ($\sigma_U(t, t) = 0$). Second, multiple factor schemes may be developed in a fairly straightforward way. These topics and examples of common error processes that can be one-factor analyzed are discussed in appendix 3.18, where certain restrictions inherent in a one-factor scheme are noted and a multiple factor model is introduced.

3.6 A Fixed Effect Bernoulli Model

Earlier $\tau(i)$, the person specific effect, was treated as a random variable. Following Mundlak's interpretation of the fixed effect regression model (1978), it is possible to derive conditional (on $\tau(i)$) fixed effect versions of the random effect and one-factor models. A fixed effect logit model has been considered by E. B. Andersen (1973). The advantages of such models are threefold: they are simple to compute; they provide one solution to the problem of initial conditions (discussed in chapter 4); and they permit the analyst to estimate rather than impose the population density of τ.

The essential ingredients of the fixed effect model are to be found in equation (3.16). The probability of sequence $\mathbf{d}(i)$ given $\mathbf{Z}(i)$ and $\tilde{\tau}(i)$ is

$$\text{Prob}[\mathbf{d}(i) \mid \mathbf{Z}(i), \tilde{\tau}(i)]$$

$$= \prod_{t=1}^{T} \Phi\left\{\left[\mathbf{Z}(i,t)\tilde{\boldsymbol{\beta}} + \tilde{\tau}(i)\left(\frac{\rho}{1-\rho}\right)^{1/2}\right][2d(i,t) - 1]\right\}.$$

The sample likelihood formed from the probabilities can be maximized with respect to $\tilde{\boldsymbol{\beta}}$ and $\tilde{\tau}(i)(\rho/1 - \rho)^{1/2} = l(i), i = 1, \ldots, I$. Note, however, that the constant term in $\tilde{\boldsymbol{\beta}}$ and the correlation parameter $(\rho/1 - \rho)^{1/2}$ are absorbed into the estimated fixed effect $l(i)$. However, it is possible to estimate the correlation parameter from the square root of the sample variance of the estimated $l(i)$. (Recall that $\tilde{\tau}(i)$ is restricted to have unit variance in the population.) From the mean of the estimated $l(i)$ one can retrieve the intercept or constant term in $\tilde{\boldsymbol{\beta}}$.[13] If $I \to \infty$ and $T \to \infty$, these estimators are consistent and asymptotically normally distributed. Estimates of $l(i)$ can be used to construct an empirical density that converges to the population density of person specific effects.

This model is very simple to compute. Holding $\tilde{\boldsymbol{\beta}}$ fixed, $l(i)$ can be estimated for each person. The log likelihood function is globally concave for $l(i)$ and hence tends to converge rapidly to an optimum in practice. Note, however, that if individual i does not change state in the course of the sample, so that $\Sigma_t d(i, t) = T$ or $\Sigma_t d(i, t) = 0$, the estimated value of $l(i)$ is $\pm\infty$, respectively. As $T \to \infty$, this becomes an improbable event (assuming that $\mathbf{Z}(i, t), t = 1, \ldots, T, i = 1, \ldots, I$, are bounded exogenous variables).

Given $l(i)$, the likelihood is an ordinary probit likelihood function and so is concave in the parameters in $\tilde{\boldsymbol{\beta}}$ (with constant term absorbed in $l(i)$). Sequential estimation of $l(i)$ and $\tilde{\boldsymbol{\beta}}$ results in rapid convergence to an optimum.[14]

The principal disadvantage of the fixed effects estimator is that if T does not become large, maximum likelihood estimators of $l(i)$ are inconsistent (Neyman and Scott 1948). Due to the nonlinearity of the model, the estimator of $\tilde{\boldsymbol{\beta}}$ is solved jointly with that of $l(i)$ to secure estimates. The inconsistency in $l(i)$ is transmitted to $\tilde{\boldsymbol{\beta}}$, unlike the situation in linear regression theory in which an estimator of $\tilde{\boldsymbol{\beta}}$ that does not depend on the estimated fixed effect can be found (Andersen 1973). Further discussion of this point is deferred to chapter 4.

3.7 Models with General Correlation in the Errors: The Concept of Heterogeneity Extended

A great advantage of the multivariate probit models considered in this chapter is that they admit a more general characterization of heterogeneity than is conventional in the literature (e.g. see Singer and Spilerman 1976).

13. Note that if there are exogenous variables that are constant for the person over the sample period (e.g., education), these variables and their coefficients are absorbed into the estimated fixed effect. One can regress the estimated $l(i)$ on an intercept and the means of all exogenous variables to estimate the coefficients of such variables. Under the conditions stated in the text such estimators are consistent and asymptotically normally distributed.

14. A copy of the fixed effects probit program is available from the author on request for a fee covering duplication and processing charges.

The standard treatment of heterogeneity assumes a components of variance scheme with $f(\tau)$ as a mixing distribution (see equation 3.16) or empirical Bayes density (e.g., see Maritz 1970). Although this treatment is generalized, somewhat, in the one-factor model (see equation 3.19) it is clearly possible, and in many economic models desirable, to entertain a more general correlation structure for the unobservables that generate discrete choices.[15] For example, a simple first-order Markov model for the unobservables is ruled out by a components of variance or a one-factor scheme (for $T > 3$, see appendix 3.18). Yet it is natural in many economic contexts to assume that the unobserved variables obey such a correlation scheme.

The errors $\varepsilon(i, t)$ can be given an unrestricted covariance structure, more general than that described by the one-factor model. Both stationary and nonstationary distributions of the error process may be entertained. Using the multivariate probit model of Ashford and Sowden (1970), Domencich and McFadden (1975), or Dutt (1976), it is possible to estimate the unrestricted $T \times T$ correlation matrix $\tilde{\Sigma}$, and, if regressors (or just a time invariant intercept) are present, $\sigma(t, t)$, $t = 2, \ldots, T$, where the first disturbance variance ($\sigma(1, 1)$) is normalized to unity. A general nonstationary error process can thus be estimated, and it is possible to test specific models of the error structure against the unrestricted general model.[16]

To illustrate these points, an example is given. Consider a stationary Markov process of order one with a permanent component for the disturbances of the model. This error process was first considered by Balestra and Nerlove (1966):

$$\varepsilon(i, t) = \rho\varepsilon(i, t-1) + \tau(i) + U(i, t),$$

$I = 1, \ldots, I$, $t = 1, \ldots, T$, where $E(\tau(i)) = 0$, $E(U(i, t)) = 0$, $E(\tau(i)^2) = \sigma_\tau^2$, $E(U(i, t)^2) = \sigma_U^2$, and $E(U(i, t)\tau(i)) = 0$, $|\rho| < 1$ and stationarity is assumed.

15. The restrictions imposed by the one-factor model are investigated in appendix 3.18. For $T > 3$, a one-factor model implies a nonstationary error process unless a random effects model is assumed. Many interesting processes, such as first-order Markov, cannot be analyzed by the one-factor scheme for $T > 3$.

16. Consistent estimators of the ratio of disturbance variances are achieved if $I \to \infty$. One does not require $T \to \infty$.

$$E(\varepsilon(i,t)\varepsilon(i,t')) = \frac{\sigma_\tau^2}{1-\rho^2} + \frac{\sigma_U^2 \rho^{|t-t'|}}{1-\rho^2};$$

$$\tilde{\sigma}(t,t') = \left[\frac{\sigma_\tau^2}{\sigma_\tau^2 + \sigma_U^2}\right] + \left[\frac{\sigma_U^2}{\sigma_\tau^2 + \sigma_U^2}\right]\rho^{|t-t'|}.$$

The correlation matrix $\tilde{\boldsymbol{\Sigma}}$ can be parameterized in terms of $\sigma_\tau^2/(\sigma_\tau^2 + \sigma_U^2)$ and ρ, and these two combinations of parameters can be estimated. Since the disturbance variance is assumed to be identical in all time periods, no further parameters can be estimated. This restriction on the correlation matrix can be tested against the unrestricted covariance matrix. For $T > 3$, this error scheme cannot be transformed into one-factor form (see appendix 3.18). Hence heterogeneity cannot be treated by classical mixing distribution methods. Nonetheless a model with this error structure can be estimated by multivariate probit analysis.[17]

The probability that randomly selected person i experiences an event at time period $t(d(i,t) = 1)$ in a population with identical and constant values of the exogenous variables $(V(i, t) = \bar{V} = \mathbf{Z}(i, t)\boldsymbol{\beta} \neq 0)$ is

$$\bar{P}(t) = \text{Prob}[\varepsilon(i,t) \geq -\bar{V}] = \Phi\left[\frac{\bar{V}}{\sigma(t,t)^{1/2}}\right].$$

17. As a second example, a nonstationary first-order Markov process is considered. The process starts up with initial disturbance $W(i)$ assumed independent of $U(i, t)$. $E(U(i, t)) = E(W(i)) = 0$. $E(W(i)^2) = \sigma_W^2$. Thus

$$\varepsilon(i, t) = \sum_{j=0}^{t-1} U(i, t-j)\rho^j + \rho^{t-1} W(i).$$

For $t' < t$,

$$E(\varepsilon(i, t)\varepsilon(i, t')) = \rho^{|t-t'|}\sigma_U^2 \sum_{j=0}^{t'-1} \rho^{2j} + \sigma_W^2 \rho^{t'+t-2},$$

$$\tilde{\sigma}(t, t') = \frac{\rho^{|t-t'|}\sigma_U^2 \sum_{j=0}^{t'-1} \rho^{2j} + \sigma_W^2 \rho^{t'+t-2}}{\left[\sigma_U^2 \sum_{j=0}^{t-1} \rho^{2j} + \sigma_W^2 \rho^{2t-2}\right]^{1/2}\left[\sigma_U^2 \sum_{j=0}^{t'-1} \rho^{2j} + \sigma_W^2 \rho^{2t'-2}\right]^{1/2}}.$$

The covariance matrix can be parameterized in terms of ρ and σ_W^2/σ_U^2. These combinations of parameters can be consistently estimated by multivariate probit analysis as $I \to \infty$, irrespective of the value of T so long as $T > 2$. Note that $\rho = 1$ (a random walk process) is a special case of this model. It is possible to test this hypothesis using classical likelihood ratios or Wald statistics (Rao 1973) based on the estimated information matrix for the model.

This probability can be estimated from a single cross section (at time t). Panel data are required to estimate the temporal correlation pattern among the unobservables. A series of successive cross sections can be used to estimate the ratio of error variances. The expected number of periods in the state over panel period T for a randomly sampled individual is

$$\sum_{t=1}^{T} \bar{P}(t).$$

The average duration in the state cannot be estimated from cross section estimates of $\bar{P}(t)$. If the intertemporal correlations among all disturbances are positive,[18] the true average duration exceeds the duration estimated from cross section data under the assumption of no intertemporal correlation in the errors.

In T trials the probability of J successes $(\Sigma d(i, t) = J)$ and $T - J$ failures is not the same for any sequence with J successes, even if $V(i, t) = \bar{V} = \mathbf{Z}(i, t)\boldsymbol{\beta}$. Hence the random variables $d(i, t)$, $t = 1, \ldots, T$, are not exchangeable. However, if the latent variables that generate the process are stationary (in the weak sense, e.g., see Koopmans 1974, p. 38), sequences of events that are reflections of each other have identical probabilities, assuming $V(i, t) = \bar{V}$. The reflection of a sequence of T outcomes $(d(i, t)$, $t = 1, \ldots, T)$ is defined as another sequence $d(i, t')$, $t' = 1, \ldots, T$, with $d(i, t') = d(i, T - t + 1)$.[19] For example, a sequence of trials recorded as (1, 0, 1, 1) has as its reflection sequence (1, 1, 0, 1).

To establish this point on reflection sequences, array $\varepsilon(i, t)$, $t = 1, \ldots, T$, into a $1 \times T$ vector $\boldsymbol{\varepsilon}(i)$, assumed to be normally distributed with mean zero and variance $\boldsymbol{\Sigma}$. As a consequence of assumed stationarity $\sigma(t, t') = \sigma(|t - t'|)$ and $\sigma(t, t) = \sigma$. The reflection of $\boldsymbol{\varepsilon}$ is $\boldsymbol{\varepsilon}^R$ defined by

$$\boldsymbol{\varepsilon}^R = \mathbf{P}\boldsymbol{\varepsilon},$$

where $\mathbf{P}$ is a traverse diagonal permutation matrix ($P(i, j) = 1$ for $j = T - i + 1$, $P(i,j) = 0$ otherwise). The covariance matrix of $\boldsymbol{\varepsilon}$ is $\mathbf{P\Sigma P'}$. From stationarity, $\mathbf{P\Sigma P'} = \boldsymbol{\Sigma}$, since $\sigma(T - i, T - j) = \sigma(|\, i - j\,|) = \sigma(i, j)$. Thus any dichotomization of the elements of $\boldsymbol{\varepsilon}$ that generates an observed sequence of events $d(i, t)$, $t = 1, \ldots, T$, has the same probability as the

18. This condition is sufficient but not necessary.

19. The term "mirror image" is more suggestive. Imagine holding the first sequence up to a mirror and noting its reflection.

identical dichotomization applied to the elements of $\boldsymbol{\varepsilon}^R$. Hence a sequence and its reflection have equal probability.[20]

Runs tests can thus be used to distinguish between the exchangeable models considered in sections 3.4 and 3.5 and the general stationary model considered here. In the former models all sequences with J successes in T trials have equal probability. In the general model for stationary disturbances only those subsequences that are reflections of each other have identical probability.[21] In a general nonstationary model reflection sequences do not have identical probability. Runs tests to distinguish between exchangeable, stationary, and nonstationary models are developed more completely elsewhere (Heckman 1978b).

Observable characteristics that determine choices can be incorporated into the model with general heterogeneity in precisely the same way as has been done in the models developed in the previous sections. $V(i, t)$ may be parameterized, so that $V(i, t) = \mathbf{Z}(i, t)\boldsymbol{\beta}$ (thus $V(i, t)$ in equation 3.6 is equal to $\mathbf{Z}(i, t)\boldsymbol{\beta}$). Given an intercept (or other exogenous variables), it is possible to estimate $\sigma(t, t)$, $t = 2, \ldots, T$, subject to the normalization that $\sigma(1, 1) = 1$.

3.8 Models with Structural State Dependence

The structural relationship between discrete outcomes in different periods is termed structural state dependence. All of the models considered in the previous sections assume no structural state dependence once heterogeneity is properly accounted for.

This is not to say that in the preceding models the conditional probability that $d(i, t) = 1$ given $d(i, t') = 1 (t' \neq t)$ is the same as the marginal probability that $d(i, t) = 1$. If there are unmeasured, serially correlated components in the errors, or measured, serially correlated components not adequately controlled for, such a conditional relationship will arise. However, controlling for the serially correlated components in the error and in the measured variables, no conditional relationship will arise.

20. The assumption of weak stationarity and normality implies strong stationarity (Koopmans 1974, p. 38). The results in the text are a consequence of strong stationarity. Any strongly stationary series has a time reversibility property required to establish the results.

21. Thus in an exchangeable model the sequences (1, 0, 1), (1, 1, 0), and (0, 1, 1) have equal probability of occurrence, but in the stationary model in general only the last two sequences have equal probability of occurrence.

To illustrate this point, consider the random effect model developed in section 3.5. Assume that there is no variation in measured exogenous variables in the population. However, assume that the probability of experiencing the event is a function of an unobserved component $P = P(\tau)$.

The probability that $d(i, 2) = 1$, given $d(i, 1) = 1$, is

$$\text{Prob}[d(i,2) = 1 \mid d(i,1) = 1] = \frac{\int_{-\infty}^{\infty} P^2(\tau) f(\tau) d\tau}{\int_{-\infty}^{\infty} P(\tau) f(\tau) d\tau},$$

which is not the same as the marginal probability $\text{Prob}[d(i, 2) = 1] = \int_{-\infty}^{\infty} P(\tau) f(\tau) d\tau$. However, the probability that $d(i, 2) = 1$ given $d(i, 1)$ and $\tau(i)$ is the same as the probability that $d(i, 2) = 1$ given $\tau(i)$:

$$\text{Prob}[d(i,2) = 1 \mid d(i,1) = 1 \text{ and } \tau(i)] = \frac{P^2(\tau(i))}{P(\tau(i))}$$

$$= P(\tau(i)) = \text{Prob}[d(i,2) = 1 \mid \tau(i)].$$

Controlling for temporally correlated unobserved components (the τ), there is no conditional relationship between the probability that $d(i, 2) = 1$ and the value of $d(i, 1)$. It is in this sense that the models developed in the preceding sections do not generate structural relationships between outcomes in different periods. The models presented in this section do.[22]

To focus on essential ideas, assume initially that there is no heterogeneity in measured or unmeasured variables, so that $\mathbf{Z}(i, t)\boldsymbol{\beta} = \beta_0$ and the $\varepsilon(i, t)$ are independently identically distributed random variables and $E[\varepsilon(i, t)^2] = 1$. To commence the analysis, assume that only previous outcomes affect current choice. This leads to the following expression for $Y(i, t)$, the difference in remaining lifetime utilities at time t:

$$Y(i,t) = \beta_0 + \sum_{j=1}^{\infty} \gamma(t-j, j) d(i, t-j) + \varepsilon(i,t). \tag{3.20}$$

22. The example offered in this section is simple and thus has considerable pedagogical appeal. The validity of the point is not confined to a simple random effect or one-factor model. The general models developed in the preceding section also generate a conditional relationship between events in different periods, solely as a consequence of temporal correlation in the errors.

Presample values of $d(i, t')$, $t' = 0, -1, \ldots$, assume fixed, nonstochastic values. If $Y(i, t) \geq 0$, $d(i, t) = 1$. Otherwise $d(i, t) = 0$. The second term on the right-hand side is assumed to be finite.

The probability that $d(i, t) = 1$, given $d(i, t-1), \ldots$, is

$$\text{Prob}[d(i,t) = 1 \mid d(i,t-1), d(i,t-2), \ldots]$$
$$= \Phi\left[\beta_0 + \sum_{j=1}^{\infty} \gamma(t-j, j) d(i, t-j)\right].$$

Thus the sample likelihood for a given sequence of outcomes arrayed in a $1 \times T$ vector $\mathbf{d}(i)$ is

$$\mathscr{L} = \prod_{i=1}^{I} \prod_{t=1}^{T} \Phi\left\{\left[\beta_0 + \sum_{j=1}^{\infty} \gamma(t-j, j) d(i, t-j)\right](2d(i,t) - 1)\right\}.$$

If $\gamma(t-j, j) = \gamma(1)$ for $j = 1$, and $\gamma(t-j, j) = 0$ for $j > 1$, the model generates a first-order Markov process.[23]

$$\text{Prob}[d(i,t) = 1 \mid d(i,t-1)] = \Phi[\beta_0 + \gamma d(i,t-1)].$$

If $\gamma(t-j, j) = \gamma(j)$ for $j \leq K$, $\gamma(t-j, j) = 0$ for $j > K$, a Kth-order Markov process is generated. If $\gamma(t-j, j) = \gamma$, a generalization of a Pólya process (e.g., see Feller 1957) is generated in which the entire history of the process is relevant to current choices.[24] Allowing for geometric decay of effects in the generalized Pólya model, one may parameterize $\gamma(t-j, j) = \gamma_0(\sigma)^j$, $0 < \sigma < 1$.

Permitting the γ coefficients to depend on calendar time t as well as age generates time inhomogeneous versions of the Markov and generalized Pólya models. Clearly the γ coefficients may be parameterized to depend on values of the exogenous variables at the time the event occurs and on current values of the exogenous variables (or for that matter values in other periods).

23. For logit Φ Boskin and Nold (1975) have presented a Markov model with exogenous variables. They ignore heterogeneity in unmeasured, serially correlated components. See also Amemiya (1978) who investigates the properties of maximum likelihood estimators for this model.

24. A related model for the Pólya type process has been developed by Chaddha (1963). I am indebted to Jerzy Neyman for this reference. The Pólya model is similar to the linear-learning probability model of Bush and Mosteller (1955). See also Massy, Montgomery, and Morrison (1970) and Wilson (1977). I am indebted to Frank O'Connnor and Abel Jeuland for these references.

Conditions for identification of parameters in Markov models (both time homogenous and time inhomogenous) are well known (c. f., Anderson and Goodman 1957). Without invoking special assumptions, such as stationarity of the process, panel data are required to estimate the model. Runs tests can be performed to discriminate between Bernoulli and Markov models (e.g., see David 1947, Goodman 1958, and Denny and Yakowitz 1978).

The parameters of the generalized Pólya model can be estimated from data available from a single cross section, provided that the number of past events ($\Sigma_{j=1}^{\infty} d(i, t-j)$) is known. One does not need to know when the past events occurred. For the generalized Pólya process with geometric decay one requires knowledge of the entire past history of the process to identify the parameters of the model.

In T trials the probability of J successes ($\Sigma_{t=1}^{T} d(i, t) = J$) and $T - J$ failures is not the same for any sequence of J successes in any order. Because of the time irreversability inherent in the nonstationary process induced by the random variable $\Sigma_{j=1}^{\infty} d(i, t-j)$, reflection sequences do not have identical probabilities. In the generalized Pólya model (without decay), if $\gamma > 0$, a sequence $\mathbf{d}(i) = (1, 0, 1, 1)$ is more probable than a sequence $(1, 1, 0, 1)$. (Recall that the sequences are ordered in time from left to right, starting with the earliest outcome.) Since occupancy of a state raises the probability of future occupancy, a later failure is less likely than an earlier one.

To see this, note that

$$\text{Prob}(1,0,1,1) = \Phi[\beta_0]\Phi[-(\beta_0 + \gamma)]\Phi[\beta_0 + \gamma]\Phi[\beta_0 + 2\gamma],$$

$$\text{Prob}(1,1,0,1) = \Phi[\beta_0]\Phi[\beta_0 + \gamma]\Phi[-(\beta_0 + 2\gamma)]\Phi[\beta_0 + 2\gamma]. \tag{3.21}$$

Since $\gamma > 0$, the first sequence is more probable. (Compare the second term in the first sequence with the third term in the second sequence.) Runs tests can be used to distinguish among exchangeable models, a model with stationary errors, and the generalized Pólya process (see Heckman 1978b).

Heterogeneity in unmeasured variables can be introduced into the models considered in this section in exactly the same way it has been introduced in the models considered in sections 3.5 through 3.7. No new idea is introduced by merging models that allow for heterogeneity with models that allow for structural state dependence. For example, in each of the models considered here, the components of variance error structure given in equation (3.22),

$$\varepsilon(i,t) = \tau(i) + U(i,t), \tag{3.22}$$

can be specified. This error structure generates to the mixing distribution representation of heterogeneity which leads to the probability for $\mathbf{d}(i)$ (given the fixed nonstochastic initial conditions of the process) of

$$\text{Prob}[\mathbf{d}(i) \mid d(i,0), d(i,-1), \ldots]$$

$$= \int_{-\infty}^{\infty} \prod_{t=1}^{T} \Phi\left\{\left[\beta_0 + \sum_{j=1}^{\infty} \gamma(t-j,j)d(i,t-j) + \left[\frac{\rho}{1-\rho}\right]^{1/2} \tilde{\tau}\right]\right.$$

$$\left. \cdot [2d(i,t) - 1]\right\} f(\tilde{\tau})d\tilde{\tau}, \tag{3.23}$$

where ρ and $\tilde{\tau}$ are as defined in section 3.5.

The one-factor model given in equation (3.17) can be applied to the disturbances of the models considered in this section in a straightforward way, as can the fixed effect and fixed factor models considered in section 3.6. Nonstationary disturbances of the sort considered in sections 3.4 and 3.5 can also be introduced in these models, and ratios of disturbance variances in different periods can be estimated if $\beta_0 \neq 0$, even for general values of $\gamma(j, t-j)$.[25]

The results on runs patterns established for the generalized Pólya process (see equation 3.21 and the surrounding discussion) remain intact if heterogeneity of the components of variance type is introduced. To see this, note that in equation (3.23), if $\gamma(t-j, j) = \gamma$, $d(i, t') = 0$, $t' \leq 0$ (so that the generalized Pólya process is generated), the ordering among the probabilities of runs patterns previously established continues to be valid, since the relative ranking in probability of any two runs sequences is not affected by integration with respect to $f(\tilde{\tau})$.

The preceding analysis does not require that $\varepsilon(i, t)$ be normally distributed. Φ can be the cumulative distribution of any latent variable (symmetry can be relaxed at the cost of minor notational inconvenience). The principal advantage of the normality assumption is that it generates a model that can readily be generalized to accommodate a rich variety of error structures for serially correlated unobserved components.

25. With more structure on the $\gamma(j, t-j)$, $j = 1, \ldots$, the ratio of disturbance variances can be identified even if $\beta_0 = 0$.

General heterogeneity, of the sort considered in section 3.7, can be introduced into the models considered in this section. The probability of $\mathbf{d}(i)$ given $\mathbf{Z}(i)$ and the nonstochastic initial conditions of the process is given by the general cumulative normal density; the expression for it is given in equation (3.6), with $V(i, t) = \beta_0 + \Sigma_{j=1}^{\infty}\gamma(t-j, t)d(i, t-j)$. Given $\beta_0 \neq 0$ (or specific structure on the $\gamma(t-j, t)$ coefficients), a nonstationary version of the model can be identified. In all of the models with nonindependent disturbances, panel data are required to estimate the serial correlation structure of the unobservables.

Introducing exogenous variables into the models considered in this section does not involve any new principle. In place of β_0 in the preceding expressions, one can substitute $\mathbf{Z}(i, t)\boldsymbol{\beta}$.

It is important to stress that the assumption made throughout this section that initial conditions are known and nonstochastic is neither innocuous nor especially plausible. In many contexts the analyst has access to data on a process that is sampled midstream, so that the initial conditions are determined by the same stochastic process that generates the panel data. In this case it is inappropriate to assume that the initial conditions are nonstochastic. Maximum likelihood estimators of the parameters of the models conditioned on presample realizations of the process are not consistent unless the disturbances are truly independent. This problem and various solutions to it are considered in chapter 4.

In all of the models considered in this section, it is possible to reverse the sense of the j subscript (in equation 3.20) and allow for future outcomes to determine current choices. This sort of structural dependence arises in certain life cycle models of decision making under perfect certainty. For example, in an analysis of labor supply behavior future work may determine the current probability of working if current labor supply raises future wage rates. The greater the volume of future labor supply, the more profitable is current work activity.[26]

26. For a discussion of certain technical problems that arise from simultaneous introduction of the effect of all past and future outcomes on current choices, see Heckman (1978a, pp. 936 and 957) and Schmidt (chapter 12). The basic problem is one of internal inconsistency in probit probability statements. The requirement for internal consistency of the model is that, through a suitable permutation of subscripts of the coefficients of the dummy variables denoting state occupancy, the equation system generating the model can be brought into lower triangular form for the coefficients of the dummy variables denoting state occupancy. The models given in the text satisfy this requirement.

3.9 A Renewal Model

The essential feature of the renewal model of structural state dependence is that the only effect of previous state occupancy on current choices is from the most recent current spell in the state. In an analysis of specific human capital of the sort considered by Jovanovic (1978), workers acquire wage-enhancing experience which makes them less likely to leave the work state. However, once the worker leaves the state, the experience is lost and hence is irrelevant to his future choices. The simplest way to capture this effect is with the term

$$\lambda \sum_{j=1}^{\infty} \prod_{l=1}^{j} d(i,t-l). \tag{3.24}$$

Closely related to the concept of specific capital is the concept of fixed costs. Such costs may be incurred once an individual enters a state (e.g., retraining costs for a woman who has entered the labor market). Having incurred the cost, the individual's choice set for subsequent decisions changes, in the sense that the fact she no longer has to incur the cost as long as she remains in the state is taken into account in her subsequent sequential decision making. This concept may be captured by the term

$$\lambda d(i,t-1).$$

This term also generates a renewal process.

Introduction of such effects into the preceding models raises no new conceptual issues, apart from those just discussed. A general expression for relative utility that captures both of these effects in a simple choice theoretic model is

$$Y(i,t) = \sum_{j=1}^{\infty} \lambda(t-j,j) \prod_{l=1}^{j} d(i,t-l) + \varepsilon(i,t).$$

The case of fixed costs corresponds to $\lambda(t-j,j) = \lambda(1)$, $j = 1$, $\lambda(t-j,\ j) = 0, j \geq 2$. The simplest model of specific human capital accumulation sets $\lambda(t-j,j) = \lambda$ for all j. Depreciation of these effects can be accommodated in the general model.

The fixed cost model is indistinguishable from a first-order Markov model.[27] The general renewal model is distinguishable from the general finite state Markov models and the generalized Pólya models considered in the preceding section. Heterogeneity and the effect of exogenous variables on choices may be introduced into the renewal models in exactly the same way as discussed in the preceding sections.

3.10 A Model with Habit Persistence

The key feature of the models with structural state dependence is that occupancy of a state in another period determines current choices, controlling for the effect of unmeasured heterogeneity. The model considered in this section ignores this form of dependence but permits relative utility evaluations in other periods ($Y(i, t')$, $t \neq t'$) to determine current choices. Models with habit formation have been considered by Pollak (1970) and are implicit in Coleman's latent Markov model (1964). The model considered here is the discrete data analogue of the classical distributed lag model in econometrics.

The basic idea of habit persistence can be captured by the following model for current relative utility, $Y(i, t)$,

$$Y(i,t) = G(L)Y(i,t) + \varepsilon(i,t), \qquad (3.25)$$

where $G(0) = 0$, and $G(L)$ is a polynomial lag of order K. ($G(L) = g_1 L + g_2 L^2 + \cdots + g_K L^K$, $L^K Y(i, t) = Y(i, t - K)$.) One can introduce distributed leads as well, but this is not done here. Assuming that $(1 - G(L))$ is invertible (e.g., see Granger and Newbold 1977), the model may always be rewritten as

$$Y(i,t) = [1 - G(L)]^{-1}\varepsilon(i,t).$$

If the $\varepsilon(i, t)$ are iid, the coefficients of $G(L)$ may be estimated (up to an unknown factor of proportionality) by multivariate probit analysis, provided the available panel is of suitable length ($T \geq K$) and that the initial conditions for $Y(i, t')$, $t' < 0$, are specified. If the $\varepsilon(i, t)$ are not iid, and the process determining $\varepsilon(i, t)$ is unknown, the model is not identified. This identification problem is exactly the same problem that arises in

27. Indeed the fixed cost model provides a rationalization for a first-order Markov model.

estimating a distributed lag model in the presence of serial correlation (see Griliches 1967, p. 35).

Introduction of exogenous variables into the model aids in identification. If the model of equation (3.25) is augmented to include exogenous variables,

$$Y(i,t) = \mathbf{Z}(i,t)\boldsymbol{\beta} + G(L)Y(i,t) + \varepsilon(i,t), \tag{3.26}$$

it is possible to estimate (variance normalized) elements of $G(L)$ and $\boldsymbol{\beta}$ as well as the correlations among the disturbances. This is so because in reduced form

$$Y(i,t) = [1 - G(L)]^{-1}\mathbf{Z}(i,t)\boldsymbol{\beta} + [1 - G(L)]^{-1}\varepsilon(i,t), \tag{3.27}$$

so that from the estimated coefficients on the lagged values of the $\mathbf{Z}(i, t)$ variables it is possible to solve for the normalized coefficients of $G(L)$, provided that the $\mathbf{Z}(i,t)$, $t = 1, \ldots, T$, are not linear combinations of each other for all i, and initial conditions $Y(i, t')$, $t \leq 0$, are specified.[28]

It is interesting to note that, if at least one variable in $\mathbf{Z}(i, t)$ changes over time, and exact linear dependency among the $\mathbf{Z}(i, t)$ does not exist, a probit model fit on one cross section can be used to test for habit persistence. The test consists of entering lagged values of $\mathbf{Z}(i, t)$ into the probit model based on equation (3.27). If the lagged values of $\mathbf{Z}(i, t)$ are statistically significantly different from zero, one can reject the hypothesis of no habit persistence. Cross section probit models can be used to estimate the normalized coefficients of $G(L)$, provided the analyst has access to lagged values of the $\mathbf{Z}(i, t)$.

The model for habit persistence may be grafted onto the models with structural state dependence developed earlier. General conditions for identification in this model are presented elsewhere (Heckman 1978a, p. 956). The important point to note is that subject to exclusion (or other identification) restrictions, even though $Y(i, t')$ is never observed, its effect on current choice can be estimated and distinguished from the effect of structural state dependence. Thus one can separate the effect of past propensities to occupy a state on current choices from the effect of past occupancy of a state on current choices.

28. A model with lagged latent variables appears in Heckman (1978a, pp. 932 and 956).

3.11 Computation in the General Model[29]

One factor and fixed effect schemes have already been proposed. In the appendix, multifactor schemes are discussed as well. All of these models are fairly cheap to compute and on these grounds are recommended.

In the random effect model it is only necessary to use two periods of data, not necessarily adjacent, to estimate ρ and $\tilde{\boldsymbol{\beta}} = \boldsymbol{\beta}/\sigma_U$ (see equation 3.16). All the parameters in this model may be estimated by standard bivariate probit programs. Estimates obtained from this procedure are presumably good starting values for optimization of the full likelihood function.

Even cheaper estimates are possible. From each cross section, $t = 1, \ldots, T$, it is possible to estimate $\tilde{\boldsymbol{\beta}}(1 - \rho^2)^{1/2}$ by probit analysis (recall that $(1 - \rho^2)^{1/2} = [\sigma_U^2/(\sigma_\tau^2 + \sigma_U^2)]^{1/2}$). Substituting for $\tilde{\boldsymbol{\beta}}$ in likelihood function (3.16), and optimizing the function with respect to ρ conditional on $\tilde{\boldsymbol{\beta}}(1 - \rho^2)^{1/2}$, reduces the computational task to a one-parameter problem. (In practice it is preferable to use an average of cross-sectional estimates of $\tilde{\boldsymbol{\beta}}(1 - \rho^2)^{1/2}$). Estimates of ρ obtained in this fashion are consistent but inefficient. Such estimates of $\tilde{\boldsymbol{\beta}}$ and ρ are consistent starting values for full system optimization. One can further simplify this procedure by optimizing only a two-period likelihood function (for any two periods of data) with respect to ρ conditional on $\tilde{\boldsymbol{\beta}}$.

These principles can also be applied to the other models considered earlier. For example, in the random factor model developed in section 3.5, one can utilize any two periods of data (say, for time t and t') to estimate $\tilde{\boldsymbol{\beta}}(t)$ and $\tilde{\boldsymbol{\beta}}(t')$, as well as $\tilde{\alpha}(t)\tilde{\alpha}(t')(= \tilde{\sigma}(t, t'))$, by bivariate probit analysis. These estimators are inefficient but can be used to compute all the parameters of the model by estimating all possible two-period models. (The periods need not be adjacent.)

It is possible to use cross section probit exactly as in the random factor model to estimate $\tilde{\boldsymbol{\beta}}(t)(1 - \eta^2(t))^{1/2}$, $t = 1, \ldots, T$, in the one-factor model. Bivariate probit (conditional on estimated values of $\tilde{\boldsymbol{\beta}}(t)(1 - \eta^2(t))^{1/2}$ can be used to estimate $\tilde{\alpha}(t)\tilde{\alpha}(t')(= \tilde{\sigma}(t, t'))$ for any two periods of data t and t'. This requires optimization of a bivariate probit model with respect to one parameter. By this bootstrap method, it is possible to estimate inexpensively all the parameters of the model. Of course, given estimated values of $\tilde{\boldsymbol{\beta}}(t)(1 - \eta^2(t))^{1/2}$, it is possible (but more

29. This section draws on Heckman (1976, pp. 245–246).

costly) to estimate the $\tilde{\alpha}(t)$ parameters from the likelihood function for the complete sample.

In a similar fashion bivariate probit may be used to compute the parameters of the model with general heterogeneity given in section 3.7. Again the full correlation matrix, $\tilde{\mathbf{\Sigma}}$, $\sigma(t, t)$, $t = 2, \ldots, T$, and $\boldsymbol{\beta}$ can be estimated from all possible combinations of bivariate calculations, and cross section probit used to compute $\tilde{\boldsymbol{\beta}}(t) = \boldsymbol{\beta}/\sigma(t, t)^{1/2}$, $t = 1, \ldots, T$. The bivariate probit computations can be made conditional on the estimated values of $\tilde{\boldsymbol{\beta}}(t)$, so that only optimization with respect to a single parameter (the correlation coefficient for the disturbances of the two periods selected) is required. Application of these methods to the model with habit persistence (section 3.10) is straightforward (see also Heckman 1976, pp. 245–246).

Fewer shortcut methods are available for the models with structural state dependence considered in sections 3.8 and 3.9. Given nonstochastic initial conditions, it is possible to use the first cross section in the panel data to estimate (variance normalized) structural coefficients. Given the (normalized) structural parameters, it is possible to use the remainder of the available panel data to estimate the correlation structure and the variances ($\sigma(t, t)$, $t = 2, \ldots, T$).

Recent advances in computing the multivariate normal integral (Albright, Lerman, and Manski 1977) make direct maximum likelihood estimation of the general model feasible for T as large as 10. The consistent estimators proposed in this section provide good starting values for this maximum likelihood algorithm. It is well known that, starting with consistent estimators, one Newton step toward the likelihood optimum yields asymptotically efficient estimators.

3.12 A Summary of Sections 3.2 through 3.11

A general model for the analysis of discrete choices made over time has been presented and special cases have been considered in detail. A variety of discrete time-discrete data stochastic processes emerges as special cases of the general model of section 3.3. The cases likely to be of interest in applied work are presented in table 3.1. The restrictions on the general model required to generate the special models are presented under the appropriate column headings.

Table 3.1
Restrictions on parameters required to generate some specific models from the general model

General model: $Y(i,t) = Z(i,t)\boldsymbol{\beta} + \sum_{j=1}^{\infty} \gamma(j,t-j)d(i,t-j) + \lambda \sum_{j=1}^{\infty} \prod_{l=1}^{j} d(i,t-l) + G(L)Y(i,t) + \varepsilon(i,t)$

$Y(i,t) \geq 0$ iff $d(i,t) = 1$
$Y(i,t) < 0$ iff $d(i,t) = 0$.

	Bernoulli model		Markov model (Kth order)		Renewal model		Polya-type model		Model with habit persistence	
	Homogeneous	Heterogeneous[a]	Homogeneous	Heterogeneous[a]	Homogeneous	Heterogeneous[a]	Homogeneous	Heterogeneous[a]	Homogeneous	Heterogeneous[a]
$\boldsymbol{\beta}$	0[e]	Free[b]	0[e]	Free[b]	0[e]	Free[b]	0[e]	Free[b]	0[e]	Free[b]
$\gamma(j,t-j)$	0	0	$\gamma(j)$[f]	$\gamma(j)$[f]	0	0	Free	Free	0	0
λ	0	0	0	0	λ	λ	0	0	0	0
$G(L)$	0	0	0	0	0	0	0	0	Free	Free[c]
$\varepsilon(i,t)$	iid[d]	Free	iid[d]	Free	iid[d]	Free	iid[d]	Free	iid[d]	Free

[a] Heterogeneous in this table refers to heterogeneity in measured variables and heterogeneity in unobserved serially correlated components.
[b] "Free" means that the parameter may assume unrestricted finite values. Thus one may replace $\boldsymbol{\beta}$ with $\mathbf{Z}(i,t)\,\tilde{\boldsymbol{\beta}}(t)$.
[c] As noted in the text, one requires regressors to distinguish between $G(L)$ and an arbitrary correlation pattern for the $\varepsilon(i,t)$, except in special cases in which $G(L)$ and/or the error process are restricted.
[d] As noted in the text, nonstationary, independently nonidentically distributed versions of these models can be estimated.
[e] Except for intercept which may be zero.
[f] $\gamma(j)$, $j \leq K$, zero otherwise.

The concept of heterogeneity has been generalized in these models beyond the mixing distribution, or convolution, concept which appears in the literature to a broader definition of serial correlation among unobservable variables.[30] Each of the models considered here can accommodate heterogeneity of a very general sort, as well as time-varying explanatory variables. It is possible to test for nonstationarity of the errors as well as special hypotheses about the correlation structure of the unobservables.

Given current computing technology, the models are estimable. The one-factor and fixed effect models are particularly simple to implement.

3.13 Heterogeneity versus Structural State Dependence: An Application of the Preceding Models[31]

In the introduction to this chapter the following empirical regularity is noted: individuals who experience an event in the past are more likely to experience the event in the future than are individuals who have not experienced the event in the past. This observation is based on many studies of series of discrete events taken from individual histories, such as records of illness, unemployment, accidents, or labor force participation. There are two conceptually distinct explanations for this empirical regularity. One is that individuals who experience the event are altered by their experience in that the constraints, preferences, or prices (or any combination of the three) that govern future outcomes are altered by past outcomes. Such an effect of past outcomes on future outcomes is termed structural state dependence. A second explanation is that individuals differ in some unmeasured propensity to experience the event and this propensity is either stable over time or, if it changes, values of the propensity are autocorrelated. Broadly defined, the second explanation is a consequence of population heterogeneity.

The problem of distinguishing between these two explanations for the empirical regularity has a long history. The earliest systematic discussion of this problem appears in the analysis of accident proneness. The seminal work on this topic is due to Feller (1940) and Bates and Neyman (1951).[32] Bates and Neyman are especially clear in pointing out the need for panel

30. The two concepts of mixing distribution and convolution, while equivalent in the models considered in this chapter, are not always identical. See Blischke (1963).

31. The comments of Zvi Griliches and Tom MaCurdy have been very helpful in preparing the revision to the remaining sections of the chapter.

32. I am indebted to Jan Hoem for the Feller reference.

data on individuals to distinguish between the two explanations. Work that preceded the Feller and Bates-Neyman papers attempted to use cross section distributions of accident counts to distinguish between true and spurious state dependence. (See Feller for references to this work.)

In the balance of this chapter the apparatus developed in the preceding sections is applied to address this problem. Before becoming absorbed in the details of the solution, it is important to distinguish the solution, which relies on special techniques and assumptions, from the problem, which can be defined more generally.

To this end it is useful to consider four simple urn models which provide a useful framework within which to introduce intuitive notions about heterogeneity and state dependence. In the first scheme there are I individuals who possess urns with the same content of red and black balls. On T independent trials individual i draws a ball and then puts it back in the urn. If a red ball is drawn at trial t, person i experiences the event ($d(i, t) = 1$). If a black ball is drawn, person i does not experience the event ($d(i, t) = 0$). This model corresponds to the simple Bernoulli model presented in section 3.4 and captures the essential idea underlying the choice process in McFadden's (1976) work on discrete choice. From data generated by this urn scheme, one would not observe the empirical regularity previously described.

The second urn scheme generates data that would give rise to the empirical regularity solely due to heterogeneity. In this model individuals possess distinct urns which differ in their composition of red and black balls. As in the first model sampling is done with replacement. However, unlike the first model information concerning an individual's past experience of the event provides information on the composition of his urn.

The person's past record can be used to estimate the person specific urn composition. The conditional probability that individual i experiences the event at time t is a function of past experience of the event. The contents of each urn are unaffected by actual outcomes and in fact are constant. There is no true state dependence. This model corresponds to the random effect model presented in section 3.5.

The third urn scheme generates data characterized by true state dependence. In this model individuals start out with identical urns. On each trial the contents of the urn change *as a consequence of the outcome of the trial*. For example, if a person draws a red ball, and experiences the event, additional new red balls are added to his urn. If he draws a black ball, no new black balls are added to his urn. Subsequent outcomes are affected by previous outcomes because the choice set for subsequent trials is altered as a consequence of experiencing the event. This model corresponds to the generalized Pólya model described in section 3.8.[33]

A variant of the third urn scheme can be constructed that corresponds to the renewal model presented in section 3.9. In this scheme new red balls are added to an individual's urn on successive drawings until a black ball is drawn, and then all of the red balls added in the most recent continuous run of drawings of red balls are removed from the urn. The composition of the urn is the same as it was before the first red ball in the run was drawn. The fixed cost model is a variant of the renewal scheme in which new red balls are added to an individual's urn only on the first draw of a red ball.

The crucial concept that distinguishes the third scheme from the second is that the contents of the urn (the choice set) are altered as a consequence of previous experience. The key point is not that the choice set changes across trials but that it changes in a way that depends on previous outcomes of the

33. For a complete description of the Pólya process and its generalizations see Johnson and Kotz (1977, chapter 4). They note (pp. 180–181) that, in the special case in which a person draws a ball and receives the *same number* of the balls of the color drawn whether a black or red ball is drawn, urn model three (in this case a strict Pólya model) generates sequences of outcomes *identical* in probability with the same sequences generated from urn model two provided that the population distribution of the proportion of red and black balls in the urn is *Beta*. In this case panel data cannot be used to distinguish between the two urn models. In a stationary environment, in which urn contents are not exogenously changed, as long as the number of red balls placed in the urn differs from the number of black balls placed in the urn when a black ball is drawn, it is possible to use panel data to discriminate between the two models. This observation is one of the key insights in the Bates-Neyman paper (1951).

A similar result appears in the multivariate probit model. For example, consider the following generalization of the model of equation (3.20) with β_0 replaced by $\beta_0 t$ where $t < \infty$ is the length of time the process has been in operation. Assume $\gamma(t-j, j) = \gamma$. Suppose that if individual i does not experience the event in time period $t'(<t)$, so that $d(i, t') = 0$, he receives a "dose" γ'. The relative utility evaluation for this model may be written as

$$Y(i, t) = \beta_0 t + \gamma \sum_{j=1}^{t} d(i, t-j) + \gamma' \sum_{j=1}^{t} (1 - d(i, t-j)) + \varepsilon(i, t)$$

$$= \beta_0 t + (\gamma - \gamma') \sum_{j=1}^{t} d(i, t-j) + \gamma' t + \varepsilon((i, t),$$

$d(i, t) = 1$ if $Y(i, t) \geq 0$, $d(i, t) = 0$ otherwise. If $\gamma = \gamma'$, there is no structural state dependence as defined in the text, although there is a trend effect (so long as $\beta_0 + \gamma' \neq 0$). Thus even though the individual receives a "dose" of γ when he experiences the event and a dose of γ' when he does not, if the doses are of equal strength there is no way to measure the dose. In the special case of a stationary environment ($\beta_0 = 0$), it is clearly possible to estimate $\gamma(=\gamma')$ from the coefficient on t.

choice process. To clarify this point, it is useful to consider a fourth urn scheme that corresponds to the models with more general types of heterogeneity considered in sections 3.5 and 3.7.

In this model individuals start out with identical urns, exactly as in the first urn scheme. After each trial, but independent of the outcome of the trial, the contents of each person's urn are changed by discarding a randomly selected portion of balls and replacing the discarded balls with a randomly selected group of balls from a larger urn (say, with a very large number of balls of both colors). Assuming that the individual urns are not completely replenished on each trial, information about the outcomes of previous trials is useful in forecasting the outcome of future trials, although the information from a previous trial declines with its remoteness in time. Like the situation in the second and third urn models, previous outcomes give information about the contents of each urn. Unlike the situation in the second model, the information depreciates since the contents of the urn are changed in a random fashion. Unlike the third model the contents of the urn do not change as a consequence of any outcome of the choice process.

The general model presented in section 3.3 is sufficiently flexible that it can be specialized to generate data on the time series of individual choices consistent with samplings from each of the four urn schemes just mentioned as well as more general schemes (including combinations of the four). The principal advantage of this model over models considered in previous work is that it accommodates very general sorts of heterogeneity and state dependence as special cases of the general model and permits the introduction of explanatory exogenous variables in a natural way. The generality of the framework proposed here permits the analyst to combine models and test among competing specifications within a unified framework.

In section 3.14 a simple example is offered to illustrate how the models presented in sections 3.2 through 3.12 can be used to distinguish betweeen heterogeneity and state dependence. Section 3.15 examines the superficially appealing analogy between the problem of distinguishing heterogeneity from state dependence and the classical time-series problem of distinguishing a distributed lag model from a model with serial correlation. The analogy is found to be somewhat misleading. A more appropriate analogy is proposed. The final section 3.16 offers three examples of how structural state dependence may arise. The most interesting example is one with state dependence generated in an environment of perfect certainty.

3.14 Testing for Heterogeneity versus State Dependence

Suppose that there is access to a sample of I randomly selected individuals who are observationally identical at time $t = 1$. There are two observations per person, so that $T = 2$. The process is assumed to start up with no history at $t = 1$. Equivalently $d(i, t') = 0$, $t' \leq 0$, and these values are fixed and independent of the process.

Utilizing the notation established in section 3.3, individual i experiences an event ($d(i, 1) = 1$) if and only if $Y(i, 1) \geq 0$, where

$$Y(i,1) = \bar{V} + \varepsilon(i,1),$$
$$E(\varepsilon(i,1)) = 0,$$
$$E(\varepsilon(i,1)^2) = \sigma(1,1).$$

Thus $Y(i, 1) \geq 0$ iff $d(i, 1) = 1$. $Y(i, 1) < 0$ iff $d(i, 1) = 0$. The utility function consists of a deterministic component $\bar{V}$ and a stochastic component $\varepsilon(i, 1)$. The probability that $d(i, 1) = 1$ is

$$\text{Prob}[\varepsilon(i,1) \geq -\bar{V}] = \Phi\left[\frac{\bar{V}}{\sigma(1,1)^{1/2}}\right].$$

The hypothesis that there is a real effect of occupancy of a state on future behavior requires that individuals who experience the event in time period one have their relevant second-period choice set changed in a way that directly depends on choice in the preceding period so that second-period choice probabilities are altered.

One way to capture this idea which is a natural extension of the choice theoretic models of McFadden (1973, 1975, 1976); is to define random variable $Y(i, 2)$ in the following way:

$$Y(i,2) = \bar{V} + \gamma d(i,1) + \varepsilon(i,2).$$

If $Y(i, 2) \geq 0$, $d(i, 2) = 1$. If $Y(i, 2) < 0$, $d(i, 2) = 0$. $E(\varepsilon(i, 2)) = 0$, $E(\varepsilon(i, 2)^2) = \sigma(2, 2)$. $E(\varepsilon(i, 1)\varepsilon(i, 2)) = \sigma(1, 2)$, and $\rho = \sigma(1, 2)/[\sigma(1, 1)\sigma(2, 2)]^{1/2}$. In this specification the act of choosing $d(i, 1) = 1$ shifts up the mean utility function of the next period by an amount γ.

If $\gamma > 0$, or $\rho > 0$, or both, individuals who experience the event in the first period are more likely to experience the event in the second period. The ρ generates this effect because on average individuals with a high value of $\varepsilon(1)$ in the first period have a high value of $\varepsilon(2)$ in the second period. The γ in the expression has this effect because of the shift in the choice set that arises from occupancy of the state in the past.

To see how $\rho > 0$ generates a conditional relationship between events, set $\gamma = 0$, and note that the conditional probability that a person experiences the event in the second period, given that he experiences the event in the first period, is

$$\mathrm{Prob}[d(i,2) = 1 \mid d(i,1) = 1] = \frac{\int_{-\bar{V}}^{\infty} \int_{-\bar{V}}^{\infty} f(\varepsilon(1), \varepsilon(2))\, d\varepsilon(1)\, d\varepsilon(2)}{\int_{-\infty}^{\infty} \int_{-\bar{V}}^{\infty} f(\varepsilon(1), \varepsilon(2))\, d\varepsilon(1)\, d\varepsilon(2)},$$

where $f(\varepsilon(1), \varepsilon(2))$ is a bivariate density. If $\varepsilon(i, 1)$ and $\varepsilon(i, 2)$ are independent, so that $\rho = 0$,

$$\mathrm{Prob}[d(i,2) = 1 \mid d(i,1) = 1] = \mathrm{Prob}[d(i,2) = 1] = \Phi\left[\frac{\bar{V}}{\sigma(2,2)^{1/2}}\right].$$

Assuming normality, the conditional probability is a monotonically increasing function of ρ, so that the dependence grows with the value of ρ. If $\rho = 1$, individuals who experience the event in period one are certain to experience the event in period two. Even if the correlation is not perfect, the information that an individual has experienced the event at $t = 1$ conveys information about his likelihood of experiencing the event at $t = 2$.

If $\rho > 0$, $d(i, 1)$ and $\varepsilon(i, 2)$ are positively correlated, so that a simple probit model applied to the second period data would lead to upward biased estimates of γ. To estimate γ consistently, and to test for true state dependence, one must control for the effect of correlated disturbances.

The data at the analyst's disposal can be summarized in the following contingency table. Sample proportions are entered in each cell. I is assumed to be sufficiently large that sample proportions closely approximate population probabilities.

	$d(2) = 1$	$d(2) = 0$
$d(1) = 1$	P_{11}	P_{10}
$d(1) = 0$	P_{01}	P_{00}

The probability of the four events in the general case is

$$P_{11} = \text{Prob}[d(i,1) = 1 \wedge d(i,2) = 1]$$
$$= \int_{-\bar{V}-\gamma}^{\infty} \int_{-\bar{V}}^{\infty} f(\varepsilon(1), \varepsilon(2))\, d\varepsilon(1)\, d\varepsilon(2),$$

$$P_{10} = \text{Prob}[d(i,1) = 1 \wedge d(i,2) = 0]$$
$$= \int_{-\infty}^{-\bar{V}-\gamma} \int_{-\bar{V}}^{\infty} f(\varepsilon(1), \varepsilon(2))\, d\varepsilon(1)\, d\varepsilon(2),$$

$$P_{01} = \text{Prob}[d(i,1) = 0 \wedge d(i,2) = 1]$$
$$= \int_{-\bar{V}}^{\infty} \int_{-\infty}^{-\bar{V}} f(\varepsilon(1), \varepsilon(2))\, d\varepsilon(1)\, d\varepsilon(2),$$

$$P_{00} = \text{Prob}[d(i,1) = 0 \wedge d(i,2) = 0]$$
$$= \int_{-\infty}^{-\bar{V}} \int_{-\infty}^{-\bar{V}} f(\varepsilon(1), \varepsilon(2))\, d\varepsilon(1)\, d\varepsilon(2).$$

Assuming $\upsilon(1, 1) = \upsilon(2, 2) = 1$, and $|\rho| < 1$, one can utilize the three independent cells of data from the contingency table to estimate the parameters $\bar{V}$, γ, and ρ, by either the method of maximum likelihood or minimum chi-square. The restriction on ρ is necessary in order to get observations in both off diagonal cells. (Recall that $|\rho| = 1$ induces either a perfect positive or perfect negative correlation in status over time, and so in general results in empty cells and lack of identification for parameters of the model.)

To see how the method works, note that the probability density of $\varepsilon(2)$ given $d(i, 1) = 1$ is

$$g(\varepsilon(2) \mid d(i,1) = 1) = \frac{\int_{-\bar{V}}^{\infty} f(\varepsilon(1), \varepsilon(2))\, d\varepsilon(1)}{\int_{-\bar{V}}^{\infty} f_1(\varepsilon(1))\, d\varepsilon(1)},$$

where $f_1(\varepsilon(1))$ is the marginal density of $\varepsilon(1)$. The probability of the event $d(i, 2) = 1$ given $d(i, 1) = 1$ is generated by

$$\text{Prob}[d(i,2) = 1 \mid d(i,1) = 1] = \int_{-\bar{V}-\gamma}^{\infty} g(\varepsilon(2) \mid d(i,1) = 1)\, d\varepsilon(2).$$

Evaluating the probability of the event that $d(i, 2) = 1$ with respect to the conditional distribution of $\varepsilon(2)$ given $d(i, 1) = 1$ avoids the spurious correlation between $d(i, 1)$ and $\varepsilon(1)$ that arises from correlation between $\varepsilon(1)$ and $\varepsilon(2)$: this procedure "controls" for the sample selection bias that causes the mean disturbance (and general distribution) of $\varepsilon(2)$ to be different for people who have experienced different period one events.

In estimating the parameters $\bar{V}$, ρ, and γ, it is desirable to utilize all available information to secure efficient estimators. The contribution to sample likelihood of an observation with $d(i, 1) = 1$ and $d(i, 2) = 1$ is

$$\text{Prob}[d(i,2) = 1 \mid d(i,1) = 1]\text{Prob}[d(i,1) = 1] = P_{11}.$$

A similar argument for other sequences of events justifies the other cell probabilities. By correctly conditioning the period two distribution, the sample likelihood "controls" for spurious correlation running from $\varepsilon(i, 1)$ to $d(i, 2)$ via $\varepsilon(i, 2)$.

The source of the identification of the parameter γ comes from the following insight: from the outcomes of the choice process in the first period it is possible to estimate $\bar{V}$. Given $\bar{V}$, and hence $P_{1.}(= 1 - P_{0.})$ the probability that the event is experienced in time period one, it is possible to use the conditional probabilities that individuals in state zero in time period one transit to states one and zero in time period two ($P_{01}/P_{0.}$ and $P_{00}/P_{0.}$, respectively) to estimate ρ. Given ρ and $\bar{V}$, it is possible to estimate γ from the transit proportions from state one in period one from $P_{11}/P_{1.}$ and $P_{10}/P_{1.}$. If there is no true state dependence, $P_{01} = P_{10}$, and the proportion of the population in state one is the same in period one and period two, since the same proportion of the population leaves state zero as enters it in period two. Starting from arbitrary initial conditions, the process is always in equilibrium if $\gamma = 0$.[34]

34. Of course, if the process were started in equilibrium, and $\gamma \neq 0$, $P_{01} = P_{10}$. This case requires a different example and has been ruled out here by the assumption that presample values of $d(t')$, $t' \leq 0$, are fixed nonstochastic constants. As noted in chapter 4, first-period equilibrium probabilities are not probit probabilities. One does not require disequilibrium to identify γ.

Another way to show how an estimate of γ is secured in this example is to consider the regions of integration for the density $f(\varepsilon(1), \varepsilon(2))$ used to define the probabilities P_{01} and P_{10}. Figure 3.1 corresponds to the case of $\gamma = 0$. The area under the density in region DBC yields P_{01}. The area under the density in region $D'BC'$ yields P_{10}. Under the assumption that the variance of $\varepsilon(1)$ is the same as that of $\varepsilon(2)$, an assumption consistent with the assumption of underlying stationarity in the distribution of the latent variables, B lies on a 45° line from the origin, and $P_{01} = P_{10}$.

Next consider the case in which $\gamma > 0$, figure 3.2. The appropriate regions of integration are DBC (for P_{01}), which is the same as in the previous diagram, and $C'B'D''$ (for P_{10}), which has a smaller area than $D'BC'$ in figure 3.1. The reduction in area is given by the strip $DBB'D''$. Accordingly $P_{01} > P_{10}$. (Clearly if $\gamma < 0$, $P_{01} < P_{10}$.)

At the heart of the definition of true state dependence in this chapter is the nonlinear shift term $\gamma d(i, 1)$ which captures the notion that occupancy of a state affects the subsequent choice set. The distinction between true and spurious state dependence rests on the distinction between the association that arises from correlation between $\varepsilon(1)$ and $\varepsilon(2)$, giving rise to spurious state dependence and the association $(\gamma d(i, 1))$ between the event in the preceding period and utility levels in the current period. Note that in the example just given, if $\rho = 1$, it is not possible to estimate γ. There is no innovation in $\varepsilon(2)$ that permits one to identify γ. The outcome in the first period perfectly predicts the outcome in the second period whether or not $\gamma = 0$.

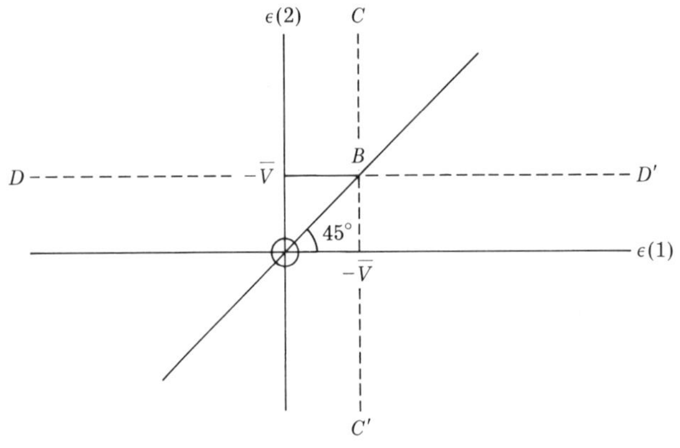

Figure 3.1
$\gamma = 0$

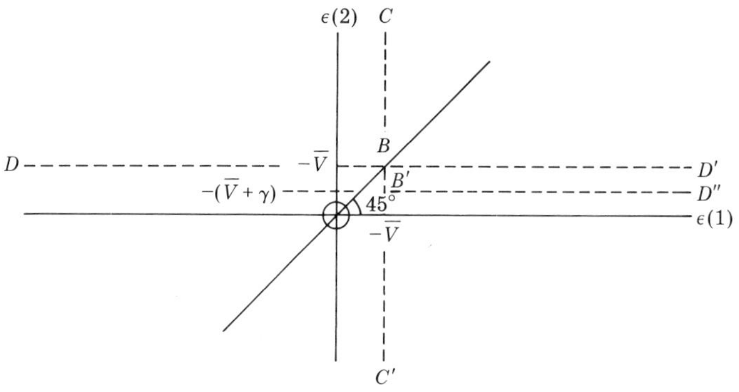

Figure 3.2
$\gamma > 0$

This example illustrates how the techniques developed in sections 3.1 through 3.12 can be used to address an important substantive problem. However, since the example is somewhat special, it is useful to separate the essential from the inessential assumptions that underlie it.

The assumptions in the example are (1) ρ is less than one in absolute value, (2) only two periods of data are available for each person, (3) the variance in $\varepsilon(2)$ is the same as that of $\varepsilon(1)$, an assumption of stationarity of the distribution of the disturbances, (4) everyone is observationally identical in terms of exogenous variables, and (5) the initial conditions of the process are fixed, nonstochastic constants, and the same for everyone.

The assumption that ρ is less than one in absolute value is essential. Without it the contingency table has empty cells, and state dependence parameters cannot be estimated. The restriction to two periods of data is made solely for convenience. If three periods of data are available, one has access to seven independent pieces of information, and a less restrictive model can be fit. It is straightforward to show that, if there are no empty cells, one can estimate the variances $\sigma(2, 2)$, $\sigma(3, 3)$ ($\sigma(1, 1) = 1$ is a required normalization), the correlation coefficients, $\tilde{\sigma}(1, 2)$, $\tilde{\sigma}(1, 3)$, $\tilde{\sigma}(2, 3)$, and γ from the seven cells of data.[35] With four periods of data one has fifteen independent cells that can be used to estimate six correlation coefficients, three variances (setting $\sigma(1, 1) = 1$), $\bar{V}$, and γ. In the four-period case more general forms of state dependence may be entertained (e.g., a fourth-order Markov process).

35. This statement and the following assume that $\beta_0 \neq 0$.

Thus, if $T > 3$, and there are no empty cells, one can separate out the effect of nonstationarity in the error process from state dependence so that the stationarity assumption invoked in the example is not essential.

The assumption that everyone is observationally identical with respect to the exogenous variables can be relaxed, and with profit. A linear combination of exogenous regressor variables, $\mathbf{Z}(i, t)\boldsymbol{\beta}$, may be substituted in place of $\bar{V}$. Assuming that the regressor matrix is of full rank, the addition of these variables permits identification of $\sigma(2, 2)$ even if $T = 2$.[36]

The assumption that initial conditions of the process are fixed and nonstochastic is essential and difficult to relax. Discussion of the important problem of initial conditions is deferred to chapter 4.

The entire discussion in this section has been conducted within the convenient framework of the normal distribution for the disturbances of the model. A parallel analysis could be performed within the general multivariate t family or for more general distributions. For example, first-order Markov state dependence could be generated in a logit model with a components of variance structure.

A complete analysis of the general, non-normal case is beyond the scope of this chapter. The normal framework is sufficiently flexible to accommodate behavior consistent with the urn schemes discussed and so is useful for testing among competing specifications. However, the concept of structural state dependence does not require the normal framework for its definition, although such a framework is convenient for measuring its effect.

The normality assumption is convenient primarily because the normal distribution can be parameterized to accommodate nonstationarity in the distribution of the disturbances in such a way that the nonstationarity can be removed or accounted for (e.g., one can estimate $\sigma(t, t)$ or introduce time trends as exogenous variables).

In the general case of a non-normal arbitrarily nonstationary distribution with unknown parameters, the measurement of state dependence effects will be a hopeless task.[37] In general for any contingency table with

36. Thus identification conditions in this model are analogous to identification conditions in a time-series model with first-order serial correlation, and a lagged value of the dependent variable. Identification of correlation and lag coefficients in that model is secured through sample variation in the exogenous variables. The proposition in the text follows from Heckman (1978a, part III).

37. This problem closely resembles the equally hopeless task of estimating parameters of distributed lag models in the presence of arbitrary serial correlation in the errors without the benefit of any a priori information (Hatanaka 1975).

choice process, any distribution with $2^T - 1$ or more parameters will in general fit the table. The methods proposed here secure identification of the state dependence effect by restricting the nonstationarity effect to operate through shifts in covariances and means of the distribution of the errors generating the model.

3.15 Analogies with Time-Series Models[38]

The analogy between the problem of distinguishing heterogeneity from state dependence and the classical time-series problem of distinguishing a serial correlation model from a distributed lag model, although superficially appealing, is not precise. As noted in section 3.10, an exact analogy can be made between the problem of distinguishing heterogeneity from habit persistence and the classical time-series problem.

A model with habit persistence is

$$Y(i,t) = G(L)\,Y(i,t) + \varepsilon(i,t),$$

$G(0) = 0$, $Y(i, t) \geq 0$ iff $d(i, t) = 1$. $Y(i, t) < 0$ otherwise. This model is exactly in the form of the classical time-series problem, except in that problem $Y(i, t)$ is observed. As noted in section 3.10, if regressors are present, it is possible to distinguish between the effects of habit persistence and serial correlation. Thus let

$$Y(i,t) = \mathbf{Z}(i,t)\boldsymbol{\beta} + G(L)\,Y(i,t) + \varepsilon(i,t).$$

Provided that the regressors in different periods for individual i $(i = 1, \ldots, I)$ are not linear combinations of each other, one can compute the marginal probability that $d(i, t) = 1$ and determine if past values of $\mathbf{Z}(i, t)$ are determinants of current period choices. If they are, one can reject the hypothesis of no habit persistence. This is so because

$$Y(i,t) = [1 - G(L)]^{-1}\mathbf{Z}(i,t)\boldsymbol{\beta} + [1 - G(L)]^{-1}\varepsilon(i,t).$$

Only if $G(L) \equiv 0$ for all L will lagged $\mathbf{Z}$ not determine the current marginal probability that $d(i, t) = 1$. In principle one can approximate the marginal probability by a linear probability model (e.g., see Heckman 1978b) so that this test does not require a normality assumption for $\varepsilon(i, t)$.

38. This section has benefited from discussions with Zvi Griliches and Tom MaCurdy, and the incisive remarks of Marc Nerlove (1978).

A model with structural state dependence may be written as a nonlinear time series. For example, consider

$$Y(i,t) = \sum_{j=1}^{\infty} \gamma(j)d(i,t-j) + \varepsilon(i,t),$$

with $Y(i, t) \geq 0$ iff $d(i, t) = 1$, $Y(i, t) < 0$ otherwise. Unlike the autoregressive habit persistence model, an effect of past Y on current Y arises only if a threshold is crossed. In a model of discrete choice in which $Y(i, t) \geq 0$ corresponds to occupancy of a different state than that occupied when $Y(i, t) < 0$, this sort of nonlinearity is natural, although in an ordinary time-series model it may appear to be artificial.

Assuming no habit persistence, a test of state dependence against heterogeneity can be based on the marginal probability that $d(i, t) = 1$, provided that regressors are available that satisfy the conditions given in the test for habit persistence against serial correlation. If lagged $\mathbf{Z}(i, t)$ determine current marginal choice probabilities, state dependence is present.[39]

In the general case with habit persistence and state dependence, the finding that lagged values of $\mathbf{Z}(i, t)$ determine current marginal choice probabilities suggests that habit persistence or state dependence, or both, are present, except in the unusual case where the two effects cancel. The finding that lagged $\mathbf{Z}(i, t)$ does not determine current marginal choice probabilities is, except for the unusual case just stated, evidence against both habit persistence and state dependence.

The identification of habit persistence effects requires exogenous variables.[40] The identification of state dependence effects does not, as the example of the preceding section has shown. For this reason the analogy between the problem of distinguishing between heterogeneity and state dependence and the problem of distinguishing between a distributed lag and serial correlation model is inexact.

39. This test for state dependence against heterogeneity presented in this paragraph was suggested to me by Gary Chamberlain and Tom MaCurdy.

3.16 Examples of Models that Generate Structural State Dependence

This section briefly considers how models with structural state dependence can be generated from well-defined economic models. Three examples are discussed: a model of stimulus-response conditioning of the sort developed by mathematical psychologists, a model of decision making under uncertainty, and a model of decision making under perfect foresight.

In the stimulus-response model developed by behavioral psychologists (e.g., see Bush and Mosteller 1955, Restle and Greeno 1970, or Johnson and Kotz 1977) the individual who makes a given "correct" response is rewarded so that he is more likely to make the response in the future. Decision making is myopic. This model closely resembles the generalized Pólya process discussed in sections 3.8 and 3.13. General heterogeneity can be introduced into the model along the lines discussed in sections 3.3 through 3.12. Models that resemble the stimulus-response model have been proposed by dual labor market economists who assume that individuals who are randomly allocated to one market are rewarded for staying in the market and are conditioned by institutions in that market so that their preferences are altered. The more time one has spent in a particular type of market, the more likely one is to stay in it.

The model of myopic sequential decision making just presented is unlikely to prove attractive to many economists. Nonmyopic sequential models of decision making under imperfect information also generate structural state dependence. Such models have been extensively developed in the literature on dynamic programming (e.g., see Dreyfus 1965, pp. 213–215, or Astrom 1970). An example is a model in which an agent at time t maximizes expected utility over the remaining horizon, given all the information at his disposal and his constraints as of time t. Transition to a state may be uncertain. As a consequence of being in a state, costs may be incurred or information may be acquired that alters the information set or opportunity set, or both, relevant for future decisions. In such cases the outcome of the process affects subsequent decision making, and structural state dependence is generated.

The disturbance in this model consists of unmeasured variables known to the agent but unknown to the observing economist as well as

40. See Hatanaka (1975). Restrictions on error covariances and/or admissible habit persistence effects can also secure identification of these effects.

unanticipated random components unknown to both the agent and the observing economist.

Structural state dependence can also be generated as *one representation* of a model of decision making under perfect certainty. In such a model there are no surprises. Given the inital conditions of the process, the full outcome of the process is perfectly predictable from information available to the agent (but not necessarily available to the observing economist).

Consider the following three-period model of consumer decision making under perfect certainty with indivisibility in purchase quantities: a consumer's strictly concave utility function is specified as

$$U(a(1)d(1), a(2)d(2), a(3)d(3)),$$

where the $a(i)$ are the fixed amounts that can be consumed in each period. The consumer purchases amount $a(i)$ if $d(i) = 1$, otherwise $d(i) = 0$. Resources are fixed so that

$$\sum a(i)d(i) \leq M.$$

The agent has full information and selects the $d(i)$ optimally. Optimal solutions are denoted by $d^*(i)$.

An alternative characterization of the problem is the following sequential interpretation. Given $d^*(1)$, maximize utility with respect to remaining choices.

Thus

$$\max_{d(2),\, d(3)} \quad U(a(1)d^*(1), a(2)d(2), a(3)d(3))$$

subject to

$$\sum_{i=2}^{3} a(i)d(i) \leq M - a(1)d^*(1).$$

The demand functions (really the demand inequalities) for $d(2)$ and $d(3)$ may be written in terms of $d^*(1)$ and available resources $(M - a(1)d^*(1))$. This characterization is a discrete choice analogue of the Hotelling (1935), Samuelson (1960), Pollak (1969) treatment of ordinary consumer choice and demonstrates that the demand function for a good can be expressed as a function of quantities consumed of some goods, the "prices" of the remaining goods and income. (Pollak's term "conditional demand function" is felicitous.)

Either past choices $d^*(1)$ or past $a(1)$ determine current choices in conjunction with future prices and current resources.[41] The choice of which characterization of the decision problem to use is a matter of convenience. When the analyst knows current disposable resources $(M - a(1)d^*(1))$ and past choices $(d^*(1))$ but not $a(1)$ or M, the second form of the problem is econometrically more convenient. The conditional demand function gives rise to structural state dependence, in the sense that past choices influence current decisions. The essential point in this example is that past choices serve as a legitimate proxy for missing M and $a(1)$ variables known to the consumer but unknown to the observing econometrician. The conditional demand function is a legitimate structural equation.[42]

Both a model of decision making under uncertainty and a model of decision making under perfect foresight may be brought into sequential form so that past outcomes of the choice process may determine future outcomes. In principle one can distinguish between a certainty model and an uncertainty model if one has access to all the relevant information at the agent's disposal. In a model of decision making under perfect certainty, if all past prices are known and entered as explanatory variables for current choice, past outcomes of the choice process contribute no new information relevant to determining current choices. In a model of decision making under uncertainty, past outcomes would contribute information on current choices not available from past prices, since uncertainty necessarily makes the prediction of past outcomes from past prices inexact, and the unanticipated components of past outcomes alter the budget set and cause a revision of initial plans.[43] In practice it is difficult to distinguish between the two models given limitations of data. The observing economist usually has less information at his disposal than the agent being analyzed has at his disposal when he makes his decisions.

41. In this example, if the utility function is additive, $d^*(1)$ would have no effect on future choices except through its effect on current resources $(M - a(1)d^*(1))$. Thus a test of structural state dependence in this model is a test of intertemporal independence in preferences.

42. Another model that generates structural state dependence in an environment of perfect certainty is a model with fixed costs. In some dynamic models of labor supply, training costs are assumed to be incurred by labor force entrants. Once these costs are incurred, they are not incurred again until re-entry occurs. Labor force participation decisions taken by labor force participants take account of such costs. In this way structural state dependence is generated.

43. If the uncertainty comes in the form of price uncertainty, *ex ante* prices are required to perform the test.

The key point to extract from these examples is that structural state dependence as defined in this chapter may be generated from a variety of models. It is not necessary to assume myopic decision making to generate structural dependence. Nor does empirical evidence in support of structural state dependence prove that agents make their decisions myopically.

3.17 Summary and Conclusion

This chapter presents a general model for the analysis of discrete panel data. The model is sufficiently flexible that it can be used to generate a variety of models useful in applied work as special cases of the general model. Bernoulli, Pólya, Markov, and renewal models are produced by imposing restrictions on the general model. Time-varying exogenous variables and unobserved variables with a general serial correlation structure can be introduced into the model. The definition of heterogeneity used in previous work is generalized in this model.

Special cases of the model likely to be used in applied work are considered in detail. Issues of identification and data requirements needed to estimate these models are addressed. Simply computed versions of the models receive considerable attention. A fixed effect probit model and one-factor probit model are presented, and their strengths and limitations are evaluated. Inexpensive methods for estimating the general model are discussed.

A great advantage of the models developed in this chapter is that they can be used to generate choice theoretic discrete data models. The apparatus developed here extends the atemporal choice models of McFadden (1974, 1976) to an intertemporal setting. Structural dependence among time-ordered discrete events can be investigated by the models. Certain models widely used in the analysis of discrete data, such as Goodman's log linear probability model, defy structural interpretation and so are not useful for the analysis of structural discrete data models (Heckman 1978a, part IV, pp. 950–954).

The methodology developed here can be put to use to address a longstanding statistical problem: distinguishing between true and false contagion (Bates and Neyman 1951) or, in the language of this chapter, distinguishing between spurious and true state dependence. The problem can be stated simply. The existence of a conditional probability relationship between the occurrence of an event in one period and its occurrence in previous periods may be due to serial correlation in the unobservables that generate the event or because past experience of the event affects the choice set and preferences relevant to choices taken in subsequent periods. The first reason for the existence of the conditional relationship is termed spurious state dependence. The second reason for the conditional relationship is termed structural state dependence. Methods for estimating structural relationships among time-ordered outcomes can be used to test for the presence of true state dependence and to measure the quantitative significance of the two sources of dependence.

Intuitively appealing analogies between this problem and the classical time-series problem of distinguishing between a distributed lag model and a serial correlation model are examined and are found to be somewhat misleading. Examples of choice theoretic models that generate structural state dependence are presented. It is demonstrated that it is possible to produce structural state dependence as one representation of a model of consumer decision making under perfect certainty.

Empirical work based on these models has been performed in other work. In Heckman (1981) data on the labor force participation of women are analyzed. A one-factor model is fit to three periods of panel data drawn from the Michigan Panel Survey of Income Dynamics. Tests for the existence of heterogeneity and state dependence are conducted. The major findings of the empirical analysis of female labor force activity are (1) Heterogeneity is not characterized by a components of variance scheme; a first-order Markov process for the unobserved variables fits the data better. (2) There is evidence of true state dependence. For an application of these models to the analysis of unemployment data, see Cave (1981). Heckman and Willis (1975) apply a simple version of these models to analyze dynamic fertility behavior.

3.18 Appendix: Factor Analytic Probit Models

Four topics are addressed: first, a more general treatment of the one-factor model is given. Equation 3.19 is derived, and the requirement that $\sigma_U(t, t) > 0$, $t = 1, \ldots, T$, is relaxed. Second, implicit restrictions inherent in the one-factor scheme are presented. It is demonstrated that in the general case the one-factor model implies that the disturbances generating the stochastic process are nonstationary. Third, specific examples of one-factor representations are given. Fourth, a multifactor model is considered.

A General One-Factor Model

The reader is referred to the text, especially the discussion following equation (3.17). The error structure is written as

$$\varepsilon(i,t) = \alpha(t)\tau(i) + U(i,t), \tag{3.28}$$

$t = 1, \ldots, T, i = 1, \ldots, I$. A key concept is the term $\tilde{\alpha}(t)$, the normalized factor loading,

$$\tilde{\alpha}(t) \equiv \frac{\alpha(t)\sigma_\tau}{[\alpha^2(t)\sigma_\tau^2 + \sigma_U(t,t)]^{1/2}}.$$

In this notation the following proposition can be verified:

Proposition 3.1: Given the one-factor structure, and the assumption $\sigma_U(t, t) > 0$, the probability of $\mathbf{d}(i)$ given $\mathbf{Z}(i)$ may be written as

$$\text{Prob}[\mathbf{d}(i) \mid \mathbf{Z}(i)]$$

$$= \int_{-\infty}^{\infty} \prod_{t=1}^{T} \Phi\{[\mathbf{Z}(i,t)\tilde{\boldsymbol{\beta}}(t) + \eta(t)\tilde{\tau}][2d(i,t) - 1]\} f(\tilde{\tau})\, d\tilde{\tau}, \tag{3.29}$$

where $\eta(t) = [\tilde{\alpha}(t)^2/1 - \tilde{\alpha}(t)^2]^{1/2}$, $\tilde{\boldsymbol{\beta}}(t) = \boldsymbol{\beta}/\sigma_U(t, t)^{1/2}$, and $\tilde{\tau}$ is a standardized variate with variance one. (Positive square roots are to be used.)

PROOF: The probability that $d(i, t) = 1$ given $\tau(i)$ and $\mathbf{Z}(i, t)$ is

$$\text{Prob}[U(i,t) \geq -\mathbf{Z}(i,t)\tilde{\boldsymbol{\beta}}(t) - \alpha(t)\tau(i) \mid \tau(i), \mathbf{Z}(i,t)]$$
$$= \Phi[\mathbf{Z}(i,t)\tilde{\boldsymbol{\beta}}(t) + \frac{\alpha(t)}{\sigma_U(t,t)^{1/2}}\tau(i)],$$

where $\tilde{\boldsymbol{\beta}}(t) = \boldsymbol{\beta}/\sigma_U(t, t)^{1/2}$.

Define $\tilde{\tau}(i) = \tau(i)/\sigma_\tau$, and note that

$$\eta(t) = \left[\frac{(\tilde{\alpha}(t))^2}{(1 - (\tilde{\alpha}(t)^2)}\right]^{1/2} = \frac{\alpha(t)\sigma_\tau}{\sigma_U(t,t)^{1/2}}.$$

Thus the probability that $d(i, t) = 1$ given $\tilde{\tau}(i)$ and $\mathbf{Z}(i, t)$ is

$$\Phi[\mathbf{Z}(i,t)\tilde{\boldsymbol{\beta}}(t) + \eta(t)\tilde{\tau}(i)].$$

Expressing the model in general form, and integrating with respect to the density of $\tilde{\tau}$, the result follows immediately. Q.E.D.

Note that, if $\sigma_U(t', t') = 0$, so that $\tilde{\alpha}(t') = 1$, the probability that $d(i, t') = 1$ given $\mathbf{Z}(i, t')$ and $\tau(i)$ is either zero or one. Thus $d(i, t') = 1$ imposes the condition that

$$\alpha(t')\tau(i) \geq -\mathbf{Z}(i, t')\boldsymbol{\beta},$$

which is a restriction on $\tilde{\tau}(i)$, with

$$\tilde{\tau}(i) \geq -\frac{\mathbf{Z}(i, t')\boldsymbol{\beta}}{\alpha(t')\sigma_\tau}, \quad \alpha(t') > 0.$$

If $\sigma_U(t', t') = 0$, $\sigma_U(t, t) > 0$, $t \neq t'$, the probability of $\mathbf{d}(i)$, the vector of the $d(i, t)$, given $\mathbf{Z}(i)$, the vector of Z(i, t), *is*

$$\text{Prob}[\mathbf{d}(i) \mid \mathbf{Z}(i)]$$

$$= \left[\int_{-\mathbf{Z}(i,t')\boldsymbol{\beta}/\alpha(t')\sigma_\tau}^{\infty} \prod_{\substack{t=1 \\ t \neq t'}}^{T} \Phi\{(\mathbf{Z}(i, t)\tilde{\boldsymbol{\beta}}(t) + \eta(t)\tilde{\tau})(2d(i, t) - 1)\} f(\tilde{\tau})\, d\tilde{\tau} \right]^{d(i, t')}$$

$$\cdot \left[\int_{-\infty}^{-\mathbf{Z}(i,t')\boldsymbol{\beta}/\alpha(t')\sigma_\tau} \prod_{\substack{t=1 \\ t \neq t'}}^{T} \Phi\{(\mathbf{Z}(i, t)\tilde{\boldsymbol{\beta}}(t) + \eta(t)\tilde{\tau})(2d(i, t) - 1)\} f(\tilde{\tau})\, d\tilde{\tau} \right]^{(1 - d(i, t'))}.$$

Under general conditions for $T \geq 3$, the $\tilde{\boldsymbol{\beta}}(t)$, $\eta(t)$, $t = 1, \ldots, T$, $t \neq t'$, and $\boldsymbol{\beta}/\alpha(t')\sigma_\tau$ can be estimated by the method of maximum likelihood. Normalizing $\sigma_U(1, 1) = 1$ (so that $t' \neq 1$), it is thus possible to estimate $\boldsymbol{\beta}$, $\alpha(t)\sigma_\tau$, $t = 1, \ldots, T$, and $\sigma_U(t, t)$, $t = 2, \ldots, T$. Other normalizations are possible (e.g., $\alpha(t)\sigma_\tau = 1$).[44]

If there are two zero variances ($\sigma_U(t', t') = 0$ and $\sigma_U(t'', t'') = 0$), two restrictions on the single factor are generated, and a special dependency between the $d(i, t')$ and $d(i, t'')$ is implied. For example, suppose

44. It is interesting to note that the extra information $\sigma_{U}(t', t') = 0$ does not permit any more parameters to be identified than if $\sigma_U(t', t') > 0$. This is because, if $\sigma_U(t', t') = 0$, $\tilde{\alpha}(t')$ is equal to one and is no longer a source of information on the parameters of the model.

$$\tilde{\tau}(i) \geq -\frac{\mathbf{Z}(i,t')\boldsymbol{\beta}}{\alpha(t')\sigma_\tau} = k(t'),$$

$$\tilde{\tau}(i) \geq -\frac{\mathbf{Z}(i,t'')\boldsymbol{\beta}}{\alpha(t'')\sigma_\tau} = k(t''), \quad \alpha(t'), \quad \alpha(t'') > 0,$$

where $k(t') < k(t'')$. Then, if $d(i, t'') = 1$, $d(i, t') = 1$. If $d(i, t') = 0$, $d(i, t'') = 0$. The only possibilities are $(d(i, t'') = 1, d(i, t') = 1; d(i, t') = 1, d(i, t'') = 0; d(i, t') = 0, d(i, t'') = 0)$. The outcome $d(i, t') = 0, d(i, t'') = 1$ is ruled out. The probability statement (3.19) must be modified in a nontrivial way to incorporate such possibilities. Such a modification, and also the modification required for more than two zero variances, are topics left for another occasion.

The General One-Factor Model Imposes Nonstationarity

The one-factor model imposes restrictions on the admissible error process. For $T > 3$, it implies nonstationarity. Only the permanent-transitory error process and a peculiar relative are stationary and one-factor analyzable.

Proposition 3.2: In the general case of weak stationarity of the process, if $T > 3$, no one-factor model is stationary except the process

$$\varepsilon(i,k) = b\tau(i) + U(i,k), \tag{3.30}$$

$k = 2t - 1,\ t = 1, \ldots, [T/2,\ T \text{ even};\ (T+1)/2,\ T \text{ odd}]$;

$$\varepsilon(i,k) = -b\tau(i) + U(i,k),$$

$k = 2t,\ t = 1, \ldots, [T/2,\ T \text{ even};\ (T-1)/2,\ T \text{ odd}]$; or the process

$$\varepsilon(i,t) = \tau(i) + U(i,t), \tag{3.31}$$

$t = 1, \ldots, T$, where $E(\tau) = 0 = E(U(i,t))$, $E(\tau^2) = \sigma_\tau^2$, $E(U(i,t)^2) = \sigma_U^2$, and $E(U(i, t)\tau(i)) = 0$.

PROOF: For a weakly stationary sequence of random variables, $\varepsilon(i, t)$, $t = 1, \ldots, T$, the autocovariances $(\tilde{\sigma}(t, t'))$ must satisfy $\tilde{\sigma}(t, t') = \tilde{\sigma}(|t - t'|)$ and $E(\varepsilon(i, t)^2) = \sigma_\varepsilon^2$ for all t, t'.

For a stationary process to be one-factor analyzable, it must be the case that

$$\tilde{\sigma}(j,j+1) = \tilde{\alpha}(j)\tilde{\alpha}(j+1) = \tilde{\alpha}(j+1)\tilde{\alpha}(j+2) = \tilde{\sigma}(j+1,j+2)$$

for $j = 1, \ldots, T-2$. Thus $\tilde{\alpha}(j) = \tilde{\alpha}(j+2), j = 1, \ldots, T-2$, so that all even- and odd-normalized factor loadings are equal, but the odd-numbered loadings need not equal the even-numbered loadings.

Stationarity also implies

$$\tilde{\sigma}(j,j+2) = \tilde{\alpha}(j)\tilde{\alpha}(j+2) = \tilde{\alpha}(j+1)\tilde{\alpha}(j+3) = \tilde{\sigma}(j+1,j+3)$$

for $T > 3$. Since $\tilde{\alpha}(j) = \tilde{\alpha}(j+2)$, it must be the case that $\tilde{\alpha}(j) = \pm\tilde{\alpha}(j+1)$. Thus either all normalized factor loadings are equal, or the odd-numbered normalized factor loadings are minus the even-numbered normalized factor loadings.

Stationarity also requires that the variances in each period be the same or

$$\alpha(t)^2\sigma_\tau^2 + \sigma_U(t,t) = \alpha(t')^2\sigma_\tau^2 + \sigma_U(t',t').$$

Since by the previous argument $\tilde{\alpha}(t)^2 = (\tilde{\alpha})^2, \alpha(t)\sigma_\tau = k$ from the definition of $\tilde{\alpha}(t)$. Hence $\sigma_U(t,\ t) = \sigma_U$ for all t.

Therefore the error process must be either the ordinary permanent-transitory process, given by equation (3.31) or the alternating permanent-transitory process, given in equation (3.30). Q.E.D.

This result is discouraging. Many interesting error structures cannot be one-factor analyzed. Note, however, if $T = 3$, the proposition is not true.

Some Examples

This subsection considers some examples of error structures that can be one-factor analyzed. The first example is a stationary first-order Markov process for $T = 3$. This process can be one-factor analyzed and provides an interesting case in which $\sigma_U(t,\ t) = 0$.

Thus $E(\varepsilon(i,\ t)\varepsilon(i,\ t')) = \rho^{|t-t'|}\sigma_\varepsilon^2$, $E(\varepsilon(i,\ t)^2) = \sigma_\varepsilon^2$, $\tilde{\alpha}(1) = \tilde{\alpha}(3) = \rho = [E(\varepsilon(i,\ 1)\varepsilon(i,\ 2))]/E(\varepsilon(i,\ 1))^2$, $\tilde{\alpha}(2) = 1$. The joint probability of $d(i,\ 1) = 1$, $d(i,\ 2) = 0$, and $d(i,\ 3) = 1$ is

$$\text{Prob}[d(i,1) = 1, d(i,2) = 0, d(i,3) = 1 \mid \mathbf{Z}(i)]$$

$$= \int_{-\infty}^{-\mathbf{Z}(i,\,2)\boldsymbol{\beta}} \Phi[\mathbf{Z}(i,1)\boldsymbol{\beta} + \tilde{\tau}\eta]\,\Phi[\mathbf{Z}(i,3)\boldsymbol{\beta} + \tilde{\tau}\eta]\,f(\tilde{\tau})\,d\tilde{\tau}$$

where $\eta = (\rho/1-\rho)^{1/2}$.

As another example, consider the scheme of Balestra and Nerlove (1966):

$$\varepsilon(i,t) = \tau(i) + \frac{U(i,t)}{1 - \rho L},$$

$t = 1, \ldots, 3$. For this model

$$\tilde{\alpha}(1) = \tilde{\alpha}(3) = \left(\frac{1 + \rho^2 k}{1 + k}\right)^{1/2},$$

$$\tilde{\alpha}(2) = \frac{1}{\tilde{\alpha}(1)}\left(\frac{1 + \rho k}{1 + k}\right),$$

where $k = \sigma_U^2/\sigma_\tau^2$.

It is easily verified that no first-order moving average scheme can be one-factor analyzed, but a first-order moving average scheme with a permanent component can be one-factor analyzed for the case $T = 3$.

A Model with Multiple Factors

The principal advantage of the one-factor model is that it is simple to compute. However, for $T > 3$, it imposes restrictions on the error process that may be inappropriate in certain applications. Higher-factor schemes are less restrictive and yet reduce the scale of the computing problem in comparison with the scale in the general case of an unrestricted correlation matrix. Assuming $Q < T$ independent factors, the probability integral can be written as Q univariate integrations of products of functions available on most computers. The general form of the Q-factor model is the topic of this subsection.

The disturbance $\varepsilon(i, t)$ can be Q factor analyzed if it can be written

$$\varepsilon(i,t) = \sum_{q=1}^{Q} \alpha(t,q)\tau(i,q) + U(i,t),$$

$t = 1, \ldots, T$, $i = 1, \ldots, I$, $Q < T$, where
$E(\tau(i, q)) = 0$,
$E(U(i, t)) = 0, \quad i = 1, \ldots, I, t = 1, \ldots, T, q = 1, \ldots, Q,$

$$\begin{aligned} E(\tau(i,j)\tau(i'',j')) &= \sigma_{jj'}, \quad i = i'', j = j', \\ &= 0, \quad i \neq i'' \text{ or } j \neq j', \end{aligned}$$

$$E(U(i, t)\tau(i', j)) = 0 \quad \text{for all } i, t, i', \text{ and } j,$$
$$E(U(i, t)^2) = \sigma_U(t, t), \quad t = 1, \ldots, T.$$

By analogy with the one-factor case, define the normalized factor loading for factor q at time t as

$$\tilde{\alpha}(t, q) = \frac{\alpha(t, q)\sigma_{qq}}{\left[\sum_{q=1}^{Q} \alpha^2(t, q)\sigma_{qq} + \sigma_U(t, t)\right]^{1/2}}.$$

The square of $\tilde{\alpha}(t, q)$ is the proportion of the variance in $\varepsilon(i, t)$ that is due to factor q. Array the $\tilde{\alpha}(t, q)$ into a $1 \times Q$ vector $\tilde{\boldsymbol{\alpha}}(t)$. Then $\tilde{\boldsymbol{\alpha}}(t)\tilde{\boldsymbol{\alpha}}(t)'$ is the proportion of the variance in $\varepsilon(i, t)$ due to all Q factors.

In this notation it is straightforward to establish the following proposition:

Proposition 3.3: If the disturbances can be Q-factor analyzed, and if $\sigma_U(t, t) > 0$, $t = 1, \ldots, T$, the probability of $\mathbf{d}(i)$ given $\mathbf{Z}(i)$ may be written as

$$\text{Prob}[\mathbf{d}(i) \mid \mathbf{Z}(i)]$$
$$= \int_{-\infty}^{\infty} \cdots \int_{-\infty}^{\infty} \prod_{t=1}^{T} \Phi\left\{\left[\mathbf{Z}(i, t)\tilde{\boldsymbol{\beta}}(t) + \frac{\tilde{\boldsymbol{\alpha}}(t)\mathbf{l}}{(1 - \tilde{\boldsymbol{\alpha}}(t)\tilde{\boldsymbol{\alpha}}(t)')^{1/2}}\right] (2d(i, t) - 1)\right\} f(\mathbf{l})d\mathbf{l},$$

where $\mathbf{l}$ is a $Q \times 1$ vector of independent standard normal variates, $f(\mathbf{l})$ is a product of Q standard normal densities, and $\tilde{\boldsymbol{\beta}}(t) = \boldsymbol{\beta}/\sigma_U(t, t)^{1/2}$.

PROOF: The probability that $d(i, t) = 1$ given $\mathbf{Z}(i, t)$ and $\tau(i, q)$, $q = 1, \ldots, Q$, may be written as

$$\text{Prob}[d(i, t) = 1 \mid \mathbf{Z}(i), \tau(i, q), q = 1, \ldots, Q]$$
$$= \text{Prob}[U(i, t) \geq -\mathbf{Z}(i, t)\boldsymbol{\beta} - \sum_{q-1}^{Q} \alpha(t, q)\tau(i, q)]$$
$$= \text{Prob}\left[\frac{U(i, t)}{\sigma_U(t, t)^{1/2}} \geq -\mathbf{Z}(i, t)\tilde{\boldsymbol{\beta}}(t) - \sum_{q=1}^{Q} \frac{\tilde{\alpha}(t, q)l(i, q)}{(1 - \tilde{\boldsymbol{\alpha}}(t)\tilde{\boldsymbol{\alpha}}(t)')^{1/2}}\right]$$
$$= \Phi\left[\mathbf{Z}(i, t)\tilde{\boldsymbol{\beta}}(t) + \frac{\tilde{\boldsymbol{\alpha}}(t)\mathbf{l}(i)}{(1 - \tilde{\boldsymbol{\alpha}}(t)\tilde{\boldsymbol{\alpha}}(t)')^{1/2}}\right],$$

where $l(i, q) = \tau(i, q)/\sigma_{qq}^{1/2}$ and $\mathbf{l}(i)$ is a $Q \times 1$ vector of the $l(i, q)$.

Removing the conditioning on $\mathbf{l}(i)$, which in this problem is equivalent to integrating out the $\mathbf{l}(i)$ with respect to $f(\mathbf{l})$(the product of the Q independent standardized variates) and considering the probability of a given sequence of outcomes (a given value of $\mathbf{d}(i)$) leads to the expression given in proposition 3.3. The crucial point to note is that, given values of $\mathbf{l}(i)$, the random variables $d(i, t)$, $t = 1, \ldots, T$, are independent.

Note that it is not required that the components of $\mathbf{l}$ be normally distributed, nor is it necesssary for $U(i, t)$ to be normally distributed. In principle each component of $\mathbf{l}$ and $U(i, t)$ may have functionally different (independent) distributions. The expression in the proposition assumes that the $U(i, t)$ are distributed symmetrically around zero. Symmetry can be relaxed at the cost of only minor notational inconvenience.

For a fixed T any correlation matrix $\tilde{\boldsymbol{\Sigma}}$ can be factor analyzed, provided a sufficiently large number of factors are used. Utilizing the results of Anderson and Rubin (1956), it is straightforward to develop a likelihood ratio test for the appropriate number of factors in order to specify a parsimonious approximation to the true correlation matrix.

As in the one-factor case the restriction that $\sigma_U(t, t) > 0$ can be relaxed. The analysis of this case resembles that in the one-factor case, except that in the general case up to Q of the period specific variances may be zero before problems arise with regard to special dependence among outcomes of the sort discussed at the beginning of this appendix, in which the occurrence of one event may imply (with probability one) the occurrence of another event. Intuitively, if Q or fewer of the T disturbances have no period specific variance ($\sigma_U(t, t) = 0$), the events associated with those periods (the $d(i, t)$) are generated by (linear combinations of) the Q independent components. Hence in this case no special dependence among outcomes is created.[45]

A complete discussion of identification in the general Q-factor model is beyond the scope of this chapter. Identification conditions for the $\tilde{\boldsymbol{\alpha}}(t)$, $t = 1, \ldots, T$, follow from standard theorems on factor representations of correlation matrices (Anderson and Rubin 1956). Note further, assuming $\sigma_U(1, 1) = 1$, it is possible to estimate $\sigma_U(t, t)$, $t = 2, \ldots, T$, as long as $\boldsymbol{\beta} \neq 0$. This follows from the discussion in section 3.4.

45. This conclusion holds provided that no linear dependencies exist among the column vectors of normalized factor loadings for the periods with zero-period specific variances, $\{t \mid \sigma_U(t, t) = 0\}$, and provided that the system of Q equations generated by the column vectors is indecomposable. If the system of equations is decomposable, and there are no linear dependencies among the equations, the statement in the text must be altered in an obvious way.

References

Albright, R. L., S. R. Lerman, and C. F. Manski. 1977. Report on the Development of an Estimation Program for the Multinomial Probit Model. Carnegie-Mellon University, Pittsburgh, Pa. Prepared for Federal Housing Administration.

Amemiya, T. 1975. Qualitative Response Models. *Annals of Economic and Social Measurement*. 4: 363–372.

Amemiya, T. 1978. A Note on the Estimation of a Time Dependent Markov Chain Model. Stanford University, Stanford, Calif.

Andersen, E. B. 1973. *Conditional Inference and Models for Measuring*. Mentalhygiejnisk Forsknings Institut, Copenhagen.

Anderson, T. W., and L. Goodman. 1957. Statistical Inference about Markov Chains. *Annals of Mathematical Statistics*. 28: 89–110.

Anderson, T. W., and H. Rubin. 1956. Statistical Inference in Factor Analysis. *Proceedings of the Third Berkeley Symposium on Mathematical Statistics and Probability*. 5: 111–150.

Ashford, J. R., and R. R. Sowden. 1970. Multivariate Probit Analysis. *Biometrics*. 26: 535–546.

Astrom, K. J. 1970. *Introduction to Stochastic Control Theory*. New York: Academic Press.

Balestra, P., and M. Nerlove. 1966. Pooling Cross Section and Time Series Data in the Estimation of a Dynamic Model. *Econometrica*. 34: 585–612.

Bates, G., and J. Neyman. 1951. Contributions to the Theory of Accident Proneness II: True or False Contagion. *University of California Publications in Statistics*. 1: 215–253.

Blischke, W. R. 1965. Mixtures of Discrete Distributions. In *Classical and Contagious Discrete Distributions*, ed. G. Patil. Calcutta: Statistical Publishing Society.

Boskin, M., and F. Nold. 1975. A Markov Model of Turnover in Aid to Families with Dependent Children. *Journal of Human Resources*. 10: 467–481.

Bush, R., and F. Mosteller. 1955. *Stochastic Models for Learning*. New York: Wiley.

Cave, G. 1981. The Incidence and Duration of Youth Unemployment: Human Capital Theory and Longitudinal Analysis. Ph.D. dissertation. University of Chicago.

Chaddha, R. 1965. A Case of Contagion in Binomial Distribution. In *Classical and Contagious Discrete Distribution*, ed. G. Patil. Calcutta: Statistical Publishing Society.

Coleman, J. 1964. *Models of Change and Response Uncertainty*. Englewood Cliffs, N. J.: Prentice Hall.

Cripps, T. F., and R. J. Tarling. 1974. An Analysis of the Duration of Male Unemployment in Great Britain 1932–1973. *The Economic Journal* 84: 289–316.

David, F. N. 1947. A Power Function for Tests for Randomness in a Sequence of Alternatives. *Biometrika*. 34: 335–339.

Denny, J., and S. Yakowitz. 1978. Admissible Run-Contingency Type Tests of Independence and Markov Dependence. *Journal of the American Statistical Association*. 73: 171–181.

Domencich, T., and D. McFadden. 1975. *Urban Travel Demand: A Behavioral Analysis*. Amsterdam: North Holland.

Dreyfus, S. E. 1965. *Dynamic Programming and the Calculus of Variations*. New York: Academic Press.

Dutt, J. 1976. Numerical Aspects of Multivariate Normal Probabilities in Econometric Models. *Annals of Economic and Social Measurement*. 5: 547–562.

Fase, M. G. 1971. Estimation of Lifetime Income. *Journal of the American Statical Association*. 66: 686–693.

Feller, W. 1957. *An Introduction to Probability Theory and Its Applications, vol 1*. New York: Wiley.

Feller, W. 1943. On a General Class of Contagious Distributions. *Annals of Mathematical Statistics*. 14: 389–400.

Goodman, L. 1961. Statistical Methods for the Mover-Stayer Model. *Journal of the American Statistical Association*. 56: 841–868.

Goodman, L. 1958. Simplified Runs Tests and Likelihood Ratio Tests for Markov Chains. *Biometrika*. 45: 181–197.

Granger, C. W. J., and P. Newbold. 1977. *Forecasting Economic Time Series*. New York: Academic Press.

Griliches, Z. 1967. Distributed Lags: A Survey. *Econometrica*. 35: 16–49.

Gupta, S. 1963. Probability Integrals of Multivariate Normal and Multivariate *t*. *Annals of Mathematical Statistics*. 34: 792–828.

Hatanaka, M. 1975. On the Global Identification of the Dynamic Simultaneous Equations Model with Stationary Disturbances. *International Economic Review*. 16: 545–554.

Heckman, J. 1976. Simultaneous Equations Models with Continuous and Discrete Endogenous Variables and Structural Shifts. *Studies in Nonlinear Estimation*, ed. S. Goldfeld and R. Quandt. Cambridge, Mass.: Ballinger.

Heckman, J. 1978a. Dummy Endogenous Variables in a Simultaneous Equation System. *Econometrica*. 46: 931–959.

Heckman, J. 1978b. Simple Statistical Models for Discrete Panel Data Developed and Applied to Test the Hypothesis of True State Dependence against the Hypothesis of Spurious State Dependence. *Anals de Insee*, Paris. 30-31: 227–270.

Heckman, J. 1981. Heterogeneity and State Dependence. In *Studies in Labor Markets*, ed. S. Rosen. Chicago: University of Chicago Press.

Heckman, J., and T. MaCurdy. 1980. A Dynamic Model of Female Labor Supply. *Review of Economic Studies*, in press.

Heckman, J., and R. Willis. 1975. Estimation of a Stochastic Model of Reproduction: An Econometric Approach. In *Household Production and Consumption*, ed. N. Terleckyj. National Bureau of Economic Research, Stanford, Calif.

Heckman, J., and R. Willis. 1977. A Beta Logistic Model for the Analysis of Sequential Labor Force Participation of Married Women. *Journal of Political Economy*. 85: 27–58.

Heckman, J., and B. Singer, 1980, eds. *Longitudinal Labor Market Studies; Theory, Methods and Empirical Results*. Social Science Research Council Monograph. New York: Academic Press, in press.

Hotelling, H. 1935. Demand Functions with Limited Budgets. *Econometrica*. 3: 66–78.

Johnson, N., and S. Kotz. 1972. *Distributions in Statistics; Continuous Multivariate Distributions*. New York: Wiley.

Johnson, N., and S. Kotz. 1977. *Urn Models and Their Application; An Approach to Modern Discrete Probability Theory*. New York: Wiley.

Joreskog, K., and A. Goldberger. 1975. Estimation of a Model with Multiple Indicators and Multiple Causes of a Single Latent Variable Model. *Journal of the American Statistical Association*. 70: 631–639.

Jovanovic, B. 1978. State Dependence in a Continuous Time Stochastic Model of Worker Behavior. Mimeographed. Columbia University, New York.

Karlin, S., and H. Taylor. 1975. *A First Course in Stochastic Processes*. 2nd ed. New York: Academic Press.

Koopmans, L. H. 1974. *The Spectral Analysis of Time Series*. New York: Academic Press.

Lawley, D., and A. Maxwell. 1971. *Factor Analysis as a Statistical Method*. 2nd ed. London: Buttersworths.

Layton, L. 1978. *Unemployment over the Work History*. Ph.D. dissertation. Department of Economics, Columbia University, New York.

Malinvaud, E. 1970. *Statistical Methods of Econometrics*. 2nd ed. Amsterdam: North Holland.

Mandelbrot, B. 1962. Paretian Distributions and Income Maximization. *Quarterly Journal of Economics*. 76: 57–83.

Maritz, J. 1970. *Empirical Bayes' Methods*. London: Metheun.

Massy, W. F., D. B. Montgomery, and D. G. Morrison. 1970. *Stochastic Models of Buying Behavior*. Cambridge, Mass.: The MIT Press.

Mundlak, Y. 1978. On the Pooling of Time Series and Cross Section Data. *Econometrica*. 46: 69–86.

McFadden, D. 1973. Conditional Logit Analysis of Qualitative Choice Behavior. In *Frontiers in Econometrics*, ed. P. Zarembka. New York: Academic Press.

McFadden, D. 1976. Quantal Choice Analysis: A Survey. *Annals of Economic and Social Measurement*. 5: 363–390.

Nerlove, M. 1978. Econometric Analysis of Longitudinal Data: Approaches, Problems and Prospects. *The Econometrics of Panel Data. Annals de Insee*, Paris. 30-31: 7–22.

Neyman, J., and E. Scott. 1948. Consistent Estimates Based on Partially Consistent Observations. *Econometrica*. 16: 1–32.

Phelps, E. 1972. *Inflation Policy and Unemployment Theory*. New York: Norton.

Polachek, S. 1975. Differences in Expected Post School Investment as a Determinant of Market Wage Differentials. *International Economic Review*. 16: 451–470.

Pollak, R. 1968. Conditional Demand Functions and Consumption Theory. *Quarterly Journal of Economics*. 83: 209–227.

Pollak, R. 1970. Habit Formation and Dynamic Demand Functions. *Journal of Political Economy*. 78: 745–763.

Rao, C. R. 1973. *Linear Statistical Inference and Its Applications*. 2nd ed. New York: Wiley.

Restle, F., and J. G. Greeno. 1970. *Introduction to Mathematical Psychology*. Reading, Mass.: Addison-Wesley.

Samuelson, P. 1960. Structure of Minimum Equilibrium Systems. In *Essays in Economics and Econometrics; A Volume in Honor of Harold Hotelling*, ed. R. Pfouts. Chapel Hill, N. C.: University of North Carolina Press.

Singer, B., and S. Spilerman. 1976. Some Methodological Issues in the Analysis of Longitudinal Surveys. *Annals of Economic and Social Measurement*. 5: 447–474.

Wilson, R. D. 1977. Generalized and Embedded Versions of Heterogeneous Stochastic Models of Consumer Choice Behavior: An Empirical Test and Statistical Evaluation in a Dynamic Store Selection Context. Ph.D. dissertation. University of Iowa, Iowa City.

4 The Incidental Parameters Problem and the Problem of Initial Conditions in Estimating a Discrete Time-Discrete Data Stochastic Process

James J. Heckman

4.1 Introduction

This chapter considers two problems: the first, and most important, is the problem of inital conditions that arises in estimating a discrete time-discrete data stochastic process; the second problem considered is the problem of incidental parameters that besets one potentially attractive solution to the problem of initial conditions.

Before parameters generating a stochastic process with dependence among time-ordered outcomes can be estimated, the process must somehow be initialized. In much applied work in the social sciences, this problem is treated casually. Two assumptions are typically invoked: either the initial conditions or relevant presample history of the process are assumed to be truly exogenous variables, or else the process is assumed to be in equilibrium.

The first assumption is valid only if the disturbances that generate the process are serially independent or if a genuinely new process is fortuitously observed at the beginning of the sample at the analyst's disposal. If the process has been in operation prior to the time it is sampled, and if the disturbances of the model are serially dependent, the initial conditions are not exogenous variables. Treating them as exogenous variables results in inconsistent parameter estimates. The confluence of serial dependence in unobservables and state dependence in the process results in an important and neglected problem that is considered in this chapter.

The second assumption—initial stationarity of the process—does lead to a tractable solution to the problem. But this assumption is unattractive in many applications, especially when time-varying exogenous variables drive the stochastic process.

This chapter proposes exact and approximate solutions to the problem of initial conditions that arises in the class of discrete-time, discrete-data stochastic processes considered in chapter 3. Limited Monte Carlo

This research was supported by NSF Grant SOC77-27136 and Grant 10-P-90748/9-01 from the Social Security Administration. I have benefited from discussions with Tom MaCurdy and Guilherme Sedlacek on the material in this chapter. I am indebted to Gary Chamberlain for the reference to the dissertation of E. B. Andersen which guided some of my thinking and to my colleague R. D. Bock for other valuable references cited. Ralph Shnelvar and Guilherme Sedlacek gave invaluable assistance in programming the Monte Carlo studies reported here. I am solely responsible for any errors.

evidence is presented on the performance of certain estimators that are simple to use.

One potentially attractive solution to the problem of initial conditions that does not require a stationarity assumption is based on the fixed effect probit estimator proposed in chapter 3, section 3.6. However, this solution gives rise to another problem also discussed in this chapter: the problem of incidental parameters first considered by Neyman and Scott (1948).

For any panel of finite length estimators of individual fixed effects are necessarily inconsistent. As Neyman and Scott have demonstrated, the inconsistency in estimating fixed effects does not necessarily give rise to inconsistency for estimators of the structural parameters of interest, provided that estimators for these parameters can be derived that do not depend on the incidental parameters (e.g., first difference estimators in linear regression). However, it is not always possible to derive such estimators, and in such a case the inconsistency in the estimator for the fixed effect is transmitted to the estimator for the structural parameters. In particular the fixed effect probit estimator suffers from this defect.

All empirical samples are of finite size. All estimators based on necessarily finite samples are inconsistent. The issue here, as always, is whether or not the asymptotic theory provides a good guide in practical work.

In this chapter a limited set of Monte Carlo sampling experiments is conducted as a first step toward evaluating the properties of the fixed effect estimator. Two main conclusions emerge from these experiments. First, for a panel of length eight the inconsistency for the fixed effect estimator is found to be small for a multivariate probit model with strictly exogenous variables. This conclusion is in general agreement with results from a set of Monte Carlo experiments for a fixed effect logit model performed by Wright and Douglas (1976). Second, for a panel of length eight the inconsistency for the fixed effect estimator is found to be disturbingly large for a multivariate probit model with fixed effect that generates a discrete data first-order Markov process.

Additional limited Monte Carlo evidence is presented on the performance of certain alternative simple approximate procedures for the solution of the problem of initial conditions that do not rely on the fixed effect probit model. These procedures are found to produce more attractive estimates than those derived from the multivariate probit model with fixed effect.

This chapter is in four sections. In sections 4.2 and 4.3 the problem of initial conditions and some solutions to it are discussed in the specific context of a first-order Markov model generated from the latent variable models presented in chapter 3. In sections 4.4 and 4.5 results from some limited Monte Carlo sampling experiments are presented. The chapter concludes with a brief summary.

4.2 The Problem of Initial Conditions and Some Formal Solutions

In order to focus the discussion on the essential aspects of the problem of initial conditions and its solution, consider the estimation of a discrete data first-order Markov process generated as a special case of the general model presented in chapter 3. For present purposes few new points arise in a discussion of the general model, and an analysis of the Markov model, which is widely used in applied work, is of interest in its own right. For simplicity exogenous variables are initially assumed to be absent, and it is further assumed that the disturbance that generates the process has a components of variance structure.

The process is defined by dichotomization of latent variable $Y(i, t)$:

$$\begin{aligned}
&Y(i,t) = \beta_0 + \gamma d(i,t-1) + \varepsilon(i,t), \quad i = 1, \ldots, I, t = 1, \ldots, T,\\
&Y(i,t) \geq 0 \quad \text{iff } d(i,t) = 1,\\
&Y(i,t) < 0 \quad \text{iff } d(i,t) = 0,\\
&\varepsilon(i,t) = \tau(i) + U(i,t),
\end{aligned} \tag{4.1}$$

where

$$\begin{aligned}
E(U(i,t)) = 0 = E(\tau(i)), E(\tau(i)^2) = \sigma_\tau^2,\\
E(U(i,t)^2) = \sigma_U^2 = 1, E(U(i,t)U(i',t'')) = 0, t \neq t'',\\
E(\tau(i)U(i',t'')) = 0, \text{for all } i, t', \text{and } t'',\\
d(i, 0) = \text{a fixed nonstochastic constant for individual } i.
\end{aligned}$$

Assuming that $U(i, t)$ is normally distributed, an inessential assumption in the present context, the transition probability for individual i at time t given $\tau(i)$ is

$$\begin{aligned}
&\text{Prob}[d(i,t) \mid d(i,t-1), \tau(i)]\\
&\qquad = \Phi\{[\beta_0 + \gamma d(i,t-1) + \tau(i)]\cdot[2d(i,t) - 1]\},
\end{aligned} \tag{4.2}$$

where $\mathbf{\Phi}$ is the unit normal cumulative distribution function.

The marginal probability of $d(i, J)$, $T \geq J$ given $\tau(i)$ is

$$P[d(i,J) \mid \tau(i)] = \left(\sum_{d(i,J-1)=0}^{1} \Phi\{[\beta_0 + \gamma d(i,J-1) + \tau(i)][2d(i,J)-1]\} \right) \cdot \left(\sum_{d(i,J-2)=0}^{1} \Phi([\beta_0 + \gamma d(i,J-2) + \tau(i)][2d(i,J-1)-1]\} \right) \cdots \left(\sum_{d(i,1)=0}^{1} \Phi\{[\beta_0 + \gamma d(i,0) + \tau(i)][2d(i,1)-1]\} \right). \tag{4.3}$$

In other words, it is the sum of the probabilities of all possible sequences of events prior to J that leads to a specific value for $d(i, J)$.

The process is ergodic for bounded γ, β_0, and $\tau(i)$. The limiting marginal probability for the state $d(i, t) = 1$ for all t (assuming an infinite past) is

$$\Pi_1(\tau(i)) = \frac{\Phi(\beta_0 + \tau(i))}{1 - \Phi(\beta_0 + \gamma + \tau(i)) + \Phi(\beta_0 + \tau(i))}, \tag{4.4}$$

and the limiting probability for state 0 is $\Pi_0(\tau(i)) = 1 - \Pi_1(\tau(i))$.[1] Π_1 and Π_0 are the equilibrium population proportions in state 1 and state 0, respectively. Note that, if the transition probabilities are of the probit functional form, the limiting probabilities are not of that form.

Further, if the process is in equilibrium,

$$P[d(i,J) \mid \tau(i)] = \Pi_1(\tau(i))^{d(i,J)} \Pi_0(\tau(i))^{1-d(i,J)},$$

so that it is possible to write a closed form expression for the probability.

The likelihood function for a sample of T observations per person, given nonstochastic initial condition $d(i, 0)$, is

$$\mathscr{L} = \prod_{i=1}^{I} \int_{-\infty}^{\infty} \prod_{t=1}^{T} \Phi\{[\beta_0 + \gamma d(i,t-1) + \tau][2d(i,t)-1]\} f(\tau) d\tau, \tag{4.5}$$

where $f(\tau)$ is the population density of τ. It is not necessary to assume that τ is normally distributed, although it is convenient to do so, and for that reason this assumption is maintained for the rest of the chapter.

1. The equilibrium probabilities are obtained by solving the equation for equilibrium $\Pi_1(\tau(i)) = \Phi(\beta_0 + \gamma + \tau(i))\Pi_1(\tau(i)) + \Phi(\beta_0 + \tau(i))\Pi_0(\tau(i))$ and using the fact that $\Pi_0(\tau(i)) = 1 - \Pi_1(\tau(i))$; see, e.g., Karlin and Taylor (1975).

Maximum likelihood estimators of β_0, γ, and the variance of τ are consistent if $T \to \infty$ and $I \to \infty$ or just $I \to \infty$. If the $\tau(i)$ are treated as parameters rather than integrated out, maximum likelihood estimators of β_0, γ, and $\tau(i)$ are consistent as $T \to \infty$, whether or not I is fixed or tends to infinity.

Thus far it has been assumed that the analyst has access to the entire history of the process. Suppose, however, that the analyst only has access to the last $T - J$ observations on the process, so that he knows $d(i, t')$, $t' = J, \ldots, T$. In this case the initial state for individual i, $d(i, J)$, is not fixed or exogenous. It is determined by the process generating the panel sample. Unless $f(\tau)$ is degenerate, random variable $d(i, J)$ is not exogenous and is in fact stochastically dependent on τ.[2] This gives rise to the problem of initial conditions.

The sample conditional likelihood function for $d(i, T), \ldots, d(i, J + 1)$ given $d(i, J)$ is

$$\mathscr{L} = \prod_{i=1}^{I} \left[\left[\int_{-\infty}^{\infty} \prod_{t=J+1}^{T} \Phi\{[\beta_0 + \gamma d(i,t-1) + \tau][2d(i,t) - 1]\} \cdot P[d(i,J) \mid \tau] f(\tau) d\tau \right] \Big/ \int_{-\infty}^{\infty} P[d(i,J) \mid \tau] f(\tau) d\tau \right], \tag{4.6}$$

where the term inside the large brackets is the conditional probability of $d(i, T), \ldots, d(i, J + 1)$ given $d(i, J)$ for observation i. The sample likelihood for $d(i, T), \ldots, d(i, J)$ is

$$\mathscr{L} = \prod_{i=1}^{I} \int_{-\infty}^{\infty} \prod_{t=J+1}^{T} \Phi\{[\beta_0 + \gamma d(i,t-1) + \tau][2d(i,t) - 1]\} \cdot P[d(i,J) \mid \tau] f(\tau) d\tau. \tag{4.7}$$

2. In the case of a degenerate $f(\tau)$ distribution, maximum likelihood estimators of the parameters of the model are consistent. Amemiya (1978) proves this for a logit first-order Markov case, and his proofs carry over fully to the probit case considered in this chapter. For a discussion about estimating a Markov model without serially dependent unobservable variables, see Anderson and Goodman (1957) and Anderson (1976).

Maximizing either the conditional likelihood function (4.6) or the unconditional likelihood function (4.7) with respect to parameters β_0, γ, and σ_τ^2 generates consistent parameter estimators that are asymptotically normally distributed if $I \to \infty$ and $T \to \infty$ or just $I \to \infty$ (provided $T \geq 2$). Recall from equation (4.3) that $P[d(i, J) \mid \tau]$ depends on β_0, γ, and $d(i, 0)$.

Unless $f(\tau)$ is degenerate, so that there is no serial dependence in the disturbance of the model, maximizing the likelihood function treats $d(i, J)$ as a fixed nonstochastic constant, that is, the function

$$\mathscr{L} = \prod_{i=1}^{I} \int_{-\infty}^{\infty} \prod_{t=J+1}^{T} \Phi\{[\beta_0 + \gamma d(i, t-1) + \tau][2d(i, t) - 1]\} f(\tau) d\tau \tag{4.8}$$

leads to inconsistent estimators for β_0, γ, and σ_τ^2.[3] Intuitively this is so because $d(i, J)$ is stochastically dependent on τ.

Maximizing likelihood (4.6) or (4.7) is a computationally forbidding task, even in the case where initial stationarity of the process can be assumed, so that

$$P[d(i, J) \mid \tau(i)] = \Pi_2\,(\tau(i))^{d(i, J)}\,\Pi_0\,(\tau(i))^{1-d(i, J)}.$$

Further, without the assumption of stationarity it is necessary to determine $d(i, 0)$, and this information is hard to come by, although in certain contexts it is plausible to assume a specific value for this variable. These difficulties become more pronounced when exogenous variables are added to the model, so that β_0 is replaced by $\mathbf{Z}(i, t)\boldsymbol{\beta}$, where the $\mathbf{Z}(i, t)$, $i = 1, \ldots, I$, $t = 1, \ldots, T$, are bounded exogenous variables. In this case two additional problems arise.

First, it is generally untenable to assume stationarity for the marginal probabilities $P[d(i, t) \mid \tau(i)]$, $t = 1, \ldots, T$, without stringent additional restrictions on the process generating the exogenous variables, such as an assumption that the exogenous variables are generated by a stationary stochastic process—an assumption that excludes time and age trends. Second, the analyst typically will not know the values of the relevant exogenous variables in the presample period $t = 1, \ldots, J - 1$. (If these values are known, they may be substituted into the expression for $P[d(i, t) \mid \tau(i)]$ given in (4.3), replacing β_0 by $\mathbf{Z}(i, t)\boldsymbol{\beta}$.)

3. The proof of this assertion is straightforward and amounts to showing that the expectations of the partials of the log likelihood (equation 4.8) with respect to the structural parameters do not vanish at the true parameter value.

If the presample exogenous variables are not available to the analyst, in principle the parameters of the distribution of the missing data can be estimated, provided that such a distribution exists. This procedure is a straightforward application of the work of Kiefer and Wolfowitz (1956). Thus, if the joint distribution of the presample values of $\mathbf{Z}(i, t)$, $t = 1, \ldots, J-1$, is a finite parameter distribution $g[\mathbf{Z}(1), \ldots, \mathbf{Z}(J-1)]$, and $P^*[d(i, J) \mid \tau(i), \mathbf{Z}(1), \ldots, \mathbf{Z}(J)]$ is defined as the marginal probability of $d(i, J)$ conditional on $\mathbf{Z}(i, t)$, $t = 1, \ldots, J$, and $\tau(i)$ (obtained by substituting $\mathbf{Z}(i, t)\boldsymbol{\beta}$ for β_0 in equation 4.3), one can define

$$\begin{aligned} P[d(i, J) \mid \tau(i), \mathbf{Z}(J)] \\ &= \int \ldots \int P^*[d(i, J) \mid \tau(i), \mathbf{Z}(1), \ldots, \mathbf{Z}(J)] \\ &\cdot g[\mathbf{Z}(1), \ldots, \mathbf{Z}(J-1)] d\mathbf{Z}(1), \ldots, d\mathbf{Z}(J-1), \end{aligned}$$

and with this modification likelihood functions (4.6) and (4.7) remain valid. Those likelihood functions, suitably modified, can be maximized with respect to the structural parameters of the g distribution.[4] Note that in general due to the fact that the regressors enter $P^*[d(i, J) \mid \tau(i), \mathbf{Z}(1), \ldots, \mathbf{Z}(J)]$ in a nonlinear fashion, it is not correct to use estimated sample means to replace the missing values of the exogenous variables.

This procedure is not as complicated as it appears to be. If the analyst has access to other data from which it is possible to estimate g consistently, he can use the estimated distribution to form $P[d(i, J) \mid \tau(i), \mathbf{Z}(1), \ldots, \mathbf{Z}(J)]$ for each set of values of β, γ, and $\tau(i)$. Therefore it is not necessary to estimate the parameters of the g distribution simultaneously with the structural parameters of interest.

4.3 Simpler Solutions and the Problem of Incidental Parameters

The preceding section presents the problem of initial conditions and sketches some formal solutions to it. The solutions presented there are somewhat computationally forbidding. In this section some alternative, simply computed estimators are considered.

Following a suggestion made by Mundlak (1978) for a linear regression model, it is possible to estimate a model with a components of variance structure conditional on error component $\tau(i)$ and to estimate the $\tau(i)$, $i = 1, \ldots, I$. The advantage of this approach is especially clear in the

4. Kiefer and Wolfowitz (1956) also consider a case of nonparametric estimation of the g function.

context of estimating conditional likelihood function (4.6). Treating $\tau(i)$ as a parameter, the conditional likelihood function for $d(i, T), \ldots, d(i, J+1)$ given $d(i, J)$ is

$$\mathscr{L} = \prod_{i=1}^{I} \prod_{t=J+1}^{T} \frac{\Phi\{[\beta_0 + \gamma d(i,t-1) + \tau(i)][2d(i,t)-1]\} P(d(i,J) \mid \tau(i))}{P(d(i,J) \mid \tau(i))}$$

$$\mathscr{L} = \prod_{i=1}^{I} \prod_{t=J+1}^{T} \Phi\{[\beta_0 + \gamma d(i,t-1) + \tau(i)][2d(i,t)-1]\}. \qquad (4.9)$$

This model is the discrete data analogue of the linear regression model with fixed effects, and it is very easy to compute.[5] Maximizing function (4.9) with respect to $\tau(i), i = 1, \ldots, I, \beta_0$, and γ, as $T \to \infty$, these parameters are consistently estimated.[6] For further discussion of this model see chapter 3, section 3.6.

The principal advantage of this procedure is that presample information about the process is not required to estimate the structural parameters. In a model with exogenous variables, the analyst can avoid estimating the distribution of missing data and computing the marginal probability $P[d(i, J) \mid \tau(i)]$. Another advantage of this procedure is that it is not necessary to assume an arbitrary distribution of the τ to estimate the model.[7]

There are two problems with the fixed effect model.[8] First, for any observation i that does not change state over the sample period the estimated fixed effect is $\pm\infty$. A fixed effect can be chosen that perfectly explains the data for such observations. For those observations for which $\Sigma d(i, t) = T - J$, $\tau(i)$ is estimated to be ∞. For those observations for which $\Sigma d(i, t) = 0$, $\tau(i)$ is estimated to be $-\infty$. The effective sample for estimating parameters is the subsample of individuals who change state. While this may be intuitively displeasing, because it apparently manufac-

5. A copy of a computer program that computes this model is available at cost.

6. Note that β_0 may be absorbed into the estimated fixed effects and recovered by invoking the requirement that the mean of the fixed effects is zero.

7. As discussed in note 3, Kiefer and Wolfowitz (1956) suggest nonparametric estimation of the density of τ. In most work in econometrics arbitrary parametric schemes are imposed. Estimating the fixed effect permits one to estimate the density of τ. This procedure is not the one proposed by Kiefer and Wolfowitz.

8. A third disadvantage is that for large $T (> 3)$. the fixed effect estimator is not a conditional version of a model with arbitrary serial correlation in the disturbances. An assumption of a components of variance error structure is required to justify the method.

tures a form of small sample selection bias, as $T \to \infty$ this problem becomes unimportant.

Second, for fixed T, estimates of structural coefficients are inconsistent. This conclusion follows from the analyses of Neyman and Scott (1948) and Andersen (1973, pp. 68–78). Andersen explicitly considers a fixed effect logit model. The inconsistency of the maximum likelihood estimator for the structural parameters arises for the following reason. Estimators of $\tau(i)$ are necessarily inconsistent. Since the roots of the likelihood equation involve the joint solution of structural parameters and fixed effects, the inconsistency of the estimator for the fixed effects is transmitted to the estimator for the structural parameters.[9]

For these reasons the fixed effect scheme appears to be unattractive. However, the analysis of Andersen's model (as it applies to the multivariate

9. Using Andersen's example (1973, pp. 68–71), it is possible to examine these difficulties more closely. Andersen assumes $\gamma = 0$ and lets $T = 2$. Define a dummy $\eta(t)$ that equals zero in period 1 and one in period 2. The likelihood function is thus

$$\mathscr{L} = \prod_{i=1}^{I} \prod_{t=1}^{2} \Phi\{[\tau(i) + \beta\eta(t)](2d(i, t) - 1)\}.$$

Maximize the logarithm of $\mathscr{L}$ with respect to $\tau(i)$ and β. Then for observation i for which $d(i, 1) = 1$ and $d(i, 2) = 1$, $\tau(i) \to \infty$. For observation i for which $d(i, 1) = 0$ and $d(i, 2) = 0$, $\tau(i) \to -\infty$. For the other observations the likelihood function may be concentrated in the $\tau(i)$ and then maximized with respect to β.

From the symmetry of the derivative of Φ it is obvious that $\tau(i) = -\beta/2$. (This is true for any symmetric Φ, not just the probit. Thus Andersen's analysis for the logit yields the same result.)

Substituting this expression into the likelihood function, it is straightforward to prove that if $\sigma_\tau^2 \to 0$, plim $\hat{\beta} = 2\beta$. If $\sigma_\tau^2 \to \infty$, plim $|\hat{\beta}| \to \infty$. The proof in the normal case for the first result closely parallels Andersen's proof. The second proof is trivial and hence is not given here.

Andersen (1973) demonstrates that conditioning the likelihood function on the event $\Sigma d(i, t) = 1$ eliminates the fixed effect in a logit model, so that conditional maximum likelihood estimators are consistent. (This result is originally due to Rasch 1960. See also the analysis of Haberman 1977.) This result is specific to a logit model. In a probit model such conditioning does not eliminate the fixed effect. In fact for the probit model the conditional maximum likelihood estimator generates unbounded estimators of the fixed effect for certain subsets of the observations.

Thus while conditional likelihood methods are helpful in a logit model, they are not helpful in a probit model, or in a general qualitative choice model. Conditioning the likelihood function in a logit model eliminates the fixed effect. First differences in a linear probability model eliminate the fixed effect, and thus the natural estimator for that model is linear regression. At this point the transformation of the probit function that eliminates the fixed effect is not known. The key point for the present discussion is that the lesson to extract from the binary logit case is *not* that conditional likelihood methods are a general approach in fixed effect models but that conditional likelihood methods in that case happen to be a convenient representation (or transformation) that eliminates fixed effects.

probit model with fixed effect) gives no guide to the performance of the fixed effect estimator when T is as large as 8, a feasible sample size in many data sets currently available. Recent Monte Carlo evidence by Wright and Douglas (1976) for the fixed effect Rasch-Andersen logit model finds that for T as small as 20 a fixed effect logit estimator performs as well as alternative consistent estimators.[10]

In Monte Carlo results reported in section 4.4 the fixed effect probit estimator performs well for T as small as 8 as long as no lagged values of dummy variables are included in the model. When lagged values are included, as is required to generate a first-order Markov model for discrete data, the fixed effect estimator performs badly.

In view of these results it is of interest to consider alternative solutions to the problem of initial conditions. An easily computed approximate solution to the problem of initial conditions is considered in the Monte Carlo experiments. This solution, which turns out to be relatively successful, approximates the reduced form marginal probability of the initial state in the sample by a probit function which has as its argument as much presample information on the exogenous variables as is available. The disturbance in the index variable that generates the reduced form probit function is left freely correlated with the structural errors over the sample period. This estimator works well in the Monte Carlo experiments, even though the probability of the initial state is not a probit function.

Specifically the following procedure is proposed and examined:

1. Approximate the probability of $d(i, J)$, the initial state in the sample, by a probit with index function

$$Y(i, J) = \sum_{l=0}^{J} D(l)[\mathbf{Z}(i,l)] + \mu(i,J)$$

$$Y(i,J) \geq 0 \text{ iff } d(i,J) = 1, \; Y(i,J) < 0 \quad \text{otherwise},$$

where $D(l)[\mathbf{Z}(i, l)]$ is a general function of the $\mathbf{Z}(i, l)$, $l = 0, \ldots, J$, and $\mu(i, J)$ is assumed to be normally distributed with mean zero.[11]

2. Permit $\mu(i, J)$ to be freely correlated with $\varepsilon(i, t)$, $t = J + 1, \ldots, T$.

3. Estimate the model by the method of maximum likelihood without

10. Their alternative consistent estimator is the conditional maximum likelihood estimator proposed by Rasch and Andersen and mentioned in the preceding note.

11. In practice polynomials in $\mathbf{Z}(i, l)$ are used to form the $D(l)$ functions.

imposing any restrictions between the parameters of the structural system and the parameters of the approximate reduced form probability function for the initial state of the sample.

Assuming that the model is exact as $I \to \infty$, and for fixed T, the maximum likelihood estimator is consistent.

4.4 Some Monte Carlo Evidence

This section presents results from a limited set of Monte Carlo experiments. In each experiment with fixed effect estimators, 25 samples of 100 individuals ($I = 100$) are selected for 8 periods ($T = 8$). Results are presented for both a probit model with only exogenous explanatory variables and the first-order Markov model. The exogenous variables are assumed to follow a Nerlove process (Nerlove 1971):

$$Z(i,t) = 0.1t + 0.5Z(i,t-1) + \omega(i,t),$$

where $\omega(i, t)$ is a uniform random variable with mean zero and range $-1/2$ to $1/2$. This process well approximates the age-trended variables found in many microdata panel sets, especially in labor market analysis.

Results for the multivariate probit model with fixed effect but without lagged dummy variables are presented in table 4.1. Maximum likelihood fixed effect estimates are presented in the first three rows. The model generating the data is given at the bottom of the table. Samples are generated from a normal random number generator. The variance of $U(i, t)$ is set at one. The variance of the fixed effect, σ_τ^2, is changed for different experiments. For $\beta = 0.1$ the fixed effect estimator does well. The estimated value (denoted $\hat{\beta}$) comes very close to the true value. For $\beta = -1$, or $\beta = 1$, the estimator does not perform as well, but the bias is never more than 10 percent and is always toward zero. As the variance in the fixed effects decreases, so does the bias.[12]

These results are consistent with the findings of Wright and Douglas (1976) who use Monte Carlo methods to investigate the performance of the fixed effect logit estimator for the Rasch-Andersen model. In a study with panels of length $T = 20$ per person, they find that the fixed effect logit

12. One unusual feature of these experiments is the consistent finding of a bias toward zero when a bias occurs. Andersen's two-period analysis would suggest an upward bias. The exogenous variables in the model investigated in the text have a much more complex character than the simple treatment effect variable used by Andersen.

estimator is virtually unbiased and its distribution is well described by a limiting normal distribution with variance-covariance matrix based on the estimated information matrix.

To judge the importance of the bias, one requires a benchmark. The benchmark selected in this chapter is a random effect estimator that integrates out the fixed effect. This is a multivariate probit model with random effect as presented in Heckman and Willis (1975) or chapter 3, section 3.5.

For each set of parameter values 25 samples with 100 observations of 3 periods are generated. The random effect estimator with $T = 3$ costs roughly the same to compute as the fixed effect estimator with $T = 8$. In terms of computational cost, the two estimators are equivalent.

The results with this model are presented in the final two rows of table 4.1. For a variance of $\sigma_\tau^2 = 3$, the random effect estimator displays more bias than the fixed effect estimator. For $\sigma_\tau^2 = 1$, the two estimators do about equally well. These experiments suggest that there is no clear ranking of the two estimators.

Test statistics for the random effect estimator (not given in the table) based on the estimated information matrix lead to rejection of the false null hypothesis that $\beta = 0$ far more often than test statistics based on the information matrix for the fixed effect estimator. On the basis of this limited evidence, if the estimators are to be used to make inference, the random effect estimator seems preferable.

Next consider some Monte Carlo experiments with the fixed effect estimator for a first-order Markov process. The results from these experiments are displayed in the first part of table 4.2. The same Nerlove process that generates the exogenous variables used in the preceding experiments is used in these experiments. The process operates for 25 periods before samples of 8 periods for each of the 100 individuals used in the 25 samples for each parameter set are selected.

The fixed effect probit estimator performs badly. The bias is greatest for large values of the variance in person effects (σ_τ^2) and when there are no exogenous variables in the model. But even the smallest bias reported in the table is still bad. The t statistics based on the estimated information matrix result in misleading inferences. From experimental results not reported in the table, one does not reject the false null hypothesis of $\gamma = \beta = 0$ in the vast majority of samples.

Note that estimates of γ are downward biased and estimates of β are upward biased. These results are very similar to Nerlove's Monte Carlo

Table 4.1
Monte Carlo results for models without lagged variables[a]

Values of $\hat{\beta}$ for the fixed effect probit model[b]

	$\beta = 1$	$\beta = -0.1$	$\beta = -1$
$\sigma_\tau^2 = 3$	0.90	−0.10	−0.94
$\sigma_\tau^2 = 1$	0.91	−0.09	−0.95
$\sigma_\tau^2 = 0.5$	0.93	−0.10	−0.96

Values of $\hat{\beta}$ for the random effect probit model[c]

	$\beta = 1$	$\beta = -1$
$\sigma_\tau^2 = 3$	1.15	−0.85
$\sigma_\tau^2 = 1$	1.04	−0.92

[a]The model generating the data is
$Y(i,t) = Z(i,t)\beta + \tau(i) + U(i,t)$,
$i = 1, \ldots, I$; if $Y(i,t) \geq 0$, $d(i,t) = 1$, $t = 1, \ldots, T$, otherwise, $d(i,t) = 0$.
$Z(i,t)$ is generated by the Nerlove (1971) process,
$Z(i,t) = 0.1t + 0.5Z(i,t-1) + \omega(i,t)$
$\omega(i,t) \sim U[-0.5, 0.5]$.
[b]$I = 100$, $T = 8$.
[c]$I = 100$, $T = 3$.

results in a linear equation model analogue of the Markov model (Nerlove 1971). Fixed effect estimators generate a downward-biased estimate of the coefficient of the lagged value of the endogenous variable in that model, just as they do for the state dependence coefficient in the Markov model.

In view of the poor performance of the fixed effect estimator as a solution to the problem of initial conditions, it is of some interest to examine the performance of some alternative estimators. The middle section of table 4.2 reports the results of a limited Monte Carlo study of the approximate random effect estimator proposed in section 4.3. The samples used to generate these estimates are the first three periods of the data utilized in the samples of the Monte Carlo study of the Markov model estimated by the fixed effect probit scheme. The first-period marginal probability is assumed to depend solely on first-period values of the exogenous variables. The proposed approximate random effect estimator discussed in section 4.3 does somewhat better than the fixed effect estimator. The $\hat{\gamma}$ consistently overstates the true γ and $\hat{\beta}$ understates the true β. As σ_τ^2 declines, so does the bias in the estimator. In results not reported here, t statistics are much more reliable in this model than in the fixed effect probit model since they lead to correct inference in a greater proportion of the samples.[13]

As in the discussion of the fixed effect probit model with strictly exogenous explanatory variables, it is natural to seek a suitable benchmark with which to compare the performance of the proposed estimators. One benchmark that provides an ideal case is a model with known nonstochastic initial conditions. Twenty-five samples with 100 observations of 3 periods are generated for each set of parameter values. Random effect maximum likelihood estimates for this model are presented in the final section of table 4.2. While this estimator is less biased than the approximate estimator, it is nonetheless biased. The difference between the results for the approximate random effect estimator for the case of stochastic initial conditions and the results for the estimator with known initial conditions

13. Another ad hoc estimator was tried. This estimator fits a linear probability function to predict the marginal probability of the first sample period state. The predicted value is substituted in place of the actual value, and the γ parameter associated with the state in the first period is permitted to be distinct from the γ parameter for the sample transition. In terms of bias the performance of this estimator is intermediate between the fixed effect estimator and the proposed approximate random effect estimator given in the text, even when several years of presample data on the exogenous variables are used to predict the probability of the first sample period state. The estimator works well for the special problem of testing the null hypothesis of no state dependence ($\gamma = 0$).

Table 4.2
Monte Carlo results for models with lagged variables[a]

Values of $\hat{\gamma}$ and $\hat{\beta}$ for the fixed effects estimator[b]

		$\sigma_\tau^2 = 3$			$\sigma_\tau^2 = 1$		
		$\beta = -0.1$	$\beta = 1$	$\beta = 0$	$\beta = -0.1$	$\beta = 1$	$\beta = 0$
$\gamma = 0.5$	$\hat{\gamma}$	0.14	0.19	0.03	na[d]	0.25	0.17
	$\hat{\beta}$	−0.07	1.21	—	na[d]	1.17	—
$\gamma = 0.1$	$\hat{\gamma}$	−0.34	−0.21	−0.04	−0.28	−0.15	−0.01
	$\hat{\beta}$	−0.06	1.14	—	−0.08	1.12	—

Values of $\hat{\gamma}$ and $\hat{\beta}$ for the proposed approximate random effect estimation[c]

		$\sigma_\tau^2 = 3$			$\sigma_\tau^2 = 1$		
		$\beta = -0.1$	$\beta = 1$	$\beta = 0$	$\beta = -0.1$	$\beta = 1$	$\beta = 0$
$\gamma = 0.5$	$\hat{\gamma}$	0.63	0.60	0.70	na[d]	0.54	0.62
	$\hat{\beta}$	−0.131	0.91	—	na[d]	0.93	—
$\gamma = 0.1$	$\hat{\gamma}$	0.14	0.13	0.17	0.11	0.11	0.13
	$\hat{\beta}$	−0.12	0.92	—	−0.12	0.95	—

Values of $\hat{\gamma}$ and $\hat{\beta}$ for the random effect estimator with known nonstochastic initial conditions[c]

		$\sigma_\tau^2 = 3$		
		$\beta = -0.1$	$\beta = 1$	$\beta = 0$
$\gamma = 0.5$	$\hat{\gamma}$	na[d]	0.57	na[d]
	$\hat{\beta}$	na[d]	0.94	—
$\gamma = 0.1$	$\hat{\gamma}$	0.13	0.12	0.14
	$\hat{\beta}$	−0.11	1.10	—

[a]The model generating the data is
$Y(i,t) = Z(i,t)\beta + \gamma d(i,t-1) + \tau(i) + U(i,t)$
$Y(i,t) \geq 0 \Leftrightarrow d(i,t) = 1$ and $Y(i,t) = 0 \Leftrightarrow d(i,t) = 0$.
The process operates 25 periods before samples are generated. $Z(i,t)$ is generated by the Nerlove proces (see table 4.1).
[b]$I = 100,\ T = 8$.
[c]$I = 100,\ T = 3$.
[d]Data are not available because the model was not estimated.

indicates that the approximate estimator is not badly biased relative to an ideal alternative.

There is one disquieting feature in the results presented in table 4.2. All of the maximum likelihood estimators exhibit considerable bias. This point deserves much further examination in view of the increasingly widespread use of maximum likelihood methods for the analysis of discrete data models.

4.5 Conclusions

This chapter has examined the problem of initial conditions that arises in estimating a discrete time-discrete data stochastic process when serially correlated unobservable variables generate the process. The analysis has been confined to a first-order Markov process, although the issues discussed here apply to the general class of models with structural state dependence considered in chapter 3. Exact and approximate solutions are proposed, and Monte Carlo evidence is presented on the performance of certain simple estimators likely to be used in applied work.

One solution based on a fixed effect probit model is simple to compute and hence is attractive. However, a limited set of Monte Carlo experiments reveals that the fixed effect probit model performs badly in panels of length eight when lagged dummy variables are included as explanatory variables, as is required to generate the general stochastic process proposed in chapter 3. When the explanatory variables of the model are all strictly exogenous, the fixed effect probit estimator performs well.

An alternative approximate simple estimator is proposed and examined, and this estimator is found to perform well in a limited set of Monte Carlo experiments. A disquieting finding in most of the experiments is that for panels with 100 observations of 3 periods, which are large samples by current standards, the method of maximum likelihood produces biased estimators even under ideal conditions. This finding deserves much further study.

More than the usual cautionary note is required to qualify the results of the Monte Carlo experiments reported in this chapter. Only a limited set of experiments has been performed. Accordingly the Monte Carlo evidence reported here is best thought of as suggestive rather than definitive. Much further work is required and would be very desirable.

References

Amemiya, T. 1978. A Note on the Estimation of a Time Dependent Markov Chain Model. Stanford University.

Andersen, E. B. 1973. *Conditional Inference and Models for Measuring*. Copenhagen: Mentalhygiejnisk Forsknings Institut.

Anderson, T. W. 1976. Panels and Time Series Analysis: Markov Chains and Autoregressive Processes. Technical report 24. Department of Statistics, Stanford University.

Anderson, T. W., and L. Goodman. 1957. Statistical Inference about Markov Chains. *Annals of Mathematical Statistics*. 28: 89–110.

Haberman, S. 1977. Maximum Likelihood Estimates in Exponential Response Models. *The Annals of Statistics*. 5: 815–841.

Heckman, J., and R. Willis. 1975. Estimation of a Stochastic Model of Reproduction: An Econometric Approach. In *Household Production and Consumption*, ed. N. Terleckyj. National Bureau of Economic Research, New York.

Karlin, S., and H. Taylor. 1975. *A First Course in Stochastic Processes*. 2nd ed. New York: Academic Press.

Kiefer, J., and J. Wolfowitz. 1956. Consistency of the Maximum Likelihood Estimator in the Presence of Infinitely Many Incidental Parameters. *Annals of Mathematical Statistics*. 27: 887–906.

Mundlak, Y. 1978. On the Pooling of Time Series and Cross Section Data. *Econometrica*. 46: 69–86.

Nerlove, M. 1971. Further Evidence on the Estimation of Dynamic Economic Relations from a Time Series of Cross Sections. *Econometrica*. 39: 359–382.

Neyman, J., and E. Scott. 1948. Consistent Estimates Based on Partially Consistent Observations. *Econometrica*. 16: 1–32.

Rasch, G. 1960. *Probabilistic Models for Some Intelligence and Attainment Tests*. Copenhagen: Danish Institute of Educational Research.

Wright, B. D., and G. Douglas. 1976. Better Procedures for Sample-Free Item Analysis. Research memorandum 20. Statistical Laboratory, Department of Education, University of Chicago.

III STRUCTURAL DISCRETE PROBABILITY MODELS DERIVED FROM THEORIES OF CHOICE

5 Econometric Models of Probabilistic Choice

Daniel McFadden

An object can have no value unless it has utility. No one will give anything for an article unless it yield him satisfaction. Doubtless people are sometimes foolish, and buy things, as children do, to please a moment's fancy; but at least they think at the moment that there is a wish to be gratified.
—F. M. Taussig, *Principles of Economics*, 1912

5.1 Economic Man

The classical economists made the assumption of *homus economicus* virtually tautological: if an object were chosen, then it must have maximized the utility of the decision maker. By contrast, contemporary economic analysis of consumer behavior has focused on the objective market environment of economic decisions and has excluded whim and perception from any formal role in the utility maximization process.[1]

From the standpoint of the observer unmeasured psychological factors introduce a random element in economic decisions. The result is a probabilistic theory of choice which has many features in common with psychophysical models of judgment (Coombs 1964, Luce and Suppes 1965, Bock and Jones 1968, Krantz, Luce, Suppes, and Tversky 1971, Krantz 1974).

Probabilistic choice models lend themselves readily to econometric implementation, particularly for choices among discrete alternatives. This chapter develops and compares a number of these models in forms suitable for econometric applications.

This research was supported in part by the National Science Foundation, through grant SOC75-22657 to the University of California, Berkeley. Portions of this chapter were written while the author was an Irving Fisher Visiting Professor of Economics at the Cowles Foundation for Research in Economics, Yale University. An early version was presented at the Third World Congress of the Econometric Society, Toronto, Canada, 1975. The author has benefited greatly from discussions with Amos Tversky at the formative stage of this chapter and has borrowed freely from his ideas. Charles Manski and Steven Cosslett have also provided useful comments. The author retains sole responsibility for errors.

1. Also excluded in the conventional consumer analysis is consideration of procedural rationality, the question of how an organism with perceptual and computational limits makes a decision; see Simon (1978). This chapter will not take up the question of probabilistic choice theory in the presence of bounded rationality. However, we note that the distributions of demand attributed in this chapter to taste variation or errors in judgment could often be reinterpreted as a consequence of bounded rationality, and vice versa.

5.2 Discrete Choice

Many empirically important economic decisions involve choice among discrete alternatives. Examples are decisions on labor force participation, occupation, educational level, marital status, family size, residential and work location, travel mode, and brands of commodity purchases. The problem of economic discrete choice parallels the decision context in which psychophysical models have been applied successfully. On the other hand, analysis of discrete choice behavior using conventional marginalist consumer theory is quite awkward. For these reasons we concentrate on a probabilistic consumer theory for discrete choice.

An example helps to clarify the conceptual and empirical issues involved in the study of discrete choice. Consider the choice by commuters of auto or bus mode to work. For the example assume the number of commuters is fixed, so that we can concentrate on the proportion of commuters choosing bus. We expect this proportion to be a function of the relative travel times and costs of the two modes. An empirical approach to forecasting, say, the effect of transit fares on bus patronage, would be to fit a demand function to aggregate time-series data, disregarding theoretical foundations. However, a priori information on the form and structure of the demand function implied by an analysis of decision behavior may permit sharper forecasts. In particular, if the relationship between individual decisions and aggregate demand is understood, then extensive data on individual choices can be used to refine estimates of the aggregate demand function.

An approach to such problems often used by the new home economists is to assume that individual demand is the result of utility maximization by a representative consumer whose decision variable is the proportion of trips taken by bus. Since this decision variable is continuous, conventional marginal analysis applies. Market demand is pictured as the aggregate of a population of identical representative consumers, so that market demand is just individual demand writ large.[2]

While the single representative consumer model may be a useful analytic device under appropriate assumptions (see section 5.6), it provides a poor description of individual behavior. What we observe is a population split into mostly full-time auto users or full-time bus users. The effect of rising

2. See, for example, Becker and Stigler (1977), where the conceptual foundation for common tastes is advocated with scant attention to the practicalities of econometric demand analysis with limited data on consumer characteristics.

transit fares is felt primarily at the extensive margin where some individuals are switching from bus to auto. The conceptual implausibility of a model of identical consumers with fractional consumption rates is even more obvious for decisions such as level of education or family size.

These comments on the difficulty of using the concept of identical representative consumers as a basis for modeling discrete choice behavior provide the kernel of a solution for the problem. Suppose we introduce a population of consumers in which tastes vary explicitly. For example, we might consider a population of consumers with quadratic utility functions whose coefficients are distributed in the population according to some specific parametric probability distribution. Then, we can express proportions such as the share of bus commuters in our example as the probability that an individual drawn randomly from the population will have tastes such that the utility of traveling by bus exceeds that for auto. The parameters of the aggregate demand function will then be the parameters of the underlying probability distribution of taste coefficients.

The idea of taste variation in a population influencing aggregate demand behavior is an old one. Many of the classical consumer demand studies, such as Prais and Houthakker (1971), discuss this as a nuisance to be eliminated by assumption. Seminal studies by Tobin (1958), Warner (1962), and Quandt (1968) use the idea explicitly in the analysis of specific problems of discrete and limited choice. More recently the analysis of econometic models with random parameters has been motivated by the presence of unobserved variations among economic agents. The topics discussed in this chapter are a natural extension of the idea of taste variation to general questions in discrete choice analysis.

The demand behavior of populations of consumers can be analyzed at two distinct levels. At a theoretical level we can examine the general implications for the structure of aggregate demands that can be drawn from the hypothesis of a population of preference-maximizing consumers. The most basic question is whether individual preference maximization has any implications for aggregate demand structure. A related question is whether the model of individual utility maximization is identifiable from the observed distributions of demands, or whether other simpler or less restrictive models could generate the same observations. These topics are discussed in sections 5.3 through 5.8. These sections also consider sufficient conditions for an aggregate demand system to be consistent with the hypothesis of a population of preference-maximizing consumers.

At a practical level we can take as given the hypothesis of a population of preference maximizers and seek parametric demand structures suitable for econometric analysis. Sections 5.9 through 5.16 survey a number of alternative model structures and summarize their features. Sections 5.17 through 5.19 treat in more detail the estimation of a proposed model structure, the tree extreme value, or nested multinomial logit model. Appendixes give computational formulae for several of the models.

5.3 Probabilistic Consumer Theory

In sections 5.4 through 5.8 we shall first define a probabilistic choice system, describing the observable distributions of demands by a population of consumers. Second, we shall state the hypothesis of random preference maximization, which postulates that the distribution of demands in a population is the result of individual preference maximization, with preferences influenced by unobserved variables. Third, we consider the features of the observable distributions of demands that are necessary or sufficient for their consistency with the hypothesis of random preference maximization.

The development of population demand behavior parallels exactly the conventional treatment of the individual consumer, with distributions of observed demands and preferences replacing a single demand system and preference order. The usual necessary conditions for consistency of an individual demand system with preference maximization have population analogues, as does a stochastic version of the theory of revealed preference. Sufficient (integrability) conditions for an observed demand distribution to be consistent with a distribution of preferences are much less complete than the analogous treatment of individual demand.

5.4 Probabilistic Choice Systems

A probabilistic choice system (PCS) is defined formally by a vector $(\mathbf{I}, \mathbf{Z}, \xi, \mathscr{B}, \mathbf{S}, P)$, where $\mathbf{I}$ is a set indexing alternatives, $\mathbf{Z}$ is the universe of vectors of measured attributes of alternatives, $\xi : \mathbf{I} \to \mathbf{Z}$ is a mapping specifying the observed attributes of alternatives, $\mathscr{B}$ is a family of finite, nonempty choice (or budget) sets from $\mathbf{I}$, $\mathbf{S}$ is the universe of vectors of measured characteristics of individuals, and $P : \mathbf{I} \times \mathscr{B} \times \mathbf{S} \to [0, 1]$ is a choice probability.

The index set **I** is imposed by the analyst and is assumed to be external to the actual choice process. Any natural or intrinsic indexing of alternatives which may affect choice is included in the vector of measured attributes $\mathbf{z} \in \mathbf{Z}$. The universe of measured attributes **Z** will be treated here as an abstract set; in later applications it will usually be assumed to be a rectangle, or else a countable dense set, in finite-dimensional Euclidean space. The choice probability $P(i \mid \mathbf{B}, \mathbf{s})$ specifies the probability of choosing $i \in \mathbf{I}$, given that a selection must be made from the choice set $\mathbf{B} \in \mathscr{B}$ and that the decision-maker has characteristics $\mathbf{s} \in \mathbf{S}$. We use the notation $P(\mathbf{C} \mid \mathbf{B}, \mathbf{s}) = \Sigma_{i \in \mathbf{C}} P(i \mid \mathbf{B}, \mathbf{s})$. Choice probabilities are assumed to satisfy the following two conditions:

PCS **5.1:** Choice probabilities are nonnegative and sum to one, with $P(\mathbf{B} \mid \mathbf{B}, \mathbf{s}) = 1$.

PCS **5.2:** Choice probabilities depend only on the measured attributes of alternatives and individual characteristics; if $\mathbf{B} = \{i_1, \ldots, i_n\}$ and $\mathbf{B}' = \{i'_1, \ldots, i'_n\}$ have $\mathbf{z}_k = \xi(i_k) = \xi(i'_k)$ for $k = 1, \ldots, n$, then $P(i_k \mid \mathbf{B}, \mathbf{s}) = P(i'_k \mid \mathbf{B}', \mathbf{s})$.

It should be noted that a PCS is analogous to a conventional econometric specification of a demand system, with the functional specification of the demand structure and the distribution of errors combined to specify the distribution of demand.

5.5 The Random Utility Maximization Hypothesis

The hypothesis of random utility maximization (RUM) is defined formally by a vector $(\mathbf{I}, \mathbf{Z}, \xi, \mathbf{S}, \mu)$, where $(\mathbf{I}, \mathbf{Z}, \xi, \mathbf{S})$ are defined as for a PCS, and μ is a probability measure depending on $\mathbf{s} \in \mathbf{S}$, on the space of utility functions on **I**.[3] The probability μ gives the distribution of tastes in the population of individuals with characteristics $\mathbf{s} \in \mathbf{S}$.[4]

3. The space of utility functions is $\mathbf{R}^{\mathbf{I}}$, where **R** is the real line. Give $\mathbf{R}^{\mathbf{I}}$ the product topology, and define the measurable sets in $\mathbf{R}^{\mathbf{I}}$ to be the Borel sets in this topology.

4. Each utility function is a specified ordinal representation of a preference relation on **I**. One could alternately start from a probability measure η on the set of preference relations on **I**. From this random preference maximization model, choice probabilities could be deduced directly. When the preference relations are representable by utility functions, the measure η on preferences and the representation mapping induce a measure μ on the space of utility functions. Technically a preference relation on **I** is defined as a subset ρ of $\mathbf{I} \times \mathbf{I}$ containing all the pairs (i, j) with i at least as desirable as j, and having the properties that $(i, j) \in \rho$ and $(j, k) \in \rho \Rightarrow (i, k) \in \rho$. Let **T** be the set of all

Let $\mathscr{B}$ denote a family of nonempty, finite choice sets, as earlier. Let $\mu^{\mathbf{B}}$ denote the restriction of μ to $\mathbf{B} \in \mathscr{B}$.[5] The following assumptions are imposed on μ:

RUM 5.1: The restriction of μ to the space of utility values on a finite set of alternatives $\mathbf{B} \in \mathscr{B}$ depends on the measured attributes of these alternatives; if $\mathbf{B} = \{i_1, \ldots, i_n\}$ and $\mathbf{B}' = \{i'_1, \ldots, i'_n\}$ have $\mathbf{z}_k = \xi(i_k) = \xi(i'_k)$ for $k = 1, \ldots, n$, then $\mu^{\mathbf{B}} = \mu^{\mathbf{B}'}$.

RUM 5.2: The probability of "ties" is zero;

$$\mu(\{\mathbf{U} \in \mathbf{R}^{\mathbf{I}} \mid u(i_1) = u(i_2)\}, \mathbf{s}) = 0.$$

The next assumption states that choice is determined by utility maximization.

RUM 5.3: Each RUM $(\mathbf{I}, \mathbf{Z}, \xi, \mathbf{S}, \mu)$ and family of choice sets $\mathbf{B} \in \mathscr{B}$ generates a PCS $(\mathbf{I}, \mathbf{Z}, \xi, \mathscr{B}, \mathbf{S}, P)$ via the following mapping: for $\mathbf{B} = \{i_1, \ldots, i_n\} \in \mathscr{B}$, $\mathbf{s} \in \mathbf{S}$, and $k = 1, \ldots, n$,

$$P(i_k \mid \mathbf{B}, \mathbf{s}) = \mu(\{\mathbf{U} \in \mathbf{R}^{\mathbf{I}} \mid U(i_k) \geqq U(i_j) \text{ for } j = 1, \ldots, n\}, \mathbf{s}). \tag{5.1}$$

The assumption RUM 5.2 guarantees that there is almost always a unique utility-maximizing alternative, so that (5.1) is well defined, with $P(\mathbf{B} \mid \mathbf{B}, \mathbf{s}) = 1$.

When the restriction of μ to $\mathbf{B} = \{i_1, \ldots, i_n\} \in \mathscr{B}$ can be represented by a probability density $f^{\mathbf{B}}$, so that $\mu^{\mathbf{B}}(\mathbf{A}, \mathbf{s}) = \int_{\mathbf{A}} f^{\mathbf{B}}(u_1, \ldots, u_n; \mathbf{s}) du_1 \ldots du_n$ for each measurable subset $\mathbf{A}$ of $\mathbf{R}^n$, then the choice probabilities can be rewritten

preference relations on $\mathbf{I}$, and $\mathscr{I}$ a Boolean σ-algebra of subsets of $\mathbf{T}$. Then $\eta: \mathscr{I} \times \mathbf{S} \to [0, 1]$ is a probability measure provided $\eta(\cdot, \mathbf{s})$ is nonnegative and countably additive on $\mathscr{I}$, with $\eta(\mathbf{T}) = 1$. Suppose a subset $\mathbf{T}_0 \subseteq \mathbf{T}$ is measurable and has $\eta(\mathbf{T}_0) = 1$, and that there exists a measurable mapping $\psi: \mathbf{T}_0 \to \mathbf{R}^{\mathbf{I}}$, giving an ordinal representation of each $\rho \in \mathbf{T}_0$. The probability measure μ will obviously depend on the choice of the representation mapping ψ. In many applications $\mathbf{I}$ can be assumed countable. Then every preference relation on $\mathbf{I}$ has a representation $U: \mathbf{I} \times \mathbf{T} \to [0, 1]$ defined by $U(i, \rho) = \bigcup_{j \in \mathbf{A}(i,\rho)} 2^{-j}$, where $\mathbf{A}(i, \rho) = \{i \in \mathbf{I} \mid (i, j) \in \rho\}$.
More general representation theorems are discussed in Debreu (1962). Note that the range of ordinal utility can be restricted without loss of generality to the unit interval, so that all positive moments can be assumed to exist.

5. For $\mathbf{B} = \{i_1, \ldots, i_n\} \in \mathscr{B}$, $\mu^{\mathbf{B}}$ is a probability measure on the finite-dimensional space $\mathbf{R}^n$ of vectors $(u(i_1), \ldots, u(i_n))$ of utility levels for the alternatives in $\mathbf{B}$.

$$P(i_1 \mid \mathbf{B},\mathbf{s}) = \int_{u_1=-\infty}^{+\infty} \int_{u_2=-\infty}^{u_1} \cdots \int_{u_n=-\infty}^{u_1} f^{\mathbf{B}}(u_1,\ldots,u_n;\mathbf{s})\,du_1 \ldots du_n$$

$$= \int_{u=-\infty}^{+\infty} F_1^{\mathbf{B}}(u,\ldots,u;s)\,du, \tag{5.2}$$

where $F^{\mathbf{B}}$ is the cumulative distribution function of $f^{\mathbf{B}}$, and $F_1^{\mathbf{B}}$ denotes the derivative of $F^{\mathbf{B}}$ with respect to its first argument. Alternately, letting $G^{\mathbf{B},1}(w_2,\ldots,w_n;\mathbf{s})$ denote the cumulative distribution function of $(w_2,\ldots,w_n) = (u(i_2) - u(i_1),\ldots,u(i_n) - u(i_1))$, the choice probability satisfies[6]

$$P(i_1 \mid \mathbf{B},\mathbf{s}) = G^{\mathbf{B},1}(0,\ldots,0;\mathbf{s}). \tag{5.3}$$

The problem of finding econometrically feasible PCS consistent with RUM is attacked by using (5.2) to generate choice probabilities constructively from parametric families of probabilities μ, or by demonstrating constructively or indirectly that candidate PCS are consistent with some probability μ.

5.6 Stochastic Revealed Preference

Does the hypothesis of a population of utility-maximizing consumers imply any restrictions on the distributions of observed demands? An affirmative answer was given by Marschak (1960) and Block and Marschak (1960), who established the necessity of conditions such as regularity and the triangle inequality.[7] A necessary and sufficient condition for consistency with random preference maximization, analogous to the strong axiom of revealed preference for the individual consumer, has been established by McFadden and Richter (1970). Let $(\mathbf{B},\mathbf{C})$ be a pair of sets with $\mathbf{B} \in \mathscr{B}$ and $\mathbf{C} \subseteq \mathbf{B}$. If an individual offered an alternative from $\mathbf{B}$ makes

6. The relation of $F^{\mathbf{B}}$ and $G^{\mathbf{B},1}$ is

$$G^{\mathbf{B},1}(w_2,\ldots,w_n) = \int_{u=-\infty}^{+\infty} F_1^{\mathbf{B}}(u, u+w_2,\ldots,u+w_n)\,du.$$

7. A PCS satisfies regularity if $\mathbf{C} \subseteq \mathbf{B} \subseteq \mathbf{B}' \Rightarrow P(\mathbf{C} \mid \mathbf{B},\mathbf{s}) \geqq P(\mathbf{C} \mid \mathbf{B}',\mathbf{s})$, and the triangle inequality if $P(i \mid \{i,j\},\mathbf{s}) \leqq P(i \mid \{i,k\},\mathbf{s}) + P(k \mid \{k,j\},\mathbf{s})$.

a selection in $\mathbf{C}$, call $(\mathbf{B}, \mathbf{C})$ a successful trial. Then the strong axiom of revealed stochastic preference states that for any finite sequence of trials $(\mathbf{B}^1, \mathbf{C}^1), \ldots, (\mathbf{B}^M, \mathbf{C}^M)$, with repetitions permitted,

$$\sum_{m=1}^{M} P(\mathbf{C}^m \mid \mathbf{B}^m, \mathbf{s}) \leqq N((\mathbf{B}^1, \mathbf{C}^1), \ldots, (\mathbf{B}^M, \mathbf{C}^M)), \tag{5.4}$$

where $N((\mathbf{B}^1, \mathbf{C}^1), \ldots, (\mathbf{B}^M, \mathbf{C}^M))$ is the maximum number of successful trials in the sequence consistent with a single preference order. This axiom implies a variety of necessary conditions that can be used to screen PCS for consistency;[8] however, it does not provide a practical sufficient condition for consistency.

Suppose a PCS is consistent with RUM. Are there alternative theories of individual behavior which can generate the same PCS, but which for reasons of generality are to be preferred to the classical model of individual utility maximization? One more general alternative is immediate. We might view the individual himself as drawing a utility function from a random distribution each time a decision is made. Then the individual is a classical utility maximizer given his state of mind, but his state of mind varies randomly from one choice situation to the next.[9] Intraindividual and interindividual variations in tastes are indistinguishable in their effect on the observed distribution of demand.

The hypothesis of intrapersonal random utility is appealing on methodological grounds, since it fits the same data as the conventional theory,

8. Consider, for example, the PCS known as the maximum model (McFadden 1974) with $\mathbf{I} = \{1, 2, 3, 4\}$. Let $\mathbf{I}_1 = \{1, 2\}$ and $\mathbf{I}_2 = \{3, 4\}$. The binary choice probabilities satisfy $P(i \mid ij) = v_i/(v_i + v_j)$, with $v_1 = 3$, $v_2 = 2$, $v_3 = 4$, $v_4 = 3$ for the example. For choice sets of more than two alternatives, only the available alternative in $\mathbf{I}_1$ with the highest scale value is retained, and similary for $\mathbf{I}_2$, with choice between the retained alternatives satisfying the binary choice probabilities; for example, $P(1 \mid 123) = v_1/(v_1 + v_3)$ and $P(2 \mid 123) = 0$. For the trials (12, 1), (34, 3), (234, 2), and (124, 4), equation (5.4) yields $P(1 \mid 12) + P(3 \mid 34) + P(2 \mid 234) + P(4 \mid 124) = 421/210 > 2 =$ the maximum number of successes consistent with RUM. Hence the maximum model can fail to satisfy the axiom of revealed stochastic preference.

9. We confine our attention to the case where the drawings of utility functions for successive decisions are independent. More generally one could introduce learning, experience, and habit by making the probability distribution over utility functions dependent on history. Data collected on series of decisions by cross sections of individuals would permit the identification of intraindividual and interindividual components of variation in tastes. Some of the econometric analysis for this extension is given in Heckman, chapters 3 and 4. A general treatment of the topic awaits future research.

with weaker postulates.[10] The intrapersonal random utility model is in fact of considerable historical and contemporary importance in psychological theories of individual choice. It was first suggested by Thurstone (1927), and it forms the basis for many current models of individual choice behavior put forward in psychology by Luce (1959), Tversky (1972), and others, and tested with reasonable success. In addition to providing evidence on the plausibility of the intrapersonal random utility model as a theory of individual choice behavior, the psychological literature provides analytic results and functional forms that can be adapted for economic applications.

5.7 Aggregation of Preferences

One useful method for examining the consistency of PCS with RUM is to test compatibility with sufficient conditions for consistency. The author is unaware of any general analogue for RUM of the simple sufficient (integrability) conditions of individual utility theory. A restricted, but useful, result of this sort is obtained when individual preferences have sufficient structure to aggregate to a social (indirect) utility function yielding aggregate demands. In this case the home economist's traditional representative consumer with fractional consumption rates can be assigned the social utility function, justifying this approach as an analytic shortcut consistent with some underlying population of utility maximizers who make discrete choices.

Suppose the consumption of an individual is defined by a vector $\mathbf{x}$ of the quantities consumed of divisible commodities and choice of a discrete alternative i which has a vector of measured intrinsic attributes $\mathbf{w}$. The individual has a utility function $\tilde{U}:\tilde{\mathbf{X}} \times \mathbf{W} \times \mathbf{I} \rightarrow [0, 1]$, where $\tilde{\mathbf{X}} \times \mathbf{W}$ is the space of pairs of vectors $(\mathbf{x}, \mathbf{w})$. The utility function is assumed to satisfy the direct utility (DU) assumption

DU: $\tilde{\mathbf{X}}$ is the nonnegative orthant of a finite-dimensional real vector space, and $\mathbf{W}$ is a closed set in a finite-dimensional real vector space. The utility function $\tilde{U}(\cdot, \cdot, i)$ is continuous on $\tilde{\mathbf{X}} \times \mathbf{W}$ for each $i \in \mathbf{I}$. $\tilde{U}(\cdot, \mathbf{w}, i)$ is twice continuously differentiable on $\tilde{\mathbf{X}}$, with $\partial\tilde{U}/\partial\mathbf{x} \geqq 0$ and

10. A particular attraction is that the hypothesis permits retention of much of the apparatus of classical welfare economics. If a criterion for interpersonal comparisons exists in the theory, then it can be applied to intrapersonal comparisons as well.

$|\partial\tilde{U}/\partial\mathbf{x}| > 0$, and is strictly differentially quasi-concave, for each $\mathbf{w} \in \mathbf{W}$ and $i \in \mathbf{I}$.[11]

The individual has income y and faces a vector of prices $\mathbf{r} \gg \mathbf{0}$ for divisible commodities and a cost q associated with the discrete alternative. For a specified discrete alternative i with measured attributes $\mathbf{w}$, the individual chooses $\mathbf{x}$ to maximize utility subject to the budget constraint $\mathbf{r}\cdot\mathbf{x} + q = y$. The result is a conditional indirect utility function $V(y - q, \mathbf{r}, \mathbf{w}, i; \tilde{U})$ defined for $y - q > 0$, $\mathbf{r} \gg \mathbf{0}$, $\mathbf{w} \in \mathbf{W}$, $i \in \mathbf{I}$, and $\tilde{U}$ satisfying assumption DU by

$$V(y - q, \mathbf{r}, \mathbf{w}, i; \tilde{U}) = \max_{\mathbf{x}} \ \{\tilde{U}(\mathbf{x}, \mathbf{w}, i) \mid \mathbf{r}\cdot\mathbf{x} \leqq y - q\}. \tag{5.5}$$

This function has the indirect utility (IU) properties:[12]

IU 5.1: For $\mathbf{r} \gg \mathbf{0}$, $y - q > 0$, $\mathbf{w} \in \mathbf{W}$, $i \in \mathbf{I}$, and $\tilde{U}$ satisfying the utility conditions of DU $V(y - q, \mathbf{r}, \mathbf{w}, i; \tilde{U})$ is continuous in $(y - q, \mathbf{r}, \mathbf{w})$, twice continuously differentiable and homogeneous of degree zero in $(y - q, \mathbf{r})$, strictly differentiably quasi-convex in $\mathbf{r}$, and has $\partial V/\partial(y - q) > 0$.[13]

IU 5.2: (Roy's identity): The maximum of $\tilde{U}(\mathbf{x}, \mathbf{w}, i)$ subject to $\mathbf{r}\cdot\mathbf{x} \leqq y - q$ is achieved at a unique vector $\mathbf{x} = \mathbf{X}(y - q, \mathbf{r}, \mathbf{w}, i; \tilde{U})$ which satisfies

$$\mathbf{X}(y - q, \mathbf{r}, \mathbf{w}, i; \tilde{U}) = -\frac{\partial V/\partial\mathbf{r}}{\partial V/\partial y}. \tag{5.6}$$

When $\mathbf{r} \gg \mathbf{0}$ and $y - q > 0$ are confined to a compact set, there exists a monotone transformation of $\tilde{U}$, given by by $\hat{U} = (e^{\alpha U} - 1)/(e^{\alpha} - 1)$, which for α sufficiently large implies the corresponding transformation of V is convex in $\mathbf{r}$.[14] Thus for most applications V can be assumed without further loss of generality to be convex in $\mathbf{r}$.

Suppose the consumer faces a finite set of discrete alternatives $\mathbf{B} \in \mathscr{B}$. With alternative $i \in \mathbf{B}$ is associated a vector of measured attributes, $\mathbf{z}_i =$

11. $\tilde{U}(\mathbf{x})$ is strictly differentiably quasi-concave if $\mathbf{t}\cdot\partial\tilde{U}/\partial\mathbf{x} = 0$ and $\mathbf{t}\cdot\mathbf{t} = 1$ imply $\mathbf{t}'[\partial^2\tilde{U}/\partial\mathbf{x}\partial\mathbf{x}']\mathbf{t} < 0$; see McFadden (1978b, pp. 30, 368).

12. See, particularly, Diewert (1977), and also McKenzie (1957) and McFadden (1978b, p. 34).

13. Strict differential quasi-convexity requires if $\mathbf{t}\cdot\partial V/\partial\mathbf{r} = 0$ and $\mathbf{t}\cdot\mathbf{t} = 1$, then $\mathbf{t}'(\partial^2 V/\partial\mathbf{r}\partial\mathbf{r}')\mathbf{t} > 0$.

14. The hessian of $\hat{V} = (e^{\alpha V} - 1)/(e^{\alpha} - 1)$ is $\hat{V}_{\mathbf{rr}} = (V_{\mathbf{rr}} + \alpha V_{\mathbf{r}}V_{\mathbf{r}}')\alpha e^{\alpha V}/(e^{\alpha} - 1)$, where $V_{\mathbf{rr}} \equiv \partial^2 V/\partial\mathbf{r}\partial\mathbf{r}'$. A sequence $(y - q, \mathbf{r})_k$ in the compact set, $\alpha_k \to +\infty$, $\mathbf{t}_k\cdot V_{\mathbf{r}} = 0$, $\mathbf{t}_k\cdot\mathbf{t}_k = 1$, and $\mathbf{t}_k'\hat{V}_{\mathbf{rr}}\mathbf{t}_k \leqq 0$ has a subsequence converging to $\mathbf{t}^*$ and $(y - q, \mathbf{r})_*$ at which $\mathbf{t}^*\cdot V_{\mathbf{r}} = 0$ and $\mathbf{t}^{*\prime}V_{\mathbf{rr}}\mathbf{t}^* \leqq 0$, contradicting the strict differential quasi-convexity of V in $\mathbf{r}$. Hence there exists a finite positive α for which the result holds.

$(q_i, \mathbf{r}, \mathbf{w}_i) = \xi(i)$ in our earlier terminology. Income y is a component of the vector $\mathbf{s}$ of consumer characteristics. The unconditional indirect utility function of the consumer is then

$$V^*(y - q_{\mathbf{B}}, \mathbf{r}, \mathbf{w}_{\mathbf{B}}, \mathbf{B}; \tilde{U}) = \max_{i \in \mathbf{B}} \; V(y - q_i, \mathbf{r}, \mathbf{w}_i, i, \tilde{U}), \tag{5.7}$$

where $y - \mathbf{q}_{\mathbf{B}}$ denotes a vector with a component $y - q_j$, and $\mathbf{w}_{\mathbf{B}}$ a vector with a component w_j, for each $j \in \mathbf{B}$. For almost all $y - \mathbf{q}_{\mathbf{B}}$, consumer demand for the discrete alternatives is given by Roy's identity,[15]

$$\delta_j = D(j \mid \mathbf{B}, \mathbf{s}; \tilde{U}) \equiv -\frac{\dfrac{\partial V^*}{\partial q_j}}{\dfrac{\partial V^*}{\partial y}}$$

$$\equiv \begin{cases} 1 & \text{if } j \in \mathbf{B} \text{ and } v_j \geqq v_k \text{ for } k \in \mathbf{B}, \\ 0 & \text{otherwise,} \end{cases} \tag{5.8}$$

where $v_k = V(y - q_k, \mathbf{r}, \mathbf{w}_k, k; \tilde{U})$. The population choice probabilities then satisfy[16]

$$\begin{aligned} P(j \mid \mathbf{B}, \mathbf{s}) &= E_{U|\mathbf{s}} D(j \mid \mathbf{B}, \mathbf{s}; \tilde{U}) \\ &= \int D(j \mid \mathbf{B}, \mathbf{s}; \tilde{U}) \mu(d\tilde{\mathbf{U}}, \mathbf{s}) \\ &= \mu(\{ \tilde{U} \in \mathbf{R}^{\mathbf{I}} \mid V(y - q_j, \mathbf{r}, \mathbf{w}_j, j; \tilde{U}) \\ &\qquad \geqq V(y - q_k, \mathbf{r}, \mathbf{w}_k, k; \tilde{U}) \text{ for } k \in \mathbf{B}\}, \mathbf{s}). \end{aligned} \tag{5.9}$$

We shall now seek sufficient conditions on preferences such that a social utility function can be defined, with fractional consumption rates for the discrete alternatives, which yields the PCS (5.9). This problem is closely related to the classical analysis of community preferences by Gorman (1953); see also Chipman (1974), Muellbauer (1976), Shapiro (1975), and Lau (1977).

15. Except for $\mathbf{q}_{\mathbf{B}}$ in a closed set of Lebesgue measure zero and (by RUM 5.2) μ-probability zero, the maximum in (5.7) is achieved at a unique alternative. On the open set where $k \in \mathbf{B}$ is the unique maximum, $V^*(y - \mathbf{q}_{\mathbf{B}}, \mathbf{r}, \mathbf{w}_{\mathbf{B}}, \mathbf{B}; \tilde{U}) = V(y - q_k, \mathbf{r}, \mathbf{w}_k; \tilde{U})$, and V^* shares the regularity and differentiability properties of V given in IU 5.1, for almost all price vectors.

16. Given $(q_i, \mathbf{r}, \mathbf{w}_i) = \xi(i)$ and the maximizing vector $\mathbf{X}(y - q_i, \mathbf{r}, \mathbf{w}_i, i; \tilde{U})$, one obtains for each i the conditional indirect utility $U(i; \tilde{U}) \equiv \tilde{U}(\mathbf{X}(\xi(i), i; \tilde{U}), i) \equiv V(\xi(i), i; \tilde{U})$. Thus there is a mapping from the set of $\tilde{U}$ to the set of $U : \mathbf{I} \to [0, 1]$. With a slight abuse of notation, we write $\mu(d\tilde{U}, \mathbf{s})$ rather than $\mu(dU, \mathbf{s})$, with the understanding that the mapping above is applied.

First, we define a utility function with fractional consumption rates. Define $\Delta = \{\boldsymbol{\delta} \in \mathbf{R}^{\mathbf{I}} \mid \delta_i \geqq 0 \text{ and } \Sigma_i \delta_i = 1\}$ and $\boldsymbol{\Delta}_{\mathbf{B}} = \{\boldsymbol{\delta} \in \boldsymbol{\Delta} \mid \delta_i = 0 \text{ for } i \notin \mathbf{B}\}$ for $\mathbf{B} \in \mathscr{B}$. Consider $\bar{U}: \bar{\mathbf{X}} \times \boldsymbol{\Delta} \times \mathbf{S} \to [0,\ 1]$. For $\mathbf{r} \gg \mathbf{0}$, $\mathbf{B} \in \mathscr{B}$, $y - \mathbf{q}_{\mathbf{B}} \gg \mathbf{0}$, and $\mathbf{w}_{\mathbf{B}} \in \mathbf{W}$, with $(y - q_i, \mathbf{r}, \mathbf{w}_i) = \xi(i)$, define

$$\bar{V}(y - q_{\mathbf{B}}, \mathbf{r}, \mathbf{w}_{\mathbf{B}}, \mathbf{B}, \mathbf{s}) = \max_{\mathbf{x}, \boldsymbol{\delta}} \{\bar{U}(\mathbf{x}, \boldsymbol{\delta}, \mathbf{s}) \mid \mathbf{x} \in \mathbf{X}, \boldsymbol{\delta} \in \boldsymbol{\Delta}_{\mathbf{B}}, \mathbf{r} \cdot \mathbf{x} + \mathbf{q}_{\mathbf{B}} \cdot \boldsymbol{\delta}_{\mathbf{B}} \leqq y\}. \tag{5.10}$$

We term $\bar{U}$ a social utility function, and $\bar{V}$ a social indirect utility function, if the choice probabilities satisfy Roy's identity,

$$P(i \mid \mathbf{B}, \mathbf{s}) = -\frac{\dfrac{\partial \bar{V}}{\partial q_i}}{\dfrac{\partial \bar{V}}{\partial y}}\ . \tag{5.11}$$

Suppose individual conditional indirect utility functions have the form

$$V(y - q, \mathbf{r}, \mathbf{w}, i; \tilde{U}) = \frac{y - q - \alpha(\mathbf{r}, \mathbf{w}, i; \tilde{U})}{\beta(\mathbf{r})}, \tag{5.12}$$

where $y > q + \alpha(\mathbf{r}, \mathbf{w}, i; \tilde{U})$ and α and β are homogeneous of degree one, concave, and nondecreasing in $\mathbf{r}$.[17] The linearity of V in $(y - q)$ implies that V^* in (5.7) is additively separable into a term independent of $\tilde{U}$ and a term independent of y. Consider the function $\bar{V}$ defined by[18]

$$\begin{aligned} \bar{V}(y - \mathbf{q}_{\mathbf{B}}, \mathbf{r}, \mathbf{w}_{\mathbf{B}}, \mathbf{B}, \mathbf{s}) &= E_{U \mid \mathbf{s}} \max_{i \in \mathbf{B}} V(y - q_i, \mathbf{r}, \mathbf{w}_i, i; \tilde{U}) \\ &\equiv \frac{1}{\beta(\mathbf{r})} \left\{ y + E_{U \mid \mathbf{s}} \max_{i \in \mathbf{B}} [-q_i - \alpha(\mathbf{r}, \mathbf{w}_i, i; \tilde{U})] \right\}. \end{aligned} \tag{5.13}$$

17. That (5.12) is an indirect utility function follows immediately from the concavity of the associated expenditure function, $y = q + \alpha(\mathbf{r}, \mathbf{w}, i; \tilde{U}) + u\beta(\mathbf{r})$, for $u \geqq 0$. The quasi-convexity of V in $(y - q, \mathbf{r})$ can also be demonstrated by a direct calculus argument. The aggregation properties of (5.12) were first noted by Gorman (1953), who provided the following characterization of the direct preference map: $\tilde{U}(\mathbf{x}, \mathbf{w}, i) = \operatorname{Max}_{\hat{\mathbf{x}}} \{U^0(\hat{\mathbf{x}}) \mid U^1(\mathbf{x} - \hat{\mathbf{x}}, \mathbf{w}, i) = 1\}$, where U^0 and U^1 are concave in $\hat{\mathbf{x}}$, U^1 is homogeneous of degree zero in $\mathbf{x} - \hat{\mathbf{x}}$, and U^0 does not vary over the population. This dual structure can also be derived from composition rules for concave conjugate functions; see McFadden (1978b, p. 49–60).

18. It is assumed here that the expectation exists. Note however that, while the ordinal utility function $\tilde{U}$ can be assumed to have a range contained in the unit interval, and thus have an expectation, the transformation of utility necessary to achieve additive separability in (5.12) may yield a function whose expectation (5.13) does not exist. In section 5.8, a modified definition of $\bar{V}$ is employed which precludes this possibility.

The terms $[-q_i - \alpha(\mathbf{r}, \mathbf{w}, i; \tilde{U})]$ are convex in $(\mathbf{q_B}, \mathbf{r})$. Since the maximum of convex functions is convex, and a nonnegative linear combination of convex functions is convex,

$$G(\mathbf{q_B}, \mathbf{r}, \mathbf{w_B}, \mathbf{B}, \mathbf{s}) \equiv E_{U|\mathbf{s}} \max_{i \in \mathbf{B}} [-q_i - \alpha(\mathbf{r}, \mathbf{w}_i, i; \tilde{U})] \tag{5.14}$$

is convex in $(\mathbf{q_B}, \mathbf{r})$. Then $\bar{V} = (y + G(\mathbf{q_B}, \mathbf{r}, \mathbf{w_B}, \mathbf{B}, \mathbf{s})/\beta(\mathbf{r})$ is invertible to a concave expenditure function $y = u\beta(\mathbf{r}) - G(\mathbf{q_B}, \mathbf{r}, \mathbf{w_B}, \mathbf{B}, \mathbf{s})$ for $u \geqq 0$ and is therefore an indirect utility function.

Applying (5.8) to this preference structure yields

$$D(j \mid \mathbf{B}, \mathbf{s}; \tilde{U}) = -\frac{\partial}{\partial q_j} \max_{i \in \mathbf{B}} [-q_i - \alpha(\mathbf{r}, \mathbf{w}_i, i; \tilde{U})], \tag{5.15}$$

and hence from (5.9)

$$\begin{aligned} P(j \mid \mathbf{B}, \mathbf{s}) &= E_{U|\mathbf{s}} D(j \mid \mathbf{B}, \mathbf{s}; \tilde{U}) \\ &\equiv -\frac{\partial G(\mathbf{q_B}, \mathbf{r}, \mathbf{w_B}, \mathbf{B}, \mathbf{s})}{\partial q_j} \\ &\equiv -\frac{\partial \bar{V}/\partial q_j}{\partial \bar{V}/\partial y} \quad . \end{aligned} \tag{5.16}$$

Therefore $\bar{V}$ is a social indirect utility function yielding the PCS.[19]

When this conclusion holds, the demand distribution can be analyzed as if it were generated by a population with common tastes, with each (representative) consumer having fractional consumption rates for the discrete alternatives and the social indirect utility function $\bar{V}$.

It should be noted that the utility structure (5.12) yields choice probabilities that are independent of current income. However, tastes (the distribution of $\tilde{U}$) may depend on individual characteristics that are correlates of current income such as historical wage rates, income levels, or occupation. Then these variables may enter the PCS.

5.8 The Williams-Daly-Zachary Theorem

The conclusion derived from the preference structure (5.12), that the resulting choice probabilities are given by the gradient of a surplus function

19. The associated direct utility function $\bar{U}$ satisfies

$$\bar{U}(\mathbf{x}, \boldsymbol{\delta}, \mathbf{s}) = \operatorname*{Inf}_{y, \mathbf{q}, \mathbf{r}, \mathbf{B}} \{\bar{V}(y - \mathbf{q_B}, \mathbf{r}, \mathbf{w_B}, \mathbf{B}, \mathbf{s}) \mid \mathbf{r} \cdot \mathbf{x} + \mathbf{q_B} \cdot \boldsymbol{\delta}_{\mathbf{B}} \leqq y, \mathbf{B} \in \mathscr{B}\}.$$

G satisfying (5.14) and (5.16), can be strengthened by giving necessary and sufficient conditions on G for (5.14) and (5.16) to hold. These conditions will then provide practical criteria for the derivation of PCS consistent with RUM having the structure (5.12). The essential elements of the following arguments are due to Williams (1977) and to Daly and Zachary (1976).

Consider a preference structure satisfying RUM and representable in the additively separable form (5.12). For $\mathbf{B} \in \mathscr{B}$, let $F(\boldsymbol{\varepsilon}_\mathbf{B}; \mathbf{r}, \mathbf{w}_\mathbf{B}, \mathbf{B}, \mathbf{s})$ denote the cumulative distribution function, induced by the probability measure on the set of $\tilde{U}$, of the random vector $\boldsymbol{\varepsilon}_\mathbf{B}$ with components $\varepsilon_i = -\alpha(\mathbf{r}, \mathbf{w}_i, i; \tilde{U})$ for $i \in \mathbf{B}$. If F can be characterized by a density $f(\boldsymbol{\varepsilon}_\mathbf{B}, \mathbf{r}, \mathbf{w}_\mathbf{B}, \mathbf{B}, \mathbf{s})$, then this random preference structure will be said to be of additive income random utility maximizing, AIRUM, form.[20]

A function $G(\mathbf{q}_\mathbf{B}, \mathbf{r}, \mathbf{w}_\mathbf{B}, \mathbf{B}, \mathbf{s})$ will be termed a social surplus, SS, function if it has the following properties:

SS 5.1: For $\mathbf{B} = \{1, \ldots, m\} \in \mathscr{B}$, G is a real-valued function of $\mathbf{q}_\mathbf{B} \in \mathbf{R}^m$, $\mathbf{r} \in \tilde{\mathbf{X}}$ with $\mathbf{r} \gg \mathbf{0}$, $\mathbf{w}_\mathbf{B} \in \mathbf{W}^m$, and $\mathbf{s} \in \mathbf{S}$.

SS 5.2: G is a positively linear homogeneous, convex function of $(\mathbf{q}_\mathbf{B}, \mathbf{r})$.

SS 5.3: G has the additivity property that $G(\mathbf{q}_\mathbf{B} + \theta, \mathbf{r}, \mathbf{w}_\mathbf{B}, \mathbf{B}, \mathbf{s}) = G(\mathbf{q}_\mathbf{B}, \mathbf{r}, \mathbf{w}_\mathbf{B}, \mathbf{B}, \mathbf{s}) - \theta$, where θ is any real scalar and $\mathbf{q}_\mathbf{B} + \theta$ denotes a vector with components $q_i + \theta$.

SS 5.4: All mixed partial derivatives of G with respect to $\mathbf{q}_\mathbf{B}$ exist, are nonpositive and independent of the order of differentiation, and satisfy $G(\mathbf{q}_\mathbf{B}, \mathbf{r}, \mathbf{w}_\mathbf{B}, \mathbf{B}, \mathbf{s}) - G(\mathbf{0}_\mathbf{B}, \mathbf{r}, \mathbf{w}_\mathbf{B}, \mathbf{B}, \mathbf{s}) = \int_0^1 (d/dt) G(\psi(t), \mathbf{r}, \mathbf{w}_\mathbf{B}, \mathbf{B}, \mathbf{s})\, dt$, where ψ is any path between $\psi(0) = \mathbf{0}_\mathbf{B}$ and $\psi(1) = \mathbf{q}_\mathbf{B}$.[21]

SS 5.5: $\lim_{q_i \to -\infty} G_i(\mathbf{q}_\mathbf{B}, \mathbf{r}, \mathbf{w}_\mathbf{B}, \mathbf{B}, \mathbf{s}) = -1$ for $i \in \mathbf{B}$.

SS 5.6: Suppose $\mathbf{B} = \{i_1, \ldots, i_m\} \in \mathscr{B}$, and $\mathbf{B}' = \{i'_1, \ldots, i'_m, \ldots, i'_{m+n}\} \in \mathscr{B}$ satisfy $(q_{i_k}, \mathbf{w}_{i_k}) = (q_{i'_k}, \mathbf{w}_{i'_k})$ for $k = 1, \ldots, m$. Then $G(\mathbf{q}_\mathbf{B}, \mathbf{r}, \mathbf{w}_\mathbf{B}, \mathbf{B}, \mathbf{s}) = G((\mathbf{q}_{\mathbf{B}'}, +\infty, \ldots, +\infty), \mathbf{r}, \mathbf{w}_{\mathbf{B}'}, \mathbf{B}', \mathbf{s})$.

20. The condition for F to be characterized by a density is that it be absolutely continuous with respect to Lebesgue measure on $\mathbf{R}^m$. Note that the linear homogeneity of $\alpha(\mathbf{r}, \mathbf{w}_i, i; \tilde{U})$ in $\mathbf{r}$ implies that $F(\lambda\boldsymbol{\varepsilon}_\mathbf{B}, \lambda\mathbf{r}, \mathbf{w}_\mathbf{B}, \mathbf{B}, \mathbf{s}) = F(\boldsymbol{\varepsilon}_\mathbf{B}, \mathbf{r}, \mathbf{w}_\mathbf{B}, \mathbf{B}, \mathbf{s})$ for $\lambda > 0$. When there is no ambiguity, the abbreviated notation $F(\boldsymbol{\varepsilon}_\mathbf{B})$ and $f(\boldsymbol{\varepsilon}_\mathbf{B})$ will be used. Note that in the utility structure (5.12), β can in general be a function of $\mathbf{r}$ and $\mathbf{s}$.

21. The partial derivative of a function G with respect to its ith argument is denoted G_i. Then $G_{1,2,\ldots,m}$ denotes the mixed partial derivative of G with respect to $(q_1, \ldots, q_m)$. ($\mathbf{0}_\mathbf{B}$ is an m-vector of zeroes.)

Consider a PCS with choice probabilities given by functions $P(i \mid \mathbf{B}, \mathbf{s}) = \pi_i(\mathbf{q_B}, \mathbf{r}, \mathbf{w_B}, \mathbf{B}, \mathbf{s})$. This will be termed a translation-invariant probabilistic choice system, TPCS, if it satisfies PCS and the following conditions:

TPCS 5.1: The functions π_i are defined for $i \in \mathbf{B} = \{1, \ldots, m\} \in \mathscr{B}$, $\mathbf{q_B} \in \mathbf{R}^m$, $\mathbf{r} \in \tilde{\mathbf{X}}$ with $\mathbf{r} \gg \mathbf{0}$, $\mathbf{w} \in \mathbf{W}^m$, and $\mathbf{s} \in \mathbf{S}$.

TPCS 5.2: π_i is homogeneous of degree zero in $(\mathbf{q_B}, \mathbf{r})$.

TPCS 5.3: For a real scalar θ, $\pi_i(\mathbf{q_B} + \theta, \mathbf{r}, \mathbf{w_B}, \mathbf{B}, \mathbf{s}) = \pi_i(\mathbf{q_B}, \mathbf{r}, \mathbf{w_B}, \mathbf{B}, \mathbf{s})$.

TPCS 5.4: $\lim_{q_i \to -\infty} \pi_i(\mathbf{q_B}, \mathbf{r}, \mathbf{w_B}, \mathbf{B}, \mathbf{s}) = 1$.

TPCS 5.5: All mixed partials of π_i with respect to components of $\mathbf{q_B}$ other than q_i exist, are nonnegative and independent of order of differentiation, and satisfy

$$\pi_1(\mathbf{q_B}, \mathbf{r}, \mathbf{w_B}, \mathbf{B}, \mathbf{s})$$

$$= \int_{-\infty}^{q_2} \cdots \int_{-\infty}^{q_m} \pi_{1,2,\ldots,m}(q_1, \hat{q}_2, \ldots, \hat{q}_m, \mathbf{r}, \mathbf{w_B}, \mathbf{B}, \mathbf{s})\, d\hat{q}_2, \ldots, d\hat{q}_m,$$

with analogous conditions for $\pi_2, \ldots, \pi_m$.[22]

TPCS 5.6: $\pi_{i,j}(\mathbf{q_B}, \mathbf{r}, \mathbf{w_B}, \mathbf{B}, \mathbf{s}) = \pi_{j,i}(\mathbf{q_B}, \mathbf{r}. \mathbf{w_B}, \mathbf{B}, \mathbf{s})$.

TPCS 5.7: Suppose $\mathbf{B} = \{i_1, \ldots, i_m\} \in \mathscr{B}$ and $\mathbf{B}' = \{i'_1, \ldots, i'_m, \ldots, i'_{m+n}\} \in \mathscr{B}$ satisfy $(q_{i_k}, \mathbf{w}_{i_k}) = (q_{i'_k}, \mathbf{w}_{i'_k})$ for $k = 1, \ldots, m$. Then, for $k = 1, \ldots, m$,

$$\pi_k(\mathbf{q_B}, \mathbf{r}, \mathbf{w_B}, \mathbf{B}, \mathbf{s}) = \pi_k((\mathbf{q}'_{\mathbf{B}'}, +\infty, \ldots, +\infty), \mathbf{r}, \mathbf{w}_{\mathbf{B}'}, \mathbf{B}', \mathbf{s}).$$

The following theorem links additive-income random utility-maximizing forms, social surplus functions, and translation-invariant probabilistic choice systems.

THEOREM 5.1: Consider $\mathbf{B} = \{1, \ldots, m\} \in \mathscr{B}$.

1. Suppose AIRUM holds, with individual indirect utility having the form $u(i) = (y - q_i + \varepsilon_i)/\beta(\mathbf{r})$, with $\boldsymbol{\varepsilon}_\mathbf{B}$ distributed in the population with

22. The partial derivative of π_i with respect to its jth argument is denoted $\pi_{i,j}$. Then $\pi_{1,2,\ldots,m}$, denotes the mixed partial derivative of π_1 with respect to $(q_2, \ldots, q_m)$.

cumulative distribution function $F(\boldsymbol{\varepsilon}_{\mathbf{B}}, \mathbf{r}, \mathbf{w}_{\mathbf{B}}, \mathbf{B}, \mathbf{s})$ and density $f(\boldsymbol{\varepsilon}_{\mathbf{B}}, \mathbf{r}, \mathbf{w}_{\mathbf{B}}, \mathbf{B}, \mathbf{s})$. Define

$$G(\mathbf{q}_{\mathbf{B}}, \mathbf{r}, \mathbf{w}_{\mathbf{B}}, \mathbf{B}, \mathbf{s}) = \int_{t=-\infty}^{+\infty} [F(\mathbf{0}_{\mathbf{B}} + t, \mathbf{r}, \mathbf{w}_{\mathbf{B}}, \mathbf{B}, \mathbf{s}) - F(\mathbf{q}_{\mathbf{B}} + t, \mathbf{r}, \mathbf{w}_{\mathbf{B}}, \mathbf{B}, \mathbf{s})]\, dt. \tag{5.17}$$

Then G exists and is a social surplus function satisfying SS. Further

$$\bar{V}(y - \mathbf{q}_{\mathbf{B}}, \mathbf{r}, \mathbf{w}_{\mathbf{B}}, \mathbf{B}, \mathbf{s}) = (y + G(\mathbf{q}_{\mathbf{B}}, \mathbf{r}, \mathbf{w}_{\mathbf{B}}, \mathbf{B}, \mathbf{s}))/\beta(\mathbf{r}) \tag{5.18}$$

is a social indirect utility function; that is, the PCS associated with this AIRUM form satisfies

$$P(i \mid \mathbf{B}, \mathbf{s}) \equiv \pi_i(\mathbf{q}_{\mathbf{B}}, \mathbf{r}, \mathbf{w}_{\mathbf{B}}, \mathbf{B}, \mathbf{s}) = -G_i(\mathbf{q}_{\mathbf{B}}, \mathbf{r}, \mathbf{w}_{\mathbf{B}}, \mathbf{B}, \mathbf{s}) \tag{5.19}$$

and satisfies TPCS.

2. Suppose $G(\mathbf{q}_{\mathbf{B}}, \mathbf{r}, \mathbf{w}_{\mathbf{B}}, \mathbf{B}, \mathbf{s})$ is a social surplus function satisfying SS. Then (5.19) defines a PCS satisfying TPCS. Further there exists an AIRUM form such that G satisfies (5.17) and (5.18).

3. Suppose $P(i \mid \mathbf{B}, \mathbf{s}) = \pi_i(\mathbf{q}_{\mathbf{B}}, \mathbf{r}, \mathbf{w}_{\mathbf{B}}, \mathbf{B}, \mathbf{s})$ is a PCS, satisfying TPCS. Then there exist an AIRUM form and a social surplus function that satisfy SS and (5.17) through (5.19).

LEMMA 5.1: If AIRUM holds, and the distribution $F(\boldsymbol{\varepsilon}_{\mathbf{B}}, \mathbf{r}, \mathbf{w}_{\mathbf{B}}, \mathbf{B}, \mathbf{s})$ has first moments, then G defined by (5.17) also equals

$$G(\mathbf{q}_{\mathbf{B}}, \mathbf{r}, \mathbf{w}_{\mathbf{B}}, \mathbf{B}, \mathbf{s}) = \int_{-\infty}^{+\infty} \left\{ \max_{i \in \mathbf{B}} (\varepsilon_i - q_i) - \max \varepsilon_i \right\} f(\boldsymbol{\varepsilon}_{\mathbf{B}})\, d\boldsymbol{\varepsilon}_{\mathbf{B}}. \tag{5.20}$$

Because the definition (5.17) of the social surplus function normalizes its value to zero for $\mathbf{q}_{\mathbf{B}} = \mathbf{0}_{\mathbf{B}}$, for any nonprice attributes $\mathbf{w}_{\mathbf{B}}$, the social indirect utility function (5.18) cannot be used to make welfare comparisons when nonprice attributes change. The following result gives a modified definition of the social surplus function which permits such comparisons.

LEMMA 5.2: Suppose AIRUM holds. If the distribution $F(\mathbf{q}_{\mathbf{B}}, \mathbf{r}, \mathbf{w}_{\mathbf{B}}, \mathbf{B}, \mathbf{s})$ has first moments, then

$$G(\mathbf{q_B}, \mathbf{r}, \mathbf{w_B}, \mathbf{B}, \mathbf{s}) = \int_{-\infty}^{+\infty} \max_{i \in \mathbf{B}} \ (\varepsilon_i - q_i) f(\boldsymbol{\varepsilon}_\mathbf{B}) d\boldsymbol{\varepsilon}_\mathbf{B}$$

is a social surplus function, satisfying SS, which when substituted in (5.18) yields a social indirect utility function, permitting welfare comparisons for nonprice attribute changes.

Alternately suppose nonprice attributes are compensable in the sense that given $\mathbf{w_B}$, $\delta > 0$, there exists $\theta > 0$ such that $F(\boldsymbol{\varepsilon}_\mathbf{B} + \theta, \mathbf{r}, \mathbf{w_B}, \mathbf{B}, \mathbf{s}) \geqq F(\boldsymbol{\varepsilon}_\mathbf{B}, \mathbf{r}, \mathbf{w}'_\mathbf{B}, \mathbf{B}, \mathbf{s}) \geqq F(\boldsymbol{\varepsilon}_\mathbf{B} - \theta, \mathbf{r}, \mathbf{w_B}, \mathbf{B}, \mathbf{s})$ for all $\boldsymbol{\varepsilon}_\mathbf{B}$ and $\mathbf{w}'_\mathbf{B}$ with $| \mathbf{w}'_\mathbf{B} - \mathbf{w_B} | < \delta$. Then $G(\mathbf{q_B}, \mathbf{r}, \mathbf{w_B}, \mathbf{B}, \mathbf{s}) = \int_{-\infty}^{+\infty} [F(\mathbf{0_B} + t, \mathbf{r}, \bar{\mathbf{w}}_\mathbf{B}, \mathbf{B}, \mathbf{s}) - F(\mathbf{q_B} + t, \mathbf{r}, \mathbf{w_B}, \mathbf{B}, \mathbf{s})]\,dt$, where $\bar{\mathbf{w}}_\mathbf{B}$ is a fixed vector of nonprice attributes, is a social surplus function satisfying SS. When this function is substituted in (5.18), the social indirect utility function permits welfare comparisons for a fixed set **B** and subsets of **B** (choice sets formed by letting $q_i \to +\infty$ for some $i \in \mathbf{B}$), and for nonprice attribute changes.

The proofs of the theorem and lemmas are lengthy and are deferred to section 5.23. Several comments on this theorem are in order. First, the conditions TPCS are usually easy to check for an empirical PCS. If they hold, the PCS is consistent with RUM. Thus TPCS is a useful set of sufficient conditions for consistency. Note, however, that, while TPCS is necessary and sufficient for an AIRUM form, there are many PCS consistent with RUM that fail to satisfy TPCS and AIRUM. Second, a useful way to generate PCS consistent with RUM is to start from a social surplus function satisfying SS. A variety of functional forms are known that satisfy SS; several are given in the remainder of this chapter.

A third comment is on welfare analysis of alternative policies involving discrete choice. When preferences have an AIRUM form, the social indirect utility function (5.18), incorporating a social surplus function defined by (5.17) or by lemma 5.2, permits ready comparison of the social desirability of alternative policies. When the vector of prices **r** of nondiscrete commodities is unchanged under alternative policies, welfare comparisons can also be made using the social surplus function G. Then G yields an analytic expression for Hicksian consumer's surplus and (since income effects are absent) Marshallian consumer's surplus: for any path $\psi : [0, 1] \to \mathbf{R}^m$ with $\psi(0) = \mathbf{0_B}$, $\psi(1) = \mathbf{q_B}$,

$$G(\mathbf{q_B}, \mathbf{r}, \mathbf{w_B}, \mathbf{B}, \mathbf{s}) \equiv - \int_{t=0}^{1} \sum_{i=1}^{m} \pi_i(\psi(t), \mathbf{r}, \mathbf{w_B}, \mathbf{B}, \mathbf{s}) \psi_i'(t)\, dt, \tag{5.21}$$

the usual sum of areas under demand curves. Since consistent use of consumer surplus welfare comparisons is grounded on utility structures of the additively separable form (5.12) in conventional problems, we conclude that the presence of discrete choice places no new restrictions on the validity of consumer surplus methods. For further discussion of consumer welfare judgments involving discrete choice, see Rosen and Small (1979).

A fourth comment regards the definition of the variables $\mathbf{q_B}$. In the argument surrounding (5.12), q_i was interpreted as the price of alternative i. The utility function (5.12) was interpreted as the indirect utility function resulting from maximization of a translated homothetic utility function subject to a budget constraint. However, (5.12) can alternately be given the interpretation of a utility function that is additively separable and linear in some physical attribute of the discrete alternative. Consider a utility function with the general structure of (5.12),

$$u = -\frac{q_i + \alpha(\mathbf{r}, \mathbf{w}_i, i, \mathbf{s}; \tilde{U})}{\beta(\mathbf{r}, \mathbf{s})}. \tag{5.22}$$

Take q_i to be the level of some physical attribute of alternative i, and $\mathbf{w}_i$ to be a vector of the remaining attributes of the alternative, including its price. Let α and β depend on the vector $\mathbf{s}$ of individual characteristics, including income. Then theorem 5.1 can be applied to establish the existence of a social surplus function G and probabilistic choice system π_i which satisfy (5.17), (5.19), and all the conditions SS and TPCS except the homogeneity properties SS 5.2 and TPCS 5.2. With suitable added assumptions on α and β, (5.21) will be an indirect utility function satisfying IU, and hence will be dual to a direct utility function satisfying DU.[23] This interpretation permits a very general dependence of the PCS on income and prices. However, the logic of the interpretation requires that it be sensible to consider alternatives in which the attribute q_i varies, with all other attributes remaining unchanged. The additively separable utility structure

23. An example that satisfies IU 5.1 for all real values of q_i is $\beta(\mathbf{r}, \mathbf{s})$ a (positive) constant and α a quasi-concave, zero-degree homogeneous function of $\mathbf{r}$ and the income component y of $\mathbf{s}$ which is twice continuously differentiable in $(\mathbf{r}, y)$, has $\partial\alpha/\partial y < 0$ and $\partial\alpha/\partial\mathbf{r} \geqq 0$, and is strictly differentiably quasi-concave.

also requires that marginal rates of substitution between attributes other than q_i not depend on the level of q_i.

The reinterpretation of (5.22) can also be made for noneconomic choice contexts, with $(\mathbf{r}, \mathbf{s})$ interpreted as individual characteristics, $(q_i, \mathbf{w}_i)$ as physical attributes of the alternative, and u as the direct utility associated with the alternative.

Finally, note that q_i may itself be a function of underlying raw attributes of the alternatives. This function may be parametric; however, it cannot depend on tastes $\tilde{U}$.

Suppose $(\mathbf{L}, \mathscr{L}, J)$ is a probability space, and G^j is a social surplus function and π_i^j the associated PCS, for each $j \in \mathbf{L}$. Then it is obvious that the probability mixture $G^* = \int_{\mathbf{L}} G^j J(dj)$ is again a social surplus function, with a probabilistic choice system given by the corresponding probability mixture $\pi_i^* = \int_{\mathbf{L}} \pi_i^j J(dj)$. This observation can be used to derive a variety of PCS obtained as mixtures of simpler PCS.[24]

Suppose $\pi_i(\mathbf{r}, \mathbf{w_B}, \mathbf{B}, \mathbf{s})$ is an arbitrary probabilistic choice system depending on individual and economic characteristics $(\mathbf{s}, \mathbf{r})$ and alternative attributes $\mathbf{w_B}$. Then the choice system

$$\tilde{\pi}_i(\mathbf{q_B}, \mathbf{r}, \mathbf{w_B}, \mathbf{B}, \mathbf{s}) = \frac{e^{-q_i}\pi_i(\mathbf{r}, \mathbf{w_B}, \mathbf{B}, \mathbf{s})}{\sum_{j \in \mathbf{B}} e^{-q_j}\pi_j(\mathbf{r}, \mathbf{w_B}, \mathbf{B}, \mathbf{s})}, \tag{5.23}$$

where the $\mathbf{q_B}$ are artificial variables, satisfies all the conditions TPCS except the homogeneity condition TPCS 5.2 and the condition TPCS 5.7 that the choice probabilities of a set depend only on the measured attributes of the alternatives in that set. The proof of theorem 5.1 then implies the existence of a social surplus function

$$G(\mathbf{q_B}) = \ln \sum_{j \in \mathbf{B}} e^{-q_j}\pi_j(\mathbf{r}, \mathbf{w_B}, \mathbf{B}, \mathbf{s}), \tag{5.24}$$

satisfying (5.19). This function fails to satisfy SS 5.6. We conclude that TPCS 5.7, or SS 5.6, are essential if the condition for a probabilistic choice system to be consistent with RUM is to be nonvacuous.

24. An example is the DOGIT model of Gaudry (1977), obtainable as a mixture of a multinomial logit and captive population PCS.

5.9 Criteria for Parametric Probabilistic Choice Systems

Assuming a population of random utility maximizers as a maintained hypothesis, the practical question is how to construct parametric PCS suitable for econometric and policy analysis. The criteria one may wish to impose on parametric PCS, beyond consistency with RUM, are (1) sufficient flexibility to capture patterns of substitution between alternatives and (2) a structure and parameterization facilitating estimation and computation. One approach to generating parametric PCS is to start from a parametric RUM model and derive the choice probabilities constructively. The primary drawback to this approach is that for many parametric RUM, the construction of the choice probabilities is analytically intractable, or results in functional forms that are impractical for empirical computation and analysis.

A second approach to specifying parametric PCS is to start from a practical system of choice probabilities and verify constructively or indirectly its consistency with RUM. One useful method is to test consistency with the sufficient conditions TPCS given in the preceding section.

5.10 Specification of Variables

Continuing the terminology of section 5.7, we consider an individual with a vector of measured individual characteristics $\mathbf{s}$, one component of which is income y. The individual faces alternatives characterized by vectors of measured nonprice attributes $\mathbf{w}_i$ and a budget constraint $q_i + \mathbf{r} \cdot \mathbf{x} = y$, where q_i and $\mathbf{r}$ are the prices of the discrete alternatives and divisible commodities, respectively. The individual has a utility function of $(\mathbf{x}, \mathbf{w}_i)$ which varies over the population. Without loss of generality, we can attribute this variation in utility to a vector of unmeasured nonprice attributes $\boldsymbol{\omega}_i$ and a vector of unmeasured individual characteristics $\boldsymbol{\sigma}$. Let $U(\mathbf{x}, \mathbf{w}_i, \mathbf{s}, \boldsymbol{\omega}_i, \boldsymbol{\sigma})$ denote this utility function.

The vector $\mathbf{w}_i$ contains information on real, or intrinsic, properties of the alternative, and in addition, nominal, or extrinsic, information such as labels attached by the observer for identification purposes. For example, a travel mode may be described by real variables such as time and number of transfers, as well as nominal labels such as bus, express, or alternative 4. It is reasonable to postulate that behavior depends solely on real properties of an alternative. However, an observed nominal label which is correlated with an unobserved real variable may appear in the population to be related to choice behavior. For example, a label that identifies a transportation mode as "bus" may be correlated with an unobserved real variable measuring the schedule flexibility of alternative modes and thus may act as a proxy for the unobserved real variable. The similarity of alternatives should also be perceived by individuals in real terms, but nominal classifications may act as proxies for the unmeasured real variables.

Some analyses of choice behavior, such as tests of the RUM hypothesis and the nature of similarity perceptions, can be carried out in PCS where alternatives are characterized partially or completely in nominal terms. This is particularly true in experimental applications where the universe of distinct alternatives is finite and saturated models are used where each alternative has a nominal label. However, analysis of economic behavior and forecasting is best done in real models. For example, knowledge of the historical effect of nominal variables, reflecting underlying unobserved real effects, is of little use in forecasting when unmeasured real variables change.

Empirical experience in travel demand forecasting (McFadden et al. 1977) suggests that it is difficult to construct purely real models using conventional market data alone. In terms of research strategy this suggests that most models using existing data will require nominal variables, but with their use limited, and that data collection should emphasize more extensive measurement of real variables.

5.11 Functional Form

The primary issues in choice of a functional form for a PCS are computational practicality and flexibility in representing patterns of similarity across alternatives. Practical experience suggests that functional forms that allow similar patterns of interalternative substitution will give comparable fits to existing economic data sets. Of course, laboratory experimentation or more comprehensive economic observations may make it possible to differentiate the fit of functional forms with respect to characteristics other than flexibility.

Currently three major families of concrete functional forms for PCS have been developed in the literature. These are logit models based on the work of Luce (1959), probit models based on the work of Thurstone (1927), and elimination models based on the work of Tversky (1972). Figure 5.1 outlines these families; the members are defined in sections 5.12 through 5.18.

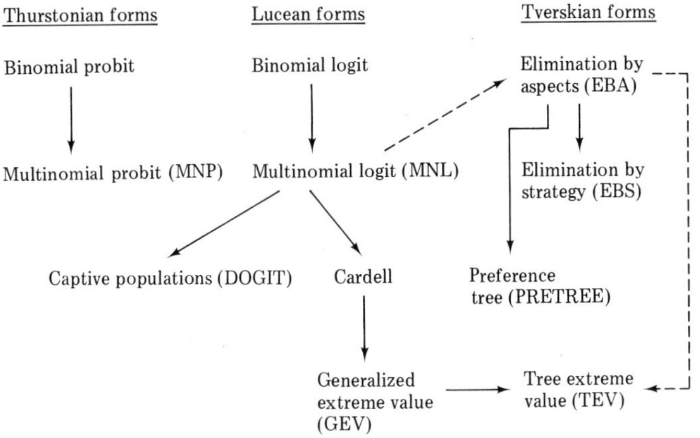

Figure 5.1
Concrete functional forms

In considering probit, logit, and related models, it is useful to quantify the random utility-maximizing hypothesis in the following terms: consider a choice set $\mathbf{B} = \{1, \ldots, m\} \in \mathscr{B}$. Alternative i has a column vector of observed attributes $\mathbf{z}_i$ and an associated utility $u_i = \boldsymbol{\alpha}'\mathbf{z}_i$, where $\boldsymbol{\alpha}$ is a vector of taste weights. Assume $\boldsymbol{\alpha}$ to have a parametric probability distribution with parameter vector $\boldsymbol{\theta}$, and let $\boldsymbol{\beta} = \boldsymbol{\beta}(\boldsymbol{\theta})$ and $\boldsymbol{\Omega} = \boldsymbol{\Omega}(\boldsymbol{\theta})$ denote the mean and covariance matrix of $\boldsymbol{\alpha}$. Let $\mathbf{z_B} = (\mathbf{z}_1, \ldots, \mathbf{z}_m)$ denote the array of observed attributes of the available alternatives. Then the vector of utilities $\mathbf{u_B} = (u_1, \ldots, u_m)$ has a multivariate probability distribution with mean $\boldsymbol{\beta}'\mathbf{z_B}$ and covariance matrix $\mathbf{z}'_\mathbf{B}\boldsymbol{\Omega}\mathbf{z_B}$. The choice probability $P(i \mid \mathbf{B}, \mathrm{s})$ for alternative i, also written $P(i \mid \mathbf{z_B}, \boldsymbol{\theta})$, then equals the probability of drawing a vector $\mathbf{u_B}$ from this distribution such that $u_i \geqq u_j$ for $j \in \mathbf{B}$. For calculation note that $\mathbf{u}_{\mathbf{B}-i} = (u_1 - u_i, \ldots, u_{i-1} - u_i, u_{i+1} - u_i, \ldots, u_m - u_i)$ has a multivariate distribution with mean $\boldsymbol{\beta}'\mathbf{z}_{\mathbf{B}-i}$ and covariance matrix $\mathbf{z}'_{\mathbf{B}-i}\boldsymbol{\Omega}\mathbf{z}_{\mathbf{B}-i}$, where $\mathbf{z}_{\mathbf{B}-i} = (\mathbf{z}_1 - \mathbf{z}_i, \ldots, \mathbf{z}_{i-1} - \mathbf{z}_i, \mathbf{z}_{i+1} - \mathbf{z}_i, \ldots, \mathbf{z}_m - \mathbf{z}_i)$, and that $P(i \mid \mathbf{z_B}, \boldsymbol{\theta})$ equals the nonpositive orthant probability for this $(m-1)$-dimensional distribution.[25]

The vector of attributes $\mathbf{z}_i$ of an alternative in this formulation is a function of the raw data $(\mathbf{q}_i, \mathbf{w}_i, \mathbf{r}, \mathbf{s})$, where $(q_i, \mathbf{w}_i)$ measure characteristics of the alternative and $(\mathbf{r}, \mathbf{s})$ characteristics of the individual and the background economic environment. Since any continuous (indirect) utility function can be approximated on a compact set to any desired degree of accuracy by an appropriate linear-in-parameters specification, and $\mathbf{z}_i$ can incorporate complex transformations and interactions of the raw data, there is virtually no loss of generality in assuming the utility structure $u_i = \boldsymbol{\alpha}'\mathbf{z}_i$.[26] Note that if $\mathbf{z}_i$ includes a (nominal) dummy variable specific to alternative i, then the corresponding component of $\boldsymbol{\alpha}$ can be interpreted as the contribution to utility of unobserved attributes of this alternative. The condition that u_i be homogeneous of degree zero in the prices $(q_i, \mathbf{r})$ will be met by requiring that $\mathbf{z}_i$ be homogeneous of degree zero

25. Suppose $\boldsymbol{\alpha}$ has a multivariate density $g(\boldsymbol{\alpha})$, with characteristic function

$$\gamma(\mathbf{t}) = \int_{-\infty}^{+\infty} e^{i\mathbf{t}'\boldsymbol{\alpha}} g(\boldsymbol{\alpha})d\boldsymbol{\alpha}.$$

Then $\mathbf{u}_{\mathbf{B}-j} = \boldsymbol{\alpha}'\mathbf{z}_{\mathbf{B}-j}$ has the characteristic function $Ee^{i\boldsymbol{\alpha}'\mathbf{z}_{\mathbf{B}-j}\boldsymbol{\tau}} = \gamma(\mathbf{z}_{\mathbf{B}-j}\boldsymbol{\tau})$, and associated density

$$h(\mathbf{u}_{\mathbf{B}-j}) = (2\pi)^{-m+1} \int_{-\infty}^{+\infty} e^{-i\boldsymbol{\tau}'\mathbf{u}_{\mathbf{B}-j}} \gamma(\mathbf{z}_{\mathbf{B}-j}\boldsymbol{\tau})d\tau$$

Then

$$P(j \mid \mathbf{z_B}, \boldsymbol{\theta}) = (2\pi)^{-m+1} \int_{\mathbf{u}_{\mathbf{B}-j}=-\infty}^{0} \int_{-\infty}^{+\infty} e^{-i\boldsymbol{\tau}'\mathbf{u}_{\mathbf{B}-j}} \gamma(\mathbf{z}_{\mathbf{B}-j}\boldsymbol{\tau})d\tau \, d\mathbf{u}_{\mathbf{B}-j}.$$

Starting from a density g with a closed form characteristic function, these formulas can be used in a few cases to obtain simple closed forms or expansions for the choice probabilities. More generally these formulas can be used, with suitable transformations of variables, to obtain numerical integrals of dimension $2(m-1)$ or less for the choice probabilities. However, some special structure is usually needed to make this approach practical.

26. Suppose indirect utility can be written in the form $U(\mathbf{t}_i, \boldsymbol{\tau}_i)$, with $\mathbf{t}_i = (q_i, \mathbf{w}_i, \mathbf{r}, \mathbf{s})$ and $\boldsymbol{\tau}_i$ a vector of unobserved attributes of alternatives and individual characteristics that

in $(q_i, \mathbf{r})$, and that the distribution of $\boldsymbol{\alpha}$ be invariant with respect to price level.

5.12 The Luce Model

A PCS that permits easy computation and interpretation but has a very restrictive pattern of interalternative substitution is the multinomial logit, MNL, form

$$P(i \mid \mathbf{z_B}, \boldsymbol{\beta}) = \frac{e^{\boldsymbol{\beta}'\mathbf{z}_i}}{\sum_{j \in \mathbf{B}} e^{\boldsymbol{\beta}'\mathbf{z}_j}}. \tag{5.25}$$

This form was first suggested by Luce (1959) as a psychological choice model derived from an axiom of independence from irrelevant alternatives, IIA:[27] If $i \in \mathbf{A} \subseteq \mathbf{B}$; then[28]

$$P(i \mid \mathbf{z_B}, \boldsymbol{\beta}) = P(i \mid \mathbf{z_A}, \boldsymbol{\beta}) P(\mathbf{A} \mid \mathbf{z_B}, \boldsymbol{\beta}). \tag{5.26}$$

determine the utility function. As noted earlier, variations in the utility functions of individuals can always be attributed to an unobserved vector $\boldsymbol{\tau}_\mathbf{I}$. Suppose $\mathbf{T}$ and $\mathbf{T}^*$ are compact sets of $\mathbf{t}_i$ and $\boldsymbol{\tau}_i$, respectively. Suppose U is uniformly Lipschitzian in $\mathbf{t}_i$ on $\mathbf{T} \times \mathbf{T}^*$ with constant M; that is, $| U(t_i, \tau_i) - U(t_i', \tau_i) | \leqq M | t_i - t_i' |$ for $t_i, t_i' \in \mathbf{T}$ and $\tau_i \in \mathbf{T}^*$. Suppose $\mathbf{T}$ is defined—by translation, scaling, and extension if necessary—to equal $\mathbf{T} = \{\mathbf{t}_i \in \mathbf{R}^n \mid t_i \geqq 0, \Sigma_{j=1}^n t_{ij} \leqq 1\}$. Let $\mathbf{K}$ be the set of integer vectors $(k_1, \ldots, k_n)$ with $(k_1/N, \ldots, k_n/N) \in \mathbf{T}$, and define

$$z_{k_1 \cdots k_n}(\mathbf{t}_i) = t_{i1}^{k_1} \cdots t_{in}^{k_n} (1 - t_{i1} - \cdots - t_{in})^{N - k_1 - \cdots - k_n} N!/k_1! \ldots k_n!$$

Consider an approximation $\hat{U}$ to U defined by

$$\hat{U}(\mathbf{t}_i, \boldsymbol{\tau}_i) = \sum_{(k_1, \cdots, k_n) \in \mathbf{K}} \alpha_{k_1 \cdots k_n}(\boldsymbol{\tau}_i) z_{k_1 \cdots k_n}(\mathbf{t}_i),$$

with $\alpha_{k_1 \ldots k_n}(\tau_i) = U((k_1/N, \ldots, k_n/N), \tau_i)$. Given $\varepsilon > 0$, if $N \geqq nM^2/\varepsilon^2$, then $| U(\mathbf{t}_i, \tau_i) - \hat{U}(\mathbf{t}_i, \tau_i) | < \varepsilon$ on $\mathbf{T} \times \mathbf{T}^*$ (see McFadden 1978b, p. 236). Since $\mathbf{T}^*$ can be chosen so that the probability of unobserved variables falling outside $\mathbf{T}^*$ is as small as we please, the RUM $\hat{U}$ will yield a PCS which is as close as we please to the PCS generated by U. Note that this justification from approximation theory for a linear-in-parameters form does not imply that this approach is efficient, or even practical, for all applications.

27. The binary logistic curve is of much earlier vintage.

28. $P(\mathbf{A} \mid \mathbf{z_B}, \boldsymbol{\theta}) = \sum_{j \in \mathbf{A}} P(j \mid \mathbf{z_B}, \boldsymbol{\theta})$.

This system satisfies TPCS and can be derived from a social surplus function

$$G(\mathbf{q_B}) = \ln \sum_{j \in \mathbf{B}} e^{-q_j} \tag{5.27}$$

where $q_j = -\boldsymbol{\beta}'\mathbf{z}_j$.

The Luce model was shown by Marschak (1960) to be consistent with RUM. A constructive demonstration due to Marley is reported in Luce and Suppes (1965); see also McFadden (1973) and Yellot (1977). Specifically, if the u_i are independently distributed, with

$$\text{Prob}[u_i \leqq \mu] = e^{-e^{-\mu - \boldsymbol{\beta}'\mathbf{z}_i}}, \tag{5.28}$$

then (5.2) yields (5.25) by an easy integration.[29] The distribution (5.28) is called a type I extreme value, or Weibull, distribution.

An implication of the MNL form is that all cross elasticities are equal; that is, for $i \neq j$,

$$\frac{\partial \ln P(i \mid \mathbf{z_B}, \boldsymbol{\theta})}{\partial \ln z_{jk}} = \beta_k z_{jk} P(j \mid \mathbf{z_B}, \boldsymbol{\theta}), \tag{5.29}$$

and the elasticity does not depend on i. This property is not plausible in some choice situations; see Debreu (1960) and McFadden, Tye, and Train (1977). The lack of flexibility of the Luce model is characteristic of a wider class of models satisfying the following property, called order independence: if $i, j \in \mathbf{A}$, $i, j \notin \mathbf{B}$, and $k \in \mathbf{B}$, then $P(i \mid \mathbf{A}) \geqq P(j \mid \mathbf{A})$ if and only if $P(k \mid \mathbf{B} \cup \{i\}) \leqq P(k \mid \mathbf{B} \cup \{j\})$.[30] A classic example shows that models satisfying order independence yield implausible conclusions when there are strong contrasts in the similarity of the alternatives. Suppose the alternatives are trips by auto (1), red bus (2), or blue bus (3). Suppose individuals treat the two buses as virtually equivalent and at prevailing travel times and costs divide evenly between auto and bus, so that $p_{12} = p_{13} = p_{23} = 0.5$, $p_{123} = 0.5$, and $p_{213} = p_{312} = 0.25$.[31] Consider

29. In the terminology of the preceding section with $u_i = \boldsymbol{\alpha}'\mathbf{z}_i$ and $\boldsymbol{\alpha}$ random, assume that the first m components of $\mathbf{z}$ are dummy variables for the m alternatives, that $\alpha_{m+1}, \ldots$ are nonrandom, and that $(\alpha_1, \ldots, \alpha_m)$ are independently distributed, with $E\alpha_i = \beta_i$ and $\text{Prob}[\alpha_i - \beta_i \leqq \mu] = \exp[-e^{-\mu}]$. Note that at least one normalization, say, $\Sigma_{i=1}^m \beta_i = 0$, is needed for identification. In applications some or all of these β_i may be restricted to zero.

30. We assume with little loss of empirical generality that all choice probabilities are positive. This property was introduced by Tversky (1972a).

31. Define $p_{ij} = P(i \mid \{i, j\})$ and $p_{ijk} = P(i \mid \{i, j, k\})$.

$\mathbf{A} = \{1, 2, 3\}$ and $\mathbf{B} = \{3\}$. By order independence $p_{123} > p_{213}$ implies $p_{31} < p_{32}$, contradicting the probabilities we have constructed in light of the pattern of similarity of the alternatives.

Tversky (1972) has shown that order independence is equivalent to a property of PCS termed simple scalability: for $\mathbf{B} = \{1, \ldots, m\}$ the choice probabilities can be written as functions $P(i \mid \mathbf{B}, \mathbf{s}) = \pi_i(q_1(\mathbf{r}, \mathbf{w}_1, \mathbf{s}), \ldots, q_m(\mathbf{r}, \mathbf{w}_m, \mathbf{s}))$ of scale values (undesirability indices) $q_i(\mathbf{r}, \mathbf{w}_i, \mathbf{s})$ of the alternatives, with π_i increasing in q_j for $j \neq i$, and decreasing in q_i, π_i going to zero when $q_i \to +\infty$, and the form of the function π_i depending on the attributes of the alternatives solely through the scale values. Then clearly functional forms that are sufficiently flexible to accommodate cases of the red bus/blue bus type must depend on the orientation of alternatives in attribute space, as well as scalar measures of their desirability. For example, choice systems satisfying TPCS will be simply scalable if the social surplus function has the weakly separable form $G(h_1(q_1, \mathbf{w}_1, \mathbf{r}, \mathbf{s}), \ldots, h_m(q_m, \mathbf{w}_m, \mathbf{r}, \mathbf{s}), \mathbf{r}, \mathbf{s})$. Similarly PCS derived from RUM of the form described in the preceding section will be simply scalable when the attributes of alternatives shift only the mean of the distribution of utility levels.

Estimation of the multinomial logit model is discussed in McFadden (1973). A method for guaranteeing convergence of maximum likelihood estimation algorithms is discussed in section 5.20.

Because of its computational simplicity, the multinomial logit model has been a primary focus of attempts at functional generalizations. Some of these are discussed in section 5.15.

5.13 Thurstone's Model V

Thurstone (1927) proposed a random utility model for psychometric choice in which the utility levels of the alternatives are normally distributed. For binary choice this yields the probit model widely used in analysis of binary data; see Finney (1964) and Cox (1970). Multinomial probit, MNP, models are discussed in Bock and Jones (1968), McFadden (1976), Hausman and Wise (1976), Daganzo, Bouthelier, and Sheffi (1976), and Lerman and Manski, chapter 7.

Supose the utility of alternative i is $u_i = \boldsymbol{\alpha}'\mathbf{z}_i$, where $\boldsymbol{\alpha}$ is multivariate normal with mean $\boldsymbol{\beta}$ and covariance matrix $\mathbf{AA}'$. Additive normal variations in utility are incorporated in this formulation as random coefficients of alternative specific dummy variables contained in $\mathbf{z}$. The vector $\mathbf{u}_{\mathbf{B}}$ is multivariate normal with mean $\mathbf{z}_{\mathbf{B}}\boldsymbol{\beta}$ and covariance matrix $\mathbf{z}_{\mathbf{B}}\mathbf{A}\mathbf{A}'\mathbf{z}_{\mathbf{B}}'$. The choice probabilities satisfy

$$P(i \mid \mathbf{z}_{\mathbf{B}}, \boldsymbol{\beta}, \mathbf{A}) = N(-\mathbf{z}_{\mathbf{B}-i}\boldsymbol{\beta}, \mathbf{z}_{\mathbf{B}-i}\mathbf{A}\mathbf{A}'\mathbf{z}_{\mathbf{B}-i}'), \tag{5.30}$$

where $N(\boldsymbol{\varepsilon}_{\mathbf{B}}, \boldsymbol{\Omega}_{\mathbf{B}})$ is the multivariate normal cumulative distribution function, with zero mean and covariance matrix $\boldsymbol{\Omega}_{\mathbf{B}}$, evaluated at $\boldsymbol{\varepsilon}_{\mathbf{B}}$, for any set of alternatives $\mathbf{B}$. This general structure and notation for the PCS follow from section 5.11 and the property that linear transformations of normal vectors are again normal.

In the case that alternative-specific dummies are included among the attributes, it is convenient to redefine $u_i = -q_i + \boldsymbol{\alpha}'\mathbf{z}_i$, where $-q_i$ is the mean of the alternative-specific effect. Then

$$P(i \mid \mathbf{z}_{\mathbf{B}}, \mathbf{q}_{\mathbf{B}}, \boldsymbol{\beta}, \mathbf{A}) = N(\mathbf{q}_{\mathbf{B}-i} - \mathbf{z}_{\mathbf{B}-i}\boldsymbol{\beta}, \mathbf{z}_{\mathbf{B}-i}\mathbf{A}\mathbf{A}'\mathbf{z}_{\mathbf{B}-i}'), \tag{5.31}$$

and the choice probabilities satisfy TPCS, with a social surplus function [32]

$$\begin{aligned} G(\mathbf{q}_{\mathbf{B}}, \mathbf{z}_{\mathbf{B}}\boldsymbol{\beta}, \mathbf{z}_{\mathbf{B}}\mathbf{A}\mathbf{A}'\mathbf{z}_{\mathbf{B}}') &= \int_{t=-\infty}^{+\infty} [N(-\mathbf{z}_{\mathbf{B}}\boldsymbol{\beta} + t, \mathbf{z}_{\mathbf{B}}\mathbf{A}\mathbf{A}'\mathbf{z}_{\mathbf{B}}') \\ &\qquad - N(\mathbf{q}_{\mathbf{B}} - \mathbf{z}_{\mathbf{B}}\boldsymbol{\beta} + t, \mathbf{z}_{\mathbf{B}}\mathbf{A}\mathbf{A}'\mathbf{z}_{\mathbf{B}}')]\,dt \\ &= -q_1 - \int_{t=0}^{\infty} [N(\mathbf{q}_{\mathbf{B}-1} - \mathbf{z}_{\mathbf{B}-1}\boldsymbol{\beta} + t, \mathbf{z}_{\mathbf{B}-1}\mathbf{A}\mathbf{A}'\mathbf{z}_{\mathbf{B}-1}') \\ &\qquad - N(-\mathbf{z}_{\mathbf{B}-1}\boldsymbol{\beta} + t, \mathbf{z}_{\mathbf{B}-1}\mathbf{A}\mathbf{A}'\mathbf{z}_{\mathbf{B}-1}')]\,dt. \end{aligned} \tag{5.32}$$

Evaluation of the choice probabilities or the social surplus function requires numerical integration or approximation of $(m-1)$-dimensional multivariate normal orthant probabilities. This is practical with conventional expansions for $m \leqq 3$ but generally impractical for $m > 5$; see Hausman and Wise (1978). A procedure due to Clark (1961) that

32. Recall that in the notation adopted beginning in section 5.11 the attributes $(\mathbf{z}_i, \mathbf{q}_i)$ are assumed to be homogeneous of degree zero in economic prices. Thus, if q_i is the price of the discrete alternative, it is here assumed to be a relative price. The conditions SS and TPCS in section 2.6 are stated in terms of a vector of absolute prices and impose the restrictions that the social surplus function and choice probabilities be homogeneous of degree one and zero, respectively, in these prices. For the current application the prices in SS and TPCS should be reinterpreted as being relative, and the homogeneity conditions in SS 5.2 and TPCS 5.2 should be ignored.

approximates the maximum of two normal variates by a normal variate is reasonably accurate for $m \leqq 10$ when the underlying variates have comparable variances and nonnegative correlations; see Daganzo, Bouthelier, and Sheffi (1977), Lerman and Manski, chapter 7, and Horowitz (1979).

When the MNP model has the form (5.31) with only the coefficients of alternative-specific dummy variables distributed randomly, the covariance matrix $\mathbf{z}_{\mathbf{B}-i}\mathbf{A}\mathbf{A}'\mathbf{z}_{\mathbf{B}-i'}$ depends only on the nominal labels of alternatives contained in $\mathbf{z}$, by PCS 5.2. If in this case there is no plausible link between nominal labels and degree of similarity, the covariance matrix will have a structure independent of the alternatives in the choice set, making the model simply scalable, and hence subject to the criticisms given the Luce model. More generally, with stochastic variation in coefficients of $\boldsymbol{\alpha}$ other than dummy coefficients, the MNP model permits quite flexible patterns of substitution across alternatives and components of variance structure for taste variations. The primary difficulty in application of the MNP model is the lack of practical, accurate methods for approximating the choice probabilities when the number of alternatives is large. There are also some technical issues in formulating iterative algorithms for maximum likelihood estimation in MNP models; see section 5.20.

5.14 Tversky Elimination Models

Choice can be viewed as a process in which alternatives are eliminated from the choice set until a single alternative remains. Formally, an elimination model is defined by a transition probability $Q: \mathscr{B} \times \mathscr{B} \times \mathbf{S} \times \mathbf{T} \to [0, 1]$, with $\mathbf{T} = \{1, 2, \ldots\}$ and with $Q(\mathbf{A} \mid \mathbf{B}, \mathbf{s}, t)$ interpreted as the probability that, starting from a set of alternatives $\mathbf{B}$ at step t, decision makers will reach in the next step the set $\mathbf{A}$ by eliminating some alternatives. The transition probabilities must satisfy $Q(\mathbf{A} \mid \mathbf{B}, \mathbf{s}, \mathbf{t}) \geqq 0$, $Q(\varnothing \mid \mathbf{B}, \mathbf{s}, t) = 0$, $Q(\mathbf{B} \mid \mathbf{B}, \mathbf{s}, t) < 1$, and $\Sigma_{\mathbf{A} \in \mathscr{B}}^{\mathbf{A} \subseteq \mathbf{B}} Q(\mathbf{A} \mid \mathbf{B}, \mathbf{s}, t) = 1$. Choice probabilities equal the sum, over all possible chains, of transition probabilities for the chain. When the transition probabilities are stationary (independent of t), the choice probabilities are given by the recursion formula

$$P(i \mid \mathbf{B}, \mathbf{s}) = \sum_{\mathbf{A} \in \mathscr{F}_{\mathbf{B}}^{*}} Q(\mathbf{A} \mid \mathbf{B}, \mathbf{s}) P(i \mid \mathbf{A}, \mathbf{s}), \tag{5.33}$$

where $\mathscr{F}_{\mathbf{B}}^{*} = \{\mathbf{A} \in \mathscr{B} \mid \mathbf{A} \subseteq \mathbf{B}, \emptyset \neq \mathbf{A}\}$.

Concrete elimination models are specified by parameterizing the transition probabilities Q. Tversky (1972a, 1972b) has introduced an important class of elimination by aspect, EBA, models in which there is associated with each $\mathbf{A} \in \mathscr{B}$ a nonnegative scale value $v_{\mathbf{A}} = V(\mathbf{z}_{\mathbf{A}})$, and the transition probabilities satisfy

$$Q(\mathbf{A} \mid \mathbf{B}, \mathbf{s}) = \frac{v_{\mathbf{A}}}{\sum_{\mathbf{C} \in \mathscr{F}^*_{\mathbf{B}}} v_{\mathbf{C}}} \tag{5.34}$$

for $\mathbf{A} \in \mathscr{F}^*_{\mathbf{B}}$. Tversky shows that this model can be interpreted as the result of a choice process in which decision makers sample from some distribution over aspects of alternatives, eliminating alternatives that fail to have the sampled aspect. The scale value $v_{\mathbf{A}}$ is interpreted as the probability of drawing an aspect that is unique to $\mathbf{A}$ and common within $\mathbf{A}$. The EBA model is consistent with a population of preference maximizers, each with lexicographic preferences over aspects.

The Luce model is a special case of the EBA family, obtained when $v_{\mathbf{A}} = 0$ for $\mathbf{A}$ containing more than one element. More generally the EBA model can accommodate complex patterns of substitutability of alternatives, with $v_{\mathbf{A}}$ measuring the similarity of the alternatives in $\mathbf{A}$. An even more general family of elimination models that are consistent with random preference maximization and permit nonstationary transition probabilities can be defined by considering strategies for selecting aspects. These elimination-by-strategy, EBS, models are discussed in section 5.24.

The EBA functional form has considerable potential for econometric applications. When the scale functions V are log-linear in parameters, $\ln V(\mathbf{z}_{\mathbf{A}}) = \boldsymbol{\beta}'_{\mathbf{A}}\mathbf{z}_{\mathbf{A}}$, the choice probabilities can be written as sums of products of MNL forms. Maximum likelihood estimation could be carried out for such systems with relatively minor modifications of current MNL computer programs. One drawback of EBA for econometric applications is that the motivation for the model provides little guidance for parametric specification of the scale function V.

5.15 Generalized Extreme Value Models

A number of authors have sought variants of the MNL form that retain its computational advantages while permitting more flexible patterns of substitution. Most of these variants must be rejected because they are inconsistent with RUM or fail to accommodate substitution patterns of the red bus/blue bus type.[33]

The MNL model can be derived from a RUM with independently extreme value-distributed utility levels. One approach to generalizing the MNL model is to start from a more general multivariate extreme value distribution. Suppose alternative i has a scale value $q_i = -\boldsymbol{\beta}'\mathbf{z}_i$. The following result gives a large class of logitlike PCS. These are termed generalized extreme value, GEV, models:

THEOREM 5.2: For $\mathbf{B} = \{1, \ldots, m\} \in \mathscr{B}$, consider $H(\mathbf{y_B}, \mathbf{z_B}, \mathbf{s})$ satisfying

GEV 5.1: $H(\mathbf{y_B}, \mathbf{z_B}, \mathbf{s})$ is a nonnegative, linear homogeneous function of $\mathbf{y_B} \geqq \mathbf{0}$.

GEV 5.2: $\lim\limits_{y_i \to +\infty} H(\mathbf{y_B}, \mathbf{z_B}, \mathbf{s}) = +\infty.$

GEV 5.3: The mixed partial derivatives of H exist and are continuous, with nonpositive even and nonnegative odd mixed partial derivatives.

GEV 5.4: If $\mathbf{B} = \{i_1, \ldots, i_m\} \in \mathscr{B}$ and $\mathbf{B}' = \{i_1', \ldots, i_m', \ldots, i_{m+n}'\} \in \mathscr{B}$ satisfies $\mathbf{z}_{i_k} = \mathbf{z}_{i_k'}$ for $k = 1, \ldots, m$, then

$$H(\mathbf{y_B}, \mathbf{z_B}, \mathbf{s}) = H((\mathbf{y_B}, 0, \ldots, 0), \mathbf{z_{B'}}, \mathbf{s}).$$

If H satisfies GEV and $\mathbf{B} = \{1, \ldots, m\}$, then

$$F(\boldsymbol{\varepsilon}_\mathbf{B}, \mathbf{z_B}, \mathbf{s}) = \exp\{-H(e^{-\varepsilon_1}, \ldots, e^{-\varepsilon_m}, \mathbf{z_B}, \mathbf{s})\} \tag{5.35}$$

is a multivariate extreme value distribution. A random utility-maximizing model in which utility levels are distributed $F(\mathbf{u_B} + \mathbf{q_B}, \mathbf{z_B}, \mathbf{s})$ for $\mathbf{B} \in \mathscr{B}$ satisfies AIRUM and has a social surplus function

$$G(\mathbf{q_B}, \mathbf{z_B}, \mathbf{s}) = E \max_{i \in \mathbf{B}} u_i - \gamma$$

$$= \ln H(e^{-q_1}, \ldots, e^{-q_m}, \mathbf{z_B}, \mathbf{s}), \tag{5.36}$$

where γ is a constant independent of $\mathbf{B}$, and choice probabilities satisfying

33. Models that may fail to be consistent with RUM are the cascade and maximum models of McFadden (1974), the universal logit model of McFadden (1975), and the fully competitive model of McLynn (1973). Models with insufficient flexibility to accommodate reasonable patterns of substitution are the cascade and fully competitive models and the DOGIT model of Gaudry (1977).

$$\pi_i(\mathbf{q_B}, \mathbf{z_B}, \mathbf{s}) = -\frac{\partial}{\partial q_i} \ln H(e^{-q_1}, \ldots, e^{-q_m}, \mathbf{z_B}, \mathbf{s}). \tag{5.37}$$

This theorem is proved by first showing that F in (5.35) is a cumulative probability distribution; that is, the range of F is the unit interval and the density f of F is nonnegative. The range condition follows from GEV 5.1 and GEV 5.2, and the nonnegativity of f can be established by induction on the order of a mixed partial derivative of F, using GEV 5.3. The formulae (5.36) and (5.37) for the social surplus function and for the choice probabilities follow by direct integration from (5.35). A formal proof is given in McFadden (1978a).

Property GEV 5.1 of H implies that the function G defined in (5.35) satisfies SS 5.1 and SS 5.3. Property SS 5.6 is a consequence of GEV 5.4. An induction argument using GEV 5.3 establishes SS 5.4. To show SS 5.5, note that

$$G_i = \frac{-H_i(\mathbf{y_B}, \mathbf{z_B}, \mathbf{s})}{H(\mathbf{y_B}, \mathbf{z_B}, \mathbf{s})} \tag{5.38}$$

with $y_j = e^{-q_j + q_i}$. As $q_i \to -\infty$, $\mathbf{y_B}$ converges to a vector $\mathbf{y'_B}$ with one in component i, zeroes elsewhere. Since $H(\mathbf{y'_B}, \mathbf{z_B}, \mathbf{s}) = H_i(\mathbf{y'_B}, \mathbf{z_B}, \mathbf{s}) > 0$ by GEV 5.2, (5.38) has the limit -1 as $q_i \to -\infty$. Under the assumptions of this section the q_i are homogeneous of degree zero in absolute prices and SS 5.2 need not be imposed. Then G is a social surplus function, and theorem 5.1 gives an alternative, nonconstructive proof that an AIRUM model exists with PCS satisfying (5.37).

When the social surplus function (5.36) depends on the $\mathbf{z}_i$ only through the terms $\boldsymbol{\beta}'\mathbf{z}_i = -q_i$, the PCS is simply scalable. Hence GEV models with flexible crossalternative substitution require dependence of $H(\mathbf{y_B}, \mathbf{z_B}, \mathbf{s})$ on the orientation of alternatives $\mathbf{z_B}$.

The GEV model reduces to the Luce model when

$$H(\mathbf{y_B}, \mathbf{z_B}, \mathbf{s}) = \left[\sum_{i \in \mathbf{B}} y_i^{1/1-\sigma}\right]^{1-\sigma},$$

$0 \leqq \sigma < 1$. An example of a more general function satisfying GEV is

$$H(\mathbf{y_B}, \mathbf{z_B}, \mathbf{s}) = \sum_{\mathbf{C} \in \mathscr{F}^*_{\mathbf{B}}} a(\mathbf{z_C}) \left[\sum_{i \in \mathbf{C}} y_i^{1/1-\sigma(\mathbf{z_C})}\right]^{1-\sigma(\mathbf{z_C})}, \tag{5.39}$$

with $a(\mathbf{z_C}) \geqq 0$ and $0 \leqq \sigma(\mathbf{z_C}) < 1$.[34] The PCS for (5.39) can be written

$$P(i \mid \mathbf{B}, \mathbf{s}) = \sum_{\mathbf{C} \in \mathscr{F}^*_{\mathbf{B}}} P(i \mid \mathbf{C}, \mathbf{s}) Q(\mathbf{C} \mid \mathbf{B}, \mathbf{s}), \tag{5.40}$$

where

$$P(i \mid \mathbf{C}, \mathbf{s}) = \frac{e^{\boldsymbol{\beta}'\mathbf{z}_i/1-\sigma(\mathbf{z_C})}}{\sum_{j \in \mathbf{C}} e^{\boldsymbol{\beta}'\mathbf{z}_j/1-\sigma(\mathbf{z_C})}} \quad \text{for } i \in \mathbf{C}, \tag{5.41}$$

and

$$Q(\mathbf{C} \mid \mathbf{B}, \mathbf{s}) = \frac{a(\mathbf{z_C}) e^{(1-\sigma(\mathbf{z_C}))h_{\mathbf{C}}}}{\sum_{\mathbf{A} \in \mathscr{F}^*_{\mathbf{B}}} a(\mathbf{z_A}) e^{(1-\sigma(\mathbf{z_A}))h_{\mathbf{A}}}}, \tag{5.42}$$

with

$$h_{\mathbf{C}} = \ln \sum_{j \in \mathbf{C}} e^{\boldsymbol{\beta}'\mathbf{z}_j/1-\sigma(\mathbf{z_C})}. \tag{5.43}$$

This can be interpreted as a PCS in which decision makers invoke a subset of alternatives **C** from **B** and then select an alternative from **C**. Conditional choice of an alternative from a set **C** has choice probabilities (5.41) of the MNL form. Associated with a set **C** is an inclusive value $h_{\mathbf{C}}$ which equals the social surplus obtained from the MNL form (5.41). Choice probabilities for the invoked set **C** are multinomial logit functions of the inclusive values. The function $\sigma(\mathbf{z_C})$ is a measure of the similarity of alternatives within **C**. When the alternatives in **C** are very similar and $\sigma(\mathbf{z_C})$ is near one, the conditional choice probability (5.41) selects with high probability the alternative with the highest value in **C** of $\boldsymbol{\beta}'\mathbf{z}_i$. Then $h_{\mathbf{C}}$ is approximately $\max_{i \in \mathbf{C}} \boldsymbol{\beta}'\mathbf{z}_i/(1-\sigma(\mathbf{z_C}))$, and in the choice of an invoked set using the probabilities (5.42), the set **C** is assessed approximately as if it contained a single alternative with a scale value $\max_{i \in \mathbf{C}} \boldsymbol{\beta}'\mathbf{z}_i$.

Functions of the form (5.39) can also be nested to multiple levels to yield a broader class of functions. For example, the two-level nested function

34. GEV 5.2 requires for each $i \in \mathbf{B}$ that $a(\mathbf{z_C}) > 0$ for some subset **C** of **B** containing i. A similar condition is required on (5.44).

$$H(\mathbf{y_B}, \mathbf{z_B}, \mathbf{s}) = \sum_{\phi \neq \mathbf{C} \subseteq \mathbf{B}} a_1(\mathbf{z_C}) \cdot \left[\sum_{\emptyset \neq \mathbf{D} \subseteq \mathbf{C}} a_2(\mathbf{z_D}) \left[\sum_{i \in \mathbf{D}} y_i^{1/1 - \sigma_2(\mathbf{z_D})} \right]^{(1 - \sigma_2(\mathbf{z_D}))/1 - \sigma_1(\mathbf{z_C})} \right]^{1 - \sigma_1(\mathbf{z_C})} \tag{5.44}$$

satisfies GEV when $a_1(\mathbf{z_C}) \geqq 0$, $a_2(\mathbf{z_D}) \geqq 0$, and $0 \leqq \sigma_2(\mathbf{z_D}) \leqq \sigma_1(\mathbf{z_C}) < 1$ for $\mathbf{D} \subseteq \mathbf{C}$. The PCS generated by (5.44) can be written, analogously to (5.40) through (5.43), as a sum of products of transition probabilities, with each transition probability corresponding to a level in the nest and expressable in an MNL form giving the choice at the next level of the nest, conditioned on the invoked set at this level. The variables in this transition probability are inclusive values of the next stage alternatives. The bounds on the parameters in (5.44) imply that the coefficients of inclusive value at each level lie in the unit interval; this condition can also be shown using theorem 5.1 to be necessary for consistency of the PCS, from (5.37) and (5.44), with AIRUM.

Choice probabilities of the form (5.40) through (5.43) were apparently first derived for a special case by Cardell (1977). Alternative derivations of PCS with the nested MNL structure (5.40) through (5.43) have been given independently by Ben-Akiva and Lerman (1977) and Daly and Zachary (1976).

As the example (5.40) through (5.43) and its obvious extensions make clear, GEV models can be interpreted as elimination models with nonstationary transition probabilities, or elimination-by-strategy models in the terminology of section 5.24. The transition probabilities have MNL forms as in the elimination-by-aspect model (5.34) but with a different definition of the scale values. Inspection suggests that EBA and GEV models are roughly comparable in flexibility and complexity.

5.16 Preference Trees

The elimination-by-aspects and generalized extreme value models both permit very general patterns of similarities between alternatives. Psychological analysis suggests that judgments of similarity often exhibit a more restricted structure in which statements such as "*A* is more like *B* than it is like *C*" have behavioral meaning; see particularly Sattath and Tversky

(1977), and also Rumelhart and Greeno (1971), Edgell et al. (1973), and Sjöberg (1975). With this structure alternatives can be arrayed in a preference tree with the least similar alternatives on the most distant branches; an example is given in figure 5.2. In economic choice it is reasonable to postulate that crossalternative substitutability is related to perceived similarity, so that alternatives on distant branches are the least substitutable. This suggests that choice in a tree be modeled as a process of transitions through a fixed hierarchy of nodes, eliminating undesirable branches until a single alternative is reached.[35] It is clear from figure 5.2 that preference trees can accommodate examples of red bus/blue bus type by making the bus alternatives very similar to each other.

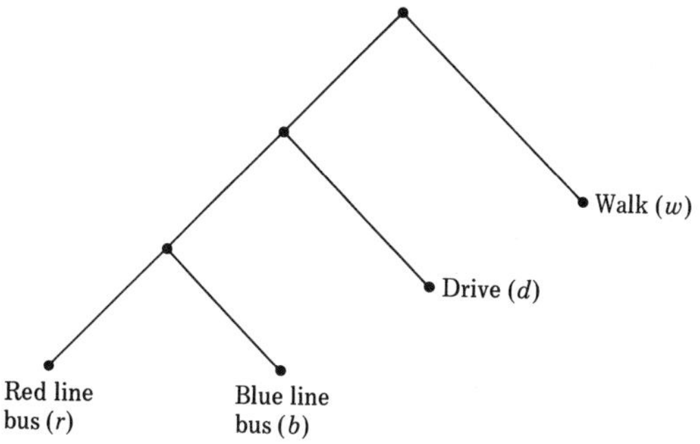

Figure 5.2
A preference tree for transportation modes

The general notation used in sections 5.14 and 5.15 to describe transitions specializes readily to preference trees and will be used for the model definition. (Later, for convenience in applications, we introduce an index notation for nodes.) A node in a preference tree is identified by the set of elemental alternatives at the ends of the branch below this node. This characterization can be applied to the tree formed by pruning away all branches not containing an alternative in a specified set of elemental alternatives.

35. When data are observed only on final choices, as is usual in economic applications, it is impossible to determine whether this elimination heuristic describes decision processes used by individuals. There is some evidence from verbal protocols in laboratory experiments supporting hierarchical elimination as a description of the cognitive choice process.

Any set $\mathbf{B} \in \mathscr{B}$ can be identified as the stem, or uppermost node, of the tree formed by pruning all branches not containing elements of $\mathbf{B}$. Define $\mathscr{F}_{\mathbf{B}}$ to be the family of nodes immediately below the stem of the pruned tree and $\mathscr{F}^*_{\mathbf{B}}$ to be the family of all nodes in the branch starting from $\mathbf{B}$. In figure 5.2, for example, $\mathscr{F}_{\{r,b,d,w\}} = \{\{w\}, \{r,b,d\}\}$ and $\mathscr{F}^*_{\{r,b,d,w\}} = \{\{w\}, \{r,b,d\}, \{d\}, \{r, b\}, \{r\}, \{b\}, \{r, b, d, w\}\}$, while $\mathscr{F}_{\{r,b,w\}} = \{\{w\}, \{r, b\}\}$ and $\mathscr{F}^*_{\{r,b,w\}} = \{\{w\}, \{r, b\}, \{r\}, \{b\}, \{r, b, w\}\}$.

We shall define a hierarchical elimination system, HES, for a specified preference tree to be one in which the PCS satisfies a recursion relation

$$P(i \mid \mathbf{B}, \mathbf{s}) = \sum_{\mathbf{C} \in \mathscr{F}_{\mathbf{B}}} P(i \mid \mathbf{C}, \mathbf{s}) Q(\mathbf{C} \mid \mathbf{B}, \mathbf{s}) \tag{5.45}$$

for some family of transition probabilities betwen adjacent nodes. For each $\mathbf{B} \in \mathscr{B}$ and $i \in \mathbf{B}$, the preference tree identifies a unique sequence of nodes $\{i\} \equiv \mathbf{B}_0 \subseteq \mathbf{B}_1 \subseteq \cdots \subseteq \mathbf{B}_J \equiv \mathbf{B}$ with $\mathbf{B}_{j-1} \in \mathscr{F}_{\mathbf{B}_j}$. The choice probability can be written

$$P(i \mid \mathbf{B}, \mathbf{s}) = Q(\mathbf{B}_0 \mid \mathbf{B}_1, \mathbf{s}) Q(\mathbf{B}_1 \mid \mathbf{B}_2, \mathbf{s}) \ldots Q(\mathbf{B}_{J-1} \mid \mathbf{B}_J, \mathbf{s}). \tag{5.46}$$

Then observations on choices are equivalent to observations on transitions, and maximum likelihood estimation of the parameters of an HES can be interpreted as maximum likelihood estimation of the parameters of the transition probabilities using observations on transitions. If the transition probabilities have computationally practical functional forms, fully efficient (full information) maximum likelihood estimation of the system parameters may be feasible. More generally it may be possible to formulate a sequence of computationally simple conditional maximum likelihood procedures, corresponding to levels in the tree, which yield consistent, but not in general efficient, estimators. These observations will apply to the two parametric specifications of HES based on the EBA and GEV models.

First consider the EBA model applied to preference trees. This specialization has been developed by Tversky and Sattath (1979), who derive its properties and report experimental evidence on its validity. Let $v_{\mathbf{C}} = V(\mathbf{z}_{\mathbf{C}})$ be a nonnegative scale value associated with a node $\mathbf{C}$, where $\mathbf{z}_{\mathbf{C}}$ is a vector of observed attributes of the alternatives in $\mathbf{C}$.[36] One can

36. The vector $\mathbf{z}$ is defined as in section 5.12 to incorporate the effects of attributes of alternatives, individual characteristics, and their interactions. We interpret $\mathbf{z}_{\mathbf{C}}$ as the vector of attributes common to or representative of the alternatives in $\mathbf{C}$.

interpret $v_{\mathbf{C}}$ as a measure of the set of aspects of alternatives that are unique to **C** and common within **C**. Define a nonnegative scale value $v_{\mathbf{C}}^*$ associated with the branch with stem **C**,

$$v_{\mathbf{C}}^* = \sum_{\mathbf{A} \in \mathscr{F}_{\mathbf{C}}^*} v_{\mathbf{A}}. \tag{5.47}$$

For $\mathbf{C} \in \mathscr{F}_{\mathbf{B}}$ define the transition probabilities

$$Q(\mathbf{C} \mid \mathbf{B}, \mathbf{s}) = \frac{v_{\mathbf{C}}^*}{\sum_{\mathbf{A} \in \mathscr{F}_{\mathbf{B}}} v_{\mathbf{A}}^*}. \tag{5.48}$$

We term a PCS satisfying (5.45) through (5.48) a hierarchical elimination-by-aspects, HEBA, model.

The EBA model (5.33) through (5.34) applied to a preference tree, with the specified scale values $v_{\mathbf{C}}$ for nodes in the tree and zero scale values for other subsets of the choice set, permits direct transitions from a node to any node in the branch below it, in contrast to the hierarchical protocol employed in HEBA. Despite this apparent difference the two models yield the same PCS. This can be seen for the example in figure 5.2. by writing out the choice probabilities. A general equivalence theorem has been proved by Tversky and Sattath. Since EBA is consistent with random preference maximization, this theorem estabishes that HEBA is also consistent. These authors refer to HEBA in either of its equivalent forms as a PRETREE model.

For econometric applications the scale functions V can be assumed with little loss of generality to be log-linear in parameters, $\ln V(\mathbf{z}_{\mathbf{C}}) = \boldsymbol{\beta}'_{\mathbf{C}}\mathbf{z}_{\mathbf{C}}$ for nodes **C** in the tree. Then, as in the general EBA model, the transition probabilities can be written as sums of MNL functional forms, with $Q(\mathbf{B}_0 \mid \mathbf{B}_1, \mathbf{s})$ a simple MNL form, and the transition probability at a node $\mathbf{B}_j$ at level j in the tree depending on $\boldsymbol{\beta}_{\mathbf{B}_j}$ and on terms appearing in the transition probabilities at levels $1, \ldots, j-1$. Then a sequential procedure that will yield consistent parameter estimates under normal regularity conditions is to first estimate the parameters of $\boldsymbol{\beta}_{\mathbf{B}_0}$ by conditional maximum likelihood estimation applied to level 1 transitions, then estimate the parameters of $\boldsymbol{\beta}_{\mathbf{B}_1}$ using level 2 transitions, substituting the estimate of $\boldsymbol{\beta}_{\mathbf{B}_0}$ obtained at level 1, and so on. Computational formulae for this procedure can be developed analogously to the formulae given in section 5.22 for the following model.

Next consider the GEV model applied to preference trees. Define scale values $v_i = e^{-q_i} \equiv e^{\boldsymbol{\beta}'\mathbf{z}_i}$, where we assume with little loss of generality that v_i is log-linear in parameters $\boldsymbol{\beta}$ and use the notation $q_i = -\boldsymbol{\beta}'\mathbf{z}_i$. Define a function $\sigma(\mathbf{z_C})$ measuring the similarity of alternatives at node $\mathbf{C}$. Assume $0 \leqq \sigma(\mathbf{z_C}) < 1$, with increasing σ denoting greater similarity, or correlation of attributes. Let $\boldsymbol{\theta}_\mathbf{C} = 1 - \sigma(\mathbf{z_C})$. Assign scale values to nodes using the recursion

$$v_\mathbf{A} = \left[\sum_{\mathbf{C} \in \mathscr{F}\mathbf{A}} v_\mathbf{C}^{1/\theta_\mathbf{A}} \right]^{\theta_\mathbf{A}}. \tag{5.49}$$

The probabilistic choice system for this model then satisfies the recursion (5.45) for hierarchical elimination, with transition probabilities

$$Q(\mathbf{C} \mid \mathbf{B}, \mathbf{s}) = \frac{v_\mathbf{C}^{1/\theta_\mathbf{B}}}{\sum_{\mathbf{A} \in \mathscr{F}\mathbf{B}} v_\mathbf{A}^{1/\theta_\mathbf{B}}}. \tag{5.50}$$

The conditions GEV require $\theta_\mathbf{A} \leqq \theta_\mathbf{B}$ for $\mathbf{A} \in \mathscr{F}_\mathbf{B}$. We term (5.45), (5.49), and (5.50) the tree extreme value, TEV, model. For $\mathbf{B} = \{1, \ldots, m\} \in \mathscr{B}$, this model has a social surplus function

$$G(\mathbf{q_B}, \mathbf{z_B}, \mathbf{B}) = \ln H(e^{-q_1}, \ldots, e^{-q_m}, \mathbf{z_B}, \mathbf{B}), \tag{5.51}$$

where H is defined recursively by $H(y_i, \mathbf{z}_i, \{i\}) = y_i$ and for any node $\mathbf{A}$,

$$H(\mathbf{y_A}, \mathbf{z_A}, \mathbf{A}) = \left[\sum_{\mathbf{C} \in \mathscr{F}\mathbf{A}} H(\mathbf{y_C}, \mathbf{z_C}, \mathbf{C})^{1/\theta_\mathbf{A}} \right]^{\theta_\mathbf{A}}. \tag{5.52}$$

Estimation of the TEV model is discussed in sections 5.17 through 5.18.

Since the HEBA and TEV models have similar structures and possible levels of parameterization, one would expect them to give similar fits to data. To test this conjecture numerically, we considered the simple three-alternative preference tree illustrated in figure 5.3. The HEBA and TEV models are fitted to binary choice probabilities that come from this tree; HEBA and TEV are each just identified by the binary probabilities. Then the multinomial choice probabilities implied by the models are compared. A simple MNP model is included in the comparison.

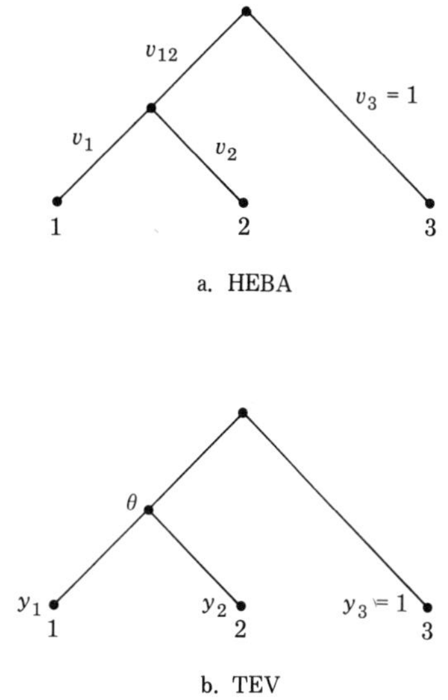

Figure 5.3
Simple HEBA and TEV preference trees

Let p_{ij} denote the binary choice probability of i over j, and P_i the multinomial choice probability. Assume the alternatives are numbered so that $p_{12} > 0.5$. Tversky and Sattath show that the preference tree configuration in figure 5.3 then implies a trinary condition,

$$\frac{p_{12}}{p_{21}} > \frac{\dfrac{p_{13}}{p_{31}}}{\dfrac{p_{23}}{p_{32}}} > 1. \tag{5.53}$$

The TEV model for this preference tree must also satisfy (5.53). Hence we compare these models for the set of binary choice probabilities satisfying (5.53).

The HEBA model for figure 5.3 can be written

$$p_{12} = \frac{v_1}{v_1 + v_2},$$

$$p_{13} = \frac{v_1 + v_{12}}{v_1 + v_3 + v_{12}},$$

$$p_{23} = \frac{v_2 + v_{12}}{v_1 + v_3 + v_{12}},$$

$$P_1 = \frac{v_1 + v_{12}\, p_{12}}{v_1 + v_2 + v_3 + v_{12}},$$

$$P_2 = \frac{v_2 + v_{12}\, p_{21}}{v_1 + v_2 + v_3 + v_{12}}, \tag{5.54}$$

where v_1, v_2, v_3, v_{12} are treated as parameters, with the normalization $v_3 = 1$. The TEV model is generated by the function

$$H(y_1, y_2, y_3) = (y_1^{1/\theta} + y_2^{1/\theta})^\theta + y_3, \tag{5.55}$$

with $p_{12} = \partial \ln H(y_1, y_2, 0)/\partial \ln y_1$, $P_1 = \partial \ln H(y_1, y_2, y_3)/\partial \ln y_1$, and so on. The parameters of the model are y_1, y_2, y_3, and θ, with the normalization $y_3 = 1$.

To form an MNP model with a similarity structure mimicing figure 5.3, we assume the multivariate normal random utility vector (u_1, u_2, u_3) has u_3 independent of u_1 and u_2. Imposing the trinary condition (5.53) implies a common variance for u_1 and u_2. Then this model also has three independent parameters.

Table 5.1 compares the multinomial probabilities from these three models for a selection of values of the binary probabilities. For the MNP model both the exact probabilities and approximate values obtained by the Clark method are given. Appendix 5.21 gives computational formulas.

The most striking feature of table 5.1 is the closeness of the multinomial probabilities predicted by HEBA, TEV, and MNP. The absolute deviation of HEBA and TEV for these cases is at most 0.0074, and the maximum relative deviation is 6 percent. The absolute deviation of TEV and MNP is at most 0.016. The relative deviation of TEV and MNP can rise to 22 percent for small probabilities but for probabilities over 0.1 is under 6 percent. We conclude that at least for simple preference trees such as figure 5.3, these models are for all practical purposes indistinguishable. Cases 4, 5, and 6 parallel the red bus/blue bus example, with case 4 corresponding to high similarity of the bus alternatives and case 6 to low similarity. All three models generate the intuitively plausible multinomial probabilities for these cases.

The Clark approximation to the MNP probabilities is quite inaccurate in a few cases, with absolute deviations as high as 0.1 and relative deviations

Table 5.1
A comparison of HEBA, TEV, and MNP choice probabilities for a simple preference tree

	Case			Nonsimilarity		P_1				P_2			
	p_{12}	p_{13}	p_{23}	θ	$1-\rho$	HEBA	TEV	MNP	Clark	HEBA	TEV	MNP	Clark
1	0.5238	0.0917	0.0909	0.1044	0.0071	0.0523	0.0511	0.0508	0.0685	0.0476	0.0464	0.0461	0.0675
2	0.5238	0.0950	0.0909	0.5119	0.1726	0.0703	0.0668	0.0636	0.0731	0.0639	0.0607	0.0569	0.0685
3	0.5238	0.0983	0.0909	0.9042	0.5415	0.0869	0.0857	0.0761	0.0799	0.0790	0.0779	0.0672	0.0718
4	0.5238	0.5025	0.5000	0.1044	0.0109	0.2756	0.2720	0.2715	0.2523	0.2505	0.2473	0.2464	0.2465
5	0.5238	0.5122	0.5000	0.5119	0.2620	0.3184	0.3110	0.3094	0.2896	0.2895	0.2828	0.2793	0.2713
6	0.5238	0.5215	0.5000	0.9042	0.8175	0.3486	0.3466	0.3477	0.3451	0.3169	0.3151	0.3127	0.3107
7	0.5238	0.9099	0.9091	0.1044	0.0071	0.4805	0.4794	0.4793	0.4255	0.4368	0.4359	0.4357	0.4062
8	0.5238	0.9130	0.9091	0.5119	0.1702	0.4921	0.4903	0.4913	0.4838	0.4473	0.4457	0.4462	0.4405
9	0.5238	0.9160	0.9091	0.9042	0.5282	0.4988	0.4983	0.5020	0.5006	0.4534	0.4530	0.4558	0.4546
10	0.6667	0.0991	0.0909	0.1375	0.0127	0.0714	0.0695	0.0696	0.0750	0.0357	0.0347	0.0337	0.0657
11	0.6667	0.1304	0.0909	0.5850	0.2404	0.1111	0.1065	0.1047	0.1059	0.0556	0.0533	0.0458	0.0613
12	0.6667	0.1597	0.0909	0.9260	0.6228	0.1458	0.1444	0.1381	0.1380	0.0729	0.0722	0.0561	0.0617
13	0.6667	0.5238	0.5000	0.1375	0.0192	0.3636	0.3585	0.3593	0.2832	0.1818	0.1792	0.1768	0.2265
14	0.6667	0.6000	0.5000	0.5850	0.3455	0.4444	0.4369	0.4425	0.4193	0.2222	0.2185	0.2099	0.2123
15	0.6667	0.6552	0.5000	0.9260	0.8593	0.4912	0.4896	0.5035	0.5000	0.2456	0.2448	0.2361	0.2354
16	0.6667	0.9167	0.9091	0.1375	0.0124	0.6154	0.6139	0.6144	0.5107	0.3077	0.3069	0.3063	0.3349
17	0.6667	0.9375	0.9091	0.5850	0.2140	0.6349	0.6334	0.6362	0.6289	0.3175	0.3167	0.3158	0.3152
18	0.6667	0.9500	0.9091	0.9260	0.5184	0.6437	0.6434	0.6483	0.6469	0.3218	0.3217	0.3219	0.3212

for small probabilities as high as 50 percent. This approximation generally follows the pattern of overpredicting small probabilities and underpredicting large ones. For this example the HEBA and TEV models provide better approximations to MNP than the Clark method.

Table 5.1 includes the nonsimilarity measure θ from the TEV model and $1 - \rho$ from the MNP model. Each measure lies in the unit interval, with smaller values corresponding to a greater degree of similarity. There is no simple relationship between the two scales.

5.17 Estimation of Tree Extreme Value Models

The tree extreme value (TEV) model introduced in section 5.16 generalizes the functional form of the Luce, or multinomial logit, model to accommodate the patterns of interalternative substitution found in preference tree similarity structures, while retaining many of the computatonal advantages of the MNL model. In particular the TEV model can be written as a nested sequence of multinomial logit models, and consistent parameter estimates can be obtained from a sequence of MNL estimators.

For econometric analysis it is convenient to introduce an index notation for the TEV form and write it as a nested multinomial logit (NMNL) model.

Suppose a tree has nodes at H levels, indexed $h = 1, \ldots, H$, with H denoting the stem of the tree; see figure 5.4. A node at level h in the tree is indexed by a pair (i_h, σ_h), where $\sigma_h = (i_{h+1}, \ldots, i_H)$ is the index of the adjacent node at level $h + 1$ in the tree. Thus the elemental alternatives, at level 1 in the tree, are indexed by vectors $(i_1, \ldots, i_H)$, while the alternative nodes at level H are indexed by integers i_H. For a choice set $\mathbf{B}$ let $\mathbf{B}_{\sigma_h}$ denote the set of elemental alternatives contained in $\mathbf{B}$ which are in the branch of the tree below node σ_h. We shall also use $\mathbf{B}_{\sigma_h}$ to denote the set of indices i_h such that (i_h, σ_h) is a node immediately below σ_h in the preference tree pruned to the set of elemental alternatives in $\mathbf{B}$; the interpretation will be clear from the context. Note that $\mathbf{B}_{\sigma_H} \equiv \mathbf{B}$, $\mathbf{B}_{\sigma_0}$ is the singleton σ_0 when $\sigma_0 \in \mathbf{B}$, and $\mathbf{C} = \mathbf{B}_{\sigma_h}$ can be interpreted as a choice set whose alternatives are confined to the branch below the node σ_h, with $\mathbf{C}_{\sigma_k} = \mathbf{B}_{\sigma_k}$ for $k \leqq h$ and $\mathbf{C} = \mathbf{C}_{\sigma_k} = \mathbf{C}_{\sigma_H}$ for $k > h$.

Let $\mathbf{x}^h_{i_h\sigma_h}$ denote the vector of observed variables common to the alternatives below node $i_h\sigma_h$, and let γ^h be a commensurate vector of taste weights. Associate with alternative σ_0 the scale value

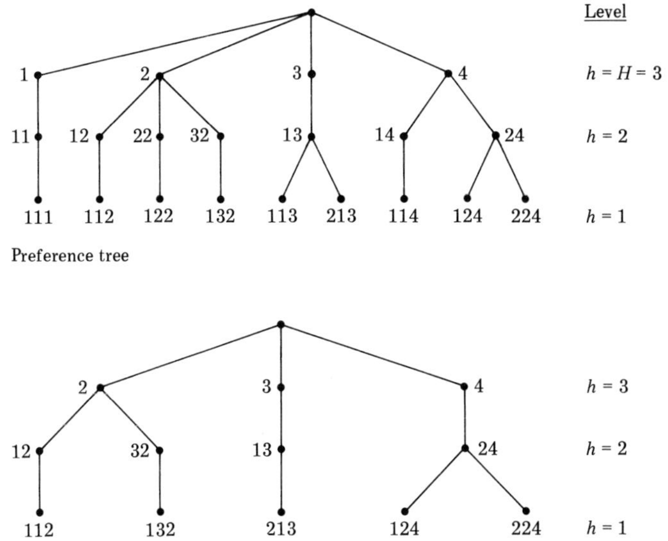

Decision tree pruned to $B = \{112, 132, 213, 124, 224\}$

$B_1 = \phi$ $\quad B_{11} = B_{22} = B_{14} = \phi$

$B_2 = \{112, 132\}$ $\quad B_{12} = \{112\}$

$B_3 = \{213\}$ $\quad B_{13} = \{213\}$

$B_4 = \{124, 224\}$ $\quad B_{24} = \{124, 224\}$

$B_{32} = \{132\}$

Figure 5.4
Index notation for preference and decision trees

$$v_{\sigma 0} = \exp\left[\sum_{h=1}^{H} \gamma^h \cdot \mathbf{x}^h_{\sigma h-1} \right], \tag{5.56}$$

where $\sigma_0 \in \mathbf{B}_{\sigma_{h-1}}$. Let $\theta_{\sigma_1}, \ldots, \theta_{\sigma_H}$ be dissimilarity parameters at the nodes on the path leading to σ_0, with

$$0 < \theta_{\sigma_1} \leqq \theta_{\sigma_2} \leqq \ldots \leqq \theta_{\sigma_H} \equiv 1. \tag{5.57}$$

Then (5.49) and (5.50) imply

$$Q(\mathbf{B}_{\sigma_0} \mid \mathbf{B}_{\sigma_1}, \mathbf{s}) = \frac{\exp[\mathbf{x}^h_{i_1\sigma_1}\gamma^1/\theta_{\sigma_1}]}{\sum_{i_1' \in \mathbf{B}_{\sigma_1}} \exp[\mathbf{x}^h_{i_1'}\gamma^1/\theta_{\sigma_1}]}. \tag{5.58}$$

For $\sigma_1 = i_2\sigma_2$ define

$$y_{i_2\sigma_2} = \ln \sum_{i_1 \in \mathbf{B}_{\sigma_1}} \exp\left[\mathbf{x}^h_{i_1\sigma_1}\frac{\gamma^1}{\theta_{\sigma_1}}\right]. \tag{5.59}$$

Recursive application of (5.49) and (5.50) for $h = 2, \ldots, H$ yields

$$Q[\mathbf{B}_{i_h\sigma_h} \mid \mathbf{B}_{\sigma_h}, \mathbf{s}] = \frac{\exp[\mathbf{x}^h_{i_h\sigma_h}\gamma^h/\theta_{\sigma_h} + y_{i_h\sigma_h}\theta_{i_h\sigma_h}/\theta_{\sigma_h}]}{\sum_{i \in \mathbf{B}_{\sigma_h}} \exp[\mathbf{x}^h_{i\sigma_h}\gamma^h/\theta_{\sigma_h} + y_{i\sigma_h}\theta_{i\sigma_h}/\theta_{\sigma_h}]} \tag{5.60}$$

and

$$y_{i_{h+1}\sigma_{h+1}} = \ln \sum_{i \in \mathbf{B}_{\sigma_h}} \exp\left[\frac{\mathbf{x}^h_{i\sigma_h}\gamma^h}{\theta_{\sigma_h}} + \frac{y_{i\sigma_h}\theta_{i\sigma_h}}{\theta_{\sigma_h}}\right]. \tag{5.61}$$

The expression $y_{i_h\sigma_h}$ is termed the inclusive value of the branch below node $i_h\sigma_h$. A necessary and sufficient condition for this model to be consistent with GEV is that (5.57) hold, or equivalently that the coefficient of each inclusive value, $\theta_{i_h\sigma_h}/\theta_{\sigma_h}$, lie in the unit interval.

For some estimation methods, it is convenient to introduce the notation

$$\boldsymbol{\beta}^h_{\sigma_h} = \left[\frac{\gamma^h}{\theta_{\sigma_h}}, \frac{\theta_{1\sigma_h}}{\theta_{\sigma_h}}, \ldots, \frac{\theta_{m\sigma_h}}{\theta_{\sigma_h}}\right], \tag{5.62}$$

where $\mathbf{B}_{\sigma_h} = \{1, \ldots, m\}$, and commensurately

$$\mathbf{z}^h_{i_h\sigma_h} = [\mathbf{x}^h_{i_h\sigma_h}, 0, \ldots, 0, y_{i_h\sigma_h}, 0, \ldots, 0]. \tag{5.63}$$

Then the model can be written

$$Q[i_h \mid \sigma_h, \mathbf{z}^h_{\cdot\sigma_h}, \boldsymbol{\beta}^h_{\sigma_h}] = \frac{\exp[\mathbf{z}^h_{i_h\sigma_h}\boldsymbol{\beta}^h_{\sigma_h}]}{\sum_{i \in \mathbf{B}_{\sigma_h}} \exp[\mathbf{z}^h_{i\sigma_h}\boldsymbol{\beta}^h_{\sigma_h}]}; \tag{5.64}$$

$$y_{\sigma h} = \ln \sum_{i \in \mathbf{B}_{\sigma_h}} \exp[\mathbf{z}^{h}_{i\sigma h} \boldsymbol{\beta}^{h}_{\sigma h}].$$

The social surplus function for this PCS, from (5.36) and either (5.60) or (5.64), is

$$\begin{aligned} y_{\sigma H} &= \ln \sum_{i_H \in \mathbf{B}} \exp[\mathbf{x}^{H}_{i_H} \gamma^{H} + y_{i_H} \theta_{i_H}] \\ &= \ln \sum_{i_H \in \mathbf{B}} \exp[\mathbf{z}^{H}_{i_H} \boldsymbol{\beta}^{H}]. \end{aligned} \tag{5.65}$$

These formulae use the conditions that σ_H is empty and $\theta_{\sigma_H} = 1$.

It should be noted that the form (5.60) implies that the coefficients of variables other than the inclusive values will differ across nodes at the same level in the tree by scale factors inversely proportional to the dissimilarity coefficients for these nodes.[37]

5.18 Sequential Estimation

Suppose a sample of T independent observations on choices from a set $\mathbf{B}$ is observed. Let $\mathbf{z}^{ht}_{\sigma_{h-1}}$ denote the vector of variables for observation t associated with h-level node σ_{h-1}. Let $m_{\sigma_{h-1}t}$ equal the number of times the choice at observation t lies in the branch below node σ_{h-1}. (Repetitions at an observation are permitted but not required.)

The conditional log likelihood of the observed transitions from the node σ_h at level $h+1$ in the tree is

$$L_{\sigma h} = \sum_{t} \sum_{i_h \in \mathbf{B}_{\sigma_h}} m_{i_h \sigma_h t} \ln Q[\mathbf{B}_{i_h \sigma_h} \mid \mathbf{B}_{\sigma_h}, \mathbf{z}^{ht}_{\cdot \sigma h}, \boldsymbol{\beta}^{h}_{\sigma h}], \tag{5.66}$$

and from all the nodes at level $h+1$ is

$$L^{h} = \sum_{\sigma_h} L_{\sigma h}. \tag{5.67}$$

The unconditional (or full information) log likelihood of the sample is

$$L = \sum_{h=1}^{H} L^{h}. \tag{5.68}$$

37. When all the variables in $x_{\cdot \sigma_h}$ enter as interactions with a dummy variable for node σ_h, and hence are specific to node σ_h, the parameter restrictions implied by (5.60) are satisfied trivially.

Direct maximization of the full information log likelihood yields efficient estimators of the parameters $\gamma^1, \ldots, \gamma^H$ and θ_{σ_h}, $h = 1, \ldots, H$, under standard regularity conditions.[38] While this approach presents a few technical problems, it appears to be practical when the preference tree is not too complex.[39]

An alternative estimation procedure is sequential: estimate $\boldsymbol{\beta}^1_{\sigma_1}$ by maximizing L_{σ_1}, use the estimated value of $\boldsymbol{\beta}^1_{\sigma_1}$ to compute the inclusive value variable at level 2, then estimate $\boldsymbol{\beta}^2_{\sigma_2}$ by maximizing L_{σ_2}, conditioned on the estimate of $\boldsymbol{\beta}^1_{\sigma_1}$, and so on. At each step one is estimating an MNL model by the maximum likelihood method, a standard problem for which fast and reliable algorithms exist. Since the estimation at step h involves only the parameter subvector $\boldsymbol{\beta}^h_{\sigma_h}$ rather than the full parameter vector $(\boldsymbol{\beta}^h_{\sigma_h} : h = 1, \ldots, H)$, computation costs are further reduced. Amemiya (1976) has pointed out that the use of estimators from previous steps to construct variables in the conditional likelihood at step h modifies the asymptotic covariance matrix of the estimators of $\boldsymbol{\beta}^h_{\sigma_h}$, so that standard errors produced by conventional MNL programs are incorrect. Computational formulae for the corrected covariances are given in section 5.22.

The sequential estimation procedure may be considerably less efficient than full information maximum likelihood estimation, particularly where the first-stage conditioning selects a small subsample with limited variation in some explanatory variables. A hybrid procedure is to use sequential estimation to obtain consistent estimators and then carry out one Berndt-Hausman-Hall-Hall (1974) step for the full-information log likelihood function to obtain efficient estimates. The gradients and hessians required for sequential or full-information maximum likelihood estimation are given in section 5.22.

5.19 An Application

The author and his associates have investigated work-trip choice among four travel modes (auto alone, bus, rapid transit, carpool) in the San Francisco Bay Area; see McFadden (1974), Train (1978), Train and McFadden (1978), and McFadden, Talvitie, and Associates (1977). We

38. See, for example, the conditions given by Manski and McFadden in chapter 1.

39. Unlike the simple MNL model the full information log likelihood function is not concave in parameters, complicating the numerical analysis problem of seeking and verifying a global maximum. In particular, the function is highly nonlinear in θ_{σ_h} near zero, creating problems of overflow and roundoff.

consider here estimation of nested multinomial logit models for several preference tree structures used for a sample taken in 1975 of 616 commuters. Table 5.2 gives estimates of the Luce (MNL) model. Estimates of alternative two-level trees, obtained by the sequential method, are given in table 5.3. Two of these structures have also been estimated by Cosslett (1978), using the full-information method; his results are reproduced in table 5.4.

The MNL model in table 5.2 indicates that commuters are adverse to time and cost of travel, with access (walk plus wait) time valued at 146 percent of the decision maker's wage, and on-vehicle time at 30 percent of the wage. Specification analysis of alternative models (McFadden, Talvitie, and Associates 1977) suggests that improved models are obtained by disaggregating alternatives by access mode, allowing interactions of on-vehicle times with mode dummies (to capture differential degrees of unpleasantness of time on different modes), and including socioeconomic and auto access variables in interaction with the alternatives. Assessment of the results given here on tree preference structures should be made with the limitations of the basic variable specification in mind.

Table 5.3 considers the seven possible two-level preference trees for mode choice. The names given these trees suggest aspects which when used in making similarity judgments will yield these trees; for example, "own auto access" is an attribute of the drive-alone mode and (because access is normally by auto) the rail mode, but not the remaining modes. The parameter estimates are obtained by the sequential procedure; corrected standard errors are given, using the formulae of section 5.22.[40] Variable definitions are as in table 5.2, except that "left-branch dummy" indicates a second-stage dummy variable and "inclusive value" indicates the variable defined in (5.59). For the NMNL model to be consistent with GEV or AIRUM, it is necessary that the coefficient of inclusive value lie in the unit

40. The coefficients of cost/wage, on-vehicle time, access time, and the identified mode-specific dummies are estimated in the first stage. Then inclusive values are calculated at these coefficients. In models 2, 5, and 6, there are two inclusive value coefficients, which in these models are constrained to be equal. The coefficients of inclusive value and the left-branch dummy are estimated in the second stage. Then corrected standard errors are calculated using the formulae of section 5.22. The magnitude of the correction is indicated by the following list of standard errors for the coefficient of inclusive value:

Model	2	3	4	5	6	7	8
Correct SE	0.109	0.217	0.270	0.162	0.446	0.283	0.304
Uncorrected SE	0.091	0.102	0.178	0.153	0.176	0.151	0.266

Table 5.2
An MNL model for travel mode choice (model a)[a]

Variable	Symbol	Parameter estimate (standard error)
Cost/wage, in minutes per round trip	C/W	−0.037 (0.006)
On-vehicle time, minutes per round trip	OVT	−0.010 (0.009)
Access time, minutes per round trip	AT	−0.054 (0.010)
Auto alone dummy	DA	−0.03 (0.37)
Rail transit dummy	DR	−1.06 (0.28)
Carpool dummy	DC	−1.74 (0.37)
Log likelihood[b]		−505.10

[a]The alternatives and sample for this and following models are

Mode	Number	Percent share
A: Auto, driven alone	378	61.4
B: Bus	68	11.0
R: Rail rapid transit	33	5.4
C: Carpool	137	22.2
	616	

[b]The log likelihood with dummies only is −567.60.

Table 5.3
Nested MNL models of travel mode choice

Model	2	3	4	5	6	7	8
Preference tree	 *A R C B*	 *B R C A*	 *A B R C*	 *A B R C*	 *A C B R*	 *A R C B*	 *A B C R*
	Own auto access	Drive alone distinct	Carpool distinct	Schedule conven-ience	Transit distinct	Bus distinct	Rail distinct
Parameter estimates[a] (standard errors)							
C/W	−0.066 (0.011)	−0.051 (0.019)	−0.037 (0.007)	−0.017 (0.007)	−0.024 (0.007)	−0.040 (0.007)	−0.026 (0.006)
OVT	−0.018 (0.011)	−0.021 (0.011)	−0.063 (0.010)	−0.022 (0.011)	−0.022 (0.021)	0.002 (0.015)	−0.014 (0.010)
AT	−0.052 (0.011)	0.053 (0.011)	−0.053 (0.012)	−0.067 (0.014)	−0.047 (0.022)	−0.058 (0.023)	−0.056 (0.011)
AD	1.90 (0.54)		0.34 (0.45)	−0.45 (0.46)	1.20 (0.31)	0.90 (0.75)	−0.39 (0.41)
RD		−1.33 (0.33)	0.83 (0.45)	1.22 (0.54)	−1.08 (0.68)		
CD	−1.81 (0.44)	−1.85 (0.44)				−0.90 (0.83)	−1.83 (0.40)
Left-branch dummy	−0.30 (0.27)	−1.12 (0.34)	0.92 (0.27)	1.43 (0.28)	3.01 (0.77)	−1.37 (0.70)	0.94 (0.45)
Inclusive value	0.47 (0.09)	0.67 (0.22)	0.50 (0.18)	0.51 (0.16)	1.62 (0.45)	1.25 (0.28)	1.27 (0.30)
Log likelihood[b]	−501.83	−502.02	−502.55	−510.32	−502.89	−503.26	−505.05

[a]For definitions of variables and modes, see table 5.2.
[b]The log likelihood with dummies only is −567.60.

interval.[41, 42] In models 2, 5, and 6, the coefficients of inclusive values in the two branches are constrained to be the same. This is not required by the TEV model; however, differing values can be accommodated in the sequential estimation procedure only by imposing a nonlinear constraint that the coefficients in one branch be a scalar multiple of the coefficients in the other branch, or else by treating the coefficients in the two branches as independent.

The alternative models 1 through 8 yield coefficients of cost, on-vehicle time, and access time of expected sign.[43] There is considerable variation between the models in the magnitude of coefficients, with models 2 and 3 implying a sharper discrimination among costs than the remainder. Estimated values of on-vehicle time range from 27 percent of the wage in model 2 to 92 percent in model 6. Extimated values of access time range from 79 percent of the wage in model 2 to 394 percent in model 5, with most values in the 100 to 200 percent range. Thus the value of time estimates are quite sensitive to model specification.

Full information maximum likelihood estimates of models 2 and 6 have been calculated by Cosslett (1978), and are given in table 5.4. In these models the coefficients of inclusive value in the two branches are allowed to differ. Thus the log likelihood is larger for these estimates both because of full model maximization and because of an additional parameter. Cosslett's estimates of model 2 do not reduce the log likelihood substantially compared to sequential estimation. However, there are substantial changes in coefficient values, implying a sensitivity to estimation method not reflected in the asymptotic standard errors. Thus caution should be exercised in interpreting these coefficients. In the FIML estimates of model 2, the coefficients of inclusive values in the two branches are not significantly different.[44] FIML estimation of model 6 results in a sub-

41. The inclusive value coefficients in models 2, 4, and 5 are significantly different from one at the 1 percent confidence level, and in model 3 at the 15 percent confidence level. In all four models the coefficient of inclusive value is significantly different from zero at the 1 percent level. It should be remembered that these tests are not independent.

42. The test statistic $T = 2[L(k) - L(1)]$, where $L(k)$ is the log likelihood for model k, has an asymptotic distribution satisfying $\text{Prob}[T \leqq t] \geqq \alpha$ for $X_1^2(\alpha) = t$. Hence $T > X_1^2(\alpha)$ implies that the null hypothesis model 1 holds can be rejected with significance level at least α. By this criterion model 1 is rejected at least at the 5 percent level in (nonindependent) tests against models 2, 3, 4, and 6.

43. The coefficient of on-vehicle time in model 7 is reversed in sign but insignificant.

44. Under the null hypothesis that these coefficients are the same, the difference in the estimated coefficients is asymptotically normal with mean zero and variance equal to left coefficient variance + right coefficient variance − 2 (covariance of coefficients).

Table 5.4
Full information estimates of MNML models

Model	2	6
Preference tree	Own auto access	Transit distinct
Parameter estimates[a] **(standard errors)**		
C/W	−0.029 (0.006)	−0.056 (0.009)
OVT	−0.007 (0.006)	−0.015 (0.010)
AT	−0.032 (0.010)	−0.055 (0.013)
AD	0.37 (0.29)	0.09 (0.47)
RD	−0.30 (0.31)	1.21 (0.38)
CD	−1.11 (0.34)	3.48 (0.66)
Left inclusive value	0.48 (0.14)	2.60 (0.42)
Right inclusive value	0.59 (0.16)	1.35 (0.46)
Log likelihood[b]	−501.1	−491.1

Source: From Cosslett (1978).
[a]For definitions of variables and modes, see table 5.2.
[b]The log likelihood with dummies only is −567.60.

stantial rise in log likelihood relative to sequential estimation, again with substantial changes in parameters. For this model the coefficients of the left and right inclusive prices are significantly different, and the left coefficient is significantly greater than one. This may indicate a failure of the AIRUM specification, or may be a consequence of shortcomings in the variable specification in the model or measurement problems associated with the carpool alternative.[45]

Model 6 fitted by the FIML method yields the highest log likelihood among the models investigated. [46] This may indicate a failure of the AIRUM specification; however, more extensive FIML estimation of alternative preference trees with a more realistic variable specification would be required before a conclusion in either direction could be drawn with confidence.

The econometric models of probabilistic choice developed in this paper permit much more general patterns of similarities between alternatives than does the commonly used MNL model, while remaining reasonably practical for estimation and forecasting. The application above suggests that these models can provide significantly better fits than the MNL models. Sequential estimation of the NMNL model is practical even for relatively large and complex trees, while the FIML method is practical for problems of moderate size. The relatively large differences in coefficient estimates obtained by the two methods suggests a need for further research on the numerical and statistical properties of these methods. Finally, the numerical example in section 5.16 suggests that the MNP, HEBA, and TEV functional forms, when restricted to the same numbers of parameters, permit closely comparable fits to data generated by various patterns of similarities.

45. See McFadden, Talvitie, et al. (1977). It should be noted that, while a negative coefficient of inclusive value leads to a local failure of the GEV conditions, a coefficient of an inclusive value exceeding one will fail to satisfy GEV only for some values of the variables. Thus it is possible that an empirical fit yielding a coefficient greater than one will be consistent with GEV over the range of the data and can be combined with a second function outside the range of the data to yield a system that satisfies GEV globally. However, this chapter has not attempted to develop a test for local consistency with GEV at the observations, or for consistency with some function that satisfies GEV globally.

46. FIML estimates have not been calculated for models 3, 4, 5, 7, or 8, and no estimates have been calculated for the twelve possible three-level preference trees.

5.20 Appendix: Normalization in MNL and MNP Models

Consider the MNL model

$$P(i \mid \mathbf{z_B}, \boldsymbol{\beta}) = \frac{e^{\boldsymbol{\beta} \cdot \mathbf{z}_i}}{\sum_{j \in \mathbf{B}} e^{\boldsymbol{\beta} \cdot \mathbf{z}_j}} \tag{5.69}$$

and the MNP model

$$P(i \mid \mathbf{z_B}, \boldsymbol{\beta}, \mathbf{A}) = \text{Prob}[\boldsymbol{\alpha}'\mathbf{z}_i \geqq \boldsymbol{\alpha}'\mathbf{z}_j \text{ for } j \in \mathbf{B}] \tag{5.70}$$

with $\boldsymbol{\alpha} \sim N(\boldsymbol{\beta}, \mathbf{AA}')$. The parameters of these models are usually fitted by iterative maximum likelihood algorithms. A practical problem in computation is that the domain of the parameters is unbounded, making it difficult to detect unbounded maxima or avoid false solutions. This problem can be avoided by a normalization which compactifies the parameter space.

Consider first the MNL model. Let $\boldsymbol{\beta}^{(k)}$ denote the vector obtained at iteration (k), and define

$$\lambda^{(k)} = [1 + \boldsymbol{\beta}^{(k)} \cdot \boldsymbol{\beta}^{(k)}]^{-1/2} > 0 \quad \text{and} \quad \bar{\boldsymbol{\beta}}^{(k)} = \lambda^{(k)}\boldsymbol{\beta}^{(k)}. \tag{5.71}$$

Then $(\lambda^{(k)}, \bar{\boldsymbol{\beta}}^{(k)})$ lies in the unit sphere and has a limit point $(\lambda^*, \bar{\boldsymbol{\beta}}^*)$. If $\lambda^* > 0$, then the likelihood attains a maximum at $\boldsymbol{\beta} = \bar{\boldsymbol{\beta}}^*/\lambda^*$. If $\lambda^* = 0$, then the likelihood has no finite maximum, and choice can be explained by nonstochastic maximization of $\bar{\boldsymbol{\beta}}^* \cdot \mathbf{z}_i$, with $\bar{\boldsymbol{\beta}}^* \cdot \bar{\boldsymbol{\beta}}^* = 1$. Termination of the iterative algorithm for sufficiently small changes in $(\lambda^{(k)}, \bar{\boldsymbol{\beta}}^{(k)})$ yields a reliable convergence criterion.

Consider the MNP model, and let $(\boldsymbol{\beta}^{(k)}, \mathbf{A}^{(k)})$ denote the parameter values at iteration k. Suppose that as a result of normalization $\boldsymbol{\beta}^{(k)} \cdot \boldsymbol{\beta}^{(k)} + \text{tr}[\mathbf{A}^{(k)}\mathbf{A}^{(k)\prime}] = 1$, and suppose that the diagonal elements of $\mathbf{A}^{(k)}$ are positive. Fix the element $A_{11}^{(k)}$ (and other normalizations as necessary for nonsingularity), and iterate to new values $\tilde{\boldsymbol{\beta}}^{(k+1)}$ and $\tilde{\mathbf{A}}^{(k+1)}$, constraining the algorithm to keep the diagonal of $\tilde{\mathbf{A}}^{(k+1)}$ positive. Define

$$(\boldsymbol{\beta}^{(k+1)}, \mathbf{A}^{(k+1)}) = (\tilde{\boldsymbol{\beta}}^{(k+1)}, \tilde{\mathbf{A}}^{(k+1)}) \cdot [\tilde{\boldsymbol{\beta}}^{(k+1)} \cdot \tilde{\boldsymbol{\beta}}^{(k+1)} + \text{tr}\, \tilde{\mathbf{A}}^{(k+1)} \tilde{\mathbf{A}}^{(k+1)\prime}]^{-1/2}. \tag{5.72}$$

Then the parameter values at iteration $k + 1$ again lie in the unit sphere and have the diagonal of $\mathbf{A}^{(k+1)}$ positive. The sequence $(\boldsymbol{\beta}^{(k)}, \mathbf{A}^{(k)})$ has a (possibly nonunique) limit point $(\boldsymbol{\beta}^*, \mathbf{A}^*)$ at which the likelihood function has a local maximum. Note that $\mathbf{A}^*$ may be degenerate, in which case the likelihood is defined on the linear subspace spanned by $\mathbf{A}^*$. This poses no difficulty in the algorithm or in the interpretation of $(\boldsymbol{\beta}^*, \mathbf{A}^*)$. Termination of the iterative algorithm for sufficiently small changes in $(\boldsymbol{\beta}^{(k)}, \mathbf{A}^{(k)})$ should identify (local) maxima.

5.21 Appendix: Computational Formulas for a Simple Model

Consider the preference tree of figure 5.3, with choice probabilities satisfying the trinary condition (5.53), and the HEBA, TEV, or MNP models. The HEBA model specification (5.54) can be inverted to

$$v_1 = \frac{r_{13} - r_{23}}{r_{12}}, \quad v_2 = \frac{r_{23} - r_{13}}{r_{21}},$$

$$v_3 = 1, \qquad v_{12} = \frac{r_{23} - r_{13} r_{21}}{r_{12}}, \tag{5.73}$$

where $r_{ij} = p_{ij}/p_{ji}$. The multinomial probabilities are then determined from the binary probabilities using the last equations in (5.54).

The TEV model with the generating function (5.55) has

$$p_{12} = \frac{y_1^{1/\theta}}{y_1^{1/\theta} + y_2^{1/\theta}},$$

$$p_{13} = \frac{y_1}{y_2 + y_3},$$

$$p_{23} = \frac{y_2}{y_2 + y_3}. \tag{5.74}$$

Inverting

$$y_1 = r_{13}, \quad y_2 = r_{23}, \quad y_3 = 1,$$

$$\theta = \frac{\ln y_1/y_2}{\ln r_{12}}. \tag{5.75}$$

The trinary condition requires that $r_{12} > 1$ $(y_1 > y_2)$ imply $r_{12} > r_{13}/r_{23} > 1$, or $(y_1/y_2)^{1/\theta} > y_1/y_2 > 1$. This holds if and only if $0 < \theta < 1$. From (5.55) the multinomial choice probabilities satisfy

$$P_3 = [1 + (y_1^{1/\theta} + y_2^{1/\theta})^{\theta}]^{-1},$$
$$P_1 = p_{12}(1 - P_3),$$
$$P_2 = p_{21}(1 - P_3). \tag{5.76}$$

Consider the MNP model with a random utility vector $(u_1, u_2, u_3) \sim N((\mu_1, \mu_2, 0), \Omega)$, where

$$\Omega = \begin{bmatrix} \sigma_{11} & \sigma_{12} & 0 \\ \sigma_{21} & \sigma_{22} & 0 \\ 0 & 0 & \sigma_{33} \end{bmatrix}.$$

The condition $\mu_3 = 0$ is a normalization; the independence of u_3 and (u_1, u_2), and $\sigma_{12} > 0$, is assumed in correspondence with the tree structure in figure 5.3. The binary choice probabilities then satisfy

$$p_{13} = \Phi\left[\frac{\mu_1}{\sqrt{\sigma_{11} + \sigma_{33}}}\right],$$

$$p_{23} = \Phi\left[\frac{\mu_2}{\sqrt{\sigma_{22} + \sigma_{33}}}\right],$$

$$p_{12} = \Phi\left[\frac{\mu_1 - \mu_2}{\sqrt{\sigma_{11} + \sigma_{22} - 2\sigma_{12}}}\right]. \tag{5.77}$$

The trinary condition requires that $r_{12} > 1$ $(\mu_1 > \mu_2)$ imply

$$\frac{r_{13}}{r_{23}} > 1 \Rightarrow \left(\frac{\mu_1}{\sqrt{\sigma_{11} + \sigma_{33}}} > \frac{\mu_2}{\sqrt{\sigma_{22} + \sigma_{33}}}\right),$$

and hence $\sigma_{11} = \sigma_{22}$. Then by standardizing the variance of utility differences, one can show that there is no loss of generality in imposing as normalizing restrictions $\sigma_{11} = \sigma_{22} = \sigma_{33} = 1/2$ and $\sigma_{12} = \rho/2$, with $0 < \rho < 1$. Hence

$$p_{13} = \Phi(\mu_1), \quad p_{23} = \Phi(\mu_2), \quad p_{12} = \Phi\left[\frac{\mu_1 - \mu_2}{\sqrt{1 - \rho}}\right]. \tag{5.78}$$

After some manipulation the multinomial choice probabilities can be written

$$P_1 = \int_{(\mu_2-\mu_1)/\sqrt{1-\rho}}^{\infty} \phi(t)\Phi\left[\frac{2\mu_1}{\sqrt{3+\rho}} + t\sqrt{\frac{1-\rho}{3+\rho}}\right]dt, \tag{5.79}$$

$$P_2 = \int_{(\mu_1-\mu_2)/\sqrt{1-\rho}}^{\infty} \phi(t)\Phi\left[\frac{2\mu_2}{\sqrt{3+\rho}} + t\sqrt{\frac{1-\rho}{3+\rho}}\right]dt.$$

The Clark approximation to these probabilities is

$$P_1 \approx \Phi\left[\frac{\mu_1 - p_{13}\mu_2 - \phi(\mu_2)}{[1 - \rho p_{13} + \mu_2^2 p_{13}p_{31} + \mu_2\phi(\mu_1) - \phi(\mu_1)^2 - 2\mu_2 p_{13}\phi(\mu_2)]^{1/2}}\right],$$

$$P_2 \approx \Phi\left[\frac{\mu_2 - p_{23}\mu_1 - \phi(\mu_1)}{[1 - \rho p_{23} + \mu_1^2 p_{23}p_{32} + \mu_1\phi(\mu_2) - \phi(\mu_2)^2 - 2\mu_1 p_{23}\phi(\mu_1)]^{1/2}}\right]. \tag{5.80}$$

5.22 Appendix: Computational Formulas for the Nested Multinomial Logit Model

This section first describes a method for calculating asymptotic covariance matrices for sequential or full-information maximum likelihood estimates of an NMNL model. Second, formulae are given for the required derivatives. Finally, there is some discussion of algorithms for implementing the computation.

The log likelihood function for NMNL can be written in the general schematic form

$$\begin{aligned} L^0(\mathbf{x}_1, \ldots, \mathbf{x}_m \mid \psi_1, \ldots, \psi_m) \equiv\; & L^1(\mathbf{x}_1 \mid \mathbf{x}_2, \ldots, \mathbf{x}_m, \psi_1) \\ & + L^2(\mathbf{x}_2 \mid \mathbf{x}_3, \ldots, \mathbf{x}_m, \psi_1, \psi_2) \\ & + \ldots + L^m(\mathbf{x}_m \mid \psi_1, \ldots, \psi_m), \end{aligned} \tag{5.81}$$

where each ψ_i is a parameter vector, $\mathbf{x}_i$ is a data vector, and L^i is the conditional log likelihood associated with transitions at one level of the decision tree.

Full information maximum likelihood (FIML) estimators satisfy

$$L_\psi^0(\mathbf{x}_1, \ldots, \mathbf{x}_m \mid \hat{\psi}_1, \ldots, \hat{\psi}_m) = 0, \tag{5.82}$$

where $\psi = (\psi_1, \ldots, \psi_m)$ and $L^0_\psi = \partial L^0/\partial\psi$. A Taylor's expansion of (5.82) about the true parameter vector ψ^* yields

$$\left[\frac{1}{N} L^0_{\psi\psi}\right]\sqrt{N}\,(\hat{\psi} - \psi^*) = -\frac{1}{\sqrt{N}} L^0_\psi, \tag{5.83}$$

where N is the sample size, L^0_ψ is evaluated at ψ^*, and the rows of $L^0_{\psi\psi}$ are evaluated at points between $\hat{\psi}$ and ψ^*. Using the conventional asymptotic development for maximum likelihood estimation, one has under standard regularity conditions that $\hat{\psi}$ is consistent for ψ^*, by the law of large numbers that plim $(1/N)L^0_{\psi\psi} = \lim E(1/N)L^0_{\psi\psi} \equiv \mathbf{B}_0$, and by a central limit theorem that $(1/\sqrt{N})L^0_\psi$ is asymptotically normal with mean $\mathbf{0}$ and covariance matrix $\lim E(1/N)L^0_\psi L^{0\prime}_\psi \equiv \mathbf{A}_0$. Further, differentiation of the identity $\mathrm{E}e^{L^0} \equiv 1$ yields $\mathbf{A}_0 = -\mathbf{B}_0$. Then $\sqrt{N}(\hat{\psi} - \psi^*)$ is asymptotically normal with zero mean and covariance matrix $\mathbf{\Omega}_0 \equiv \mathbf{B}_0^{-1}\mathbf{A}_0\mathbf{B}_0^{-1} \equiv \mathbf{B}_0^{-1}$.

The sequential estimation procedure first determines $\tilde{\psi}_1$, satisfying

$$L^1_{\psi_1}(\mathbf{x}_1 \mid \mathbf{x}_2, \ldots, \mathbf{x}_m, \tilde{\psi}_1) = 0, \tag{5.84}$$

and then recursively determines $\tilde{\psi}_i$, satisfying

$$L^i_{\psi_i}(\mathbf{x}_i \mid \mathbf{x}_{i+1}, \ldots, \mathbf{x}_m, \tilde{\psi}_1, \ldots, \tilde{\psi}_{i-1}, \tilde{\psi}_i) = \mathbf{0}, \tag{5.85}$$

given the previously estimated values of $\tilde{\psi}_1, \ldots, \tilde{\psi}_{i-1}$, for $i = 2, \ldots, m$. The development of the asymptotic properties of the sequential estimator parallels that of the FIML estimator. A series of Taylor's expansions of (5.84) and (5.85) yield

$$\frac{1}{N}\begin{bmatrix} L^1_{\psi_1\psi_1} & \mathbf{0} & \ldots & \mathbf{0} \\ L^2_{\psi_1\psi_2} & L^2_{\psi_2\psi_2} & \ldots & \mathbf{0} \\ \vdots & \vdots & & \vdots \\ L^m_{\psi_1\psi_m} & L^m_{\psi_2\psi_m} & \ldots & L^m_{\psi_m\psi_m} \end{bmatrix}\begin{bmatrix} \sqrt{N}\,(\tilde{\psi}_1 - \psi^*_1) \\ \sqrt{N}\,(\tilde{\psi}_2 - \psi^*_2) \\ \vdots \\ \sqrt{N}\,(\tilde{\psi}_m - \psi^*_m) \end{bmatrix} = -\frac{1}{\sqrt{N}}\begin{bmatrix} L^1_{\psi_1} \\ L^2_{\psi_2} \\ \vdots \\ L^m_{\psi_m} \end{bmatrix}, \tag{5.86}$$

or in matrix notation

$$\mathbf{B}_N\sqrt{N}\,(\tilde{\psi} - \psi^*) = -\frac{1}{\sqrt{N}}\boldsymbol{\lambda}_N. \tag{5.87}$$

Analogously to the FIML case $\mathbf{B}_N$ converges in probability to a lower block triangular matrix $\mathbf{B}_* = \lim E\mathbf{B}_N$ and, $(1/\sqrt{N})\boldsymbol{\lambda}_N$ converges in distribution to an asymptotically normal random variable with zero mean and covariance matrix $\mathbf{A}_* = \lim E(1/N)\boldsymbol{\lambda}_N\boldsymbol{\lambda}_N'$. Then $\sqrt{N}(\tilde{\psi} - \psi^*)$ is asymptotically normal with zero mean and covariance matrix $\mathbf{B}_*^{-1}\mathbf{A}_*\mathbf{B}_*^{-1}$. Computation of this covariance matrix is facilitated by noting first that at ψ^*

$$\lim E\frac{1}{N}L^i_{\psi_{i-k}\psi_i} = -\lim E\frac{1}{N}L^i_{\psi_{i-k}}L^i_{\psi_k}, \tag{5.88}$$

and second that the block triangular matrix $\mathbf{B}_*^{-1}$ can be calculated using a recursion formula which requires inverting only matrices of the order of the blocks $L^i_{\psi_i\psi_i}$.

The following paragraphs give formulae for the derivatives of the log likelihood function of the NMNL model. From (5.64) define $i = i_h$, $\sigma = \sigma_h$, and

$$\begin{aligned}\ln q(i \mid \sigma) &\equiv \ln Q[i \mid \sigma_h, \mathbf{z}^h_{\cdot\sigma_h}, \boldsymbol{\beta}_{\sigma_h}]\\ &= \mathbf{x}^h_{i\sigma}\frac{\gamma^h}{\theta_\sigma} + \frac{\theta_{i\sigma}}{\theta_\sigma}y_{i\sigma}\\ &\quad - \ln \sum_{j\in\mathbf{B}_\sigma} \exp\left(\frac{\mathbf{x}^h_{j\sigma}\gamma^h}{\theta_\sigma} + \frac{\theta_{j\sigma}}{\theta_\sigma}y_{j\sigma}\right).\end{aligned} \tag{5.89}$$

Then

$$\frac{\partial \ln q(i \mid \sigma)}{\partial \gamma^{h-r}} = \frac{(\mathbf{x}^{h-r}_{i\sigma} - \mathbf{x}^{h-r}_{\sigma})}{\theta_\sigma} \tag{5.90}$$

for $r = 0, \ldots, h-1$, where

$$\mathbf{x}^{h-r}_\sigma = \sum_{i_{h-r}} \cdots \sum_{i_h} q(i_{h-r}\ldots i_h \mid \sigma)\mathbf{x}^{h-r}_{i_{h-r}\cdots i_h\sigma} \tag{5.91}$$

and

$$q(i_{h-r}\ldots i_h \mid \sigma) = q(i_{h-r} \mid i_{h-r+1}\ldots i_h\sigma)\ldots q(i_h \mid \sigma). \tag{5.92}$$

Further

$$\begin{aligned}\frac{\partial \ln q(i \mid \sigma)}{\partial(1/\theta_\sigma)} &= (\mathbf{x}^h_{i\sigma} - \mathbf{x}^h_\sigma)\gamma^h + y_{i\sigma}\theta_{i\sigma}\\ &\quad - \sum_j q(j \mid \sigma)y_{j\sigma}\theta_{j\sigma},\end{aligned} \tag{5.93}$$

and

$$\frac{\partial \ln q(i \mid \sigma)}{\partial(1/\theta_{i_{h-r}\cdots i_h\sigma})}$$

$$= [\delta_{i_h i} - q(i_h \mid \sigma)]\,\alpha[i_{h-r}\ldots i_h\sigma], \tag{5.94}$$

with $\delta_{ij} = 1$ if $i = j$ and

$$\alpha(i_{h-r}\ldots i_h\sigma) = q(i_{h-r}\ldots i_{h-1} \mid i_h\sigma)$$

$$\cdot \frac{\theta_{i_{h-r}\cdots i_h\sigma}}{\theta_\sigma}\Bigg\{\mathbf{x}^{h-r-1}_{i_{h-r}\cdots i_h\sigma}\gamma^{h-r-1}$$

$$+ \sum_j q(j \mid i_{h-r}\ldots i_h\sigma)\,y_{j i_{h-r}\cdots i_h\sigma}\,\theta_{j i_{h-r}\cdots i_h\sigma}$$

$$- y_{i_{h-r}\cdots i_h\sigma}\,\theta_{i_{h-r}\cdots i_h\sigma}\Bigg\}. \tag{5.95}$$

Consider the conditional log likelihood function for transition from node σ, which from (5.66) satisfies

$$L_\sigma = \sum_t \sum_{i\in\mathbf{B}_\sigma} m_{i\sigma t}\ln q(i \mid \sigma, t), \tag{5.96}$$

with $m_{i\sigma t}$ the number of choices of $i\sigma$ at case t and $q(i \mid \sigma, t)$ the transition probability for case t.

Then

$$\frac{\partial L_\sigma}{\partial \gamma^{h-r}} = \frac{\sum_t\left[\sum_{i\in\mathbf{B}_\sigma} m_{i\sigma t}\mathbf{x}^{h-r,t}_{i\sigma} - m_{\sigma t}\mathbf{x}^{h-r,t}_{\sigma}\right]}{\theta_\sigma}; \tag{5.97}$$

$$\frac{\partial L_\sigma}{\partial(1/\theta_\sigma)} = \sum_t \sum_{i\in\mathbf{B}_\sigma} (m_{i\sigma t} - m_{\sigma t}q(i \mid \sigma, t))[\mathbf{x}^{ht}_{i\sigma}\gamma^h + y^t_{i\sigma}\theta_{i\sigma}]; \tag{5.98}$$

$$\frac{\partial L_\sigma}{\partial[1/\theta_{i_{h-r}\cdots i_h\sigma}]} = \sum_t [m_{i_h\sigma t} - m_{\sigma t}q(i_h \mid \sigma t)]\,\alpha(i_{h-r}\cdots i_h\sigma, t). \tag{5.99}$$

The distribution of $m_{i\sigma t}$, conditioned on $m_{\sigma t}$, is multinomial, statistically independent of transitions at nodes other than σ and by assumption independent across t. The gradients (5.97) through (5.99) have zero means, when evaluated at the true parameter vector, and covariances

$$E\left[\frac{\partial L_\sigma}{\partial \gamma^{h-r}}\right]\left[\frac{\partial L_\sigma}{\partial \gamma^{h-s}}\right]' = \sum_t \sum_{i \in \mathbf{B}_\sigma} q(i \mid \sigma, t)(\mathbf{x}_{i\sigma}^{h-r,t} - \mathbf{x}_\sigma^{h-r,t}) \cdot \frac{(\mathbf{x}_{i\sigma}^{h-s,t} - \mathbf{x}_\sigma^{h-s,t})'}{\theta_\sigma^2}; \tag{5.100}$$

$$E\left[\frac{\partial L_\sigma}{\partial[1/\theta_\sigma]}\right]^2 = \sum_t m_{\sigma t}\left\{\sum_{i \in \mathbf{B}_\sigma} q(i \mid \sigma, t)(\mathbf{x}_{i\sigma}^{ht}\gamma^h + y_{i\sigma}^t \theta_{i\sigma})^2 - \left[\sum_{i \in \mathbf{B}_\sigma} q(i \mid \sigma, t)(\mathbf{x}_{i\sigma}^{ht}\gamma^h + y_{i\sigma}^t \theta_{i\sigma})\right]^2\right\}; \tag{5.101}$$

$$E\frac{\partial L_\sigma}{\partial[1/\theta_{i_{h-r}\cdots i_h\sigma}]}\frac{\partial L_\sigma}{\partial[1/\theta_{i'_{h-s}\cdots i'_h\sigma}]} = \sum_t m_{\sigma t} q(i_h \mid \sigma, t)[\delta_{i_h i'_h} - q(i'_h \mid \sigma, t)] \cdot \alpha(i_{h-r}\cdots i_h\sigma, t)\alpha(i'_{h-s}\cdots i'_h\sigma, t); \tag{5.102}$$

$$E\frac{\partial L_\sigma}{\partial \gamma^{h-r}}\frac{\partial L_\sigma}{\partial[1/\theta_\sigma]} = \sum_t m_{\sigma t}\left\{\left[\sum_i q(i \mid \sigma, t)\mathbf{x}_{i\sigma}^{h-r,t}\mathbf{x}_{i\sigma}^{h,t'} - \mathbf{x}_\sigma^{h-r,t}\mathbf{x}_\sigma^{h'}\right]\gamma^h + \sum_i q(i \mid \sigma, t) y_{i\sigma}^t \theta_{i\sigma}(\mathbf{x}_{i\sigma}^{h-r,t} - \mathbf{x}_\sigma^{h-r,t})/\theta_\sigma\right\}; \tag{5.103}$$

$$E\frac{\partial L_\sigma}{\partial \gamma^{h-r}}\frac{\partial L_\sigma}{\partial[1/\theta_{i_{h-s}\cdots i_h\sigma}]} = \sum_t m_{\sigma t} q(i_h \mid \sigma, t)\alpha(i_{h-s}\cdots i_h\sigma, t) \cdot \frac{[\mathbf{x}_{i_h\sigma}^{h-r,t} - \mathbf{x}_\sigma^{h-r,t}]}{\theta_\sigma}; \tag{5.104}$$

$$E\frac{\partial L_\sigma}{\partial[1/\theta_\sigma]}\frac{\partial L_\sigma}{\partial[1/\theta_{i_{h-s}\cdots i_h\sigma}]} = \sum_t m_{\sigma t} q(i_h \mid \sigma, t)\alpha(i_{h-s}\cdots i_h\sigma, t) \cdot \left\{[\mathbf{x}_{i_h\sigma}^{ht} - \mathbf{x}_\sigma^{ht}]\gamma^h + y_{i_h\sigma}^t \theta_{i_h\sigma} - \sum_i q(i \mid \sigma, t) y_{i\sigma}^t \theta_{i\sigma}\right\}. \tag{5.105}$$

The covariance matrices for FIML or sequential maximum likelihood estimators are constructed from (5.100) through (5.105), using the asymptotic methods given at the beginning of this section and the definitions (5.66) through (5.68) of the conditional and unconditional log likelihood functions. The FIML log likelihood is the sum over the nodes σ in the decision tree of the terms L_σ. The gradients of L_σ and $L_{\sigma'}$ have zero covariance for $\sigma \neq \sigma'$; hence the information matrix for FIML has elements equal to the sum over σ of terms like (5.100) or (5.105). This matrix is readily estimated by substituting the FIML estimates of the parameters in (5.100) through (5.105), and its inverse yields an estimate of the asymptotic covariance matrix of the maximum likelihood estimator.

The structure of sequential estimation is simplified substantially if either the dissimilarity parameters θ_{σ_h} at level h in the tree are constrained a priori to be equal or the proportionality constraints on parameters across nodes at the same level of the tree are ignored. In the first case estimation can be carried out sequentially over the levels of the tree. At each level the parameters are estimated by applying a multinomial logit maximum likelihood procedure to the choice data for all the transitions at this level. For this procedure it is convenient to use the parameterization (5.62) with a common dissimilarity parameter θ_h at level h, writing

$$\boldsymbol{\beta}^h \equiv (\boldsymbol{\beta}_1^h, \boldsymbol{\beta}_2^h) = \left(\frac{\gamma^h}{\theta_h}, \frac{\theta_{h-1}}{\theta_h}\right) \tag{5.106}$$

$$\mathbf{z}_{i_h\sigma_h}^h = [\mathbf{x}_{i_h\sigma_h}^h, y_{i_h\sigma_h}]$$

$$Q[i_h \mid \sigma_h, \mathbf{z}_{\cdot\sigma_h}^h, \boldsymbol{\beta}^h] = \frac{\exp[\mathbf{z}_{i_h\sigma_h}^h \boldsymbol{\beta}^h]}{\sum_{i\in\mathbf{B}_{\sigma_h}} \exp[\mathbf{z}_{i\sigma_h}^h \boldsymbol{\beta}^h]}.$$

Then the log likelihood function satisfies

$$L^h = \sum_t \sum_{\sigma_h} \sum_{i\in\mathbf{B}_{\sigma_h}} m_{i\sigma_h t} \ln q(i \mid \sigma_h, t); \tag{5.107}$$

$$\frac{\partial L^h}{\partial \boldsymbol{\beta}^{h-r}} = \sum_t \sum_{\sigma_h} \lambda_r^h \left[\sum_{i\in\mathbf{B}_{\sigma_h}} \mathbf{z}_{i\sigma_h}^{h-r,t} m_{i\sigma_h t} - \mathbf{z}_{\sigma_h}^{h-r,t} m_{\sigma_h t}\right], \tag{5.108}$$

with $\lambda_0^h = 1$ and $\lambda_r^h = \beta_2^{h-r+1} \cdots \beta_2^h$ for $r > 0$; and

$$E\left[\frac{\partial L^h}{\partial \boldsymbol{\beta}^{h-r}}\right]\left[\frac{\partial L^h}{\partial \boldsymbol{\beta}^{h-s}}\right]'$$

$$= \sum_t \sum_{\sigma_h} \lambda_r^h \lambda_s^h m_{\sigma_h t}\left[\sum_{i \in \mathbf{B}_{\sigma_h}} q(i \mid \sigma_h, t)\mathbf{z}_{i\sigma_h}^{h-r,t}\mathbf{z}_{i\sigma_h}^{h-s,t'} - \mathbf{z}_{\sigma_h}^{h-r,t}\mathbf{z}_{\sigma_h}^{h-s,t'}\right]. \tag{5.109}$$

The parameters γ^h and θ_h can be obtained from the $\boldsymbol{\beta}$'s using the transformations

$$\theta_h = \beta_2^{h+1} \cdots \beta_2^H \tag{5.110}$$

$$\gamma^h = \boldsymbol{\beta}_1^h \theta_h.$$

Consider the case where the dissimilarity parameters are not constrained to be equal across nodes at the same level of the tree and the proportionality restrictions across these nodes on the coefficients of variables other than inclusive values are ignored. Note that failure to impose these conditions entails some loss of information, except in the case where all variables are defined by interactions with alternative or branch-specific dummies. In this case the estimation procedure using (5.107) through (5.109) can be applied to each branch separately; the formulae are modified solely by dropping the summation over σ_h.

The general case of sequential estimation, where dissimilarity parameters at each level of the tree are not constrained to be equal, and parameter restrictions across nodes are imposed, can be treated in the same framework as the FIML analysis. However, the estimation problem at each level no longer has a simple multinomial logit structure, and there appears to be little reason, except possibly the scale of the problem, to use a sequential rather than FIML estimation.

Consider algorithms for implementing the computation of sequential or FIML estimators of the NMNL model, and estimators of the covariance matrix of the estimates. Letting $L(\boldsymbol{\psi})$ denote the log likelihood function for FIML or for one step of sequential estimation, a practical and relatively efficient search algorithm chooses the direction of search from a trial parameter vector $\boldsymbol{\psi}^{(k)}$, satisfying

$$\boldsymbol{\psi}^{(k+1)} - \boldsymbol{\psi}^{(k)} = \lambda\left[E\left[\frac{\partial L}{\partial \boldsymbol{\psi}}\right]\left[\frac{\partial L}{\partial \boldsymbol{\psi}}\right]'\right]^{-1}\frac{\partial L}{\partial \boldsymbol{\psi}}, \tag{5.111}$$

with the right-hand side derivatives evaluated at $\psi^{(k)}$ and λ a positive step size. In a neighborhood of the optimum, this algorithm has quadratic convergence for $\lambda = 1$. The search direction will always be a line of ascent, even if the function is not locally concave. These properties are discussed further in Berndt-Hausman-Hall-Hall (1974). It is often efficient to carry out an interpolation along the direction of search, choosing λ, so that an approximate optimum is obtained and the following search direction will be nearly orthogonal. Using the calculated levels and gradients of the function at points along the direction of search which straddle the maximum permits a fairly accurate interpolation.

In the sequential estimation procedure the asymptotic covariance structure can be utilized to give recursive formulae for the covariance matrices at each stage. In the case where dissimilarity coefficients within each level of the tree are constrained to be equal, let

$$\mathbf{M}^{h}_{h-r,h-s} = E\left[\frac{\partial L^h}{\partial \boldsymbol{\beta}^{h-r}}\right]\left[\frac{\partial L^h}{\partial \boldsymbol{\beta}^{h-s}}\right]', \quad r, s = 0, \ldots, h-1. \tag{5.112}$$

$$\mathbf{B}_N = \frac{1}{N}\begin{bmatrix} \mathbf{M}^1_{11} & \mathbf{0} & \cdots & \mathbf{0} \\ \mathbf{M}^2_{21} & \mathbf{M}^2_{22} & \cdots & \mathbf{0} \\ \vdots & \vdots & & \\ \mathbf{M}^H_{H1} & \mathbf{M}^H_{H2} & \cdots & \mathbf{M}^H_{HH} \end{bmatrix}, \tag{5.113}$$

and

$$\mathbf{A}_N = \frac{1}{N}\begin{bmatrix} \mathbf{M}^1_{11} & \mathbf{0} & \cdots & \mathbf{0} \\ \mathbf{0} & \mathbf{M}^2_{22} & \cdots & \mathbf{0} \\ \vdots & \vdots & & \\ \mathbf{0} & \mathbf{0} & \cdots & \mathbf{M}^H_{HH} \end{bmatrix}$$

Then the asymptotic covariance matrix of

$$\sqrt{N}\,(\tilde{\boldsymbol{\beta}} - \boldsymbol{\beta}^*) \equiv \sqrt{N}\,(\tilde{\boldsymbol{\beta}}^1 - \boldsymbol{\beta}^{1*}, \ldots, \tilde{\boldsymbol{\beta}}^H - \boldsymbol{\beta}^{H*}) \tag{5.114}$$

is $\mathbf{B}_N^{-1}\mathbf{A}_N\mathbf{B}_N^{-1}$. Let

$$\mathbf{B}_N^{-1} \equiv \mathbf{C}_N = \begin{bmatrix} \mathbf{C}_{11} & \mathbf{0} & \cdots & \mathbf{0} \\ \mathbf{C}_{21} & \mathbf{C}_{22} & \cdots & \mathbf{0} \\ \vdots & \vdots & \vdots & \\ \mathbf{C}_{H1} & \mathbf{C}_{H2} & \cdots & \mathbf{C}_{HH} \end{bmatrix}. \tag{5.115}$$

Then recursion formulae for the asymptotic covariance matrix are

$$\mathbf{C}_{hh} = (\mathbf{M}_{hh}^{h})^{-1}; \tag{5.116}$$

$$\mathbf{C}_{h,h-r} = -\mathbf{C}_{hh} \sum_{l=h-r}^{h-1} \mathbf{M}_{h-1,l}^{h-1} \mathbf{C}_{l,h-r} \quad \text{for} \quad r > 0; \tag{5.117}$$

$$\mathbf{V}_{h,h-r} = \sum_{l=1}^{h-r} \mathbf{C}_{hl} \mathbf{M}_{ll}^{l} \mathbf{C}_{h-r,l}', \tag{5.118}$$

where

$$\mathbf{B}_N^{-1} \mathbf{A}_N \mathbf{B}_N^{-1} = \begin{bmatrix} \mathbf{V}_{11} & \cdots & \mathbf{V}_{1H} \\ \vdots & & \vdots \\ \mathbf{V}_{H1} & \cdots & \mathbf{V}_{HH} \end{bmatrix}. \tag{5.119}$$

5.23 Appendix: Proof of Theorem 5.1

i. Supose an AIRUM form is given, with individual indirect utility having the form $u(i) = (y - q_i + \varepsilon_i)/\beta(\mathbf{r})$, and $\boldsymbol{\varepsilon}_{\mathbf{B}}$ distributed in the population with a cumulative distribution function $F(\boldsymbol{\varepsilon}_{\mathbf{B}})$ and density $f(\boldsymbol{\varepsilon}_{\mathbf{B}})$. Define

$$G(\mathbf{q}_{\mathbf{B}}) = \int_{-\infty}^{+\infty} [F(t + \mathbf{0}_{\mathbf{B}}) - F(t + \mathbf{q}_{\mathbf{B}})]\, dt. \tag{5.120}$$

First, we will show that G exists and is differentiable. Let F^i denote the marginal cumulative distribution function of ε_i. If $\lambda = \max_{i \in \mathbf{B}} |q_i - q_i'|$, then

$$\begin{aligned} F(t + \mathbf{q}_{\mathbf{B}}) - F(t + \mathbf{q}_{\mathbf{B}} + \lambda) &\leqq F(t + \mathbf{q}_{\mathbf{B}}) - F(t + \mathbf{q}_{\mathbf{B}}') \\ &\leqq F(t + \mathbf{q}_{\mathbf{B}}) - F(t + \mathbf{q}_{\mathbf{B}} - \lambda), \end{aligned} \tag{5.121}$$

implying $|F(t + \mathbf{q}_{\mathbf{B}}) - F(t + \mathbf{q}_{\mathbf{B}}')| \leqq F(t + \mathbf{q}_{\mathbf{B}} + \lambda) - F(t + \mathbf{q}_{\mathbf{B}} - \lambda)$. Since F is a cumulative distribution function,

$$\begin{aligned} &F(t + \mathbf{q}_{\mathbf{B}} + \lambda) - F(t + \mathbf{q}_{\mathbf{B}} - \lambda) \\ &\qquad \leqq \sum_{i=1}^{m} [F^i(t + q_i + \lambda) - F^i(t + q_i - \lambda)]. \end{aligned} \tag{5.122}$$

For any scalar $M \geqq 0$ and positive integer K,

$$\int_{M}^{M+K\lambda} [F^i(t+q_i+\lambda) - F^i(t+q_i-\lambda)]\,dt$$

$$= \sum_{k=1}^{K} \int_{M+(k-1)\lambda}^{M+k\lambda} [F^i(t+q_i+\lambda) - F^i(t+q_i-\lambda)]\,dt$$

$$= \int_{M+(K-1)\lambda}^{M+(K+1)\lambda} F^i(t+q_i)\,dt - \int_{M-\lambda}^{M+\lambda} F^i(t+q_i)\,dt$$

$$\leqq 2\lambda\{F^i(M+(K+1)\lambda+q_i) - F^i(M-\lambda+q_i)\}. \tag{5.123}$$

Letting $K \to +\infty$, (5.121) through (5.123) imply

$$\int_{M}^{\infty} |F(t+\mathbf{q_B}) - F(t+\mathbf{q'_B})|\,dt \leqq 2\lambda \sum_{i=1}^{m} (1 - F^i(M-\lambda+q_i)). \tag{5.124}$$

A similar argument yields

$$\int_{-\infty}^{-M} |F(t+\mathbf{q_B}) - F(t+\mathbf{q'_B})|\,dt \leqq 2\lambda \sum_{i=1}^{m} F^i(-M+\lambda+q_i). \tag{5.125}$$

Taking $\mathbf{q'_B} = \mathbf{0_B}$ and $M = 0$ implies

$$\int_{-\infty}^{+\infty} |F(t+\mathbf{q_B}) - F(t)|\,dt \leqq 4m \max|q_i|. \tag{5.126}$$

Hence G defined by (5.120) exists.

For $\theta > 0$,

$$G(\mathbf{q_B}) - G(\mathbf{q_B}+\theta) = \lim_{K\to\infty} \sum_{i=-K}^{K-2} \int_{i\theta}^{(i+1)\theta} [F(t+\mathbf{q_B}+\theta) - F(t+\mathbf{q_B})]\,dt$$

$$= \lim_{K \to \infty} \left\{ \int_{(K-1)\theta}^{K\theta} F(t + q_{\mathbf{B}})\, dt - \int_{-K\theta}^{(1-K)\theta} F(t + q_{\mathbf{B}})\, dt \right\}$$

$$= \theta. \tag{5.127}$$

An analogous argument establishes (5.127) for $\theta < 0$. Hence SS 5.3 holds.

Next the differentiability of G is established. For $\mathbf{q_B} = \mathbf{q'_B} + \theta \mathbf{q''_B}$ and $\lambda = \max_i |q''_i|$,

$$\left| \frac{G(\mathbf{q'_B} + \theta \mathbf{q''_B}) - G(\mathbf{q'_B})}{\theta} + \int_{-M}^{M} \frac{F(\mathbf{q'_B} + \theta \mathbf{q''_B} + t) - F(\mathbf{q'_B} + t)}{\theta} dt \right|$$

$$\leqq 2\lambda \sum_{i=1}^{m} [1 - F^i(M - \lambda + q'_i) + F^i(-M + \lambda + q'_i)]. \tag{5.128}$$

The right-hand side of this inequality converges to zero as $M \to +\infty$, uniformly in θ. For each M the left-hand side converges to

$$\left| \lim_{\theta \to 0} \frac{G(\mathbf{q'_B} + \theta \mathbf{q''_B}) - G(\mathbf{q'_B})}{\theta} + \int_{-M}^{M} \sum_{i=1}^{m} F_i(\mathbf{q'_B} + t) q''_i \, dt \right|,$$

since F has a density and is therefore differentiable. This establishes that G is differentiable, with

$$\begin{aligned} G_i(\mathbf{q_B}) &= - \int_{-\infty}^{+\infty} F_i(\mathbf{q_B} + t)\, dt \\ &= - \int_{-\infty}^{+\infty} F_i(\mathbf{q_B} - q_i + t)\, dt \\ &= - \int_{\varepsilon_i = -\infty}^{+\infty} \int_{\varepsilon_2 = -\infty}^{\varepsilon_i - q_i + q_2} \cdots \int_{\varepsilon_m = -\infty}^{\varepsilon_i - q_i + q_m} f(\boldsymbol{\varepsilon}_{\mathbf{B}})\, d\boldsymbol{\varepsilon}_{\mathbf{B}} \\ &= - \operatorname{Prob}[\varepsilon_i - q_i \geqq \varepsilon_j - q_j \text{ for } j \in \mathbf{B}] \\ &= - P(i \mid \mathbf{B}, \mathbf{s}), \end{aligned} \tag{5.129}$$

with the second equality following by a change in the variable of integration from t to $t - q_i$ and the last inequality following from (5.2). Then (5.19) holds, and $\Sigma_{i=1}^{m} G_i(\mathbf{q_B}) = -1$. From (5.129) the mixed partial derivatives of G exist and are nonpositive and independent of order of differentiation. Thus we have established SS 5.1, SS 5.3, and SS 5.4.

The linear homogeneity of G in $(\mathbf{q_B}, \mathbf{r})$ follows from the linear homogeneity of the functions α_i in (5.12) which imply $F(\lambda\boldsymbol{\varepsilon}_\mathbf{B}, \lambda\mathbf{r}, \mathbf{w_B}, \mathbf{B}, \mathbf{s}) = F(\boldsymbol{\varepsilon}_\mathbf{B}, \mathbf{r}, \mathbf{w_B}, \mathbf{B}, \mathbf{s})$ for $\lambda > 0$. The convexity of G follows by noting that $\Sigma_{i=1}^{M} G_i = -1$ and $G_{ij} \leqq 0$ for $i \neq j$ imply $G_{ii} = -\Sigma_{j \neq i} G_{ij} \geqq 0$. Hence the hessian of G has a weakly dominant positive diagonal. Then SS 5.2 holds.

To establish SS 5.5, note from (5.129) that

$$\lim_{q_i \to -\infty} G_i(\mathbf{q_B}) = -\lim_{q_i \to -\infty} \int_{\varepsilon_i = -\infty}^{+\infty} \int_{\varepsilon_2 = -\infty}^{\varepsilon_i - q_i + q_2} \cdots \int_{\varepsilon_m = -\infty}^{\varepsilon_i - q_i + q_m} f(\boldsymbol{\varepsilon}_\mathbf{B})\, d\boldsymbol{\varepsilon}_\mathbf{B}$$

$$= -\int_{\boldsymbol{\varepsilon}_\mathbf{B} = -\infty}^{+\infty} f(\boldsymbol{\varepsilon}_\mathbf{B})\, d\boldsymbol{\varepsilon}_\mathbf{B} = -1. \tag{5.130}$$

Finally SS 5.6 follows from RUM 5.1. Hence G is a social surplus function.

It is immediate from the definition (5.18) of $\bar{V}$, and the previously established condition (5.19), that $\bar{V}$ is a social indirect utility function, since $\bar{V}$ inverts to an expenditure function which is concave in prices.

Note finally that the conditions SS for a social surplus function imply immediately that the PCS system defined by (5.19) satisfies TPCS.

ii. Suppose G is a social surplus function satisfying SS. Then SS 5.4 and the condition $\Sigma_{i=1}^{m} G_i = -1$ implied by SS 5.3 establish that (5.19) defines a PCS system. It is immediate from SS that this PCS satisfies TPCS.

We next will establish the existence of an AIRUM form such that G satisfies (5.17). Define

$$F(\boldsymbol{\varepsilon}_\mathbf{B}) = \int_{-\infty}^{\varepsilon_1} \pi_1(0, \varepsilon_2 - t, \ldots, \varepsilon_m - t)\psi(t)\, dt, \tag{5.131}$$

where ψ is an arbitrary density. From TPCS 5.4 $\lim_{\varepsilon_i \to -\infty} F(\boldsymbol{\varepsilon}_\mathbf{B}) = 0$. Also, $\lim_{\boldsymbol{\varepsilon}_\mathbf{B} \to +\infty} \pi_1(0, \varepsilon_2, \ldots, \varepsilon_m) = 1$,

$$\lim_{\varepsilon_{\mathbf{B}} \to +\infty} F(\varepsilon_{\mathbf{B}}) = \int_{-\infty}^{+\infty} \pi_1(0, +\infty, \ldots, +\infty)\psi(t)\,dt = \int_{-\infty}^{+\infty} \psi(t)\,dt = 1.$$

From TPCS 5.5 and TPCS 5.6

$F_{1\ldots m}(\varepsilon_{\mathbf{B}}) = \pi_{1,2,\ldots,m}(0, \varepsilon_2 - \varepsilon_1, \ldots, \varepsilon_m - \varepsilon_1)\psi(\varepsilon_1) \geqq 0.$

Hence (5.131) defines a cumulative distribution function characterizing an AIRUM form.

Consider the function

$$\tilde{G}(\mathbf{q_B}) = \int_{-\infty}^{+\infty} [F(t + \mathbf{0_B}) - F(t + \mathbf{q_B})]\,dt$$

$$= -q_1 - \int_{-\infty}^{+\infty} [F(t + \mathbf{q_B} - q_1) - F(t + \mathbf{0_B})]\,dt, \tag{5.132}$$

where the existence of $\tilde{G}$ and the second equality were established in the proof of part i. Then

$$\tilde{G}(\mathbf{q_B}) = -q_1 - \int_{t=-\infty}^{+\infty} \int_{\tau=-\infty}^{t} [\pi_1(0, t + q_2 - q_1 - \tau, \ldots, t + q_m - q_1 - \tau)$$
$$- \pi_1(0, t - \tau, \ldots, t - \tau)]\psi(\tau)\,d\tau\,dt$$
$$= -q_1 - \int_{\tau=-\infty}^{+\infty} \int_{t=\tau}^{+\infty} [\pi_1(0, q_2 - q_1 + t - \tau, \ldots, q_m - q_1 + t - \tau)$$
$$- \pi_1(0, t - \tau, \ldots, t - \tau)]\psi(\tau)\,dt\,d\tau$$
$$= -q_1 - \int_{t=0}^{\infty} [\pi_1(0, q_2 - q_1 + t, \ldots, q_m - q_1 + t)$$
$$- \pi_1(0, t, \ldots, t)]\,dt \int_{\tau=-\infty}^{+\infty} \psi(\tau)\,d\tau$$

$$= -q_1 - \int_{t=0}^{\infty} [\pi_1(-t, q_2 - q_1, \ldots, q_m - q_1)$$

$$- \pi_1(-t, 0, \ldots, 0)]\, dt. \tag{5.133}$$

Since $\pi_1 = -G_1$,

$$\begin{aligned} \tilde{G}(\mathbf{q_B}) &= -q_1 + [G(-t, 0, \ldots, 0) - G(-t, q_2 - q_1, \ldots, q_m - q_1)]_0^{+\infty} \\ &= -q_1 + G(0, q_2 - q_1, \ldots, q_m - q_1) = G(\mathbf{q_B}). \end{aligned} \tag{5.134}$$

Thus $\tilde{G}$ defined by (5.17) from this AIRUM form equals G.

iii. Suppose $\pi_i(\mathbf{q_B})$ is a PCS satisfying TPCS. Define $F(\boldsymbol{\varepsilon}_\mathbf{B})$ and $\tilde{G}(\mathbf{q_B})$ as in (5.131) and (5.132). Then F characterizes an AIRUM form, and

$$F(t + \mathbf{q_B} - q_1) = \int_{-\infty}^{t} \pi_1(0, t + q_2 - q_1 - \tau, \ldots, t + q_m - q_1 - \tau)\psi(\tau)\, d\tau$$

$$= \int_{-\infty}^{0} \pi_1(q_1, q_2 - \tau, \ldots, q_m - \tau)\psi(\tau + t)\, d\tau. \tag{5.135}$$

Hence

$$F_j(t + \mathbf{q_B} - q_1) = \int_{-\infty}^{0} \pi_{1,j}(q_1, q_2 - \tau, \ldots, q_m - \tau)\psi(\tau + t)\, d\tau, \tag{5.136}$$

implying from (5.132) that for $j > 1$

$$\tilde{G}_j(\mathbf{q_B}) = -\int_{t=-\infty}^{+\infty} \int_{\tau=-\infty}^{0} \pi_{1,j}(q_1, q_2 - \tau, \ldots, q_m - \tau)\psi(\tau + t)\, d\tau\, dt$$

$$= -\int_{\tau=-\infty}^{0} \pi_{1,j}(q_1 + \tau, q_2, \ldots, q_m) \int_{-\infty}^{+\infty} \psi(\tau + t)\, dt\, d\tau$$

$$= -\int_{\tau=-\infty}^{0} \pi_{j,1}(q_1 + \tau, q_2, \ldots, q_m)\, d\tau$$

$$= -\pi_j(\mathbf{q_B}) + \pi_j(-\infty, q_2, \ldots, q_m) = -\pi_j(\mathbf{q_B}) \tag{5.137}$$

and

$$\tilde{G}_1(\mathbf{q_B}) = -1 - \sum_{j=2}^{m} \tilde{G}_j(\mathbf{q_B}) = -1 + \sum_{j=2}^{m} \pi_j(\mathbf{q_B}) = -\pi_1(\mathbf{q_B}). \tag{5.138}$$

In (5.137) the third equality is a consequence of TPCS 5.6, and the last equality is a consequence of TPCS 5.4.

The foregoing argument establishes the existence of an AIRUM generating the PCS and of a function $\tilde{G}$, satisfying (5.17) and (5.18). The argument in part i then establishes that $\tilde{G}$ is a social surplus function satisfying SS and $\bar{V}$ defined by (5.18) is a social indirect utility function. This completes the proof of theorem 5.1.

To establish lemma 5.1, note that the existence of first moments of F implies

$$E \max_{i \in \mathbf{B}} (\varepsilon_i - q_i) = \int_{-\infty}^{+\infty} t \frac{d}{dt} F(\mathbf{q_B} + t)\, dt$$

exists, and hence

$$0 = \lim_{M \to \infty} \int_{-\infty}^{-M} t \frac{d}{dt} F(\mathbf{q_B} + t)\, dt \leqq \lim_{M \to \infty} [-MF(\mathbf{q_B} - M)] \leqq 0.$$

Similarly $\lim_{M \to \infty} M[1 - F(\mathbf{q_B} + M)] = 0$. Applying integration by parts to (5.17),

$$G(\mathbf{q_B}) = \lim_{M \to \infty} \int_{-M}^{M} [F(\mathbf{0_B} + t) - F(\mathbf{q_B} + t)]\, dt$$

$$= -\lim_{M \to \infty} t[F(\mathbf{q_B} + t) - F(\mathbf{0_B} + t)]\Big|_{-M}^{M}$$

$$+ \lim_{M \to \infty} \int_{-M}^{M} t \frac{d}{dt}[F(\mathbf{q_B} + t) - F(\mathbf{0_B} + t)]\, dt$$

$$= \int_{-\infty}^{+\infty} t \frac{d}{dt} F(\mathbf{q_B} + t)\, dt - \int_{-\infty}^{+\infty} t \frac{d}{dt} F(\mathbf{0_B} + t)\, dt$$

$$= E \max_{i \in \mathbf{B}} (\varepsilon_i - q_i) - E \max_{i \in \mathbf{B}} \varepsilon_i, \tag{5.139}$$

where the third equality follows from the existence of moments and the last equality from the definition of the expectation of the maximum component of a random vector. This proves lemma 5.1.

We next prove lemma 5.2. Suppose the first moments of F exist. Then, using the proof of lemma 5.1, and letting $G(\mathbf{q_B}, \mathbf{r}, \mathbf{w_B}, \mathbf{B}, \mathbf{s}) = E \max_{i \in \mathbf{B}} (\varepsilon_i - q_i)$, one has

$$G(\mathbf{q_B}, \mathbf{r}, \mathbf{w_B}, \mathbf{B}, \mathbf{s}) = G(\mathbf{0_B}, \mathbf{r}, \mathbf{w_B}, \mathbf{B}, \mathbf{s}) + \int_{-\infty}^{+\infty} [F(t + \mathbf{0_B}) - F(t + \mathbf{q_B})]\, dt, \tag{5.140}$$

and the proof of theorem 5.1 implies that G satisfies SS.

Alternately suppose nonprice attributes are compensatable in the sense that, given $\mathbf{w_B}$ and $\delta > 0$, there exists $\theta > 0$, such that $F(\boldsymbol{\varepsilon}_\mathbf{B} + \theta, \mathbf{r}, \mathbf{w_B}, \mathbf{B}, \mathbf{s}) \geqq F(\boldsymbol{\varepsilon}_\mathbf{B}, \mathbf{r}, \mathbf{w}'_\mathbf{B}, \mathbf{B}, \mathbf{s}) \geqq F(\boldsymbol{\varepsilon}_\mathbf{B} - \theta, \mathbf{r}, \mathbf{w_B}, \mathbf{B}, \mathbf{s})$ for all $\boldsymbol{\varepsilon}_\mathbf{B}$ and $|\mathbf{w}'_\mathbf{B} - \mathbf{w_B}| < \delta$. Let $\bar{\mathbf{w}}_\mathbf{B}$ denote a fixed vector of nonprice attributes, and define

$$G(\mathbf{q_B}, \mathbf{r}, \mathbf{w_B}, \mathbf{B}, \mathbf{s}) = \int_{-\infty}^{+\infty} [F(t + \mathbf{0_B}, \mathbf{r}, \bar{\mathbf{w}}_\mathbf{B}, \mathbf{B}, \mathbf{s}) - F(t + \mathbf{q_B}, \mathbf{r}, \mathbf{w_B}, \mathbf{B}, \mathbf{s})]\, dt. \tag{5.141}$$

Theorem 5.1 implies that $G(\mathbf{q_B}, \mathbf{r}, \bar{\mathbf{w}}_\mathbf{B}, \mathbf{B}, \mathbf{s})$ exists and satisfies SS. Given $\mathbf{w}'_\mathbf{B}$ with $|\mathbf{w}'_\mathbf{B} - \mathbf{w_B}| < \delta$. one has

$$\begin{aligned} &F(t + \mathbf{0_B}, \mathbf{r}, \bar{\mathbf{w}}_\mathbf{B}, \mathbf{B}, \mathbf{s}) - F(t - \theta + \mathbf{q_B}, \mathbf{r}, \bar{\mathbf{w}}_\mathbf{B}, \mathbf{B}, \mathbf{s}) \\ &\quad \geqq F(t + \mathbf{0_B}, \mathbf{r}, \bar{\mathbf{w}}_\mathbf{B}, \mathbf{B}, \mathbf{s}) - F(t + \mathbf{q_B}, \mathbf{r}, \mathbf{w}'_\mathbf{B}, \mathbf{B}, \mathbf{s}) \\ &\quad \geqq F(t + \mathbf{0_B}, \mathbf{r}, \bar{\mathbf{w}}_\mathbf{B}, \mathbf{B}, \mathbf{s}) - F(t + \theta + \mathbf{q_B}, \mathbf{r}, \bar{\mathbf{w}}_\mathbf{B}, \mathbf{B}, \mathbf{s}). \end{aligned} \tag{5.142}$$

By dominated convergence $G(\mathbf{q_B}, \mathbf{r}, \mathbf{w}'_\mathbf{B}, \mathbf{B}, \mathbf{s})$ exists, with

$$G(\mathbf{q_B}, \mathbf{r}, \bar{\mathbf{w}}_\mathbf{B}, \mathbf{B}, \mathbf{s}) + \theta \geqq G(\mathbf{q_B}, \mathbf{r}, \mathbf{w}'_\mathbf{B}, \mathbf{B}, \mathbf{s})$$
$$\geqq G(\mathbf{q_B}, \mathbf{r}, \bar{\mathbf{w}}_\mathbf{B}, \mathbf{B}, \mathbf{s}) - \theta. \tag{5.143}$$

Then one can write

$$G(\mathbf{q_B}, \mathbf{r}, \mathbf{w}'_\mathbf{B}, \mathbf{B}, \mathbf{s}) = G(\mathbf{0_B}, \mathbf{r}, \mathbf{w}'_\mathbf{B}, \mathbf{B}, \mathbf{s}) + \int_{-\infty}^{+\infty} [F(t + \mathbf{0_B}, \mathbf{r}, \mathbf{w}'_\mathbf{B}, \mathbf{B}, \mathbf{s}) - F(t + \mathbf{q_B}, \mathbf{r}, \mathbf{w}'_\mathbf{B}, \mathbf{B}, \mathbf{s})]\, dt. \tag{5.144}$$

Since the integral in (5.144) has the form (5.17), the proof of theorem 5.1 establishes that G satisfies SS.

5.24 Appendix: The Elimination-by-Strategy Model

Tversky (1972b) has given examples showing that not all PCS satisfying RUM can be written as EBA models. However, one can establish an equivalence between models satisfying random preference maximization and a more general family of elimination models called elimination-by-strategy, EBS, models.

Let $\mathbf{H}$ be an abstract space of aspects, and $\mathscr{H}$ a σ-algebra of subsets of $\mathbf{H}$. Let $\mathbf{T}$ be a well-ordered set with an order relation $\prec$. Let $(\mathbf{K}, \mathscr{K})$ be a measurable space of functions from $\mathbf{T}$ into $\mathbf{H}$. Each $k \in \mathbf{K}$ is interpreted as a selection strategy.

Each alternative $i \in \mathbf{I}$ owns a set of aspects $\mathbf{D}_i \in \mathscr{H}$. Suppose a decision maker with strategy k and choice set $\mathbf{B}$ has remaining at $t \in \mathbf{T}$ a set $\mathbf{B}_t \subseteq \mathbf{B}$ of noneliminated alternatives. Then $i, j \in \mathbf{B}_t$ implies $k(t') \notin \mathbf{D}_i \Delta \mathbf{D}_j \equiv (\mathbf{D}_i - \mathbf{D}_j) \cup (\mathbf{D}_j - \mathbf{D}_i)$ for $t' \prec t$, and $i \in \mathbf{B}_{t'}$, $j \in \mathbf{B} - \mathbf{B}_t$ implies $k(t') \in \mathbf{D}_i - \mathbf{D}_j$ for some $t' \prec t$ and $k(t'') \notin \mathbf{D}_i \Delta \mathbf{D}_j$ for $t'' \prec t'$. Since $\mathbf{T}$ is well ordered, $\mathbf{B}_t$ is well defined and monotonically nonincreasing to a nonempty limit set. A probability measure v on $(\mathbf{K}, \mathscr{K})$ then determines choice probabilities, provided there is probability one of selecting a strategy for which the limit set of $\mathbf{B}_t$ is a singleton.

The EBS model is a random preference model: each $k \in \mathbf{K}$ corresponds to a lexicographic preference order on $\mathbf{H}$, and v gives the distribution of preferences. To show that every random preference model can be rewritten as an EBS model, suppose $(\mathbf{J}, \mathscr{J}, \mu)$ is a probability space of preferences on

$\mathbf{I}$, and suppose that $\mathbf{T} = \mathbf{I}$, with $\prec$ ordering $\mathbf{I}$. Define $\mathbf{H} = \mathbf{J} \times \mathbf{I}$ and $\mathscr{H} = \mathscr{J} \otimes 2^{\mathbf{I}}$. Define $\mathbf{D}_i = \{(\succsim, l) \in \mathbf{J} \times \mathbf{I} \mid i \succsim l\}$ to be the set of aspects owned by i. Define $\mathbf{K}$ to be the set of functions $k: \mathbf{I} \to \mathbf{H}$ with $k(i) = (\succsim, i)$, where $\succsim \in \mathbf{J}$ is independent of i. Let $\succsim_k$ denote the preference relation in $\mathbf{J}$ determined by $k \in \mathbf{K}$, and define a measure v on $\mathbf{K}$ by $v(\mathbf{K}_1) = \mu(\{\succsim_k \in \mathbf{J} \mid k \in \mathbf{K}_1\})$ for each $\mathbf{K}_1 \in \mathscr{K}$. Given a choice set $\mathbf{B} \in \mathscr{B}$, suppose $k \in \mathbf{K}$ induces an elimination process that leads to choice of alternative $i \in \mathbf{B}$. Then for each $j \in \mathbf{B}, j \neq i$, there exists $l' \in \mathbf{I}$ such that $k(l') \in \mathbf{D}_i - \mathbf{D}_j$ and for $l'' \in \mathbf{I}, l'' \prec l'$, $k(l'') \notin \mathbf{D}_i \Delta \mathbf{D}_j$. This implies $i \succsim_k l'$ and not $j \succsim_k l'$, so that $i \succ_k j$. Let $\mathbf{K}_1 = \{k \in \mathbf{K} \mid i \succsim_k j \text{ for } j \in \mathbf{B}, j \neq i\}$. Then $v(\mathbf{K}_1) = \mu(\{\succsim \in \mathbf{J} \mid i \succsim j \text{ for } j \in \mathbf{B}, j \neq i\}) = P(i \mid \mathbf{B}, \mathbf{s})$, and the EBS model implies the same PCS as the random preference model.

Tversky's EBA model is a special case of the EBS model, corresponding to $\mathbf{K} = \mathbf{H}^{\infty}$ and v the product measure induced by independent sampling from a probability measure η on $\mathbf{H}$.

References

Amemiya, T. 1976. Specification and Estimation of a Multinomial Logit Model. Technical report 211. Institute of Mathematical Studies in the Social Sciences, Stanford University.

Becker, G., and G. Stigler. 1977. De Gustubus Non Est Disputandum. *American Economic Review*. 67: 76–90.

Berndt, E., J. Hausman, B. Hall, and R. Hall. 1974. Estimation and Inference in Non-Linear Structural Models. *Annals of Economic and Social Measurement*. 3: 653–665.

Ben-Akiva, M., and S. Lerman. 1977. Disaggregate Travel and Mobility Choice Models and Measures of Accessibility. Third International Conference on Behavioural Travel Modelling, Tanenda, Australia.

Block, H., and J. Marschak. 1960. Random Orderings and Stochastic Theories of Response. In *Contributions to Probability and Statistics*, ed. I. Olkin. Stanford, Calif.: Stanford University Press.

Bock, R., and L. Jones. 1968. *The Measurement and Prediction of Judgment and Choice*. San Francisco: Holden-Day.

Cardell, S. 1977. Multinomial Logit with Correlated Stochastic Terms. Working paper. Charles River Associates, Boston, Mass.

Chipman, J. 1974. Homothetic Preferences and Aggregation. *Journal of Economic Theory*. 8: 26–38.

Clark, C. 1961. The Greatest of a Finite Set of Random Variables. *Operations Research*. 9: 145–162.

Coombs, C. 1964. A Theory of Data. New York: Wiley.

Corbin, R., and A. Marley. 1974. Random Utility Models with Equality. *Journal of Mathematical Psychology*. 3: 174–193.

Cosslett, S. 1978. Efficient Estimation of Discrete-Choice Models from Choice-Based Samples. Ph.D. dissertation. Department of Economics, University of California, Berkeley.

Cox, D. 1970. *Analysis of Binary Data*. London: Methuen.

Daganzo, C., F. Bouthelier, and Y. Sheffi. 1977. Multinomial Probit and Qualitative Choice: A Computationally Efficient Algorithm. *Transportation Science*. 11: 338–358.

Daly, A., and S. Zachary. 1979. Improved Multiple Choice Models. In *Identifying and Measuring the Determinants of Mode Choice*. ed. D. Hensher and Q. Dalvi. London: Teakfield.

Debreu, G. 1960. Review of R. D. Luce *Individual Choice Behavior*. *American Economic Review*. 50: 186–188.

Debreu, G. 1962. New Concepts and Techniques for Equilibrium Analysis. *International Economic Review*. 3: 257–273.

Diewert, E. 1977. Generalized Slutsky Conditions for Aggregate Consumer Demand Functions. *Journal of Economic Theory*. 15: 353–362.

Edgell, S., W. Geisler, and J. Zinnes. 1973. A Note on a Paper by Rumelhart and Greeno. *Journal of Mathematical Psychology*. 10: 86–90.

Finney, D. 1964. *Statistical Method in Bioassay*. London: Griffin.

Fuss, M., D. McFadden, and Y. Mundlak. 1978. A Survey of Functional Forms in the Economic Analysis of Production. In *Production Economics; A Dual Approach to Theory and Applications*, vol. 1, ed. M. Fuss and D. McFadden. Amsterdam: North-Holland.

Gaudry, M., and M. Dagenais. 1977. The DOGIT Model. Centre de Recherche sur les Transports, University of Montreal.

Gorman, W. 1953. Community Preference Fields. *Econometrica*. 21: 63–80.

Hausman, J., and D. A. Wise. 1978. A Conditional Probit Model for Qualitative Choice: Discrete Decisions Recognizing Interdependence and Heterogeneous Preferences. *Econometrica*. 46: 403–426.

Hausman, J. 1978. Alternative Specifications of Probit Models of Qualitative Choice. Mimeographed Massachusetts Institute of Technology, Cambridge.

Heckman, J. 1978. Simple Statistical Models for Discrete Panel Data. *Annales de L'Insee*. 30–31: 227–270.

Horowitz, J. 1979. A Note on the Accuracy of the Clark Approximation for the Multinomial Probit Model. Mimeographed. Massachusetts Institute of Technology, Cambridge.

Krantz, D. 1974. Measurement Theory and Qualitative Laws in Psychophysics. In *Measurement, Psychophysics, and Neural Information Processing*, vol. 2, ed. D. Krantz et al. San Francisco: Freeman.

Krantz, D., D. Luce, P. Suppes, and A. Tversky. 1971. *Foundations of Measurement*, vol. 1: *Additive and Polynomial Representations*. New York: Academic Press.

Lau, L. 1977. Existence Conditions for Aggregate Demand Functions. Technical report 248. Institute for Mathematical Studies in the Social Sciences, Stanford University.

Luce, R. D. 1959. *Individual Choice Behavior; A Theoretical Analysis*. New York: Wiley.

Luce, R. D. 1977. The Choice Axiom after Twenty Years, *Journal of Mathematical Psychology*, 15: 215–233.

Luce, R. D., and P. Suppes. 1965. Preference, Utility, and Subjective Probability. In *Handbook of Mathematical Psychology*, vol. 3, ed. R. D. Luce, R. Bush, and E. Galanter. New York: Wiley.

Marschak, J. 1960. Binary-Choice Constraints and Random Utility Indicators. In *Mathematical Methods in the Social Sciences*. ed. K. Arrow, S. Karlin, and P. Suppes. Stanford: Stanford University Press.

McFadden, D. 1973. Conditional Logit Analysis of Qualitative Choice Behavior. In *Frontiers in Econometrics*, ed. P. Zarembka. New York: Academic Press.

McFadden, D. 1974. The Measurement of Urban Travel Demand. *Journal of Public Economics*. 3: 303–328.

McFadden, D. 1975. On Independence, Structure, and Simultaneity in Transportation Demand Analysis. Working paper 7511. Urban Travel Demand Forecasting Project, Institute of Transportation Studies, University of California, Berkeley.

McFadden, D. 1976. Quantal Choice Analysis: A Survey. *Annals of Economic and Social Measurement*. 5: 363–390.

McFadden, D. 1978a. Modelling the Choice of Residential Location. In *Spatial Interaction Theory and Residential Location*, ed. A Karlgvist et al. North Holland: Ansterdam, pp. 75–96.

McFadden, D. 1978b. Cost, Revenue, and Profit Functions. In *Production Economics; A Dual Approach to Theory and Applications*, vol. 1, ed. M. Fuss and D. McFadden. Amsterdam: North-Holland.

McFadden, D., and M. Richter. 1970. Revealed Stochastic Preference. Mimeographed. Department of Economics, Massachusetts Institute of Technology.

McFadden, D., A. Talvitie, and Associates. 1977. *Demand Model Estimation and Validation*. Urban travel demand forecasting project, final report, vol. 5. Institute of Transportation Studies, University of California, Berkeley.

McFadden, D., W. Tye, and K. Train. 1977. An Application of Diagnostic Tests for the Independence from Irrelevant Alternatives Property of the Multinomial Logit Model. *Transportation Research Record*. 637: 39–45.

McKenzie, L. 1957. Demand Theory without a Utility Index. *Review of Economic Studies*. 24: 185–189.

McLynn, J. 1973. A Technical Note on a Class of Fully Competitive Modal Choice Models. DIM Corporation, Bethesda, Md.

Muellbauer, J. 1976. Community Preferences and the Representative Consumer. *Econometrica*. 44: 979–999.

Prais, S., and H. Houthakker. 1971. *The Analysis of Family Budgets*. Cambridge, England: Cambridge University Press.

Quandt, R. 1968. Estimation of Modal Splits. *Transportation Research*. 2: 41–50.

Rosen, H., and K. Small. 1979. Applied Welfare Economics with Discrete Choice Models. Working paper 319. National Burean of Economic Research, Cambridge, Mass.

Rumelhart, D., and J. Greeno. 1971. Similarity between Stimuli: An Experimental Test of the Luce and Restle Choice Models. *Journal of Mathematical Psychology*. 8: 370–381.

Sattath, S., and A. Tversky. 1977. Additive Similarity Trees. *Psychometrika*. 42: 319–345.

Shapiro, P. 1975. Aggregation, Social Choice, and the Existence of a Social Utility Function. Working paper 55. U. S. Bureau of Labor Statistics, Washington, D.C.

Simon, H. 1977. On How to Decide What to Do. C.I.P. working paper. Carnegie-Mellon University, Pittsburgh.

Sjöberg, L. 1977. Choice Frequency and Similarity. *Scandinavian Journal of Psychology*. 18: 103–115.

Thurstone, L. 1927. A Law of Comparative Judgment. *Psychological Review*. 34: 273–286.

Tobin, J. 1958. Estimation of Relationships for Limited Dependent Variables. *Econometrica*. 26.

Train, K. 1978. A Validation Test of a Disaggregate Mode Choice Model. *Transportation Research*. 12: 167–174.

Train, K., and D. McFadden 1978. The Goods-Leisure Tradeoff and Disaggregate Work Trip Mode Choice Models. *Transportation Research;* 12: 349–353.

Tversky, A. 1972a. Elimination-by-Aspects: A Theory of Choice. *Psychological Review*. 79: 281–299.

Tversky, A. 1972b. Choice-by-Elimination. *Journal of Mathematical Psychology*. 9: 341–367.

Tversky, A., and S. Sattath. 1979. Preference Trees. *Psychological Review*. 86: 542–573.

Warner, S. 1962. *Stochastic Choice of Mode in Urban Travel; A Study in Binary Choice*. Evanston: Northwestern University Press.

Williams, H. 1977. On the Formation of Travel Demand Models and Economic Evaluation Measures of User Benefit. *Environment Planning*. A.9: 285–344.

Yellot, J. 1977. The Relationship between Luce's Choice Axiom, Thurstone's Theory of Comparative Judgment, and the Double Exponential Distribution. *Journal of Mathematical Psychology*. 15: 109–144.

6 Random versus Fixed Coefficient Quantal Choice Models

Gregory W. Fischer and Daniel Nagin

6.1 Introduction

A large class of decision problems is most appropriately characterized as a choice dilemma in which an individual selects one element from a discrete set of decision alternatives. Examples of such dilemmas are almost limitless, ranging from the relatively profound (selection of a job or a spouse) to the relatively mundane (selection of a brand of toothpaste or shaving cream). Quantal choice theory attempts to explain and predict the behavior of individuals confronted by such decision dilemmas.[1] To date, quantal choice models have been most widely employed in transportation demand studies. Here the models have been used to examine such issues as the selection of transportation modes for home-to-work trips (e.g., Ben-Akiva and Haus 1973, Charles Rivers Associates 1972) and automobile ownership decisions (Lerman and Ben-Akiva 1975). A key motivation for all of these studies has been the development of models that predict the impact of changes in certain factors which can be manipulated by policy makers (e.g., gasoline prices, travel time). In view of the potential significance of these applications of quantal choice models, it is essential that the statistical procedures used in developing these models lead to accurate inferences and predictions.

6.2 Quantal Choice Theory and Variation in Tastes

Notationally let $\mathbf{R} = (\mathbf{X}^1, \ldots, \mathbf{X}^r)$ be a mutually exclusive and exhaustive set of r choice alternatives, where each alternative is characterized by a vector of m value relevant attributes. That is, $\mathbf{X}^i = (x_1^i, \ldots, x_m^i)$. For example, if the alternatives are transportation modes, the attribute vector might include such factors as time per trip, cost per trip, and so forth. Further let $\mathbf{Y}^j = (y_1^j, \ldots, y_n^j)$ be a vector of attributes characterizing the jth individual choosing from choice set $\mathbf{R}$. These might include the

This research was supported by a grant from the Duke University Research Council. The authors are indebted to Charles Manski for numerous insights which have greatly enhanced our analysis. The observations of several anonymous reviewers were also of substantial value in preparing the final draft. Any errors remain the responsibility of the authors alone.

1. For general historical reviews of quantal choice theory see Bock and Jones (1968) and Luce and Suppes (1965). For more recent developments in quantal choice theory see Hausman and Wise (1978), McFadden (1973), Manski (1973), and Tversky (1972).

individual's age, sex, income, and so forth. Then for any such choice set **R**, and for any individual described by the set of attributes $\mathbf{Y}^j$, quantal choice models generate a vector of choice probabilities $(P^{1j}, \ldots, P^{rj})$. Here P^{ij} is the probability that a person characterized by $\mathbf{Y}^j$ will choose alternative $\mathbf{X}^i$ from choice set **R**. Thus $\Sigma_{i=1}^{r} P^{ij} = 1$.

The models considered here assume that each individual is a utility maximizer. Thus $P^{ij} = Pr(U^{ij} \geq U^{kj}$, for all $k \neq i)$, where U^{ij} is the subjective utility of alternative $\mathbf{X}^i$ to the jth individual. Statistically the models considered here assume that U^{ij} is a linear function of the attributes of alternative $\mathbf{X}^i$ and the individual's attributes, $\mathbf{Y}^j$. More precisely let $\mathbf{Z}^{ij} = (z_1^{ij}, \ldots, z_s^{ij})$ be a vector of arithmetic combinations of $\mathbf{X}^i$ and $\mathbf{Y}^j$. This **Z**-vector might include simple attributes (say, income or price per trip), transformations of attributes (say, the log of income or price), or explicit interactions of the attributes of the alternatives and the individual (e.g., price/income).

The first statistical specification we consider here is the linear in parameters, independent and identically distributed (LPIID) disturbances model

$$U^{ij} = \mathbf{Z}^{ij}\boldsymbol{\beta} + \varepsilon^{ij}. \tag{6.1}$$

Here U^{ij} is the unobservable utility of the ith alternative to the jth individual. This utility is assumed to be linear in the elements of $\mathbf{Z}^{ij}$. Thus the coefficient vector $\boldsymbol{\beta}$ reflects the tastes of the individuals in the population. Random variation in the U^{ij} is introduced through the additive disturbance term ε^{ij} which is assumed to be independently and identically distributed across individuals and alternatives. Manski (1973) provides an insightful analysis of the possible sources of apparent random variation in behavior. For our purposes two relatively straightforward interpretations seem adequate. First the ε^{ij} may arise due to choice relevant but unobserved attributes of alternatives or individuals. Such factors are necessarily excluded from the attribute vector $\mathbf{Z}^{ij}$ and are, with the LPIID specification, assumed to be independent of the elements of $\mathbf{Z}^{ij}$. A second (and not incompatible) possibility is that the ε^{ij} reflect true random variation in choice behavior, an interpretation that is commonly invoked by psychologists (see Coombs, Dawes, and Tversky 1970).

Although the U^{ij} are unobservable, the coefficients of equation (6.1) are estimable. Consider a binary choice situation in which an individual described by the vector $\mathbf{Y}^j$ is choosing between two alternatives described by the vectors $\mathbf{X}^1$ and $\mathbf{X}^2$. Then $\mathbf{Z}^{1j}$ and $\mathbf{Z}^{2j}$ are the vectors of the appropriate arithmetic combinations of the attributes of the alternatives and of the individual choosing between them. According to equation (6.1) the probability that the individual will choose alternative $\mathbf{X}^1$ is given by

$$\begin{aligned} Pr(U^{1j} \geq U^{2j}) &= Pr[\mathbf{Z}^{1j}\boldsymbol{\beta} + \varepsilon^{1j} \geq \mathbf{Z}^{2j}\boldsymbol{\beta} + \varepsilon^{2j}] \\ &= Pr[(\mathbf{Z}^{1j} - \mathbf{Z}^{2j})\boldsymbol{\beta} \geq \varepsilon^{2j} - \varepsilon^{1j}]. \end{aligned}$$

Thus if the ε^{ij} are assumed to be normally distributed, and if a sample of binary choices has been observed, $\boldsymbol{\beta}$ can be estimated using IID probit estimation procedures (Albright, Lerman, and Manski 1977, Hausman and Wise 1978); if the ε are assumed to be extreme value distributed, then β can be estimated using IID logit estimation methods (McFadden 1972). Here we consider only the probit specification of the LPIID model.

Note that the LPIID model assumes that all individuals' tastes are identical with respect to the observed attributes embodied in the $\mathbf{Z}^{ij}$ vectors. Consequently the LPIID formulation implies that all individuals of identical observed characteristics have identical tastes with respect to the observed attributes of alternatives (except for random additive disturbances). Empirically, this need not be the case. For example, two individuals of identical observed characteristics may attach different disutilities to price per trip and time per trip when making transportation mode choices. If this is the case, the specification in equation (6.1) is incorrect, for apparently random variation in behavior is due not only to an additive disturbance effect but also to variation in tastes, that is, to variation in the elements of $\boldsymbol{\beta}$.

Recognizing this difficulty, Hausman and Wise (1978), and Albright, Lerman and Manski (1977) have developed the random coefficients, covarying disturbances (RCCD) model, a quantal choice model that explicitly incorporates variation in the tastes of individuals with identical observed characteristics. The RCCD model is given by

$$U^{*ij} = \mathbf{Z}^{ij}\boldsymbol{\beta}^* + \mathbf{Z}^{ij}\boldsymbol{\delta}^j + \gamma^{ij}, \tag{6.2}$$

where $\boldsymbol{\beta}^*$ is the mean coefficient vector for the population of interest, $\boldsymbol{\delta}^j$ is a coefficient vector describing the deviations of the jth individual's tastes from the tastes embodied in the mean coefficient vector, and γ^{ij} is an additive disturbance term assumed to be independently and identically distributed across individuals but possibly correlated across alternatives. In general RCCD models assume that the $\boldsymbol{\delta}^j$ and $\boldsymbol{\gamma}^j = (\gamma^{1j}, \ldots, \gamma^{rj})$ are multivariate normally distributed with $\boldsymbol{\delta}^j \sim \text{MVN}(\mathbf{0}, \boldsymbol{\Sigma})$ and $\gamma^j \sim \text{MVN}(\mathbf{0}, \boldsymbol{\Sigma}_\gamma)$. The parameters $\boldsymbol{\beta}^*$, $\boldsymbol{\Sigma}$, and $\boldsymbol{\Sigma}_\gamma$ are not jointly identified. The necessary identification restrictions are generally imposed on the components of $\boldsymbol{\Sigma}_\gamma$, and the remaining parameters are estimated up to these restrictions. Referring again to the binary choice example used earlier, the probability that an individual described by the attribute vector $\mathbf{Y}^j$ will prefer alternative $\mathbf{X}^1$ to $\mathbf{X}^2$ is

$$\begin{aligned} Pr(U^{*1j} \geq U^{*2j}) &= Pr[\mathbf{Z}^{1j}(\boldsymbol{\beta}^* + \boldsymbol{\delta}^j) + \gamma^{1j} \geq \mathbf{Z}^{2j}(\boldsymbol{\beta}^* + \boldsymbol{\delta}^j) + \gamma^{2j}] \\ &= Pr[(\mathbf{Z}^{1j} - \mathbf{Z}^{2j})(\boldsymbol{\beta}^* + \boldsymbol{\delta}^j) \geq \gamma^{2j} - \gamma^{1j}]. \end{aligned}$$

If the distribution assumptions are satisfied, then $\boldsymbol{\beta}^*$ and $\boldsymbol{\Sigma}$, the covariance matrix for the $\boldsymbol{\delta}^j$, can be estimated using maximum likelihood random coefficients probit estimation procedures (Hausman and Wise 1978).

With the RCCD formulation the total disturbance term for the ith alternative and jth individual is given by

$$\varepsilon^{*ij} = \mathbf{Z}^{ij}\boldsymbol{\delta}^j + \gamma^{ij}.$$

Note that, because $\boldsymbol{\delta}^j$ is constant for all alternatives evaluated by the jth individual, the total disturbances for all alternatives evaluated by the jth individual will covary.

This study uses the results of a choice experiment to address the following questions:

1. To what extent do taste parameters vary across individuals?

2. Is RCCD probit more immune to specification errors than LPIID probit?

3. Does the RCCD estimator provide a better fit to choice data?

4. Does the RCCD estimator lead to more accurate predictions concerning the impact of marginal changes in attributes on choice probabilities?

5. How precise are the RCCD estimates of the mean tastes coefficient vector? Of the variation in tastes?

6. Do the RCCD and LPIID estimators yield similar estimates of the elements of the mean tastes vector?

Question 1 addresses the fundamental premise motivating the development of the RCCD estimator. Taste variations undoubtedly exist, but to our knowledge no empirical studies have assessed the magnitude of such taste variations. Nor, to our knowledge, has any empirical study examined the shape of taste distributions (e.g., normal, exponential). It is apparent that the extent to which the RCCD estimator yields improved predictive accuracy will be directly related to the magnitude of the variation in taste parameters, and also to their distribution.

This speculation suggests a corollary speculation addressed in question 2. The degree to which RCCD estimation procedures are superior to LPIID procedures should be inversely related to the extent to which we are able to explicitly model the sources of variation in tastes. To illustrate this argument, suppose that attribute x_1 is a quality measure, attribute x_2 a price measure, and y is a measure of income.

Consider the following RCCD specifications:

$$U_1^{*ij} = (\beta_1^* x_1^i + \beta_2^* x_2^i) + (\delta_1^j x_1^i + \delta_2^j x_2^i) + \gamma_1^{ij},$$

$$U_2^{*ij} = \left[\alpha_1^* x_1^i + \alpha_2^* \left(\frac{x_2^i}{y^j}\right)\right] + \left[\theta_1^j x_1^i + \theta_2^j \left(\frac{x_2^i}{y^j}\right)\right] + \gamma_2^{ij}.$$

On a priori grounds we would expect much of the variation in the disutility of price to be explained by income. Consequently we expect Var $(\theta_2) <$ Var (δ_2). Also the covariance of the total disturbance term across alternatives should be smaller for the second specification, since one important source of this covariation (namely, income) is now explicitly incorporated in the utility model. The parallel LPIID models are

$$U_1^{ij} = \beta_1 x_1^i + \beta_2 x_2^i + \varepsilon_1^{ij},$$

$$U_2^{ij} = \alpha_1 x_1^i + \alpha_2 \left(\frac{x_2^i}{y^j}\right) + \varepsilon_2^{ij}.$$

Both are misspecified if these RCCD models hold. Nevertheless it would appear that the problems associated with incorrectly using an LPIID estimator should be greater in the first case. For here there is greater variation in tastes and greater covariation of the ε^{ij}. Thus the relative superiority of an RCCD estimator should be greater in the first case (where we do not model the source of taste variation) than in the second (where in part we do).

This observation has important practical implications for the potential usefulness of RCCD estimators. Whether through ignorance or lack of data, an analyst will frequently be unable to model explicitly the major sources of taste variation. Under such circumstances RCCD estimators may prove a useful tool for reducing the resulting losses in explanatory power and predictive accuracy. We hasten to add that we are not advocating the use of RCCD estimators as a remedy to excuse sloppy or ill-considered analyses. It must be recognized, however, that our understanding of the sources of taste variation is extremely limited. Consequently our ability to model explicitly the sources of taste variation is also extremely limited. Even in the most careful analyses numerous specification errors are almost certain to arise. Even though each of these errors may be small in its impact, the total effect may still be large. Because RCCD estimators may reduce the costs of such unavoidable specification errors, they are deserving of careful scrutiny.

Questions 3 and 4 address closely related, but not identical, issues. The LPIID model is a special case of the RCCD model that arises when $\mathbf{\Sigma}_\gamma = \sigma^2\mathbf{I}$ and $\mathbf{\Sigma}$ is a zero matrix. Thus it is apparent that the RCCD model will provide a better fit to a set of data than will the corresponding LPIID model. In principle one should not go wrong by obtaining maximum likelihood (ML) estimates of the RCCD model parameters. For when there is in fact random variation in tastes, ML estimators of the RCCD parameters are consistent.[2] If there is no variation in tastes, the ML estimators will still be consistent and will asymptotically reveal the true LPIID structure. By contrast ML estimators of the LPIID model parameters are consistent only in the absence of variation in tastes. The degree to which RCCD estimators are superior is clearly an empirical matter, depending both on the criterion one uses and on the amount of taste variation present in the empirical context studied. And if the speculation embodied in question 2 is correct, the superiority of the RCCD model should be inversely related to the extent to which we are able to explicitly model the source of variation in tastes.[3] With regard to predicting the effect of changes in choice relevant attributes (question 4), it is not obvious to what extent RCCD estimators will be superior, or even that they will be superior at all. Because RCCD models have more coefficients than the corresponding LPIID models, the standard errors of the RCCD model coefficients are likely to be larger. Predictions of the effects of changes in

2. Provided of course that variations in the taste parameters are multivariate normally distributed as assumed in the RCCD specification.

3. In general we explicitly model variation in tastes by including terms in the utility function constructed from explicit interactions of the attributes of alternatives and the attributes of individuals, for example, price/income.

choice relevant attributes that are based on imprecisely measured coefficients may be correspondingly imprecise. Also actual estimation of the parameters of either LPIID or RCCD models depends on ML search procedures that provide no assurance of attaining the global maximum. The fallibility of these search procedures, in conjunction with the greater complexity of RCCD models, may in practice more than offset the theoretical advantages of RCCD estimators.[4]

Questions 5 and 6 address related issues. Note that the first part of question 5 does not involve a comparison of the RCCD and LPIID estimators. We state it in this form because we are confident (even absent a formal proof) that the LPIID estimator of $\boldsymbol{\beta}$ is not a consistent estimator of $\boldsymbol{\beta}^*$, the population tastes vector. If the true total disturbance terms are of the form

$$\varepsilon^{*ij} = \mathbf{Z}^{ij}\boldsymbol{\delta}^j + \gamma^{ij},$$

then these ε^{*ij} are not independently distributed as assumed by the LPIID model. Under these conditions we conjecture that application of LPIID estimation procedures to choice data generated by an RCCD process will result in inconsistent estimates of $\boldsymbol{\beta}^*$, the true mean tastes coefficient vector. In particular we speculate that the probability limit of elements of the LPPID estimator $\boldsymbol{\beta}$ will be too small in absolute value terms (relative to the true mean tastes vector $\boldsymbol{\beta}^*$).[5] The reasoning behind this speculation is briefly outlined here and developed more fully in section 6.9. The unit of the utility measure (and consequently $\boldsymbol{\beta}$) in quantal choice models is arbitrary. In statistical applications the standard procedure has been to normalize coefficients with respect to the variance of the independent additive disturbance term. In the LPIID model this disturbance is ε^{ij}. In the RCCD model it is γ^{ij}. Note that, when tastes do in fact vary, Var (ε^{ij}) = Var (ε^{*ij}) > Var (γ^{ij}), for under these circumstances, Var (ε^{ij}) = Var $(\mathbf{Z}^{ij}\boldsymbol{\delta}^j + \gamma^{ij})$. Consequently the elements of the LPIID estimator $\boldsymbol{\beta}$ should be too small in absolute value (relative to $\boldsymbol{\beta}^*$). The reasoning behind this speculation leads to a related speculation addressed in question 6. The unit of measure cancels out when we look at the ratios of coefficients. Thus we

4. Also, RCCD estimation procedures are much more costly. These costs must also be weighed in any decision to use RCCD methods.

5. This argument, and the one which immediately follows, were suggested to us by Charles Manski.

suspect that on the average the ratios of the LPIID estimated coefficients should be close to the ratios of the RCCD coefficients, that is,

$$\frac{\hat{\beta}_s}{\hat{\beta}_t} \cong \frac{\hat{\beta}^*_s}{\hat{\beta}^*_t}, \quad \text{for all } s, t.$$

6.3 An Empirical Comparison of the LPIID and RCCD Models

The experiment described in this section was designed to provide a data base appropriate for addressing the six questions. The general design follows. To answer these questions we asked a group of respondents to choose between pairs of alternatives, with each alternative defined by two attributes. Each respondent made a relatively large number of hypothetical choices between pairs of alternatives, thus permitting us to estimate (for each respondent) the coefficients of the LPIID model:

$$U(x_1^i, x_2^i) = \beta_1 x_1^i + \beta_2 x_2^i + \varepsilon^i.$$

That is, we assumed that apart from an additive disturbance term each respondent's tastes were fixed (for the duration of the experiment) and linear in the attributes x_1 and x_2. The coefficients obtained from these individual choice models were used first to assess the degree of variation in tastes and second as a benchmark for evaluating the LPIID and RCCD models when they were applied to the group data.

We are of course aware that the data used in this study involve hypothetical choices. But given our objective of precisely modeling each individual's choice process, we need to observe many choices by each individual. It is extremely difficult to do this in a real choice setting. The hypothetical choices made by the individuals studied here are systematic and sensible. Thus we believe that they provide an appropriate basis for evaluating the statistical properties of the two estimation procedures.

6.4 Details of the Experiment

In implementing the experimental strategy outlined in section 6.3, we sought a choice task that was realistic, interesting, and yet involved alternatives described by only two major attributes. At the time we conducted the study, Duke University was embroiled in a debate over procedures for allocating parking permits. Some participants in that debate suggested that a pricing mechanism be used, with higher prices being levied for parking spots closer to the center of the campus. We exploited this situation by recruiting twenty respondents from the faculty, administration, and secretarial staff of Duke University's Institute of Policy Sciences and Public Affairs. Each respondent was asked to consider 60 pairs of parking lot alternatives, with each alternative being characterized by the attributes price per year and walking distance (in minutes) from the parking lot to the building where the respondent worked. The respondents were asked to choose one option from each pair. In constructing alternatives we used five price levels ($20, $40, $60, $90, and $120) and four walking distances (1.5, 2.5, 4 to 5, and 9 to 10 minutes).[6] From the 20 basic alternatives we created 60 pairs of alternatives in which, for every pair, the less expensive lot always involved the greater walking distance. The order of alternatives within pairs was randomly determined, with the low price-long distance option being presented first in half the pairs, and second in the other half. After the respondent had worked through all 60 pairs of alternatives, he or she was asked to complete a short questionnaire which elicited background information on age, position, income, and some details concerning where the respondent typically parked.

6.5 Results

The analysis proceeds in two stages. In the first stage a linear stochastic utility function is estimated for each respondent. In the second the observations for all respondents are pooled and stochastic utility functions for the entire sample are estimated. The alternative model specifications estimated in the second stage include both LPIID and RCCD models.[7]

The results of the first stage analyses will serve several functions. First, they will provide some empirical evidence on the magnitude of taste variations in the respondent population and on shape of the distributions

6. Since three of the four lots in question were real, we gave ranges for the more distant lots to avoid an aura of phony precision.

7. The first-stage models were estimated using a well-tested LPIID probit program developed by Richard McKelvey of Carnegie-Mellon University. The second-stage models (both LPIID and RCCD) were estimated using a program developed by Cambridge Systematics, Inc., Cambridge, Mass. In fact we could also have used the latter program to obtain the first-stage estimates. The decision to estimate the first-stage models with the McKelvey program was purely pragmatic. We had that program first and used it to complete the first stage analyses before receiving the Cambridge Systematics program.

of taste coefficients (question 1). Additionally, summary statistics characterizing the taste distribution estimated in the first stage analysis provide a useful basis for evaluating the parameter estimates from the second stage analysis. For example, are the second stage RCCD parameter estimates of $\boldsymbol{\beta}^*$ close to some measure of the central tendency of the estimated distribution of tastes (question 5)? How well does the estimation method allowing for taste variation capture the estimated distribution in tastes from the first stage analysis (question 5)? Finally, the models estimated in the first stage can be used as the basis for an analysis of the predictive accuracy of the models estimated in the second stage (question 4).

6.6 Analysis of Individual Respondents

A linear stochastic utility function (eq. 6.3) for each respondent was estimated under the assumption that the disturbance term in the utility function was normally distributed:[8]

$$U(D,F) = \beta_1 D + \beta_2 F + \varepsilon, \tag{6.3}$$

where

D = distance,
F = fee,
$\varepsilon \sim N(0, \sigma^2)$.

The results are summarized in table 6.1. No coefficient estimates are given for three respondents. The reasons for β_1 and β_2 being unestimable for these respondents are discussed in detail in section 6.9. In brief model (6.3) is unestimable for these respondents because their choice behavior is perfectly explained by a model of the form:

$$U(D,F) = \beta_1 D + \beta_2 F. \tag{6.4}$$

Model (6.4) is a special case of model (6.3) where the disturbance has zero variance (there is no stochastic component, ε, in the utility function). When

8. A log-linear utility model was also estimated for each respondent. The explanatory power (the log likelihood) of model (6.3) was almost always greater than the log-linear model.

Table 6.1
The model estimates for the individual respondents

Respondent	β_1	β_2	Percentage of choices correctly predicted
1	−4.57	−0.635	98
	(1.07)	(1.05)	
2	−0.623	−0.0509	85
	(3.89)	(3.89)	
3	−0.858	−0.0675	90
	(3.66)	(3.66)	
4	−0.230	−0.0751	92
	(1.92)	(3.01)	
5	−0.543	−0.0340	87
	(4.37)	(3.85)	
6	−0.266	−0.101	93
	(1.71)	(2.59)	
7	—	—	100
8	−0.0614	−0.0730	97
	(0.42)	(2.22)	
9	−1.75	−0.0924	95
	(2.80)	(2.89)	
10	−1.70	−0.0730	87
	(2.83)	(2.74)	
11	−0.569	−0.0366	83
	(4.04)	(3.75)	
12	−0.218	−0.0892	93
	(1.55)	(2.65)	
13	−0.628	−0.146	93
	(2.71)	(2.92)	
14	−0.476	−0.0381	83
	(4.24)	(4.17)	
15	−0.905	−0.0620	90
	(3.61)	(3.45)	
16	−0.382	−0.0133	82
	(3.82)	(2.30)	
17	−0.452	−0.0283	80
	(4.24)	(3.75)	
18	—	—	100
19	−1.73	−0.0887	93
	(2.83)	(2.83)	
20	—	—	100

Note: Ratio of parameter estimate to its standard error in parenthesis.

$\sigma^2 = 0$, only the ratio β_1/β_2 is potentially identifiable; β_1 and β_2 cannot be individually estimated.[9]

For the respondents with estimable models, the ratios of the parameter estimates to their standard errors are generally greater than two which suggests that the estimates are reasonably precise. The explanatory power of the models is also excellent. The percentage of choices predicted correctly ranges from 80 to 100 percent. For 70 percent of the individuals the percentage of correct predictions is 90 percent or better.

The results are examined from a different perspective in table 6.2. In this table the estimates of β_1, β_2, and β_1/β_2 (the value of time) are rank ordered from smallest to largest. (The basis for including the respondents with unestimable models in the ranking is discussed in section 6.9.)

These rankings can be interpreted as estimates of the distribution of tastes in the respondent population. The results suggest that the taste variations in the respondent population are large. The interquartile range (the difference between 25th and 75th percentile values) for each distribution is greater than the distribution's median value. (Because some respondent's models are not estimable, we cannot calculate sample means for the taste coefficients. But for reasons discussed in section 6.9 we are able to confidently estimate the sample medians.) While the results in table 6.2 may exaggerate the magnitude of the actual taste variations due to statistical variations in the parameter estimates for each respondent, the estimated distributions are sufficiently dispersed to leave little question that the actual taste variations are large. The results thus imply that in principle the idea of developing estimation methods that account for taste variations is well founded and that, if these methods can successfully capture the actual variation, they would be of considerable value.

Under an assumption of the number of trips made per year, the estimated values of β_1/β_2 can be transformed into estimates of the value of time (in a restricted sense) on a scale of dollars per hour. Assuming 500 trips to and from a lot per year, the median value of time is \$1.53; the 25th to 75th percentile range is \$.50 to \$2.27.

Information on the demographic and economic characteristics of each respondent was collected to assess which individual characteristics, if any, are systematically related to taste variation. The results of this analysis were used as a basis for properly specifying the population models

9. The parameters β_1, β_2, and σ^2 are not jointly identifiable. β_1 and β_2 are only estimable up to some assumed value of $1/\sigma$.

Table 6.2
β_1, β_2, and β_1/β_2 rank ordered from smallest to largest

	β_1		β_2		β_1/β_2	
1	—	(7, 18)	—	(8, 20)	—	(20)
2	—		—		0.842	(8)
3	−4.57	(1)	−0.635	(1)	2.44	(12)
4	−1.75	(9)	−0.146	(13)	2.64	(6)
5	−1.73*	(19)	−0.101*	(6)	3.06	(4)
					3.68*	
6	−1.70	(10)	−0.0924	(9)	4.29	(13)
7	−0.905	(15)	−0.0892	(12)	4.50	(18)
8	−0.858	(3)	−0.0887	(19)	7.20	(1)
9	−0.628	(13)	−0.0751	(4)	12.3	(2)
10	−0.623*	(2)	−0.0730*	(10)	12.5	(14)
					12.6*	
11	−0.569	(11)	−0.0730	(8)	12.7	(3)
12	−0.544	(5)	−0.0675	(3)	14.6	(15)
13	−0.476	(14)	−0.0620	(15)	15.6	(11)
14	−0.452	(17)	−0.0509	(2)	16.0	(17)
15	−0.382*	(16)	−0.0381*	(14)	16.0	(5)
					17.5*	
16	−0.266	(6)	−0.0366	(17)	18.9	(9)
17	−0.230	(4)	−0.0340	(5)	19.5	(19)
18	−0.218	(12)	−0.0283	(17)	23.2	(10)
19	−0.0614	(8)	−0.0133	(16)	28.6	(16)
20					95.0	(7)

Note: Respondent number in parentheses. Asterisks indicate 25th, 50th, and 75th percentile values.

estimated in the second stage analysis. Regressions of β_1/β_2 on respondent characteristics suggested that the only significant determinant of β_1/β_2 is income.[10] The income effect is positive as expected. The distributions of β_1 and β_2 (income adjusted) are shown in figures 6.1 and 6.2. (The method

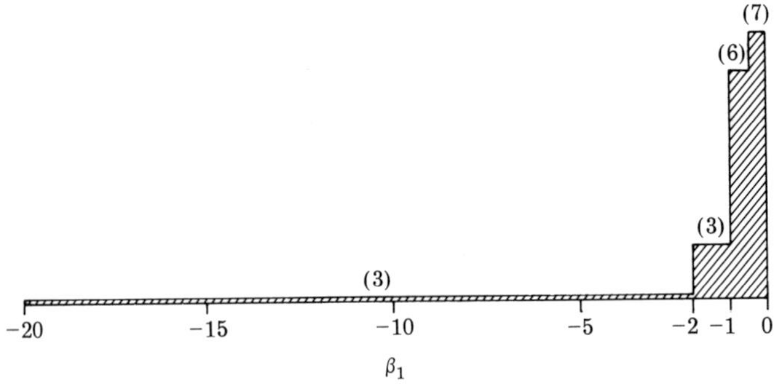

Figure 6.1
Relative frequency distribution for β_1 (the distance coefficient). Ths histogram is drawn so that areas are proportional to relative frequencies. At point (3) one respondent has an estimable coefficient value of 4.57. Two respondents have unestimable coefficients. Arbitrarily --20 is used as the lower bound for the interval.

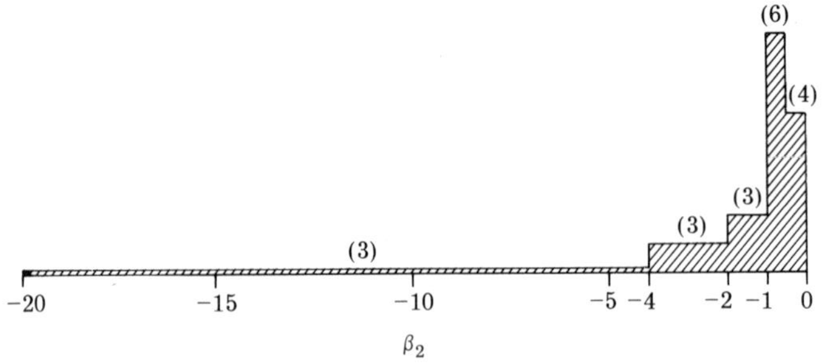

Figure 6.2
Relative frequency distribution for β_2 (the income adjusted fee coefficient). The histogram is drawn so that areas are proportional to relative frequency. At (3) one respondent has an estimable coefficient value of 15.88. Two others have unestimable coefficients. Arbitrarily −20 is used as the lower bound for the interval.

10. Regressions of β_1 and β_2 individually on respondent characteristics were not estimated because estimates of β_1 and β_2 are not available for the three respondents with unestimable models. Regressions involving only the β's of respondents with estimable models would yield inconsistent parameter estimates because, in effect, we would be sampling on the basis of the value of the dependent variable. Regressions involving the ratio of β_1/β_2 were feasible because an estimate was available for 19 of 20 respondents (see section 6.9). For the remaining respondent (number 20) β_1/β_2 could safely be approximated as zero.

used to make the income adjustment is described in section 6.7.) Note that even with the income adjustment there is still appreciable variation in both β_1 and β_2. This result suggests that attempts to model explicitly the sources of variation in tastes will meet with limited success at best. The potential usefulness of RCCD probit is enhanced accordingly.

6.7 A Comparison of LPIID Probit and RCCD Probit Estimation

To examine the merits of RCCD probit estimation relative to LPIID probit extimation, the responses for the entire respondent population were pooled, and several model specifications were estimated on the pooled data set using both estimation methods.[11]

Using the simulated cross section, we estimate model (6.3) using LPIID probit and a generalized version of model (6.3) that allows for taste variation using RCCD probit. The generalized model is of the form

$$U(D, F) = (\beta_1 + \delta_1)D + (\beta_2 + \delta_2)F + \gamma, \tag{6.5}$$

where

$$\delta_1, \delta_2 \sim N(\mathbf{0}, \boldsymbol{\Sigma}),$$
$$\gamma \sim N(0, \sigma^2).$$

In view of our finding that β_1/β_2 is significantly associated with the respondent's income, neither models (6.3) nor (6.5) are actually appropriate specifications for analyzing the pooled data set. Nevertheless we estimate the coefficients of models (6.3) and (6.5) in order to empirically evaluate the speculation that RCCD probit may offer valuable protection against the ill effects of specification error.

11. In estimating the various models with the pooled data, all responses were treated as independent. The responses are of course not independent since the 1,200 observations in the data set were not the responses of 1,200 different respondents but of 20 respondents making 60 choices. The LPIID and RCCD probit estimation algorithms are not designed to allow for the possibility that successive observations might be nonindependent, and we therefore made no attempt to account for the probable absence of independence among observations. While we have not analytically examined the impact of the nonindependence of the observations, standard results for least squares regression provide some insights into the probable impact. The estimated standard errors of the parameters are almost certainly incorrect because they are computed under the assumption that the observations are independent. It is unclear whether the parameter estimates themselves are inconsistent due to failure of the independence assumption. Standard regression results concerning the effect of correlation among the disturbances are probably not transferable because knowledge of the distribution of the disturbances is generally not necessary to make consistent estimates of the structural parameters.

To model the income effect we interact β_2 with income (I) as follows:

$$\text{Without taste variations: } U(D, F; I) = \beta_1 D + \frac{\beta_2}{I} F + \gamma \quad (6.6)$$

$$= \beta_1 D + \beta_2 \frac{F}{I} + \gamma,$$

$$\text{With taste variations: } U(D, F; I) = (\beta_1 + \delta_1) D + \left(\frac{\beta_2 + \delta_2}{I}\right) F + \gamma$$

$$= (\beta_1 + \delta_1) D + (\beta_2 + \delta_2) \frac{F}{I} + \gamma. \quad (6.7)$$

The parameter estimates for the four models are shown in table 6.3. Also included in the table are the median values of β_1, β_2, β_2/I, β_1/β_2, and $\beta_1/(\beta_2/I)$ from the first stage analysis of the individual respondents.

For the distance-fee specification the explanatory power of the RCCD probit model estimate is substantially greater than that for the LPIID probit model estimate. The log likelihood of the former is nearly twice as large as for the latter. While the RCCD probit model estimate has appreciably greater explanatory power than the LPIID probit model estimate, the estimated values of β_1 and β_2 from the LPIID probit model are much closer to the sample median estimates of β_1 and β_2. For the reasons discussed in the introduction, and elaborated upon in section 6.10, we believe the seemingly greater precision of the LPIID estimates is merely coincidental. In section 6.10 we argue that the LPIID estimates of β_1 and β_2 are probably not comparable to the estimated population medians because the LPIID estimates are made under an incorrect assumption about the variance of the disturbance.

While we suspect that the LPIID estimates of β_1 and β_2 are not comparable to the population medians, we do believe that their ratio, β_1/β_2, is comparable to the estimated population median ratio. The results in table 6.3 reveal that the LPIID ratio is moderately closer to the sample median ratio than the RCCD ratio. But the RCCD and LPIID estimates of β_1/β_2 are very similar, and both provide reasonably precise estimates of the median ratio in the sample.

Table 6.3
Parameter estimates for models estimated from the pooled data[a]

	Median value among respondents	Distance, fee model		Distance, fee/income model	
		LPIID probit	RCCD probit	LPIID probit	RCCD probit
β_1 (distance)	−0.623	−0.590 (−85.61)	−1.38 (−1.58)	−0.421 (−18.40)	−0.764 (−2.94)
β_2 (fee)	−0.07512	−0.0502 (−65.88)	−0.135 (−1.59)	—	—
β_1/β_2	12.71	11.77	10.21	—	—
β_2 (fee/income)	−1.20	—	—	−0.597 (−21.74)	−1.09 (−2.99)
β_1/β_2 (with income interaction)	0.639	—	—	0.705	0.702
Log likelihood	−224[b]	−1168	−641	−596	−559

[a]Ratio of parameter estimate with its standard error in parentheses.
[b]Sum of the log likelihoods for the models estimated for each respondent.

Turning to the more appropriate income interaction specification the difference in the explanatory power of the LPIID and RCCD probit estimation is greatly diminished; the log likelihood of the RCCD probit model estimate is only 10% greater than that for the LPIID probit model estimate. The improvement in explanatory power resulting from the introduction of the income interaction displays an interesting pattern. For the models estimated with LPIID probit the log likelihood increases by a factor of two with the introduction of the income interaction. In contrast for the models estimated with RCCD probit the introduction of the income interaction improves the log likelihood by less than 20%. This result is consistent with our speculation that RCCD probit estimation may be more immune to specification error than estimation methods that do not allow for taste variations.

While there is only a moderate difference in the explanatory power of LPIID and RCCD probit estimation for the income interaction model, the resulting parameter estimates differ appreciably. The RCCD probit estimates of β_1 and β_2 (income adjusted) are quite close to the corresponding median values of the individual taste coefficients from the first stage analysis. By contrast, the LPIID estimates of β_1 and β_2 are only slightly more than half as large (in absolute magnitude) as the corresponding RCCD estimates. This latter finding may be due to the fact that even when the income effect is explicitly modeled, substantial taste variation remains to be accounted for (see figure 6.1).

We next examine the ability of RCCD probit estimation to capture the taste variation in the population. Table 6.4 gives the RCCD probit estimates of Σ, the variance-covariance matrix of tastes, for both RCCD model specifications. As can be seen in table 6.4, the estimate of Σ for the fee-distance model is very imprecise; the ratios of the estimated parameters to their standard errors are never greater than one. The estimate of the population variance of β_2 is particularly poor; the ratio of the estimate to its standard error is nearly zero. Albright, Lerman, and Manski (1977) and Hausman and Wise (1978) experienced similar difficulties in estimating the variances of taste parameters.

The estimates of Σ for the income-adjusted model appear to be moderately precise. Nevertheless the more important question is how well do the point estimates of the population variance of β_1 and β_2 for the income-adjusted model capture the variation measured in the first-stage analysis. Since RCCD probit estimation assumes that tastes are normally distributed, the 25th to 75th percentile range, the interquartile range, of the estimated taste distributions from the first-stage analyses should be approximately equal to

$$\beta_i^{25\text{th}} = \beta_1 - 0.667\sigma_i,$$
$$\beta_i^{75\text{th}} = \beta_i + 0.667\sigma_i,$$

where

$\beta_i^{25\text{th}}, \beta_i^{75\text{th}}$ = respectively, the 25th and 75th percentile estimates of β_i,
β_i = RCCD probit estimate of the mean (or median) β_i,
σ_i = RCCD probit estimate of the standard deviation of the taste distribution.

In table 6.5 the interquartile range of β_1 and β_2 (income adjusted) estimated from the first-stage analysis is compared with the estimate of that

Table 6.4
Estimates of Σ for RCCD models

	Fee distance	Income adjusted
Population variance β_1	0.518 (0.73)	0.277 (1.20)
Population variance β_2	0.00358 (0.01)	0.247 (1.18)
Population covariance β_1 and β_2	−0.0574 (−0.75)	0.0689 (0.47)

Note: Ratio of estimate to its standard error in parentheses.

Table 6.5
The 25th to 75th percentile range of taste parameters

	β_1		β_2 (income adjusted)	
	25th	75th	25th	75th
From first-stage analysis	−1.72	−0.38	−3.11	−0.58
From RCCD probit parameter estimates	−1.11	−0.41	−1.42	−0.76

range generated from the RCCD probit parameter estimates of the income-adjusted model.

As can be seen in table 6.5, the RCCD probit estimate of the 75th percentile value of β_1 corresponds quite closely with the estimate from the first stage analysis. There is also a reasonably close correspondence between the two estimates of the 75th percentile value of β_2 (income adjusted). In contrast the RCCD probit estimates of the 25th percentile values of β_1 and β_2 differ markedly from the first-stage estimates. The reason for the lack of correspondence between the RCCD probit and first-stage estimates of the 25th percentile values of β_1 and β_2 is due to the marked leftward skew in the distribution of each in the respondent population. Histograms of the distribution of β_1 and β_2 (income adjusted) from the first-stage analysis are shown in figures 6.1 and 6.2. Since RCCD probit estimation assumes tastes to be symmetrically distributed, it is not surprising that the RCCD probit and first-stage estimates of the 25th percentile values of β_1 and β_2 (income adjusted) differ markedly.

The leftward skew of the distributions in figure 6.1 suggests that the assumption that tastes are normally distributed may not be a good approximation for taste parameters which for theoretical reasons are thought to be bounded. A more appropriate distributional approximation for β_1 and β_2 might be the negative of either a log-normal or exponential distribution. Both of these distributions are bounded from above by zero. Theoretically these two distributions are also more appealing. While it is conceivable that a small proportion of the population might value walking time positively ($\beta_1 > 0$), it is not plausible that even a minority of the population would positively value paying more for parking privileges ($\beta_2 > 0$).

We close this section with the results of an experiment comparing the predictive accuracy of the two estimation methods. Using log likelihood as a measure of explanatory power, the results suggest that, if the specification of explanatory variables is approximately correct, then LPIID and RCCD probit estimation are about equivalently powerful. However, if the explanatory variables are misspecified, then RCCD probit estimation is appreciably more powerful than LPIID probit estimation. Nevertheless, even if the explanatory variables are correctly specified, it is not clear that the predictive accuracy of the RCCD and LPIID models will be equal. The predictions of the two models may potentially be quite different. In view of the current and potential applications of RCCD and LPIID estimation, their relative predictive accuracy is a crucial test of their relative overall merits. The following experiment is intended to provide such a test.

For any given value of the fee and distance differential between two lots, A and B, the expected change in the proportion of the population choosing A because of a one unit increase in ΔF can be approximated by

$$E_{\Delta F}(\Delta P_A; \Delta F, \Delta D) = \frac{1}{n} \sum_{i=1}^{n} \frac{\partial P^i_A(\Delta F, \Delta D)}{\partial(\Delta F)}, \tag{6.8}$$

where

$E_{\Delta F}(\Delta P_A;\, \Delta F,\, \Delta D)$ = expected change in the proportion of the population choosing lot A, resulting from a one unit increase in ΔF for given values of ΔF and ΔD,

$P^i_A(\Delta F,\, \Delta D)$ = probability of individual i choosing lot A for given values of ΔF and ΔD,

n = number of individuals in the population.

Similarly the expected change in the proportion choosing A resulting from a one unit increase in ΔD can be approximated by

$$E_{\Delta D}(\Delta P_A; \Delta F, \Delta D) = \frac{1}{n} \sum_{i=1}^{n} \frac{\partial P^i_A(\Delta F, \Delta D)}{\partial(\Delta D)}. \tag{6.9}$$

For selected values of ΔF and ΔD we computed equations (6.8) and (6.9), using as our population the 20 respondents in the sample. The partial derivatives of P^i_A w.r.t. ΔD and ΔF for each respondent with an estimable model were computed on the basis of the estimated values of β_1 and β_2 for that respondent. For the respondents with unestimable models the partial derivatives of P^i_A could be assumed to be zero for the values of ΔF and ΔD used in the experiment.

Estimation of $E_{\Delta D}$ for the models estimated in the second-stage analysis can be computed as follows (we show only equations for $E_{\Delta D}$; the corresponding equations for $E_{\Delta F}$ are the same except that the partial derivatives are computed with respect to ΔF):

Fee-distance model: LPIID probit

$$E_{\Delta D} = \frac{\partial P^I_A(\Delta F, \Delta D)}{\partial(\Delta D)},$$

RCCD probit

$$E_{\Delta D} = \frac{\partial P_A^R(\Delta F, \Delta D)}{\partial(\Delta D)};$$

Income-adjusted model: LPIID probit

$$E_{\Delta D} = \sum_{i=1}^{k} \pi_k \cdot \frac{\partial P_A^I(\Delta F, \Delta D; Y_k)}{\partial(\Delta D)},$$

RCCD probit

$$E_{\Delta D} = \sum_{i=1}^{k} \pi_k \cdot \frac{\partial P_A^R(\Delta F, \Delta D; Y_k)}{\partial(\Delta D)};$$

where $P_A^I(\Delta F, \Delta D), P_A^R(\Delta F, \Delta D)$ = predicted proportion of the population choosing lot A for given ΔF and ΔD for, respectively, the LPIID and RCCD probit estimates of the fee-distance model,

$P_A^I(\Delta F, \Delta D; Y_k), P_A^R(\Delta F, \Delta D; Y_k)$ = predicted proportion of the population choosing lot A for given ΔF, ΔD and Y_k for, respectively, the LPIID and RCCD probit estimates of the income-adjusted model,

Y_k = income of respondents in income class k,

π_k = proportion of respondents in income class k.

In the experiment we treat the estimates of $E_{\Delta D}$ and $E_{\Delta F}$ from the first-stage model estimates (eqs. (6.8) and (6.9)) as the actual changes in P_A that would occur from one unit increases in ΔD and ΔF, respectively. We then compare these estimates of $E_{\Delta D}$ and $E_{\Delta F}$ with those generated from the second-stage model estimates. Estimates of $E_{\Delta D}$ and $E_{\Delta F}$ are computed for nine different values of $(\Delta F, \Delta D)$ and three different values of $(\Delta F/\Delta D)$.[12] The results are shown in tables 6.6 and 6.7.

12. One value of $-(\Delta F/\Delta D)$ used in the experiment is 12 which is about equal to the median estimate of β_1/β_2 in the population. The remaining two values of $-(\Delta F/\Delta D)$ are 8 and 16. The population estimate of the 75th percentile value of β_1/β_2 is 16, but due to the leftward skew of the distributions of β_1 and β_2 the 25th percentile estimate of β_1/β_2 is nearly 3.5. For the purpose of the experiment we chose not to use a value of $-(\Delta F/\Delta D)$ that was so far from the population median.

Table 6.6
The results of the fee-distance model prediction experiment

			$E_{\Delta F}$			$E_{\Delta D}$		
$-\dfrac{\Delta F}{\Delta D}$	ΔF	ΔD	"Actual" $E_{\Delta F}$	Deviation of LPIID probit estimates from "actual"	Deviation of RCCD probit estimates from "actual"	"Actual" $E_{\Delta D}$	Deviation of LPIID probit estimates from "actual"	Deviation of RCCD probit estimates from "actual"
8	−48	6.0	0.00212	0.00842	0.00358	0.02731	0.09662	0.01835
12	−72	6.0	0.00542	0.01456	−0.00024	0.07610	0.15888	0.03988
16	−96	6.0	0.00563	0.00324	−0.00385	0.08707	0.01727	−0.05864
8	−24	3.0	0.01168	0.00538	−0.00046	0.10432	0.09631	−0.01393
12	−36	3.0	0.00723	0.01278	−0.00123	0.10274	0.13269	−0.03097
16	−48	3.0	0.00892	0.00742	−0.00536	0.14496	0.04722	−0.08833
8	−12	1.5	0.02419	0.00495	−0.00300	0.20626	0.02005	−0.03221
12	−18	1.5	0.01323	0.00679	−0.00144	0.16321	0.07233	−0.02320
16	−24	1.5	0.01237	0.00666	−0.00526	0.18528	0.03861	−0.07376
Sum of absolute deviations				0.07020	0.02655		0.6710	0.3794

Note: Positive deviations are overpredictions, and negative deviations are underpredictions.

Table 6.7
The results of the income-adjusted model prediction experiment

			$E_{\Delta F}$			$E_{\Delta D}$		
$-\frac{\Delta F}{\Delta D}$	ΔF	ΔD	"Actual" $E_{\Delta F}$	Deviation of LPIID probit estimates from "actual"	Deviation of RCCD probit estimates from "actual"	"Actual" $E_{\Delta D}$	Deviation of LPIID probit estimates from "actual"	Deviation of RCCD probit estimates from "actual"
8	−48	6.0	0.00212	0.00459	−0.00306	0.02731	0.04105	−0.03749
12	−72	6.0	0.00542	−0.00045	−0.00169	0.07610	−0.01169	0.00105
16	−96	6.0	0.00563	−0.00172	−0.00289	0.08707	−0.02822	0.00769
8	−24	3.0	0.01168	−0.00281	0.00217	0.10432	−0.02007	−0.02237
12	−36	3.0	0.00723	−0.00011	0.00026	0.10274	−0.02422	−0.03763
16	−48	3.0	0.00892	−0.00324	0.00373	0.14496	−0.07341	−0.00049
8	−12	1.5	0.02419	−0.01422	0.00894	0.20626	−0.11602	−0.00694
12	−18	1.5	0.01323	−0.00413	0.00144	0.16321	−0.07576	−0.06039
16	−24	1.5	0.01237	−0.00435	0.00322	0.18528	−0.10217	−0.04057
Sum of absolute deviations				0.03564	0.02736		0.4926	0.2147

Note: Positive deviations are overpredictions, and negative deviations are underpredictions.

For the fee-distance model the LPIID model consistently overpredicts the magnitude of the change, whereas the RCCD model underpredicts the change in all but one trial. In terms of the absolute magnitude of the prediction errors, the predictions from the RCCD model are appreciably more precise than those of the LPIID model. The RCCD estimate of $E_{\Delta F}$ is closer to the actual value of $E_{\Delta F}$ in 8 of 9 trials. Moreover the sum of the absolute deviations of the RCCD estimate of $E_{\Delta F}$ from the actual value of $E_{\Delta F}$ across the nine trials is about 40 percent of that sum for the LPIID estimates of $E_{\Delta F}$. For $E_{\Delta D}$ the RCCD estimates are more accurate in only 5 of 9 trials. But using the sum of absolute deviations as a measure of predictive accuracy, the RCCD sum is roughly half that of the LPIID sum.

For the income-adjusted model the patterns in the direction of prediction errors is markedly different from that pattern for the fee-distance model. The LPIID estimates of $E_{\Delta F}$ and $E_{\Delta D}$ are smaller than the actual in 8 of 9 trials. In contrast the patterns in the sign of the prediction errors for the RCCD model are less distinct. A pattern of overprediction of $E_{\Delta F}$ and underprediction of $E_{\Delta D}$ does appear to be present, however. In terms of the absolute magnitudes of the prediction errors, RCCD probit again appears to be distinctly more accurate than LPIID probit estimation. The RCCD probit estimates of $E_{\Delta D}$ are more accurate than the LPIID probit estimates in 7 of 9 trials, and the sum of absolute deviations for the RCCD probit estimates is less than half that sum for the LPIID probit estimates. For $E_{\Delta F}$ the improvement in predictive accuracy offered by RCCD probit estimation is more moderate. The RCCD estimates are more accurate than the LPIID estimates in only 5 of 9 trials, but the sum of absolute deviations for the RCCD estimates is moderately smaller than the sum for the LPIID estimates.

Overall, the results of this experiment suggest that models allowing for taste variation have appreciably better predictive power than models that do not account for such variations.

6.8 Conclusions

The results discussed in section 6.7 prompt several observations. The first-stage analysis clearly indicates that the magnitude of taste variation is appreciable. Regressions of β_1/β_2 on various respondent characteristics revealed only one significant correlate—income. Yet figures 6.1 and 6.2 reveal that, even when the effects of income are explicitly modeled, substantial taste variation remains unexplained. This observation suggests that attempts to model explicitly the sources of taste variation using an LPIID formulation are unlikely to succeed. Thus the motivation underlying the development of RCCD estimation methods appears well founded.

The results of the second-stage analysis suggest that RCCD estimators are more robust than LPIID estimators against errors involving inappropriate specification of explanatory variables. Here our results are at odds with those of Albright, Lerman, and Manski (1977) and Hausman and Wise (1978). They found that the explanatory power of RCCD probit was not appreciably greater than that of LPIID logit. Thus it would be premature to conclude that RCCD probit is more robust to specification errors than the LPIID formulation (either probit or logit).

To account for the conflict between our results and those obtained in the two studies cited, we speculate that the difference may be attributable to the relative contributions of $\mathbf{Z}\boldsymbol{\delta}$ (error due to taste variation) and ε (additive error) to the total disturbance term. On the basis of our first-stage analyses we are confident that the bulk of the disturbance in our second-stage model specifications is attributable to taste variation.[13] This may well be due to the fact that in the problem studied we knew what the relevant attributes of the alternatives were. We knew because we specified them as part of our experimental design. By contrast the Albright, Lerman, and Manski (1977) and Hausman and Wise (1978) analyses used nonexperimental data concerning transportation mode selection for work commuting trips. In such nonexperimental contexts there may well be many excluded but choice relevant attributes of alternatives. These omitted variables are reflected in ε, the additive disturbance term. When important attributes of alternatives are omitted (as they are likely to be), ε will make a large contribution to the total disturbance term; and $\mathbf{Z}\boldsymbol{\delta}$ (error due to variation in tastes for observed attributes) may be a relatively minor contributor to the total disturbance term. This speculation suggests that RCCD probit will become an increasingly valuable tool as our ability to recognize and measure choice relevant attributes increases.

13. Recall the excellent explanatory power of the first-stage models of individual respondents.

6.9 Appendix: The Unestimable Models

For three respondents a model of the form

$$U(D,F) = \beta_1 D + \beta_2 F + \varepsilon \tag{6.10}$$

was not estimable. To motivate a discussion of the reasons model (6.10) is not estimable for these respondents, it is useful to consider the implications for estimating taste parameters when choice behavior is perfectly explained by a model of the form

$$U(D,F) = \beta_1 D + \beta_2 F. \tag{6.11}$$

Model (6.11) is a special case of model (6.10) where the disturbance has zero variance (there is no stochastic component, ε, in the utility function). When $\sigma_\varepsilon^2 = 0$, only the ratio β_1/β_2 is identifiable. It can be shown that, when $\sigma_\varepsilon^2 = 0$, the prefered alternative in a binary choice set (A, B) can always be predicted by the following rule: A will be chosen if

$$\begin{aligned} \frac{\beta_1}{\beta_2} &> -\frac{F_A - F_B}{D_A - D_B} \quad \text{if} \quad D_A - D_B < 0, \\ \frac{\beta_1}{\beta_2} &< -\frac{F_A - F_B}{D_A - D_B} \quad \text{if} \quad D_A - D_B > 0. \end{aligned} \tag{6.12}$$

Otherwise B will be chosen. Thus in instances where $\sigma_\varepsilon^2 = 0$, only the ratio β_1/β_2 is identifiable from actual choice behavior.

Table 6.8 shows how choice behavior predicted perfectly by (6.11) would closely identify β_1/β_2.

The choice behavior of the three respondents with unestimable models is consistent with the predictions of model (6.10). The choice behavior of respondent 18 is fully consistent with that predicted by model (6.11), and accordingly β_1/β_2 could confidently be estimated at 4.15.

Respondent 7 picked the most convenient lot in all except one trial. In that trial the choice of the most convenient lot required the individual to pay an additional \$105 annually to reduce walking time by about 1 minute per trip; this trial involved the largest $(\Delta F/\Delta D)$ in the experiment. Although respondent 7 demonstrated a willingness to sacrifice convenience for a savings in the parking fee in only one instance, his behavior is fully consistent with model (6.10), and we estimate β_1/β_2 for this respondent to be about 95.

Table 6.8
Estimating β_1/β_2 when model (6.11) is the applicable utility function

(ranked from largest to smallest) $-\frac{F_A - F_B}{D_A - D_B}$	$D_A - D_B < 0$ (chosen alternative)	$D_A - D_B > 0$ (chosen alternative)
K_1	B	A
K_2	B	A
K_3	B	A
K_4	B	A
$\frac{\beta_1}{\beta_2} = \frac{(K_4 + K_5)}{2}$		
K_5	A	B
K_6	A	B
K_7	A	B

Respondent 20 displayed lexicographic type behavior; the individual always picked the most inexpensive lot. If this respondent actually used a lexicographic choice rule, then neither models (6.10) nor (6.11) would be an appropriate specification. However, his behavior is not inconsistent with model (6.11). It is possible that the reason we observed no trade-offs between D and F is that the individual's value of time was sufficiently small that it was not detected by the experiment. Indeed this interpretation seems more plausible than the lexicographic interpretation, since the lexicographic interpretation implies that the individual would be unwilling to pay a trivial sum (e.g., 1 cent/annum) in return for any savings in walking time (e.g., 30 minutes/trip). We thus assume that a value of β_1/β_2 exists for this individual and ranked this respondent's β_1/β_2 as the smallest in the sample without specifying a value (see table 6.2).

While estimates of β_1 and β_2 for the three respondents could not be identified with the data at hand, this does not necessarily imply that a unique value for each does not exist. Estimates do not exist only if $\sigma_\varepsilon^2 = 0$. The fact that model (6.11) is sufficient for explaining the behavior of these respondents for this data set does not imply that it would be sufficient for explaining their behavior in all possible data sets. In fact it seems safe to assume that $\sigma_\varepsilon^2 \neq 0$ for these individuals. Suppose these individuals were confronted with successive choice sets where $-(F_A - F_B)/(D_A - D_B) \cong \beta_1/\beta_2$. It is highly unlikely that their choices would be predicted exactly by (6.12); human cognitive capabilities are simply not sufficiently acute to distinguish very small differences. Additionally any excluded determinants of choice that only marginally effect the utility of each alternative could become decisive for individuals close to the margin.

The observation that σ_ε^2 probably does not equal zero for these three respondents has implications for the rankings of the β_1's and β_2's for these respondents. In model (6.10) β_1 and β_2 are estimable only up to some assumed value of $1/\sigma_\varepsilon$; β_1, β_2, and σ_ε are not jointly identified. The estimated values of β_1 and β_2 should actually be interpreted as $\beta_1/\sigma_\varepsilon$ and $\beta_2/\sigma_\varepsilon$, respectively, where the value of σ_ε is arbitrarily assigned.

Suppose two respondents, X and Y, both have identical β_1 and β_2 but $\sigma_\varepsilon^X < \sigma_\varepsilon^Y$. We would thus predict that the estimates of β_1 and β_2 for X would be larger in absolute magnitude than those for Y, since

$$|E(\hat{\beta}_i^X)| = |[\beta_i^X/\sigma_\varepsilon][\sigma_\varepsilon/\sigma_\varepsilon^X]| > |E(\hat{\beta}_i^Y)| = |[\beta_i^Y/\sigma_\varepsilon][\sigma_\varepsilon/\sigma_\varepsilon^Y]|, \tag{6.13}$$

$i = 1, 2$, where

$\hat{\beta}_i^X$, $\hat{\beta}_i^Y$ = estimated value of β_i for X and Y, respectively,

σ_ε = assumed value of σ_ε^X and σ_ε^Y.

This result provides a basis for making some reasonable assumptions about the appropriate rankings of β_1 and β_2 for respondents with unestimable models. The results suggest that the value of σ_ε^2 for these respondents is probably small relative to its value for the remainder of the respondents.

In the case of respondent 18, whose β_1/β_2 is very precisely bracketed by the experiment, we are quite confident that this individual has a relatively small σ_ε^2. The result in equation (6.13) thus suggests that this individual's β_1 and β_2 are best assumed to be among the largest in the sample (see table 6.2). Also included among the largest values of β_1 and β_2 in the population are respondent 7's β_1 and 20's β_2, respectively.

We have made no assumptions about the ranking of respondent 7's β_2 and 20's β_1. Recall that respondent 7 had a very high value of time and respondent 20 a very low value of time. Loosely speaking, this implies 7's β_2 and 20's β_1 are small, since the value of time is estimated by β_1/β_2. Thus for respondent 7's β_2 and 20's β_1 to be ranked among the largest in their respective distributions, σ_ε^2 for 7 and 20 would have to be extremely small relative to the remainder of the respondents. This seemed to us to be an overly strong assumption, and we thus have chosen to exclude them from the rankings. This is an admittedly tenuous assumption but in any event the alternative of ranking each among the largest in their respective distributions does not alter any of our conclusions.

6.10 Appendix: Mean Taste Estimates in the LPIID and RCCD Models

Among the issues we had initially intended to explore in this analysis was the correspondence between the LPIID probit estimates of β and some measure of the central tendency of the taste distribution estimated in the first-stage analysis. In the course of the analysis the question arose of whether the LPIID estimates of β are theoretically comparable to the first-stage estimates of the central tendency of the taste distribution. Stated differently, is there any theoretical reason for suspecting that the LPIID estimates of β will be biased estimates of the mean (or median) of the population's taste distribution? Although we have not addressed this question in a fully rigorous fashion, we suspect that LPIID estimate of β is not comparable to the mean (or median) of the population taste distribution.

The generalized forms of the stochastic utility functions considered in this chapter are

$$\text{Without taste variations (LPIID): } U(Z) = \mathbf{Z}\boldsymbol{\beta} + \varepsilon, \tag{6.14}$$

$$\begin{aligned}\text{With taste variations (RCCD): } U(Z) &= \mathbf{Z}(\boldsymbol{\beta} + \boldsymbol{\delta}) + \gamma \\ &= \mathbf{Z}\boldsymbol{\beta} + (\mathbf{Z}\boldsymbol{\delta} + \gamma),\end{aligned} \tag{6.15}$$

where

$\mathbf{Z} = (1 \times K)$ vector of individual and alternative characteristics,
$\boldsymbol{\beta} = (K \times 1)$ vector of parameters,
$\boldsymbol{\delta} = (K \times 1)$ disturbance vector assumed to be distributed $N(0, \boldsymbol{\Sigma})$,
$\gamma, \varepsilon =$ random variables assumed to be distributed $N(0, \sigma^2)$.

In both models (6.14) and (6.15) all the parameters are not jointly identified: $\boldsymbol{\beta}$ and σ^2 in (6.14) and $\boldsymbol{\beta}$, $\boldsymbol{\Sigma}$, and σ^2 in (6.15). For both models a necessary condition for identification is that the value of one parameter be assumed; the remaining parameters are identified up to that assumed value. For both models identification is typically accomplished by assuming the value of σ^2. It can be shown that for model (6.14) the expected value of $\hat{\boldsymbol{\beta}}$ equals $\boldsymbol{\beta}/\sigma$ and that for model (6.15) the expected values of $\hat{\boldsymbol{\beta}}$ and $\hat{\boldsymbol{\Sigma}}$ are $\boldsymbol{\beta}/\sigma$ and $\boldsymbol{\Sigma}/\sigma^2$, respectively.

Now suppose model (6.14) is estimated when the true model is (6.15). The actual disturbance is thus not ε but $\alpha = \varepsilon + \mathbf{Z}\boldsymbol{\delta}$, and therefore the actual variance of the disturbance is not σ^2 but $\sigma^2 + \mathbf{Z}\Sigma\mathbf{Z}'$, where $\sigma^2 + \mathbf{Z}\Sigma\mathbf{Z}' > \sigma^2$. We thus speculate that, when model (6.14) is estimated where (6.15) is the true model, the following result will hold:

$$|E(\hat{\boldsymbol{\beta}})| = \frac{|\boldsymbol{\beta}|}{(\sigma^2 + \mathbf{Z}\Sigma\mathbf{Z}')^{\frac{1}{2}}} < \frac{|\boldsymbol{\beta}|}{\sigma}. \tag{6.16}$$

Furthermore we would predict that the absolute magnitude of each element of the LPIID estimate of $\boldsymbol{\beta}$ would be less than the corresponding element of the RCCD estimate of $\boldsymbol{\beta}$. The basis for this prediction is that in RCCD estimation, the presence of $\mathbf{Z}\boldsymbol{\delta}$ in the disturbance is explicitly taken into account in estimating $\boldsymbol{\beta}$.

While we have not formally proven these results, the empirical results in table 6.3 are consistent with our speculation. For both the fee-distance and income-adjusted models the absolute magnitude of RCCD estimates of β_1 and β_2 are greater than the corresponding LPIID estimates. An inspection of the alternative estimates of the ratio β_1/β_2 also supports our speculation. If we are correct in supposing the source of the bias in the LPIID estimate of $\boldsymbol{\beta}$ is the presence of the term $\mathbf{Z}\Sigma\mathbf{Z}'$ in the denominator of eq. (6.16), then the ratio of the LPIID estimates of β_1 and β_2 should be comparable to both the ratio of the RCCD estimates of β_1 and β_2 and to the median estimate of β_1/β_2 from the first-stage analysis. An examination of table 6.3 reveals all three estimates of the true mean value of β_1/β_2 in the population are about equal.

For these reasons we do not believe the LPIID estimates of β_1 and β_2 can be meaningfully compared with the estimates of the median values of β_1 and β_2 in the respondent population. Thus we suspect that it is only coincidental that the LPIID estimates of β_1 and β_2 in the fee-distance model are closer to the first-stage medians than the RCCD estimates. We attribute the large divergence of the RCCD estimates of β_1 and β_2 in the fee-distance model from first-stage estimates of the population medians to the absence of an income adjustment in the fee-distance model.

References

Albright, R. L., S. Lerman, and C. F. Manski. 1977. Report on the Development of an Estimation Program for Multinomial Probit Model. Prepared for the Federal Highway Administration.

Ben-Akiva, M., and P. Haus. 1973. Estimation of a Work Mode Split Model Which Includes the Carpool Mode. Working paper WP-1. U.S. Department of Transportation, Washington, D. C.

Bock, R. D., and L. V. Jones. *The Measurement and Prediction of Judgment and Choice*. San Francisco: Holden-Day.

Charles Rivers Associates. 1972. *A Disaggregate Behavioral Model of Urban Travel Demand*. Cambridge, Mass.

Coombs, C., R. Dawes, and A. Tversky. 1970. *Mathematical Psychology*. Englewood Cliffs, N. J.: Prentice-Hall.

Hausman, J. A., and D. A. Wise. 1978. A Conditional Probit Model for Qualitative Choice: Descrete Decisions Recognizing Interdependence and Heterogeneous Preferences. *Econometrica*. 46: 403–426.

Kohn, M., C. Manski, and D. Mundel. 1971. A Study of College Choice: Report on Research in Progress. Unpublished.

Lerman, S., and M. Ben-Akiva. 1975. A Disaggregate Model of Auto Ownership. Presented at the Annual meetings of the Transportation Research Board, Washington, D. C.

Luce, R. D., and P. Suppes. 1965. Preference, Utility, and Subjective Probability. In *Handbook of Mathematical Psychology*, vol. 3, ed. R. D. Luce. New York: Wiley, pp. 249–410.

Manski, C. F. 1973. The Stochastic Utility Model of Choice. School of Urban and Public Affairs, Carnegie-Mellon University, Pittsburgh.

McFadden, D. 1973. Conditional Logit Analysis of Qualitative Choice Behavior. In *Frontiers in Econometrics*, ed. P. Zarembka. New York: Academic Press.

Tversky, A. 1972. Choice by Elimination. *Journal of Mathematical Psychology*. 79: 281–299.

7 On the Use of Simulated Frequencies to Approximate Choice Probabilities

Steven R. Lerman and Charles F. Manski

7.1 Introduction

A mundane but common problem in probabilistic analysis concerns the calculation of the event probabilities generated by a random process.

To be precise, let $\boldsymbol{\alpha}$ be a real random M-vector whose distribution G has support $\mathbf{A} \subset \mathbf{R}^M$. Let $\mathbf{A}(j), j = 1, \ldots, J$ be a finite Lebesgue measureable partition of $\mathbf{A}$ such that $\boldsymbol{\alpha} \in \mathbf{A}(j)$ if and only if observable event j occurs. Then for any $j = 1, \ldots, J$, the probability that event j occurs is simply

$$P(j) = \text{Prob}\,[\boldsymbol{\alpha} \in \mathbf{A}(j)] = \int_{\mathbf{A}(j)} dG. \tag{7.1}$$

The generation of event probabilities from an underlying random process in this manner is ubiquitous in probabilistic analysis. Unfortunately unless the distribution G and the subset $\mathbf{A}(j)$ are particularly benign, the integral $\int_{\mathbf{A}(j)} dG$ will not have a closed form. A common problem then is to find a computationally practical method to adequately approximate the event probability.

A simple general solution to problem (7.1) exists. In its most basic form the procedure is to draw a set of pseudorandom realizations of $\boldsymbol{\alpha}$, observe on each draw whether the realization of $\boldsymbol{\alpha}$ lies within $\mathbf{A}(j)$, and use the frequency of such occurrences over the set of draws as an estimate of the event probability $P(j)$.

This simulated frequency Monte Carlo approach to probability calculation is well known by workers in the area of computer simulation. In particular see Hammersley and Handscomb (1964) and Fishman (1973) for discussions. The potential value of the approach in econometric applications, however, appears not to have been widely recognized.

In this chapter a version of the simulated frequency procedure is applied to solve a specific problem in discrete choice analysis. Let the events $j = 1, \ldots, J$ now be alternatives from which a decision maker must choose one. Assume that behavior is consistent with a random utility model, and let

The work reported here was performed at Cambridge Systematics, Inc., under a Federal Highway Administration contract. We would like to thank Carlos Daganzo, William Eddy, and Daniel McFadden for useful discussions. Responsibility for the contents of this chapter is the authors' alone.

$\boldsymbol{\alpha} = [\alpha(1), \ldots, \alpha(J)]$ be the random utility vector with distribution G. Then as long as G is such that ties have zero probability, the probability that alternative j is chosen is given by

$$P(j) = \text{Prob}[\alpha(j) \geq \alpha(k), k = 1, \ldots, J] = \int_{\mathbf{A}(j)} dG, \tag{7.2}$$

where $\mathbf{A}(j) = [\boldsymbol{\alpha} : \alpha(j) \geq \alpha(k), k = 1, \ldots, J]$.

A long-standing problem of some importance has been to develop practical methods to evaluate the choice probability (7.2) under alternative distributions G. In particular many researchers have been interested in evaluating (7.2) under the assumption that G is multivariate normal, when the choice probabilities have the multinomial probit form. Clearly the simulated frequency procedure offers a solution to the general problem and to that of calculating multinomial probit probabilities specifically.

7.2 The Simulated Frequency Method

This section describes the classical simulated frequency procedure for estimation of a single probability. Section 7.3 sets out a Bayesian version of the procedure. Section 7.4 discusses issues that arise when a collection of probabilities must be calculated and ultimately some function of this collection evaluated.

Let N realizations of $\boldsymbol{\alpha}$ be drawn at random, and let $N(j)$ be the number of such realizations lying in $\mathbf{A}(j)$. Then $F(j, N) = N(j)/N$ is binomially distributed with mean $P(j)$ and variance $P(j)(1 - P(j))/N$. Observe that the distribution of $F(j, N)$ depends only on $P(j)$ and N and not directly on the random process, characterized by G and $\mathbf{A}(j)$, generating event j.

As an estimate of $P(j)$, $F(j, N)$ has well-known statistical properties. It is strongly consistent, minimum variance unbiased, and is the maximum likelihood estimate. Computationally the cost of calculating $F(j, N)$ may reasonably be assumed linear in N. The marginal cost per trial has two additive components. First, there is the cost of drawing a pseudorandom realization of $\boldsymbol{\alpha}$, and second, the cost of determining whether this realization lies in $\mathbf{A}(j)$. The size of these two marginal cost components are problem specific, the former depending on the nature of the distribution G and the latter on the structure of the set $\mathbf{A}(j)$.

A comment should be made regarding the drawing of pseudorandom realizations of $\boldsymbol{\alpha}$. If $\boldsymbol{\alpha}$ is univariate, and G is strictly increasing, realizations may be relatively easily drawn by first taking a random variable $\beta \sim U[0, 1]$ and then calculating $\boldsymbol{\alpha} \equiv G^{-1}(\beta)$. See Shreider (1966) for a discussion of methods for drawing the needed uniform random numbers.

On the other hand, if $\boldsymbol{\alpha}$ is multivariate, such a simple general method seems not to be available. A very useful approach is to find M independent random variables $\gamma = [\gamma_1, \ldots, \gamma_M]$ and a function $\mathbf{H}: \mathbf{R}^M \rightarrow \mathbf{R}^M$ such that $\mathbf{H}(\gamma)$ is distributed G. Then $\boldsymbol{\alpha}$-realizations may be generated by drawing values for $\gamma_1, \ldots, \gamma_M$ and computing $\mathbf{H}(\gamma)$. For example, if $\boldsymbol{\alpha} \sim N(\boldsymbol{\mu}, \boldsymbol{\Sigma})$, let $\gamma_m \sim N(0, 1)$, $m = 1, \ldots, M$, and let $\boldsymbol{\Omega}$ be an $M \times M$ triangular matrix such that $\boldsymbol{\Sigma} = \boldsymbol{\Omega}'\boldsymbol{\Omega}$. Then $(\boldsymbol{\mu} + \boldsymbol{\Omega}'\gamma) \sim N(\boldsymbol{\mu}, \boldsymbol{\Sigma})$ as desired.

It has been speculated that for any multivariate distribution G, there exists some γ and $\mathbf{H}$ such that $\mathbf{H}(\gamma) \sim G$; so the method can be applied generally. However, no proof of this proposition is known to us.

7.3 Bayesian Approach

The classical simulated frequency method appears naive in at least two respects: the procedure provides no means for one to incorporate prior information regarding the value of $P(j)$ into the estimation process; use of the method requires one to fix ahead of time the number of simulation trials N to be performed.

The literature on simulation suggests various sophisticated but ad hoc variants on the basic classical method, including ones utilizing informative stopping rules. See Fishman (1973) for details. A more satisfactory approach is offered by Bayesian statistical decision theory. See DeGroot (1970) for a comprehensive textbook presentation.

The Bayesian approach becomes particularly convenient if it is assumed that a priori, $P(j) \sim B(a, b)$, where B designates the beta distribution. As is well known, the distribution of $P(j)$ after N simulation trials is then $B(a + N(j), b + N - N(j))$.

7.4 Estimation of a Function of a Collection of Probabilities

In many applications the concern is not merely to calculate a single probability but to compute a function of a collection of probabilities. In exploring the properties of simulated estimates of such functions, we will be concerned with two types of asymptotic behavior. First, we may be interested in the properties of the estimates when the number of probabilities in the collection becomes arbitrarily large, while the simulations per probability is held constant. Second, both the number of draws per probability and the number of probabilities in the collection can become arbitrarily large. This turns out to be a significant distinction in two problems of particular interest that follow.

In the first situation we would like to estimate the share of a population that will choose an alternative. One common approach is to calculate the expected fraction of a random sample of decision makers who will select a given alternative j from some population. Let $t = 1, \ldots, T$ be the sample of decision makers, and let $P_t(j)$ be the probability that decision maker t selects alternative j. Then our concern is to calculate $Q_T(j) = 1/T \sum_{t=1}^{T} P_t(j)$. Observe that $\operatorname{plim}_{T \to \infty} Q_T(j) = Q(j) \equiv E[P(j)]$, the population average probability of selecting j. This fact provides the basis for use of $Q_T(j)$ as an estimate for $Q(j)$ in what has come to be termed the "random sample enumeration" forecasting method.

It is easy to see that the simulated frequency approach is well suited to the task of approximating $Q_T(j)$ and, more important, of estimating $Q(j)$. The classical simulation estimate is $R_T(j, N_t, t = 1, \ldots, T) = 1/T \sum_{t=1}^{T} N_t(j)/N_t$, where $N_t \geq 1$ is the number of trials performed for decision maker t. Conditional on T, this estimate has mean $E_T(R_T) = Q_T(j)$ and variance $V_T(R_T) = 1/T^2 \sum_{t=1}^{T} [P_t(j)(1 - P_t(j))]/N_t$. Letting $T \to \infty$, and recalling that decision makers are drawn at random, one finds that $\operatorname{plim}_{T \to \infty} R_T(j, N_t, t = 1, \ldots, T) = Q(j)$ for any positive values of N_t, $t = 1, \ldots \infty$.[1]

This simple result is quite powerful, as it states that the simulated frequency method consistently (as $T \to \infty$) estimates $Q(j)$ without any requirement for consistent estimation of each $P_t(j)$. That is, we do not require that each $N_t \to \infty$. In the extreme, one simulation trial per decision maker would suffice.

The second application is not nearly so benign. Consider now the problem of calculating a sample log likelihood $L_T = 1/T \sum_{t=1}^{T} \ln P_t(j_t)$, where j_t is the alternative actually selected by the sampled decision maker t.

1. This can be readily demonstrated by noting that $\operatorname{plim}_{T \to \infty} E_T(R_T) = Q(j)$ and $\operatorname{plim}_{T \to \infty} V_T(R_T) = 0$. Chebychev's theorem implies directly that R_T is a consistent estimate for $Q(j)$ as $T \to \infty$.

In this case the classical simulation estimate is S_T $(N_t, t = 1, \ldots, T) = 1/T \; \Sigma_{t=1}^{T} \ln [N_t(j_t)/N_t]$.

Observe first that, as long as $P(j) < 1$, there is nonzero probability that alternative j will never have the greatest utility in a finite number of draws. This implies that $\operatorname{plim}_{T \to \infty} S_T = -\infty$. On the other hand, it is the case that, if we let $N_t \to \infty$, then $\ln N_t(j_t)/N_t$ is a consistent estimate for $\ln P_t(j_t)$. It follows that for any T the simulation estimate for S_T converges (as $N_t \to \infty$ for each $t = 1, \ldots, T$) to the true sample likelihood L_T. Finally, if both $N_t \to \infty$ for all t and $T \to \infty$, the simulation estimate converges to $E(L)$. Thus the classical simulated frequency method consistently estimates $E(L)$ only if the number of trials per decision maker and the number of decision makers sampled both go to infinity.

The rather extreme result that for fixed N_t values $\operatorname{plim}_{T \to \infty} S_T = -\infty$ can be avoided if each classical simulation estimate is replaced by one of the form $(a_t + N_t(j_t))/(a_t + b_t + N_t)$ for $a_t, b_t > 0$. This estimate is interpretable in Bayesian terms as the posterior mean for $P_t(j_t)$ under the assumption that the prior distribution of $P_t(j_t)$ is beta with parameters a_t and b_t. As before, consistency requires that $T \to \infty$ and that for each $t = 1, \ldots, T, N_t \to \infty$.

The foregoing discussion is of some potential consequence for the use of simulation estimates in maximum likelihood estimation. Let $\boldsymbol{\theta}$ be a real parameter vector, and for each t let $P_t(j_t \mid \boldsymbol{\theta})$ be a family of probabilities indexed by $\boldsymbol{\theta}$. Define $N_t(j_t \mid \boldsymbol{\theta})$, $a_t(\boldsymbol{\theta})$, $b_t(\boldsymbol{\theta})$, $L_T(\boldsymbol{\theta})$, and $S_T(\boldsymbol{\theta})$ in the natural way. If we use posterior means as simulation estimates, then for fixed N_t, $t = 1, \ldots, \infty$ the difference $\operatorname{plim}_{T \to \infty} S_T(\boldsymbol{\theta}) - E(L(\boldsymbol{\theta}))$ will in general be a function of $\boldsymbol{\theta}$. Consistency (as $T \to \infty$) of the ideal maximum likelihood estimator $\max_{\theta} L_T(\boldsymbol{\theta})$ therefore does not ensure consistency of the approximate estimator $\max_{\theta} S_T(\boldsymbol{\theta})$. The latter property is guaranteed only as $N_t \to \infty$, $t = 1, \ldots, T$ and $T \to \infty$.

7.5 Application to the Calculation of Multinomial Probit Choice Probabilities

The multinomial probit probabilistic choice model presumes a population of decision makers T each member t of which must select an alternative from a choice set $\mathbf{C}$ consisting of J alternatives. With each $t \in T$ there is associated a utility vector $(U_{tj}, j \in \mathbf{C})$ distributed as multivariate normal.

The probability that t selects some $i \in \mathbf{C}$ is then the normal tail probability $Pr(U_{tj} - U_{ti} \leq 0, \text{ all } j \in \mathbf{C})$.

A quite flexible parametric specification for the utilities $(U_{tj}, j \in \mathbf{C}, t \in T)$ is the random coefficients form $U_{tj} = \mathbf{Z}_{tj} \cdot \boldsymbol{\theta}_t^*$. Here $\mathbf{Z}_{tj}$ is a vector of observed attributes characterizing the decision maker and alternative, and $\boldsymbol{\theta}_t^*$ is an unobserved realization of a random vector $\boldsymbol{\theta}^* \sim N(\bar{\boldsymbol{\theta}}^*, \boldsymbol{\Sigma})$. It is assumed that for any t, $t' \in T$, $t \neq t'$, that $\boldsymbol{\theta}_t^*$ and $\boldsymbol{\theta}_{t'}^*$ are independent realizations of $\boldsymbol{\theta}^*$.

Until recently the multinomial probit model remained a theoretically attractive but empirically unused specification for discrete choice analysis. In particular the random coefficients form of the model drew attention for its great flexibility relative to the widely used conditional logit model. See for example McFadden (1976) for a discussion. The difficulty in applying the model derived from the fact that mathematically a multinomial probit choice probability is a multidimensional integral which has no closed form and in which the domain of integration is unbounded from below. As is well known, classical methods for numerical integration become quite burdensome in multiple integral contexts, with computation times for given accuracy generally increasing with the power of the integral's dimensionality.

The first advances in resolving the computational impasse were due to Dutt (1976) and Hausman and Wise (1978) who investigated series approximations to the multinomial probit choice probability. Dutt's work has never been implemented in any probit estimation program, but Hausman and Wise did succeed in developing a program capable of handling choice sets with three and four alternatives. In personal communications the latter authors have indicated a belief that the series approximation approach may be practical for choice sets of up to but not beyond five alternatives. This judgment, combined with the fact that series evaluation of choice probabilities requires a separate routine for each size choice set, persuaded us that the series approach was too limited in practical scope and too rigid in implementation for use in a general purpose program. Instead our attention turned to the simulated frequency method.

In the abstract the simulation approach appeared attractive for a variety of reasons. First, it is easily programmed and applied to choice sets of any size. Second, the method not only gives the user a measure of the accuracy of the probability calculations after any number of trials but allows him to control this accuracy through his ability to set the number of trials to be performed. Third, CPU time in the simulation approach goes up relatively slowly with choice set size. In particular for a given number of trials CPU time increases linearly with choice set size.

We have applied the simulated frequency method to the problem of calculating random coefficients—multinomial probit choice probabilities for use in a routine performing maximum likelihood estimation of the parameters $(\bar{\boldsymbol{\theta}}^*, \Sigma)$[2]. Section 7.6 describes the version of the method programmed. While in the midst of this effort we learned of an intriguing alternative probability calculation approach originated by Clark (1961) and unearthed by Daganzo, Bouthelier, and Sheffi (1977). A routine for producing Clark probabilities was subsequently added to our estimation program. Section 7.7 describes the Clark algorithm, and section 7.8 presents numerical tests comparing simulation and Clark probability calculation results. A detailed description of our probit estimation package is not given here. The interested reader should see Albright, Lerman, and Manski (1977a and 1977b).

7.6 The Simulation Routine

A certain amount of informed pragmatism has guided our design of a simulated frequency routine for use in the probit estimation package. The routine programmed has the following features:

1. The quantity $(N_t(j_t) + 1)/(N_t + J)$ is used as the estimate for $P_t(j_t)$. This quantity is interpretable as the posterior mean under the beta prior having mean $1/J$ and variance $(J - 1)/[J^2(J + 1)]$. The assumption of prior mean $1/J$ is natural as the choice set contains J alternatives. The variance assumption imposed has no particular justification.

2. For every realization $\tilde{\boldsymbol{\theta}}_t$ drawn, another one $\tilde{\tilde{\boldsymbol{\theta}}}_t = \bar{\boldsymbol{\theta}} + (\bar{\boldsymbol{\theta}} - \tilde{\boldsymbol{\theta}}_t)$ is used on the following simulation trial. Here $\bar{\boldsymbol{\theta}}$ is the mean of the $\boldsymbol{\theta}$ distribution from which draws are made. This use of antithetic variates makes the realizations of pairs of simulation trials negatively correlated, thereby increasing the precision of the simulation estimate relative to that in which independent trials are used. The use of antithetics also halves the number of times the random number generator must be invoked.

3. An informative stopping rule for determining the number of trials N_t is used. Specifically let N_0 and K be positive integers, λ be a positive real,

2. We have recently learned that a similar application has been made by Charles River Associates (1976).

and $F(j, kN_0)$ be the value of the simulation estimate for $P_t(j_t)$ after kN_0 trials, $k = 1, \ldots, K$. Now set $k = 1$, run N_0 trials and stop if $(1 - F(j, kN_0))/[F(j, kN_0)kN_0] < \lambda$ or if $k = K$. Otherwise set $k = k + 1$, run N_0 additional trials, and apply the stopping rule again. Use of this stopping rule was motivated by a concern to estimate ln P with equal precision regardless of the value of P. A more detailed but still heuristic explanation is given in Albright, Lerman, and Manski (1977a).

It should be noted that with these modifications to the classical simulation procedure, the classical variance formula $P(j)(1 - P(j))/N$ no longer is valid. We have nevertheless continued to use this formula to provide a measure of the precision with which $F(j)$ estimates $P(j)$. More precisely, since $P(j)$ is not known, the quantity $F(j)(1 - F(j))/N$ is used. An alternative, and perhaps more justifiable measure of precision is the Bayesian posterior variance $F(j)(1 - F(j))/(N + J + 1)$ obtained under the beta prior introduced above.[3]

7.7 The Clark Method

Clark (1961) suggested an approximation to the distribution of the maximum of M jointly normal random variables. The approximation rests on the fact that if x_1, x_2, and x_3 are jointly normal, the statistics $E(\max(x_1, x_2))$, VAR$(\max(x_1, x_2))$, and COV$(\max(x_1, x_2), x_3)$ can be calculated exactly in a straightforward manner. Clark then suggests the approximation that max (x_1, x_2) is itself normally distributed. Given this demonstrably false assumption, the first two moments of $\max(x_1, x_2, x_3) = \max(\max(x_1, x_2), x_3)$ can be calculated. Repeated application of the approximation allows one to approximate the distribution of the maximum of M jointly normal random variables. As evidence of the success of his approximation, Clark shows that it gives a very close estimate of $E(\max(x_1, \ldots, x_M))$ for M as large as 10. He also suggests error bounds. Clark does not provide evidence as to the suitability of the approximation in estimating higher moments of $\max(x_1, \ldots, x_M)$, or for approximating normal tail probabilities.

Daganzo, Bouthelier, and Sheffi (1977) discovered the Clark paper and applied its method to the estimation of probit choice probabilities. If **C** is a

3. It should be noted that all stopping rules in which the stopping criterion is monotonic decreasing in $F(j)$ lead to upward biased estimates of $P(j)$. Our rule has this property. However, the bias goes to zero as $\lambda \to 0$ and $KN_0 \to \infty$. See Albright, Lerman, and Manski (1977a).

choice set with utilities ($U_j, j \in \mathbf{C}$) distributed multivariate normal, and if i is the chosen alternative, then the utility differences ($U_j - U_i, j \in \mathbf{C}, j \neq i$) are multivariate normal, and the probability that i is chosen is $\text{Prob}[(\max(U_j - U_i), j \in \mathbf{C}, j \neq i) \leq 0]$. Daganzo et al. used the Clark approximation to the distribution of $(\max(U_j - U_i), j \in \mathbf{C}, j \neq i)$ to estimate this probability.

A priori the Clark method's attractiveness to us lay in its speed. The method requires the evaluation of only univariate normal tail probabilities, a task quite quickly accomplished by series approximation.[4] Moreover it is easy to show that CPU times for the Clark probabilities go up no faster than the square of choice set size.

In contrast to the simulation and series approaches where the user may control the accuracy of his approximated choice probabilities, the Clark method offers only a fixed accuracy level. The crucial question in determining the method's practical usefulness therefore was whether this accuracy was sufficient for probit estimation purposes. In particular it was important to determine whether the deviations of Clark approximation from true choice probabilities systematically vary with choice set size, true probability magnitude, disturbance covariance structure, and so on.[5] Since no analytical approach to determining the Clark properties could be found, we conducted a series of numerical tests.[6]

7.8 Numerical Test Objectives and Design

We have computed high accuracy (large number of trials) simulation probabilities for a broad range of choice problems and the corresponding probabilities approximated by the Clark algorithm. These tests serve two purposes. First, the Clark probabilities may be compared with the accurate

4. For this purpose we have used subroutine NDTR of the IBM scientific subroutine package.

5. Since the Clark method works recursively, the order in which alternatives are treated can also in principle affect the choice probabilities obtained. Daganzo et al. have, however, found that this order effect is quite small and our own tests confirm this. Hence we have not concerned ourselves with alternate orders in our programming.

6. About the only known analytical property of the Clark approach is that it uses a symmetric distribution to approximate one skewed to the right. This fact has led to the unconfirmed belief that the Clark method will overestimate true probabilities at the lower tail. Moreover, since the skewness of the true distribution increases with choice set size, it has been speculated that the accuracy of Clark probabilities decreases with choice set size. Finally, it has been asserted by some that the Clark method is most accurate when the normal covariance matrix contains only positive elements. Again no proof exists.

simulation ones to determine how the Clark accuracy depends on choice set size, the magnitude of the true choice probability and the variance-covariance structure of the utility function. Second, the tests allow us to assess the accuracy obtainable through the simulation approach when the number of trials is set so as to use the same CPU time as does the Clark method. In particular if x_s is the per trial CPU time consumed in the simulation method, and x_c is the CPU time for the Clark algorithm, then $N_c = x_c/x_s$ is the number of simulation trials that can be performed in the time taken by the Clark method.[7] The accuracy of the simulation probabilities obtainable in N_c trials can then be measured through the percent variance formula $(1 - P(j))/(P(j) \cdot N_c)$ and compared with the Clark method's accuracy as previously determined.

The tests reported here assume choice sets containing three or five alternatives.[8] The utility function is assumed to have the form $U_{ti} = \delta_t \cdot Z_{ti} + \varepsilon_{ti}$, where δ_t is a random coefficient and $(\varepsilon_{tj}, j \in \mathbf{C})$ is a set of alternative specific disturbances (random coefficients for alternative specific constants). It is assumed that $\delta_t \sim N(1, \sigma_\delta^2)$, $(\varepsilon_{tj}, j \in \mathbf{C}) \sim N(\mathbf{0}, \mathbf{\Sigma}_\varepsilon)$ and that δ is independent of the $\boldsymbol{\varepsilon}$ vector.

Within given choice sets, the attribute differences $(Z_i - Z_j)$ for $i, j \in \mathbf{C}$ lie in the range $[-4, 4]$. Across the set of tests the variances σ_δ^2 of the scalar random taste variable δ lies in the interval [0, 2]. The variance-covariance matrix $\mathbf{\Sigma}_\varepsilon$ of the $\boldsymbol{\varepsilon}$ disturbances is in some tests scalar, sometimes diagonal, and sometimes general. The $\boldsymbol{\varepsilon}$ variances (diagonal elements of $\mathbf{\Sigma}_\varepsilon$) range over the interval [1/4, 4]. The choice probabilities (as estimated by a large number of simulation drawings) resulting from the various test specifications range over the interval [0.002, 0.718].

For each test specification we calculate simulation and Clark choice probabilities for all alternatives in the relevant choice set.[9] In the simulation runs the stopping rule parameters are set at $N_0 = 1{,}000$, $K = 10$, and $\lambda = 0.0005$, so as to guarantee relatively high accuracy. In general it

7. These calculations are choice set size specific but should not depend on any other aspect of the choice problem.

8. These are a representative selection from our full series of tests, which are documented in Albright, Lerman, and Manski (1977a).

9. The simulation probability for each alternative is calculated independently. Hence over the choice set these probabilities do not in general sum exactly to one. Clark probabilities also do not usually sum to one.

can be expected that the simulation probability estimate $F(j)$ satisfies the conditions $|(F(j) - P(j))/P(j)| < 0.044$ and $|F(j) - P(j)| < 0.030$.[10]

7.9 Test Results and Analysis

Table 7.1 presents simulation and Clark choice probabilities for a set of choice problems, each choice set containing three alternatives. Table 7.2 presents similar results for choice sets containing five alternatives.

The most striking feature of the test results is the relatively high accuracy of the Clark probabilities. Not only are the simulation estimates and Clark approximations generally quite close to one another, but perhaps surprisingly, the accuracy of the Clark probabilities does not appear to systematically vary along the dimensions of concern to us. In particular the size of the choice set, magnitude of the true probability, and covariance structure of the random coefficients δ and ε have no noticeable effects.[11] We do not really understand why Clark's approximation works as well as it does. All we know is that within the domain tested it does work.[12]

The CPU times x_c required for each Clark calculation are quite reasonable, as expected. The reported average values (denoted as $\bar{x}_c$) of 0.007 and 0.009 seconds for three and five alternative choice sets allow the calculation of 8,000 and 6,000 probabilities per minute, a rate sufficiently high for economical probit estimation. The reported values of 14 and 11 for $N_c = \bar{x}_c/\bar{x}_s$ are quite small, implying that only crude simulation probabilities can be obtained in the time used by the Clark method. In fact comparison of the Clark root mean square error estimates and the simulation standard errors reported in tables 7.1 and 7.2 indicate that the

10. Assuming a classical (unmodified) simulation procedure, the standard error of $F(j)$ after N trials is $(P(j)(1 - P(j))/N)^{1/2}$, and the standard error of $F(j)/P(j)$ is $((1 - P(j))/NP(j))^{1/2}$. In our modified procedure a minimum of $N_0 = 1{,}000$ trials is performed, so it seems safe to assume that the standard error of $F(j)$ is always less than $((1/2 \cdot 1/2)/1{,}000) \cong 0.015$. Moreover setting $\lambda \cong 0.0005$ implies that $((1 - F(j)/NF(j))^{1/2} < (0.0005)^{1/2} \cong 0.022$, giving an upper bound on the standard error of $F(j)/P(j)$. Using a conservative two-standard-error criterion, we conclude that generally the fractional error $|(F(j) - P(j))/P(j)|$ will be less than 0.044 and the absolute error $|F(j) - P(j)|$ less than 0.030.

11. Note, however, that none of the tests performed have negative elements in the matrix Σ_ε.

12. Since our simulation probabilities still contain some error even with the large number of trials performed, the Clark method's accuracy may be even better than tables 7.1 and 7.2 indicate. There is a slight tendency for the simulation probabilities to be higher than the Clark ones. This may be a consequence of the simulation stopping rule we used.

Table 7.1
Probability calculation tests using choice sets with three alternatives

Case 1	$Z_1 = 0$	$Z_2 = 0$	$Z_3 = 0$	$\sigma_\delta = 0$	$\Sigma_\varepsilon = I_3$
Simulation	$P_1 = 0.320$	$P_2 = 0.348$	$P_3 = 0.330$	$\Sigma P = 0.998$	
Clark	0.332	0.332	0.332	0.996	
Case 2	$Z_1 = 1$	$Z_2 = 0$	$Z_3 = 0.75$	$\sigma_\delta = 2$	$\Sigma_\varepsilon = I_3$
Simulation	$P_1 = 0.474$	$P_2 = 0.215$	$P_3 = 0.321$	$\Sigma P = 1.010$	
Clark	0.463	0.210	0.319	0.992	
Case 3	$Z_1 = 0$	$Z_2 = 0$	$Z_3 = 0$	$\sigma_\delta = 0$	$\Sigma_\varepsilon = \begin{matrix} 0.25 & 0 & 0 \\ 0 & 1 & 0 \\ 0 & 0 & 4 \end{matrix}$
Simulation	$P_1 = 0.261$	$P_2 = 0.319$	$P_3 = 0.417$	$\Sigma P = 0.997$	
Clark	0.261	0.300	0.416	0.977	
Case 4	$Z_1 = 0$	$Z_2 = 0$	$Z_3 = 0$	$\sigma_\delta = 0$	$\Sigma_\varepsilon = \begin{matrix} 1 & 0.75 & 0 \\ 0.75 & 1 & 0 \\ 0 & 0 & 1 \end{matrix}$
Simulation	$P_1 = 0.285$	$P_2 = 0.301$	$P_3 = 0.418$	$\Sigma P = 1.004$	
Clark	0.279	0.279	0.419	0.977	
Case 5	$Z_1 = 0$	$Z_2 = 0$	$Z_3 = 0$	$\sigma_\delta = 0$	$\Sigma_\varepsilon = \begin{matrix} 0.25 & 0.38 & 0 \\ 0.38 & 1 & 0 \\ 0 & 0 & 4 \end{matrix}$
Simulation	$P_1 = 0.245$	$P_2 = 0.310$	$P_3 = 0.447$	$\Sigma P = 1.002$	
Clark	0.239	0.284	0.447	0.970	

$\bar{x}_c \cong 0.007$ $\bar{x}_s = 0.0005$ seconds $N_c = \dfrac{\bar{x}_c}{\bar{x}_s} \cong 14$

Root mean square value of (Simulation − Clark) = 0.012 $(P(1-P)/N_c)^{1/2} = 0.126$ for $P = 1/3$

Root mean square value of $\left(\dfrac{\text{Simulation} - \text{Clark}}{\text{Simulation}}\right) = 0.021$ $((1-P)/PN_c)^{1/2} = 0.379$ for $P = 1/3$

Table 7.2
Probability calculation tests using choice sets with five alternatives

Case 1	$Z_1 = 0$	$Z_2 = 0$	$Z_3 = 0$	$Z_4 = 0$	$Z_5 = 0$	$\sigma_\delta = 0$	$\Sigma_\varepsilon = I_5$
Simulation	$P_1 = 0.198$	$P_2 = 0.196$	$P_3 = 0.189$	$P_4 = 0.203$	$P_5 = 0.200$	$\Sigma P = 0.986$	
Clark	0.198	0.198	0.198	0.198	0.198	0.990	
Case 2	$Z_1 = 2$	$Z_2 = 1$	$Z_3 = 0$	$Z_4 = -1$	$Z_5 = -2$	$\sigma_\delta = 0$	$\Sigma_\varepsilon = I_5$
Simulation	$P_1 = 0.718$	$P_2 = 0.228$	$P_3 = 0.050$	$P_4 = 0.007$	$P_5 = 0.002$	$\Sigma P = 1.005$	
Clark	0.723	0.220	0.048	0.007	0.001	0.999	
Case 3	$Z_1 = 2$	$Z_2 = 1$	$Z_3 = 0$	$Z_4 = -1$	$Z_5 = -2$	$\sigma_\delta = 1$	$\Sigma_\varepsilon = I_5$
Simulation	$P_1 = 0.608$	$P_2 = 0.149$	$P_3 = 0.059$	$P_4 = 0.060$	$P_5 = 0.086$	$\Sigma P = 0.962$	
Clark	0.568	0.134	0.064	0.073	0.093	0.932	
Case 4	$Z_1 = 0$	$Z_2 = 0$	$Z_3 = 0$	$Z_4 = 0$	$Z_5 = 0$	$\sigma_\delta = 0$	$\Sigma_\varepsilon = G$
Simulation	$P_1 = 0.282$	$P_2 = 0.266$	$P_3 = 0.131$	$P_4 = 0.138$	$P_5 = 0.209$	$\Sigma P = 1.026$	
Clark	0.256	0.256	0.118	0.137	0.185	0.952	
Case 5	$Z_1 = 2$	$Z_2 = 1$	$Z_3 = 0$	$Z_4 = -1$	$Z_5 = -2$	$\sigma_\delta = 1$	$\Sigma_\varepsilon = G$
Simulation	$P_1 = 0.667$	$P_2 = 0.289$	$P_3 = 0.050$	$P_4 = 0.014$	$P_5 = 0.003$	$\Sigma P = 1.023$	
Clark	0.639	0.272	0.056	0.019	0.007	0.993	

$$G = \begin{bmatrix} 1 & 1 & 0 & 0 & 0 \\ 1 & 5 & 2 & 2 & 2 \\ 0 & 2 & 2 & 1.75 & 1.75 \\ 0 & 2 & 1.75 & 2.56 & 2.31 \\ 0 & 2 & 1.75 & 2.31 & 3.13 \end{bmatrix}$$

$\bar{x}_c \cong 0.009$ seconds $\quad \bar{x}_s \cong 0.0008$ seconds $\quad N_c = \bar{x}_c/\bar{x}_s \cong 11$

Root mean square value of (Simulation − Clark) $= 0.014$ $\quad (P(1-P)/N_c)^{1/2} = 0.120$ for $P = 1/5$

Root mean square value of $\left(\dfrac{\text{Simulation} - \text{Clark}}{\text{Simulation}}\right) = 0.032$ $\quad ((1-P)/PN_c)^{1/2} = 0.603$ for $P = 1/5$

Clark probabilities are ten to twenty times more accurate than the simulation ones achievable for the same CPU time. Conversely, since simulation accuracy increases as the square root of the number of trials, the simulation method can be seen to require more than one hundred times the Clark CPU time to achieve the same accuracy.

7.10 Conclusions

The above numerical results plus independent corroborating evidence in Daganzo et al. (1977) suggest that the Clark method should provide the preferred means for likelihood evaluation in multinomial probit estimation. While the Clark approximation seems to dominate the simulation approach in this application, our work with the latter method has still been quite valuable. First, without the ability to estimate true choice probabilities using high accuracy simulations, it would have been impossible to assess the accuracy of the Clark probabilities. Second, if some problem with the Clark method should be uncovered, the simulation approach, as programmed in our probit estimation program, will still be available. Thus the simulation approach provides some security to the empirical researcher wishing to estimate a multinomial probit choice model.

More generally the emergence of the Clark method as a successful approach for the calculation of multinomial probit probabilities may be regarded as somewhat fortuitous. Since such a powerful approximation may not exist under other distributions than the normal, it is useful to know that a generally applicable method, the simulation method, is available.

Finally, recall the findings of section 7.4 that in a forecasting situation, the simulation method works well even if the number of trials per observation is quite small. This result suggests that even when the simulation method is dominated by another in an estimation context, the method may still prove cost effective when the estimated model is used in forecasting.

References

Albright, R., S. Lerman, and C. Manski. 1977a. Compendium of Technical Memoranda on the Development and Testing of a Multinomial Probit Estimation Package. Prepared for the Federal Highway Administration.

Albright, R., S. Lerman and C. Manski. 1977b. Report on the Development of an Estimator for the Generalized Multinomial Probit Model. Prepared for the Federal Highway Administration.

Charles River Associates. 1976. Impact of Trade Policies on the U.S. Automobile Market. Report prepared for the Bureau of International Labor Affairs, U.S. Department of Labor, Washington, D.C.

Clark, C. 1961. The Greatest of a Finite Set of Random Variables. *Operations Research.* 9: 145–162.

Daganzo, C., F. Bouthelier, and Y. Sheffi. 1977. Multinomial Probit and Qualitative Choice—A Computationally Efficient Algorithm. *Transportation Science.* 11: 338–358.

DeGroot, M. 1970. *Optimal Statistical Decisions.* New York: McGraw-Hill.

Dutt, J. 1976. Numerical Aspects of Multivariate Normal Probabilities in Econometric Models. *Annals of Economic and Social Measurement.* Vol. 5.

Fishman, G. 1973. *Concepts and Methods in Discrete Event Digital Simulation.* New York: Wiley.

Hammersley, J., and D. Handscomb. 1964. *Monte Carlo Methods.* London: Methuen.

Hausman, J., and D. Wise. 1978. A Conditional Probit Model for Qualitative Choice: Discrete Decisions Recognizing Interdependence and Heterogeneous Preferences. *Econometrica.* 46: 403–426.

McFadden, D. 1976. Quantal Choice Analysis: A Survey. *Annals of Economic and Social Measurement.* 5: 363–390.

Shreider, Y. ed. 1966. *The Monte Carlo Method.* New York: Pergamon Press.

8 Application of a Continuous Spatial Choice Logit Model

Moshe Ben-Akiva and Thawat Watanatada

8.1 Introduction

Travel demand predictions require aggregation over numerous spatial alternatives and spatially distributed individuals.[1] It is customarily done by dividing the area into zones that are taken as the relevant spatial alternatives and as homogeneous market segments of individuals. However, in general unbiased aggregate predictions cannot be obtained by using only average values of the independent variables in an individual choice model. Therefore an aggregation procedure that employs information about the distributions of the variables is required.[2] An efficient aggregation procedure is particularly important in sketch-planning models that are designed for large spatial analysis units and limited input data requirements.

The methodology developed in this chapter employs continuous mathematical functions, expressed in terms of spatial coordinates, for the spatial choice models and for the distribution of individuals, spatial alternatives, and spatial attributes. The prediction of aggregate travel demand is achieved by integrating a continuous spatial choice model over the areas of the relevant zones.

The work reported in this chapter was partially supported by the Development of an Aggregate Model of Urbanized Area Travel Behavior project for the Office of the Secretary and the Federal Highway Administration, U.S. Department of Transportation and by the Understanding, Prediction, and Evaluation of Transportation-Related Consumer Behavior project for the Program of University Research, U.S. Department of Transportation. In conducting this research, we benefited from the advice of Jesse Jacobson, Frank Koppelman, Steve Lerman, Charles Manski, Dan McFadden, and Paul Roberts.

1. Travel and spatial choice models are described in many references including Domencich and McFadden (1975), Richards and Ben-Akiva (1975), Ben-Akiva et al. (1976), Ben-Akiva and Atherton (1977), and Spear (1977).

2. Procedures for aggregating choice models over individuals were investigated by Talvitie (1973), Westin (1974), McFadden and Reid (1975), Koppelman (1975) and Landau (1976). The alternative forms of representing the distributions are reviewed in Koppelman (1975) for aggregation over individuals and in Watanatada and Ben-Akiva (1977) for aggregation over alternatives and individuals.

The logit model has been extensively applied to spatial and nonspatial choice problems.[3] It is described here in its conventional discrete form and is then applied in a continuous form as a spatial choice model expressed in terms of two-dimensional coordinates to represent the location of the spatial alternatives.

The chapter concludes with a brief description of an application of the methodology to an aggregate prediction model of urbanized area travel demand using Monte Carlo simulation techniques. This model can be used in the framework of the multimodal national urban transportation policy-planning model described in Weiner (1976) and known as TRANS (transportation resource allocation study); it is referred to as MIT-TRANS (Watanatada and Ben-Akiva 1977).

8.2 Basic Definitions

Denote the probability of an individual t, choosing an elemental alternative s as $P_t(s)$.[4] The expected number of individuals choosing alternative s, T_s, is the sum of individual's choice probabilities for alternative s:

$$T_s = \sum_{t=1}^{T} P_t(s),$$

where T is the number of individuals in the aggregate group.

The foregoing relationship represents an aggregation of individuals for an elemental alternative. In the case where a group of elemental alternatives, rather than the elemental alternatives themselves, is of interest, aggregation of alternatives is performed for each individual t by summation of elemental alternatives' choice probabilities:

$$P_t(j) = \sum_{s \in j} P_t(s),$$

where $P_t(j)$ denotes the probability that individual t will choose an elemental alternative in group j.

3. The logit model and its derivation from a theory of utility maximization, properties, and econometric analysis techniques are given in McFadden (1974).

4. Elemental alternatives in a choice process are defined such that the individual chooses one and only one of them. That is, elemental alternatives are mutually exclusive in the same sense as elemental or atomic events in probability.

The aggregation of individuals for a group of alternatives j expresses the expected number of individuals choosing an elemental alternative in group j:

$$T_j = \sum_{t=1}^{T} P_t(j) = \sum_{t=1}^{T} \sum_{s \in j} P_t(s).$$

8.3 Spatial Aggregation

Spatial aggregation involves elemental alternatives and individuals that are distributed over space. Choices of residential location, workplace, shopping destination, and so on are characterized by spatially defined alternatives. The geographic distribution of individuals and spatial alternatives and their interrelationships in space in terms of transportation level-of-service attributes are essential inputs for predicting aggregate travel demand.

Consider an origin zone as a group of individuals and a destination zone as a group of elemental spatial alternatives. The elemental spatial alternatives are housing units (in the choice of residential locations), jobs (in the choice of workplace), and so on. The expected number of individuals at an origin i selecting an alternative in destination j is

$$T_{ij} = \sum_{t \in i} \sum_{s \in j} P_t(s).$$

To illustrate the relationship between spatial and nonspatial alternatives, let $P_t(m \mid s)$ be the probability of individual t choosing mode m given that he travels to spatial alternative s. The expected number of trips from origin i to destination j by mode m is given by

$$T_{ijm} = \sum_{t \in i} \sum_{s \in j} P_t(m \mid s) P_t(s).$$

8.4 The Discrete Logit Model

Assume the logit model for the spatial choice probability

$$P_t(s) = \frac{e^{V_{st}}}{\sum_{s=1}^{M} e^{V_{st}}}, \tag{8.1}$$

where

V_{st} = the average utility of elemental spatial alternative s to individual t,[5]
M = the number of available elemental spatial alternatives.

The independent variables of a spatial choice model that enter the utility functions are transportation level-of-service attributes by different modes, times of day, and facilities to the elemental spatial alternatives, L; locational attributes, or attraction variables, of the elemental alternatives, A; and socioeconomic characteristics of the individual, S.

To obtain choice probabilities for aggregate alternatives, partition the space of available alternatives into nonoverlapping subsets of elemental alternatives, or destinations, and sum the logit choice probabilities as follows:

$$P_t(j) = \frac{\sum_{s=1}^{M_j} e^{V_{st}}}{\sum_{j=1}^{J} \sum_{s=1}^{M_j} e^{V_{st}}}, \tag{8.2}$$

where

$\sum_{j=1}^{J} M_j = M,$

J = the number of destination zones,
M_j = the number of elemental spatial alternatives in zone j.

Define

$$\bar{K}_{jt} = \frac{1}{M_j} \sum_{s=1}^{M_j} e^{V_{st}} \tag{8.3}$$

and

$$\tilde{V}_{jt} = \ln \bar{K}_{jt}. \tag{8.4}$$

Substitute (8.3) and (8.4) in (8.2):

5. In the derivation of logit as a random utility model the utility of an alternative is written as $U_{st} = V_{st} + \varepsilon_{st}$, where ε_{st} is the random unobserved utility.

$$P_t(j) = \frac{e^{\tilde{V}_{jt} + \ln M_j}}{\sum_{j=1}^{J} e^{\tilde{V}_{jt} + \ln M_j}}. \tag{8.5}$$

This model for aggregate spatial alternatives was investigated by Lerman (1975) and McFadden (1977) who consider the problem of estimating $\tilde{V}_{jt}$.[6] Lerman (1975) used a Taylor series expansion around the mean

$$\bar{V}_{jt} = \frac{1}{M_j} \sum_{s=1}^{M_j} V_{st} \tag{8.6}$$

to investigate the sensitivity of the model to higher moments of the distribution of the attributes of elemental alternatives within zones. McFadden (1977) employed the transformation

$$\tilde{V}_{jt} = \bar{V}_{jt} + \ln \frac{1}{M_j} \sum_{s=1}^{M_j} e^{V_{st} - \bar{V}_{jt}} \tag{8.7}$$

to show that under the assumption that for large zones V_{st} are normally distributed the difference $\tilde{V}_{jt} - \bar{V}_{jt}$ approaches $1/2\ \sigma_{jt}^2$, where σ_{jt}^2 is the within zone variance of the utility V_{st}. Thus in all cases

$$\tilde{V}_{jt} \geq \bar{V}_{jt},$$

and the equality holds for perfectly homogeneous zones. This implies that, in order to use average zonal values for spatial aggregation, the zones should be defined to be homogeneous or to have equal within zone variances.

This also holds for the nested, or sequential, logit model described in McFadden (1977) and Ben-Akiva and Lerman (1977). The choice probability for $s \in j$ is

$$P_t(s) = \frac{e^{V_{st}}}{\sum_{s=1}^{M_j} e^{V_{st}}} \cdot \frac{e^{\mu \tilde{V}_{jt} + \mu \ln M_j}}{\sum_{j=1}^{J} e^{\mu \tilde{V}_{jt} + \mu \ln M_j}}, \tag{8.8}$$

6. An alternative approach described in Lerman (1975) is to define the utility of a zone as the maximum of the elemental alternatives' utilities. Under the logit assumption the expected value of the maximum is

$$\tilde{V}_{jt} + \ln M_j,$$

and the model in (8.5) is obtained.

where $0 \leq \mu \leq 1$ is an additional parameter, indicating the degree of similarity among unobserved attributes of elemental alternatives in the zones, or communities. The model in (8.1) is a special case of (8.8) when $\mu = 1$. The major disadvantage of this generalization for applications to spatial aggregation is the need to retain the definition of the zones used to define μ.

8.5 Spatial Aggregation Using Continuous Functions

The discrete summation form cannot be used in actual applications when the numbers of spatial alternatives and individuals are large, because complete enumeration would require astronomical amounts of data and computation. There are many possible ways to represent spatial distributions, depending on the level of detail desired. One way to generalize the definition of spatial aggregation is to employ mathematical functions expressed in terms of two-dimensional coordinates to represent the geographic distributions of the spatial alternatives, individuals, and the attributes.

Define a spatial choice function, denoted by $G_k(p, q \mid x, y)$, as the probability of an individual of type k located at point (x, y) choosing one spatial alternative located at point (p, q). This is a unique surface for individual type k located at (x, y) which is a function of[7]

$L(p, q; x, y)$ = transportation level-of-service attributes between origin point (x, y) and destination point (p, q),

$A(p, q)$ = locational attributes of the elemental alternatives at point (p, q),

S_k = socioeconomic characteristics of individual type k.

Define spatial density functions for spatial alternatives and individuals as follows:

$M(p, q)$ = density of elemental spatial alternatives at point (p, q),

$H_k(x, y)$ = density of individuals of type k at point (x, y).

The integral of the spatial choice function over all available alternatives M, must equal one. Thus the spatial choice function is defined such that

7. The derivation in McFadden (1976) implies that a unique spatial choice function exists if the choice probabilities are absolutely continuous with respect to the number of elemental spatial alternatives.

$$\iint_M G_k(p, q \mid x, y) M(p,q)\, dp dq = 1.$$

If it is only a function of the attributes of alternatives at (p, q), it is the continuous logit model. In the more general case it can be a function of the entire distribution of attributes of alternatives with respect to (x, y).

The expected number of individuals from zone i selecting alternatives in zone j can now be derived as follows:

1. by aggregation over spatial alternatives to obtain the probability that individual of type k located at (x, y) will choose an alternative in zone j:

$$P_k(j \mid x, y) = \iint_{\substack{\text{zone} \\ j}} G_k(p, q \mid x, y) M(p, q)\, dp dq, \tag{8.9}$$

2. by aggregation over individuals to obtain the expected number of individuals of type k located in zone i who will select an alternative in zone j:

$$T_{kij} = \iint_{\substack{\text{zone} \\ i}} P_k(j \mid x, y) H_k(x, y)\, dx dy. \tag{8.10}$$

The total number of trips from zone i to zone j is

$$\begin{aligned} T_{ij} &= \sum_k T_{kij} \\ &= \sum_k \iint_{\substack{\text{zone} \\ i}} \iint_{\substack{\text{zone} \\ j}} G_k(p, q \mid x, y) M(p, q) H_k(x, y)\, dp dq dx dy. \end{aligned} \tag{8.11}$$

It is also possible to repeat these steps to derive other quantities. For example, let $D(p, q\,; x, y)$ be the distance between points (p, q) and (x, y). Then the expected miles of travel for the origin/destination pair (i, j) is given by

$$MT_{ij} = \sum_k \iint_{\substack{\text{zone}\\ i}} \iint_{\substack{\text{zone}\\ j}} D(p,q;x,y)G_k(p,q \mid x,y)M(p,q)H_k(x,y)\,dpdqdxdy. \tag{8.12}$$

8.6 The Continuous Logit Model

The definition of an aggregate spatial choice probability can be rewritten as

$$P_t(j) = \iint_{\substack{\text{zone}\\ j}} G_t(p,q)M(p,q)\,dpdq, \tag{8.13}$$

where the subscript t is used to denote an individual type k at location (x, y). The continuous logit model is obtained by assuming the independence from irrelevant alternatives, IIA, property (McFadden 1976).[8] It implies that the spatial choice probabilities for any feasible subset of spatial alternatives, M^1, can be written as

$$P_t(j \mid M^1) = \frac{\iint_j K_t(p,q)M(p,q)\,dpdq}{\iint_{M^1} K_t(p,q)M(p,q)\,dpdq}, \tag{8.14}$$

where $K_t(p, q)$ is a spatial choice function defined in terms of attributes at (p, q). The spatial choice probability of an infinitesimal area $(dpdq)$ is given by

$$P_t(dpdq \mid M^1) = \frac{K_t(p,q)M(p,q)\,dpdq}{\iint_{M^1} K_t(p,q)M(p,q)\,dpdq}. \tag{8.15}$$

8. Alternatively the spatial choice function could be defined as the product $G_t(p, q)M(p, q)$ and the elemental alternative as the unit area. The continuous logit model can then be viewed as the infinitesimal limit of the discrete logit model (Ben-Akiva et al. 1976).

As in equation (8.4) define

$$V_t(p,q) = \ln K_t(p,q),$$

and substitute it in (8.15) to obtain

$$P_t(dpdq \mid M^1) = \frac{e^{V_t(p,q)} M(p,q)dpdq}{\iint\limits_{M^1} e^{V_t(p,q)} M(p,q)dpdq}$$

$$= \frac{e^{V_t(p,q) + \ln M(p,q)\, dpdq}}{\iint\limits_{M^1} e^{V_t(p,q) + \ln M(p,q)\, dpdq}}, \tag{8.16}$$

where $V_t(p, q)$ can be interpreted as the average utility to individual t of a spatial alternative at (p, q) and $M(p, q)dpdq$ the number of elemental spatial alternatives in the infinitesimal area $dpdq$.

To derive the discrete logic model, the feasible choice set is partitioned into groups of elemental alternatives as in (8.2), and the model (8.14) is rewritten as

$$P_t(j \mid M) = \frac{\iint\limits_{j} K_t(p,q)M(p,q)dpdq}{\sum\limits_{j=1}^{J} \iint\limits_{j} K_t(p,q)M(p,q)dpdq}. \tag{8.17}$$

Define

$$\bar{K}_{jt} = \frac{1}{M_j} \iint\limits_{j} K_t(p,q)M(p,q)dpdq, \tag{8.18}$$

where

$$M_j = \iint\limits_{j} M(p,q)dpdq.$$

Substitution of (8.18) and (8.4) in (8.17) yields the discrete logit model for aggregate spatial alternatives in (8.5).

8.7 A Parametric Example of Spatial Aggregation

The concept of spatial aggregation and the continuous logit model can be demonstrated by means of a specific travel demand model. The purpose of the example is to illustrate (1) the conversion of spatial choice models from their original discrete form to the continuous form, (2) the linkage between spatial choices and nonspatial choices in travel demand forecasting, and (3) the use of parametric distributions over space.

Consider a joint shopping destination-mode logit choice model of the form

$$P_t(md) = \frac{e^{V_{tmd}}}{\sum_{m'} \sum_{d'} e^{V_{tm'd'}}},$$

where

$P_t(md)$ = the probability that an individual trip maker t will travel to shop at destination d by mode m,

V_{tmd} = the average utility of mode m and destination d for individual t.

V_{tmd} is assumed to have a simplified specification, as follows:

$$V_{tmd} = a_1 S_{tm} + a_2 TC_{tmd} + a_3 IT_{tmd} + a_4 OT_{tmd} + a_5 \ln(Q_d) + \ln(A_d)$$

where

S_{tm} = a measure of socioeconomic characteristics of individual t for mode m,

TC_{tmd} = round trip out-of-pocket travel cost,

IT_{tmd} = round trip in-vehicle travel time,

OT_{tmd} = round trip out-of-vehicle travel time,

A_d = area of destination d,

Q_d = measure of attraction density at destination d—for example, retail employment per acre (the logarithmic form for Q in the utility function is used for convenience, although it is not necessary),

$a_1, \ldots, a_5$ = unknown parameters.

In this model the destinations are treated as groups of relatively homogeneous elemental spatial alternatives. Grouping of spatial alternatives is necessary for model estimation because data on spatial alternatives are only available for discrete area units (e.g., retail employment by zone). Because the notion of elemental alternatives for the shopping destination choice is not well defined, the unit area is taken as the measure of an elemental alternative. Thus the number of elemental alternatives contained in destination d is proportional to A_d, with the attraction variable Q_d representing the locational attributes of these spatial alternatives. The coefficient for $\ln(A_d)$ is constrained to unity to ensure that the model is linearly homogeneous with respect to the size of the aggregate spatial alternatives. That is, doubling the area of a destination will double the odds for choosing that destination. The property of linear homogeneity of a spatial choice model is needed to guarantee that the model will be applicable to any level of geographic aggregation.[9]

For simplicity rewrite the utility function into three groups of variables:

$$V_{tmd} = \alpha_{tm} + \beta_{tmd} + \ln(A_d \gamma_d),$$

where

$$\alpha_{tm} = a_1 S_{tm};$$
$$\beta_{tmd} = a_2 TC_{tmd} + a_3 IT_{tmd} + a_4 OT_{tmd},$$
$$\gamma_d = Q_d^{a_5}.$$

Substitute this definition of the utility function in the model to get

$$P_t(md) = \frac{e^{\alpha_{tm}} A_d \gamma_d e^{\beta_{tmd}}}{\sum_{m'} e^{\alpha_{tm'}} \sum_{d'} A_{d'} \gamma_{d'} e^{\beta_{tm'd'}}}.$$

To convert the discrete form model to the continuous form, we use a system of polar coordinates (L, θ) for the location of the spatial alternatives (the unit areas) with respect to individual t, a trip maker of type k residing at (x, y). We express the generalized travel cost (β_{tmd}) and the attraction measure (γ_d) in terms of (L, θ): β_{tmd} is replaced by $\beta_{tm}(L, \theta)$, and γ_d is replaced by $\gamma(L, \theta)$. Furthermore, because the unit area is the measure of an

9. To maintain this property when there are two or more size variables, it is necessary to replace the variable A_d with a linear function of size variables with unknown parameters. This results in a logit model with utility functions that are not linear in the parameters. An estimator for this case was developed by Daly (1978).

elemental alternative, we take the infinitesimal area ($LdLd\theta$) as the measure of the number of elemental alternatives. Then the probability of the individual traveling to the infinitesimal area ($LdLd\theta$) by mode m is given by

$$P_t(m, LdLd\theta) = G_t[m, (L, \theta)]\, LdLd\theta$$

$$= \frac{e^{\alpha_{tm}} \gamma(L, \theta) e^{\beta_{tm}(L, \theta)}\, LdLd\theta}{\sum_{m'} e^{\alpha_{tm'}} \int_0^B \int_0^{2\pi} \gamma(L, \theta) e^{\beta_{tm'}(L, \theta)}\, LdLd\theta},$$

where the summation in the denominator is replaced by an area integral over θ and L with an upper limit on travel distance B which could be set to infinity if the space of alternatives is not constrained.

The function $G_t[m, (L, \theta)]$ is the joint choice function for mode m and destination at point (L, θ). The spatial choice function for the model, expressed as the probability of the trip maker t choosing one spatial alternative at (L, θ), is derived as the sum of $G_t[m, (L, \theta)]$ over all modes:

$$G_t(L, \theta) = \sum_m G_t[m, (L, \theta)]$$

$$= \frac{\sum_m e^{\alpha_{tm}} \gamma(L, \theta) e^{\beta_{tm}(L, \theta)}}{\sum_m e^{\alpha_{tm}} \int_0^B \int_0^{2\pi} \gamma(L, \theta) e^{\beta_{tm}(L, \theta)}\, LdLd\theta}.$$

These functions can be used to derive required predictions. For example, to predict the probability of choosing mode m, we integrate $G_t[m, (L, \theta)]$ over the spatial alternatives space:

$$P_t(m) = \int_0^B \int_0^{2\pi} G_t[m, (L, \theta)]\, LdLd\theta.$$

To predict the trip length distribution by specific mode m, we first obtain the spatial choice function for (L, θ) conditional on mode m:

$$G_t[(L, \theta) \mid m] = \frac{G_t[m, (L, \theta)]}{P_t(m)}.$$

Then the trip length distribution by mode m is given by

$$f_t(L \mid m) = \int_0^{2\pi} G_t[(L,\theta) \mid m] L d\theta, \quad 0 \le L \le B,$$

and the expected trip length by mode m is

$$\bar{L}_{tm} = \int_0^B L f_t(L \mid m) dL.$$

Note that the expressions for mode choice probability and trip length distribution entail integrals in a generally intractable form which requires numerical integration

8.8 Continuous Logit with Featureless Plane

Under simplifying assumptions on the functional forms of the independent variables, a solution exists in closed form. Consider the following continuous spatial choice logit model without mode choice:

$$P(LdLd\theta) = \frac{e^{\beta(L,\theta) + \ln \gamma(L,\theta)} LdLd\theta}{\int_0^B \int_0^{2\pi} e^{\beta(L,\theta) + \ln \gamma(L,\theta)} LdLd\theta},$$

$0 \le L \le B$ and $0 \le \theta \le 2\pi$, and assume that the attraction measure is constant across all destinations,

$$\gamma(L,\theta) = \gamma,$$

and the transportation level of service is a linear function of distance,

$$\beta(L,\theta) = -bL.$$

Under these assumptions the following results are derived:

1. Consumer surplus, or the expected utility from the choice, equals the natural logarithm of the denominator of the model (Ben-Akiva and Lerman 1977):

$$CS = \ln \int_0^{2\pi} \int_0^B e^{-bL+\ln\gamma} L dL d\theta = \ln \frac{2\pi\gamma}{b^2}[1 - e^{-bB}(bB+1)],$$

$$\lim_{B\to\infty} CS = \ln \frac{2\pi\gamma}{b^2}.$$

If the term CS is divided by the cost coefficient in the utility function (e.g., coefficient a_2 in the parametric example), the consumer surplus will become expressable in monetary units.

2. Spatial choice function

$$G(L,\theta) = \frac{e^{-bL+\ln\gamma}}{\int_0^{2\pi} \int_0^B e^{-bL+\ln\gamma} L dL d\theta} = \frac{b^2 e^{-bL}}{2\pi[1 - e^{-bB}(bB+1)]},$$

$$\lim_{B\to\infty} G(L,\theta) = \frac{b^2}{2\pi} e^{-bL}.$$

3. Trip length probability density function[10]

$$f(L) = \int_0^{2\pi} G(L,\theta) L d\theta = \frac{b^2 L e^{-bL}}{1 - e^{-bB}(bB+1)},$$

$$\lim_{B\to\infty} f(L) = b^2 L e^{-bL}.$$

4. Trip length cumulative distribution function

$$F(L) = \frac{1 - e^{-bL}(bL+1)}{1 - e^{-bB}(bB+1)},$$

$$\lim_{B\to\infty} F(L) = 1 - e^{-bL}(bL+1).$$

5. Average trip length

$$\bar{L} = \frac{1}{b}[2 - Bf(B)],$$

10. This result for $B \to \infty$ was also obtained by Goodwin (1975) in a similar derivation.

$$\lim_{B \to \infty} \bar{L} = \frac{2}{b}.$$

6. The effect of B on CS and $\bar{L}$, or the effect of time/distance budget B on consumer surplus, is given by

$$\frac{\partial CS}{\partial B} = f(B) \geq 0,$$

and

$$\frac{\partial^2 CS}{\partial B^2} = \frac{f(B)}{B}[1 - bB - f(B)] \leq 0,$$

where the second inequality is derived from the condition that $\bar{L} \leq B$. Thus as B increases, the CS increases monotonically at a diminishing rate. The effect on average trip length is given by

$$\frac{\partial \bar{L}}{\partial B} = -\frac{f(B)}{B}[2 - bB - f(B)] \geq 0,$$

where the term in brackets can be shown to be nonpositive from the condition that $\bar{L} \leq B$.

For the parametric example with mode choice consider the following transportation level of service

$$\beta_{tm}(L, \theta) = -a_{tm} - b_{tm}L,$$

where a_{tm} is the generalized fixed travel cost and b_{tm} is the generalized marginal travel cost per unit distance for mode m. These generalized travel costs include both out-of-pocket costs and travel times weighted by model parameters.

The (marginal) probability for mode m becomes

$$P_t(m) = \frac{b_{tm}^{-2} e^{\alpha_{tm} - a_{tm}}[1 - e^{-b_{tm}B}(b_{tm}B + 1)]}{\sum_{m'} b_{tm'}^{-2} e^{\alpha_{tm'} - a_{tm'}}[1 - e^{-b_{tm'}B}(b_{tm'}B + 1)]}.$$

The trip length distribution by mode m is

$$f_t(L \mid m) = Lb_{tm}^2 e^{-b_{tm}L}[1 - e^{-b_{tm}B}(b_{tm}B + 1)]^{-1},$$

and the expected trip length is

$$\bar{L}_{tm} = 2b_{tm}^{-1}\left[1 - \frac{B}{2} f_t(B \mid m)\right].$$

In other words, the average trip length by mode is inversely proportional to the mode's generalized marginal travel cost per unit trip length. (The generalized travel costs not only vary with mode but also with trip purpose and socioeconomic characteristics.) For B approaching infinity, the elasticity of average modal trip length with respect to the unit generalized travel cost for the mode is equal to minus one. It should be noted, however, that in this rudimentary analysis we have ignored the elasticities of trip frequency and mode shares.

The resulting trip length distribution by mode for B equal to infinity is a gamma two distribution of familiar shape, as shown in figure 8.1 (for $B < \infty$ the gamma distribution becomes truncated), that was observed for a number of urban areas (A. M. Voorhees and Associates 1968, 1970). This indicates that even highly simplifying assumptions for the distributions may still result in qualitatively meaningful predictions. The behavioral implications of the conditional trip length distribution can be seen by plotting it for modes with significantly different level-of-service characteristics, for example, walk and auto, as shown in figure 8.2.

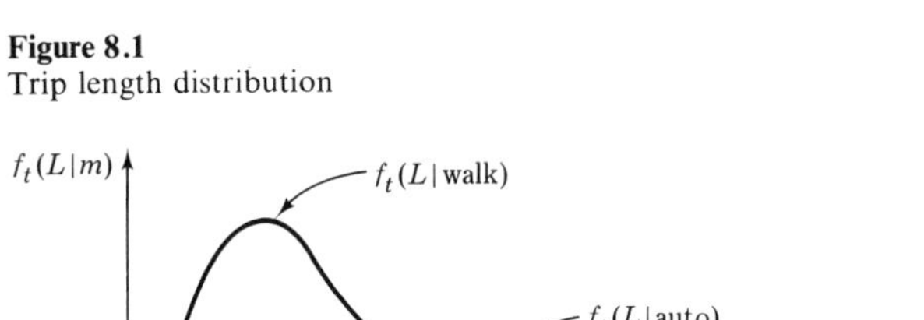

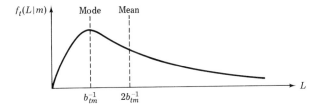

Figure 8.1
Trip length distribution

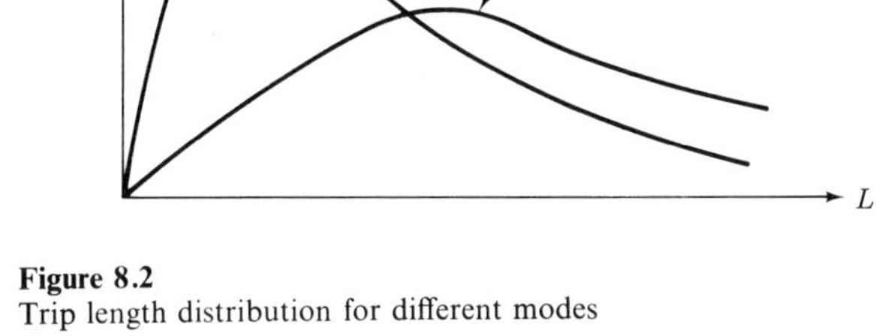

Figure 8.2
Trip length distribution for different modes

This example is intended for illustrative purposes only, since the assumed attractiveness and level-of-service distributions for the spatial alternatives are clearly unlikely to be even approximate in real urban situations. To achieve more accurate predictions, more realistic mathematical functions should be used to describe these distributions. However, because solutions to the integrals rarely exist in closed form, the general approach to perform spatial aggregation must be based on numerical integration techniques.

8.9 Basic Operations of the MIT-TRANS Model[11]

The MIT-TRANS model represents an extreme form of test for the feasibility and validity of the spatial aggregation methodology, because it treats an entire urban area as a single zone. The model is based on the application of Monte Carlo simulation, as the main numerical integration technique, to forecast trip generation, trip distribution, and modal split, with a system of disaggregate travel demand models. There are seven disaggregate models for both work and nonwork trips linked together (outputs from one model become inputs to lower-hierarchy models). Examples of predictions are the number of trips made, mode shares, person-miles of travel, vehicle-miles, and average vehicle occupancy rates for both work and nonwork trips, number of automobiles per family, and so on. These predictions are policy-sensitive, as reflected by the fact that they embody elastic travel demand models for the choices of workplace, auto ownership, mode to work, nonwork travel frequency, destination, and mode.

It should be noted that the MIT-TRANS model in its present form represents only the demand component of an overall policy evaluation package which must also include a supply component and evaluation procedures. Future extensions of the MIT-TRANS model include the development of network abstract transportation supply and traffic assignment models and the integration of these models and the aggregation procedure into an equilibrium framework. (In lieu of a complete supply-demand equilibrium framework, a set of level-of-service relationships describing a spatial distribution of the equilibrium conditions of an existing transportation system with externally specified parameters is being used in the current MIT-TRANS model.)

11. A detailed description of this model is given in Watanatada and Ben-Akiva (1977).

The operations of the MIT-TRANS model are summarized schematically in figure 8.3. It accepts three sets of inputs: (1) the aggregate city geometry and land use distribution parameters, (2) the urbanized area's socioeconomic characteristics, and (3) the specifications of a transportation policy alternative. These policy specifications are used to modify the level-of-service relationships which have been calibrated for the base conditions. The Monte Carlo aggregation procedure—a numerical integration procedure—operates on these inputs, the disaggregate choice models, and the (modified) level-of-service relationships to produce aggregate travel demand forecasts for the urbanized area. The forecasts can be disaggregated by market segments such as by income group.

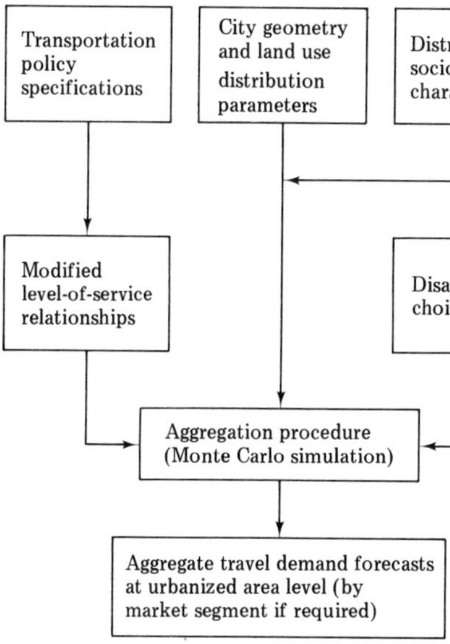

Figure 8.3
Basic operations of MIT-TRANS model

The urbanized area is modeled as a quasi-circular shape with the origins (home ends of trips) and destinations (nonhome ends) defined by sets of coordinates (R, λ) and (r, ϕ), or $(L, \theta \mid R, \lambda)$, respectively, as depicted in figure 8.4. For each of three income classes the household density function such as negative exponential is assumed (figure 8.5). The spatial alternatives—jobs, shopping destinations, and social recreational facilities—are also represented by employment density functions (negative exponential) and other functions describing locational attributes. The parameters of these density functions can be easily estimated from total counts of population and employment for a central city and its entire metropolitan area.

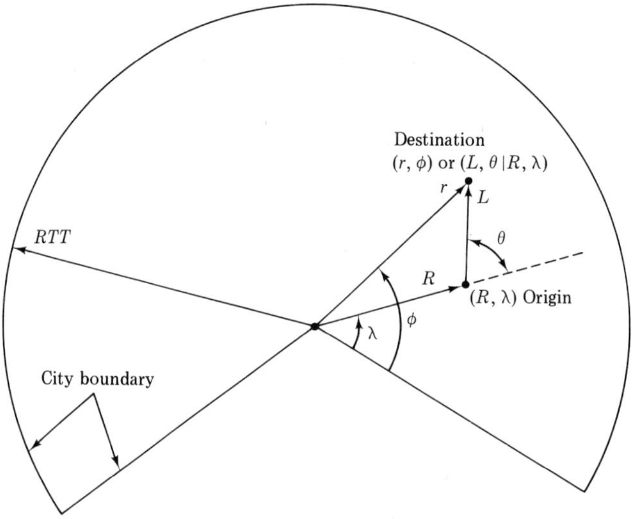

Figure 8.4
City geometry and system of coordinates

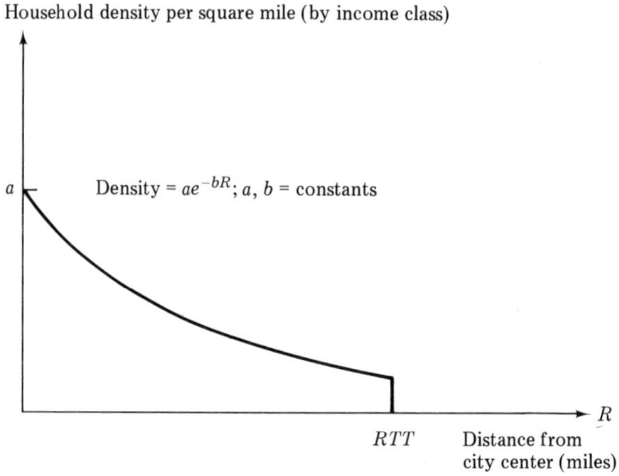

Figure 8.5
Negative exponential distribution of households

The transportation level-of-service functions by mode and time of day are expressed in terms of trip geometry variables, which are in turn functions of the coordinates of the trip ends.

MIT-TRANS also includes a procedure, similar to the one used by Duguay et al. (1976), to obtain the distribution of socioeconomic characteristics of the urban area population by generating a sample of households from available data. The procedure can operate on samples of disaggregate observations from the census public use sample, or any other household survey, and available aggregate data from surveys or published sources for the past years, from forecasts, or from explicit future scenarios.

The operations of the Monte Carlo aggregation procedure, summarized in figure 8.6, include the following basic steps:

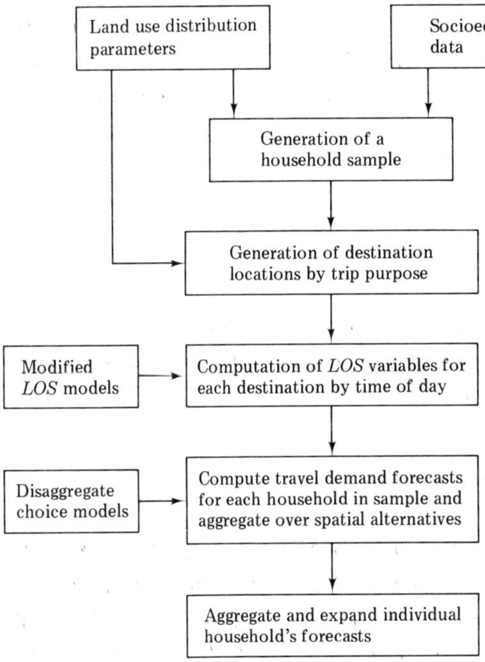

Figure 8.6
Monte Carlo aggregation procedure

1. Determine household sample size.

2. Generate sample of households for forecast year, characterizing each household by (R, λ) location and a set of socioeconomic attributes.

3. Determine sample size of spatial alternatives by purpose.

4. Generate sample of spatial alternatives by purpose for each household in the sample, defining each destination by (L, θ) coordinates.

5. Modify appropriate attributes of the alternatives for policy analysis.

6. Apply linked demand models for each household in the sample.

7. Expand sample forecasts to population market segments.

8. Compare forecasts against base case for policy analysis.

The Monte Carlo approach was selected to circumvent the extreme complexity of setting the bounds of the integrals for L and θ and to allow the use of alternative parametric distributions. The flexibility of the technique is demonstrated for an integral taken from a continuous logit model for an individual at (R, λ), which for simplicity is written as

$$I_j = \iint_j K(L,\theta) M(L,\theta) L dL d\theta,$$

where the origin of the coordinates (L, θ) is at (R, λ).

The most simple technique is to draw points $(L, \theta)_n$ uniformly over the area j and obtain the following unbiased estimator:

$$\hat{I}_j = \frac{A_j}{N_j} \sum_{n=1}^{N_j} K(L,\theta)_n M(L,\theta)_n,$$

where A_j is the area of zone j and N_j the number of points drawn in zone j.

Alternatively, since the input distribution of spatial alternatives is given in terms of (r, ϕ), it is possible, for example, to draw directly from the negative exponential distributions shown in fig. 8.5. (It involves drawing from a gamma distribution.) In this case

$$\hat{I}_j = \frac{M_j}{N_j} \cdot \sum_{n=1}^{N_j} K(L,\theta)_n.$$

However, with regard to shopping trips most destinations are expected to be 4 to 5 miles from the trip maker's home. Uniform sampling or sampling from an urbanized area employment distribution generate many locations outside the potential destination area with a very low value of $K(L, \theta)$. Therefore a more efficient sampling technique based on the knowledge of the entire integrand is also employed. The basic principle of importance sampling is to find a probability density function $f_j(L, \theta)$, such that

$$\frac{K(L,\theta)M(L,\theta)L}{f_j(L,\theta)}$$

varys as little as possible (Hammersley and Handscomb 1965). Drawing from $f_j(L, \theta)$ results in

$$\hat{I}_j = \frac{1}{N_j} \sum_{n=1}^{N_j} \frac{K(L,\theta)_n M(L,\theta)_n L_n}{f_j(L,\theta)_n}.$$

It is necessary, however, to find $f_j(L, \theta)$ that is simple enough to allow locations $(L, \theta)_n$ to be drawn conveniently. The featureless plane example presented earlier suggests for the entire urbanized area the gamma distribution with a parameter

$$b = \frac{2}{\bar{L}}$$

which can be calculated from generally available information on average trip lengths. In the implementation of this procedure some efficiency was lost because locations were sampled from a gamma distribution over an infinite space and therefore some fell outside the urbanized area.

The MIT-TRANS model was programmed in Fortran for an IBM 370/168 computer. It required about 0.6 CPU minutes per policy run with a standard error of about 1 percent of predicted average passenger miles of travel.

The model was calibrated for the 1968 metropolitan Washington, D.C., area and then used to forecast 1975 conditions as a validation test. Between 1968 and 1975 there were substantial changes in the metropolitan Washington area. The major changes in travel behavior include increased auto ownership, increased vehicle miles of travel per household, and decreased transit patronage. All the forecasted changes agree with these trends.

Apart from Washington, D.C., the model was also calibrated for the Minneapolis-St. Paul area, which has two central business districts. The elasticities produced by the model for both the Washington, D.C., and the Twin Cities are comparable to before-and-after empirical evidence and forecasts obtained from other more detailed studies.

Several Monte Carlo sampling experiments were conducted to investigate the statistical properties of the model. It was found empirically that a small number of sampled destinations would result in minimal bias and optimal efficiency.

The empirical results have led to the basic conclusion with respect to the applicability of disaggregate travel demand models and Monte Carlo techniques for aggregate sketch-planning predictions. The travel demand-forecasting methodology proposed operates with readily available aggregate input data, while still maintaining the full degree of policy sensitivity available in recently developed systems of disaggregate models. The most important future extensions of the methodology are the incorporation of supply and traffic assignment models and the development of a version of MIT-TRANS for multiple zones of varying sizes.

References

Alan M. Voorhees and Associates. 1968. *Factors and Trends in Trip Lengths*. NCHRP report 48. Washington, D.C.

Alan M. Voorhees and Associates. 1970. *Factors, Trends and Guidelines Related to Trip Length*. NCHRP report 89. Washington, D.C.

Ben-Akiva, M., and T. Atherton. 1977. Methodology for Short Range Travel Demand Predictions. *Journal of Transport Economics and Policy*. 11: 224–261.

Ben-Akiva, M., F. S. Koppelman, and T. Watanatada. 1976. Development of an Aggregate Model of Urbanized Area Travel Behavior. Phase I report, prepared for the U.S. Department of Transportation. Center for Transportation Studies, Massachusetts Institute of Technology.

Ben-Akiva, M., and S. R. Lerman. 1977. Disaggregate Travel and Mobility Choice Models and Measures of Accessibility. Presented at the International Conference on Behavioral Travel Demand Modelling, Australia, March, 1977. In *Behavioral Travel Modelling*, ed. D. A. Hensher and P. R. Stopher. London: Croom Helm, in press.

Ben-Akiva, M., S. R. Lerman, and M. L. Manheim. 1976. Disaggregate Models: An Overview of Some Recent Research Results and Practical Applications. *PTRC, Transportation Models*. P142: 289–329.

Daly, A. 1978. Estimating Attraction Variables. Cambridge Systematics, Inc., Cambridge, Mass.

Domencich, T., and D. McFadden. 1975. *Urban Travel Demand; A Behavioral Analysis*. Amsterdam; North Holland.

Duguay, G., Woo Jung, and D. McFadden. 1976. SYNSAM: A Methodology for Synthesizing Household Transportation Survey Data. Working paper 7618. Travel Demand Forecasting Project. Institute of Transportation Studies, University of California, Berkeley.

Goodwin, P. B. 1975. Variations in Travel Between Individuals Living in Areas of Different Population Density. *PTRC, Urban Traffic Models.* P122: 357–370.

Hammersley, J. M., and D. C. Handscomb. 1965. *Monte Carlo Methods.* London: Methuen.

Koppelman, F. S. 1975. *Travel Prediction with Models of Individual Travel Behavior.* Ph.D. dissertation. Transportation Systems Division, Department of Civil Engineering, Massachusetts Institute of Technology.

Landau, U. 1976. *Sketch Planning Models in Transportation Systems Analysis.* Ph.D. dissertation. Transportation Systems Division. Department of Civil Engineering, Massachusetts Institute of Technology.

Lerman, S. R. 1975. *A Disaggregate Behavioral Model of Urban Mobility Decisions.* Ph.D. dissertation. Transportation Systems Division. Department of Civil Engineering, Massachusetts Institute of Technology.

McFadden, D. 1974. Conditional Logit Analysis of Quantitative Choice Behavior. In *Frontiers in Econometrics*, ed. P. Zarembka. New York; Academic Press.

McFadden, D. 1976. The Mathematical Theory of Demand Models. In *Behavioral Travel-Demand Models*, ed. P. R. Stopher and A. M. Meyburg. Lexington, Mass.; Lexington Books.

McFadden; D. 1977. Modelling the Choice of Residential Location. Department of Economics, University of California, Berkeley.

McFadden, D., and F. Reid. 1975. Aggregate Travel Demand Forecasting from Disaggregated Behavioral Models. *Transportation Research Record.* 534: 24–37.

Richards, M. G., and M. E. Ben-Akiva. 1975. *A Disaggregate Travel Demand Model.* Lexington, Mass.: D. C. Heath.

Spear, B. D. 1977. *A Study of Individual Choice Models; Applications of New Travel Demand Forecasting Techniques to Transportation Planning.* Federal Highway Administration, U.S. Dept. of Transportation, Washington, D.C.

Talvitie, A. 1973. Aggregate Travel Demand Analysis with Disaggregate or Aggregate Travel Demand Models. *Transportation Research Forum Proceedings.* 14: 583–603.

Watanatada, T., and M. Ben-Akiva. 1977. *Development of an Aggregate Model of Urbanized Area Travel Behavior.* Final report prepared for the U.S. Dept. of Transportation Center for Transportation Studies, Massachusetts Institute of Technology.

Weiner, E. 1976. Assessing National Urban Transportation Policy Alternatives. *Transportation Research.* 10; 159–178.

Westin, R. B. 1974. Prediction from Binary Choice Models. *Journal of Econometrics.* 2: 1–16.

IV SIMULTANEOUS EQUATIONS MODELS WITH DISCRETE ENDOGENOUS VARIABLES

9 Simultaneous Equations Models with Discrete and Censored Dependent Variables

Lung-Fei Lee

9.1 Introduction

Recently a class of econometric models involving dichotomous, limited, and censored dependent variables was introduced by Amemiya (1974), Heckman (1976a, 1976b, 1977), Lee (1976, 1977), Nelson and Olsen (1977), and others in econometrics literature. In this chapter we will investigate the estimation principle posed by Amemiya, using a unified general simultaneous equation model. The simultaneous equation model includes censored simultaneous equation models, switching simultaneous equation models, and Nelson-Olson and Heckman models without structural change as special cases. Estimation methods that are computationally simple and consistent are also proposed. Alternative estimates can be derived from Amemiya's principle (Amemiya 1977a, 1977b). The Amemiya principle is a general principle used to derive structural parameter estimates from estimated reduced form parameters. Amemiya proved that his principle can lead to simple estimators more efficient than the estimators derived in Nelson-Olsen (1977) and Heckman (1977).[1] Since Amemiya only demonstrated the efficiency of his approach in a case-by-case basis, one may wonder whether it still holds in more general and complicated models.

9.2 Two-Stage Methods and Amemiya's Principle

To provide an unified framework, let us consider the following simultaneous equation model

This chapter is a shortened version of a paper prepared for the NBER-NSF Conference on Decision Rules and Uncertainty, Carnegie-Mellon University, March 29–April 1, 1978, with a slightly different title: "On the Estimation of Probit Choice Model with Censored Dependent Variables and Amemiya's Principle." I would like to thank Jerry Hausman, James Heckman, G.S. Maddala, Charles F. Manski, Daniel McFadden, Randall Olsen, Richard Westin, and a referee for their comments. Any errors remaining are solely my own.

1. In the Nelson-Olson model he used one limited dependent and one continuous endogenous variable (Amemiya 1977a) and in Heckman's model a continuous and dichotomous dependent variable (Amemiya 1977b).

$$\mathbf{Y}_i = \mathbf{Y}_i\mathbf{B} + \mathbf{X}_i\boldsymbol{\Gamma} + \boldsymbol{\varepsilon}_i, \tag{9.1}$$

$i = 1, \ldots, N$, where $\mathbf{Y}_i$ is a $1 \times G$ row vector of endogenous variables, $\mathbf{X}_i$ is a $1 \times k$ vector of exogenous variables, $\mathbf{I} - \mathbf{B}$ is a $G \times G$ nonsingular matrix, $\boldsymbol{\Gamma}$ is a $k \times G$ matrix, $\boldsymbol{\varepsilon}_i \sim N(\mathbf{0}, \boldsymbol{\Sigma})$ and are i.i.d. The model differs from the usual simultaneous equation model in that $\mathbf{Y}_i$ may consist of latent variables and limited and censored dependent variables as well as observable continuous variables. Without loss of generality, we assume that $0 \leq G_1 \leq G_2 \leq G_3 \leq G$ and

1. the first G_1 variables $Y_{1i}, \ldots, Y_{G_1 i}$ are observable continuous variables,

2. the next $G_2 - G_1$ variables $Y_{G_1+1i}, \ldots, Y_{G_2 i}$ are limited dependent variables, that is, one can observe it only when $Y_{ji} > 0$,

3. the next $G_3 - G_2$ variables $Y_{G_2+1i}, \ldots, Y_{G_3 i}$ are unobservable latent variables. However binary indicators I_{ji} are observable and are determined by the latent variable Y_{ji} as follows;

$I_{ji} = 1$ iff $Y_{ji} > 0$,
$I_{ji} = 0$ otherwise,
$j = G_2 + 1, \ldots, G_3$.

4. the last $G - G_3$ variables are censored dependent variables. The variables $Y_{G_3+1i}, \ldots, Y_{Gi}$ are censored by a subset of latent variables in the preceding assumption. Specifically the index set $\{G_3 + 1, \ldots, G\}$ can be partitioned into finite mutually exclusive and exhausted nonempty subsets $\mathbf{S}_k$, that is, $\{G_3 + 1, \ldots, G\} = U_{l=1}^{L}\mathbf{S}_l$ where $L \leq G_3 - G_2$. For each $1 \leq l \leq L$ there is a unique latent variable Y_{G_2+li} activating it; $Y_{j_l i}$ is observed if $Y_{G_2+li} > 0$, for all $j_l \in \mathbf{S}_l^*$, and $Y_{j_l i}$ is observed if $Y_{G_2+li} < 0$, for $j_l \in \mathbf{S}_l/\mathbf{S}_l^*$, where $\mathbf{S}_l^*$ is a subset of $\mathbf{S}_l$ which may be empty or equal $\mathbf{S}_l$.

The model in (9.1) is well defined and contains models developed by Lee (1976, 1977) as well as Heckman's models without structural shifts (1976, 1977) and Nelson and Olson (1977) models as special cases.

The $\mathbf{B}$ and $\boldsymbol{\Gamma}$ can be identified under rank conditions and suitable normalization rules. However, in general only certain nonlinear transformation of $\boldsymbol{\Sigma}$ will be identifiable when $G_3 < G$ and $\phi \neq \mathbf{S}_l^* \subsetneqq \mathbf{S}_l$ for some l. The analysis of identification conditions will be similar to that in Lee (1977), but the details will be omitted here.

To estimate model (9.1), maximum likelihood methods are too complicated to be useful. However, consistent methods proposed by Heckman (1976, 1977), Lee (1977), Maddala and Lee (1976), and Nelson and Olson (1977) can be easily extended. Alternative estimates can also be derived from Amemiya's principle (Amemiya 1977a, 1977b). All those methods require estimation of reduced form parameters in the first stage. For the model in (9.1) reduced form equations always exist:

$$\mathbf{Y}_i = \mathbf{X}_i\boldsymbol{\Pi} + \mathbf{u}_i, \tag{9.2}$$

where $\boldsymbol{\Pi} = \boldsymbol{\Gamma}(\mathbf{I} - \mathbf{B})^{-1}$ and $\mathbf{u}_i = \boldsymbol{\varepsilon}_i(\mathbf{I} - \mathbf{B})^{-1}$. Equation (9.2) can be estimated by a single equation method such as probit or tobit maximum likelihood methods, depending on the nature of the dependent variable. The variables are defined in terms of the four specified categories.

The second stage is to estimate the structural parameters. To simplify notations, each single equation is specified as

$$Y_i = \mathbf{R}_i\boldsymbol{\delta}_0 + \mathbf{Y}_i^*\boldsymbol{\delta}_1 + \varepsilon_i, \tag{9.3}$$

where $\mathbf{Y}_i^*$ is a subvector of endogenous variables other than Y_i in $\mathbf{Y}_i$. Equation (9.3) can be modified to

$$Y_i = \mathbf{R}_i\boldsymbol{\delta}_0 + (\mathbf{X}_i\boldsymbol{\Pi}^*)\boldsymbol{\delta}_1 + v_i, \tag{9.4}$$

where $\mathbf{Y}_i^* = \mathbf{X}_i\boldsymbol{\Pi}^* + \mathbf{u}_i^*$. With consistent estimates $\hat{\boldsymbol{\Pi}}^*$ derived in the first stage, the second stage in the methods proposed by Lee (1976, 1977), Maddala and Lee (1976) and Nelson and Olson (1977) is to estimate $(\boldsymbol{\delta}_0, \boldsymbol{\delta}_1)$ from

$$Y_i = \mathbf{R}_i\boldsymbol{\delta}_0 + (\mathbf{X}_i\hat{\boldsymbol{\Pi}}^*)\boldsymbol{\delta}_1 + w_i, \tag{9.5}$$

where $w_i = v_i + \mathbf{X}_i(\boldsymbol{\Pi}^* - \hat{\boldsymbol{\Pi}}^*)\boldsymbol{\delta}_1$. Equation (9.5) is estimated by probit, tobit, and so on, depending on the nature of Y_i in (9.5).

Instead of estimating (9.5), Amemiya suggests one should solve by regression methods the structural parameters from the estimated reduced form parameters. Based on this principle, one can derive alternative estimates. Let $\mathbf{R} = \mathbf{X}\mathbf{J}_1$, where $\mathbf{J}_1$ consists of unit and zero column vectors. From (9.4) one has

$$Y_i = \mathbf{X}_i(\mathbf{J}_1\boldsymbol{\delta}_0 + \boldsymbol{\Pi}^*\boldsymbol{\delta}_1) + v_i. \tag{9.6}$$

Let $\mathbf{c}$ be the corresponding reduced form parameter vector of Y_i in (9.2). It is obvious that

$$\mathbf{c} = \mathbf{J}_1\boldsymbol{\delta}_0 + \boldsymbol{\Pi}^*\boldsymbol{\delta}_1. \tag{9.7}$$

The estimates suggested by Amemiya are ordinary least squares, OLS, or generalized least squares, GLS, estimates derived from

$$\hat{\mathbf{c}} = \mathbf{J}_1\boldsymbol{\delta}_0 + \hat{\boldsymbol{\Pi}}^*\boldsymbol{\delta}_1 + \xi, \tag{9.8}$$

where $\xi = \hat{\mathbf{c}} - \mathbf{c} - (\hat{\boldsymbol{\Pi}}^* - \boldsymbol{\Pi}^*)\boldsymbol{\delta}_1$.

Under general conditions all these estimation methods give consistent and asymptotic normal estimates. Amemiya in the two mentioned cases showed that his GLS estimates are more efficient. The question remaining is to compare his GLS estimates with the other consistent methods in the general model with arbitrary number of equations and different type of endogenous variables.

9.3 Structural Equations with Probit Structure

The $G_3 - G_2$ equations have unobservable latent variables at the left-hand side that belong to this category. In our model the endogenous variable Y_i is an unobservable latent variable. The two-stage estimates are derived from maximizing the function $\ln L$ in (9.9) w.r.t. $\boldsymbol{\Theta}_1' = (\boldsymbol{\delta}_0', \boldsymbol{\delta}_1')$ which are the identifiable parameters under the normalization $\sigma_v^2 = 1$.

$$\ln L = \sum_{i=1}^{N} \{I_i \ln \Phi(\mathbf{R}_i\boldsymbol{\delta}_0 + (\mathbf{X}_i\hat{\boldsymbol{\Pi}}^*)\boldsymbol{\delta}_1)$$
$$+ (1 - I_i)\ln(1 - \Phi(\mathbf{R}_i\boldsymbol{\delta}_0 + (\mathbf{X}_i\hat{\boldsymbol{\Pi}}^*)\boldsymbol{\delta}_1))\}, \tag{9.9}$$

where I_i is the observed dichotomous indicator of Y_i, Φ is the standard normal c.d.f. Let $\mathbf{P} = [\mathbf{X}\delta_{11}, \ldots, \mathbf{X}\delta_{1M}]$, $\boldsymbol{\Theta}_2' = (\boldsymbol{\Pi}_1^{*\prime}, \ldots, \boldsymbol{\Pi}_M^{*\prime})$, $\mathbf{S} = [\mathbf{RX\Pi^*}]$, where $\boldsymbol{\delta}_1' = [\delta_{11}, \ldots, \delta_{1M}]$ and $\boldsymbol{\Pi}^* = (\boldsymbol{\Pi}_1^*, \ldots, \boldsymbol{\Pi}_M^*)$. Let

$$\boldsymbol{\Lambda}_1 = \begin{bmatrix} \dfrac{\phi_1}{1 - \Phi_1} & & 0 \\ & \ddots & \\ 0 & & \dfrac{\phi_N}{1 - \Phi_N} \end{bmatrix}$$

and

$$\mathbf{\Lambda} = \begin{bmatrix} \frac{\phi_1^2}{1-\Phi_1} & & 0 \\ & \ddots & \\ 0 & & \frac{\phi_N^2}{1-\Phi_N} \end{bmatrix},$$

where ϕ_i and Φ_i are standard normal density and distribution functions evaluated at $\mathbf{R}_i\boldsymbol{\delta}_0 + \mathbf{X}_i\boldsymbol{\Pi}^*\boldsymbol{\delta}_1$. Following Amemiya, the asymptotic distribution of this two-stage estimator $\hat{\boldsymbol{\Theta}}_1$ can be derived from

$$\hat{\boldsymbol{\Theta}}_1 - \boldsymbol{\Theta}_1 \triangleq (\mathbf{S}'\mathbf{\Lambda}\mathbf{S})^{-1}(\mathbf{S}'\mathbf{\Lambda}_1(\mathbf{I}-\boldsymbol{\Phi}) - \mathbf{S}'\mathbf{\Lambda}\mathbf{P}(\hat{\boldsymbol{\Theta}}_2 - \boldsymbol{\Theta}_2)), \tag{9.10}$$

where $\triangleq$ means both sides have the same asymptotic distributions and $\mathbf{I}-\boldsymbol{\Phi}$ is a $N \times 1$ vector consisting of $I_i - \Phi_i$. The detailed expression for the asymptotic variance matrix is lengthy but can be derived in a straightforward manner. The two-stage estimates can then be compared with Amemiya's GLS estimates.

PROPOSITION 9.1: For equation (9.3) with unobservable latent variable Y_i and its dichotomous realization I_i, the two-stage estimate $\hat{\boldsymbol{\Theta}}_1$ derived from maximizing equation (9.9) is asymptotically less efficient than the GLS estimate $\hat{\boldsymbol{\Theta}}_1^A$ derived from Amemiya's principle.

PROOF: From (9.10), the asymptotic variance of $\hat{\boldsymbol{\Theta}}_1$ is

$$\begin{aligned}\mathbf{V}_{\boldsymbol{\Theta}_1} = (\mathbf{S}'\mathbf{\Lambda}\mathbf{S})^{-1}\{&\mathbf{S}'\mathbf{\Lambda}\mathbf{S} + \mathbf{S}'\mathbf{\Lambda}\mathbf{P}\mathbf{V}_{\boldsymbol{\Theta}_2}\mathbf{P}'\mathbf{\Lambda}\mathbf{S} - \mathbf{S}'\mathbf{\Lambda}_1\mathbf{E}_2'\mathbf{P}'\mathbf{\Lambda}\mathbf{S} \\ &- \mathbf{S}'\mathbf{\Lambda}\mathbf{P}\mathbf{E}_2\mathbf{\Lambda}_1\mathbf{S}\}(\mathbf{S}'\mathbf{\Lambda}\mathbf{S})^{-1},\end{aligned}$$

where $\mathbf{E}_2$ is the asymptotic covariance of $(\hat{\boldsymbol{\Theta}}_2 - \boldsymbol{\Theta}_2)$ and $(\mathbf{I}-\boldsymbol{\Phi})$. The asymptotic variance matrix of $\hat{\boldsymbol{\Theta}}_1^A$ is

$$\mathbf{V}_{\boldsymbol{\Theta}_1^A} = (\mathbf{Z}'\boldsymbol{\Omega}_\xi^{-1}\mathbf{Z})^{-1},$$

where $\mathbf{Z} = [\mathbf{J}_1\ \boldsymbol{\Pi}^*]$ and $\boldsymbol{\Omega}_\xi$ in this probit structural equation is

$$\boldsymbol{\Omega}_\xi = [\mathbf{I}\ \mathbf{P}_1]\begin{bmatrix}(\mathbf{X}'\mathbf{\Lambda}\mathbf{X})^{-1} & * \\ -\mathbf{E}_2\mathbf{\Lambda}_1\mathbf{X}(\mathbf{X}'\mathbf{\Lambda}\mathbf{X})^{-1} & \mathbf{V}_{\boldsymbol{\Theta}_2}\end{bmatrix}\begin{bmatrix}\mathbf{I} \\ \mathbf{P}_1'\end{bmatrix},$$

with $\mathbf{P} = \mathbf{X}\mathbf{P}_1$. The two expressions $\mathbf{V}_{\boldsymbol{\Theta}_1}$ and $\boldsymbol{\Omega}_\xi$ follow, because $\mathbf{c}$ is the probit maximum likelihood estimate of the reduced form equation and $\hat{\mathbf{c}} - \mathbf{c} \triangleq (\mathbf{X}'\mathbf{\Lambda}\mathbf{X})^{-1}\mathbf{X}'\mathbf{\Lambda}_1(\mathbf{I}-\boldsymbol{\Phi})$. On the other hand, $\mathbf{V}_{\boldsymbol{\Theta}_1}$ can be rewritten as

$$\mathbf{V}_{\mathbf{\Theta}_1} = (\mathbf{Z}'\mathbf{X}'\mathbf{\Lambda}\mathbf{X}\mathbf{Z})^{-1}\mathbf{Z}'\mathbf{X}'\mathbf{\Lambda}\mathbf{X}\mathbf{\Omega}_\xi\mathbf{X}'\mathbf{\Lambda}\mathbf{X}\mathbf{Z}(\mathbf{Z}'\mathbf{X}'\mathbf{\Lambda}\mathbf{X}\mathbf{Z})^{-1}.$$

It follows that $\mathbf{V}_{\mathbf{\Theta}_1} - \mathbf{V}_{\mathbf{\Theta}_1{}^A}$ is nonnegative definite.

9.4 Structural Equations with Observable Continuous Endogenous Variables

The first G_1 equations in our model (9.1) are in this category. Y_i in (9.3) is an observable continuous variable. Let $\mathbf{\Theta}_1' = (\boldsymbol{\delta}_0', \boldsymbol{\delta}_1')$, $\mathbf{S} = [\mathbf{R} \quad \mathbf{X}\mathbf{\Pi}^*]$ be a matrix with $(\mathbf{R}_i \quad \mathbf{X}_i\mathbf{\Pi}^*)$ in its ith row, and $\tilde{\mathbf{S}}$ be its estimated value. An OLS procedure can be applied to (9.5). The two-stage estimate is thus

$$\hat{\mathbf{\Theta}}_1 = (\tilde{\mathbf{S}}'\tilde{\mathbf{S}})^{-1}\tilde{\mathbf{S}}'\mathbf{Y}. \tag{9.11}$$

This two-stage method is similar to Theil's two-stage least squares method (1971) and was used in Heckman (1976, 1977). Amemiya GLS estimate derived from (9.8) is

$$\hat{\mathbf{\Theta}}_1^A = (\tilde{\mathbf{Z}}'\tilde{\mathbf{\Omega}}_\xi^{-1}\tilde{\mathbf{Z}})^{-1}\tilde{\mathbf{Z}}'\tilde{\mathbf{\Omega}}'^{-1}_\xi\hat{\mathbf{c}}, \tag{9.12}$$

where $\mathbf{Z} = [\mathbf{J}_1 \quad \mathbf{\Pi}^*]$, $\mathbf{\Omega}_\xi$ is the variance matrix of ξ, and $\tilde{\mathbf{Z}}$ and $\tilde{\mathbf{\Omega}}_\xi$ are their estimated values.

Using the two-equation Nelson-Olson and Heckman models, Amemiya derived the asymptotic variance matrices for $\hat{\mathbf{\Theta}}_1$ and $\hat{\mathbf{\Theta}}_1^A$. He also gave separate proofs in the two models that $\hat{\mathbf{\Theta}}_1^A$ is more efficient than $\hat{\mathbf{\Theta}}_1$. For our model the asymptotic covariance matrices are quite lengthy but can be derived in a straightforward manner. The interesting thing is to compare their efficiency. This follows in proposition 9.2.

PROPOSITION 9.2: For equation (9.3) with observable continuous variable Y_i the estimate $\hat{\mathbf{\Theta}}_1^A$ in (9.12) is asymptotically more efficient than the estimate $\hat{\mathbf{\Theta}}_1$ in (9.11).

PROOF: Let $\mathbf{P} = [\mathbf{X}\delta_{11}, \ldots, \mathbf{X}\delta_{1M}]$, $\mathbf{\Theta}_2' = (\mathbf{\Pi}_1^{*\prime}, \ldots, \mathbf{\Pi}_M^{*\prime})$, where $\boldsymbol{\delta}_1' = [\delta_{11}, \ldots, \delta_{1M}]$ and $\mathbf{\Pi}^* = (\mathbf{\Pi}_1^*, \ldots, \mathbf{\Pi}_M^*)$. Denote the asymptotic variance matrix of $\hat{\mathbf{\Theta}}_2' = (\hat{\mathbf{\Pi}}_1^{*\prime}, \ldots, \hat{\mathbf{\Pi}}_M^{*\prime})$ by $\mathbf{V}_{\mathbf{\Theta}_2}$ and the asymptotic covariance of $\hat{\mathbf{\Theta}}_2$ and v by $\mathbf{E}_1$. From (9.5) it is obvious that the variance matrix of $\hat{\mathbf{\Theta}}_1$ is

$$\mathbf{V}_{\mathbf{\Theta}_1} = (\mathbf{S}'\mathbf{S})^{-1}\mathbf{S}'\{\sigma_v^2\mathbf{I} + \mathbf{P}\mathbf{V}_{\mathbf{\Theta}_2}\mathbf{P}' - \mathbf{P}\mathbf{E}_1 - \mathbf{E}_1'\mathbf{P}'\}\mathbf{S}(\mathbf{S}'\mathbf{S})^{-1}.$$

The asymptotic variance matrix of $\hat{\mathbf{\Theta}}_1^A$ is

$$\mathbf{V}_{\mathbf{\Theta}_1{}^A} = (\mathbf{Z}'\mathbf{\Omega}_\xi^{-1}\mathbf{Z})^{-1}.$$

To compare $\mathbf{V}_{\mathbf{\Theta}_1}$ and $\mathbf{V}_{\mathbf{\Theta}_1{}^A}$, one notes from (9.8) that

$$\mathbf{\Omega}_\xi = [\mathbf{I} - \mathbf{P}_1]\begin{bmatrix} \sigma_v^2(\mathbf{X}'\mathbf{X})^{-1} & (\mathbf{X}'\mathbf{X})^{-1}\mathbf{X}'\mathbf{E}_1' \\ * & \mathbf{V}_{\mathbf{\Theta}_2} \end{bmatrix}\begin{bmatrix} \mathbf{I} \\ -\mathbf{P}_1' \end{bmatrix},$$

where $\mathbf{P}_1 = \boldsymbol{\delta}_1' \otimes \mathbf{I}$, $\otimes$ being the Kronecker product. Since $\mathbf{P} = \mathbf{X}\mathbf{P}_1$ and $\mathbf{S} = \mathbf{X}\mathbf{Z}$,

$$\begin{aligned}\mathbf{V}_{\mathbf{\Theta}_1} &= (\mathbf{Z}'\mathbf{X}'\mathbf{X}\mathbf{Z})^{-1}\mathbf{Z}'\mathbf{X}'\{\sigma_v^2\mathbf{I} + \mathbf{X}\mathbf{P}_1\mathbf{V}_{\mathbf{\Theta}_2}\mathbf{P}_1'\mathbf{X}' - \mathbf{X}\mathbf{P}_1\mathbf{E}_1 \\ &\quad - \mathbf{E}_1'\mathbf{P}_1'\mathbf{X}'\}\mathbf{X}\mathbf{Z}(\mathbf{Z}'\mathbf{X}'\mathbf{X}\mathbf{Z})^{-1} \\ &= (\mathbf{Z}'\mathbf{X}'\mathbf{X}\mathbf{Z})^{-1}\mathbf{Z}'\mathbf{X}'\mathbf{X}\mathbf{\Omega}_\xi\mathbf{X}'\mathbf{X}\mathbf{Z}(\mathbf{Z}'\mathbf{X}'\mathbf{X}\mathbf{Z})^{-1}.\end{aligned}$$

It follows $\mathbf{V}_{\mathbf{\Theta}_1} - \mathbf{V}_{\mathbf{\Theta}_1{}^A}$ is nonnegative definite, and $\hat{\mathbf{\Theta}}_1^A$ is more efficient.

It is interesting to note that the proposition holds no matter how $\hat{\mathbf{\Theta}}_2$ is derived so far as the asymptotic variance $\hat{\mathbf{\Theta}}_2 - \mathbf{\Theta}_2$ exists and $\hat{\mathbf{\Theta}}_2$ is consistent.

9.5 Structural Equations with Censored Dependent Variables

The last $G - G_3$ equations belong to this category. The variable Y_i is censored. When $\mathbf{S}_l^*$ and its complement set $\mathbf{S}_l/\mathbf{S}_l^*$ are nonempty, there are switching systems. For the variable Y in $\mathbf{S}_l^*$ which is observed when $Y_{G_2+l,i} > 0$, based on observed subsamples, equation (9.4) can be rewritten

$$Y_i = \mathbf{R}_i\boldsymbol{\delta}_0 + (\mathbf{X}_i\mathbf{\Pi}^*)\boldsymbol{\delta}_1 + \lambda\frac{\phi(\mathbf{X}_i\boldsymbol{\alpha})}{\Phi(\mathbf{X}_i\boldsymbol{\alpha})} + \xi_i, \tag{9.13}$$

where $E(\xi_i \mid I_i = 1) = 0$, I_i is the dichotomous indicator of the underlying latent variable that activates the censoring, and $\boldsymbol{\alpha}$ is the reduced form parameters of that latent variable. The two-stage estimator is to find $\boldsymbol{\alpha}$ and $\mathbf{\Pi}^*$ in the first stage from probit maximum likelihood and similar equations in (9.19) and estimate $\mathbf{\Theta}_1' = (\boldsymbol{\delta}_0', \boldsymbol{\delta}_1', \lambda)$ in the second stage from

$$Y_i = \mathbf{R}_i\boldsymbol{\delta}_0 + (\mathbf{X}_i\hat{\mathbf{\Pi}}^*)\boldsymbol{\delta}_1 + \lambda\frac{\phi(\mathbf{X}_i\hat{\boldsymbol{\alpha}})}{\Phi(\mathbf{X}_i\hat{\boldsymbol{\alpha}})} + \eta_i, \tag{9.14}$$

where

$$\eta_i = \xi_i - \lambda\left(\frac{\phi(\mathbf{X}_i\hat{\boldsymbol{\alpha}})}{\Phi(\mathbf{X}_i\hat{\boldsymbol{\alpha}})} - \frac{\phi(\mathbf{X}_i\boldsymbol{\alpha})}{\Phi(\mathbf{X}_i\boldsymbol{\alpha})}\right) - \mathbf{X}_i(\hat{\mathbf{\Pi}}^* - \mathbf{\Pi}^*)\boldsymbol{\delta}_1.$$

For the variable Y in $\mathbf{S}_l/\mathbf{S}_l^*$, (9.14) should be modified to

$$Y_i = \mathbf{R}_i\boldsymbol{\delta}_0 + (\mathbf{X}_i\hat{\mathbf{\Pi}}^*)\boldsymbol{\delta}_1 + \lambda\frac{\phi(\mathbf{X}_i\hat{\boldsymbol{\alpha}})}{1 - \Phi(\mathbf{X}_i\hat{\boldsymbol{\alpha}})} + \eta_i, \tag{9.15}$$

where

$$\eta_i = \xi_i - \lambda\left(\frac{\phi(\mathbf{X}_i\hat{\boldsymbol{\alpha}})}{1 - \Phi(\mathbf{X}_i\hat{\boldsymbol{\alpha}})} - \frac{\phi(\mathbf{X}_i\boldsymbol{\alpha})}{1 - \Phi(\mathbf{X}_i\boldsymbol{\alpha})}\right) - \mathbf{X}_i(\hat{\mathbf{\Pi}}^* - \mathbf{\Pi}^*)\boldsymbol{\delta}_1.$$

All these expressions can be represented as

$$Y_i = \mathbf{R}_i\boldsymbol{\delta}_0 + (\mathbf{X}_i\hat{\mathbf{\Pi}}^*)\boldsymbol{\delta}_1 + \lambda G(\mathbf{X}_i\hat{\boldsymbol{\alpha}}) + \eta_i, \tag{9.16}$$

where $G(\mathbf{X}_i\boldsymbol{\alpha})$ is a nonlinear function of $\mathbf{X}_i\boldsymbol{\alpha}$ and

$$\eta_i = \xi_i - \lambda(G(\mathbf{X}_i\hat{\boldsymbol{\alpha}}) - G(\mathbf{X}_i\boldsymbol{\alpha})) - \mathbf{X}_i(\hat{\mathbf{\Pi}}^* - \mathbf{\Pi}^*)\boldsymbol{\delta}_1.$$

Let $\mathbf{S} = [\mathbf{R} \quad \overline{\mathbf{X\Pi}^*} \quad \mathbf{G}]$ and $\tilde{\mathbf{S}}$ be its estimated value, where $\mathbf{G}$ is the vector consisted of $G(\mathbf{X}_i\boldsymbol{\alpha})$. The two-stage estimator $\hat{\mathbf{\Theta}}_1$ from (9.16) is

$$\hat{\mathbf{\Theta}}_1 = (\tilde{\mathbf{S}}'\tilde{\mathbf{S}})^{-1}\tilde{\mathbf{S}}'\mathbf{Y}. \tag{9.17}$$

Let $\mathbf{P} = \mathbf{X}(\boldsymbol{\delta}_1' \otimes \mathbf{I})$ and $\rho = \xi - \lambda\mathbf{D}_1(\hat{\boldsymbol{\alpha}} - \boldsymbol{\alpha})$, where $\mathbf{D}_1$ is the gradient matrix of G evaluated at $\boldsymbol{\alpha}$. The asymptotic covariance matrix can be derived from

$$\hat{\mathbf{\Theta}}_1 - \mathbf{\Theta}_1 \triangleq (\tilde{\mathbf{S}}'\tilde{\mathbf{S}})^{-1}\tilde{\mathbf{S}}'(\rho - \mathbf{P}(\hat{\mathbf{\Theta}}_2 - \mathbf{\Theta}_2)). \tag{9.18}$$

To derive the Amemiya's GLS, one has to estimate the reduced form parameter $\mathbf{c}' = (\mathbf{c}_1', \mathbf{c}_2')$ for Y_i from

$$Y_i = \mathbf{X}_i\mathbf{c}_1 + G(\mathbf{X}_i\hat{\boldsymbol{\alpha}})\mathbf{c}_2 + \rho_i. \tag{9.19}$$

It is $\hat{\mathbf{c}} = (\mathbf{W}'\mathbf{W})^{-1}\mathbf{W}'\mathbf{Y}$, where $\mathbf{W} = [\mathbf{X} \quad \mathbf{G}]$. Let $\mathbf{Z} = [\mathbf{J}_1 \quad \mathbf{J}_2\mathbf{\Pi}^* \quad \mathbf{J}_3]$ be defined from $\mathbf{S} = \mathbf{W}[\mathbf{J}_1 \quad \mathbf{J}_2\mathbf{\Pi}^* \quad \mathbf{J}_3]$. The GLS derived from Amemiya's principle is

$$\hat{\mathbf{\Theta}}_1{}^A = (\tilde{\mathbf{Z}}'\tilde{\mathbf{\Omega}}_\omega^{-1}\tilde{\mathbf{Z}})^{-1}\tilde{\mathbf{Z}}'\tilde{\mathbf{\Omega}}_\omega^{-1}\hat{\mathbf{c}}, \tag{9.20}$$

where $\mathbf{\Omega}_\omega$ is the asymptotic covariance matrix of $\omega = \hat{\mathbf{c}} - \mathbf{c} + \mathbf{J}_2(\mathbf{\Pi}^* - \hat{\mathbf{\Pi}}^*)\boldsymbol{\delta}_1$. The comparisons of $\hat{\mathbf{\Theta}}_1$ and $\hat{\mathbf{\Theta}}_1^A$ follow from proposition 9.3.

PROPOSITION 9.3: In the equation with censored dependent variable Y_i, the GLS estimate (9.20) derived from Amemiya's principle is asymptotically more efficient than the two-stage estimator $\hat{\mathbf{\Theta}}_1$ in (9.17)

PROOF: From (9.18) the asymptotic covariance matrix of $\hat{\mathbf{\Theta}}_1$ is

$$\mathbf{V}_{\mathbf{\Theta}_1} = (\mathbf{Z}'\mathbf{W}'\mathbf{W}\mathbf{Z})^{-1}\mathbf{Z}'\mathbf{W}'(\mathbf{V}_\rho + \mathbf{P}\mathbf{V}_{\mathbf{\Theta}_2}\mathbf{P}' - \mathbf{P}\mathbf{E} - \mathbf{E}'\mathbf{P}')\mathbf{W}\mathbf{Z}(\mathbf{Z}'\mathbf{W}'\mathbf{W}\mathbf{Z})^{-1},$$

where $\mathbf{V}_{\boldsymbol{\rho}}$ is the asymptotic variance matrix of $\boldsymbol{\rho}$, $\mathbf{E}$ is the asymptotic covariance matrix of $\hat{\mathbf{\Theta}}_2 - \mathbf{\Theta}_2$ and $\boldsymbol{\rho}$. On the other hand, $\mathbf{V}_{\mathbf{\Theta}_1^A} = (\mathbf{Z}'\mathbf{\Omega}_\omega^{-1}\mathbf{Z})^{-1}$ from (9.20). Since $\hat{\mathbf{c}} - \mathbf{c} \triangleq (\mathbf{W}'\mathbf{W})^{-1}\mathbf{W}'\boldsymbol{\rho}$, it implies

$$\begin{aligned}\mathbf{\Omega}_\omega = {} & (\mathbf{W}'\mathbf{W})^{-1}\mathbf{W}'\mathbf{V}_\rho\mathbf{W}(\mathbf{W}'\mathbf{W})^{-1} + \mathbf{J}_2(\boldsymbol{\delta}_1' \otimes \mathbf{I})\mathbf{V}_{\theta_2}(\boldsymbol{\delta}_1 \otimes \mathbf{I})\mathbf{J}_2' \\ & - \mathbf{J}_2(\boldsymbol{\delta}_1' \otimes \mathbf{I})\mathbf{E}\mathbf{W}(\mathbf{W}'\mathbf{W})^{-1} - (\mathbf{W}'\mathbf{W})^{-1}\mathbf{W}'\mathbf{E}'(\boldsymbol{\delta}_1 \otimes \mathbf{I})\mathbf{J}_2'.\end{aligned}$$

Since $\mathbf{P} = \mathbf{W}\mathbf{J}_2(\boldsymbol{\delta}_1' \otimes \mathbf{I})$, $\mathbf{V}_{\mathbf{\Theta}_1}$ can be rewritten as

$$\mathbf{V}_{\mathbf{\Theta}_1} = (\mathbf{Z}'\mathbf{W}'\mathbf{W}\mathbf{Z})^{-1}\mathbf{Z}'\mathbf{W}'\mathbf{W}\mathbf{\Omega}_\omega\mathbf{W}'\mathbf{W}\mathbf{Z}(\mathbf{Z}'\mathbf{W}'\mathbf{W}\mathbf{Z})^{-1}.$$

It follows that $\mathbf{V}_{\mathbf{\Theta}_1} - \mathbf{V}_{\mathbf{\Theta}_1^A}$ is nonnegative definite.

It is interesting to point out that this conclusion applies not only to the censored dependent variables in (9.14) and (9.15) but also to other models. Amemiya (1977b) derives the asymptotic covariance matrix for a two-equation Heckman model with structural shift but fails to apply his principle to that model. Consider the following equation with structural shift;

$$Y_{2i} = \mathbf{R}_i\boldsymbol{\delta}_0 + Y_{1i}\delta_1 + I_i\delta_2 + \varepsilon_i, \tag{9.21}$$

where Y_{1i} is an unobservable latent variable with dichotomous realization I_i and Y_{2i} is an observable continuous variable. From the reduced form equation for Y_{1i},

$$Y_{1i} = \mathbf{X}_i\mathbf{c} + u_i. \tag{9.22}$$

Equation (9.21) is modified to

$$Y_{2i} = \mathbf{R}_i\boldsymbol{\delta}_0 + (\mathbf{X}_i\mathbf{c})\delta_1 + \Phi(\mathbf{X}_i\mathbf{c})\delta_2 + \xi_i, \tag{9.23}$$

where Φ is standard normal c.d.f. With consistent estimates $\hat{\mathbf{c}}$ available, Heckman's two-stage estimator for $\mathbf{\Theta}_1' = (\boldsymbol{\delta}_0', \boldsymbol{\delta}_1', \boldsymbol{\delta}_2)$ is derived by least squares applied to

$$Y_{2i} = \mathbf{R}_i\boldsymbol{\delta}_0 + (\mathbf{X}_i\hat{\mathbf{c}})\delta_1 + \Phi(\mathbf{X}_i\hat{\mathbf{c}})\delta_2 + \eta_i. \tag{9.24}$$

It is obvious that equation (9.24) is a special case of (9.16). Hence it is possible to apply Amemiya's principle to equation (9.21), and more efficient estimates can be derived.

9.6 Structural Equations with Tobit Structure

This is the case where Y_i in (9.3) is limited dependent. Equations $G_1 + 1, \ldots, G_2$ in the general model (9.2) are in this category. A two-stage estimator $\hat{\boldsymbol{\Theta}}_1$ was proposed by Nelson and Olson (1977). This estimation method can be generalized to our model. The two-stage estimators are derived by maximizing the following function:

$$\ln L(\boldsymbol{\Theta}_1) = \sum_{i=1}^{N} \left\{ -\frac{1}{2} I_i \ln \sigma_v^2 - \frac{1}{2\sigma^2} I_i (Y_i - \mathbf{R}_i \boldsymbol{\delta}_0 - (\mathbf{X}_i \hat{\boldsymbol{\Pi}}^*) \boldsymbol{\delta}_1)^2 \right.$$

$$\left. + (1 - I_i) \ln (1 - \Phi(\mathbf{R}_i \boldsymbol{\delta}_0 + (\mathbf{X}_i \hat{\boldsymbol{\Pi}}^*) \boldsymbol{\delta}_1)) \right\}. \tag{9.25}$$

Define

$$a_{11i} = \frac{\dfrac{S_i \Theta_1}{\sigma_v} \phi_i - \dfrac{\phi_i^2}{1 - \Phi_i} - \Phi_i}{\sigma_v^2},$$

$$a_{22i} = \frac{1}{4\sigma_v^4} \left(\phi_i \left(\frac{S_i \Theta_1}{\sigma_v} \right)^3 + \frac{S_i \Theta_1}{\sigma_v} \phi_i - \left(\frac{S_i \Theta_1}{\sigma_v} \right)^2 \frac{\phi_i^2}{1 - \Phi_i} - 2\Phi_i \right),$$

$$a_{12i} = \frac{-\phi_i}{2\sigma_v^3} \left(\left(\frac{S_i \Theta_1}{\sigma_v^2} \right)^2 + 1 - \frac{S_i \Theta_1}{\sigma_v} \frac{\phi_i}{1 - \Phi_i} \right),$$

where $S_i = [\mathbf{R}_i \mathbf{X}_i \boldsymbol{\Pi}^*]$ and $\boldsymbol{\Theta}_1' = (\boldsymbol{\delta}_0', \boldsymbol{\delta}_1')$.

Let $\mathbf{A}_{ij}$ be the $N \times N$ diagonal matrix whose kth diagonal element is a_{ijk}, $i, j = 1, 2$, and

$$\mathbf{A} = \begin{bmatrix} \mathbf{A}_{11} & \mathbf{A}_{12} \\ \mathbf{A}_{12} & \mathbf{A}_{22} \end{bmatrix}.$$

It is easy to show that

$$E\left(\frac{\partial^2 \ln L(\boldsymbol{\Theta}_1)}{\partial \boldsymbol{\Theta}_1 \partial \boldsymbol{\Theta}_1'} \right) = \mathbf{Z}^{*\prime} \mathbf{X}^{*\prime} \mathbf{A} \mathbf{X}^* \mathbf{Z}^*,$$

$$E\left(\frac{\partial^2 \ln L(\boldsymbol{\Theta}_1, \boldsymbol{\Theta}_2)}{\partial \boldsymbol{\Theta}_1 \partial \boldsymbol{\Theta}_2'} \right) = -\mathbf{Z}^{*\prime} \mathbf{X}^{*\prime} \mathbf{A} \mathbf{P}^*,$$

and

$$\frac{\partial \ln L(\mathbf{\Theta}_1)}{\partial \mathbf{\Theta}_1} = \mathbf{Z}^{*\prime}\mathbf{X}^*\mathbf{u},$$

where

$$\mathbf{X}^* = \begin{bmatrix} \mathbf{X} & \mathbf{0} \\ \mathbf{0} & \mathbf{l} \end{bmatrix}, \quad \mathbf{Z}^* = \begin{bmatrix} \mathbf{Z} & \mathbf{0} \\ \mathbf{0} & \mathbf{1} \end{bmatrix}, \quad \mathbf{P}^* = \begin{bmatrix} \mathbf{P} \\ \mathbf{0} \end{bmatrix}, \quad \mathbf{P} = \mathbf{X}\mathbf{P}_1, \quad \mathbf{P}_1 = \delta_1' \otimes \mathbf{I},$$

$\mathbf{l}$ is $N \times 1$ vector with unity in all the components, $\mathbf{0}$ is the appropriate zero matrix, or vector, and $\mathbf{u}$ is a $2N \times 1$ vector,

$$\mathbf{u}' = \Bigg[\frac{1}{\sigma_v}\frac{\phi_1}{1-\Phi_1}(1-I_1) + \frac{1}{\sigma_v^2}I_1 v_1, \ldots, \frac{1}{\sigma_v}\frac{\phi_N}{1-\Phi_N}(1-I_N) + \frac{1}{\sigma_v^2}I_N v_N,$$

$$\frac{S_1\Theta_1}{2\sigma_v^3}\frac{\phi_1}{1-\Phi_1}(1-I_1) - \frac{1}{2\sigma_v^2}I_1 + \frac{1}{2\sigma_v^4}I_1 v_1^2,$$

$$\ldots, \frac{S_N\Theta_N}{2\sigma_v^3}\frac{\phi_N}{1-\Phi_N}(1-I_N) - \frac{1}{2\sigma_v^2}I_N + \frac{1}{2\sigma_v^4}I_N v_N^2\Bigg].$$

It follows from the Taylor series expansion

$$\hat{\mathbf{\Theta}}_1 - \mathbf{\Theta}_1 \triangleq \mathbf{L}_1[\mathbf{Z}^{*\prime}\mathbf{X}^{*\prime}\mathbf{A}\mathbf{X}^*\mathbf{Z}^*]^{-1}(\mathbf{Z}^{*\prime}\mathbf{X}^{*\prime}\mathbf{u} - \mathbf{Z}^{*\prime}\mathbf{X}^{*\prime}\mathbf{A}\mathbf{P}^*(\hat{\mathbf{\Theta}}_2 - \mathbf{\Theta}_2)), \tag{9.26}$$

where $\mathbf{L}_1 = [\mathbf{I}, \mathbf{0}]$ is an identity matrix augmented with a column of zeros. The detailed expression for $\mathbf{V}_{\mathbf{\Theta}_1}$ is quite lengthy but can be derived in a straightforward manner as in Amemiya (1977a).

With consistent estimator $\hat{\mathbf{\Theta}}_2$ from the first stage and $\hat{\mathbf{c}}$ from the tobit maximum likelihood, one can compare the two-stage estimate in (9.26) with Amemiya's generalized least squares estimate $\hat{\mathbf{\Theta}}_1^A$.

PROPOSITION 9.4: For equation (9.3) with limited dependent variable Y_i, the two-stage estimator $\hat{\mathbf{\Theta}}_1$ derived by maximizing equation (9.25) is asymptotically less efficient than $\hat{\mathbf{\Theta}}_1^A$.

PROOF: From (9.26) the asymptotic variance of $\hat{\mathbf{\Theta}}_1$ is

$$\begin{aligned}\mathbf{V}_{\mathbf{\Theta}_1} = {} & \mathbf{L}_1(\mathbf{Z}^{*\prime}\mathbf{X}^{*\prime}\mathbf{A}\mathbf{X}^*\mathbf{Z}^*)^{-1}\mathbf{Z}^{*\prime}\mathbf{X}^{*\prime}\mathbf{A}\mathbf{X}^*\{(\mathbf{X}^{*\prime}\mathbf{A}\mathbf{X}^*)^{-1} \\ & + \mathbf{P}_1^*\mathbf{V}_{\theta_2}\mathbf{P}_1^{*\prime} - (\mathbf{X}^{*\prime}\mathbf{A}\mathbf{X}^*)^{-1}\mathbf{X}^{*\prime}\mathbf{E}\mathbf{P}_1^* \\ & - \mathbf{P}_1^*\mathbf{E}'\mathbf{X}^*(\mathbf{X}^{*\prime}\mathbf{A}\mathbf{X}^*)^{-1}\}\mathbf{X}^{*\prime}\mathbf{A}\mathbf{X}^*\mathbf{Z}^*(\mathbf{Z}^{*\prime}\mathbf{X}^{*\prime}\mathbf{A}\mathbf{X}^*\mathbf{Z}^*)^{-1}\mathbf{L}_1',\end{aligned}$$

where $\mathbf{P}_1^* = \left[\begin{smallmatrix}\mathbf{P}_1\\ \mathbf{0}\end{smallmatrix}\right]$ and $\mathbf{E}$ is the asymptotic covariance matrix of $\mathbf{u}$ and $(\hat{\mathbf{\Theta}}_2 - \mathbf{\Theta}_2)'$. To compare the asymptotic variance of $\hat{\mathbf{\Theta}}_1^A$, one notes that $\hat{\mathbf{c}}$ is a tobit maximum likelihood estimate, and hence

$$\hat{\mathbf{c}} - \mathbf{c} \stackrel{\Delta}{=} -\mathbf{L}_2(\mathbf{X}^{*\prime}\mathbf{A}\mathbf{X}^*)^{-1}\mathbf{X}^{*\prime}\mathbf{u},$$

where $\mathbf{L}_2$ is an appropriate identity matrix augmented with a zero column.

It follows that the asymptotic variance of $\hat{\mathbf{\Theta}}_1^A$ is

$$\mathbf{V}_{\mathbf{\Theta}_1{}^A} = (\mathbf{Z}'\mathbf{\Omega}_\xi^{-1}\mathbf{Z})^{-1},$$

where

$$\begin{aligned}\mathbf{\Omega}_\xi = {} & \mathbf{L}_2(\mathbf{X}^{*\prime}\mathbf{A}\mathbf{X}^*)^{-1}\mathbf{L}_2' + \mathbf{P}_1\mathbf{V}_{\mathbf{\Theta}_2}\mathbf{P}_1' - \mathbf{P}_1\mathbf{E}'\mathbf{X}^*(\mathbf{X}^{*\prime}\mathbf{A}\mathbf{X}^*)^{-1}\mathbf{L}_2' \\ & - \mathbf{L}_2(\mathbf{X}^{*\prime}\mathbf{A}\mathbf{X}^*)^{-1}\mathbf{X}^{*\prime}\mathbf{E}\mathbf{P}_1'.\end{aligned}$$

To compare $\mathbf{V}_{\mathbf{\Theta}_1}$ with $\mathbf{V}_{\mathbf{\Theta}_1{}^A}$, one has to evaluate $\mathbf{L}_1(\mathbf{Z}^{*\prime}\mathbf{X}^{*\prime}\mathbf{A}\mathbf{X}^*\mathbf{Z}^*)^{-1}$ and $\mathbf{L}_2(\mathbf{X}^{*\prime}\mathbf{A}\mathbf{X}^*)^{-1}\mathbf{L}_2'$. This can be done with the well-known formulas for finding the inverse of a partitioned matrix: let

$$\mathbf{B} = \mathbf{A}_{11} - \mathbf{A}_{12}\mathbf{l}(\mathbf{l}'\mathbf{A}_{22}\mathbf{l})^{-1}\mathbf{l}'\mathbf{A}_{21}.$$

It is easy to check that the following equalities hold:

$$\begin{gathered}\mathbf{L}_1(\mathbf{Z}^{*\prime}\mathbf{X}^{*\prime}\mathbf{A}\mathbf{X}^*\mathbf{Z}^*)^{-1} = \\ (\mathbf{Z}'\mathbf{X}'\mathbf{B}\mathbf{X}\mathbf{Z})^{-1}[\mathbf{I} - \mathbf{Z}'\mathbf{X}'\mathbf{A}_{12}\mathbf{l}(\mathbf{l}'\mathbf{A}_{22}\mathbf{l})^{-1}];\end{gathered} \tag{9.27}$$

$$\begin{gathered}\mathbf{L}_2(\mathbf{X}^{*\prime}\mathbf{A}\mathbf{X}^*)^{-1} = \\ (\mathbf{X}'\mathbf{B}\mathbf{X})^{-1}[\mathbf{I} - \mathbf{Z}'\mathbf{X}'\mathbf{A}_{12}\mathbf{l}(\mathbf{l}'\mathbf{A}_{22}\mathbf{l})^{-1}];\end{gathered} \tag{9.28}$$

$$\begin{gathered}\mathbf{L}_2(\mathbf{X}^{*\prime}\mathbf{A}\mathbf{X}^*)^{-1}\mathbf{X}^{*\prime} = \\ (\mathbf{X}'\mathbf{B}\mathbf{X})^{-1}[\mathbf{X}' - \mathbf{Z}'\mathbf{X}'\mathbf{A}_{12}\mathbf{l}(\mathbf{l}'\mathbf{A}_{22}\mathbf{l})^{-1}\mathbf{l}'];\end{gathered} \tag{9.29}$$

$$[\mathbf{I} - \mathbf{Z}'\mathbf{X}'\mathbf{A}_{12}\mathbf{l}(\mathbf{l}'\mathbf{A}_{22}\mathbf{l})^{-1}]\mathbf{Z}^{*\prime}\mathbf{X}^{*\prime}\mathbf{A}\mathbf{X}^{*\prime}\mathbf{P}_1^* = \mathbf{Z}'\mathbf{X}'\mathbf{B}\mathbf{X}\mathbf{P}_1; \tag{9.30}$$

$$[\mathbf{I} - \mathbf{Z}'\mathbf{X}'\mathbf{A}_{12}\mathbf{l}(\mathbf{l}'\mathbf{A}_{22}\mathbf{l})^{-1}]\mathbf{Z}^{*\prime}\mathbf{X}^{*\prime} = \mathbf{Z}'\mathbf{X}'\mathbf{B}\mathbf{X}\mathbf{L}_2(\mathbf{X}^{*\prime}\mathbf{A}\mathbf{X}^*)^{-1}\mathbf{X}^{*\prime}. \tag{9.31}$$

It follows from (9.27) through (9.31) that

$$\mathbf{V}_{\mathbf{\Theta}_1} = (\mathbf{Z}'\mathbf{X}'\mathbf{B}\mathbf{X}\mathbf{Z})^{-1}\mathbf{Z}'\mathbf{X}'\mathbf{B}\mathbf{X}\mathbf{\Omega}_\xi\mathbf{X}'\mathbf{B}\mathbf{X}\mathbf{Z}(\mathbf{Z}'\mathbf{X}'\mathbf{B}\mathbf{X}\mathbf{Z})^{-1},$$

and hence $\mathbf{V}_{\mathbf{\Theta}_1} - \mathbf{V}_{\mathbf{\Theta}_1{}^A}$ is nonnegative definite.

9.7 Switching and Censored Models with Sample Separation Information

Switching and censored simultaneous equations systems with sample separation are special cases of the general model introduced in section 9.2. These models correspond to the cases in which $G_2 = 0$, $G_3 = 1$, $\mathbf{S}_1 = \{G_3 + 1, \ldots, G\}$, and the unobserved latent variable Y_1 does not appear explicitly in other equations. The system is a switching simultaneous equation model when $\mathbf{S}_1^*$ is nonempty; $\mathbf{S}_1^* \neq \mathbf{S}_1$, the endogenous variables in $\mathbf{S}_1^*$ and $\mathbf{S}_1/\mathbf{S}_1^*$, form a complete simultaneous equation system in each regime; and the endogenous variables in one regime do not appear in another one. This switching simultaneous equation model differs from the models studied in Goldfeld and Quandt (1972, 1973, 1976), since the sample separation information is available.[2] The censored simultaneous equation model introduced by Heckman (1974, 1976) can also be regarded as a special case in which either $\mathbf{S}_1^*$ is empty or $\mathbf{S}_1^* = \mathbf{S}_1$.

In this section we would consider procedures such as two-stage least squares, instrumental variables methods, and Amemiya's principle in the estimation of single structural equations in the system.[3] For each structural equation (9.3) in regime $\mathbf{S}_1^*$, based on observed subsamples corresponding to that regime, equation (9.3) can be rewritten as

$$Y_i = \mathbf{R}_i\boldsymbol{\delta}_0 + \mathbf{Y}_i^*\boldsymbol{\delta}_1 + \lambda\frac{\phi(\mathbf{X}_i\boldsymbol{\alpha})}{\Phi(\mathbf{X}_i\boldsymbol{\alpha})} + \varepsilon_i^*, \tag{9.32}$$

where $E(\varepsilon_i^* \mid I_i = 1) = 0$. For the structural equation in the other regime

$$Y_i = \mathbf{R}_i\boldsymbol{\delta}_0 + \mathbf{Y}_i^*\boldsymbol{\delta}_1 + \lambda\frac{\phi(\mathbf{X}_i\boldsymbol{\alpha})}{1 - \Phi(\mathbf{X}_i\boldsymbol{\alpha})} + \varepsilon_i^*, \tag{9.33}$$

where $E(\varepsilon_i^* \mid I_i = 0) = 0$. These two expressions can be represented by

$$Y_i = \mathbf{R}_i\boldsymbol{\delta}_0 + \mathbf{Y}_i^*\boldsymbol{\delta}_1 + \lambda G(\mathbf{X}_i\boldsymbol{\alpha}) + \varepsilon_i^*, \tag{9.34}$$

2. These two approaches have many different aspects in identification, estimation and empirical applications. In our model the structural equations in each regime can be identified under the usual rank conditions. This is not the case when sample separation information is not available, see Goldfeld and Quandt (1975). More discussions on the value of sample separation can be found in Goldfeld and Quandt (1975), Kiefer (1978), and Lee (1977).

3. Instrumental variables methods on the estimation of usual simultaneous equation models can be found in Theil (1971), Sargan (1958), Brundy and Jorgensen (1974), and Hendry (1976).

and therefore it is enough to consider the estimation of (9.34). Let $\hat{\boldsymbol{\alpha}}$ be the probit maximum likelihood estimator of the reduced form Y_1. Equation (9.34) can be modified to

$$Y_i = \mathbf{R}_i\boldsymbol{\delta}_0 + \mathbf{Y}_i^*\boldsymbol{\delta}_1 + \lambda G(\mathbf{X}_i\boldsymbol{\alpha}) + \eta_i. \tag{9.35}$$

Let $\mathbf{H}$ be a matrix consisting of $(\mathbf{R}_i, \mathbf{Y}_i^*, G(\mathbf{X}_i\boldsymbol{\alpha}))$ as its ith row and $\tilde{\mathbf{H}}$ be its estimated value evaluated at $\hat{\boldsymbol{\alpha}}$. In matrix form equation (9.35) is

$$\mathbf{Y} = \tilde{\mathbf{H}}\boldsymbol{\Theta} + \boldsymbol{\eta}, \tag{9.36}$$

where $\boldsymbol{\Theta}' = (\boldsymbol{\delta}_0', \boldsymbol{\delta}_1', \lambda)$. The disturbances η_i in (9.36) are heteroscedastic and autocorrelated as pointed out in Lee, Maddala, and Trost (1977). There are several methods to estimate equation (9.36).

METHOD 9.1: Let $\tilde{\mathbf{X}}$ be a matrix with $(\mathbf{X}_i, G(\mathbf{X}_i\hat{\boldsymbol{\alpha}}))$ as its rows. Premultiply (9.36) by $\tilde{\mathbf{X}}$:

$$\tilde{\mathbf{X}}'\mathbf{Y} = \tilde{\mathbf{X}}'\tilde{\mathbf{H}}\boldsymbol{\Theta} + \tilde{\mathbf{X}}'\boldsymbol{\eta}. \tag{9.37}$$

This equation can then be estimated by GLS as if $\tilde{\mathbf{X}}'\tilde{\mathbf{X}}$ were the covariance matrix. The estimator is

$$\hat{\boldsymbol{\Theta}}_{(1)} = [\tilde{\mathbf{H}}'\tilde{\mathbf{X}}(\tilde{\mathbf{X}}'\tilde{\mathbf{X}})^{-1}\tilde{\mathbf{X}}'\tilde{\mathbf{H}}]^{-1}\tilde{\mathbf{H}}'\tilde{\mathbf{X}}(\tilde{\mathbf{X}}'\tilde{\mathbf{X}})^{-1}\tilde{\mathbf{X}}'\mathbf{Y},$$

with the asymptotic covariance matrix

$$V(\hat{\boldsymbol{\Theta}}_{(1)}) = [\tilde{\mathbf{H}}'\tilde{\mathbf{X}}(\tilde{\mathbf{X}}'\tilde{\mathbf{X}})^{-1}\tilde{\mathbf{X}}'\tilde{\mathbf{H}}]^{-1}\tilde{\mathbf{H}}'\tilde{\mathbf{X}}(\tilde{\mathbf{X}}'\tilde{\mathbf{X}})^{-1} \\ \tilde{\mathbf{X}}'\tilde{\mathbf{V}}_\eta\tilde{\mathbf{X}}(\tilde{\mathbf{X}}'\tilde{\mathbf{X}})^{-1}\tilde{\mathbf{X}}'\tilde{\mathbf{H}}[\tilde{\mathbf{H}}'\tilde{\mathbf{X}}(\tilde{\mathbf{X}}'\tilde{\mathbf{X}})^{-1}\tilde{\mathbf{X}}'\tilde{\mathbf{H}}]^{-1},$$

where $\mathbf{V}_\eta$ is the covariance matrix of $\boldsymbol{\eta}$ and $\tilde{\mathbf{V}}_\eta$ is a consistent estimate of $\mathbf{V}_\eta$. Method 9.1 is similar to the usual two-stage least squares procedures; this method has been discussed in Heckman (1976) and Lee et al. (1977).

METHOD 9.2: Equation (9.37) is estimated by GLS with covariance matrix $\tilde{\mathbf{X}}'\tilde{\mathbf{V}}_\eta\tilde{\mathbf{X}}$. The estimator is

$$\hat{\boldsymbol{\Theta}}_{(2)} = [\tilde{\mathbf{H}}'\tilde{\mathbf{X}}(\tilde{\mathbf{X}}'\tilde{\mathbf{V}}_\eta\tilde{\mathbf{X}})^{-1}\tilde{\mathbf{X}}'\tilde{\mathbf{H}}]^{-1}\tilde{\mathbf{H}}'\tilde{\mathbf{X}}(\tilde{\mathbf{X}}'\tilde{\mathbf{V}}_\eta\tilde{\mathbf{X}})^{-1}\tilde{\mathbf{X}}'\mathbf{Y},$$

with the asymptotic covariance matrix $V(\hat{\boldsymbol{\Theta}}_{(2)}) = [\tilde{\mathbf{H}}'\tilde{\mathbf{X}}(\tilde{\mathbf{X}}'\tilde{\mathbf{V}}_\eta\tilde{\mathbf{X}})^{-1}\tilde{\mathbf{X}}'\tilde{\mathbf{H}}]^{-1}$. Method 9.2 differs from method 9.1 in that the correct asymptotic covariance matrix of $\tilde{\mathbf{X}}'\boldsymbol{\eta}$ is used.

METHOD 9.3: Premultiply equation (9.36) by $\tilde{\mathbf{X}}'\tilde{\mathbf{V}}_\eta^{-1}$;

$$\tilde{\mathbf{X}}'\tilde{\mathbf{V}}_\eta^{-1}\mathbf{Y} = \tilde{\mathbf{X}}'\tilde{\mathbf{V}}_\eta^{-1}\tilde{\mathbf{H}}\boldsymbol{\Theta} + \tilde{\mathbf{X}}'\tilde{\mathbf{V}}_\eta^{-1}\boldsymbol{\eta}. \tag{9.38}$$

The GLS procedure is then applied to (9.38). The estimator is

$$\hat{\mathbf{\Theta}}_{(3)} = [\tilde{\mathbf{H}}'\tilde{\mathbf{V}}_{\eta}^{-1}\tilde{\mathbf{X}}(\tilde{\mathbf{X}}'\tilde{\mathbf{V}}_{\eta}^{-1}\tilde{\mathbf{X}})^{-1}\tilde{\mathbf{X}}'\tilde{\mathbf{V}}_{\eta}^{-1}\tilde{\mathbf{H}}]^{-1}\tilde{\mathbf{H}}'\tilde{\mathbf{V}}_{\eta}^{-1}\tilde{\mathbf{X}}(\tilde{\mathbf{X}}'\tilde{\mathbf{V}}_{\eta}^{-1}\tilde{\mathbf{X}})^{-1}\tilde{\mathbf{X}}'\tilde{\mathbf{V}}_{\eta}^{-1}\mathbf{Y},$$

with the asymptotic covariance matrix $V(\hat{\mathbf{\Theta}}_{(3)}) = [\tilde{\mathbf{H}}'\tilde{\mathbf{V}}_{\eta}^{-1}\tilde{\mathbf{X}}(\tilde{\mathbf{X}}'\tilde{\mathbf{V}}_{\eta}^{-1}\tilde{\mathbf{X}})^{-1}\tilde{\mathbf{X}}'\tilde{\mathbf{V}}_{\eta}^{-1}\tilde{\mathbf{H}}]^{-1}$. This method is similar to a two-stage generalized least squares procedure.

METHOD 9.4: Choose an instrumental variables matrix $\tilde{\mathbf{V}}_{\eta}^{-1}\tilde{\mathbf{X}}(\tilde{\mathbf{X}}'\tilde{\mathbf{X}})^{-1}\tilde{\mathbf{X}}'\tilde{\mathbf{H}}$. The following instrumental variables (IV) estimator can be derived;

$$\hat{\mathbf{\Theta}}_{(4)} = [\tilde{\mathbf{H}}'\tilde{\mathbf{X}}(\tilde{\mathbf{X}}'\tilde{\mathbf{X}})^{-1}\tilde{\mathbf{X}}'\tilde{\mathbf{V}}_{\eta}^{-1}\tilde{\mathbf{H}}]^{-1}\tilde{\mathbf{H}}'\tilde{\mathbf{X}}(\tilde{\mathbf{X}}'\tilde{\mathbf{X}})^{-1}\tilde{\mathbf{X}}'\tilde{\mathbf{V}}_{\eta}^{-1}\mathbf{Y}.$$

The asymptotic covariance matrix of $\hat{\mathbf{\theta}}_{(4)}$ is

$$V(\hat{\mathbf{\Theta}}_{(4)}) = [\tilde{\mathbf{H}}'\tilde{\mathbf{X}}(\tilde{\mathbf{X}}'\tilde{\mathbf{X}})^{-1}\tilde{\mathbf{X}}'\tilde{\mathbf{V}}_{\eta}^{-1}\tilde{\mathbf{H}}]^{-1}\tilde{\mathbf{H}}'\tilde{\mathbf{X}}(\tilde{\mathbf{X}}'\tilde{\mathbf{X}})^{-1}\tilde{\mathbf{X}}'\tilde{\mathbf{V}}_{\eta}^{-1}$$
$$\tilde{\mathbf{X}}(\tilde{\mathbf{X}}'\tilde{\mathbf{X}})^{-1}\tilde{\mathbf{X}}'\tilde{\mathbf{H}}[\tilde{\mathbf{H}}'\tilde{\mathbf{V}}_{\eta}^{-1}\tilde{\mathbf{X}}(\tilde{\mathbf{X}}'\tilde{\mathbf{X}})^{-1}\tilde{\mathbf{X}}'\tilde{\mathbf{H}}]^{-1}.$$

It is of interest to compare these various estimators. Since $\mathbf{H} = \tilde{\mathbf{X}}\mathbf{Z} + [\mathbf{0}, \mathbf{V}^*, \mathbf{0}]$, with $\mathbf{Z} = [\mathbf{J}_1, \mathbf{\Pi}^*, \mathbf{J}_3]$ as in (9.6), it can be easily shown that

$$\text{p}\lim \frac{1}{N_1}\tilde{\mathbf{X}}'\mathbf{H} = \text{p}\lim \frac{1}{N_1}\tilde{\mathbf{X}}'\tilde{\mathbf{X}}\mathbf{Z},$$

$$\text{p}\lim \frac{1}{N_1}\tilde{\mathbf{X}}'\mathbf{V}_{\eta}^{-1}\mathbf{H} = \text{p}\lim \frac{1}{N_1}\tilde{\mathbf{X}}'\mathbf{V}_{\eta}^{-1}\tilde{\mathbf{X}}\mathbf{Z},$$

where N_1 is the number of sample observations in the relevant regime. It follows that

$$\text{p}\lim N_1 V(\hat{\mathbf{\Theta}}_{(4)}) = \text{p}\lim N_1 V(\hat{\mathbf{\Theta}}_{(3)}) = \text{p}\lim N_1[\mathbf{Z}'\tilde{\mathbf{X}}'\mathbf{V}_{\eta}^{-1}\tilde{\mathbf{X}}\mathbf{Z}]^{-1},$$

$$\text{p}\lim N_1 V(\hat{\mathbf{\Theta}}_{(2)}) = \text{p}\lim N_1[\mathbf{Z}'\tilde{\mathbf{X}}'\tilde{\mathbf{X}}(\tilde{\mathbf{X}}'\mathbf{V}_{\eta}\tilde{\mathbf{X}})^{-1}\tilde{\mathbf{X}}'\tilde{\mathbf{X}}\mathbf{Z}]^{-1},$$

and

$$\text{p}\lim N_1 V(\hat{\mathbf{\Theta}}_{(1)}) = \text{p}\lim N_1[\mathbf{Z}'\tilde{\mathbf{X}}'\tilde{\mathbf{X}}\mathbf{Z}(\mathbf{Z}'\tilde{\mathbf{X}}'\mathbf{V}_{\eta}\tilde{\mathbf{X}}\mathbf{Z})^{-1}\mathbf{Z}'\tilde{\mathbf{X}}'\tilde{\mathbf{X}}\mathbf{Z}]^{-1}.$$

The estimators $\hat{\mathbf{\Theta}}_{(3)}$ and $\hat{\mathbf{\Theta}}_{(4)}$ are asymptotically equivalent. But from the computational point of view, $\hat{\mathbf{\Theta}}_{(4)}$ is relatively simpler. Since it is obvious that[4]

$$\mathbf{Z}'\tilde{\mathbf{X}}'\mathbf{V}_{\eta}^{-1}\tilde{\mathbf{X}}\mathbf{Z} \geq \mathbf{Z}'\tilde{\mathbf{X}}'\tilde{\mathbf{X}}(\tilde{\mathbf{X}}'\mathbf{V}_{\eta}\tilde{\mathbf{X}})^{-1}\tilde{\mathbf{X}}'\tilde{\mathbf{X}}\mathbf{Z} \geq \mathbf{Z}'\tilde{\mathbf{X}}'\tilde{\mathbf{X}}\mathbf{Z}(\mathbf{Z}'\tilde{\mathbf{X}}'\mathbf{V}_{\eta}\tilde{\mathbf{X}}\mathbf{Z})^{-1}\mathbf{Z}'\tilde{\mathbf{X}}'\tilde{\mathbf{X}}\mathbf{Z},$$

4. $\mathbf{A} \geq \mathbf{B}$ means that $\mathbf{A} - \mathbf{B}$ is nonnegative definite.

$\hat{\boldsymbol{\Theta}}_{(4)}$ and $\hat{\boldsymbol{\Theta}}_{(3)}$ are asymptotically more efficient than $\hat{\boldsymbol{\Theta}}_{(2)}$, and $\hat{\boldsymbol{\Theta}}_{(2)}$ is more efficient than $\hat{\boldsymbol{\Theta}}_{(1)}$.

The estimator $\hat{\boldsymbol{\Theta}}_{(4)}$ derived from method 9.4 has an optimal property. It is the most efficient IV estimator in the set of IV estimators in the estimation of equation (9.36). This can be shown as follows. let $\mathbf{W}$ be an arbitrary instrumental variables matrix. The corresponding IV estimator is

$$\hat{\boldsymbol{\Theta}}_W = (\mathbf{W}'\mathbf{H})^{-1}\mathbf{W}'\mathbf{Y},$$

with asymptotic covariance matrix $V(\hat{\boldsymbol{\Theta}}_W) = (\mathbf{W}'\mathbf{H})^{-1}\mathbf{W}'\mathbf{V}_\eta\mathbf{W}(\mathbf{H}'\mathbf{W})^{-1}$. Since

$$\text{p lim}\, N_1 V(\hat{\boldsymbol{\Theta}}_W) = \text{p lim}\, N_1[\mathbf{Z}'\tilde{\mathbf{X}}'\mathbf{W}(\mathbf{W}'\mathbf{V}_\eta\mathbf{W})^{-1}\mathbf{W}'\tilde{\mathbf{X}}\mathbf{Z}]^{-1}$$

and

$$\tilde{\mathbf{X}}'\mathbf{V}_\eta^{-1}\tilde{\mathbf{X}} \geq \tilde{\mathbf{X}}'\mathbf{W}(\mathbf{W}'\mathbf{V}_\eta\mathbf{W})^{-1}\mathbf{W}'\tilde{\mathbf{X}},$$

$\hat{\boldsymbol{\Theta}}_{(4)}$ is asymptotically more efficient than $\hat{\boldsymbol{\Theta}}_W$.

Now let us consider Amemiya's principle which is applied to

$$\hat{\mathbf{C}} = \tilde{\mathbf{Z}}\boldsymbol{\Theta} + \omega, \tag{9.39}$$

where $\tilde{\mathbf{Z}} = [\mathbf{J}_1 \quad \hat{\boldsymbol{\Pi}}^* \quad \mathbf{J}_3]$, with $\hat{\mathbf{C}} = (\tilde{\mathbf{X}}'\tilde{\mathbf{X}})^{-1}\tilde{\mathbf{X}}'\mathbf{Y}$ and $\hat{\boldsymbol{\Pi}}^* = (\tilde{\mathbf{X}}'\tilde{\mathbf{X}})^{-1}\tilde{\mathbf{X}}'\mathbf{Y}^*$. The GLS estimator derived from Amemiya's principle is

$$\hat{\boldsymbol{\Theta}}_G^A = (\tilde{\mathbf{Z}}'\tilde{\boldsymbol{\Omega}}_\omega^{-1}\tilde{\mathbf{Z}})^{-1}\tilde{\mathbf{Z}}'\tilde{\boldsymbol{\Omega}}_\omega^{-1}\hat{\mathbf{C}}.$$

As derived in section 9.4, $\tilde{\boldsymbol{\Omega}}_\omega = \tilde{\mathbf{X}}'\tilde{\mathbf{X}}(\tilde{\mathbf{X}}'\tilde{\mathbf{V}}_\eta\tilde{\mathbf{X}})^{-1}\tilde{\mathbf{X}}'\tilde{\mathbf{X}}$. It is obvious that $\tilde{\mathbf{X}}(\tilde{\mathbf{X}}'\tilde{\mathbf{X}})^{-1}\tilde{\mathbf{X}}'\mathbf{H} = \tilde{\mathbf{X}}\tilde{\mathbf{Z}}$. It follows $\hat{\boldsymbol{\Theta}}_G^A = \hat{\boldsymbol{\Theta}}_{(2)}$, that is Amemiya's GLS procedure is exactly method 9.2. Therefore one concludes that the estimators $\hat{\boldsymbol{\Theta}}_{(3)}$ and $\hat{\boldsymbol{\Theta}}_{(4)}$ are asymptotically more efficient than the GLS estimator derived from Amemiya's principle. Let us now analyze the OLS estimator derived from Amemiya's principle. The OLS estimator is

$$\hat{\boldsymbol{\Theta}}_L^A = (\tilde{\mathbf{Z}}'\tilde{\mathbf{Z}})^{-1}\tilde{\mathbf{Z}}'\hat{\mathbf{C}}.$$

It follows

$$\begin{aligned}\hat{\boldsymbol{\Theta}}_L^A &= [\tilde{\mathbf{Z}}'\tilde{\mathbf{X}}'\tilde{\mathbf{X}}(\tilde{\mathbf{X}}'\tilde{\mathbf{X}})^{-1}(\tilde{\mathbf{X}}'\tilde{\mathbf{X}})^{-1}\tilde{\mathbf{X}}'\tilde{\mathbf{X}}\tilde{\mathbf{Z}}]^{-1}\tilde{\mathbf{Z}}'\tilde{\mathbf{X}}'\tilde{\mathbf{X}}(\tilde{\mathbf{X}}'\tilde{\mathbf{X}})^{-1}\hat{\mathbf{C}}\\ &= [\mathbf{H}'\tilde{\mathbf{X}}(\tilde{\mathbf{X}}'\tilde{\mathbf{X}})^{-2}\tilde{\mathbf{X}}'\mathbf{H}]^{-1}\mathbf{H}'\tilde{\mathbf{X}}(\tilde{\mathbf{X}}'\tilde{\mathbf{X}})^{-2}\tilde{\mathbf{X}}'\mathbf{Y},\end{aligned}$$

which is the GLS procedure applied to 9.37 as if $(\tilde{\mathbf{X}}'\tilde{\mathbf{X}})$ is the covariance matrix. This estimator is less efficient than $\hat{\boldsymbol{\Theta}}_{(2)}$, $\hat{\boldsymbol{\Theta}}_{(3)}$, and $\hat{\boldsymbol{\Theta}}_{(4)}$, but in general $\hat{\boldsymbol{\Theta}}_L^A$ and $\hat{\boldsymbol{\Theta}}_{(1)}$ will not dominate each other.

As a final remark we would like to point out that $\hat{\boldsymbol{\theta}}_{(3)}$ and $\hat{\boldsymbol{\theta}}_{(4)}$ are computationally as simple as the GLS estimator derived from Amemiya's principle. As demonstrated in Lee et al. (1977), $\mathbf{V}_\eta$ in the first regime is a sum of two matrices;

$$\mathbf{V}_\eta = \mathbf{V}_1 + \mathbf{D}_1(\mathbf{X}'\mathbf{\Lambda}\mathbf{X})^{-1}\mathbf{D}_1',$$

where $\mathbf{V}_1$ is a diagonal matrix. Hence the following inversion relation can be used;

$$\mathbf{V}_\eta^{-1} = \mathbf{V}_1^{-1} - \mathbf{V}_1^{-1}\mathbf{D}_1(\mathbf{X}'\mathbf{\Lambda}\mathbf{X} + \mathbf{D}_1'\mathbf{V}_1^{-1}\mathbf{D}_1)^{-1}\mathbf{D}_1'\mathbf{V}_1^{-1},$$

and we do not need to invert numerically an $N_1 \times N_1$ matrix. Similarly this is true for $\mathbf{V}_u$ in the second regime.

9.8 Conclusion

We have analyzed an estimation principle of Amemiya in a general simultaneous equation model. The model consists of observable continuous endogenous variables, unobservable latent endogenous variables with dichotomous indicator, and limited and censored dependent variables in a simultaneous equation framework. This general model contains the Nelson and Olson simultaneous tobit model, the Heckman simultaneous dummy endogenous variables model, the censored simultaneous equation model, and the switching simultaneous equations models as special cases. Various consistent two-stage estimation methods are generalized. Amemiya's principles are investigated in this general model, using an arbitrary number of equations. Amemiya's generalized two-stage estimators are compared with the other two-stage estimators. It was shown that Amemiya's estimators are more efficient in all the cases. Contrary to Amemiya (1977a) his principle can also be applied to Heckman's model with structural shift. A generalized two-stage estimator derived from his principle is also found to be more efficient than Heckman's approach. The proofs are general and do not depend on a case-by-case analysis.

In the censored simultaneous equation models and switching simultaneous equation models, GLS and OLS estimators derived from Amemiya's principle can be identified as instrumental variables methods. Two estimation methods that give more efficient estimators than the GLS estimator derived from Amemiya's principle are found. These two estimators are shown to be asymptotically equivalent and are computationally simple.

References

Amemiya, T. 1974. Multivariate Regression and Simultaneous Equation Models When the Dependent Variables are Truncated Normal. *Econometrica.* 42; 999–1012.

Amemiya, T. 1976. The Specification and Estimation of A Multivariate Logit Model. Technical report 211. Institute for Mathematical Studies in the Social Sciences, Stanford University.

Amemiya, T. 1977a. The Estimation of a Simultaneous Equation Tobit Model. Technical report 236. Institute for Mathematical Studies in the Social Sciences, Stanford University. *International Economic Review*, in press.

Amemiya, T. 1977b. The Estimation of a Simultaneous Equation Generalized Probit Model. *Econometrica.* 46; 1193–1205.

Brundy, J. M., and D. W. Jorgenson. 1974. Consistent and Efficient Estimation of Systems of Simultaneous Equations by Means of Instrumental Variables. In *Frontiers in Econometrics*, ed. P. Zarembka. New York: Academic Press; pp. 215–244.

Goldfeld, S. M., and R. E. Quandt. 1972. *Nonlinear Methods in Econometrics.* Amsterdam; North-Holland.

Goldfeld, S. M., and R. E. Quandt. 1975. Estimation in a Disequilibrium Model and the Value of Information. *Journal of Econometrics.* 3; 325–348.

Goldfeld, S. M., and R. E. Quandt. 1976. Estimation of Structural Change in Simultaneous Equation Models. In *Studies in Nonlinear Estimation*, ed. S. M. Goldfeld and R. E. Quandt. Cambridge, Mass.; Ballinger, chapter 2.

Heckman, J. J. 1974. Shadow-Price Market Wages and Labor Supply. *Econometrica.* 42; 679–694.

Heckman, J. J. 1976a. The Common Structure of a Statistical Models of Truncation, Sample Selection and Limited Dependent Variables and a Simple Estimator for Such Models. *Annals of Economic and Social Measurement.* 5; 475–492.

Heckman, J. J. 1976b. Simultaneous Equation Models with Both Continuous and Discrete Endogenous Variables with and Without Structural Shift in the Equations. In *Studies in Nonlinear Estimation*, ed. S. M. Goldfeld and R. E. Quandt. Cambridge, Mass.: Ballinger.

Heckman, J. J. 1977. Dummy Endogenous Variable in a Simultaneous Equation System. *Econometrica*, in Press.

Hendry, D. F. 1976. The Structure of Simultaneous Equation Estimators. *Journal of Econometrics.* 4; 51–88.

Kiefer, N. M. 1978. On the Value of Sample Separation Information. University of Chicago. *Econometrica*, in press.

Lee, L. F. 1976. Unionism and Wage Rates: A Simultaneous Equations Model with Qualitative and Limited Dependent Variables. Discussion paper 76–77–04, University of Florida. *International Economic Review*, in press.

Lee, L. F. 1977. Identification and Estimation in Binary Choice Models with Limited Dependent Variables. Discussion paper. 77–85. Center for Economic Research, University of Minnesota. *Econometrica*, in press.

Lee, L. F., G. S., Maddala and R. P. Trost. 1977. Instrumental Variable Estimation of Simultaneous Equation System with Selectivity. *Econometrica*, in press.

Lewis, H. Gregg. 1974. Comments on Selectivity Biases in Wage Comparisons. *Journal of Political Economy*. Nov./Dec.

Maddala, G. S., and L. Lee. 1976. Recursive Models with Qualitative Endogenous Variables. *Annals of Economic and Social Measurement*. 5: 525–545.

Nelson, F. D. 1977. Censored Regression Models with Unobserved, Stochastic, Censored Thresholds. *Journal of Econometrics*. 6; 309–327.

Nelson, F. D., and L. Olson. 1977. Specification and Estimation of a Simultaneous-Equation Model with Limited Dependent Variables. Social Science Working Paper 149. California Institute of Technology. *International Economic Review*; in press.

Sargan, J. D. 1958. The Estimation of Economic Relationships Using Instrumental Variables. *Econometrica*. 26; 393–415.

Theil, H. 1971. *Principles of Econometrics*. New York: Wiley.

10 Stratification on Endogenous Variables and Estimation: The Gary Income Maintenance Experiment

Jerry A. Hausman and David A. Wise

10.1 Introduction

Unbiased parameter estimates, although illusory, are thought by many researchers to be the primary objective of empirical analysis in the social sciences in general and of econometric analysis in particular. In a technical sense unbiased estimation of the parameters of a behavioral model requires that the independent measured variables of the specification be uncorrelated with unmeasured variables not explicitly accounted for in the analysis, rather captured only in spirit through a stochastic (or error) term. We normally think of correlation between independent variables and the error term as arising from improperly excluded variables, simultaneous relationships, or inaccurately measured independent variables. But such correlation may also be artificially induced, often unintended, through sample selection. Sample selection is not always random; in fact it is often systematically nonrandom. Stratification based on endogenous variables is a prevalent example.

Individual data in the social sciences are often collected by survey. The selection of persons to be surveyed is often based on a stratified sample design, with random sampling within strata. The proportions of observations within strata—for example, defined by levels of income and education—do not necessarily reflect population proportions, as they would if the sample were selected randomly from the population at large. In general this does not pose a problem for empirical analysis based on survey data if stratification is based on exogenous variables only. That is, unbiased estimates of behavioral parameters may be obtained, for example, by standard regression techniques.[1] But often variables considered as endogenous to the model whose parameters are to be estimated are also the basis for stratification.

The research was performed pursuant to contract number HEW 100-76-0073 from the Department of Health, Education, and Welfare, Washington, D.C. The opinions and conclusions expressed herein are solely those of the authors and should not be construed as representing the opinions or policy of any agency of the United States government.

This study was part of continuing analysis of the Gary experiment at Mathematica Policy Research. The authors also acknowledge research support of the National Science Foundation. Research assistance was provided by G. Burtless. We have benefited from comments by Charles Manski, John Pratt, and Roy Radner and from the comments of two referees for this volume.

1. There may, however, be questions about extrapolation of the results beyond the sample range of independent variables.

Many major surveys, some conducted in conjunction with social experiments, are characterized by endogenous stratification.[2] The selection of participants in the New Jersey negative income tax experiment is an extreme example; see Hausman and Wise (1977a). No families with incomes greater than one and one-half times the poverty level were sampled. The income maintenance experiments in Gary and Seattle–Denver followed a less extreme selection procedure. Although higher income families were not excluded from these experiments, they were undersampled. In Gary this was particularly true of families with incomes greater than 2.4 times the poverty level. Even below that level families were grouped into intervals defined by multiples of the poverty level. Sampling proportions within the intervals did not necessarily reflect population proportions.[3]

We present in this chapter alternative methods of correcting for endogenous sampling in order to obtain consistent estimates of population parameters. If sample-versus-population proportions within strata are known, either weighted least squares or a more efficient maximum likelihood procedure may be used. If these proportions are not known, they may be estimated along with behavioral parameters using our proposed maximum likelihood procedure. Although possibly not immediately transparent, it should become clear that the methods we propose here are conceptually parallel to the estimation procedures proposed by Manski and Lerman (1977) and Manski and McFadden (chapter 1) under conditions of choice-based sampling. But our procedures are directed toward estimation with continuous endogenous variables, while theirs are directed at estimation in discrete (or qualitative) choice situations. The underlying problem—the likelihood that an observation is in the sample depends on the value of an endogenous (or outcome) variable—is the same, however.

2. The 1967 survey of economic opportunity also undersampled high income families. So did the University of Michigan panel study of income dynamics that resurveyed part of the survey of economic opportunity sample. The use of any of these data sets to estimate behavioral relationships that treat earnings or components of earnings (wages and hours worked) as endogenous variables will lead to biased and inconsistent estimates of population parameters.

3. In attempting to estimate the treatment effect of this experiment, we found that there were two potentially serious statistical problems: one was attrition and the other, sample selection. We found that either of these problems could be handled individually without undue complication but that treating them simultaneously, although conceptually straightforward, would present a somewhat complicated estimation problem. Thus we have used preexperimental (baseline) data, before attrition became a matter of concern, in this chapter. A primary goal was to see whether or not correction for sample selection

10.2 The Problem of Endogenous Sampling and Estimation Methods

We shall focus the conceptual formulation of the problem on the sample selection procedure followed in the Gary income maintenance experiment. The proposed method of estimation is in no way peculiar to this experiment.

Approximately 2,600 families were drawn at random from certain geographic areas in Gary, Indiana, for the experiment.[4] But only about 1,800 families actually participated. To select the 1,800, families were stratified by income as well as by exogenous variables. Five income intervals were defined by multiples of the poverty level, and families were selected at random from within the intervals; but the within interval totals were not intended to reflect population proportions.

While for estimation purposes it is necessary to assume a precise formulation of the sampling procedure, we do not in fact have a precise description of the process followed in the Gary experiment. Consequently we obtained approximate accounts from persons knowledgeable about the early phases of the experiment and assumed a process that we think represents a good approximation to the true procedure: (1) a family was selected at random, (2) the family was classified according to five income intervals, (3) the family was retained in the sample with some probability that depended on its income interval, and (4) this procedure was followed until a sample size of 1,800 was obtained. We assume that the 1,800 was fixed by the sample design rather than the 2,600. There are several other reasonable possibilities. We shall develop a statistical model and obtain empirical estimates based on these assumptions. Then we shall discuss other plausible procedures and statistical models that correspond to them.

lead to parameter estimates that were substantially different from those obtained without correction. We previously found that the extreme form of sample selection in the New Jersey experiment lead to seriously biased estimates of behavioral parameters (see Hausman and Wise 1976, 1977). The much less severe sampling procedure followed in the Gary experiment, however, does not seem to produce large bias in parameter estimates. Thus we have concluded that evaluation of experimental results without explicit corrections for sample selection would not in this case yield substantial inaccuracies. In particular we have in another paper proposed a method of correcting for attrition bias and have presented estimates based on it that do not at the same time correct for sample selection bias (see Hausman and Wise 1977b).

4. All the families were black, and there had to be at least one dependent under the age of 18 present in the household. The majority of the families were headed by feinales. For more detail see Kehrer et al. (1975).

We shall begin by assuming only two income intervals. Assume that in the population, income $Y = \mathbf{X}\boldsymbol{\beta} + \varepsilon$, with Y given $\mathbf{X}$ distributed normally with mean $\mathbf{X}\boldsymbol{\beta}$, variance σ^2, and density function denoted by $f(Y \mid \mathbf{X})$. Assume that below some level L a proportion P_1 of a random sample of the population is in fact sampled and above L, a proportion P_2. (Note that with purely random sampling these proportions would have expected value equal to one.) These values may be thought of as the probabilities of retaining randomly sampled values. The density function h of Y given $\mathbf{X}$ in the sample can be written as

$$h(y) = \begin{cases} \dfrac{P_1 \cdot f(y)}{P_1 \cdot Pr[Y \leq L] + P_2 \cdot Pr[Y > L]}, & \text{if } y \leq L, \\[2ex] \dfrac{P_2 \cdot f(y)}{P_1 \cdot Pr[Y \leq L] + P_2 \cdot Pr[Y > L]}, & \text{if } y > L, \end{cases} \tag{10.1}$$

where f is the normal density function $N(\mathbf{X}\boldsymbol{\beta}, \sigma^2)$. The distribution of Y for any given $\mathbf{X}$, say $\mathbf{X}^*$, would not be smooth like that of the normal. The distribution might look something like the one in figure 10.1, where the solid line represents a normal distribution and the dashed line the distribution in our sample. There is a discontinuity at the point L with

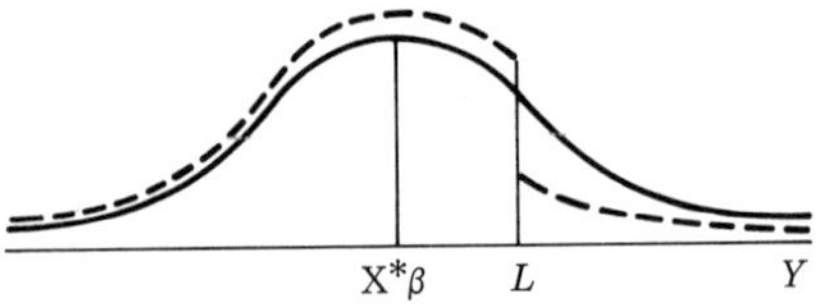

Figure 10.1

greater density relative to the normal below L and less density above. The denominator in (10.1) can be thought of as a normalizing constant, assuring that the integral over $h(y)$ with respect to y is one. Note that we cannot identify both P_1 and P_2, only their ratio. We divide through by P_1 and let $P_2/P_1 = P$ and rewrite the probabilities in the denominator, giving

$$h(y) = \begin{cases} \dfrac{f(y)}{\int_{-\infty}^{L} f(y)dy + P \cdot \int_{L}^{\infty} f(y)dy}, & \text{if } y \leq L, \\[2ex] \dfrac{P \cdot f(y)}{\int_{-\infty}^{L} f(y)dy + P \cdot \int_{L}^{\infty} f(y)dy}, & \text{if } y > L. \end{cases} \tag{10.2}$$

Note that, if no persons are sampled above L, so that $P_2 = 0$ (and thus P), equation (10.2) reduces to the density of a truncated distribution (as shown in Hausman and Wise 1977, equation 1.4). Thus complete truncation can be seen to be a special case of this more general possibility.

The expected value of Y given $\mathbf{X}$ can be obtained in a straightforward manner by integration over the density function shown in equation (10.2). It is

$$E(Y \mid \mathbf{X}) = \mathbf{X}\boldsymbol{\beta} - \sigma \frac{(1 - P)\phi[(L_i - \mathbf{X}_i\boldsymbol{\beta})/\sigma]}{(1 - P)\Phi[(L_i - \mathbf{X}_i\boldsymbol{\beta})/\sigma] + P}, \tag{10.3}$$

where ϕ is a unit normal density function and Φ the corresponding distribution function. Note that this expression reduces to the expected value of a truncated distribution when $P = 0$, which of course indicates complete truncation of the distribution at L. We see also that it equals $\mathbf{X}\boldsymbol{\beta}$ when sample selection is random.[5]

If we write $Pr[Y_i \leq L]$, as $\Phi[(L - \mathbf{X}_i\boldsymbol{\beta})/\sigma] = \Phi_i$, and divide the sample into N_1 persons with $Y \leq L$ and N_2 with $y > L$, we can write the log likelihood function as

5. The form of equation (10.3) suggests an estimator not discussed in the text. If P_1 and P_2 were known, a probit specification could be used to estimate $\boldsymbol{\beta}/\sigma$, allowing estimation of values for ϕ and Φ in equation (10.3). Using the fitted value of $\{(1 - P)\phi[\cdot]\}/\{(1 - P)\Phi[\cdot] + P\}$, consistent estimates of both $\boldsymbol{\beta}$ and σ could be obtained by ordinary least squares regression of Y on $\mathbf{X}$ and the fitted value. This procedure is related to those proposed by Heckman (1976) and Lee, chapter 9, for censored models. The extension of this approach to more groups (strata) is outlined in note 7.

$$L = \sum_{i=1}^{N_1} \ln f(y_i) - \sum_{i=1}^{N_1} \ln (\Phi_i + P(1 - \Phi_i))$$
$$+ \sum_{i=1}^{N_2} \ln P + \sum_{i=1}^{N_2} \ln f(y_i) - \sum_{i=1}^{N_2} \ln (\Phi_i + P(1 - \Phi_i))$$
$$= \sum_{i=1}^{N} \ln f(y_i) - \sum_{i=1}^{N} \ln (P + (1 - P)\Phi_i) + N_2 \ln P. \quad (10.4)$$

For convenience we let the index i begin at 1 in both groups, instead of letting it run from 1 to N_1 and from $N_1 + 1$ to N_2, for example. We use this convention throughout the chapter. It should be clear from the context what the more precise notation would be. Maximization of this function would lead to a maximum likelihood estimate for P as well as for $\boldsymbol{\beta}$ and σ. Or, if P were known, it could be maximized with respect to $\boldsymbol{\beta}$ and σ only.[6]

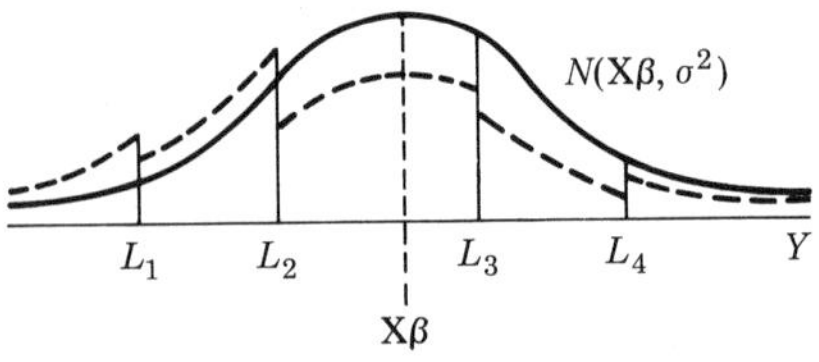

Figure 10.2

It is easy to extend the idea to more income groups. Assume that the five groups in the Gary experiment are defined by the points $L_1, L_2, \ldots, L_4$. Then, given $\mathbf{X}$, the distribution of Y might look something like the dashed representation in figure 10.2. Let the proportion of a random sample of the population below L_1, that is, selected, be P_1 between L_1 and L_2 be P_2, and so on, and above L_4 be P_5. Again we normalize by dividing each proportion by P_1. In the following we will use P_2, P_3, P_4, and P_5 but understand them to be P_2/P_1, P_3/P_1, and so on. Then the density function of Y is given by

6. N_1 and $N_2 = N - N_1$ are assumed random in the sampling procedure. $N = N_1 + N_2$ is given. An alternative sampling procedure is to fix N_1 and N_2. That is, N_1 values are sampled below L and N_2 above. This possibility is discussed in some detail in section 10.5.

$$h(y) = \begin{cases} \dfrac{f(y)}{\int_{-\infty}^{L_1} f(y)dy + P_2 \int_{L_1}^{L_2} f(y)dy + \cdots + P_5 \int_{L_4}^{\infty} f(y)dy}, & \text{if } y \le L_1, \\ \dfrac{P_2 f(y)}{\int_{-\infty}^{L_1} f(y)dy + P_2 \int_{L_1}^{L_2} f(y)dy + \cdots + P_5 \int_{L_4}^{\infty} f(y)dy}, & \text{if } L_1 < y \le L_2, \\ \vdots & \\ \dfrac{P_5 f(y)}{\int_{-\infty}^{L_1} f(y)dy + P_2 \int_{L_1}^{L_2} f(y)dy + \cdots + P_5 \int_{L_4}^{\infty} f(y)dy}, & \text{if } L_4 < y. \end{cases} \tag{10.5}$$

If we let $\Phi[(L_1 - \mathbf{X}\boldsymbol{\beta})/\sigma] = \Phi_1$, and so on, we can again write the expected value of Y given $\mathbf{X}$ as

$$E(Y \mid \mathbf{X}) = \mathbf{X}\boldsymbol{\beta} - \sigma \frac{(1 - P_2)\phi_1 + (P_2 - P_3)\phi_2 + (P_3 - P_4)\phi_3 + (P_4 - P_5)\phi_4}{(1 - P_2)\Phi_1 + (P_2 - P_3)\Phi_2 + (P_3 - P_4)\Phi_3 + (P_4 - P_5)\Phi_4 + P_5}. \tag{10.6}$$

The last term of course is an indicator of sample selection bias; if all proportions were 1, the expected value would be $\mathbf{X}\boldsymbol{\beta}$.[7] We see that it is no longer straightforward to evaluate the direction of the bias. It depends on the relative values of the proportions $P_2, \ldots, P_5$. They may have

7. The estimator suggested in note 6 could be extended to this more complex situation as well, if P_1 through P_5 were known. Let the bias term in equation (10.6) be $\sigma\mathbf{V}$. Then the elements of $\mathbf{V}$ could be estimated using ordered probit analysis, and next $\boldsymbol{\beta}$ and σ by regressing Y on $\mathbf{X}$ and the fitted value of $\mathbf{V}$. Probit analysis can be used here, even though there are several groups, because the groups are ordered. Let

$\Pi_1 = Pr(y \text{ is observed and } -\infty < y \le L_1 \mid \mathbf{X})$

offsetting effects, for example. But we can observe that, if the sampling proportions decrease consistently with income, the bias will be negative.[8]

In practice both y and L would be indexed by i to indicate the ith family. If we let $\Phi[(L_{1i} - \mathbf{X}_i\boldsymbol{\beta})/\sigma] = \Phi_{1i}$, and so on, and N_1 be the number of observations below L_1, N_2 the number between L_1 and L_2, and so on, we can write the log likelihood function for this case as

$$L = \sum_{i=1}^{N} \ln f(y_i) - \sum_{i=1}^{N} \ln [(1 - P_2)\Phi_{1i} + (P_2 - P_3)\Phi_{2i} + (P_3 - P_4)\Phi_{3i} + (P_4 - P_5)\Phi_{4i} + P_5] + N_2 \ln P_2 + N_3 \ln P_3 + N_4 \ln P_4 + N_5 \ln P_5. \quad (10.7)$$

As in the first example maximization of L would yield estimates for $\boldsymbol{\beta}$, σ^2. and the proportions P_2 through P_5, if they were unknown.

Note that one could test the hypothesis of population proportions under the normality assumptions by testing the hypothesis that P_2 through P_5 are all equal to one. Each could also be tested individually. If the hypothesis that they are all equal to one cannot be rejected, then it seems reasonable to assume random sampling.

The proportions P_2 through P_5 are often known, at least approximately. For example, for each income interval of the Gary data it is possible to calculate the approximate ratio of the number of persons in the actual sample to the number in a larger random sample. In some instances one could make use of population-versus-sample frequencies within intervals.

$$= P_1 \cdot \int_{-\infty}^{(L_1 - X\boldsymbol{\beta})/\sigma} \phi(u)\, du,$$

$$\Pi_2 = Pr(y \text{ is observed and } L_1 < y \leq L_2 \mid \mathbf{X})$$
$$= P_2 \cdot \int_{(L_1 - X\boldsymbol{\beta})/\sigma}^{(L_2 - X\boldsymbol{\beta})/\sigma} \phi(u)\, du,$$

and so on through Π_5. Construct the likelihood function

$$L = \sum_{i=1}^{N} \sum_{j=1}^{5} \ln \boldsymbol{\Pi}_{ij}^{y_{ij}},$$

where y_{ij} equals 1 if y is in the jth income interval and 0 otherwise. Maximization of L will yield estimates of $\boldsymbol{\beta}/\sigma$, which can in turn be used to estimate the elements of $\mathbf{V}$.

8. Equation (10.6) does not of course indicate the magnitude of the bias in individual elements of the vector of parameters $\boldsymbol{\beta}$. In practice, however, the bias in individual parameters tends toward 0.

But if the proportions are known, it seems intuitively plausible that weighted least squares would also yield consistent estimates. The idea can be motivated by referring again to figure 10.1. Consider a particular value of **X**, say **X***. Because a random sample would include approximately two times as many observations above L as there in fact are, we would like to fill in these missing points. This can be done by using inverse sampling weights. If P is the proportion of observations above L in a random sample actually sampled, then $1/P$ would be the expected number of observations in a random sample. If again we divide the sample into two groups, with N_1 below and N_2 above L, we minimize the expression

$$S = \sum_{i=1}^{N_1} (Y_i - \mathbf{X}_i\boldsymbol{\beta})^2 + \frac{1}{P} \sum_{i=1}^{N_2} (Y_i - \mathbf{X}_i\boldsymbol{\beta})^2. \tag{10.8}$$

More generally, if for each value Y_i we associate a sampling proportion P_i—by determining in which income interval Y_i falls—we minimize the expression

$$S = \sum_{i=1}^{N} \frac{1}{P_i} (Y_i - \mathbf{X}_i\boldsymbol{\beta})^2, \tag{10.9}$$

which is of course equivalent to weighted least squares with the weights given by $1/\sqrt{P_i}$. As with the maximum likelihood estimates we can normalize by dividing each P_i by the value of P associated with values of Y below L_1, P_1 in our terminology. To draw an explicit comparison with the likelihood function in equation (10.7), the sample can be broken into five groups and S written as

$$S = \sum_{j=1}^{5} \sum_{i=1}^{N_j} \frac{1}{P_j} (Y_i - \mathbf{X}_i\boldsymbol{\beta})^2, \tag{10.10}$$

where $1/P_1 = 1$. The log likelihood function analogous to this expression is[9]

9. Estimates of $\boldsymbol{\beta}$ could be obtained by weighted least squares in the usual way or by maximizing this function.

$$L = \sum_{j=1}^{5} \frac{1}{P_j} \sum_{i=1}^{N_j} \ln f(y_i)$$
$$= \sum_{j=1}^{5} \left\{ -\frac{N_j}{P_j} \ln \sqrt{2\pi} - \frac{N_j}{P_j} \ln \sigma - \sum_{i=1}^{N_j} \frac{1}{2P_j} \left(\frac{Y_i - \mathbf{X}_i \boldsymbol{\beta}}{\sigma} \right)^2 \right\}. \tag{10.11}$$

The relative efficiency of maximum likelihood versus weighted least squares estimates is discussed in the next section. Both are consistent. We shall show, however, that the maximum likelihood estimates based on the density function shown in equation (10.5), and the corresponding likelihood function of equation (10.7), are likely to be more efficient than the weighted least squares estimates, or identical estimates obtained from maximization of the analogous likelihood function shown in equation (10.11). If the sampling ratios are not known, as at first appeared to be the case with the Gary data, a maximum likelihood procedure must of course be used, with the weights estimated along with the behavioral parameters.

The maximum likelihood procedure proposed in this section can easily be extended to accomodate two time periods, or a two-equation—wages and hours worked—model. But because our empirical results based on pre-experimental data do not suggest substantial sample selection bias, we have not extended the analysis here. We have, however, sketched out the density and corresponding likelihood functions applicable to these extensions in the appendix.

10.3 Relative Efficiencies of Weighted Least Squares versus Maximum Likelihood Estimates

Only when the sampling proportions P_i are known can weighted least squares estimates be obtained. Thus only in this case does it make sense to compare the variances of weighted least squares with maximum likelihood estimates. In practice these proportions or their approximate values are likely to be known.

Although the weighted least squares estimates do not depend on distributional assumptions, because of the stratification of the endogenous variable, both their expected value and variance do. Not surprisingly, standard errors calculated from a weighted least squares regression are not consistent estimates of the true standard errors, even asymptotically.[10] On

10. We have reported the calculated weighted least squares standard errors in the results, however.

the other hand, the maximum likelihood estimates themselves depend on distributional assumptions. Given that the distributional assumptions are correct, however, the maximum likelihood estimates are more efficient than weighted least squares. And standard errors are provided easily by applying asymptotic distribution theory relevant to maximum likelihood estimates. But because the weighted least squares estimates are distribution free, they provide a check on the distributional assumptions used to obtain maximum likelihood estimates. Both estimates are asymptotically unbiased.

As we will see, the relative efficiencies of these two estimators depend on several parameters. To obtain some idea of the orders of magnitude that one might expect, we consider a case with only two strata and in which only the expected value of the dependent variable is to be estimated, without variables X. This gives a reasonable indication of relative efficiencies when the expected value depends on a vector of parameters.

The model we consider is of the form

$$Y_i = \beta + \varepsilon_i, \tag{10.12}$$

where the ε_i are independently distributed as $N(0, \sigma^2)$. Assume that Y is divided into two strata defined by point L as shown in figure 10.1 and as discussed in section 10.2. For convenience we continue to use both P_1 and P_2 (as opposed to their ratio P). Recall that because ordinary least squares, OLS, yields an unbiased estimate of the sample mean, the expectation of the OLS estimate, $\bar{Y}$, is

$$E\hat{\beta}_{\mathrm{OLS}} = \beta - \sigma\frac{(P_1 - P_2)\phi((L-\beta)/\sigma)}{P_2 + (P_1 - P_2)\Phi(L - \beta/\sigma)}, \tag{10.13}$$

which is analogous to equation (10.2) with P relaced by P_2/P_1. Note that, if P_2 is greater than P_1 (values of Y greater than L are oversampled), the bias is positive. It is negative if values less than L are oversampled, so that P_1 is greater than P_2.

The weighted least squares, WLS, estimate of β is found by minimizing the expression

$$S = \sum_{i=1}^{N} \frac{1}{P_i}(Y_i - \beta)^2 = \sum_{i=1}^{N_1} \frac{1}{P_1}(Y_i - \beta)^2 + \sum_{i=1}^{N_2} \frac{1}{P_2}(Y_i - \beta)^2, \tag{10.14}$$

where N_1 of the values in the sample fall below L and N_2 above. This is a special case of equation (10.9). The estimate is given by

$$\hat{\beta}_{\mathrm{WLS}} = \left(\frac{N_1}{P_1} + \frac{N_2}{P_2}\right)^{-1} \left[\sum_{i=1}^{N_1} \frac{Y_i}{P_1} + \sum_{i=1}^{N_2} \frac{Y_i}{P_2}\right]. \tag{10.15}$$

If the Y_i are normally distributed, the expected value of Y_i for $Y_i \leq L$ is given by $\beta - \sigma(\phi/\Phi)$, and for $Y_i > L$ by $\beta + \sigma(\phi/(1 - \Phi))$, where both ϕ and Φ are functions of $(L - \beta)/\sigma$. Although the weighted least squares estimator of β is not unbiased, in general it is consistent and asymptotically unbiased. Given N_1 (and thus $N_2 = N - N_1$), its expected value is given by

$$E(\hat{\beta}_{\mathrm{WLS}} \mid N_1) = \beta + \left(\frac{N_1}{P_1} + \frac{N_2}{P_2}\right)^{-1} \left[-\frac{N_1}{P_1}\sigma\frac{\phi}{\Phi} + \frac{N_2}{P_2}\sigma\frac{\phi}{1 - \Phi}\right]. \tag{10.16}$$

As N gets large, N_1 goes to $P_1\Phi N/D$, and $N_2 = N - N_1$ to $P_2(1 - \Phi)N/D$, where $D = P_1\Phi + P_2(1 - \Phi)$. The second term of (10.16) is zero when these values are substituted for N_1 and N_2.[11]

The derivation of the variance of the weighted least squares estimator is complicated by the fact that N_1 (and N_2), as well as the Y_i are random variables. If we use the property that the variance of $\hat{\beta}$ is equal to $E[\mathrm{Var}(\hat{\beta} \mid N_1)] + \mathrm{Var}[E(\hat{\beta} \mid N_1)]$, we can write it as

$$\begin{aligned}
\mathrm{Var}(\hat{\beta}_{\mathrm{WLS}}) = {} & E\left\{\left(\frac{N_1}{P_1} + \frac{N_2}{P_2}\right)^{-2} \left[\frac{N_1}{P_1^2}\left(\sigma^2 - \sigma^2\left(\frac{L - \beta}{\sigma} \cdot \frac{\phi}{\Phi} + \frac{\phi^2}{\Phi^2}\right)\right)\right.\right. \\
& \left.\left. + \frac{N_2}{P_2^2}\left(\sigma^2 + \sigma^2\left(\frac{L - \beta}{\sigma} \cdot \frac{\phi}{1 - \Phi} - \frac{\phi^2}{(1 - \Phi)^2}\right)\right)\right]\right\} \\
& + \mathrm{Var}\left\{\beta + \left(\frac{N_1}{P_1} + \frac{N_2}{P_2}\right)^{-1} \left[-\frac{N_1}{P_1}\sigma\frac{\phi}{\Phi} + \frac{N_2}{P_2}\sigma\frac{\phi}{1 - \Phi}\right]\right\} \\
= {} & E\{f(N_1)\} + \mathrm{Var}\{g(N_1)\},
\end{aligned} \tag{10.17}$$

where f and g are defined by the last equality. By using appropriate asymptotic Taylor expansions of both f and g, the variance can be approximated by

11. By expanding the second term in (10.16) around the expected value of N_1, it can be shown that the expected value of this term with respect to N_1 goes to zero at the rate of $1/N$.

$$\operatorname{Var}(\hat{\beta}_{\mathrm{WLS}}) = \frac{D\Phi}{P_1 N}\left[\sigma^2 - \sigma^2\left(\frac{L-\beta}{\sigma}\cdot\frac{\phi}{\Phi} + \frac{\phi^2}{\Phi^2}\right)\right]$$
$$+ \frac{D(1-\Phi)}{P_2 N}\left[\sigma^2 + \sigma^2\left(\frac{L-\beta}{\sigma}\cdot\frac{\phi}{1-\Phi} - \frac{\phi^2}{(1-\Phi)^2}\right)\right]$$
$$+ \frac{P_1\Phi\cdot P_2(1-\Phi)\cdot\phi^2\cdot\sigma^2}{N}\left(\frac{1-\Phi}{P_1} + \frac{\Phi}{P_2}\right)^2\left(\frac{1}{\Phi} + \frac{1}{1-\Phi}\right)^2, \tag{10.18}$$

where the first two terms come from $E\{f(N_1)\}$ and the third from $\operatorname{Var}\{g(N_1)\}$. The last term essentially represents the variance in the estimate due to the randomness of N_1.

The correct variance is not given when a standard regression program is used to calculate the weighted least squares estimates. The correct variance is also considerably more difficult to calulate than the maximum likelihood variance.

A maximum likelihood, ML, estimate for β may be obtained by maximization of a function analogous to (10.4).[12] The variance of the asymptotic distribution of the maximum likelihood estimator of β is given by

$$\operatorname{Var}(\hat{\beta}_{\mathrm{ML}}) = \frac{\sigma^2}{N}\left[1 - \frac{(P_1-P_2)\phi}{P_2 + (P_1-P_2)\Phi}\left(\frac{L-\beta}{\sigma} + \frac{(P_1-P_2)\phi}{P_2+(P_1-P_2)\Phi}\right)\right]^{-1}, \tag{10.19}$$

using the appropriate term from the information matrix. Note that it equals σ^2/N when $P_1 = P_2$ and increases as P_2 approaches zero.

To compare the relative efficiencies of maximum likelihood and weighted least squares estimates, we need to make some simplifications, since both estimators depend on L, β, and σ, as well as P_1 and P_2. As discussed in the previous section, we need only consider the ratio of P_1 and P_2; we accomplish this by setting $P_1 = 1$. We also set $L = 0$ and $\sigma = 1$. Ratios of the weighted least squares to the maximum likelihood variance for various values of P_1 and β are given in table 10.1.

12. The case of known P_i yields a likelihood function very similar to those corresponding to tobit and standard truncation situations. Amemiya's (1973) proofs of the properties of maximum likelihood estimators can be altered in a straightforward way and applied here. His proofs, however, cannot be as easily extended to cover the case of unknown P_i.

Table 10.1
Relative efficiency of maximum likelihood versus weighted least squares estimates for selected values of P_2 and β

P_2	$\beta = 0$	$\beta = 0.5$	$\beta = 1$	$\beta = 2$
0.01	9.906	5.439	3.818	4.506
0.10	1.736	1.524	1.696	1.748
0.20	1.291	1.256	1.379	1.325
0.30	1.148	1.149	1.225	1.172
0.50	1.045	1.053	1.080	1.054
0.70	1.012	1.015	1.022	1.014
0.80	1.005	1.006	1.009	1.006
0.90	1.001	1.001	1.002	1.001
0.99	1.000	1.000	1.000	1.000
1.00	1.000	1.000	1.000	1.000

The gain in efficiency from using maximum likelihood instead of weighted least squares is small, as long as P_2 is greater than 0.5. But the relative efficiency of maximum likelihood becomes substantial if P_2 is less than 0.3, say. It should be emphasized, however, that the maximum likelihood asymptotic variance is much easier to calculate for any values of P_2 (as well as the other parameters), although weighted least squares estimates themselves may be easier to obtain. The relative efficiencies are not affected very much by β except at very low levels of P_2. One might conclude that weighted least squares would give a good indication of the importance of endogenous stratification, when compared to least squares estimates, as long as P_2 were not very small.

Relative efficiencies in the more general case with $Y_i = \mathbf{X}_i\boldsymbol{\beta} + \varepsilon_i$, where $\boldsymbol{\beta}$ is a vector of parameters, would be developed analogously, with β replaced by the conditional expectation $\mathbf{X}_i\boldsymbol{\beta}$. But in this case the conditional expectation depends on $\mathbf{X}$ as well as $\boldsymbol{\beta}$, and the variance calculations depend on the values of $\mathbf{X}$ in the sample. Thus it is impossible to present simple comparisons like those in table 10.1. Presumably the same considerations apply, however. For P_2 close to one, weighted least squares should entail little loss of efficiency. The analysis also could be extended to more strata and associated values P_i. There seems to be no straightforward way to compare efficiencies in this case either, and in addition our results for two strata may provide a less reliable guide for this more complicated case. However, one might suspect that very low values of P_i with respect to any strata tend to lower the relative efficiency of weighted least squares.

10.4 Empirical Results of the Selection Bias in the Gary Income Maintenance Experiment

We will first describe briefly the sample selection procedure followed in the Gary experiment. (For a more detailed discussion see Kehrer et al. 1975.) Then we will compare maximum likelihood and weighted least squares estimates—that correct for sample selection—with least squares estimates obtained with no attempt to correct for selection bias.

Recall that after some preliminary screening a random sample of approximately 2,600 black families was selected from specified geographic areas of Gary. The families had to include at least one dependent child under the age of 18; more than half were female-headed households. This group was stratified by income as well as by exogenous variables. Families were then selected at random within the income intervals defined by multiples of the poverty level, which depends on family size. The government poverty line for a family of four was $4,275 in 1972, when the experiment began.

Only the male-headed households, of which about 730 were selected for the experiment, are used in our analysis. The proportions of the random sample of male-headed households in each income interval that were included in the selected sample of 730 are shown in the third column of table 10.2. Normalized ratios—the P values in equations (10.5) through (10.7)—are shown in the last column. The first two columns define the income groups. (The last four numbers are the values of P_2 through P_5, which follow the definitions applied in equation 10.4, in particular the bias expression in equation 10.6.) We see that relative to families in the first income interval those in the third and fourth intervals are slightly oversampled, while those in the highest income group are substantially undersampled. In a random sample we would expect to find about two and one-half times as many observations in the high income group as we in fact have. By referring back to equation (10.6), we see that of the four terms in the numerator of the bias expression the first is approximately zero, while the second and third are positive, and the fourth is negative. Thus we cannot a priori evaluate the direction of the bias. But it seems clear that the bias should be much less than in the New Jersey negative income tax experiment. The New Jersey sample excluded altogether families in the two highest income intervals as defined here. As one might expect, the estimates indicate much less bias using the Gary sample than was found using data from the New Jersey experiment.

Table 10.2
Sampling proportions and ratios

Group	Income (Y) interval (multiple of poverty line)	Proportion of random sample selected for experiment	Normalized ratios
1	$Y \leq 0.5$	0.7273	$P_1 = 1.0000$
2	$0.5 < Y \leq 1.0$	0.7381	$P_2 = 1.0148$
3	$1.0 < Y \leq 1.5$	0.8061	$P_3 = 1.1083$
4	$1.5 < Y \leq 2.4$	0.8594	$P_4 = 1.1816$
5	$2.4 < Y$	0.2966	$P_5 = 0.4078$

To evaluate the extent of sample selection bias in the Gary data, we estimated earnings equations using pre-experimental (baseline) data rather than experimental data, because a large number of families dropped out of the experiment over time. We wanted to avoid the somewhat more complex specification that would be required to correct for sample selection and attrition bias simultaneously. The results indicate that sample selection bias was not severe. Therefore in evaluating the extent of attrition bias (Hausman and Wise 1977b), we have not at the same time made a correction for sample selection bias.

We will compare four sets of estimates:

1. ordinary least squares,
2. weighted least squares using inverse sample ratios,
3. maximum likelihood with known sample ratios,
4. maximum likelihood with unknown sample ratios.[13]

The weights used in the second and third approaches are those listed in the last column of table 10.2. Estimates using the last two methods are obtained by maximization of a likelihood function similar to equation (10.7), but the third uses the known normalized sample ratios and estimates only $\boldsymbol{\beta}$ and σ^2, while the fourth estimates the ratios P_2 through P_5 along with $\boldsymbol{\beta}$ and σ^2. If the maintained assumptions of the model are in accord with empirical evidence—in particular that given $\mathbf{X}$ income is distributed

13. The maximum likelihood estimates were obtained using the Berndt, Hall, Hall, and Hausman modified scoring algorithm. The costs were approximately twice the cost of the weighted least squares estimates.

log normal—then the estimated ratios should be close to the those shown in the table.

The dependent variable in each case is the logarithm of labor income. The independent variables are

Constant
Education: years of education,
Experience: years of work experience,
Income: log of nonlabor family income, including foodstamps, AFDC payments, public assistance, and earnings of other family members,
Union: a dummy variable that is one for union members and zero otherwise.

A total of 585 black males were used in the analysis, comprising both controls and experimentals (persons ultimately assigned an experimental income guarantee and tax rate).[14] Note the limits $L_1, \ldots, L_4$ that define the income intervals depend on family size and must therefore be calculated for each observation. The ratios, however, are the same over all observations. The limits have been adjusted slightly because they pertain to family income, whereas our data pertain to earnings of the male head only.[15]

Parameter estimates are presented in table 10.3. Ratios of the other estimates to least squares estimates are shown in table 10.4. In this case we find that least squares estimates do not differ substantially from those that correct for sample selection bias and do not seem to be systematically biased in one direction or another. In general the estimates obtained by weighted least squares and by the two maximum likelihood methods agree rather closely with one another. The estimated coefficients on income, however, differ substantially, with the weighted least squares estimates tending considerably closer to zero than the maximum likelihood estimates.

14. Although there were about 730 male-headed households in the sample, we had complete data for only 585 of them. This could of course affect the relationship between the estimated P values and the sampling proportions as shown in table 10.2. Based on evidence reported elsewhere (Hausman and Wise 1977b), we believe that these missing observations would not have a substantial affect on the parameter estimates.

15. Other income was assumed given, and the limits were related to the earnings of the male head by determining individual earnings limits corresponding to the specified limits. For example, if other family income is 0.5 times the poverty level, then the male head would have to earn between 0.5 and 1.0 times the poverty level to be in group 3. In practice family income not included in labor income of the male head was very small on the average.

Table 10.3
Parameter estimates (and standard errors) by method of estimation

Variable	Least squares	Weighted least squares[a]	Maximum likelihood (ratios known)	Maximum likelihood (ratios unknown)
Constant	5.916	5.8424	5.9300	5.7355
	(0.0879)	(0.0899)	(0.1047)	(0.1196)
Education	0.0190	0.0270	0.0252	0.0281
	(0.0068)	(0.0068)	(0.0079)	(0.0083)
Experience	0.0042	0.0048	0.0050	0.0053
	(0.0018)	(0.0018)	(0.0020)	(0.0023)
Income	−0.0162	−0.0056	−0.0189	−0.0231
	(0.0068)	(0.0069)	(0.0092)	(0.0101)
Union	0.2596	0.2314	0.2021	0.2881
	(0.0519)	(0.0407)	(0.0386)	(0.0647)
P_2	—	—	—	1.4831
	—	—	—	(0.1836)
P_3	—	—	—	0.8267
	—	—	—	(0.1983)
P_4	—	—	—	2.3916
	—	—	—	(0.2361)
P_5	—	—	—	0.2429
	—	—	—	(0.0570)

[a]The standard errors shown in this column are those reported from a regression program. They understimate the true standard errors.

Table 10.4
Ratios of other estimates to least squares estimates by method of estimation

Variable	Weighted least squares	Maximum likelihood (ratios known)	Maximum likelihood (ratios unknown)
Constant	0.99	1.00	0.97
Education	1.42	1.33	1.48
Experience	1.14	1.19	1.26
Income	0.35	1.17	1.43
Union	0.89	0.78	1.11

The estimated ratios P_2 through P_5 do differ from their sample counterparts shown in table 10.2, but the general pattern of the estimates is similar to the sample ratios. That is, they suggest that persons in the highest income group were undersampled relative to persons in the other groups. But they also suggest a much larger oversampling of persons in the fourth interval than the sample ratios indicate and a somewhat larger oversampling in the second interval. We can see nonetheless that, if these estimates were in fact accurate reflections of empirical ratios, the undersampling in the highest interval would tend to be offset by oversampling in the fourth.[16] Thus the bias resulting from one is offset by the other.

We note also that these sampling ratios are estimated with considerable precision. Each of the standard errors is less than one-fourth of the corresponding estimate. We have not formally tested the hypothesis that all are equal to one, indicating random sampling, but it is clear from the standard errors that this hypothesis would be rejected.

Finally we emphasize that in principle it is not possible to distinguish deviations from random sampling from deviations from normality in the population. We have maintained the hypothesis of a log normal distribution of income in the population, given **X**. On the other hand, it seems unlikely that deviations from normality in the population would follow the pattern of the estimates we have obtained.

10.5 Alternative Sampling Procedures

The sampling process assumed in the foregoing analysis was intended to reflect as closely as possible the process actually used in the Gary experiment, as we understand it. There are of course several other possibilities. We will briefly discuss two others, to the point of presenting appropriate likelihood functions. Recall that we assumed that the total number of observations retained was fixed, but the number of retained observations within each stratum was random. One alternative is to stratify the population (or a random sample from the population) and draw a fixed number of observations within each stratum. A second alternative is to *fix the number of retained plus unretained observations*, letting both the number of observations within each stratum and the number of observations actually observed be random.

16. We note that the calculated ratios are subject to error.

Consider first sampling within strata, with N_1 observations taken from the first, N_2 from the second, and so on. The density function for observations in the sample is given by

$$h(y) = \begin{cases} \dfrac{f(y)}{\Phi_1}, & \text{if } y \leq L_1, \\[2ex] \dfrac{f(y)}{\Phi_2 - \Phi_1}, & \text{if } L_1 < y \leq L_2, \\ \vdots & \vdots \\ \dfrac{f(y)}{1 - \Phi_4}, & \text{if } L_4 < y. \end{cases} \tag{10.20}$$

Within each stratum the values of y have truncated normal density functions. The appropriate log likelihood function is then

$$L = \sum_{j=1}^{5} \left\{ \sum_{i=1}^{N_j} \ln f(y_i) - \sum_{i=1}^{N_j} \ln (\Phi_{ji} - \Phi_{j-1,i} \right\}, \tag{10.21}$$

where $\Phi_0 = 0$ and $\Phi_5 = 1$. This is a straightforward generalization of our earlier work (Hausman and Wise 1977a).

A variant of this possibility arises if we know the proportions of the population with values of y within each of the strata. Let the values be $Q_1, \ldots, Q_5$. Then, for example,

$$Q_1 \equiv \int_{\mathbf{X}} \Phi_1 \cdot g(\mathbf{X}) d\mathbf{X},$$

where $g(\mathbf{X})$ is the multivariate density function defined over population values of the vector $\mathbf{X}$. Similar expressions apply to Q_2 through Q_5. Presumably more efficient estimates could then be obtained by maximizing (10.21) subject to these identity constraints. In general, however, they seem to be intractable.[17]

17. A possible exception is to suppose that $\mathbf{X}$ is distributed multivariate normal with mean $\boldsymbol{\mu}_X$ and covariance matrix $\boldsymbol{\Sigma}_X$. Then, for example,

$$Q_1 \equiv \Phi\left[\frac{L_1 - \mu_X \boldsymbol{\beta}}{1 + \boldsymbol{\beta}' \boldsymbol{\Sigma}_X \boldsymbol{\beta}}\right],$$

and analogous expressions define Q_2 through Q_5. Alternatively $g(\mathbf{X})$ could be replaced by

Next suppose that the total sample size is fixed but that some values of y are unobserved. Each value of $\mathbf{X}$ is observed. Whether y is observed or not depends on the stratum in which the randomly selected observation of y falls. If it falls in the first stratum, it is retained in the sample with probability P_1. It is retained with probability P_2 if it falls in the second, and so forth.

To develop a likelihood function for this case, consider the pairs of values $(y, \mathbf{X})$ and the sample selection probability P. The likelihood that a pair $(y, \mathbf{X})$ will be in the sample is given by

$$l(y,\mathbf{X})\cdot P(y)=f(y\mid \mathbf{X})g(\mathbf{X})P(y). \tag{10.22}$$

It is the likelihood that the pair $(y, \mathbf{X})$ is randomly selected multiplied by the probability that it is retained in the sample, once selected. The probability of retention depends only on y. As shown in (10.22), $P(y)$ equals P_1 for $y < L$, P_2 for $L_1 < y < L_2$, and so on.

The likelihood of a pair $(y, \mathbf{X})$ with y unobserved is given by

$$l(y,\mathbf{X})(1-P(y))=f(y\mid \mathbf{X})g(\mathbf{X})(1-P(y)). \tag{10.23}$$

But only the stratum of y is known if y is unobserved, not y itself. The likelihood of observing $\mathbf{X}$ with unobserved y in the first stratum, for example, is given by

$$\begin{aligned}\int_{-\infty}^{L_1} f(y\mid \mathbf{X})g(\mathbf{X})(1-P(y))\,dy &= \Phi\left[\frac{L_1-\mathbf{X}\beta}{\sigma}\right]g(\mathbf{X})\cdot P_1\\ &= \Phi_1 g(\mathbf{X})P_1.\end{aligned}$$

The analogous expression for unobserved y in the second stratum is given by

$$(\Phi_2-\Phi_1)g(\mathbf{X})P_2,$$

and so forth.

If there are N_1 observed values of y in the first stratum, and $N_{1'}$ unobserved, N_2 observed values in the second and $N_{2'}$ unobserved, and so forth, the likelihood function for N observations is

weights corresponding to empirical observations and (10.21) maximized with respect to these weights as well as the other parameters of the likelihood function (see Cosslett 1977).

$$L = \sum_{j=1}^{5} \left\{ N_i \ln P_j + \sum_{i=1}^{N_j} \ln (f(y_i \mid \mathbf{X}_i) + N_{j'} \ln (1 - P_j) \right.$$
$$\left. + \sum_{i=1}^{N_{j'}} \ln (\Phi_{ji} - \Phi_{j-1,i}) \right\}, \tag{10.24}$$

where $\Phi_0 = 0$ and $\Phi_5 = 1$.

The term $\Sigma_{i=1}^{N} \ln g(\mathbf{X}_i)$ has been deleted because it does not include any of the parameters of (10.24). Presumably this formulation would provide more efficient estimates of P_1 through P_5, because within any stratum the number of unobserved as well as observed values of y is known. The expected value of each of these numbers is determined by the corresponding value of P. The estimates of the β parameters would also be more efficient because, although given $N_1 + \cdots + N_5$, we have the same number of observations of y; the observations with y unobserved are represented explicitly by $N_{1'} + \cdots + N_{5'}$ probit functions in (10.24). Each indicates the probability that y falls in the indicated interval, given $\mathbf{X}$, and provides additional information on the value of β.

A variant of this case is to suppose that for y unobserved, $\mathbf{X}$ is also unobserved; the observations are completely missing. This was the assumption in sections 10.2 through 10.4. But we assume somewhat more information here, namely, the number of observations that are discarded in each stratum, and we make explicit use of this information.

The likelihood for retained observations is the same as in equation (10.22). But to get expressions for the likelihoods of unobserved values, we must integrate out $\mathbf{X}$ as well as y, since neither is observed in this case. For example, the probability of an unobserved pair $(y, \mathbf{X})$ with y in the first stratum is given by

$$\int_{\mathbf{X}} \int_{-\infty}^{L_1} f(y \mid \mathbf{X}) g(\mathbf{X})(1 - P(y))\, dy\, d\mathbf{X} = \int_{\mathbf{X}} \Phi_1 g(\mathbf{X})(1 - P_1)\, d\mathbf{X}$$
$$\equiv (1 - P_1) Q_1.$$

Note this expression is identical to $(1 - P_1)Q_1$. Similar expressions pertain to unobserved pairs in the other strata.

The log likelihood function for N observations would be

$$L = \sum_{j=1}^{5} \left\{ N_j \ln P_j + \sum_{i=1}^{N_j} \ln f(y_i \mid \mathbf{X}_i) + \sum_{i=1}^{N_j} \ln g(\mathbf{X}_i) \right.$$

$$\left. + N_{j'} [\ln (1 - P_j) + \ln Q_j] \right\}, \tag{10.25}$$

where

$$Q_1 = \int_{\mathbf{X}} \Phi_1 g(\mathbf{X}) \, d\mathbf{X}, \tag{10.26}$$

$$Q_2 = \int_{\mathbf{X}} (\Phi_2 - \Phi_1) g(\mathbf{X}) \, d\mathbf{X},$$

$$\vdots$$

$$Q_5 = \int_{\mathbf{X}} (1 - \Phi_4) g(\mathbf{X}) \, d\mathbf{X}.$$

One could think of this function as the likelihood of $N_1, N_2, \ldots, N_5$ observed values in the five strata; $N_{i'}, N_{2'}, \ldots, N_{5'}$ unobserved values; $y_{11}, \ldots, y_{1N_1}$ in strata 1; $y_{21}, \ldots y_{2N_2}$ in strata 2; and so on to $y_{51}, \ldots,$ y_{5N_5} in strata 5. Because more information is retained in this procedure than the one described in section 10.3, it yields more efficient estimates. In fact, if the Q_i were known, (10.25) could be maximized subject to (10.26) and considered as a series of identity constraints. Maximization of this likelihood function, with or without the constraint, appears to be impractical at this time, however.

10.6 Conclusion

Sample selection for panel surveys is often based on a stratified sample design with random sampling within strata. The proportions of observations within strata do not necessarily correspond to population proportions. This is usually not a serious problem if stratification is based on exogenous variables. But often variables we would like to treat as endogenous are also the basis for stratification. For example, the New Jersey negative income tax experiment excluded entirely all families with income greater than 1.5 times the poverty level. The income maintenance experiments in Gary and Seattle–Denver, although not excluding higher income families, undersampled them. The 1967 survey of economic opportunity also undersampled high income families, as did the University of Michigan panel study of income dynamics that resurveyed part of the SEO sample. Any uses of these data sets that treat earnings or components of earnings as endogenous variables in behavioral relationships will lead to biased estimates of population parameters.

We have presented alternative methods of correcting for endogenous sample selection when faced with rather general stratification designs. If relevant sample versus population proportions are known, either weighted least squares or a more efficient maximum likelihood procedure can be used. If the proportions are not known, they can be estimated along with behavioral parameters using our proposed maximum likelihood procedure. We have demonstrated the technique through estimation of earnings functions using data from the Gary income maintenance experiment. In this case we find that, although the sampling was not random, undersampling of the highest income families tended to be offset by oversampling of the next highest group. Thus parameter estimates were not seriously biased. All of the methods of correcting for endogenous sampling produced similar results.

We note in particular that estimation of sampling ratios when they are unknown is quite practical. In fact we obtained very precise estimates. The general pattern of the estimates was consistent with a priori knowledge about actual ratios, although some of the individual estimates differed significantly from their empirical counterparts.

10.7 Appendix: Extension of the Analysis to Two Time Periods and to Two Equations

The idea embodied in equations (10.5) and (10.7) can easily be extended to earnings, for example, in two time periods such as before and during an experiment, by noting that, if Y_1 and Y_2 are jointly normal, with $Y_1 = \mathbf{X}_1\boldsymbol{\beta} + \varepsilon_1$ and $Y_2 = \mathbf{X}_2\boldsymbol{\beta} + \varepsilon_2$, the appropriate density function would now be

$$h(y_1, y_2) = \begin{cases} \dfrac{f(y_1, y_2)}{\int_{-\infty}^{L_1} f_1(y_1)dy_1 + P_2 \int_{L_1}^{L_2} f_1(y_1)dy_1 + \ldots + P_5 \int_{L_4}^{\infty} f_1(y_1)dy_1}, \\ \text{if} \quad y_1 \leq L_1, \qquad \vdots \\ \dfrac{P_5 f(y_1, y_2)}{\int_{-\infty}^{L_1} f_1(y_1)dy_1 + P_2 \int_{L_1}^{L_2} f_1(y_1)dy_1 + \ldots + P_5 \int_{L_4}^{\infty} f_1(y_1)dy_1}, \\ \text{if} \quad L_4 < y_1, \end{cases} \tag{10.27}$$

where $f(y_1, y_2)$ is a bivariate normal density function with appropriate mean vector and covariance matrix and $f_1(y_1)$ is the marginal density function for y_1. This would lead to a log likelihood function of the form

$$\begin{aligned} L = {} & \sum_{i=1}^{N} f(y_{1i}, y_{2i}) \\ & - \sum_{i=1}^{N} \ln[(P_1 - P_2)\Phi_{1i} + (P_2 - P_3)\Phi_{2i} \\ & + (P_3 - P_4)\Phi_{3i} + (P_4 - P_5)\Phi_{4i} + P_5] \\ & + N_2 \ln P_2 + N_3 \ln P_3 + N_4 \ln P_4 + N_5 \ln P_5, \end{aligned} \tag{10.28}$$

where the functions $\Phi_{1i}, \Phi_{2i}, \ldots$, are defined as shown and refer to the cumulative distribution function of Y_1.

The extension of this approach to estimation of simultaneous hourly wage rate and hours-worked equations is also straightforward. Without going through the details here, it can be shown that the appropriate density function would be of the form

$f(\ln w, \ln h) =$

$$\frac{\tilde{\phi}(\ln w, \ln h)}{(P_1 - P_2)\Phi[d_1] + (P_2 - P_3)\Phi[d_2] + \ldots + (P_4 - P_5)\Phi[d_4] + P_5}, \quad \text{if} \quad y \leq L_1,$$

$$\frac{P_5 \cdot \tilde{\phi}(\ln w_i, \ln h_i)}{(P_1 - P_2)\Phi[d_1] + (P_2 - P_3)\Phi[d_2] + \ldots + (P_4 - P_5)\Phi[d_4] + P_5}, \quad \text{if} \quad L_4 \leq y, \tag{10.29}$$

where $\tilde{\phi}(\cdot)$ is a bivariate normal density function, and

$$d_1 = \frac{\ln L_1 - X_1\delta_1 - X_1\delta_1\beta - X_2\delta_2}{\sqrt{\omega_{11} + \omega_{22} + 2\omega_{12}}},$$

$$d_2 = \frac{\ln L_2 - X_1\delta_1 - X_1\delta_1\beta - X_2\delta_2}{\sqrt{\omega_{11} + \omega_{22} + 2\omega_{12}}},$$

$$d_4 = \frac{\ln L_4 - X_1\delta_1 - X_1\delta_1\beta - X_2\delta_2}{\sqrt{\omega_{11} + \omega_{22} + 2\omega_{12}}}.$$

The notation is the same as that in Hausman and Wise (1977a), and the development leading to equation (10.29) is analogous to the approach followed there. Again the resulting likelihood function has a rather simple form.

Finally, extension to two equations and two time periods is also straightforward but somewhat tedious and therefore not carried out here.

References

Amemiya, T. 1973. Regression Analysis when the Dependent Variable is Truncated Normal. *Econometrica*. 41: 997–1016.

Cosslett, Stephen R. 1977. Choice-Based Sampling and Disaggregate Demand Forecasting. Mimeograph. Department of Economics, University of California, Berkeley.

Hausman, J. A., and Wise, D. A. 1976. The Evaluation of Results from Truncated Samples: The New Jersey Negative Income Tax Experiment. *Annals of Economic and Social Measurement*. 5: 421–445.

Hausman, J. A., and Wise, D. A. 1977a. Social Experimentation, Truncated Distributions, and Efficient Estimation. *Econometrica*. 45: 319–339.

Hausman, J. A., and Wise, D. A. 1977b. Attrition Bias in Experimental and Panel Data: The Gary Income Maintenance Experiment. Discussion paper 47D. John F. Kennedy School of Government, Harvard University.

Heckman, J. 1976. The Common Structure of Statistical Models of Truncation, Sample Selection, and Limited Dependent Variables and a Simple Estimator for Such Models. *Annals of Economic and Social Measurement*. 5: 475–492.

Kehrer, K. C., E. K. Bruml, G. T. Burtless, and D. N. Richardson. 1975. The Gary Income Maintenance Experiment: Design, Administration, and Data Files Mimeograph.

Manski, C. F., and S. R. Lerman. 1977. The Estimation of Choice Probabilities from Choice Based Samples. *Econometrica*. 45: 1977–1988.

11 A Switching Simultaneous Equations Model of Physician Behaviour in Ontario

Dale J. Poirier

11.1 Introduction

This study provides an econometric model of physician behavior utilizing a switching regression framework.[1] Briefly it assumes that various measures of physician behavior (e.g., hours worked, number of patients, quantity of labor employed) are determined in a simultaneous equations framework belonging to one of two regimes. Assignment of a particular physician to one of these two regimes is based on the physician's choice to "opt-in" or "opt-out" of the Ontario Health Insurance Plan (OHIP).[2] The switching equation intended to explain this discrete binary choice depends on various exogenous variables (e.g., number of dependents, school of graduation) and an additive stochastic term.

Recognition of this discrete choice aspect of the model suggests its numerous connections with the limited dependent variable, LDV, literature. The eclectic nature of our model will become obvious as an estimation scheme is devised. Because the econometric machinery needed in this estimation is substantial, it is not possible to fully discuss the underlying theory of physician behavior for which this model provides a statistical framework. (See Wolfson and Tuohy 1980 for a detailed discussion.) We instead discuss this model's econometric implications. However, we provide in this section brief overview of the behavioral model employed by Wolfson et al. (1980) which should help to motivate the econometric discussion in section 11.2.

This study describes the econometric model developed by the author for use by Wolfson and Tuohy (1980). While thanks are owed to Alan Wolfson, Carolyn Tuohy, and Stewart Iglesias for their comments, the author accepts the sole responsibility for the results reported here.

1. For surveys dealing with switching regression models, see Goldfeld and Quandt (1973, 1976), Lee and Trost (1978), Maddala and Nelson (1975) and Poirier (1976, chapter 7).

2. For readers who are not familiar with OHIP a brief description may be helpful. OHIP is a comprehensive government-sponsored health insurance plan for the residents of Ontario. It provides a wide scope of benefits for medical and hospital services plus additional benefits for the services of certain other health practitioners. The plan pays 90 percent of the Ontario Medical Association (OMA) schedule of fees for all physicians' services that are medically required. Those physicians who have opted-in submit their fee billings directly to OHIP and accept the plan's allowance as full payment. Those physicians who have opted-out usually bill their patients directly and also submit a claim to OHIP on behalf of the patient. OHIP then reimburses the patient based on 90 percent of the OMA Schedule of Fees, and the patient supplements this amount accordingly in paying the physician. Physicians who have opted-out generally charge higher fees; however, they lose the advantage of having payments guaranteed.

The major goal of the study undertaken by Wolfson and Tuohy (1980) was to obtain the understanding of physician practice behavior required for planning and policy development in the physician sector. Insofar as some of the variables that are influential determinants of practice behavior are instruments of public policy, or susceptible to policy actions, planning agencies can both forecast and effect change in physician behavior by adjusting these determining variables in an appropriate fashion.

Briefly the underlying theoretical model hypothesizes that a physician's utility is positively related to net income, the amount of leisure time, the extent to which there exists excess demand for services, the quality of care provided, the extent to which the practice can be independent (free from scrutiny and control by either government or peers), and the degree to which peer group standards are met. These variables are in turn related to various instruments under the physician's control. For example, the physician has some control over three basic classes of discretionary services: (1) services provided by the physician, (2) services provided by other parts of the system but complimentary to the physician's own services in that they generate more services for the physician such as laboratory tests, and (3) services provided by others that substitute for those of the physician such as referrals. The physician also has control over auxiliary inputs such as labor (e.g., nurses) or capital (e.g., waiting rooms) inputs. Further the physician has control over the number of hours and speed at which to work and most important whether or not to opt-out of OHIP.

As will be seen in the following sections, the physician's option decision will play a central role in the econometric model that follows. This is convenient for policy purposes because the option decision is of great concern to politicians. Politically the existence of the option has both advantages and disadvantages for government. To the extent that government incurs the dissatisfaction of voters faced with out-of-pocket costs for medical care under a government health insurance program, it is politically costly. To the extent, however, that it eases government-professional relationships, it has political advantages.

11.2 Econometric Model

The purpose of this section is to lay out a general switching simultaneous equations model. So as to simplify partly the elaborate notation that must follow, only the case of two regimes will be considered—although extensions to more than two regimes can be easily incorporated. Furthermore, while the physician behavior context of our model will be dealt with throughout, we will abstract in sections 11.2 and 11.3 from many of the pertinent problems (such as nonrandom sampling) covered later in section 11.4. This decision does not reflect their secondary importance but rather only the fact that their econometric implications will be difficult to grasp until the basic underlying model has been specified.

To begin, for a sample of size T, consider the following quantities for the tth physician. Let J_t be an observed dichotomous variable denoting sample separation into two groups or regimes: physicians who have opted-in ($J_t = 1$) and physicians who have opted-out ($J_t = 2$). Let $\mathbf{z}_t$ be a $1 \times m$ vector of fixed exogenous variables, let $\boldsymbol{\alpha}$ be a $m \times 1$ vector of unknown coefficients, and suppose

$$\begin{aligned} J_t &= 1, \quad \text{iff } \mathbf{z}_t\boldsymbol{\alpha} < u_t, \\ J_t &= 2, \quad \text{iff } \mathbf{z}_t\boldsymbol{\alpha} \geq u_t, \end{aligned} \tag{11.1}$$

where $u_t \sim$ i.i.d. $N(0, 1)$ for $t = 1, 2, \ldots, T$. Note that in terms of the binary variable

$$I_t = \begin{cases} 0, & \text{iff } J_t = 1, \\ 1, & \text{otherwise,} \end{cases} \tag{11.2}$$

specification (11.1) implies the familiar probit model

$$\begin{aligned} \text{Prob}(I_t = 0) &= 1 - \Phi(\mathbf{z}_t\boldsymbol{\alpha}), \\ \text{Prob}(I_t = 1) &= \Phi(\mathbf{z}_t\boldsymbol{\alpha}), \end{aligned} \tag{11.3}$$

where $\Phi(\cdot)$ denotes the standard normal distribution function.

Based on (11.1) define the index sets

$$\mathbf{S}_j = \{t \mid J_t = j\}, \tag{11.4}$$

$j = 1, 2$, containing T_1 and $T_2 = T - T_1$ observations, respectively, and suppose that the overall model has the following structure

$$\begin{aligned} \text{Regime 1:} \quad & \mathbf{y}_{1t}\mathbf{B}_1 + \mathbf{x}_{1t}\boldsymbol{\Gamma}_1 + \boldsymbol{\varepsilon}_{1t} = \mathbf{0}, \\ \text{Regime 2:} \quad & \mathbf{y}_{2t}\mathbf{B}_2 + \mathbf{x}_{2t}\boldsymbol{\Gamma}_2 + \boldsymbol{\varepsilon}_{2t} = \mathbf{0}, \end{aligned} \tag{11.5}$$

where for $j = 1, 2$, $\mathbf{y}_{jt}$ is a $1 \times G_j$ vector corresponding to the tth observation on the G_j endogenous variables in regime j, $\mathbf{x}_{jt}$ is a $1 \times K_j$ vector corresponding to the tth observation on the K_j exogenous variables in regime j, $\mathbf{B}_j$ and $\boldsymbol{\Gamma}_j$ are $G_j \times G_j$ and $K_j \times G_j$ matrices of unknown coefficients, with all diagonal elements of $\mathbf{B}_j$ equal to minus one, and

$$\boldsymbol{\varepsilon}_{jt} \sim \text{i.i.d. } N(\mathbf{0}, \boldsymbol{\Sigma}_j). \tag{11.6}$$

In matrix notation (11.5) can alternatively be written as

$$\mathbf{Y}_j\mathbf{B}_j + \mathbf{X}_j\boldsymbol{\Gamma}_j + \boldsymbol{\varepsilon}_j = 0, \tag{11.7}$$

$j = 1, 2$, where $\mathbf{Y}_j$ is a $T_j \times G_j$ matrix with row t equal to $\mathbf{y}_{jt}$, $\mathbf{X}_j$ is a $T_j \times K_j$ matrix with row t equal to $\mathbf{x}_{jt}$, and $\boldsymbol{\varepsilon}_j$ is a $T_j \times G_j$ matrix with row t equal to $\boldsymbol{\varepsilon}_{jt}$. Imposing any exclusion restrictions, the g th equation of (11.7) can be concisely expressed as

$$\mathbf{y}_{jg} = \mathbf{Y}_{jg}\boldsymbol{\beta}_{jg} + \mathbf{X}_{jg}\boldsymbol{\gamma}_{jg} + \boldsymbol{\varepsilon}_{jg}, \tag{11.8}$$

where, for $j = 1, 2$, $\mathbf{y}_{jg}$ and $\boldsymbol{\varepsilon}_{jg}$ are the g th columns of $\mathbf{Y}_j$ and $\boldsymbol{\varepsilon}_j$, respectively, $\boldsymbol{\beta}_{jg}$ is the g th column of $\mathbf{B}_j$ omitting the g th element which has been normalized to equal minus one and any zero elements, $\mathbf{Y}_{jg}$ is a matrix consisting of the columns of $\mathbf{Y}_j$ corresponding to the elements of $\boldsymbol{\beta}_{jg}$, $\boldsymbol{\gamma}_{jg}$ is the g th column of $\boldsymbol{\Gamma}_j$ omitting any zero elements, and $\mathbf{X}_{jg}$ is a matrix consisting of the columns of $\mathbf{X}_j$ corresponding to the elements of $\boldsymbol{\gamma}_{jg}$.

Assuming that $\mathbf{B}_j (j = 1, 2)$ is nonsingular, the reduced form corresponding to (11.5) is

$$\text{Regime 1:} \quad \mathbf{y}_{1t} = \mathbf{x}_{1t}\boldsymbol{\Pi}_1 + \mathbf{v}_{1t}, \tag{11.9}$$

$$\text{Regime 2:} \quad \mathbf{y}_{2t} = \mathbf{x}_{2t}\boldsymbol{\Pi}_2 + \mathbf{v}_{2t}, \tag{11.10}$$

or

$$\mathbf{Y}_j = \mathbf{X}_j\boldsymbol{\Pi}_j + \mathbf{V}_j \tag{11.11}$$

for $j = 1, 2$, where

$$\boldsymbol{\Pi}_j = -\boldsymbol{\Gamma}_j\mathbf{B}_j^{-1}, \tag{11.12}$$

$$\mathbf{v}_{jt} = -\boldsymbol{\varepsilon}_{jt}\mathbf{B}_j^{-1}, \tag{11.13}$$

$$\mathbf{V}_j = -\boldsymbol{\varepsilon}_j\mathbf{B}_j^{-1}. \tag{11.14}$$

If for $j = 1, 2$ the joint distribution of the structural error $\boldsymbol{\varepsilon}_{jt}$ and the switching error u_t is given by[3]

$$(\boldsymbol{\varepsilon}_{jt}, u_t)' \sim \text{i.i.d. } N(\mathbf{0}, \mathbf{C}_j), \tag{11.15}$$

3. As Lee (1976) has noted, $E(\varepsilon_{1t}\varepsilon'_{2t})$ is not identifiable.

where

$$\mathbf{C}_j = \begin{bmatrix} \boldsymbol{\Sigma}_j & \boldsymbol{\Sigma}_{ju} \\ \boldsymbol{\Sigma}'_{ju} & 1 \end{bmatrix}, \tag{11.16}$$

then it follows from (11.13) that the joint distribution of the reduced form error $\mathbf{v}_{jt}$ and the switching error u_t is given by

$$(\mathbf{v}_{jt}, u_j)' \sim \text{i.i.d.}\, N(\mathbf{0}, \boldsymbol{\Omega}_j), \tag{11.17}$$

where

$$\boldsymbol{\Omega}_j = \begin{bmatrix} (\mathbf{B}_j^{-1})'\boldsymbol{\Sigma}_j\mathbf{B}_j^{-1} & (\mathbf{B}_j^{-1})'\boldsymbol{\Sigma}_{ju} \\ \boldsymbol{\Sigma}'_{ju}\mathbf{B}_j^{-1} & 1 \end{bmatrix}. \tag{11.18}$$

The model just outlined posits that there exists two regimes, describing the determination of various measures y_{jt} of a physician's behavior under option choice j, and a binary random variable J_t, indicating the physician's actual option choice. Given exogenous variables x_{1t}, x_{2t}, and z_t, it is possible in theory to observe both y_{1t} and y_{2t} as well as J_t. However, in practice only those measures of a physician's behavior corresponding to a physician's actual choice are observed: y_{1t} is observed iff $J_t = 1$, and y_{2t} is observed iff $J_t = 2$. Thus there is a sample selectivity problem in the observed data if the unobserved determinant u_t of the option decision is correlated with the unobserved determinant ε_{jt} of the physician's behavior as measured by y_{jt}. To emphasize this partial observability, we will hereafter add whenever appropriate the condition $t \in S_j$ to denote that observation t belongs to regime j.

Since identification logically precedes estimation, it is appropriate to discuss it here before the estimation of the model described by (11.1) to (11.18). Goldfeld and Quandt (1973, p. 482) have noted that identification of the model can be achieved if the structural equations in each regime are identifiable, and if each equation in any one regime satisfies the same a priori restrictions as the corresponding equation in the other regime. However, as Lee (1979, p. 989) has noted, when sample separation information is available, this latter condition is not necessary. Thus in the following sections we will assume that a sufficient number of restrictions have been imposed on $\mathbf{B}_j$ and $\boldsymbol{\Gamma}_j$ ($j = 1, 2$) in each regime to insure identifiability.

11.3 Estimation

The gth reduced form equation of regime j in (11.9) or (11.10) can be written as

$$y_{jgt} = \mathbf{x}_{jt}\boldsymbol{\pi}_{jg} + v_{jgt}, \quad t \in \mathbf{S}_j, \tag{11.19}$$

where, for $j = 1, 2$, y_{jgt} and v_{jgt} are the gth elements of $\mathbf{y}_{jt}$ and $\mathbf{v}_{jt}$, respectively, and $\boldsymbol{\pi}_{jg}$ is the gth column of $\boldsymbol{\Pi}_j$. Using well-known properties of the truncated normal distribution, it is straightforward to derive the following properties for v_{jgt}:

$$E(v_{jgt} \mid J_t = j) = \omega_{jg,\,G_j+1}\,\delta_{jt}, \quad t \in \mathbf{S}_j, \tag{11.20}$$

$$E(v_{jgt}^2 \mid J_t = j) = \omega_{jgg} + (\omega_{jg,\,G_j+1})^2\,(\mathbf{z}_t\boldsymbol{\alpha})\delta_{jt}, \quad t \in \mathbf{S}_j, \tag{11.21}$$

where

$$\delta_{1t} = \phi(\mathbf{z}_t\boldsymbol{\alpha})\,[1 - \Phi(\mathbf{z}_t\boldsymbol{\alpha})]^{-1}, \quad t \in \mathbf{S}_1, \tag{11.22}$$

$$\delta_{2t} = -\,\phi(\mathbf{z}_t\boldsymbol{\alpha})\,[\Phi(\mathbf{z}_t\boldsymbol{\alpha})]^{-1}, \quad t \in \mathbf{S}_2, \tag{11.23}$$

and where ω_{jgi} is the element in the gth row and ith column of $\boldsymbol{\Omega}_j$, and $\phi(\cdot)$ denotes the standard normal density.

If $\omega_{jg,G_j+1} = 0$ (u_t and ε_{jgt} are independent), and we have enough sample observations for regime j, then, in the absence of any other complications, each regime can be estimated separately by one of the usual techniques such as two-stage least squares (2SLS). However, if $\omega_{jg,G_j+1} \neq 0$, then it can be seen from (11.20) that application of ordinary least squares, OLS, to (11.19), as is done in the first stage of 2SLS, will lead to inconsistent estimators.[4]

As a first step toward developing a consistent estimation scheme, define

$$\eta_{jgt} \equiv v_{jgt} - E(v_{jgt} \mid J_t = j), \quad t \in \mathbf{S}_j, \tag{11.24}$$

for $j = 1, 2$, and rewrite (11.19) as

$$y_{jgt} = \mathbf{x}_{jt}\boldsymbol{\pi}_{jg} + \omega_{jg,\,G_j+1}\,\delta_{jt} + \eta_{jgt}, \quad t \in \mathbf{S}_j. \tag{11.25}$$

Since by construction $E(\eta_{jgt} \mid J_t = j) = 0$, consistent estimators of π_{jg,G_j+1} can be obtained by applying OLS to (11.25), provided $\boldsymbol{\alpha}$ is known.

4. Note that, if (11.20) were nonzero but identical for all $t \in \mathbf{S}_j$, then only the estimator of the intercept in (11.19) would be biased. However, if the nonzero value of (11.20) varies across observations, then the estimators of all reduced form coefficients in (11.19) are biased.

The bias and inconsistency of the OLS estimator based on (11.19) arises from a specification error—namely, the exclusion of the sample selectivity regressor δ_{jt}. (The sign of this bias cannot in general be determined.) On an intuitive level the sample selectivity regression δ_{jt} is probably best thought of as an omitted variable. The sign of this omitted variable is determined solely by the observed option decision. Opted-in ($J_t = 1$) physicians have positive δ_{jt}'s and opted-out ($J_t = 2$) physicians have negative δ_{jt}'s. The magnitude (absolute value) of δ_{jt} is determined by how surprising is the observed option decision given the individual's probit score $\mathbf{z}_t\boldsymbol{\alpha}$.

While the implications for estimation of ignoring the sample selectivity regressor are fairly straightforward, it should also be pointed out that the sample selectivity regressor plays a crucial role in the interpretation of parameters in the model. To see this, suppose we wish to determine the impact, conditional on $J_t = j$, of an exogenous variable on the expected value of the g th endogenous variable in in the reduced form of regime j, that is, on

$$E(y_{jgt} \mid J_t = j) = \mathbf{x}_{jgt}\boldsymbol{\pi}_{jg} + \omega_{jg,G_j+1}\delta_{jt}. \tag{11.26}$$

Let the exogenous variable in question be the first regressor in $\mathbf{x}_{jgt}$, and denote it by $x_{jgt}^{(1)}$. Then

$$\frac{\partial[E(y_{jgt} \mid J_t = j)]}{\partial x_{jgt}^{(1)}} = \pi_{jg}^{(1)} + \omega_{jg,G_j+1}[\delta_{jt}(\delta_{jt} - \mathbf{z}_t\boldsymbol{\alpha})]\frac{\partial(\mathbf{z}_t\boldsymbol{\alpha})}{\partial x_{jgt}^{(1)}}, \tag{11.27}$$

where $\pi_{jg}^{(1)}$ is the first element in $\boldsymbol{\pi}_{jg}$, and the bracketed part of the second term is second term is $\partial\delta_{jt}/\partial x_{jgt}^{(1)}$. If $x_{jgt}^{(1)}$ is also an exogenous variable in the option decision, $[\partial(\mathbf{z}_t\boldsymbol{\alpha})/\partial x_{jgt}^{(1)}] \neq 0$, and if sample selectivity is present, $\omega_{jg,G_j+1} \neq 0$, then $\pi_{jg}^{(1)}$ cannot be interpreted as the impact of $x_{jgt}^{(1)}$ on $E(y_{jgt} \mid J_t = j)$; rather $\pi_{jg}^{(1)}$ gives the impact unconditional on the impact that works itself through the option decision.

Fortunately consistent estimators are still obtainable, even if $\boldsymbol{\alpha}$ is unknown. Heckman (1976) and Lee (1976) have shown that if $\hat{\boldsymbol{\alpha}}$ is a consistent estimator of $\boldsymbol{\alpha}$ (see section 11.4), then OLS applied to

$$\begin{aligned} y_{jgt} = {} & \mathbf{x}_{jt}\boldsymbol{\pi}_{jg} + \omega_{jg,G_j+1}\hat{\delta}_{jt} \\ & + [\eta_{jgt} + \omega_{jg,G_j+1}(\delta_{jt} - \hat{\delta}_{jt})], \quad t \in \mathbf{S}_j, \end{aligned} \tag{11.28}$$

where

$$\hat{\delta}_{1t} = \phi(\mathbf{z}_t\hat{\boldsymbol{\alpha}})[1 - \Phi(\mathbf{z}_t\hat{\boldsymbol{\alpha}})]^{-1}, \quad t \in \mathbf{S}_1, \tag{11.29}$$

$$\hat{\delta}_{2t} = -\phi(\mathbf{z}_t\hat{\boldsymbol{\alpha}})[\Phi(\mathbf{z}_t\hat{\boldsymbol{\alpha}})]^{-1}, \quad t \in \mathbf{S}_2, \tag{11.30}$$

will result in consistent estimators of π_{jg} and ω_{jg,G_j+1}. More specifically, defining the $T_j \times (K_j + 1)$ matrix,

$$W_j = [\mathbf{X}_j \mid \hat{\boldsymbol{\delta}}_j], \tag{11.31}$$

$j = 1, 2,$ where

$$\hat{\boldsymbol{\delta}}_j = [\hat{\boldsymbol{\delta}}_{j1}, \hat{\boldsymbol{\delta}}_{j2}, \ldots, \hat{\boldsymbol{\delta}}_{jT_j}]'; \tag{11.32}$$

then the OLS estimator of (11.28) is given by

$$\hat{\boldsymbol{\Pi}}_{jg} \equiv \left[\frac{\hat{\boldsymbol{\pi}}_{jg}}{\hat{\omega}_{ig,G_j+1}}\right] = (\mathbf{W}_j'\mathbf{W}_j)^{-1}\mathbf{W}_j'\mathbf{y}_{ig}. \tag{11.33}$$

Based on the results of Lee, Maddala, and Trost (1980), it can be shown that the asymptotic distribution of $\sqrt{T_j}(\hat{\boldsymbol{\Pi}}_{jg} - \boldsymbol{\Pi}_{jg})$ is normal with mean zero and covariance matrix $T_j\mathbf{T}_j$, where

$$\begin{aligned}\mathbf{T}_j = {} & \omega_{jgg}(\mathbf{W}_j'\mathbf{W}_j)^{-1} - \omega_{jg,G_j+1}^2[\mathbf{A}_j\mathbf{W}_j(\mathbf{W}_j'\mathbf{W}_j)^{-1}]' \\ & (\mathbf{A}_j^{-1} - \mathbf{Z}_j\boldsymbol{\Xi}\mathbf{Z}_j')[\mathbf{A}_j\mathbf{W}_j(\mathbf{W}_j'\mathbf{W}_j)^{-1}],\end{aligned} \tag{11.34}$$

and where $\boldsymbol{\Xi}$ is the asymptotic covariance matrix of $\hat{\boldsymbol{\alpha}}$ to be defined implicitly by (11.52). In (11.34) the $T \times m$ matrix of explanatory variables in the switching equation, namely,

$$\mathbf{Z} = \begin{bmatrix}\mathbf{z}_1\\ \mathbf{z}_2\\ \vdots\\ \mathbf{z}_T\end{bmatrix} = \left[\frac{\mathbf{Z}_1}{\mathbf{Z}_2}\right], \tag{11.35}$$

has been ordered and partitioned into two matrices $\mathbf{Z}_1$ and $\mathbf{Z}_2$, such that the first T_1 observations correspond to regime 1 and the last T_2 observations correspond to regime 2. This ordering is also utilized in defining the diagonal matrices

$$A_1 = \begin{bmatrix}\delta_{11}(\delta_{11} - \mathbf{z}_1\boldsymbol{\alpha}) & 0 & \cdots & 0\\ 0 & \delta_{12}(\delta_{12} - \mathbf{z}_2\boldsymbol{\alpha}) & \cdots & 0\\ \vdots & \vdots & & \vdots\\ 0 & 0 & & \delta_{1T_1}(\delta_{1T_1} - \mathbf{z}_{T_1}\boldsymbol{\alpha})\end{bmatrix}, \tag{11.36}$$

$$A_2 = \begin{bmatrix} \delta_{2,T_1+1}(\delta_{2,T_1+1} - \mathbf{z}_{T_1+1}\boldsymbol{\alpha}) & 0 & \cdots & 0 \\ 0 & \delta_{2,T_1+2}(\delta_{2,T_1+2} - \mathbf{z}_{T_1+2}\boldsymbol{\alpha}) & \cdots & 0 \\ \vdots & \vdots & & \vdots \\ 0 & 0 & \cdots & \delta_{2,T}(\delta_{2,T} - \mathbf{z}_T\boldsymbol{\alpha}) \end{bmatrix} \tag{11.37}$$

The unknown parameters in covariance matrix (11.34) may be estimated consistently by $\hat{\boldsymbol{\alpha}}$, $\hat{\omega}_{jg,G_j+1}$ given in (11.33), and

$$\hat{\omega}_{jgg} = T_j^{-1} \sum_{t \in \mathbf{S}_j} [\hat{\eta}_{jgt}^2 - (\hat{\omega}_{jg,G_j+1})^2(\mathbf{z}_t\hat{\boldsymbol{\alpha}} - \hat{\delta}_{jt})\hat{\delta}_{jt}], \tag{11.38}$$

where

$$\hat{\eta}_{jgt} = y_{jgt} - \mathbf{x}_{jgt}\hat{\boldsymbol{\pi}}_{jg} - \hat{\omega}_{jg,G_j+1}\hat{\delta}_{jgt}, \quad t \in S_j, \tag{11.39}$$

are the OLS residuals from (11.28).[5]

It is important to note that while (11.28) may be estimated by OLS, the usual covariance for OLS would be inappropriate, because it ignores the fact that $\hat{\boldsymbol{\alpha}}$ rather than $\boldsymbol{\alpha}$ is used in constructing the sample selectivity regressor and because, even if $\boldsymbol{\alpha}$ were known, the residuals are heteroscedastic. Ignoring this first aspect implies the incorrect covariance matrix

$$\omega_{jgg}(\mathbf{W}_j'\mathbf{W}_j)^{-1} - \omega_{jg,G_j+1}^2 [\mathbf{W}_j(\mathbf{W}_j'\mathbf{W}_j)^{-1}]'\mathbf{A}_j[\mathbf{W}_j(\mathbf{W}_j'\mathbf{W}_j)^{-1}], \tag{11.40}$$

which, as Lee, Maddala, and Trost (1980) note, underestimates all the variances. Ignoring the second aspect (the heteroscedasticity) would involve additional underestimation resulting from neglect of the second term in (11.40).

To obtain consistent estimators of the parameters in the gth ($g = 1, 2, \ldots, G_j$) structural equation in regime j ($j = 1, 2$), we can proceed as follows. Reconsider (11.8) which expresses the gth structural equation

5. Since the disturbances in (11.28) are heteroscedastic, it may be desirable on efficiency grounds to perform a two-step weighted least squares, WLS, procedure to (11.28). Similarly, since all the disturbances in (11.28) depend on $\hat{\boldsymbol{\alpha}}$, they are also serially correlated. See also Lee, Maddala, and Trost (1980) on this point.

(assumed to be identified) in regime j after imposition of all zero restrictions:

$$y_{jg} = \mathbf{Y}_{jg}\boldsymbol{\beta}_{jg} + \mathbf{X}_{jg}\gamma_{jg} + \boldsymbol{\varepsilon}_{jg}. \tag{11.41}$$

In terms of the notation just introduced, $\mathbf{Y}_{jg}$ is $T_j \times (G_{jg}^{\Delta} - 1)$, $\boldsymbol{\beta}_{jg}$ is $(G_{jg}^{\Delta} - 1) \times 1$, $\mathbf{X}_{jg}$ is $T_j \times K_{jg}^{*}$, and γ_{jg} is $K_{jg}^{*} \times 1$. Analogous to (11.28), it is easy to show that

$$E(\boldsymbol{\varepsilon}_{jg} \mid J_t = j,\ t \in S_j) = c_{jg,\,G_j+1}\boldsymbol{\delta}_j, \tag{11.42}$$

$j = 1, 2$, where c_{jg,G_j+1} is the element in the g th row and $(G_j + 1)$th column of $\mathbf{C}_j$. As in the case of reduced form estimation (11.42) indicates that (11.41) suffers from sample selectivity.

To correct this sample selectivity, define

$$\boldsymbol{\psi}_{jg} = \boldsymbol{\varepsilon}_{jg} - E(\boldsymbol{\varepsilon}_{jg} \mid J_t = j,\ t \in \mathbf{S}_j), \tag{11.43}$$

and rewrite (11.41) as

$$y_{jg} = Y_{jg}\beta_{jg} + X_{jg}\gamma_{jg} + c_{jg,\,G_j+1}\hat{\delta}_j + [\psi_{jg} + c_{jg,\,G_j+1}(\delta_j - \hat{\delta}_j)]. \tag{11.44}$$

While the inclusion of $\hat{\delta}_j$ in (11.44) removes the sample selectivity present in (11.41), (11.44) still suffers from simultaneous equations bias. However, this simultaneous equations bias in (11.44) can be handled in the usual fashion by two-stage least squares provided that instruments for the endogenous variables $\mathbf{Y}_{jg}$ are obtained from selectivity-free reduced form equation (11.28) rather than (11.19). In words, application of conventional 2SLS to the original structural equations augmented by the appropriate sample selectivity regressors will provide consistent estimators of the structural parameters. Alternatively the entire procedure may be viewed as 2SLS applied to an augmented system in which the estimated sample selectivity regressor appears in each structural equation. For further discussion, see Lee, Maddala, and Trost (1980).

From a computational standpoint, 2SLS applied to (11.54) can be equivalently viewed as OLS applied to

$$\begin{aligned} \mathbf{y}_{jg} = {} & \hat{\mathbf{Y}}_{jg}\boldsymbol{\beta}_{jg} + \mathbf{X}_{jg}\gamma_{jg} + c_{jg,\,G_j+1}\hat{\boldsymbol{\delta}}_j + [\psi_{jg} + c_{jg,\,G_j+1}(\boldsymbol{\delta}_j - \hat{\boldsymbol{\delta}}_j) \\ & + (\mathbf{Y}_{jg} - \mathbf{Y}_{jg})\boldsymbol{\beta}_{jg}], \end{aligned} \tag{11.45}$$

where $\hat{\mathbf{Y}}_{jg}$ is a $T_j \times (G_{jg}^{\Delta} - 1)$ matrix of predicted values of included endogenous variables obtained from reduced form (11.28). Defining the $T_j \times (G_{jg}^{\Delta} + K_{jg}^{*})$ matrix

$$\mathbf{D}_{jg} = [\hat{\mathbf{Y}}_{jg} \mid \mathbf{X}_{jg} \mid \hat{\boldsymbol{\delta}}_j], \tag{11.46}$$

the OLS estimator of (11.45) is defined by

$$\hat{\boldsymbol{\lambda}}_{jg} \equiv \begin{bmatrix} \hat{\boldsymbol{\beta}}_{jg} \\ \hat{\gamma}_{jg} \\ \hline \hat{c}_{jg,G_j+1} \end{bmatrix} = (\mathbf{D}'_{jg}\mathbf{D}_{jg})^{-1}\mathbf{D}'_{jg}\mathbf{y}_{jg}. \tag{11.47}$$

Based on arguments similar to those employed previously, it can be shown that the asymptotic distribution of $T_j^{1/2}(\hat{\boldsymbol{\lambda}}_{jg} - \boldsymbol{\lambda}_{jg})$ is normal with mean zero and covariance matrix $T_j\boldsymbol{\Lambda}_{jg}$, where

$$\begin{aligned}\boldsymbol{\Lambda}_{jg} = c_{jgg}(\mathbf{D}'_{jg}\mathbf{D}_{jg})^{-1} - c_{jg,G_j+1}[\mathbf{A}_j\mathbf{D}_{jg}(\mathbf{D}'_{jg}\mathbf{D}_{jg})^{-1}]' \\ (\mathbf{A}_j^{-1} - \mathbf{Z}_j\boldsymbol{\Xi}\mathbf{Z}'_j)[\mathbf{A}_j\mathbf{D}_{jg}(\mathbf{D}'_{jg}\mathbf{D}_{jg})^{-1}].\end{aligned} \tag{11.48}$$

As in the case of estimating the reduced form, the usual OLS procedure for constructing the covariance matrix will neglect the second term (11.48). A consistent estimator of the disturbance variance in structural equation g of regime j is given by

$$\hat{c}_{jgg} = T_j^{-1} \sum_{t \in \mathbf{S}_j} [\hat{\psi}_{jgt}^2 - (\hat{c}_{jg,G_{jg}+1}^2)\hat{\delta}_{jt}(\mathbf{z}_t\hat{\boldsymbol{\alpha}} - \hat{\delta}_{jt})]. \tag{11.49}$$

11.4 Estimation of the Switching (Option) Equation

The assumption in (11.1) that $u_t \sim N(0, 1)$ for $t = 1, 2, \ldots, T$ implies that a physician's decision to opt-in or opt-out can be described by the familiar probit model. Associated with this decision is the observed price charged by the physician. This price variable can be described as follows.

Consider two physicians performing an identical service, and suppose one has opted-in and the other has opted-out. The opted-in physician will bill the patient according to OHIP reimbursements which specify a rate equaling 0.9 times the Ontario Medical Association, OMA, scheduled fee for the service in question. The opted-out physician will bill at a rate in excess of 0.9 times the OMA fee. Thus the probability density for the relative price of this typical service will have a spike at 0.9 for opted-in physicians and a continuous positive segment over the range greater than

0.9 for opted-out physicians. This density is of course reminiscent of the classic model of Tobin (1958).

It would, however, seem overly restrictive to assume that the option and pricing decisions can be treated identically.[6] Thus as numerous authors (e.g., Cragg 1971) have suggested, we will treat them separately. However, we will not require the error terms in the option equation and the price equation to be statistically independent. In fact we expect them to be highly correlated, because both likely capture similar attitudinal characteristics.

Another connection with the limited dependent variable literature lies not with the model's structure but rather with the data-gathering process employed. In the qualitative choice literature exogenous sampling is distinguished from choice-based or, more appropriately here, regime-based sampling. In the present context exogenous sampling is one in which physicians are drawn and their choice behavior (e.g., option-decision) is observed. In contrast regime-based sampling is one in which a preassigned number of opted-in physicians and a preassigned number of opted-out physicians are selected, and their behavioral characteristics are observed. The statistical relevance of regime-based sampling is that it renders the usual ML estimator inconsistent. As an alternative to ML, Manski and Lerman (1977) and Manski and McFadden, chapter 1, have suggested a computationally simple weighted exogenous sampling maximum likelihood, WESML, estimator. In terms of the marginal likelihood for the option equation, the WESML of $\boldsymbol{\alpha}$ may be obtained by maximizing

$$L^*(\alpha) = \sum_{t=1}^{T} \xi_1 I_t \ln[\Phi(-\mathbf{z}_t\boldsymbol{\alpha})] + \xi_2(1 - I_t)\ln[\Phi(\mathbf{z}_t\boldsymbol{\alpha})]. \tag{11.50}$$

The weights in (11.50) are given by

$$\xi_j = \frac{Q(j)}{H(j)}, \tag{11.51}$$

$j = 1, 2$, where $Q(j)$ is the fraction of physicians in the population selecting option j and $H(j)$ is the analogous fraction for the regime-based sample.

6. If they were treated identically, then the switching equation would be analogous to the model considered by Tobin (1958). Lee, Maddala, and Trost (1980) have considered such a switching simultaneous equation in the case of random sampling, and they have outlined a two-step estimation procedure similar to that discussed in the text. Asymptotic covariance matrix (11.48) is, however, inappropriate, and it is no longer true that the usual 2SLS covariance matrix is biased downward.

The WESML estimator $\hat{\boldsymbol{\alpha}}$ is consistent and asymptotically normal; however, in general it is not asymptotically efficient. The asymptotic covariance matrix of $T^{1/2}(\hat{\boldsymbol{\alpha}} - \boldsymbol{\alpha})$ is given by $T\boldsymbol{\Xi}$, where $\boldsymbol{\Xi}$ can be consistently estimated by

$$\hat{\boldsymbol{\Xi}} = \left[\sum_{t=1}^{T} \left\{ \hat{\phi}_t(\mathbf{z}_t\hat{\boldsymbol{\alpha}})(\xi_1 - \xi_2) - \frac{\hat{\phi}_t^2(\xi_1(1 - \hat{\Phi}_t) + \xi_2\hat{\Phi}_t)}{\hat{\Phi}_t(1 - \hat{\Phi}_t)} \right\} \mathbf{z}_t'\mathbf{z}_t \right]^{-1}$$
$$\cdot \left[\sum_{t=1}^{T} \left\{ \frac{\hat{\phi}_t^2(\xi_1^2(1 - \hat{\Phi}_t) + \xi_2^2\hat{\Phi}_t)}{\hat{\Phi}_t(1 - \hat{\Phi}_t)} \right\} \mathbf{z}_t'\mathbf{z}_t \right]$$
$$\cdot \left[\sum_{t=1}^{T} \left\{ \hat{\phi}_t(\mathbf{z}_t\hat{\boldsymbol{\alpha}})(\xi_1 - \xi_2) - \frac{\hat{\phi}_t^2(\xi_1(1 - \hat{\Phi}_t) + \xi_2\hat{\Phi}_t)}{\hat{\Phi}_t(1 - \hat{\Phi}_t)} \right\} \mathbf{z}_t'\mathbf{z}_t \right]^{-1}, \tag{11.52}$$

where $\hat{\Phi}_t = \Phi(\mathbf{z}_t\hat{\boldsymbol{\alpha}})$ and $\hat{\phi}_t = \phi(\mathbf{z}_t\hat{\boldsymbol{\alpha}})$ for $t = 1, 2, \ldots, T$.

In the model specification considered here, the switching or option equation drives the model in the sense that the two regimes depend in a recursive fashion on the option equation. While we have permitted correlation between the disturbance term in the option equation and the disturbance terms in the structural equations of each regime, we have omitted any of the endogenous variables in each regime from appearing in the option equation itself. Although this specification seems reasonable given the stickiness and infrequency of the option decision, more general specifications may be employed. See Lee (1979) for a discussion.

11.5 Empirical Results

In Wolfson and Tuohy (1980) the model presently under discussion is estimated, using a survey sample of 309 Ontario physicians. Given the size of the model—a total of 26 structural equations involving 549 coefficients in addition to the option equation—the present discussion will involve only a few selected issues. Specifically section 11.6 will provide a brief discussion of the option equation, and section 11.7 will provide a similarly brief discussion of one particular structural equation appearing in both regimes, namely, the equation describing the extent to which the physician generates medical services by referring patients to other physicians (measured in terms of the dollar value of the referred services). However, before proceeding on to a discussion of these equations, a brief overview of the entire model will be given.

In the sample of $T = 309$ physicians, 82 physicians (0.2654 percent) opted-out of OHIP. The opted-out regime for these $T_2 = 82$ physicians consists of $G_2 = 9$ structural equations involving $K_2 = 43$ exogenous variables. The nine endogenous variables are (1) the total OHIP billings for the physician during the period May 1975 to January 1976, (2) the total discrete patient load for the physician during the five-month period September 1975 to January 1976, (3) the average number of days between the time a patient requests services and the time of an encounter with the physician, (4) the total hours worked per week by the physician on the provision of patient care (exclusive of teaching, administration, and research), (5) the salaries paid to office employees, (6) the total annual office expenses less salaries, (7) the dollar value of laboratory investigations and radiological tests and ordered from other physicians during the period May 1975 to January 1976, (8) the dollar value of medical services arising from referral of patients to other physicians during the period May 1975 to January 1976, and (9) a price index reflecting the average price charged by the physician relative to the price charged by an opted-in physician. In all cases these structural equations are extremely overidentified—the average degree of overidentification being approximately twenty.

For the remaining $T_1 = 227$ physicians, the opted-in regime is divided into two subregimes: one for the 128 general practitioners and one for the 99 specialists contained in the opted-in sample.[7] Both of the subregimes contain a structural equation for each of the first eight endogenous variables considered in the opted-out regime. In addition the subregime for opted-in general practitioners contains an additional structural equation describing the extent to which each general practitioner's patients use the services of other physicians on a nonreferral basis. The subregime for general practitioners involves 33 exogenous variables and the subregime for specialists involves the same 33 exogenous variables plus 6 specialist dummies. Hence there are a total of $G_1 = 17$ endogenous variables and $K_1 = 72$ exogenous variables in the overall opted-in regime. As in the opted-out regime all equations in the opted-in regime are highly overidentified.

7. The small sample size precluded a similar division for opted-out physicians.

11.6 Estimated Option Equation

In the theoretical model developed in Wolfson and Tuohy (1980) the option equation plays a central role. The overall model is predicated on the belief that physicians who opt-out of OHIP are inherently different in terms of practice behavior from those who opt-in. The option decision is viewed as disjoint from the rest of the model in the sense that it does not depend on contemporaneous characteristics of the physician's practice. Rather it depends on basic characteristics of the individual and the community in which he practices. It is not, however, fully recursive from the rest of the model because the unobserved elements that help determine the option decision are allowed to be correlated with unobserved components of the various other endogenous variables in the model.

Since the overall population proportion of Ontario physicians who opt-out is comparatively small, opted-out physicians were oversampled to guarantee that they would appear in sufficient numbers in the final sample. Specifically in terms of (11.51) the appropriate weights are

$$\xi_1 = 0.4435 \quad \text{and} \quad \xi_2 = 1.201. \tag{11.53}$$

In the results that follow both weighted and unweighted maximum likelihood estimates will be presented.

The central role of the option decision arises from a methodological position that underscores the sociopolitical factors created by government intrusion into medical care. The existence of the opting-out provision has had a major symbolic and strategic importance for organized medicine in Ontario. It symbolizes the independence of physicians, both individually and as a self-governing profession, from government, and it also enhances the bargaining power of organized medicine in negotiating the schedule of payments to physicians under the government plan.

In general the local medical community, which in many areas is coincident with the hospital medical staff association, is politically, socially, and economically cohesive. This may not be so much a matter of the exercise of political, social, and economic sanctions (although certainly these sanctions exist in the form of the granting of hospital privileges, the referral of patients, the scheduling of operating room time, and social amenities) as it is a matter of the existence of a community of shared expertise and experience within which political and economic behavior is shaped.[8]

As can be seen from table 11.1, the option decision depends on $m = 26$ variables $z_1, z_2, \ldots, z_{26}$. These twenty-six variables can be conveniently broken down into eight broad groups: family characteristics, community characteristics, teaching duties, foreign background, political orientation, attitudes toward government, specialty effects, and a catch-all miscellaneous classification. Leaving more detailed definitions to Wolfson and Tuohy (1980), it will simply be noted here that the descriptions in table 11.1 are for the most part self-explanatory. Variables z_2, z_3, z_7 through z_{22}, and z_{24} are all dummies defined in an obvious fashion. Throughout the subsequent analysis one, two, and three asterisks will be used to denote asymptotic significance at the 10, 5, and 1 percent levels, respectively.

Overall the results contained in table 11.1 are quite satisfactory. All coefficients have the sign expected a priori, and as can be seen from table 11.2, the joint effects of groups of variables are for the most part highly significant. Leaving a detailed discussion to Wolfson and Tuohy (1980), we will dwell on only one economic aspect here, namely, the crucial role played by z_6 in the option decision. The results strongly suggest that the percent of opted-out physicians in the same specialty in the community is a major determinant in a physician's own option decision. In fact this emulation of peers is so strong that it swamps most other community and specialty effects. While attitudinal characteristics do play a role, the impact of the local market for the physician's services, as reflected in z_6, is most interesting.

The most interesting econometric aspect of the estimated option equation is the effect of weighting to correct for regime-based sampling. The estimated standard errors of coefficients from WESML are uniformly smaller than their unweighted counterparts. As a result the effects of variables tend to look more significant when considering the weighted as opposed to unweighted probit estimates. While of course the inconsistency of unweighted probit estimates makes any inference based on unweighted

8. Economically this local cohesiveness facilitates the establishment and maintenance of common price structures for opted-out physicians. In most professional markets, including medicine, professionals have treated the practitioner who charges prices lower than those of his peers as suspect of offering services of a quality lower than the community standard as well. Price-cutters in medicine may find themselves in conflict with local agencies of peer review, such as hospital staff committees, who have the effective ability to award, refuse, or curtail hospital privileges.

Table 11.1
Switching (option) equation

Number	Variable descriptions	Weighted probit: Estimated coefficient	Weighted probit: Estimated Standard deviation	Unweighted probit: Estimated coefficient	Unweighted probit: Estimated standard deviation
	Family characteristics				
1	number of dependents	0.08422*	0.05070	0.08794	0.06029
2	spouse employed	0.05768	0.2149	0.1012	0.2417
	Community characteristics				
3	urban	0.8568***	0.2947	0.9793**	0.4566
4	average income per capita	0.1923	0.8731	0.2821	1.100
5	physicians per capita	−0.1983	0.2252	−0.1400	0.2689
6	percent opted-out in the physicians own speciality	0.0358***	0.007447	0.03775***	0.007530
	Teaching duties				
7	part-time	0.5646***	0.2160	0.6380***	0.2456
8	full-time	−0.2692	0.4209	−0.1458	0.4472
	Foreign background				
9	born in England	0.4601	0.3238	0.4689	0.3891
10	born outside of Canada or England	−0.1852	0.2731	−0.1964	0.3318
11	Ontario medical education	0.4940*	0.2685	0.5308*	0.3136
	Political orientation				
12	liberal	−0.3983*	0.2190	−0.4155*	0.2517
13	conservative	0.3612	0.2286	0.3893	0.2692

Table 11.1
(continued)

Number	Variable descriptions	Weighted probit: Estimated coefficient	Weighted probit: Estimated Standard deviation	Unweighted probit: Estimated coefficient	Unweighted probit: Estimated standard deviation
	Attitude toward government				
14	more power among physicians	−0.02671	0.2474	−0.02823	0.2834
15	less power in the medical review committee	0.6619***	0.2325	0.7431***	0.2781
	Specialties				
16	family practice	0.2009	0.2782	0.2079	0.3943
17	obstetrics and gynecology	0.5502	0.5072	0.3868	0.5847
18	pediatrics	−0.3473	0.4777	−0.3756	0.6296
19	anaesthesia	−0.6880*	0.3930	−0.5737	0.4755
20	psychiatry	0.1872	0.6305	0.2908	0.6938
21	surgery	0.5684	0.4531	0.4630	0.5572
22	medical specialties	1.029*	0.6023	0.8461	0.7340
	Miscellaneous				
23	years of practice in present locality	0.01656*	0.009207	0.01880	0.01211
24	member of a medical advisory committee	0.04963	0.1820	0.05657	0.2215
25	billings of physician's specialty relative to the billings of all physicians	−3.973**	1.829	−3.355	2.107
26	constant term	−0.3745	1.798	−0.7800	2.128

Note: * Significant at 10 percent level; ** significant at 5 percent level; *** significant at 1 percent level.

Table 11.2
Tests of joint effects

Test description	Degrees of freedom	Weighted probit	Unweighted probit
Family characteristics			
$\alpha_1 = \alpha_2 = 0$	2	2.773*	2.216
Community characteristics			
$\alpha_3 = \alpha_4 = 0$ (demographic)	2	10.61***	5.700**
$\alpha_5 = \alpha_6 = 0$ (medical)	2	24.19***	25.13***
$\alpha_3 = \alpha_4 = \alpha_5 = \alpha_6 = 0$ (total)	4	38.70***	33.79***
Teaching duties			
$\alpha_7 = \alpha_8 = 0$	2	7.992**	7.604**
Foreign background			
$\alpha_9 = \alpha_{10} = 0$ (birth)	2	4.373	2.893
$\alpha_9 = \alpha_{10} = \alpha_{11} = 0$ (total)	3	7.327*	5.379
Political orientation			
$\alpha_{12} = \alpha_{13} = 0$	2	7.566**	6.401**
Attitude toward government			
$\alpha_{14} = \alpha_{15} = 0$	2	8.333**	7.227**
Specialties			
$\alpha_{17} = \alpha_{18} \ldots = \alpha_{22} = 0$ (non-GP's)	6	11.23*	7.300
$\alpha_{16} = \alpha_{17} = \ldots = \alpha_{22} = 0$ (total)	7	11.89	7.500
Total			
$\alpha_1 = \alpha_2 = \ldots = \alpha_{26} = 0$	26	85.04***	85.57***

Note: *Significant at 10 percent level; ** significant at 5 percent level; ***significant at 1 percent level.

estimates tenuous at best, it is interesting to note that, unless one was overly attached to magical significance levels, then one would be led to basically the same economic conclusions using the unweighted as opposed to the weighted estimates.[9]

Table 11.3 suggests, however, that predictions of opting-out probabilities do differ substantially between the weighted and unweighted estimates. Not surprisingly, the unweighted estimates, which ignore the oversampling of opted-out physicians, yield higher predicted probabilities of opting-out than the weighted estimates. Based on a critical predicted probability of 0.5, the weighted estimates predict observed options slightly more accurately than the unweighted estimates.

Finally, the sample selectivity regressors implied by the weighted and unweighted coefficient estimates have a correlation of 0.9755 and fairly similar partial correlations with respect to other variables. Thus whether weighted or unweighted sample selectivity regressors are used in the analysis of either regime is of little practical consequence.

11.7 Estimated Referral Equation

In any publicly financed medical scheme an important consideration for policy purposes is the degree to which the medical profession generates medical services from within through referrals for consultations with other physicians. Specifically, it is of interest to determine whether various characteristics of the physician, his community, and his practice are systematically related to the referrals he generates. In addition there also exists the question of whether these systematic determinants differ in their impact on opted-in and opted-out physicians.

To assess the determinants of physician referrals the following equations were estimated. The equations in both regimes share numerous mutual determinants. As in the option equation family and community character-

9. The marginal effect of z_{ti} on the probability of the tth physician opting-out is given by

$$\frac{\partial[\text{Prob}(I_t = 1)]}{\partial z_{ti}} = \phi(\mathbf{z}_t\boldsymbol{\alpha})\alpha_i.$$

This effect may be estimated for the average physician by $\phi(\bar{\mathbf{z}}\hat{\boldsymbol{\alpha}}) \cdot \hat{\alpha}_i$. From table 11.3 it is seen that $\phi(\bar{\mathbf{z}}\hat{\boldsymbol{\alpha}}) = 0.1383$ in the case of the weighted estimates, and $\phi(\bar{\mathbf{z}}\hat{\boldsymbol{\alpha}}) = 0.2521$ in the case of unweighted estimates. As a result these marginal effects tend to be overestimated in the case of unweighted probit, since the unweighted estimates of the α_i's tend to be larger in absolute value.

Table 11.3
Descriptive statistics

Statistic	Weighted probit	Unweighted probit
Proportion of successful predictions	0.8317	0.8285
Weighted proportion of successful predictions	0.5854	0.6199
Population proportion opting-out	0.1177	0.1177
Predicted probability of opting-out at mean index	0.07272	0.1690
Mean predicted probability of opting-out	0.1736	0.2658
Density evaluated at mean index	0.1383	0.2521

istics, teaching duties, political orientation, and specialty variables reappear. The only new variables included in these groups are the number of hospitals at which the physician has privileges and the average referral rate of the physician's peer group. In addition three other groups of variables are employed: three endogenous variables, three attitudinal variables, and two practice characteristics.[10]

Table 11.4 contains the results of estimating the referral equation for opted-in general practitioners. (The results for opted-in specialists have been omitted for the sake of brevity.) Both OLS and 2SLS estimates are provided. In the case of 2SLS two estimated standard deviations are given: one is uncorrected for heteroscedasticity and the estimated nature of the

10. The three attitudinal variables are dummy variables referring to the physician's practice behavior. The first equals one if the physician takes into account the cost of treatment, besides the patients medical condition, when recommending treatment. Similarly the second equals unity if the physician takes into account the patient's wishes when recommending treatment. The third equal unity if the physician feels harassed by problem patients. The first practice characteristic variable is a dummy variable equaling unity if the physician belongs to a multispecialty group. The second is a scaled variable so that larger values indicate that the physican provides, relatively speaking, more complex services. In other words, a large value indicates that the physician's practice is concentrated in services that are themselves concentrated among relatively few physicians.

Table 11.4
Estimated referral equation for opted-in general practitioners

Number	Variable descriptions	2SLS Coefficient	2SLS Standard deviation (uncorrected)	2SLS Standard deviation (corrected)	OLS Coefficient	OLS Standard deviation
	Endogenous variables					
1	patient load	3.485***	0.7342	0.8204**	2.669***	0.3321
2	labor employed	0.5312	0.09448	0.9150	0.09997**	0.0423
3	overhead	−0.02303	0.07798	0.07489	−0.04109	0.0250
	Family characteristics					
4	number of dependents	−68.05	157.1	160.8	−34.23	129.7
5	spouse employed	654.5	570.5	688.9	682.7	479.6
	Community characteristics					
6	urban	513.4	627.9	2579.0	565.0	533.5
7	average income per capita	−0.3419	0.2465	0.6024	−0.2872	0.2060
8	physicians per capita	−2.065	674.4	907.5	−143.2	568.1
9	hospital privileges	198.6	244.8	237.9	193.7	205.6
10	average referrals of others in the physicians own speciality	9.208***	2.956	3.463**	9.534***	2.417
	Teaching duties					
11	part-time	−510.3	1056.0	2561.0	−606.8	861.0
	Political orientation					
12	liberal	442.2	571.0	1062.0	237.6	472.2
13	conservative	22.01	942.7	1017.0	−30.66	754.6

Table 11.4
(continued)

Number	Variable descriptions	2SLS Coefficient	2SLS Standard deviation (uncorrected)	2SLS Standard deviation (corrected)	OLS Coefficient	OLS Standard deviation
	Practice attitudes toward					
14	cost of treatment	170.9	531.3	970.4	320.5	434.3
15	patients' wishes	−399.9	530.8	683.2	−504.0	437.5
16	problem patients	656.1	569.7	605.6	492.5	459.4
	Practice characteristics					
17	member of a multispecialty group practice	−755.5	971.5	1320.0	−1174.0	770.2
18	complexity	−2815.0*	1678.0	2333.0	−1700.0	1255.0
	Specialty					
19	family practice	−2129.0***	783.4	908.0**	−1792.0***	625.3
	Miscellaneous					
20	sample selectivity regressor	5391.0	3416.0	47077.0	4703.0*	2842.0
21	constant term	−357.3	2231.0	7843.0	−509.4	1893.7

Note: * Significant at 10 percent level; ** significant at 5 percent level; *** significant at 1 percent level.

sample selectivity regressor, and the other is corrected for both. Joint hypothesis tests based on Wald's method are given in table 11.5. Asterisks on the corrected standard deviations indicate the significance of the coefficients when the corrected standard deviations are used.

Basically the results indicate that the principle determinants of referrals for an opted-in general practitioner are (not surprisingly) the patient load, the referral behavior of peers, and whether the physician has a certificate from the College of Family Physicians. The overall fit of the equation is indicated by the 2SLS $R^2 = 0.4255$.

Surprisingly there is little evidence of sample selectivity. Given the corrected variance estimator $\hat{c}_{1gg} = 58913.0$, it is seen that the estimated correlation between u_t and ε_{1gt} is $5391/(58913.0)^{1/2} = 2.221$, which exceeds unity by a substantial margin.[11] Hence the point estimate for $\hat{c}_{1g,G_1+1}$ is both implausible and insignificant.

Tables 11.6 and 11.7 contain estimates analogous to tables 11.4 and 11.5, but for opted-out physicians. The results indicate that the principle determinants of referrals for an opted-out physician are family characteristics, the referral behavior of his peers, and his political orientation. The strong negative effect of the number of dependents is consistent with the hypothesis that an opted-out physician with family dependents will be hesitant to make referrals and run the risk of losing patients. The nature of the employed spouse effect is somewhat unclear and does not correspond to the a priori expected sign. The negative political orientation effects indicate that opted-out physicians who consider themselves to be more liberal or more conservative than the Ontario Medical Association are also less likely to make referrals. For opted-out physicians $R^2 = 0.6922$.

Once again there is little evidence of sample selectivity. Given the corrected variance estimator $\hat{c}_{2gg} = 23274.5$, the estimated correlation between u_t and ε_{2gt} is $-35.07/(23274.5)^{1/2} = -0.02299$. Taking into account the estimated nature of the sample selectivity regressor has a negligible effect on the estimated standard deviations.

Formal testing of identical behavior across the regimes is of little consequence here since the regimes were specified to be different on a priori

11. The fact that the estimated correlation exceeds unity explains why the corrected standard deviations in table 11.4 are sometimes smaller than the uncorrected standard deviations.

Table 11.5
Test of joint effects in referral equation (opted-in general practitioners)

Test description	Degrees of freedom	2SLS (corrected)	2SLS (uncorrected)	OLS
Endogenous variables				
$\beta_{1g1} = \beta_{1g2} = \beta_{1g3} = 0$	3	23.48***	30.72***	91.35***
Family characteristics				
$\gamma_{1g1} = \gamma_{1g2} = 0$	2	0.9851	1.578	2.140
Community characteristics				
$\gamma_{1g3} = \gamma_{1g4} = 0$ (demographic)	2	0.8214	2.335	2.717
$\gamma_{1g5} = \gamma_{1g6} = \gamma_{1g7} = 0$ (medical)	3	11.84***	12.67***	19.25***
$\gamma_{1g2} = \dots = \gamma_{1g7} = 0$ (total)	5	14.96***	16.53***	27.28***
Political orientation				
$\gamma_{1g9} = \gamma_{1g,10} = 0$	2	0.1880	0.6013	0.2594
Practice attitudes				
$\gamma_{1g,11} = \gamma_{1g,12} = \gamma_{1g,13} = 0$	3	1.969	1.961	2.430
Practice characteristics				
$\gamma_{1g,14} = \gamma_{1g,15} = 0$	2	5.400*	4.936*	5.331*
Total				
$\beta_{1g1} = \dots = \beta_{1g3} = \gamma_{1g1} = \dots = \gamma_{1g1,17} = 0$	20	88.87***	94.80***	176.1***

Note: * Significant at 10 percent level; ** significant at 5 percent level; *** significant at 1 percent level.

Table 11.6
Estimated referral equation for opted-out physicians

Number	Variable descriptions	2SLS Coefficient	2SLS Standard deviation (uncorrected)	2SLS Standard deviation (corrected)	OLS Coefficient	OLS Standard deviation
	Endogenous variables					
1	patient load	0.1393	0.7337	0.7340	0.1836	0.4553
2	labor employed	0.05294	0.06784	0.06791	0.1322***	0.03123
3	overhead	0.03548	0.03817	0.03820	−0.004030	0.01785
	Family characteristics					
4	number of dependents	−319.4***	122.3	122.6***	−276.7***	104.0
5	spouse employed	−862.9*	482.6	483.6*	−1005.0**	413.4
	Community characteristics					
6	urban	1068.0	1372.0	1382.0	1099.1	1197.0
7	average income per capita	0.1841	0.2728	0.3147	0.09507	0.2171
8	physicians per capita	−837.4	603.1	603.6	−597.0	500.9
9	average referrals of others in the physicians own specialty	0.7752***	0.1530	0.1532**	0.7298***	0.1255
10	percent opted-out in physicians own specialty	−31.88	20.71	20.89	−25.51**	17.62
	Teaching duties					
11	part-time	−759.7	502.3	504.4	−664.0	422.6
12	full-time	−1679.0*	992.6	993.9	−1168.0	789.0

Table 11.6
(*continued*)

		2SLS			OLS	
Number	Variable descriptions	Coefficient	Standard deviation (uncorrected)	Standard deviation (corrected)	Coefficient	Standard deviation
	Political orientation					
13	liberal	−1391.0**	502.3	572.7**	−1257.0**	494.1
14	conservative	−1393.0***	501.9	502.5***	−1311.0***	436.1
	Practice attitudes toward:					
15	cost of treatment	53.28	504.7	505.2	−203.0	406.4
16	patients' wishes	355.4	581.5	581.8	492.9	499.5
17	problem patients	−464.4	461.4	461.8	−551.4	393.2
	Practice characteristics					
18	member of multispecialty group practice	−283.3	1088.0	1088.0	−166.5	953.0
19	complexity	−1950.0	1220.0	1221.0	−2185.0	1000.0
	Specialties					
20	family practice	1609.0	979.3	983.8	1452.0*	855.2
21	obstrics and gynecology	595.0	981.4	983.7	412.4	842.8
22	pediatrics	−154.9	1369.0	1370.0	174.0	1174.0
23	anaesthesia	−78.06	1495.0	1496.0	573.9	1228.0
24	psychiatry	−1275.0	1054.0	1057.0	−588.9	831.1
25	surgery	−240.6	1100.0	1101.0	−87.93	928.9
26	medical specialties	−984.1	1029.0	1030.0	−538.1	863.6
	Miscellaneous					
27	sample selectivity regressor	−35.07	706.9	1023.0	136.0	615.4
28	constant term	3835.0	3265.0	3792.0	388.6	2728.0

Table 11.7
Test of joint effects in referral equation for opted-out physicians

Test description	Degrees of freedom	2SLS (corrected)	2SLS (uncorrected)	OLS
Endogenous variables				
$\beta_{2g1} = \beta_{2g2} = \beta_{2g3} = 0$	3	5.117	5.120	30.94***
Family characteristics				
$\gamma_{2g1} = \gamma_{2g2} = 0$	2	9.518***	9.578***	11.87***
Community characteristics				
$\gamma_{2g3} = \gamma_{2g4} = 0$ (demographic)	2	1.278	1.707	1.564
$\gamma_{2g5} = \gamma_{2g6} = \gamma_{2g7} = 0$ (medical)	3	29.88***	30.03***	38.97***
$\gamma_{2g3} = \ldots = \gamma_{2g7} = 0$ (total)	5	32.25***	32.64***	41.29***
Teaching duties				
$\gamma_{2g8} = \gamma_{2g9} = 0$	2			
Political orientation				
$\gamma_{2g,10} = \gamma_{2g,11} = 0$	2	11.14***	11.18***	12.86***
Practice attitudes				
$\gamma_{2g,12} = \gamma_{2g,13} = \gamma_{2g,14} = 0$	3	1.397	1.398	2.633
Practice characteristics				
$\gamma_{2g,15} = \gamma_{2g,16} = 0$	2	2.552	2.554	4.839
Specialties				
$\gamma_{2g,18} = \ldots = \gamma_{2g,23} = 0$	6	3.949	3.957	2.685
$\gamma_{2g,17} = \ldots = \gamma_{2g,23} = 0$	7	8.668	8.736	8.274
Total				
$\beta_{2g1} = \ldots = \beta_{2g3} = \gamma_{2g1} = \ldots = \gamma_{2g,24} = 0$	27	167.0***	184.4***	263.4***

Note: * Significant at 10 percent level; ** significant at 5 percent level; *** significant at 1 percent level.

grounds.[12] However, one similarity stands out, namely, the predominant influence of referral practices of the physician's peer group. Such peer group effects are not isolated to the referral equation alone but rather form one of the basic founding blocks upon which the model of Wolfson and Tuohy (1980) is built.

11.8 Concluding Remarks

The development of the econometric model of physician behavior reported here and in Wolfson and Tuohy (1980) necessitated addressing three major econometric issues: (1) the regime-based nature of the sampling procedure, (2) the switching role played by the option equation, and (3) simultaneous equations bias. Here a few concluding remarks are offered concerning each of these issues.

With respect to (1) the overall impression one obtains from tables 11.1 through 11.3 is that the WESML estimator yields tangibly better results than the unweighted estimator. However, the choice between the sample selectivity regressors of the two methods had little effect on estimation in the individual regimes.

With respect to (2) the results of the overall model indicate that the sample selectivity regressor has little explanatory power in any of the structural equations. No matter whether one considers OLS estimates of the 26 reduced form equations, or either OLS or 2SLS estimates of the 26 structural equations, there are never more than 3 out of 26 sample selectivity regressors individually significant at the 10 percent significance level. The practical implication of this result is that the unobserved variables on which the option decision depends appear to be uncorrelated with the unobserved components of the various structural equations, and hence the two regimes may be analyzed separately from the option equation without fear of serious sample selectivity.

12. Such a priori specifications are of two types. First are theoretically motivated specifications such as belonging to the opted-out regime of the percent of opted-out physicians in an individual's peer group but not to the opted-in regime. This specification is premised on the grounds that the behavior of opted-out physicians is highly dependent on the market situation they face. Second are sample-motivated specifications such general practitioners and specialists combined in the opted-out regime due to small sample sizes. Despite such a priori specifications, equality across regimes of remaining coefficients may be tested by combining the two regimes in a manner reminiscent of the *D*-method of Goldfeld and Quandt (1972) and Lee (1976).

Finally, with respect to (3) the acknowledgment of simultaneity by the use of 2SLS led to somewhat different results than arose from the use of OLS; however, for the most part the differences were slight. In particular the weak explanatory power of the sample selectivity regressor persisted under both 2SLS and OLS.

References

Cragg, J. G. 1971. Some Statistical Models for Limited Dependent Variables with Application to the Demand for Durable Goods. *Econometrica*. 39: 829–844.

Goldfeld, S. M., and R. E. Quandt. 1972. *Nonlinear Methods in Econometrics* Amsterdam: North-Holland.

Goldfeld, S. M., and R. E. Quandt. 1973. The Estimation of Structural Shifts by Switching Regressions. *Annals of Economic and Social Measurement*. 2: 475–485.

Goldfeld, S. M., and R. E. Quandt. 1976. Techniques for Estimating Ssitching Regressions. In *Studies in Nonlinear Estimation*, ed. S. M. Goldfeld and R. E. Quandt. Cambridge, Mass.: Ballinger, chapter 1.

Heckman, J. J. 1976. Simultaneous Equation Models with Continuous and Discrete Endogenous Variables and Structural Shifts. In *Studies in Nonlinear Estimation*, ed. S. M. Goldfeld and R. E. Quandt. Cambridge, Mass.: Ballinger, pp. 235–272.

Lee, L. F. 1976. Two Stage Estimation of Limited Dependent Variable Models. Ph.D dissertation. Department of Economics, University of Rochester.

Lee, L. F. 1979. Identification and Estimation in Binary Choice Models with Limited (Censored) Dependent Variables. *Econometrica*. 977–996.

Lee, L. F., and R. P. Trost. 1978. Estimation of Some Limited Dependent Variable Models with Application to Housing Demand. *Journal of Econometrics*. 357–382.

Lee, L. F., G. S. Maddala, and R. P. Trost. 1980. Asymptotic Covariance Matrices of Two-Stage Probit and Two-Stage Tobit Methods for Simultaneous Equations Model with Selectivity. *Econometrica*. 48: 491–503.

Maddala, G. S., and F. D. Nelson. 1975. Switching Regression Models with Exogenous and Endogenous Switching. *Proceedings of the Business and Economics Statistics Section, American Statistical Association*, pp. 423–426.

Manski, C. F., and S. Lerman. 1977. The Estimation of Choice Probabilities from Choice Based Samples. *Econometrica*. 45: 1977–1988.

Poirier, D. J. 1976. *The Econometrics of Structural Change* Amsterdam: North-Holland.

Tobin, J. 1958. Estimation of Relationships for Limited Dependent Variables. *Econometrica*. 26: 24–36.

Wolfson, A. D., and C. Tuohy. 1980. *Opting-Out of Medicare; Private Medical Markets within the Ontario Programme*. Toronto: University of Toronto Press.

12 Constraints on the Parameters in Simultaneous Tobit and Probit Models

Peter Schmidt

12.1 Introduction

This chapter considers simultaneous tobit and probit models. When the observed (truncated or dichotomous) endogenous variables appear as right-hand side (r.h.s.) variables in some or all equations, the parameters of the model must satisfy certain constraints. It turns out that the constraints for the tobit and probit cases are similar in form. However, in the tobit case the constraints are inequalities, while in the probit case they are equalities. In the probit case these constraints rule out some models that would seem apparently reasonable, at least at first glance, and impose a degree of recursivity on the allowable models.

12.2 Simultaneous Tobit Models

Throughout this section a superscript* will represent an unobservable variable; the same variable without the asterisk will represent its observable (truncated) counterpart. In a tobit context the relationship between unobservables and observables is of course

$$y = \begin{cases} y^* & \text{if } y^* > 0, \\ 0 & \text{if } y^* \le 0, \end{cases}$$

for any variable y subject to a tobit truncation.

The models to be considered here have the observed endogenous variables as explanatory variables. For example, a simple two-equation model with one truncation could be written as follows:

$$y_1^* = \gamma_1 y_2 + \boldsymbol{\beta}_1' \mathbf{X} + \varepsilon_1, \tag{12.1}$$

$$y_2 = \gamma_2 y_1 + \boldsymbol{\beta}_2' \mathbf{X} + \varepsilon_2, \tag{12.2}$$

$$y_1 = \begin{cases} y_1^* & \text{if } y_1^* > 0, \\ 0 & \text{if } y_1^* \le 0. \end{cases} \tag{12.3}$$

(Here $\mathbf{X}$ is a vector of exogenous variables, and ε_1 and ε_2 are disturbances.) Note it is the observed y_1 (not the unobserved y_1^*) that appears on the r.h.s. of (12.2). Models of this general type have been considered by Amemiya (1974), Lee (1976), and Schmidt and Sickles (1978).

On the other hand, models in which the truncated versions of endogenous variables never appear as r.h.s. variables have been considered by Nelson and Olson (1978) and Amemiya (1979). None of the constraints of the type investigated here arise in such models.

The distinction between these two types of models is basically the distinction as to whether y_1 or y_1^* should appear on the r.h.s. of (12.2). In my opinion this should depend on whether in a particular application it is y_1 or y_1^* that has a meaningful economic interpretation.

Such issues aside, we now return to system (12.1) through (12.3). Let us add a subscript t indicating observation. Now for t such that $y_{1t}^* > 0$, $y_{1t}^* = y_{1t}$ and the reduced form for y_{1t}^* (or y_{1t}) is

$$y_{1t}^* = \frac{1}{1 - \gamma_1\gamma_2}[(\boldsymbol{\beta}_1 + \gamma_1\boldsymbol{\beta}_2)'\mathbf{X}_t + (\varepsilon_{1t} + \gamma_1\varepsilon_{2t})]. \tag{12.4}$$

On the other hand, for t such that $y_{1t}^* \leq 0$, $y_{1t} = 0$, and the reduced form for y_{1t}^* is

$$y_{1t}^* = [(\boldsymbol{\beta}_1 + \gamma_1\boldsymbol{\beta}_2)'\mathbf{X}_t + (\varepsilon_{1t} + \gamma_1\varepsilon_{2t})]. \tag{12.5}$$

From (12.4) and (12.5) it follows that we must have $1 - \gamma_1\gamma_2 > 0$. This condition ensures that for any $\mathbf{X}_t$, ε_{1t}, ε_{2t}, the model produces one and only one y_{1t}. This condition is necessary for the internal consistency (perhaps "unique solvability" would be a better phrase) of the model.

To see that this condition is indeed necessary, assume the opposite—let $1 - \gamma_1\gamma_2 < 0$. Then if the r.h.s. of (12.5) is positive, the r.h.s. of (12.4) is negative, which implies two different y_{1t}^* but no solution for y_{1t}. On the other hand, if the r.h.s. of (12.5) is negative, the r.h.s. of (12.4) is positive, which implies two different y_{1t}^* and two solutions for y_{1t}. Neither difficulty arises if $1 - \gamma_1\gamma_2 > 0$. Also neither difficulty would arise if y_1^* appeared in place of y_1 on the r.h.s. of (12.5). Then (12.4) would be the reduced form for every t.

12.3 All Endogenous Variables Truncated

As noted previously, the earliest models of this type are those of Amemiya (1974), who considers models in which each of the endogenous variables is subject to a tobit truncation. We can write his model as follows:

$$\mathbf{Y}^* = \mathbf{Y}\boldsymbol{\Gamma} + \mathbf{X}\mathbf{B} + \boldsymbol{\varepsilon}. \tag{12.6}$$

Here $\mathbf{Y}^*$, $\mathbf{Y}$, and $\boldsymbol{\varepsilon}$ are of dimension $1 \times G$; $\mathbf{X}$ is $1 \times K$; $\boldsymbol{\Gamma}$ is $G \times G$; and $\mathbf{B}$ is $K \times G$. (G is therefore the number of equations.) The relationship between $\mathbf{y}^*$ and $\mathbf{y}$ is

$$y_i = \begin{cases} y_i^* & \text{if } y_i^* > 0, \\ 0 & \text{if } y_i^* \leq 0, \end{cases} \tag{12.7}$$

$i = 1, \ldots, G$, where y_i is the ith column of $\mathbf{Y}$, and y_i^* is the ith column of $\mathbf{Y}^*$.

Amemiya (1974, p. 1006) shows (by reference to a theorem in linear programming) that the conditions for internal consistency of this model are the following:

CONDITION 12.1: All principal minors of $(\mathbf{I} - \boldsymbol{\Gamma})$ must be positive.

12.4 Some Endogenous Variables Truncated

We now consider the case in which some, but not necessarily all, endogenous variables are subject to a tobit truncation. This case has been considered by Lee (1976) and Sickles and Schmidt (1978).

The model is the same as (12.6) above, except that only the first S endogenous variables are truncated. Namely, we retain equation (12.6) but replace (12.7) with the following:

$$y_i = \begin{cases} y_i^* & \text{if } y_i^* > 0, \\ 0 & \text{if } y_i^* \leq 0, \end{cases} \tag{12.8}$$

$i = 1, \ldots, S$, and

$$y_i = y_i^*, \tag{12.9}$$

$i = S + 1, \ldots, G$. Alternatively we can write

$$(\mathbf{Y}_1^*, \mathbf{Y}_2) = (\mathbf{Y}_1, \mathbf{Y}_2)\begin{bmatrix} \boldsymbol{\Gamma}_{11} & \boldsymbol{\Gamma}_{12} \\ \boldsymbol{\Gamma}_{21} & \boldsymbol{\Gamma}_{22} \end{bmatrix} + \mathbf{X}(\mathbf{B}_1, \mathbf{B}_2) + (\boldsymbol{\varepsilon}_1, \boldsymbol{\varepsilon}_2). \tag{12.10}$$

Here $\mathbf{Y}_1^*$ represents the first S untruncated variables, which are related to $\mathbf{Y}_1$ as in (12.8).

As shown by Lee (1976), $\mathbf{Y}_2$ can be substituted out of this expression, which yields

$$\begin{aligned} \mathbf{Y}_1^* = {} & \mathbf{Y}_1[\boldsymbol{\Gamma}_{11} + \boldsymbol{\Gamma}_{12}(\mathbf{I} - \boldsymbol{\Gamma}_{22})^{-1}\boldsymbol{\Gamma}_{21}] + \mathbf{X}[\mathbf{B}_1 + \mathbf{B}_2(\mathbf{I} - \boldsymbol{\Gamma}_{22})^{-1}\boldsymbol{\Gamma}_{21}] \\ & + [\boldsymbol{\varepsilon}_1 + \boldsymbol{\varepsilon}_2(\mathbf{I} - \boldsymbol{\Gamma}_{22})^{-1}\boldsymbol{\Gamma}_{21}]. \end{aligned} \tag{12.11}$$

But this is a system form with all endogenous variables truncated, so we can simply invoke the results of the previous section. That is, the condition for internal consistency of the model given by (12.6), (12.8), and (12.9) is that all principal minors of $\mathbf{I} - [\mathbf{\Gamma}_{11} + \mathbf{\Gamma}_{12}(\mathbf{I} - \mathbf{\Gamma}_{22})^{-1}\mathbf{\Gamma}_{21}]$ be positive. This can in turn be rewritten somewhat. Define

$$\mathbf{A} \equiv \mathbf{I} - \mathbf{\Gamma}, \tag{12.12}$$

and partition it as $\mathbf{\Gamma}$ is partitioned in (12.10). (Thus $\mathbf{A}_{11} = \mathbf{I} - \mathbf{\Gamma}_{11}$, $\mathbf{A}_{22} = \mathbf{I} - \mathbf{\Gamma}_{22}$, $\mathbf{A}_{12} = -\mathbf{\Gamma}_{12}$, $\mathbf{A}_{21} = -\mathbf{\Gamma}_{21}$.) Then the condition just given can be expressed in the following way:

CONDITION 12.2: All principal minors of $(\mathbf{A}_{11} - \mathbf{A}_{12}\mathbf{A}_{22}^{-1}\mathbf{A}_{21})$ must be positive.

As noted, condition 12.2 and its derivation are due to Lee (1976). An equivalent condition, given as condition 12.3, is derived by Sickles and Schmidt (1978).

CONDITION 12.3: All principal minors of A that involve at least the last $G-S$ rows and columns must have the same sign.

The Sickles-Schmidt derivation need not be repeated here. However, it is easy to show that conditions 12.2 and 12.3 are indeed equivalent. To see this, we use the fact that

$$|\mathbf{A}_{11} - \mathbf{A}_{12}\mathbf{A}_{22}^{-1}\mathbf{A}_{21}| = \frac{|\mathbf{A}|}{|\mathbf{A}_{22}|}.$$

Now let $\mathbf{A}^*$ be formed from $\mathbf{A}$ by dropping corresponding rows and columns not involved in $\mathbf{A}_{22}$ (none of the last $G-S$ rows and columns is dropped). We therefore have

$$\mathbf{A}^* = \begin{bmatrix} \mathbf{A}_{11}^* & \mathbf{A}_{12}^* \\ \mathbf{A}_{21}^* & \mathbf{A}_{22} \end{bmatrix}$$

and

$$|\mathbf{A}_{11}^* - \mathbf{A}_{12}^*\mathbf{A}_{22}^{-1}\mathbf{A}_{21}^*| = \frac{|\mathbf{A}^*|}{|\mathbf{A}_{22}|}. \tag{12.13}$$

The l.h.s. is just a principal minor of $(\mathbf{A}_{11} - \mathbf{A}_{12}\mathbf{A}_{22}^{-1}\mathbf{A}_{21})$, while $|\mathbf{A}^*|$ is a principal minor of $\mathbf{A}$ involving at least $\mathbf{A}_{22}$. Thus the condition that all principal minors of $(\mathbf{A}_{11} - \mathbf{A}_{12}\mathbf{A}_{22}^{-1}\mathbf{A}_{21})$ be positive is equivalent to the condition that all principal minors of $\mathbf{A}$ involving at least $\mathbf{A}_{22}$ have the same sign.

12.5 Both Y and Y^* as Explanatory Variables

In section 12.2 we discussed the distinction between models in which the truncated variables appeared as r.h.s. variables and models in which only untruncated variables appeared as r.h.s. variables. We can of course allow both possibilities, although no one appears to have proposed such models so far. Suppose therefore that analogously to (12.6) we write

$$\mathbf{Y}^* = \mathbf{Y}\boldsymbol{\Gamma} + \mathbf{Y}^*\boldsymbol{\Delta} + \mathbf{X}\mathbf{B} + \boldsymbol{\varepsilon}. \tag{12.14}$$

Clearly we can solve for $\mathbf{Y}^*$ to obtain

$$\mathbf{Y}^* = \mathbf{Y}\boldsymbol{\Gamma}(\mathbf{I} - \boldsymbol{\Delta})^{-1} + \mathbf{X}\mathbf{B}(\mathbf{I} - \boldsymbol{\Delta})^{-1} + \boldsymbol{\varepsilon}(\mathbf{I} - \boldsymbol{\Delta})^{-1}. \tag{12.15}$$

But this is exactly of the form of (12.6), and the ensuing discussion still holds, with $\boldsymbol{\Gamma}$ replaced by $\boldsymbol{\Gamma}(\mathbf{I} - \boldsymbol{\Delta})^{-1}$.

What this points out is that the presence of truncated endogenous variables as r.h.s. variables is responsible for the constraints on the parameters. Whether untruncated endogenous variables appear as r.h.s. variables does not matter.

12.6 Simultaneous Probit Models

Simultaneous probit models appear to be somewhat less well worked out than simultaneous tobit models. Basically there is only the work of Heckman (1978) to refer to.

The notation of this section will be similar to that of the last section. For example, y^* will represent an unobservable variable, with observable counterpart

$$y = \begin{cases} 1 & \text{if } y^* > 0, \\ 0 & \text{if } y^* \leq 0. \end{cases}$$

Constraints on the parameters are implied whenever such dichotomous variables appear as r.h.s. variables. These constraints are very similar in form to those of the corresponding tobit model, except that they are equalities rather than inequalities.

As a simple example to illustrate the nature of the problem, consider the two-equation model

$$y_1^* = \gamma_1 y_2 + \boldsymbol{\beta}_1'\mathbf{X} + \varepsilon_1, \tag{12.16}$$

$$y_2 = \gamma_2 y_1 + \boldsymbol{\beta}_2'\mathbf{X} + \varepsilon_2, \tag{12.17}$$

$$y_1 = \begin{cases} 1 & \text{if } y_1^* > 0, \\ 0 & \text{if } y_1^* \leq 0. \end{cases} \tag{12.18}$$

(This is identical to system (12.1) through (12.3), except for the rule relating y_1 to y_1^*.) The solution for y_1^* is

$$y_1^* = (\gamma_1\gamma_2)y_1 + (\boldsymbol{\beta}_1 + \gamma_1\boldsymbol{\beta}_2)'\mathbf{X} + (\varepsilon_1 + \gamma_1\varepsilon_2). \tag{12.19}$$

From this it is easy to see that we must require $\gamma_1\gamma_2 = 0$. As in the tobit case the constraint ensures a unique outcome y_1 for any value of $\mathbf{X}$, ε_1 and ε_2. We can see this by noting that

$$\begin{aligned} y_1 &= 0 \quad \text{if } (\varepsilon_1 + \gamma_1\varepsilon_2) \leq -(\boldsymbol{\beta}_1 + \gamma_1\boldsymbol{\beta}_2)'\mathbf{X}, \\ y_1 &= 1 \quad \text{if } (\varepsilon_1 + \gamma_1\varepsilon_2) > -(\boldsymbol{\beta}_1 + \gamma_1\boldsymbol{\beta}_2)'\mathbf{X} - \gamma_1\gamma_2. \end{aligned}$$

If and only if $\gamma_1\gamma_2 = 0$, one and only one of these outcome must occur. This conclusion has previously been pointed out, for the two-equation case just considered, by Maddala and Lee (1976).

Two points are worth stressing here, in anticipation of what will come. First, the condition $\gamma_1\gamma_2 = 0$ is similar to the tobit condition $\gamma_1\gamma_2 < 1$. Second, the condition $\gamma_1\gamma_2 = 0$ imposes recursivity.

12.7 All Endogenous Variables Truncated

We consider the model

$$\mathbf{Y}^* = \mathbf{Y}\boldsymbol{\Gamma} + \mathbf{X}\mathbf{B} + \boldsymbol{\varepsilon}, \tag{12.20}$$

$$y_i = \begin{cases} 1 & \text{if } y_i^* > 0, \\ 0 & \text{if } y_i^* \leq 0, \end{cases} \tag{12.21}$$

$i = 1, 2, \ldots, G$. This is very simular to the tobit system (12.6) to (12.7), see section 12.3 for more detail on the notation.

The condition for the internal consistency of this model is essentially that it be recursive. This can be expressed more precisely by the following condition:

CONDITION 12.4: There must be no nonzero product (chain) of the form $\Gamma_{i_1i_2}\Gamma_{i_2i_3}\ldots\Gamma_{i_{r-1}i_r}\Gamma_{i_ri_1}$, where for any $r \le G$, $\{i_1, \ldots, i_r\}$ is any set of nonrepeated integers chosen from $\{1, 2, \ldots, G\}$.

To see why this condition is necessary, suppose that it does not hold. Thus we have a nonzero chain of the form

$$\Gamma_{ij}\Gamma_{jk}\cdots\Gamma_{pq}\Gamma_{qr}\Gamma_{ri}, \tag{12.22}$$

where $\{i, j, k, \ldots, p, q, r\}$ is a set of integers as before. Thus we have the situation:

$$\begin{aligned}
y_i^* &= \Gamma_{ri}y_r + \mathbf{X}\boldsymbol{\beta}_i + \varepsilon_i,\\
y_r^* &= \Gamma_{qr}y_q + \mathbf{X}\boldsymbol{\beta}_q + \varepsilon_q,\\
y_q^* &= \Gamma_{pq}y_p + \mathbf{X}\boldsymbol{\beta}_p + \varepsilon_p,\\
&\;\;\vdots\\
y_k^* &= \Gamma_{jk}y_j + \mathbf{X}\boldsymbol{\beta}_k + \varepsilon_k,\\
y_j^* &= \Gamma_{ij}y_i + \mathbf{X}\boldsymbol{\beta}_j + \varepsilon_j,
\end{aligned}$$

where for simplicity we have suppressed other endogenous r.h.s. variables. Now note that y_r depends on y_r^*, which depends on y_q, which depends on y_q^*, which depends on $y_p, \ldots$, which depends on y_k^*, which depends on y_j, which depends on y_j^*, which depends on y_i. Since y_i^* depends on y_r, we now have y_i^* depending on y_i. Explicitly we could write

$$y_i^* = \Gamma_{ri}f(y_i, \mathbf{X}, \varepsilon_j, \ldots, \varepsilon_r, \text{parameters}) + \mathbf{X}\boldsymbol{\beta}_i + \varepsilon_i,$$

where f shows that y_r depends on y_i (among other things). We then note that

$$\begin{aligned}
y_i = 1 \quad &\text{if } \varepsilon_i > -\mathbf{X}\boldsymbol{\beta}_i - \Gamma_{ri}f(1, \mathbf{X}, \varepsilon_j, \ldots, \varepsilon_r, \text{parameters}),\\
y_i = 0 \quad &\text{if } \varepsilon_i \le -\mathbf{X}\boldsymbol{\beta}_i - \Gamma_{ri}f(0, \mathbf{X}, \varepsilon_j, \ldots, \varepsilon_r, \text{parameters}).
\end{aligned}$$

If the chain in (12.22) is nonzero, we are not guaranteed that one and only one of these outcomes will occur.

Condition 12.4 is just a condition of recursivity. As such it is equivalent to the following:

CONDITION 12.5: It must be possible to reorder variables (and equations) in such a way that all elements of Γ on or below the diagonal equal zero.

It is also possible to express this condition in other equivalent ways, which more closely resemble the statements for the tobit case. For example, condition 12.4 (and hence condition 12.5) can be shown to be equivalent to the following condition:

CONDITION 12.6: All principal minors of Γ must equal zero.

It is clear that condition 12.4 implies condition 12.6. To show their equivalence, it is therefore necessary to show that condition 12.6 implies condition 12.4. This can be done by induction. Consider the case $G = 2$. The principal minors of $\mathbf{\Gamma}$ are Γ_{11}, Γ_{22}, and $\Gamma_{11}\Gamma_{22} - \Gamma_{12}\Gamma_{21}$. The requirement that these equal zero clearly implies that the chains Γ_{11}, Γ_{22}, $\Gamma_{12}\Gamma_{21}$, and $\Gamma_{21}\Gamma_{12}$ all equal zero. Hence condition 12.6 implies condition 12.4 for $G = 2$. Now assume that this implication holds for arbitrary value $G - 1$. This immediately implies that all chains of length $G - 1$ or less equal zero. What remains to be shown then is that $|\mathbf{\Gamma}| = 0$ and all chains of length $G - 1$ equal to zero (together) imply that all chains of length G must equal zero. This we show by contradiction. Suppose there is a nonzero chain of length G. Since the ordering of variables is arbitrary, we may as well suppose that this is the chain

$$\Gamma_{12}\Gamma_{23}\Gamma_{34}\ldots\Gamma_{G1} \neq 0. \tag{12.23}$$

Consider the implications of this. Since all chains of lengths of length 2 are zero, we must have

$$\Gamma_{21} = \Gamma_{32} = \Gamma_{43} = \ldots = \Gamma_{G,G-1} = \Gamma_{1G} = 0. \tag{12.24}$$

Similarly, since all chains of length 3 are zero,

$$\Gamma_{31} = \Gamma_{42} = \ldots \Gamma_{G,G-2} = \Gamma_{1,G-1} = \Gamma_{2G} = 0. \tag{12.25}$$

Since all chains of length 4 are zero,

$$\Gamma_{41} = \Gamma_{52} = \ldots = \Gamma_{G,G-3} = \Gamma_{1,G-2} = \Gamma_{2,G-1} = \Gamma_{3G} = 0, \tag{12.26}$$

and so forth. The final implication is that since all chains of length $G - 1$ equal zero,

$$\Gamma_{G-1,1} = \Gamma_{G2} = \Gamma_{13} = \ldots = \Gamma_{G-2,G} = 0. \tag{12.27}$$

Now equations (12.24) through (12.27) each imply that G off-diagonal elements of Γ must equal zero. Furthermore the coefficients appearing in these equations are all distinct. Hence (12.24) through (12.27) together set to zero all $G(G - 2)$ off-diagonal elements of $\mathbf{\Gamma}$ that do not appear in (12.23). Given that the diagonal elements of $\mathbf{\Gamma}$ also equal zero, this means that the expression in (12.23) equals $|\mathbf{\Gamma}|$. But this contradicts that fact that $|\mathbf{\Gamma}| = 0$. This completes the proof that condition 12.6 implies condition 12.4, and hence that they are equivalent.

Furthermore by the same line of proof we can show that the following requirement is equivalent to conditions 12.4 through 12.6:

CONDITION 12.7: All principal minors of $(\mathbf{I} - \mathbf{\Gamma})$ must equal one.

The similarity between this condition and condition 12.1 for the tobit model (that all principal minors must be positive) is evident.

12.8 Some Endogenous Variables Truncated

We now consider the case in which some endogenous variables, but not necessarily all of them, are of the probit type. Suppose that the first S variables are of the probit type. Then the model under consideration is as given in equation (12.20), but with (12.21) replaced by

$$y_i = \begin{cases} 1 & \text{if } y_i^* > 0, \\ 0 & \text{if } y_i^* \leq 0, \end{cases} \tag{12.28}$$

$i = 1, \ldots, S$ and

$$y_i = y_i^*, \tag{12.29}$$

$i = S + 1, \ldots, G$. Alternatively as in section 12.4 we can write

$$(\mathbf{Y}_1^*, \mathbf{Y}_2) = (\mathbf{Y}_1, \mathbf{Y}_2)\begin{bmatrix} \mathbf{\Gamma}_{11} & \mathbf{\Gamma}_{12} \\ \mathbf{\Gamma}_{21} & \mathbf{\Gamma}_{22} \end{bmatrix} + \mathbf{X}(\mathbf{B}_1, \mathbf{B}_2) + (\boldsymbol{\varepsilon}_1, \boldsymbol{\varepsilon}_2). \tag{12.30}$$

Substituting $\mathbf{Y}_2$ out of (12.30), we obtain

$$\begin{aligned} \mathbf{Y}_1^* = {} & \mathbf{Y}_1[\mathbf{\Gamma}_{11} + \mathbf{\Gamma}_{12}(\mathbf{I} - \mathbf{\Gamma}_{22})^{-1}\mathbf{\Gamma}_{21}] + \mathbf{X}[\mathbf{B}_1 + \mathbf{B}_2(\mathbf{I} - \mathbf{\Gamma}_{22})^{-1}\mathbf{\Gamma}_{21}] \\ & + [\boldsymbol{\varepsilon}_1 + \boldsymbol{\varepsilon}_2(\mathbf{I} - \mathbf{\Gamma}_{22})^{-1}\mathbf{\Gamma}_{21}], \end{aligned} \tag{12.31}$$

which is identical to (12.11) except for the relationship of $\mathbf{Y}_1$ to $\mathbf{Y}_1^*$. But this is now a system in which all endogenous variables are of the probit type, so the results of the last section apply. In particular we need to require that all principal minors of $[\mathbf{\Gamma}_{11} + \mathbf{\Gamma}_{12}(\mathbf{I} - \mathbf{\Gamma}_{22})^{-1}\mathbf{\Gamma}_{21}]$ be zero, or that all principal minors of $[\mathbf{I} - \mathbf{\Gamma}_{11} - \mathbf{\Gamma}_{12}(\mathbf{I} - \mathbf{\Gamma}_{22})^{-1}\mathbf{\Gamma}_{21}]$ equal one, and so on. This can be rewritten, as in section 12.4, by defining $\mathbf{A} = \mathbf{I} - \mathbf{\Gamma}$ (as in equation 12.12), and partitioning it conformably to $\mathbf{\Gamma}$. In this way we obtain the following:

CONDITION 12.8: All principal minors of $(\mathbf{A}_{11} - \mathbf{A}_{12}\mathbf{A}_{22}^{-1}\mathbf{A}_{21})$ must equal one.

An equivalent condition is the following:

CONDITION 12.9: All principal minors of $\mathbf{A}$ which involve at least the last $G-S$ rows columns must be equal.

The proof of the equivalence of conditions 12.8 and 12.9 follows exactly the lines of the discussion following condition 12.3 in section 12.4, with a few obvious changes. As a result there is no point in presenting it again. However, the analogy between the tobit and probit cases is again worth noting.

12.9 Both Y and Y^* as Explanatory Variables

As in the tobit case (section 12.5) we can consider models with both $\mathbf{Y}$ and $\mathbf{Y}^*$ as r.h.s. variables. (Heckman 1978 has previously considered some such models.) The model is as given in (12.14), but with the relationship between $\mathbf{Y}$ and $\mathbf{Y}^*$ given by (12.28) and (12.29). We can solve for $\mathbf{Y}^*$ in terms of $\mathbf{Y}, \mathbf{X}$, and $\boldsymbol{\varepsilon}$ to obtain

$$\mathbf{Y}^* = \mathbf{Y}\boldsymbol{\Gamma}(\mathbf{I} - \boldsymbol{\Delta})^{-1} + \mathbf{X}\mathbf{B}(\mathbf{I} - \boldsymbol{\Delta})^{-1} + \boldsymbol{\varepsilon}(\mathbf{I} - \boldsymbol{\Delta})^{-1}, \tag{12.32}$$

which is the same as (12.15), of course. But this is now of the form discussed in section 12.4 and therefore that discussion now applies.

As an example, consider the model of Heckman (1978) "translated" to the present notation:

$$\begin{aligned} y_1^* &= \gamma_{11}y_1 + \gamma_{21}y_2 + \mathbf{X}\boldsymbol{\beta}_1 + \varepsilon_1, \\ y_2 &= \gamma_{12}y_1 + \delta y_1^* + \mathbf{X}\boldsymbol{\beta}_2 + \varepsilon_2, \\ y_1 &= \begin{cases} 1 & \text{if } y_1^* > 0, \\ 0 & \text{if } y_1^* \le 0. \end{cases} \end{aligned} \tag{12.33}$$

In matrix form

$$(y_1^*, y_2) = (y_1, y_2)\begin{bmatrix} \gamma_{11} & \gamma_{12} \\ \gamma_{21} & 0 \end{bmatrix} + (y_1^*, y_2)\begin{bmatrix} 0 & \delta \\ 0 & 0 \end{bmatrix} + \mathbf{X}(\boldsymbol{\beta}_1, \boldsymbol{\beta}_2) + (\varepsilon_1, \varepsilon_2).$$

It is then easy to calculate that

$$\mathbf{I} - \boldsymbol{\Gamma}(\mathbf{I} - \boldsymbol{\Delta})^{-1} = \begin{bmatrix} 1 - \gamma_{11} & -\delta\gamma_{11} - \gamma_{12} \\ -\gamma_{21} & 1 - \delta\gamma_{21} \end{bmatrix}.$$

By condition 12.9 we must have all principal minors of this matrix involving at least the last row and column equal:

$$1 - \delta\gamma_{21} = (1 - \gamma_{11})(1 - \delta\gamma_{21}) + \gamma_{21}(-\delta\gamma_{11} - \gamma_{12}),$$

or

$$\gamma_{11} + \gamma_{12}\gamma_{21} = 0. \tag{12.34}$$

As Heckman shows, with this restriction (12.33) becomes

$$\begin{aligned} y_1^* &= \gamma_{21} y_2^l + \mathbf{X}\boldsymbol{\beta}_1 + \varepsilon_1, \\ y_2^l &= \delta y_1^* + \mathbf{X}\boldsymbol{\beta}_2 + \varepsilon_2, \end{aligned} \tag{12.35}$$

where y_1 is related to y_1^* as before, and $y_2 = y_2^l + \gamma_{12} y_1$.[1] This is a model of unusual structure: $\mathbf{X}$ and ε determine (y_1^*, y_2^l); y_1^* then determines y_1; (y_2^l, y_1) then determines y_2. One might describe this structure as "quasi-recursive," or some such phrase. Clearly, however, inclusion of both y_1 and y_1^* as r.h.s. variables in (12.33) has allowed strict recursivity to be escaped.

Similar comments apply to similar versions of the model. Consider briefly the model like (12.33) but with two probit variables:

$$\begin{aligned} y_1^* &= \gamma_{11} y_1 + \gamma_{21} y_2 + \delta_1 y_2^* + \mathbf{X}\boldsymbol{\beta}_1 + \varepsilon_1, \\ y_2^* &= \gamma_{12} y_1 + \gamma_{22} y_2 + \delta_2 y_1^* + \mathbf{X}\boldsymbol{\beta}_2 + \varepsilon_2. \end{aligned} \tag{12.36}$$

We can then derive the constraints:

$$\begin{aligned} \gamma_{11} + \delta_1\gamma_{12} &= 0, \\ \gamma_{22} + \delta_2\gamma_{21} &= 0, \\ \gamma_{12}\gamma_{21} &= 0. \end{aligned} \tag{12.37}$$

There are a number of ways that these constraints might be satisfied. Clearly in all of them either γ_{12} or γ_{21} (or both) must equal zero. We may as well consider

$$\gamma_{21} = 0,$$

since due to the symmetry of the notation this is no different than considering $\gamma_{12} = 0$. From the second line of (12.37), this implies $\gamma_{22} = 0$. With $\gamma_{21} = \gamma_{22} = 0$, we have then eliminated y_2 as a r.h.s. variable in (12.36):

1. Note that y_2^l is the value of y_2 when $y_1 = 0$. For example, if y_1 were a unionism dummy, and y_2 were a wage rate, then y_2 would be the nonunion wage rate. The first equation of (12.35) then states that the probability of unionism depends on the nonunion wage.

$$y_1^* = \gamma_{11}y_1 + \delta_1 y_2^* + \mathbf{X}\boldsymbol{\beta}_1 + \varepsilon_1,$$
$$y_2^* = \gamma_{21}y_1 + \delta_2 y_1^* + \mathbf{X}\boldsymbol{\beta}_2 + \varepsilon_2$$

(still subject to $\gamma_{11} + \delta_1\gamma_{12} = 0$). But this is essentially identical to (12.33). (It differs only in the replacement of y_2 in equation 12.34 by y_2^* here.) We can, imposing $\gamma_{11} + \delta_1\gamma_{12} = 0$, write

$$y_1^* = \delta_1 y_2^l + \mathbf{X}\boldsymbol{\beta}_1 + \varepsilon_1,$$
$$y_2^l = \delta_2 y_1^* + \mathbf{X}\boldsymbol{\beta}_2 + \varepsilon_2, \qquad (12.38)$$

where now $y_2^* = y_2^l + \gamma_{12}y_1$. The structure of the model is again quasi-recursive: $(\mathbf{X}, \varepsilon) \rightarrow (y_1^*, y_2^l)$; $y_1^* \rightarrow y_1$; $(y_2^l, y_1) \rightarrow y_2^*$; $y_2^* \rightarrow y_2$.

Similar special cases are easily worked out as well. They all have in common some element of recursivity, which limits the type of structure the model can have. More work is needed to fully understand what sorts of structures are internally consistent.

12.10 Conclusions

This chapter has derived the constraints that arise in simultaneous tobit and probit models. The constraints are necessary so that a given set of exogenous variables and disturbances yield a unique solution for the endogenous variables. They are very similar for the two cases, with the same principal minors required to be positive in the tobit case, but required to equal one in the probit case.

However, these constraints are far more interesting in the probit case, since the equality constraints essentially remove certain variables from certain equations. The result is to make simultaneous equations models recursive, in one way or another. The implications of this appear not yet to be fully understood.

It should be noted that these constraints arise when the (truncated) observable variables (y's) appear as r.h.s. variables, either in place of or in addition to the underlying unobservable variables (y^*'s). It is therefore reasonable to ask whether we might do better to avoid these problems by not using y's as r.h.s. variables. At least in the probit case, my own feeling is that this is not reasonable, since it is often natural to think of the effect of some discrete variable, quite apart from the effect of an underlying index of that variable. Indeed the fact that we observe legislatures passing laws, schools granting diplomas, and so forth, suggests that the effects of a discrete y are not always thought to be captured by its underlying y^*.

Another point worth making is that the necessity of the constraints discussed here may raise questions of whether we ought to even consider simultaneous tobit and probit models at all. It is by no means clear that the best way to model truncated and/or qualitative variables is to embed them (essentially by analogy) into the usual simultaneous equations model. At this point it is not clear what the alternatives would be. However, the difficulties one runs into, especially in the probit case, do indicate that the analogy to the usual simultaneous equations model is not completely straightforward.

Finally, it should be noted that the simultaneous tobit and probit models considered here can be viewed as special cases of a general nonlinear model with unobserved variables. In both cases we have appearing as a r.h.s. variable a function of an unobservable endogenous variable. Multimarket disequilibrium models (e.g., where observable quantity is the minimum of supply and demand) also fit this general category and necessitate similar constraints. A general treatment of this problem is an interesting topic for future work. For some recent work on such a general treatment see Gourieroux, Laffont, and Monfort (1978).

References

Amemiya, T. 1974. Multivariate Regression and Simultaneous Equation Models when the Dependent Variables are Truncated Normal. *Econometrica*. 42; 999–1012.

Amemiya, T. 1979. The Estimation of a Simultaneous Equation Tobit Model. *International Economic Review* 20: 169–182.

Gourieroux, C., J. J. Laffont, and A. Monfort. 1978. Coherency Conditions in Simultaneous Linear Equation Models with Endogenous Switching Regimes. Ecole Polytechnique Working Paper A190-0478.

Heckman. J. J. 1978. Dummy Endogneous Variables in a Simultaneous Equation System. *Econometrica*. 46; 931–959.

Lee, L. F. 1976. Multivariate Regression and Simultaneous Equations Models with Some Dependent Variables Truncated. Unpublished manuscript.

Maddala, G. S., and L. F. Lee. 1976. Recursive Models with Qualitative Endogenous Variables. *Annals of Economic and Social Measurement*. 5; 525–545.

Nelson, F. S., and L. Olson. 1978. Specification and Estimation of a Simultaneous Equation Model with Limited Dependent Variables. *International Economic Review*. 19: 695–710.

Sickles, R. C., and P. Schmidt. 1978. Simultaneous Equation Models with Truncated Dependent Variables: A Simultaneous Tobit Model. *Journal of Economics and Business*. 31: 11–21.

13 Estimating Credit Constraints by Switching Regressions

Robert B. Avery

13.1 Introduction

Congress recently passed the Equal Credit Opportunity Act, ECOA, which prohibits firms from discriminating on the basis of race, sex, or age in the granting of credit. The ultimate impact of ECOA cannot be determined until precise definitions of discrimination are decided by the judicial system. It is clear, however, that the effect of ECOA will depend largely upon the relationship between race, sex, age, and credit risk, hence credit availability. This essentially empirical issue has not yet been satisfactorily addressed. It is the intent of this chapter to investigate empirically the pre-ECOA relationship between credit availability and variables cited in the act, using a methodology that avoids many of the problems of earlier studies. Although ECOA covers all credit markets and the variables cited, we shall focus on the consumer credit market and race. We define consumer credit to include virtually all short-term, nonmortgage household borrowing. Although other types of borrowing are common, this type of lending is generally associated with durable goods purchases. Consumers are likely to owe small amounts to a number of lenders scattered among banks, stores, credit unions, and consumer finance companies.

Empirical evidence from previous studies linking race and the availability of consumer credit appears to be contradictory. Shinkel (1976), in the only comprehensive study on the effects of ECOA, examines a stratified random sample of approximately 10,000 national consumer finance company loan customers for evidence of racial effects in credit riskiness. Shinkel divides his sample into good loans (those repaid) and bad loans (those defaulted). He examines differences between the two samples with respect to a set of variables generally available at the time of the loan application, using multiple discriminate analysis. He concludes that one can discriminate between the two samples almost as well with an information set excluding race as when race is included. Excluding race increased the bad loans accepted by 0.5 percent and reduced the good loans accepted by 2.3 percent, resulting in a drop of at most 7 percent in firm profits.

Shinkel presents some other interesting evidence. He cites a survey of 100 credit-scoring systems conducted by Fair, Isaac and Company that showed neither race nor color was used by any firm. This does not necessarily imply that race is not, or never has been, used in credit screening, as many firms rely on subjective judgment even if they also use credit-scoring systems. This author conducted interviews with a number of New Jersey consumer loan officers, with the conclusion that race indeed was used. Most loan officers indicated, however, that race was not a major factor and was useful mainly in screening low-income applicants.

In contrast to the evidence that race does not play a large role in firm credit screening procedures, is the evidence that blacks, particularly in low-income classes, are observed to hold substantially lower amounts of consumer debt than comparable whites. Bell (1974) using the 1967 Survey of Economic Opportunity, SEO, data file concludes that black family renters with income less than $3,000 hold between 35 and 79 percent of the debt of comparable whites, depending on geographic location. Families with income between $3,000 and $6,000 hold between 59 and 73 percent of the debt of comparable whites. Bell also concludes that young black families in particular are likely to hold substantially less consumer debt than comparable whites.

Is the evidence that at the firm level race appears to only a small factor in the granting of credit inconsistent with evidence that in the aggregate blacks in fact receive less credit? One possible explanation is that blacks demand less credit. Kain and Quigley (1972), however, present empirical evidence that blacks pay higher per unit prices in the housing market than comparable whites. They argue that since blacks face higher housing prices, their demand for substitute goods, such as automobiles and durables may increase, altering their composition of wealth. Since durables are generally associated with short-term debt, blacks may demand higher not lower levels of consumer debt than comparable whites.

We give an alternative explanation in Avery (1977). We argue that Shinkel is measuring a firm-based decision rule that critically depends on who applies for loans. There is a cost to applicants in making loan applications, however. Those applicants with high probabilities of loan denials may not bother applying. Similarly firms may effectively screen large segments of the black community by not locating offices in black neighborhoods. We demonstrate that self-selection on the part of applicants may produce firm decision rules that differ substantially in their treatment of race from rules that would be used if all potential applicants were to apply. This suggests that Bell is in effect measuring a different concept than Shinkel. The amount of credit that ultimately flows to blacks is a function not only of explicit firm credit screening procedures and consumer credit demand but indirect credit screening via office location or induced applicant self-selection.

There is a grave danger that ECOA will only affect explicit credit screening by race and ignore the potentially more serious form of indirect screening. It is the interest of this chapter to examine and measure the latter concept. We propose to do this via a household not firm-based model. As we argued earlier, firm-based empirical models cannot be used to measure indirect screening. It would also be insufficient, however, to use household data and simply regress aggregate observed levels of debt against a series of demographic variables, isolating the sign and magnitude of a coefficient on race. The observed quantity of debt is as much a function of the demand for debt as the supply. To the extent that the demand for debt is correlated with race, the coefficient on race in such a reduced form regression would be a mixture of supply and demand effects.

As an alternative we propose to estimate a model of household behavior that combines both a demand and supply function for consumer debt. Since we believe that both the supply and demand for debt are functions of simultaneously determined household decisions, we also propose to incorporate behavioral equations thought to be closely related to consumer debt. Our broad interest is in the estimation of a consumer debt supply function, and specifically the role of race.

13.2 The Supply of Debt

The supply of consumer debt is a concept that may need further elaboration. The concept of a consumer loan supply function or credit rationing is not original with this study. Friedman (1957), Tobin (1957, 1972), Tobin and Watts (1960), Dolde and Tobin (1971), Watkins (1975), and Anderson (1976), each allude to the existence of credit constraints within the context of household demand models. None of these authors, however, specified a credit supply function, nor did they incorporate such constraints in estimation. Harris (1974) and Peterson (1976) explored aggregate credit supply functions, but neither author considers such a function at the micro level.

At the heart of the concept of a liquidity constraint or credit supply function is the view that credit is rationed, that firms fix the nominal rate of interest and deny loans to all applicants with expected net returns below a predetermined threshold. Thus all variation in applicant rates of return stems from their ability to repay the loan, not differential interest rates. One explanation for fixed interest rates is state usary laws that impose binding ceilings on consumer credit interest rates in most states. Modigliani and Jaffee (1970) also argue that rationing may arise endogenously. They argue that due to market imperfections and transactions costs it is optimal for American financial institutions to segment the lending market into a small number of segments and within each segment charge the same interest rate.

We argued in another study (Avery 1977) that faced with fixed interest rates rational profit-maximizing firms will collect data from prospective applicants. They will use this information to compute an expected return, granting loans where the expected return exceeds a predetermined threshold. This process, which we believe accurately describes much of the consumer credit market, is a loan-by-loan process. If, however, an applicant's existing stock of debt is one of the variables used in screening loans, it can easily be shown that the process reduces to a credit limit or maximum amount of debt for each applicant. Furthermore, this credit limit will be a function of other variables used in credit screening. To the extent that all firms use similar screening devices, the process yields a market credit limit.

We admit that it may be unrealistic to assume that consumers face one market credit limit. Even if interest rates are fixed within segments of the market, consumers have access to other sources of credit, for example, loan sharks, at higher interest rates. However, we see no practical way of addressing this problem, particularly given the limitations of our data. We are forced to assume that price variations are minor and that consumers face one consumer credit limit.

Finally, we argue that firms screen credit applicants by both direct and indirect means. As we argued earlier, firms may be able to indirectly screen applicants by office location. Similarly applicants may anticipate firm-screening procedures and not bother applying for loans that are likely to be turned down. Thus the implicit credit-screening procedure may differ from the process used by firms to evaluate actual credit applicants. We are interested in estimating the total credit supply function or credit limit, recognizing that it is achieved via a combination of both direct and indirect screening.

13.3 The Model and Data

We propose a cross-sectional stock demand model similar in spirit to that of Tobin (1957) and Watts and Tobin (1960). At a given point in time households are assumed to maintain equilibrium stocks of debt and durables. Household behavior is modified by wealth, income, and debt constraints. Desired household durable holdings are assumed to be functions of demographic characteristics and debt holdings and a measure of life cycle or permanent income, with stochastically distributed error terms accounting for omitted variables such as personality. Each of these is taken as exogenously given and independent of portfolio decisions. Households are assumed to be subject to debt or liquidity constraints. The maximum amount of debt allowed a household is assumed to be a function of demographic variables, durable stock holdings, income, credit history, plus errors accounting for firm discretion or omitted variables. Households are also assumed to have a well-specified demand for debt, which is a function of durable stock holdings and the same exogenous variables that affect durable demand. The actual observed household debt holding will be the minimum of debt demand and supply. Since our empirical model is to some extent shaped by the characteristics of our data, before outlining the specific model, let us briefly describe the data base.

Data were drawn from the New Jersey negative income tax experiment. The experiment was conducted primarily to measure the labor supply response of low-income families to a negative income tax system. Roughly 1,300 low income families were selected in four New Jersey cities—Trenton, Jersey City, Paterson, and Passaic—and in Scranton, Pennsylvania. Families were then assigned to a control sample, or to one of a set of negative income tax plans. The negative income tax plans were described by a guarantee—an amount paid the family whether they work or not—and a tax rate, or the fraction of a dollar that negative income tax payments are reduced for each dollar of family earnings. Families were allocated to one of eight experimental plans characterized by guarantees ranging from 50 to 125 percent of the poverty level and tax rates of 0.3, 0.5, or 0.7.

The experimental data represents a stratified sample of low-income families. This, however, offers a particularly good sample for our problem. Bell (1974) argues that black-white credit differentials were most pronounced in low-income groups. It can also be argued that low-income families are the most likely to be debt constrained. Thus such a sample offers more information on the equation of particular interest, credit supply.

The experiment ran for three years in each city, starting in Trenton in 1968 and ending in Scranton in 1972. Participants were asked a series of questions prior to enrollment and approximately every three months thereafter. Roughly half the original participants either dropped out of the experiment or had major gaps of missing data, leaving a sample of 604 for whom complete data are available for the three-year period.

Although the New Jersey experiment data base is in panel form, 13 drawings over time on each family, we shall treat it as cross-sectional. Several of the critical debt variables are available only once, near the end of the experiment. For this reason it was decided to view the sample as cross-sectional and to utilize the temporal nature of the data in constructing variables rather than directly. The specific variables used are listed in table 13.1 with sample means and standard deviations. Several of the variables, such as age and asset stocks, show considerable variation over the course of the experiment. Each of these variables therefore was taken as of the tenth quarter of the experiment when the richest set of financial variables were available. Most of the independent variables are self-explanatory.

Thirteen quarterly drawings on weekly family income and earnings were available over the course of the experiment. These were averaged to provide a measure of stable income. In addition the variance of income was computed about the three-year average. Total income comprises income from all sources, including welfare and experimental payments, other unearned income, and all family earnings.

The negative income tax experiment coincided with the 1970 census, affording access to some interesting neighborhood variables. The 604 sample families were located in roughly 100 different census tracts. Data from these census tracts were used to compute the neighborhood variables.

We choose to account for the effects of the experiment itself in two ways: first, by a 0–1 dummy variable, allowing a mean shift for the 60 percent of the sample families on one of the eight experimental plans, and second, by including experimental payments in the income variables.

Construction of the endogenous variables was a little more complex and needs further explanation. We discuss this within the context of our specific model equations.

Table 13.1
List of variables used

	Symbol	Sample mean	Sample standard deviation
Endogenous variables			
Value of automobiles stock (100's \$)	A	4.7	8.4
Value of other durables (100's \$)	O	9.9	5.8
Stock demand for consumer debt (100's \$)	D	—	—
Stock supply of consumer debt (100's \$)	S	—	—
Actual quantity of debt (100's \$)	Q	8.5	10.7
Independent variables			
Age of family head			
$\leq$ 25 years	A_1	0.04	0.19
26–35 years	A_2	0.33	0.47
36–45 years	A_3	0.37	0.48
46–55 years	A_4	0.21	0.41
56 $\leq$ years	A_5	0.05	0.23
Education of family head			
$<$ 8 years	E_1	0.27	0.44
8–11 years	E_2	0.50	0.50
12 $\leq$ years	E_3	0.23	0.42
Family demographics			
total number of persons in family	F_1	6.3	2.2
number of adults	F_2	2.6	0.9
Health			
dummy bad health family head	HL_1	0.30	0.34
dummy bad health spouse	HL_2	0.30	0.32
Homeownership dummy	H	0.23	0.42
Family income			
average total weekly income (from all sources) over three year period (\$)	I_1	141.0	41.5
average weekly head earnings (\$)	I_2	95.7	39.3
average weekly spouse earnings (\$)	I_3	7.5	18.0
ratio of average earned to total income	I_4	0.78	0.21
variance of earnings over three year period (\$)	I_5	34.1	20.2
dummy if total average income > \$100 a week	I_6	0.85	0.35
dummy if ever on welfare during three-year period	I_7	0.34	0.48

Table 13.1
(*continued*)

	Symbol	Sample mean	Sample standard deviation
Neighborhood characteristics (by census tract)			
median weekly family income ($)	N_1	146.3	23.9
dummy if neighborhood median income above poverty level	N_2	0.72	0.45
fraction of neighborhood that is black	N_3	0.28	0.31
ratio of median neighborhood housing value to income	N_4	122.5	39.1
Negative income tax experimental family	X	0.62	0.49
Race			
white	W	0.44	0.50
black	B	0.33	0.47
Spanish-speaking	SP	0.23	0.42
Credit supply function variables			
average tenure at last two jobs for head (years)	C_1	6.0	5.1
dummy if lived in residence less than one year	C_2	0.38	0.49
dummy if ever repossessed or wages garnished	C_3	0.07	0.26

Auto and Durable Stock Demand

Although there are many household asset decisions, we choose to model only those thought to be closely related to consumer debt decisions. In particular we model only durable stock decisions, which we believe are generally made simultaneously with consumer debt. Because we think they are related differently to consumer debt, particularly credit supply, we separate durables into two classes: (1) automobiles and (2) all other durables. We assume that stock holdings of autos A and other durables O will be linear functions of the same set of exogenous demographic variables, the quantity of consumer debt Q and ε_1, ε_2 stochastic normal errors. Formally

$$A = f_A(Q, A_2, A_3, A_4, A_5, E_2, E_3, F_1, F_2, HL_1, HL_2, H, I_1, I_4, I_5, N_1, N_3, N_4, X, B, SP, \text{constant}, \varepsilon_1); \tag{13.1}$$

$$O = f_O(Q, A_2, A_3, A_4, A_5, E_2, E_3, F_1, F_2, HL_1, HL_2, H, I_1, I_4, I_5, N_1, N_3, N_4, X, B, SP, \text{constant}, \varepsilon_2). \tag{13.2}$$

The stock value of automobiles was estimated as a function of the age and make of the car. Other durables include both appliances and furniture. Stock values were computed from purchase price, where available, or by extrapolation. A detailed description of the methods used to calculate stock valuations of both automobiles and other durables is available in Metcalf (1977).

Debt Demand

Households are assumed to have a stock demand for consumer debt that is a function of the same exogenous variables as autos and other durables and to be simultaneously determined with these variables. Defining consumer debt as the dollar sum of all nonmortgage household debt, we assume

$$D = f_D(A, O, A_2, A_3, A_4, A_5, E_2, E_3, F_1, F_2, HL_1, HL_2, H, I_1, I_4, I_5, N_1, N_3, N_4, X, B, SP, \text{constant}, \varepsilon_3), \quad (13.3)$$

where D is debt demand and again ε_3 is a stochastic normal error.

The assumption that debt, durable, and auto demand are functions of the same variables will be shown later to imply that the parameters of the debt demand equation are not fully identified. We will ultimately estimate a reduced form where debt demand is a function only of the exogenous variables. Thus the effects of A and O will be indistinguishable from those of the exogenous variables.

Debt Supply

Debt supply is the equation of primary interest to our study and the only one resembling a structural or behavioral equation. Consumers are assumed to face a market credit limit that varies from household to household. Firms are assumed to be able to constrain households at a fixed credit price by a combination of direct and indirect screening. Variables for the supply function were selected on the basis of interviews with a number of loan officers drawn from the experimental area. Exogenous variables mentioned most frequently as being used in credit screening were income, domestic and job stability, demographics, and credit history. We have tried to include measures of these variables similar to those seen on loan application forms. Formally we assume that the supply of debt is a linear function,

$$S = f_S(A, O, A_1, A_5, F_1, H, I_2, I_3, I_6, I_7, N_2, B, SP, C_1, C_2, C_3, \text{constant}, \varepsilon_4), \quad (13.4)$$

where ε_4 is again a normally distributed error.

We have assumed debt supply to be a function of auto and durable stocks. The inclusion of these variables dictates our particular model specification. We could have specified both credit supply and demand as reduced forms, functions only of exogenous variables. This would have made the model much simpler and avoided the necessity of estimating durable and debt equations simultaneously. However, we are interested in the effects of race on credit supply, holding other variables constant. To the extent that important variables like durable holdings may vary by race, they must be controlled for explicitly in the credit supply equation. Since we believe that durable decisions are often made simultaneously with debt decisions, this also requires us to specify the linkages between debt and durables in the durable equations we have noted.

Marketing Clearing

In most economic models we assume market clearing, supply equals demand, as an equilibrium condition. Our earlier discussions of the consumer credit market suggest, however, that this is an inappropriate condition for supply and demand as we have defined it. We argued in our discussion of debt demand that given a fixed interest rate, firms would establish a credit limit for each household. Thus credit supply is really an upper bound or constraint. Viewed this way, there is no reason to believe that supply will equal demand. This will affect the relationship between debt demand and supply and the actual amount of debt observed. If a household's debt demand were less than its market credit limit, observed debt would equal that demanded and the constraint would be irrelevant. However, if demand were to exceed the credit limit, the constraint would be binding, and we would observe actual debt equal to debt supply. This implies that

$$Q = \min(S, D), \quad (13.5)$$

where Q is the observed quantity of consumer debt. Note that this specification implies that we will observe either debt demand or debt supply for a given observation, never both.

There are a number of potential weaknesses of our model which bear some comment. First, some of the variables we call exogenous, such as income and housing stocks, cannot be said to be truly independent of portfolio decisions. Cain (1967) and Mincer (1960), for example, argue persuasively that earnings, particularly of secondary workers, may be sensitive to asset holdings, particularly constraints on debt. Housing stocks, particularly due to their dependence on mortgage debt (which is not included in consumer debt), are also likely to be influenced by consumer debt stocks. Second, households are assumed to be price-takers and to face the same prices for durables and debt. The assumption of a fixed debt price is particularly critical. To the extent that it is violated, demographic variables may pick up some price effects. Third, all households are assumed to be in equilibrium. This is perhaps the least defensible of our assumptions. Clearly at any point in time some households will be out of equilibrium. Their income may have suddenly fallen, yet there may not have been sufficient time to adjust their portfolio. We are forced to assume, however, either that all households are in equilibrium or that deviations from desired stocks are independent of the exogenous variables. Finally, and most important, is the reduced form flavor of our model. Our demand equations lack the behavioral characteristics normally found in structural economic models. To the extent that these reduced forms so not adequately explain observed variations in demand, the whole model may suffer.

The Complete Model System

The model system can be represented compactly as follows:

Autos: $$A = \mathbf{X}_1\boldsymbol{\beta}_1 + \alpha_{11}Q + \varepsilon_1 \tag{13.6}$$

Other durables: $$O = \mathbf{X}_1\boldsymbol{\beta}_2 + \alpha_{21}Q + \varepsilon_2 \tag{13.7}$$

Demand for debt: $$D = \mathbf{X}_1\boldsymbol{\beta}_3 + \alpha_{31}A + \alpha_{32}O + \varepsilon_3 \tag{13.8}$$

Supply of debt: $$S = \mathbf{X}_2\boldsymbol{\beta}_4 + \alpha_{41}A + \alpha_{42}O + \varepsilon_4 \tag{13.9}$$

Observed debt: $$Q = \min(S, D) \tag{13.10}$$

with $\mathbf{X}_1$ and $\mathbf{X}_2$ representing different exogenous variable sets. The fact that S and D are unobserved, coupled with the simultaneous determination of the five equations, creates some difficulties in estimation. In section 13.4 we address the issue of estimation and derive a procedure to compute consistent parameter estimates. Actual estimates of the model are presented in section 13.5.

13.4 Simultaneous Switching Regression and Linear Equations

The model system described in the previous section consists of two linear equations and a switching regression. For illustrative purposes consider the smaller system containing only one linear equation:

$$Y_n = \mathbf{X}'_{1n}\boldsymbol{\beta}_1 + \alpha_1 Q_n + \varepsilon_{1n}, \tag{13.11}$$

$$D_n = \mathbf{X}'_{2n}\boldsymbol{\beta}_2 + \alpha_2 Y_n + \varepsilon_{2n}, \tag{13.12}$$

$$S_n = \mathbf{X}'_{3n}\boldsymbol{\beta}_3 + \alpha_3 Y_n + \varepsilon_{3n}, \tag{13.13}$$

$$Q_n = \min(D_n, S_n), \tag{13.14}$$

$n = 1, \ldots, N$, where $\mathbf{X}_{1n}$, $\mathbf{X}_{2n}$, and $\mathbf{X}_{3n}$ are K_1, K_2, and K_3 length column vectors of independent variables, and ε_{1n}, ε_{2n}, ε_{3n} are stochastic errors, serially independent, and contemporaneously distributed $N(\mathbf{0}, \boldsymbol{\Sigma})$.

This system can be interpreted as the simultaneous solution of two demand equations, D and Y, complicated by an unobserved constraint on the value of D, S. We could also view D and S as the unobserved quantity demanded and supplied of variable Q, with only their minimum observed. The latter view is identical to the interpretation given the model presented in section 13.3.

Taken by themselves, equations (13.12), (13.13), and (13.14) resemble a switching regression or markets in disequilibrium model first introduced by Fair and Jaffee (1972) and later modified by Amemiya (1974) and Maddala and Nelson (1974). Were it not for the simultaneity, Hartley and Mallela (1977) show that strongly consistent parameter estimates for (13.14) and (13.13) could easily be derived from maximum likelihood techniques under very general conditions. However, the simultaneous determination of Q and Y necessitates the use of a more complex estimation procedure. In the remainder of this section we outline a procedure that can be used to compute consistent estimates of the parameters of (13.11) through (13.14). We start by deriving the system's reduced forms.

There are only two possible equilibrium reduced forms: either observed debt is equal to supply, or it is equal to demand. We solve (13.11) through (13.14) under each of these assumptions. Assume for the moment that Q is supply constrained, $Q_n = S_n$. Solving (13.11) and (13.13) simultaneously yields the reduced forms

$$Y_n = Y_n^s = \frac{\mathbf{X}'_{1n}\boldsymbol{\beta}_1 + \alpha_1 \mathbf{X}'_{3n}\boldsymbol{\beta}_3}{1 - \alpha_1\alpha_3} + \frac{\alpha_1\varepsilon_{3n} + \varepsilon_{1n}}{1 - \alpha_1\alpha_3}, \tag{13.15}$$

$$Q_n = S_n^s = \frac{\mathbf{X}'_{3n}\boldsymbol{\beta}_3 + \alpha_3 \mathbf{X}'_{1n}\boldsymbol{\beta}_1}{1 - \alpha_1\alpha_3} + \frac{\alpha_3\varepsilon_{1n} + \varepsilon_{3n}}{1 - \alpha_1\alpha_3}, \tag{13.16}$$

which we denote with superscript s. Furthermore we can solve for unobserved demand D_n^s as

$$D_n^s = \mathbf{X}'_{2n}\boldsymbol{\beta}_2 + \frac{\alpha_2 \mathbf{X}'_{1n}\boldsymbol{\beta}_1 + \alpha_1\alpha_2 \mathbf{X}'_{3n}\boldsymbol{\beta}_n}{1 - \alpha_1\alpha_3} + \frac{\alpha_2\varepsilon_{1n} + \alpha_1\alpha_2\varepsilon_{3n}}{1 - \alpha_1\alpha_3} + \varepsilon_{2n}. \tag{13.17}$$

Conversely suppose that the system is demand constrained, $Q_n = D_n$. Solving (13.11) and (13.12) yields the reduced forms

$$Y_n = Y_n^d = \frac{\mathbf{X}'_{1n}\boldsymbol{\beta}_1 + \alpha_1 \mathbf{X}'_{2n}\boldsymbol{\beta}_2}{1 - \alpha_1\alpha_2} + \frac{\alpha_1\varepsilon_{2n} + \varepsilon_{1n}}{1 - \alpha_1\alpha_2}, \tag{13.18}$$

$$Q_n = D_n^d = \frac{\mathbf{X}'_{2n}\boldsymbol{\beta}_2 + \alpha_2 \mathbf{X}'_{1n}\boldsymbol{\beta}_1}{1 - \alpha_1\alpha_2} + \frac{\alpha_2\varepsilon_{1n} + \varepsilon_{2n}}{1 - \alpha_1\alpha_2}, \tag{13.19}$$

which we denote with superscript d. Unobserved supply S_n^d can be solved for as

$$S_n^d = \mathbf{X}'_{3n}\boldsymbol{\beta}_3 + \frac{\alpha_3 \mathbf{X}_{1n}\boldsymbol{\beta}_1 + \alpha_1\alpha_3 \mathbf{X}_{2n}\boldsymbol{\beta}_2}{1 - \alpha_1\alpha_2} + \frac{\alpha_3\varepsilon_{1n} + \alpha_1\alpha_3\varepsilon_{2n}}{1 - \alpha_1\alpha_2} + \varepsilon_{3n}. \tag{13.20}$$

Thus the reduced form solutions imply two possible reduced form systems, (13.15) through (13.17) which hold when $Q_n = S_n$, and (13.18) through (13.20) which hold when $Q_n = D_n$.

A yet unanswered question is whether a unique equilibrium will exist for all observations: Can the demand-constrained and supply-constrained regimes occur simultaneously, or can there be regions of the error space for which neither occurs? In the simple case where $S_n = D_n = Q_n$, the two reduced forms are identical, and the system will have a unique equilibrium. However, if S_n differs from D_n, we require restrictions on the parameters for the existence of a unique equilibrium. In particular we require that $1 - \alpha_1\alpha_2$ and $1 - \alpha_1\alpha_3$ be the same sign. If and only if this condition is met, the system will have a unique equilibrium with either the demand-constrained regime or the supply-constrained regime prevailing for every observation. A proof of this assertion is omitted, because it is a straightforward algebraic exercise.

Assuming that conditions for a unique equilibrium are met, it should be possible to compute consistent parameter estimates of the two reduced form regimes simultaneously using a full information maximum likelihood. For computational simplicity and compatibility with existing computer algorithms, however, it may be desirable to consider a limited information procedure.

We have asserted that, given conditions for a unique equilibrium, we will observe either $Q_n = S_n^s$ or $Q_n = D_n^d$. We have not, however, addressed the issue of how the prevailing reduced form regime is determined. It can be shown that the determination of the prevailing reduced form depends on the sign of $1 - \alpha_1\alpha_2$ and $1 - \alpha_1\alpha_3$. If both terms are positive, the supply-constrained regime will prevail when $S_n^s < D_n^d$ and the demand-constrained regime when $D_n^d < S_n^s$. Thus we will observe Q_n equal to the minimum of D_n^d and S_n^s. If $1 - \alpha_1\alpha_2$ and $1 - \alpha_1\alpha_3$ are both negative, the observed Q_n will be equal to the maximum of D_n^d and S_n^s.

The observed value of Y_n is determined in a similar fashion, depending on the sign of α_1. If $1 - \alpha_1\alpha_2$ and $1 - \alpha_1\alpha_3$ are positive, and if α_1 is also positive, we will observe Y_n equal to the minimum of Y_n^s and Y_n^d. If α_1 is negative, we will observe the maximum of Y_n^s and Y_n^d. If $1 - \alpha_1\alpha_2$ and $1 - \alpha_1\alpha_3$ are negative, then these relationships will be reversed.

Assuming, as we shall throughout the remainder of this chapter, that $1 - \alpha_1\alpha_2$ and $1 - \alpha_1\alpha_3$ are both positive, we can thus represent the reduced forms as two switching regression models:

$$Y_n^s = \frac{\mathbf{X}_{1n}'\boldsymbol{\beta}_1 + \alpha_1\mathbf{X}_{3n}'\boldsymbol{\beta}_3}{1 - \alpha_1\alpha_3} + \frac{\alpha_1\varepsilon_{3n} + \varepsilon_{1n}}{1 - \alpha_1\alpha_3}, \tag{13.21}$$

$$Y_n^d = \frac{\mathbf{X}_{1n}'\boldsymbol{\beta}_1 + \alpha_1\mathbf{X}_{2n}'\boldsymbol{\beta}_2}{1 - \alpha_1\alpha_2} + \frac{\alpha_1\varepsilon_{2n} + \varepsilon_{1n}}{1 - \alpha_1\alpha_2}, \tag{13.22}$$

$$\begin{aligned} Y_n &= \min(Y_n^s, Y_n^d) \quad \text{if } \alpha_1 > 0, \\ Y_n &= \max(Y_n^s, Y_n^d) \quad \text{if } \alpha_1 < 0; \end{aligned} \tag{13.23}$$

and

$$S_n^s = \frac{\mathbf{X}_{3n}'\boldsymbol{\beta}_3 + \alpha_3\mathbf{X}_{1n}'\boldsymbol{\beta}_1}{1 - \alpha_1\alpha_3} + \frac{\alpha_3\varepsilon_{1n} + \varepsilon_{3n}}{1 - \alpha_1\alpha_3}, \tag{13.24}$$

$$D_n^d = \frac{\mathbf{X}_{2n}'\boldsymbol{\beta}_2 + \alpha_2\mathbf{X}_{1n}'\boldsymbol{\beta}_1}{1 - \alpha_1\alpha_2} + \frac{\alpha_2\varepsilon_{1n} + \varepsilon_{2n}}{1 - \alpha_1\alpha_2}, \tag{13.25}$$

$$Q_n = \min(D^d_n, S^s_n). \tag{13.26}$$

Hartley and Mallela (1977) show that under very general conditions MLE's of standard switching regression models will be strongly consistent. Since the reduced form equations otherwise meet the assumptions of the standard model, if they satisfy the general regularity conditions, then the ML methods can be applied to each reduced form separately. We require, however, knowledge of the sign of α_1. These estimates are likely to be less efficient than full information ML, however, since we are ignoring any cross-equation restrictions and that both reduced form systems switch at the same time. Note, even if the original structural equation errors are uncorrelated, the reduced form errors will be correlated as ε_1 enters each term.

Assuming conditions for identification are met, there may be a variety of methods that could be used to solve for structural parameters from the reduced forms. We propose a solution procedure that is computationally feasible and will produce consistent estimators. We describe our procedure and prove its properties as follows:

The reduced form equations (13.21) through (13.26) can be rewritten as

$$Y^s_n = \mathbf{X}'_{1n}\boldsymbol{\beta}_1 + \alpha_1 \bar{S}^s_n + \frac{\alpha_1\varepsilon_{3n} + \varepsilon_{1n}}{1 - \alpha_1\alpha_3}, \tag{13.27}$$

$$Y^d_n = \mathbf{X}'_{1n}\boldsymbol{\beta}_1 + \alpha_1 \bar{D}^d_n + \frac{\alpha_1\varepsilon_{2n} + \varepsilon_{1n}}{1 - \alpha_1\alpha_2}, \tag{13.28}$$

$$D^d_n = \mathbf{X}'_{2n}\boldsymbol{\beta}_2 + \alpha_2 \bar{Y}^d_n + \frac{\alpha_2\varepsilon_{1n} + \varepsilon_{2n}}{1 - \alpha_1\alpha_2}, \tag{13.29}$$

$$S^s_n = \mathbf{X}'_{3n}\boldsymbol{\beta}_3 + \alpha_3 \bar{Y}^s_n + \frac{\alpha_3\varepsilon_{1n} + \varepsilon_{3n}}{1 - \alpha_1\alpha_3}, \tag{13.30}$$

where

$$\bar{S}^s_n = \frac{\mathbf{X}'_{3n}\boldsymbol{\beta}_3 + \alpha_3\mathbf{X}'_{1n}\boldsymbol{\beta}_1}{1 - \alpha_1\alpha_3},$$

$$\bar{D}^d_n = \frac{\mathbf{X}'_{2n}\boldsymbol{\beta}_2 + \alpha_2\mathbf{X}'_{1n}\boldsymbol{\beta}_1}{1 - \alpha_1\alpha_2},$$

$$\bar{Y}^s_n = \frac{\mathbf{X}'_{1n}\boldsymbol{\beta}_1 + \alpha_1\mathbf{X}'_{3n}\boldsymbol{\beta}_3}{1 - \alpha_1\alpha_3},$$

$$\bar{Y}_n^d = \frac{\mathbf{X}'_{1n}\boldsymbol{\beta}_1 + \alpha_1 \mathbf{X}'_{2n}\boldsymbol{\beta}_2}{1 - \alpha_1\alpha_2}, \tag{13.31}$$

are the nonerror right-hand terms of the four equations (13.24), (13.25), (13.21), and (13.22), respectively.

Suppose for a moment that we could observe $\{\bar{S}_n^s, \bar{D}_n^d, \bar{Y}_n^s, \bar{Y}_n^d\}$. Assuming that the reduced forms (13.27) through (13.30) each satisfy the assumptions of a standard switching regression model, we could apply ML procedures to compute consistent estimates for the parameter set $\{\beta_1, \beta_2, \beta_3, \alpha_1, \alpha_2, \alpha_3\}$. We propose an estimation procedure similar to this except that instruments are used for the unobserved variables. Specifically we propose using ML estimates of the two reduced forms (13.21) through (13.26) to obtain instruments for $\{\bar{S}_n^s, \bar{D}_n^d, \bar{Y}_n^s, \bar{Y}_n^d\}$. The four instruments are then plugged into (13.27) through (13.30) and quasi-MLE's of $\{\beta_1, \beta_2, \beta_3, \alpha_1, \alpha_2, \alpha_3\}$ computed by maximizing the likelihood of (13.27) through (13.30) given the instruments rather than the true values $\{\bar{S}_n^s, \bar{D}_n^d, \bar{Y}_n^s, \bar{Y}_n^d\}$. We assert that if the model satisfies several very general conditions that our proposed estimators will be strongly consistent for $\{\beta_1, \beta_2, \beta_3, \alpha_1, \alpha_2, \alpha_3\}$. We prove this assertion as follows:

We need to assume that each of the reduced forms (13.21) through (13.26) and (13.27) through (13.30) individually satisfies the conditions required by Hartley-Mallela (1977) for strong consistency.

Defining $\mathbf{X}_s$ and $\mathbf{X}_d$ as the exogenous variables, ε_s and ε_d as the errors, and $\boldsymbol{\theta}_s$ and $\boldsymbol{\theta}_d$ as the unknown parameters of the supply and demand equations, respectively, these conditions require that

1. the errors are bivariate normal, have zero mean, serially independent, and independent of $\mathbf{X}_s$ and $\mathbf{X}_d$,
2. the empirical distribution of $\{\mathbf{X}_s, \mathbf{X}_d\}$ converges completely to a nondegenerate distribution function and the empirical second moment of $\{\mathbf{X}_s, \mathbf{X}_d\}$ divided by N converges to a positive definite matrix $\mathbf{M}$,
3. the parameter space $\boldsymbol{\Theta}$ is compact where $\{\boldsymbol{\theta}_s, \boldsymbol{\theta}_d\}$ is an interior point, with positive error variances and error correlation less in absolute value than one,
4. the components of $\{\boldsymbol{\theta}_s, \boldsymbol{\theta}_d\}$ are functionally independent and $\mathbf{X}_s$ or $\mathbf{X}_d$ contain at least one variable specific to it.

Assumptions 13.1 and 13.3. follow from the original specification of the model. Assumption 13.2 restricts the process generating $\mathbf{X}_s$ and $\mathbf{X}_d$. It does not require, however, that $\mathbf{X}_s$ and $\mathbf{X}_d$ be random. Assumption 13.4, when applied to (13.21) through (13.26) requires that $\mathbf{X}_2$ or $\mathbf{X}_3$ have at least one variable unique to it. When applied to (13.27) through (13.30), it requires that the structural equation parameters be identified.

Define $\hat{\pi}_Y$ and $\hat{\pi}_Q$ as the estimators that maximize the sample likelihood of the reduced forms (13.21) through (13.23) and (13.24) through (13.26), respectively. Let π_Y and π_Q be the true parameters of these equations. Furthermore let

$$L_Y(Y, \pi_Q, \boldsymbol{\theta}_Y)$$
$$L_Q(Q, \pi_Y, \boldsymbol{\theta}_Q)$$

be the sample likelihood of the structural equations (13.27) through (13.30), with parameter vectors $\boldsymbol{\theta}_Y = \{\boldsymbol{\beta}_1, \boldsymbol{\alpha}_1\}$ and $\boldsymbol{\theta}_Q = \{\boldsymbol{\beta}_2, \boldsymbol{\beta}_3, \boldsymbol{\alpha}_2, \boldsymbol{\alpha}_3\}$ (ignoring error distribution parameters), assuming we could observe $\{\bar{S}_n^s, \bar{D}_n^d, \bar{Y}_n^s, \bar{Y}_n^d\}$. Let $\hat{\boldsymbol{\theta}}_Y$ and $\hat{\boldsymbol{\theta}}_Q$ be the estimates that maximize $L_Y(Y, \pi_Q, \boldsymbol{\theta}_Y)$ and $L_Q(Q, \pi_Y, \boldsymbol{\theta}_Q)$. With these definitions, we can conclude:

THEOREM 13.1: If the reduced forms (13.21) through (13.23) and (13.24) through (13.26) and structural equations (13.27) through (13.30) each satisfy assumptions 13.1 through 13.4, then the MLE's $\{\hat{\pi}_Y, \hat{\pi}_Q, \hat{\boldsymbol{\theta}}_Y, \hat{\boldsymbol{\theta}}_Q\}$ will be strongly consistent for $\{\pi_Y, \pi_Q, \boldsymbol{\theta}_Y, \boldsymbol{\theta}_Q\}$, and the second-stage estimators $\tilde{\boldsymbol{\theta}}_Y$ and $\tilde{\boldsymbol{\theta}}_Q$ that maximize the functions

$$L_Y(Y, \hat{\pi}_Q, \boldsymbol{\theta}_Y),$$
$$L_Q(Q, \hat{\pi}_Y, \boldsymbol{\theta}_Q)$$

will also be strongly consistent for $\boldsymbol{\theta}_Y$ and $\boldsymbol{\theta}_Q$.

PROOF: The proof follows almost directly from Hartley and Mallela (1977). Details of the proof are given in section 13.7.

It would be desirable to derive an expression for the asymptotic distribution of the second-stage estimators $\tilde{\boldsymbol{\theta}}_Y$ and $\tilde{\boldsymbol{\theta}}_Q$. Unfortunately an examination of a Taylor expansion of the normal equations indicates that, unless relatively restrictive conditions are met, an expression for the asymptotic distribution of $\tilde{\boldsymbol{\theta}}_Y$ and $\tilde{\boldsymbol{\theta}}_Q$ will involve terms from the reduced forms as well as the second stage. We can, however, derive easily estimable expressions for the asymptotic distribution of the maximum likelihood estimators $\hat{\boldsymbol{\theta}}_Y$ and $\hat{\boldsymbol{\theta}}_Q$. Using $\hat{\boldsymbol{\theta}}_Y$ as an example, these can be estimated by the inverse of the information matrix of (13.27) through (13.28) as follows:

THEOREM 13.2: If conditions 13.1 through 13.4 are met, then

$$1. \sqrt{n}\,(\hat{\boldsymbol{\theta}}_Y - \boldsymbol{\theta}_Y) \rightarrow N\left(\mathbf{0}, \left[-\frac{\partial^2 G_Y(\boldsymbol{\pi}_Q, \boldsymbol{\theta}_Y)}{\partial \boldsymbol{\theta}_Y \partial \boldsymbol{\theta}'_Y}\right]^{-1}\right),$$

where

$$G_Y(\boldsymbol{\pi}_Q, \boldsymbol{\theta}_Y) = \lim_{n \to \infty} \frac{1}{n} \ln L_Y(Y, \boldsymbol{\pi}_Q, \boldsymbol{\theta}_Y).$$

Furthermore, if conditions for theorem 13.1 hold, then

2. $G_Y(\hat{\boldsymbol{\pi}}_Q, \tilde{\boldsymbol{\theta}}_Y)$ converges to $G_Y(\boldsymbol{\pi}_Q, \boldsymbol{\theta}_Y)$ a.e. the same holding for $\hat{\boldsymbol{\theta}}_Q$.

PROOF: Part 1 follows directly from Hartley-Mallela (1977). Part 2 follows from Hartley-Mallela lemma 10 (showing uniform convergence for $G_Y(\cdot))$ and lemma 13.1 of Section 13.7 (Amemiya 1973, lemma 4).

Although the asymptotic distribution of the maximum likelihood estimators is unlikely to be the same as that of $\{\tilde{\boldsymbol{\theta}}_Y, \tilde{\boldsymbol{\theta}}_Q\}$, we could interpret estimates of their standard errors as lower bounds of the standard errors of $\tilde{\boldsymbol{\theta}}_Y$ and $\tilde{\boldsymbol{\theta}}_Q$.

The major advantage of our proposed procedure is computational simplicity and feasibility. Each of the four equation systems—the two reduced forms and the two second-stage models—can be estimated separately, using computer programs for standard switching regression models. An alternative procedure, full information ML, might require estimation of a prohibitively large number of parameters. However, by not using full information ML, we are likely to be losing efficiency as we are ignoring cross-equation restrictions and common system switching points. If cross-equation restrictions are necesssary for full identification of the model, then our procedure, which ignores such restrictions, will be incapable of producing consistent structural parameter estimates.

Our proposed procedure requires the estimation of four switching regression model systems. Since these systems are relatively expensive to estimate, as a final modification we show how one of these runs can be eliminated.

The expectation of the observed dependent variable of a switching regression model, given the exogenous variables, can be computed by a straightforward method. This formula can be used to estimate an instrument for observed debt, Q, from the debt-reduced form. This instrument can then be plugged into (13.11) in place of Q and structural parameters of the Y equation estimated by OLS. This step avoids having to estimate the second-stage Y switching regressions. Formally the instrument is derived from the debt-reduced forms as follows.

Let $\hat{\sigma}_s^{*2}$, $\hat{\sigma}_d^{*2}$, $\hat{\sigma}_{sd}^{*}$ be the variance and covariance estimates of the errors of the reduced forms (13.24) and (13.25), respectively, and let $\hat{\sigma} = \sqrt{\hat{\sigma}_s^{*2} + \hat{\sigma}_d^{*2} - 2\hat{\sigma}_{sd}^{*}}$. Defining $f(\cdot)$ as the standard normal density function, and $F(\cdot)$ as the cumulative normal, a consistent estimate of the expectation of Q_n given $\mathbf{X}_{1n}$, $\mathbf{X}_{2n}$, and $\mathbf{X}_{3n}$ is

$$E(Q_n \mid \mathbf{X}_{1n}, \mathbf{X}_{2n}, \mathbf{X}_{3n}) = F\left(\frac{\hat{\bar{S}}_n^s - \hat{\bar{D}}_n^d}{\hat{\sigma}}\right)\hat{\bar{D}}_n^d + \left(1 - F\left(\frac{\hat{\bar{S}}_n^s - \hat{\bar{D}}_n^d}{\hat{\sigma}}\right)\right)\hat{\bar{S}}_n^s - \hat{\sigma}\, f\left(\frac{\hat{\bar{S}}_n^s - \hat{\bar{D}}_n^d}{\hat{\sigma}}\right), \tag{13.32}$$

where $\{\hat{\bar{S}}_n^s, \hat{\bar{D}}_n^d\}$ are estimates of $\{\bar{S}_n^s, \bar{D}_n^d\}$ calculated using the estimated reduced form parameters. It can then be shown that under very general conditions, consistent estimates of the structural parameters $\boldsymbol{\beta}_1$ and $\boldsymbol{\alpha}_1$ can be obtained by substituting $E(Q_n \mid \mathbf{X}_{1n}, \mathbf{X}_{2n}, \mathbf{X}_{3n})$ for Q_n in the original linear structural equation (13.11) and running OLS.

We propose to estimate the parameters of the model we derived in section 13.3, using a procedure based on the methods just described. We discuss our specific application and present empirical estimates in section 13.5.

13.5 The Evidence

The estimation procedure used for our model follows directly from the procedure outlined in the previous section. We can briefly summarize the process. The first step is the estimation of switching regression reduced form equations for each of the three endogenous variables—autos, other durables, and consumer debt. Parameters of the reduced forms are estimated by maximum likelihood assuming a Hartley-Mallela switching regression model with correlated equation errors. A complication of the reduced form estimation is the requirement that the sign of the debt variable in both the auto and durable structural equations be known.

The second step of the procedure is to construct instrumental variables for the three endogenous variables. Although all are not used, potentially three different instruments could be computed for each reduced form: (1) an instrument for the observed dependent variable computed using the formula given in equation (13.32), (2) an instrument for the unobserved demand dependent variable formed from the demand equaton, and (3) an instrument for the unobserved supply dependent variable.

The final step of the procedure is the estimation of structural equation parameters. Both the auto and other durable equations are estimated by OLS, using instruments for the observed dependent variables (instrument form 1). Although OLS yields consistent parameter estimates, we note that the form of equation (13.32) implies that OLS standard errors are unlikely to be consistent.

The equations of particular interest to this chapter are the structural equations for debt. Unfortunately, since debt demand is assumed to be a function of the same exogenous variables as durable and auto demand, the structural equation for debt demand is not fully identified. Thus we are forced to estimate a reduced form for the second-stage debt demand equation. The debt supply equation, however, is identified.

Estimates of the debt supply and demand equations are computed by maximizing a switching regression likelihood function of the exogenous variables and supply instruments for autos and other durables. As shown in section 13.4, these estimates will be strongly consistent.

Maximum likelihood estimates (or quasi-maximum likelihood in case of the second-stage equations) of the switching regression parameters are computed using a Davidon-Fletcher-Powell iterative procedure with two criteria for convergence. Each element of the vector of first derivatives and the change in the log likelihood function value is required to be within a preset tolerance of zero. As a check on the quality of convergence the negative of the matrix of log likelihood second derivatives is computed and, if invertible, used as an estimate of the information matrix and for standard errors. We note, however, that for the second stage, the matrix of second derivatives will not yield estimates of our actual coefficient standard errors. A correct interpretation is that they yield consistent estimates of the standard errors of the maximum likelihood estimators and hence can be considered lower bounds.

Before we report the results of our estimation, it may be useful to show a few sample statistics. Sample means of several key variables broken down by race are given in table 13.2. One statistic that stands out is the substantially higher average debt holdings for whites than for blacks or Hispanics. This difference, which supports Bell's (1974) evidence, is mirrored in auto and durable holdings but is not nearly as apparent in income.

The first step of the estimation was the three switching regression reduced forms, parameter estimates of which are given in section 13.8. It

Table 13.2
Sample statistics (means broken down by race)

	Total	White	Black	Spanish-speaking
Number	604	264	201	139
Age (years head)	39.6	41.0	38.2	39.1
Education (years head)	8.9	10.0	8.6	7.5
Number in family	6.3	5.8	7.1	6.2
Family weekly income ($)	141.0	147.0	141.0	130.0
Value automobile ($)	466.0	606.0	374.0	334.0
Value other durables ($)	991.0	1118.0	916.0	858.0
Consumer debt ($)	855.0	1191.0	627.0	546.0

was assumed that debt would enter both the auto and other durable equations with a positive sign, thus each switching regression dependent variable was assumed to be a minimum. This assumption is consistent with the view that consumers are concerned primarily with their net wealth position. The assumption is supported by positive coefficients later estimated for the second-stage structural equations. To check the robustness of this assumption, we re-estimated each of the reduced forms, assuming the dependent variables were maximums not minimums. However, the relevant second-stage coefficients again turned out to be positive, supporting our original assumption.

Satisfactory convergence of the reduced forms was achieved for the auto and debt equations but not for durable goods. Although the functional values and log likelihood first derivatives met our criteria of convergence, the negative of the matrix of second derivatives would not invert. The problem was caused by second derivatives associated with the equation error correlation coefficient, estimated to be an implausible 0.999. We computed standard errors for the durable goods equation therefore using the Davidon-Fletcher-Powell approximation to the information matrix.

The final step of the estimation procedure were the structural equations. Coefficient estimates of the OLS auto and durable goods equations are given in tables 13.3 and 13.4. Both equations show the expected positive signs for the debt instrument variable indicating that a 1 dollar increase in debt increases the stock of autos by 24 cents and other durables by 21 cents. Coefficients on race accounted for at most a $41 difference in stock levels. This contrasts with the figures of table 13.2, which showed blacks on average held only 62 percent of the auto stock and 82 percent of other

Table 13.3
Structural equation for automobile stock (100's $)

Variable		Coefficient
$\hat{Q}$	Debt instrument	0.235
A_2	Age 26–35	2.231
A_3	Age 36–45	1.875
A_4	Age 46–55	1.080
A_5	Age $\geq$ 56	1.020
E_2	Education 8–11	0.278
E_3	Education $\geq$ 12	0.525
F_1	Total in family	−0.452
F_2	Number of adults	0.250
HL_1	Bad health head	0.444
HL_2	Bad health spouse	1.394
H	Homeownership	3.110
I_1	Total weekly income	0.030
I_4	Earned/total income	2.032
I_5	Variance of earnings	0.023
N_1	Neighborhood median income	−0.002
N_3	Fraction neighborhood black	0.079
N_4	Neighborhood housing/income	−0.005
X	Negative income tax	0.945
B	Black	−0.051
SP	Spanish-speaking	0.346
	Constant	−4.712
		$R^2 = 0.1451$

Table 13.4
Structural equation for other durables (100's \$)

Variable		Coefficient
$\hat{Q}$	Debt instrument	0.213
A_2	Age 26–35	−0.292
A_3	Age 36–45	−0.906
A_4	Age 46–55	−0.952
A_5	Age $\geq$ 56	−0.642
E_2	Education 8–11	0.011
E_3	Education $\geq$ 12	0.364
F_1	Total in family	0.226
F_2	Number of adults	0.019
HL_1	Bad health head	−0.938
HL_2	Bad health spouse	0.656
H	Homeownership	0.852
I_1	Total weekly income	0.019
I_4	Earned/total income	−0.389
I_5	Variance of earnings	0.024
N_1	Neighborhood median income	0.001
N_3	Fraction neighborhood black	−1.039
N_4	Neighborhood housing/income	−0.002
X	Negative income tax	−0.554
B	Black	−0.414
SP	Spanish-speaking	−0.378
	Constant	4.820
		$R^2 = 0.1539$

durable stock as whites. A portion of this difference must be attributable to demographic differences and importantly to different expected holdings of debt.

The equations of particular interest to this chapter are the structural equations for consumer debt presented in table 13.5. Satisfactory convergence was achieved on all counts. The most striking feature of the demand equation is the significant age effects. As might be predicted by a life-cycle model, debt demand declines significantly with age. Demand increases with bad health, number in family, and homeownership as might be expected but decreases with variance in income and increases with the ratio of earned to total income. Coefficients for both black and Spanish-speaking households are positive and significant. This provides support for the view of Kain and Quigley (1972) that blacks would have higher rather than lower demands for short-term debt.

Coefficients of the supply equation contrast noticeably with those of the demand equation. Age effects are far less pronounced. Total in family enters negatively rather than positively. Garnishing and residence of less than one year enter negatively as might be expected. Somewhat surprisingly neighborhood income above the poverty level enters negatively and ever-on-welfare enters positively. The instruments for autos and durables both show expected positive signs. The larger coefficients for autos indicate firms are willing to finance a higher fraction of auto purchases than other durables. Finally, coefficients for both black and Spanish-speaking households are both large and negative, indicating these groups will be constrained at significantly lower debt levels than comparable whites. The racial coefficients are offset by the large positive constant term. This has the net effect of assigning all white observations to the demand regime and all but one of the black and Spanish-speaking observations to the supply constrained regime. Thus our procedure has in effect split the sample along racial lines.

Table 13.5
Second-stage equations for consumer debt (100's $)

Variable		Coefficient	Approximate standard errors
Demand equation			
A_2	Age 26–35	−8.768	4.668*
A_3	Age 36–45	−13.951	4.729***
A_4	Age 46–55	−16.333	4.736***
A_5	Age $\geq$ 56	−20.538	5.586***
E_2	Education 8–11	2.939	2.200
E_3	Education $\geq$ 12	3.180	2.452
F_1	Total in family	0.621	0.451
F_2	Number of adults	−0.606	0.992
HL_1	Bad health head	4.986	2.187**
HL_2	Bad health spouse	3.564	2.340
H	Homeownership	1.503	1.622
I_1	Total weekly income	0.068	0.023***
I_4	Earned/total income	3.357	3.648
I_5	Variance of earnings	−0.084	0.039**
N_1	Neighborhood median income	0.009	0.037
N_3	Fraction neighborhood black	−2.932	3.329
N_4	Neighborhood housing/income	−0.002	0.020
X	Negative income tax	−0.456	1.634
B	Black	12.040	4.026***
SP	Spanish-speaking	11.145	5.443**
	Constant	6.932	8.497

Table 13.5
(*continued*)

Variable		Coefficient	Approximate standard errors
Supply equation			
$\hat{A}$	Auto instrument	0.483	0.256*
$\hat{D}$	Durable instrument	0.277	0.730
A_1	Age < 26	2.190	2.244
A_5	Age ≥ 56	−3.371	2.095
F_1	Total in family	−0.307	0.312
H	Homeownership	0.840	1.876
I_2	Head week earnings	0.015	0.022
I_3	Spouse week earnings	−0.038	0.030
I_6	Dummy income > $100	1.792	1.492
I_7	Dummy ever welfare	0.616	1.213
N_2	Dummy neighborhood income > poverty	−0.978	0.993
B	Black	−55.064	32.580*
SP	Spanish-speaking	−56.870	32.580*
C_1	Average job tenure	−0.006	0.102
C_2	Dummy residence < 1 year	−0.308	1.415
C_3	Dummy garnished/repossessed	−0.869	4.034
	Constant	57.018	32.622*
	Standard devation demand error	11.436	0.513***
	Standard devation supply error	7.578	0.318***
	Correlation of errors	0.251	0.260
	Log of the likelihood function = − 2193.0		

Note: * Significant at 10 percent level; ** significant at 5 percent level; *** significant at 1 percent level.

13.6 Qualifications and Evaluations

We have asked a lot of our procedure. We asked it to estimate parameters of two debt equations based only on the slim information that observed debt will be the minimum of two unobserved supply and demand variables and the assumption that equation errors are normally distributed. Our problem is compounded by the fact that we use micro data subject to large stochastic noise.

A priori the above arguments suggest it is not likely we would achieve what we sought—identification of the parameters of low-income debt supply and debt demand functions. The actual empirical evidence leaves us no more optimistic. Our procedure may have done little more than divide the sample along racial lines. The implied conclusion—that debts of virtually all whites are demand determined and of all blacks and Hispanics supply constrained—seems implausible at best. We suspect that our trouble in obtaining convergence for the other durable reduced form equation was caused in part by the severity of the sample separation. Since virtually all sample observations had estimated regime probabilities of 0 or 1, there was little information to estimate the correlation of equation error terms.

Before discarding our results as a purely methodological exercise, however, let us recall the empirical inconsistency generated by Shinkel (1976) and Bell (1974). Bell found evidence, supported by our sample, that low-income blacks have substantially less debt than comparable whites. If Bell's evidence is true, and if Shinkel's conclusion that race plays a small role in direct credit screening is correct, then either (1) blacks must demand less debt or (2) blacks are indirectly screened. On this question we believe our results have some merit. It is noteworthy that the particular sample division estimated by our procedure separates white into the demand regime and blacks into the supply regime. As we suggest in section 13.5, parameter estimates suggest that debt holdings within the white population are allocated in a manner consistent with our view of cross-sectional demand. Similarly debt holdings within the black population appear to be allocated consistently with our view of a supply function. Thus although we have doubts about specific parameter estimates of our model, we believe that our evidence supports the view that observed differences in black-white debt holdings are a supply not a demand phenomena.

13.7 Appendix: Proof of Theorem 13.1

The proof of theorem 13.1 follows almost directly from lemmas proved by Hartley and Mallela (1977). We require two additional lemmas, the first of which is taken directly from lemma 4 of Amemiya (1973). Each of these lemmas is stated in terms of single parameters, although they are easily generalized to parameter vectors.

LEMMA 13.1: Let $f_n(\omega, \theta)$ be a measurable function on a measurable space $\mathbf{\Omega}$ and for ω in $\mathbf{\Omega}$ a continuous function for θ in a compact set $\mathbf{\Theta}$. If $f_n(\omega, \theta)$ converges to $f(\theta)$ a.e. uniformly for all θ in $\mathbf{\Theta}$, and if $\hat{\theta}_n(\omega)$ converges to θ^0 a.e., then $f_n[\omega, \hat{\theta}_n(\omega)]$ converges to $f(\theta^0)$ a.e. Proof of this lemma 13.1 is given in Amemiya (1973).

LEMMA 13.2: Let $f_n(\omega, \theta_1, \theta_2)$ be a measurable function on a measurable space $\mathbf{\Omega}$ and for each ω in $\mathbf{\Omega}$ a continuous function for $\{\theta_1, \theta_2\}$ in a compact set $\mathbf{\Theta}$. If

1. $f_n(\omega, \theta_1, \theta_2)$ converges to $f(\theta_1, \theta_2)$ uniformly a.e. $\forall \omega \in \mathbf{\Lambda}$ such that $\mathscr{P}(\mathbf{\Lambda}) = 1$,
2. $f(\theta_1^0, \theta_2^0)$ is a unique maximum for $\{\theta_1, \theta_2\}$ in $\mathbf{\Theta}$,
3. $\hat{\theta}_{n1}(\omega)$ converges to θ_1^0 a.e. $\forall \omega \in \mathbf{\Lambda}$ such that $\mathscr{P}(\mathbf{\Lambda}) = 1$.

Then $\hat{\theta}_{n2}(\omega)$, such that

$$f_n(\omega, \hat{\theta}_{n1}(\omega), \hat{\theta}_{n2}(\omega)) = \sup_{\theta_2 \in \boldsymbol{\theta}} f_n(\omega, \hat{\theta}_{n1}(\omega), \theta_2)$$

converges to θ_2^0 a.e.

PROOF: The proof parallels that of Hansen (1979, theorem 1). By definition

$$f_n(\omega, \hat{\theta}_{n1}(\omega), \hat{\theta}_{n2}(\omega)) \geq f_n(\omega, \hat{\theta}_{n1}(\omega), \theta_2^0).$$

Taking limits, it follows from lemma 13.1 and conditions 1 and 3, that

$$\lim_{n \to \infty} \inf f_n(\omega, \hat{\theta}_{n1}(\omega), \hat{\theta}_{n2}(\omega)) \geq f(\theta_1^0, \theta_2^0).$$

$\forall \omega \in \tilde{\mathbf{\Lambda}}$ such that $\mathscr{P}(\tilde{\mathbf{\Lambda}}) = 1$.

We now assume that lemma 13.2 is not true and show that this leads to a contradiction. If conditions 1, 2, and 3 hold, but $\hat{\theta}_2(\omega)$ does not converge to θ_2^0, a.e., then there exists $\bar{\mathbf{\Lambda}}$, a subset of $\tilde{\mathbf{\Lambda}}$, $\mathscr{P}(\bar{\mathbf{\Lambda}}) > 0$ such that for some

$\delta > 0$ there exists an unbounded subset of the positive integers, $\bar{\mathbf{I}}(\omega)$, such that for all $\omega \in \bar{\mathbf{\Lambda}}$

$$|\hat{\theta}_{n2}(\omega) - \theta_2^0| > \delta, \quad \text{for } n \in \bar{\mathbf{I}}(\omega),\ \omega \in \bar{\mathbf{\Lambda}}.$$

It also follows that

$$|\{\hat{\theta}_{n1}(\omega), \hat{\theta}_{n2}(\omega)\} - \{\theta_1^0, \theta_2^0\}| > \delta, \quad \text{for } n \in \bar{\mathbf{I}}(\omega),\ \omega \in \bar{\mathbf{\Lambda}}.$$

Consider a region $\mathbf{S}$ about $\{\theta_1^0, \theta_2^0\}$, such that $[\theta_1, \theta_2] \in \mathbf{S}$ implies $| \{\theta_1^0, \theta_2^0\} - \{\theta_1, \theta_2\} | > \delta$, then condition 2 implies

$$\inf\{f(\theta_1^0, \theta_2^0) - f(\theta_1, \theta_2)\} > 0, \quad \text{for } [\theta_1, \theta_2] \in \mathbf{S}.$$

Thus there exists $\varepsilon > 0$ such that

$$\{f(\theta_1^0, \theta_2^0) - f(\hat{\theta}_{n1}(\omega), \hat{\theta}_{n2}(\omega))\} > 2\varepsilon, \quad \forall n \in \bar{\mathbf{I}}(\omega),\ \omega \in \bar{\mathbf{\Lambda}}.$$

However, condition 1 implies that, given 2ε, there exists an $n'(\omega)$ such that

$$|f_n(\omega, \hat{\theta}_{n1}(\omega), \hat{\theta}_{n2}(\omega)) - f(\hat{\theta}_{n1}(\omega), \hat{\theta}_{n2}(\omega))| < \varepsilon, \quad \forall n > n'(\omega),\ \omega \in \bar{\mathbf{\Lambda}}.$$

Thus

$$\{f(\theta_1^0, \theta_2^0) - f_n(\omega, \hat{\theta}_{n1}(\omega), \hat{\theta}_{n2}(\omega))\} > \varepsilon, \quad \forall n > n'(\omega) \text{ and } \in \bar{\mathbf{I}}(\omega),\ \omega \in \bar{\mathbf{\Lambda}};$$

hence

$$f(\theta_1^0, \theta_2^0) \geq \varepsilon + \lim_{n \to \infty} \inf f_n(\omega, \hat{\theta}_{n1}(\omega), \hat{\theta}_{n2}(\omega)), \text{ for all } \omega \in \bar{\mathbf{\Lambda}},$$

which is a direct contradition. ■

The proof of theorem 13.1 consists of demonstrating that the second-stage estimators $\tilde{\theta}_Y$ and $\tilde{\theta}_Q$ satisfy the conditions of lemma 13.2. We demonstrate this as follows. Using $\tilde{\theta}_Q$ as an example, define

$$\begin{aligned} \theta_1^0 &= \{\pi_Y\}, \\ \theta_2^0 &= \{\theta_Q\}, \\ \hat{\theta}_{n1} &= \{\hat{\pi}_Y\}, \\ \hat{\theta}_{n2} &= \{\tilde{\theta}_Q\}. \end{aligned}$$

Hartley-Mallela (1977, theorem 4) prove that if conditions (13.1) through (13.4) of section 13.4 are satisfied for (13.21) through (13.26), $\{\hat{\pi}_Y, \hat{\pi}_Q\}$ will be strongly consistent for $\{\pi_Y, \pi_Q\}$. This is sufficient to establish condition 3 of lemma 13.2. Furthermore define

$$f_n^1(\omega, \theta_1, \theta_2) = \ln\left[\frac{\prod_{t=1}^{n} g_t^1(\omega, \theta_1, \theta_2)}{\prod_{t=1}^{n} g_t^1(\omega, \theta_1^0, \theta_2^0)}\right]^{1/n},$$

$$f_n^2(\omega, \theta_1) = \ln\left[\frac{\prod_{t=1}^{n} g_t^2(\omega, \theta_1)}{\prod_{t=1}^{n} g_t^2(\omega, \theta_1^0)}\right]^{1/n},$$

where $g_t^1(\cdot)$ and $g_t^2(\cdot)$ are the likelihood functions of the tth observation of (13.29) and (13.30) and (13.21) through (13.23), respectively. Given conditions 1 through 4 of section 13.4 are satisfied, Hartley-Mallela prove lemmas that imply

1. $f_n(\omega, \theta_1, \theta_2) = f_n^1(\omega, \theta_1, \theta_2) + f_n^2(\omega, \theta_1)$ is measurable and continuous for a compact parameter space (Hartley-Mallela, lemmas 1 and 3),

2. $f_n(\cdot)$ converges uniformly a.e. (Hartley-Mallela, lemmas 8 and 9 and Tchebyschoff's theorem),

3. $\lim_{n\to\infty} f_n^2(\cdot)$ has a unique maximum at θ_1^0, and $\lim_{n\to\infty} f_n^1(\cdot)$ has a unique maximum at θ_2^0 given $\theta_1 = \theta_1^0$ (follows immediately from Hartley-Mallela, theorem 1). This also implies that $\lim_{n\to\infty} f_n^1(\cdot)$ achieves a maximum at θ_1^0, θ_2^0 (since 13.29 and 13.30 are just rearrangements of 13.24 through 13.26). Thus $\lim_{n\to\infty} f_n(\cdot)$ has a unique maximum at θ_1^0, θ_2^0.

Noting that maximizing $f_n(\cdot)$ is equivalent to maximizing the sample likelihood function of (13.29) and (13.30), parts 1, 2, and 3, are sufficient to establish conditions 1 and 2 of lemma 13.2. Thus theorem 13.1 is proved.

13.8 Appendix: Empirical Reduced Form Equations

Tables 13.6 through 13.8 report the fitted reduced form equations for the study of consumer credit in section 13.5.

Table 13.6
Reduced form for automobile stock (100's $)

Variable		Coefficient	Standard error
Demand-constrained regime			
A_2	Age 26–35	−0.033	2.900
A_3	Age 36–45	−2.676	2.923
A_4	Age 46–55	−3.755	2.976
A_5	Age ≥ 56	−6.908	3.545*
E_2	Education 8–11	−0.095	1.416
E_3	Education ≥ 12	−0.557	1.572
F_1	Total in family	−0.608	0.289**
F_2	Number of adults	0.929	0.680
HL_1	Bad health head	1.404	1.457
HL_2	Bad health spouse	2.695	1.530*
H	Homeownership	4.286	1.127***
I_1	Total weekly income	0.064	0.015***
I_4	Earned/total income	2.336	2.477
I_5	Variance of earnings	−0.027	0.027
N_1	Neighborhood median income	0.011	0.024
N_3	Fraction neighborhood black	−0.720	2.242
N_4	Neighborhood housing/income	0.003	0.013
X	Negative income tax	0.101	1.097
B	Black	28.757	6.712***
SP	Spanish-speaking	4.830	2.072**
	Constant	−5.106	5.343

Table 13.6
(continued)

Variable		Coefficient	Standard error
Supply-constrained regime			
A_2	Age 26–35	1.611	2.484
A_3	Age 36–45	2.849	2.610
A_4	Age 46–55	1.018	2.895
A_5	Age $\geq$ 56	4.291	3.420
E_2	Education 8–11	1.963	1.193*
E_3	Education $\geq$ 12	3.203	1.673*
F_1	Total in family	−0.120	0.260
F_2	Number of adults	−0.663	0.653
HL_1	Bad health head	1.712	1.678
HL_2	Bad health spouse	2.513	1.613
H	Homeownership	1.852	1.474
I_2	Head week earnings	0.038	0.025
I_3	Spouse week earnings	0.057	0.028**
I_4	Earned/total income	−0.315	4.243
I_5	Variance of earnings	0.050	0.028*
I_6	Dummy income > \$100	−0.517	1.686
I_7	Dummy ever welfare	−0.289	1.192
N_1	Neighborhood median income	0.009	0.032
N_2	Dummy neighborhood income > poverty	−0.681	1.607
N_3	Fraction neighborhood black	0.966	2.066
N_4	Neighborhood housing/incone	−0.019	0.014
X	Negative income tax	1.649	1.380
B	Black	−129.237	240.941
SP	Spanish-speaking	−124.205	240.941
C_1	Average job tenure	0.070	0.111
C_2	Dummy residence < 1 year	−1.501	1.046
C_3	Dummy garnished/repossessed	1.371	1.967
	Constant	125.058	240.941
	Standard deviation demand error	7.948	0.328***
	Standard deviation supply error	7.802	0.429***
	Correlation of errors	−0.124	0.121
	Log of the likelihood function = − 2102.6		

Note: * Significant at 10 percent level; ** significant at 5 percent level; *** significant at 1 percent level.

Table 13.7
Reduced form for other durables (100's $)

Variable		Coefficient	Standard error
Demand-constrained regime			
A_2	Age 26–35	−3.215	2.249
A_3	Age 36–45	−5.181	2.402**
A_4	Age 46–55	−6.311	2.345***
A_5	Age ≥ 56	−4.759	3.224
E_2	Education 8–11	0.684	1.401
E_3	Education ≥ 12	1.648	1.475
F_1	Total in family	0.157	0.438
F_2	Number of adults	0.055	0.147
HL_1	Bad health head	−0.383	1.123
HL_2	Bad health spouse	2.149	2.139
H	Homeownership	0.260	0.866
I_1	Total weekly income	0.033	0.019*
I_4	Earned/total income	−0.040	0.925
I_5	Variance of earnings	0.017	0.023
N_1	Neighborhood median income	−0.008	0.005*
N_3	Fraction neighborhood black	−2.656	2.122
N_4	Neighborhood housing/income	−0.000	0.001
X	Negative income tax	−1.779	0.931*
B	Black	5.727	2.222***
SP	Spanish-speaking	5.167	2.554**
	Constant	10.405	3.484***

Table 13.7
(continued)

Variable		Coefficient	Standard error
Supply-constrained regime			
A_2	Age 26–35	−0.067	0.069
A_3	Age 36–45	−0.550	0.627
A_4	Age 46–55	−0.025	0.617
A_5	Age $\geq$ 56	−0.370	0.712
E_2	Education 8–11	0.583	0.391
E_3	Education $\geq$ 12	0.045	0.057
F_1	Total in family	0.255	0.115**
F_2	Number of adults	0.043	0.038
HL_1	Bad health head	0.322	0.858
HL_2	Bad health spouse	0.046	0.075
H	Homeownership	1.804	0.968*
I_2	Head week earnings	0.035	0.011***
I_3	Spouse week earnings	0.031	0.013**
I_4	Earned/total income	−1.267	1.991
I_5	Variance of earnings	0.020	0.017
I_6	Dummy income > $100	0.086	0.085
I_7	Dummy ever welfare	0.716	0.364**
N_1	Neighborhood median income	0.009	0.008
N_2	Dummy neighborhood income > poverty	−0.028	0.022
N_3	Fraction neighborhood black	−0.026	0.028
N_4	Neighborhood housing/income	−0.011	0.007
X	Negative income tax	0.637	0.402
B	Black	−55.162	39.458
SP	Spanish-speaking	−54.442	39.465
C_1	Average job tenure	0.037	0.048
C_2	Dummy residence < 1 year	0.980	0.692
C_3	Dummy garnished/repossessed	4.949	1.252***
	Constant	56.951	39.560
	Standard deviation demand error	6.666	0.299***
	Standard deviation supply error	3.396	0.139***
	Correlation of errors	0.999	0.050***
	Log of the likelihood function = − 1790.8		

Note: * Significant at 10 percent level; ** significant at 5 percent level; *** significant at 1 percent level.

Table 13.8
Reduced form for consumer debt (100's $)

Variable		Coefficient	Standard error
Demand-constrained regime			
A_2	Age 26–35	−8.830	4.695*
A_3	Age 36–45	−13.975	4.762***
A_4	Age 46–55	−16.368	4.766***
A_5	Age ≥ 56	−20.562	5.650***
E_2	Education 8–11	2.840	2.349
E_3	Education ≥ 12	3.170	2.563
F_1	Total in family	0.612	0.464
F_2	Number of adults	−0.624	1.019
HL_1	Bad health head	5.017	2.220**
HL_2	Bad health spouse	3.486	2.391
H	Homeownership	1.434	1.648
I_1	Total weekly income	0.069	0.024***
I_4	Earned/total income	3.199	3.693
I_5	Variance of earnings	−0.086	0.040**
N_1	Neighborhood median income	0.010	0.037
N_3	Fraction neighborhood black	−3.207	3.472
N_4	Neighborhood housing/income	−0.001	0.020
X	Negative income tax	−0.411	1.669
B	Black	12.849	4.900***
SP	Spanish-speaking	11.191	5.848*
	Constant	7.155	8.615

Table 13.8
(continued)

Variable		Coefficient	Standard error
Supply-constrained regime			
A_2	Age 26–35	−0.696	2.268
A_3	Age 36–45	−1.320	2.400
A_4	Age 46–55	−1.838	2.741
A_5	Age ≥ 56	−3.559	3.139
E_2	Education 8–11	1.577	1.087
E_3	Education ≥ 12	0.950	1.459
F_1	Total in family	−0.151	0.256
F_2	Number of adults	−0.710	0.630
HL_1	Bad health head	1.339	1.549
HL_2	Bad health spouse	0.559	1.480
H	Homeownership	2.526	1.440*
I_2	Head week earnings	0.023	0.024
I_3	Spouse week earnings	−0.011	0.027
I_4	Earned/total income	3.095	3.954
I_5	Variance of earnings	0.049	0.028*
I_6	Dummy income > $100	2.662	1.515*
I_7	Dummy ever welfare	0.384	1.117
N_1	Neighborhood median income	−0.020	0.029
N_2	Dummy neighborhood income > poverty	−0.127	1.468
N_3	Fraction neighborhood black	2.422	1.963
N_4	Neighborhood housing/income	−0.010	0.012
X	Negative income tax	0.203	1.269
B	Black	−60.550	71.557
SP	Spanish-speaking	−59.406	71.524
C_1	Average job tenure	0.084	0.106
C_2	Dummy residence < 1 year	−0.840	0.960
C_3	Dummy garnish/repossess	1.271	1.971
	Constant	63.105	71.677
	Standard deviation demand error	11.446	0.491***
	Standard deviation supply error	7.471	0.332***
	Correlation of errors	0.273	0.149*
	Log of the likelihood function = − 2187.1		

Note: * Significant at 15 percent level; ** significant at 5 percent level; *** significant at 1 percent level.

References

Amemiya, T. 1973. Regression Analysis When the Dependent Variable is Truncated Normal. *Econometrica.* 41; 997–1016.

Amemiya, T. 1974. A Note on the Fair and Jaffee Model. *Econometrica.* 42; 759–762.

Anderson, R. 1976. Durable Goods, Savings, and Consumer Credit. Research paper 148. Graduate School of Business, Columbia University.

Avery, B. 1977. Information Restrictions and Equal Credit Opportunity Legislation. Working paper. Carnegie-Mellon University.

Cain, G. C. 1967. Unemployment and Labor Force Participation of Secondary Workers. *Industrial Labor Relations Review.* 20; 275–297.

Dolde, W., and J. Tobin. 1971. Wealth, Liquidity, and Consumption. In *Consumer Spending and Monetary Policy; The Linkages.* Boston: Federal Reserve Bank of Boston, pp. 99–160.

Fair, R. C., and D. M. Jaffee. 1972. Methods of Estimation for Markets in Disequilibrium. *Econometrica.* 40; 497–514.

Friedman, M. 1957. *A Theory of the Consumption Function.* Princeton: Princeton University Press, National Bureau of Economic Research.

Hansen, L. P. 1979. Consistency Theorems for a General Class of Econometric Estimators. Working paper. Carnegie-Mellon University.

Harris, D. G. 1974. Credit Rationing at Commercial Banks. *Journal of Money Credit and Banking.* 5; 227–240.

Hartley, M. J. 1973. On the Estimation of Markets in Disequilibrium. Discussion paper 275. Economics Department, State University of New York at Buffalo.

Hartley, M. J., and P. Mallela. 1977. The Asymptotic Properties of a Maximum Likelihood Estimator for a Model of Markets in Disequilibrium. *Econometrica.* 45; 1205–1220.

Jaffee, D. M., and F. Modigliani. 1969. A Theory and Test of Credit Rationing. *American Economic Review.* 69; 850–872.

Kain, J. F., and J. M. Quigley. 1972. Housing Market Discrimination, Homeownership, and Savings Behavior. *American Economic Review.* 62; 263–277.

Laffont, T. T., and R. Garcia. 1977. Disequilibrium Econometrics for Business Loans. *Econometrica.* 45; 1187–1204.

Maddala, G. S., and F. D. Nelson. 1974. Maximum Likelihood Methods for Markets in Disequilibrium. *Econometrica.* 42; 1013–1030.

Metcalf, C. E. 1977. Consumption Behavior: Implications for a Permanent Program. In *The New Jersey Income-Maintenance Experiment, Volume III: Expenditures, Health, and Social Behavior; and the Quality of the Evidence*, ed. Harold W. Watts and Albert Rees. New York: Academic Press, pp. 93–111.

Mincer, J. 1960. Labor Supply, Family Income, and Consumption. *American Economic Review Proceedings.* 50; 574–583.

Peterson, R. L. 1976. The Impact of General Credit Restraint on the Supply of Commercial Bank Consumer Installment Credit. *Journal of Money Credit and Banking.* 7; 527–535.

Schmidt, P. 1979. Constraints on the Parameters in Simultaneous Probit and Tobit Models. In *Structural Analysis of Discrete Data: With Econometric Applications* ed. Charles F. Manski and Daniel McFadden. Cambridge, Mass.: MIT Press.

Sealey, C. W. 1978. Credit Rationing in the Commercial Loan Market: Estimates of a Structural Model under Conditions of Disequilibrium. Department of Finance, Arizona State University.

Shinkel, B. A. 1976. *The Effects of Limiting Information in the Granting of Credit.* Ph.D. dissertation. Purdue University.

Tobin J. 1957. Consumer Debt and Spending: Some Evidence from Analysis of a Survey. Comsumer Installment Credit, part 2, vol. 1, Board of Governors of the Federal Reserve System. Washington: Government Printing Office, pp. 521–545.

Tobin, J. 1972. Wealth, Liquidility, and the Propensity to Consume. In *Human Behavior in Economic Affairs: Essays in Honor of George Katona*, ed. B. Strumpel, et al. Amsterdam: Elsevier, pp. 36–56.

Watkins, T. H. 1975. The Time Allocation of Consumption under Debt Limitations. *Southern Economic Journal.* 42; 61–68.

Watts, H. W., and J. Tobin 1960. Consumer Expenditures and the Capital Account. *Proceedings of the Conference on Consumption and Savings*, vol. 2, ed. Irwin Friend and Robert Jones. Philadelphia: University of Pennsylvania Press, pp. 1–48.

Index